## CORRUPTION AND HUMAN RIGHTS LAW IN AFRICA

This important new book provides a framework for complementarity between promoting and protecting human rights and combating corruption. The book makes three major points regarding the relationship between corruption and human rights law. First, corruption per se is a human rights violation, insofar as it interferes with the right of the people to dispose of their natural wealth and resources and thereby increases poverty and frustrates socio-economic development. Second, corruption leads to a multitude of human rights violations. Third, the book demonstrates that human rights mechanisms have the capacity to provide more effective remedies to victims of corruption than can other criminal and civil legal mechanisms.

The book takes up one of the pervasive problems of governance – large-scale corruption – to examine its impact on human rights and the degree to which a human rights approach to confronting corruption can buttress the traditional criminal law response. It examines three major aspects of human rights in practice – the importance of governing structures in the implementation and enjoyment of human rights, the relationship between corruption, poverty and underdevelopment, and the threat that systemic poverty poses to the entire human rights edifice.

The book is a very significant contribution to the literature on good governance, human rights and the rule of law in Africa.

**Volume 52 in the series Studies in International Law**

**Studies in International Law**

**Recent titles in this series**

Europe and Extraterritorial Asylum
*Maarten den Heijer*

The Practice of International and National Courts and the (De) Fragmentation of International Law
*Edited by Ole Kristian Fauchald and André Nollkaemper*

The Politics of International Criminal Justice: A Spotlight on Germany
*Ronen Steinke*

Fighting Corruption in Public Procurement: A Comparative Analysis of Disqualification or Debarment Measures
*Sope Williams-Elegbe*

The Interception of Vessels on the High Seas: Contemporary Challenges to the Legal Order of the Oceans
*Efthymios Papastavridis*

Integration at the Border: The Dutch Act on Integration Abroad and International Immigration Law
*Karin de Vries*

An Equitable Framework for Humanitarian Intervention
*Ciarán Burke*

Democratic Statehood in International Law: The Emergence of New States in Post-Cold War Practice
*Jure Vidmar*

International Law and the Construction of the Liberal Peace
*Russell Buchan*

The OIC, the UN, and Counter-Terrorism Law-Making: Conflicting or Cooperative Legal Orders?
*Katja Samuel*

Statelessness: The Enigma of the International Community
*William E Conklin*

The Reception of Asylum Seekers under International Law: Between Sovereignty and Equality
*Lieneke Slingenberg*

**For the complete list of titles in this series, see 'Studies in International Law' link at www.hartpub.co.uk/books/series.asp**

# Corruption and Human Rights Law in Africa

Kolawole Olaniyan

·HART·
PUBLISHING

OXFORD AND PORTLAND, OREGON
2016

Published in the United Kingdom by Hart Publishing Ltd
16C Worcester Place, Oxford, OX1 2JW
Telephone: +44 (0)1865 517530
Fax: +44 (0)1865 510710
E-mail: mail@hartpub.co.uk
Website: http://www.hartpub.co.uk

Published in North America (US and Canada) by
Hart Publishing
c/o International Specialized Book Services
920 NE 58th Avenue, Suite 300
Portland, OR 97213-3786
USA
Tel: +1 503 287 3093 or toll-free: (1) 800 944 6190
Fax: +1 503 280 8832
E-mail: orders@isbs.com
Website: http://www.isbs.com



First published in hardback 2014
Paperback edition, 2016



Hart Publishing is an imprint of Bloomsbury Publishing plc.



British Library Cataloguing in Publication Data
Data Available

ISBN: HB: 978-1-84946-637-0
PB: 978-1-50990-845-5

Typeset by Hope Services, Abingdon
Printed and bound in Great Britain by
Lightning Source UK Ltd

For my loving wife Helen, and children,
Oluwatosin, Tolulope, and Tumininu

# Foreword

The development of international human rights law has been a process of gradual expansion, from the earliest manifestations focused on a single issue, beginning in the seventeenth century, to recognition that the treatment of all individuals within a state is a matter of international concern. Efforts to obtain religious liberty in Europe and end the regional religious wars, culminating in the Peace of Westphalia, and the later successful battle to stop the transatlantic slave trade, did not initially alter the common theory that how a government treated those within its jurisdiction was solely a domestic matter. Only the advent of the United Nations and other international institutions after World War II brought human rights generally onto the agenda of the international community. Over more than 60 years, a vast codification process has given rise to a network of global and regional treaties, institutions and procedures that aim to provide an international 'safety net' to human beings throughout the world, while still recognising that the observance of human rights is 'the first responsibility of Government', as proclaimed in the 1993 Vienna Declaration on Human Rights.

Inevitably, new issues and concerns have arisen in response to changes in technology, globalisation and the rise of powerful non-state actors. New rights and new responsibilities have been articulated. While human rights law began with specialists working in a relatively closed environment, it has been increasingly recognised that respect for human rights requires attention to be paid to nearly every aspect of governance and all domains of international law. In particular, there has been a growing interest in shifting from litigation models that respond to violations after they occur, to trying to address root causes of human rights violations in order to prevent them from occurring in the first place. This approach has in turn led to recognising the inescapable links between human rights and democratic governance, economic policies, poverty, and institutional deficits in, for example, judicial bodies and justice systems.

Kolawole Olaniyan has taken up one of the pervasive problems of governance, large-scale corruption, to examine its impact on human rights and the degree to which a human rights approach to confronting corruption can buttress the traditional criminal law response. His focus is Africa, but the valuable lessons he teaches in this comprehensive study can resonate throughout the world. This is a global issue, as the initial section of the book indicates, and it is one that has been growing in scope. Modern electronic transfers of funds make it possible to shift wealth across borders almost instantaneously. Banking secrecy laws hamper the ability to track and repatriate looted assets. As the author demonstrates, the criminal law approach to the issue, both nationally and internationally, has gaps and weaknesses that call for new approaches.

The book reveals the effects of large-scale corruption in Africa, examining the situation in a number of African states, together with their responses to the problem. Part II of the book examines national and international laws aimed at combating corruption, before turning in Part III to the potential for human rights law to address this problem more effectively. The result is a comprehensive and holistic legal framework for addressing some of the root causes of human rights violations and poverty, not only in Africa, but wherever corruption exists. The recommendations are thoughtful and serious, and should be taken up by regional and global institutions, including financial institutions. As the medical profession has long known and practised, prevention is always better than cure.

Dinah Shelton
Manatt/Ahn Professor of International Law (emeritus)
The George Washington University Law School

January 2014

# *Acknowledgements*

This book has been long in the making, and several people have offered invaluable support and encouragement along the way. The book emerged from a meeting I had in 2000 with Dinah Shelton, Manatt/Ahn Professor of International Law (emeritus), the George Washington University Law School, who was then director of the doctoral programme in international human rights law at the University of Notre Dame Law School to discuss my doctoral thesis topic. During our meeting, several ideas were discussed but one from Professor Shelton – on corruption and human rights law – truly stood out. Several meetings, discussions and periods of research afterwards helped to deepen my interest and understanding of the subject. I eventually wrote and successfully defended my doctoral thesis on the topic in August 2003. The revision and publication of the thesis had been severely delayed due to competing commitments, but Professor Shelton's constant encouragement and untiring efforts kept alive the hope of publishing the book. She generously gave her time, looking at all drafts of the manuscript, and writing the Foreword. I have been truly privileged to have had the benefit of her mentorship, enormous academic expertise and experience in the field of international human rights law.

Other people have also helped me in the accomplishment of this project. Thanks must go to Donald Kommers, Joseph and Elizabeth Robbie Professor of Political Science and Concurrent Professor Emeritus of Law, and Professor Pablo Carozza at Notre Dame Law School who together with Professor Shelton supervised my doctoral thesis. I am very grateful for their indispensable counsel, support, encouragement, and advice. Warm thanks are owed, too, to the University of Notre Dame for awarding me scholarships to pursue my postgraduate studies, and to Garth Meintjes, for his invaluable support during my stay at Notre Dame.

A considerable debt of thanks is owed to all at Hart Publishing in Oxford, in particular Richard Hart, for commendable dedication to the project, and penetrating comments on the manuscript and excellent editorial suggestions. The team at Hart Publishing has been enthusiastic and supportive throughout. I am also grateful to Merel Alstein, Senior Commissioning Editor and Anthony Hilton, Assistant Editor at Oxford University Press for obtaining insightful comments from six of Oxford's anonymous reviewers on the book, and whose comments have immensely improved the final product.

I would also like to acknowledge my indebtedness to my brothers, sisters and friends: Adetokunbo Mumuni, Eze Anaba, Sola and Temitope

Akinlade, Olalekan Saidi, Nike Balogun, Dr Abiola Akiyode-Afolabi, Katherine Ofori-Mikala, Professor 'Dejo Olowu, Dr Chidi Odinkalu, Professor Vincent Nmehielle, Professor Mashood Baderin, Justice Sanji Monangeng, Modupe Atoki, Pastor Amos Alade, Ameen Ayodele, Professor Rachel Murray, Ibrahima Kane, Chan Un Park, and to my good uncles, Femi Falana, Senior Advocate of Nigeria and Dr Bola Mustapha, for their unwavering support and encouragement. I also express my sincere appreciation to His Royal Majesty Oba Riliwanu Akiolu, the Oba of Lagos, for his generosity and assistance to Adetokunbo and myself throughout our undergraduate years. Exceptional assistance, encouragement and support of various kinds came from Professor Makau Mutua, Professor Ndiva Kofele-Kale, Lila Stromer, Salil Shetty, Galina Bradley, Tawanda Hondura, Michael Bochenek, and Pastor Glen Podd and his wife, Gillian.

Most of all, a special debt is owed to my loving wife Helen, and children – Oluwatosin, Tolulope, and Tumininu – for their unfailing love, motivation, encouragement and remarkable understanding in the years that it has taken me to complete this book. They stood by me all the way through what at times seemed a tedious and prolonged process. I appreciate the love of my junior, Olalekan, and I am especially grateful to my mum, Musiliat, for pointing the way forward down my present life path.

Finally, I owe a special vote of thanks to Almighty God for grace, wisdom and strength to complete this project.

Kolawole Olaniyan
London
February 2014

# Contents

**Part III: Human Rights Law and Corruption**

# *List of Abbreviations*

African Charter: African Charter on Human and Peoples' Rights
African Commission: African Commission on Human and Peoples' Rights
African Court: African Court on Human and Peoples' Rights
AML: Anti-money laundering
APDHE: Asociación Pro Derechos Humanos de España
APG: Asia/Pacific Group on Money Laundering
AU: African Union
BAI: Banco Africano de Investimentos
CAT: Convention against Torture and Other Cruel, Inhuman or Degrading Treatment or Punishment
CBN: Central Bank of Nigeria
CEDAW: Convention on the Elimination of All Forms of Discrimination against Women
CERD: International Convention on the Elimination of All Forms of Racial Discrimination
CFATF: Caribbean Financial Action Task Force
CICAD: Inter-American Drug Abuse Control Commission
CMW: International Convention on the Protection of the Rights of All Migrant Workers and Members of Their Families
CPI: Corruption Perceptions Index
CRC: Convention on the Rights of the Child
DPCI: Directorate of Priority Crime Investigation
DSO: Directorate of Special Operations
DRC: Democratic Republic of Congo
EAG: Eurasian Group
ECOSOC: Economic and Social Council
ECOWAS: Economic Community of West African States
ECOWAS Court: Community Court of Justice
EFCC: Economic and Financial Crime Commission
EU: European Union
FATF: Financial Action Task Force
FCPA: Foreign Corrupt Practices Act
FSIA: Foreign Sovereign Immunities Act
FIU: Financial Intelligence Unit
FNLA: National Front for the Liberation of Angola
FTAA: Free Trade Area of the Americas
GAFISUD: Financial Action Task Force of South America Against Money Laundering

GPML: Global Program against Money Laundering
GRECO: Group of States against Corruption
IACtHR: Inter-American Court of Human Rights
ICC: International Criminal Court
ICCPR: International Covenant on Civil and Political Rights
ICESCR: International Covenant on Economic, Social and Cultural Rights
ICJ: International Court of Justice
ICPC: Independent Corrupt Practices and Other Related Offences Commission
ICPC Act: Corrupt Practices and Other Related Offences Act, 2000
IMF: International Money Fund
KYC: Know Your Customer
MENAFATF: Middle East and North Africa FATF
MPLA: Popular Movement for the Liberation of Angola
NAPIMS: National Petroleum Investment Management Services
NGO: Non-govermental organisation
NNPC: Nigerian National Petroleum Corporation
NPA: National Prosecuting Authority
OAS: Organization of American States
OAS Convention: OAS Inter-American Convention against Corruption
OAU: Organization of African Unity
OECD: Organisation for Economic Co-operation and Development
OHCHR: Office of the High Commissioner for Human Rights
PALU: Pan-African Lawyers Union
PEPs: Politically exposed persons
PSNR: Permanent sovereignty over natural resources
RICO: Racketeer Influenced and Corrupt Organizations Act
SADC: Southern Africa Development Community
SAFAC: Southern African Forum against Corruption
SAHRIT: Human Rights Trust of Southern Africa
SAPS: South African Police Service
SAR: Suspicious Activity Report
SERAP: Socio-Economic Rights and Accountability Project
StAR: Stolen Asset Recovery Initiative
TI: Transparency International
UBEC: Universal Basic Education Commission
UDHR: Universal Declaration of Human Rights
UN: United Nations
UNCAC: United Nations Convention against Corruption
UNITA: National Union for the Total Independence of Angola (UNITA)
UNODC: United Nations Office on Drugs and Crime
WBCCI: World Bank Control of Corruption Index

# Table of Cases

# *Table of International Treaties and Other Instruments*

# *Table of National Laws and Legislation*

**Angola**

**African Union**



**Equatorial Guinea**

**France**



**Ghana**



**Hong Kong**



**India**



**Nigeria**

**Portugal**

**South Africa**



**Spain**



**Switzerland**



**United Kingdom**



**United States**

# Introduction

Corruption is as old as humanity, yet international recognition of its corrosive nature is relatively recent. The fight against corruption is now an important aspect of contemporary international law. The last three decades have witnessed steady and even remarkable advances in recognising corruption as an international problem that precipitates poverty and threatens both the rule of law and the foundation of a law-based state. An impressive array of international conventions, declarations, guidelines, national laws, and institutions exist to combat corruption and to establish a framework for international cooperation and assistance, in particular in the area of asset recovery. Intergovernmental organisations are constantly engaged in the fight against corruption and are issuing recommendations, directives, and codes of conduct, or more significantly, drafting legally binding international conventions.[1] These commitments have naturally grown a desire by states to address corruption within their jurisdiction, and in other territories. Furthermore, various non-state actors, such as civil society organisations, continue to insist on accountability for the crime of corruption, and the need to sensitise people as to its destructive effects.[2] There is hardly a region in the world in which there are no anti-corruption agencies, instruments, or laws in place. Post-independent Africa is one region that has actively participated in the growing trend to curb corruption,[3] and African states have overwhelmingly endorsed several United Nations anticorruption initiatives and decisions.[4] The

[1] Key intergovernmental organisations in the field include the: United Nations (UN), Organisation for Economic Cooperation and Development (OECD), African Union (AU), Organization of American States (OAS), Council of Europe, European Union (EU), Arab League, and Financial Action Task Force (FATF). International financial institutions (such as the World Bank and the International Monetary Fund), agencies, and bilateral donors are also engaged in the fight against corruption.

[2] The two most prominent and influential international non-governmental organisations are Transparency International and Global Witness. There are also several regional and national NGOs and bar associations engaged in the fight against corruption.

[3] See, for example, the Dakar Declaration on the Prevention and Control of Organised Transnational Crime and Corruption, adopted by the African Regional Ministerial Workshop on Organised Transnational Crime and Corruption, held in Dakar in July 1997, E/CN 15/1998/6/Add 1, sect I.

[4] As of February 2014, 169 countries had ratified the UN Convention against Corruption. Of these, 43 out of 54 African Union member states had ratified the Convention, the highest number of ratifications of any region, even though the African group complained of a lack of funds to facilitate and ensure full participation of all developing countries in the negotiation of the Convention. Nonetheless, while many African states have ratified this treaty and other similar instruments, not many have revised their laws to bring them into conformity with the requirements of the treaties.

proliferation of criminal law instruments against corruption shows the importance the international community has consistently attached to such measures as a way to end the problem.

Despite several years of universal consensus, cooperation, and apparent belief in the ability and effectiveness of legal rules and institutions to fight corruption, it continues to flourish in many parts of Africa, with deleterious effects on human rights, in particular of the most economically and socially disadvantaged. The question that then arises is whether criminal law instruments against corruption can provide an adequate remedy, and satisfactory sense of justice for victims. The book aims to examine the effectiveness of the criminal law instruments against corruption, and if they are unsatisfactory, to consider the role human rights law might play to address any deficiencies. It provides a framework for complementarity between promoting and protecting human rights and combating corruption. The book probes into three major aspects of human rights in practice – the importance of governing structures in the implementation and enjoyment of human rights, the relationship between corruption, poverty and underdevelopment, and the threat that systemic poverty poses to the entire human rights edifice.

Although there is widespread awareness of the adverse effects of corruption within political, economic, and social spheres, the extent of corruption in several African states is well illustrated by their constant low rankings and scores on Transparency International's (TI) Corruption Perceptions Index (CPI), published annually since 1995. Indeed the CPI 2013 shows the worsening problem of corruption in regions like Africa, with Somalia recorded as one of the three most corrupt countries in the world.[5] There is a multitude of anti-corruption indexes measuring corruption in African states, but the CPI is probably the most widely acceptable tool at the moment because it is frequently used and relied upon by academics, economists, journalists, international organisations, and civil society groups to challenge governments' record on their fight against corruption.[6] The CPI gives 177 countries a score from zero to 100, with

[5] The other two countries are Afghanistan and North Korea. Because corruption takes place in secret, it is difficult to know exactly the level of corruption in any given country. However, important anticorruption indexes like the CPI have created reliable measurements of the magnitude of corruption in various sectors and countries. Many governments worry about how they fare on the CPI. Other important anticorruption indices include the World Bank Control of Corruption Index (WBCCI) and the Global Integrity Report. These indices adopt broadly similar methodologies and are the most widely recognised and frequently cited indices in corruption research. For example, both the CPI and the WBCCI attempt to qualitatively measure the pervasiveness of corruption in a country.

[6] Many of the criticisms of the CPI have focused on the fact that it only documents *perception,* rather than real evidence of corruption as adjudged by a select few of individuals. The CPI may not be perfect, and in fact no index is. The difficulties in obtaining real evidence of corruption may be put down to the secretive (and complex) nature of corrupt acts (and the fact that those who perpetrate corruption rarely admit to doing so). Even so, while the CPI's

zero indicating high levels of corruption, and 100, low levels (that is, 'very clean'). For 2013, the CPI showed that with the exceptions of Botswana, Cape Verde, Mauritius, and Rwanda, all other African states are considered significantly corrupt. Even though some African states scored comparatively better than others, the CPI showed that public sector corruption remains embedded in the region. Moreover, the CPI also showed clear links between corruption and the weak political and administrative institutions that have resulted from prolonged periods of conflict and violence.

Moreover, whereas some early scholars[7] in the field argued that corruption in poor economies like Africa can be 'welfare enhancing', empirical evidence suggests that corruption invariably impedes sustainable development, and thus disproportionately affects the economically and socially vulnerable, weakens the rule of law, erodes public trust in government, and permeates (and undermines) critical institutions of state.[8] Corruption can be harmful across national borders – regionally and internationally – and has been stated to undermine 'economic development and political stability [of countries, while also being] a threat to international peace and prosperity, as well as facilitating drug-trafficking, money laundering, and other international criminal activity'.[9] In the light of globalisation and advanced technology, the consequences of corruption in one country are now easily felt continentally and even beyond. Underdevelopment, lack of opportunities, violence, and insecurity in one country can bring about forced migration (including economic migrants) and consequently inflows of refugees and mercenaries to other parts of the region. Economic and social migrants may for instance impose a strain on the resources of poor neighbouring countries, and lead sometimes to rivalry with local populations, resentment, violent competition for resources, and ultimately, insecurity. Furthermore, corrupt immigration and custom officials make countries' borders porous and easily accessible by, for example, drug traffickers and 'terrorists', thereby not only endangering the security and

accuracy and methodology may be debated, it has arguably been effective in building political pressure on governments to address corruption. The mere existence of perception of corruption has normative value – helping to shape public morality and sentiment against corruption – regardless of the 'real evidence'. Even perceptions may provide a pointer as to the real evidence, and if they are well publicised can generate public outrage which in turn might help to promote positive change and enhance accountability of governments. In any case, while real evidence of corruption may be difficult to obtain, its devastating effects are too glaring to ignore.

[7] These scholars include Joseph Nye, Samuel Huntington, and Nathaniel Leff. There is a detailed discussion of their views on 'cost-benefit analysis' of corruption in Ch 1.

[8] See UNDP/Global Financial Integrity, 2013, 'Illicit Financial Flows from the Least Developed Countries: 2002–2011', www://iff.gfintegrity.org/iff2013/2013report.html. The report is an annual update of the one published in 2011, which states that 'Weak governance spawns public corruption and encourages corporate malfeasance' ibid 18.

[9] Kimberly Ann Elliot, 'The Problem of Corruption: A Tale of Two Countries' (1998) 18 *Northwestern Journal of International Law & Business* 524.

well-being of individual countries in the region, but of foreign countries abroad and potentially international peace.

Yet, it is almost impossible to determine exactly how deep corruption flows (in part, because of the notorious secrecy within which corruption takes place). Even so, few will doubt its negative consequences in the forms of poverty and inequality, which are a common phenomenon in several African states. While it is true that the causes of poverty and underdevelopment in those states are complex (and no single factor causes poverty), the longstanding problem of corruption is arguably one explanation for deficits in the rule of law, a drain on public treasury, and exacerbation of existing vulnerabilities and inequalities. Inevitably, the challenge posed by corruption to the rule of law and enjoyment of human rights has raised important questions about the coherence, adequacy, and effectiveness of a criminal law response on its own to drive the legal and social changes necessary to combat corruption (and corrupt behaviour) and its increasing effects – directly or indirectly – on the rights guaranteed under the African Charter on Human and Peoples' Rights.[10]

Despite the complexities and the recognition of the harms that corruption inflicts on individuals, communities, society, and institutions of governance, especially in poor regions, each corrupt act is treated as an isolated incident. The fight against these individual acts is nearly always approached from a criminal and law enforcement dimension, presumably because this is the common approach in developed countries that have mostly effective legal and judicial systems to treat corruption solely as a crime. However, the universal application of such a restrictive approach tends to ignore the serious human (and social) consequences of corruption in several parts of Africa, a region generally lacking sound institutional and justice systems. This leaves both communities and individual victims powerless and without effective remedies.[11] While a criminal and law enforcement approach to corruption clearly has the incentive of deterring would-be corrupt officials in states where the criminal justice systems themselves are corruption-free (which is not usually the case in many African states), a 'one size fits all' approach has proved counterproductive, thus making durable and sustainable solutions to the problem elusive.

[10] African Charter on Human and Peoples' Rights, adopted 26 June 1981, OAU Doc CAB/LEG/67/3 Rev 5 (entered into force 21 Oct 1986) (1982) 21 *International Legal Materials* 58. 53 of the 54 member states of the AU have ratified the Charter.

[11] Remedies are measures (substantive reliefs or the procedures of obtaining such reliefs) that may be taken in response to an actual or threatened violation of human rights. Remedies include 'an award of damages, declaratory relief, injunctions or orders'. See Dinah Shelton, *Remedies in International Human Rights Law*, 2nd edn (Oxford: Oxford University Press, 2005), 4.

In addition, the relationship between corruption and human rights law is one of the most fundamental and yet least studied questions in the field of international law.[12] This book attempts to throw more light on the relationship. The main purposes of the book are to examine the extent to which the criminal and law enforcement framework can effectively address corruption and its effects on human rights, and to explore the potential of human rights law as a complementary legal framework to combat corruption. This book therefore aims to advance and to contribute to a comprehensive and multidisciplinary approach to corruption, and to increase awareness of the legal protections of human and peoples' rights in Africa. The book demonstrates that the effects of corruption on human rights can be debilitating. It puts forward a theoretical foundation for addressing the absence of effective legal remedies for victims of corruption in African states. The book relies heavily on the framework of the African Charter on Human and Peoples' Rights (the principal African regional human rights treaty) to analyse the effects of corruption on human rights in Africa. While arguing for the creative use and dynamic and evolutionary interpretation of the African Charter in order to achieve its 'full effects' in combating corruption, the book also proposes operational, legal, and policy frameworks to combat effectively and satisfactorily the problem.

As noted, a criminal law response, while necessary, is only a small deterrent to corruption (as for example, prosecution for corruption in practice hardly helps to remove any threat of re-offending),[13] because the absence of accountability institutions makes engaging in acts of corruption a risk worth taking. The criminal law solution to corruption is generally reactive. It is also the case that corrupt officials are mostly not deterred either by imprisonment or society's condemnation of their acts, and are instead frequently celebrated. Those who possess economic influence or strong political connections are also less likely to be deterred. The implementation and enforcement of a legal framework to combat corruption in several African states is unfortunately dependent on weak governments and corrupt public officials, leading to predictable effects in political, economic, and social spheres. One such result is the lack of full and effective enjoyment of human rights and peoples' rights.

[12] On the other hand, literature on corruption generally (and its effects on socio-economic and political development) has flourished over the years.

[13] In developed countries with limited incidents of corruption and where the justice systems are largely corruption-free, criminal law generally serves other purposes, such as prevention, punishment or retribution, which arguably can deter potential offenders. See generally, A Ashworth, *Principles of Criminal Law*, 3rd edn (Oxford: Oxford University Press, 1999) 36. Furthermore, a criminal law approach to corruption may be warranted, especially given the central values that are promoted by criminal prohibition, and the significant harms that corruption causes. The prohibition of corruption can also normatively serve to condemn and stigmatise corrupt officials. Yet, lack of effective enforcement of any such prohibition will inevitably make the purposes of criminal law completely ineffectual.

Notably, former UN Secretary General Kofi Annan aptly captured the growing international community's concern with corruption and its negative impact on human rights during the 2003 adoption by the General Assembly of the United Nations Convention against Corruption (UNCAC), stating that corruption: '[H]as a wide range of corrosive effects on societies; undermines democracy and the rule of law; *leads to violations of human rights;* erodes the quality of life, and allows organised crime, terrorism and other threats to human security to flourish; hurts the poor disproportionately by diverting funds intended for development, and undermines a state's ability to provide basic services.'[14] This viewpoint contrasted sharply to the predominant attention paid to the effects of corruption on economies and development, and triggered a remarkable tendency among human rights institutions to mention 'corruption' in their work or make a case for it to be considered a human right issue,[15] and as recently as March 2013, the UN Human Rights Council, at its 23rd Session, organised a panel discussion on the negative impact of corruption on the enjoyment of human rights (and commissioned a study on the matter).

Despite the increasing global recognition of the connection between corruption and human rights, these two concepts are still largely considered discrete and, as such, are treated separately. While the AU Convention on Preventing and Combating Corruption refers to the African Charter on Human and Peoples' Rights, it makes only passing reference to human rights and to the rule of law. It also does not articulate how exactly this notion will be operationalised in a coherent manner within the charter's provisions, nor contain any idea of justiciability. In addition, the interpretation and implementation of a legal framework for corruption and human rights law (in particular the African Charter on Human and Peoples' Rights) rarely take into account the human rights dimension of the problem. On the one hand, despite the complexities of corruption, the reactive and limited criminalisation and prosecution solutions remain the conceptual foundation of any anticorruption legal response. On the other hand, human rights law does not explicitly prohibit corruption, and

[14] Secretary-General Lauds Adoption by General Assembly of United Nations Convention against Corruption, SG/SM/8977, GA/10200, SOC/CP/271 (3 November 2003).

[15] See for example, similar statement made by UN Secretary General Ban Ki-moon during his launch of the Stolen Asset Recovery Initiative (StAR). More recently, the UN High Commissioner for Human Rights, Ms Navi Pillay, stated (at the 'panel discussion on the negative impact of corruption on human rights', held in March 2013 during the 22nd session of the Human Rights Council) pointedly: 'Let us be clear. Corruption kills . . . Corruption hits the poor first and hardest, breeds impunity of perpetrators; exacerbates inequality, weakens governance and institutions, erodes public trust, undermines the rule of law; and denies victims the right to effective redress, thus creating "a vicious cycle of crime".' See Annual report of the United Nations High Commissioner for Human Rights and reports of the Office of the High Commissioner and the Secretary-General, available at www.ohchr.org/Documents/HRBodies/HRCouncil/RegularSession/Session23/A.HRC.23.26_EN.pdf, paras 3, 4.

human rights institutions and tribunals rarely apply rigorous human rights analysis to the problem,[16] and human rights defenders and anticorruption activists rarely engage or work together on issues of common interests.

Sanji Mmasenono Monageng, former chairperson of the African Commission on Human and Peoples' Rights and now a judge (and vice president) at the International Criminal Court (ICC), stated on a questionnaire sent out by this author: 'I never used the word "corruption" throughout my time on the commission – perhaps because complainants do not raise issues of corruption.'[17] Modupe Atoki, also a former chairperson of the Commission, agrees:

> I don't use the word 'corruption' that much in my work as commissioner, although I personally believe that certain corrupt practices like large-scale corruption may violate the human rights under the African Charter. However, the closest we have come is interpreting Article 21 to mean that the resources of the state should be used to the exclusive benefit of the citizens. Corruption may very well be implied but the Commission has not ruled that this is the case. It would be interesting for a complainant to bring a case under this rubric and see how the Commission interprets large-scale corruption.[18]

The relatively recent history of the international anticorruption movement may account for the discrete treatment of the two concepts of human rights and corruption. While human rights law emerged following World War II, the anticorruption movement grew out of the 1977 Watergate scandal in the United States. Furthermore, several years after the development and expansion of human rights law as a 'fundamental aim of modern international law',[19] the use of the word corruption was still considered taboo. While human rights law has diluted the concept of state sovereignty to the point that a state's treatment of its own citizens is no longer considered a matter of only domestic concern, combating corruption is generally seen as an improper intrusion into the domestic affairs of sovereign states.

Although the legal frameworks for corruption and human rights law emerged at different times in history, and there may be some conceptual

[16] It is far less common to find detailed human rights analysis of corruption in the reports of the Office of the UN High Commissioner for Human Rights or the African Commission on Human and Peoples' Rights. For instance, former UN Special Rapporteur Christy Mbonu prepared working papers and reports on corruption and its impact on the enjoyment of human rights, but they lacked a rigorous human rights analysis and most of her recommendations were based on criminal and law enforcement solutions. While she stated that individuals, communities, and societies are often victims of corruption, she did not articulate any remedies within the framework of human rights law.

[17] This is the first of two remarks (among the responses received from former and current members of the Commission). The responses were based on questionnaires and telephone interviews conducted between April 2012 and June 2012 for the preparation of this book.

[18] This is the second remark. See 'Responses to Questionnaire', on file with the author.

[19] Shelton, *Remedies* (n 11) 1.

differences between them, there are also several common areas and complementarities. First, they both converge around a body of identifiable common principles. Several human rights obligations and principles, such as the obligations of vigilance and diligence, and the principles of accountability and participation, are central to the fight against corruption and, in fact, are deemed critical to its long-term success and sustainability. Second, the fight against corruption aims to enthrone both good governance and the rule of law, which relate directly to several foundational objectives of human rights law. Both are important to the realisation of systems that respect human rights, because political stability and sound economic management, intrinsic to the fabric of human rights law, cannot be realised without them. In many cases, violations of human rights are consequences of weak governance and a lack of the rule of law. Third, an effective fight against corruption is crucial to the realisation of human rights, because it unquestionably leads to the sound management of public resources and subsequently improves citizens' access to justice and vital public services.

Nonetheless, a coherent and consistent framework has not yet been developed to reflect and build on the relationship between corruption and human rights law. Standards and laws relating to corruption are still narrowly conceived as an infringement against the state, and not the individual victims. This is true even given the emphasis on a comprehensive and multidisciplinary approach to corruption. While the legal framework for corruption requires states to take specific measures to combat it, it does not indicate any legal responsibility or accountability on the part of states that either encourage (or condone) it or fail to effectively fight it within their territories. This lack of accountability has resulted in the sporadic and lax prosecution and punishment of officials responsible for large-scale corruption, while, conversely, imposing severe sanctions for petty corruption, so as to give the impression of justice. These behaviours clearly violate the underlying legal and moral assumptions that a government will treat all persons equally, fairly, and with respect.

In addition, although rhetoric about corruption constantly fills political speeches and the media, comparatively few high-ranking state officials are prosecuted, and corruption cases that are taken to court proceed at a snail's pace and serve no more than a symbolic purpose. Prosecutorial agencies regularly abuse their wide discretionary power, and many anti-corruption laws rarely provide for independent prosecution or counsel; where they do, as in Nigeria,[20] they are almost always paper tigers, as they have a very limited mandate, and, as such, are rarely effective in practice. In most countries the consent and approval of the attorney general or

[20] See s 52 of the Corrupt Practices and Other Related Offences Act, 2000 (commonly known as ICPC Act). There is a discussion of the ICPC Act in Ch 3.

minister of justice, who are usually political appointees, is required to bring charges of corruption (and to file *nolle prosequi,* translated as 'we shall no longer prosecute'), but political realities mean this discretionary power is regularly abused or exercised in such a manner as to achieve a political or unfair objective.[21] Yet, sometimes, public demands for government to act against corruption may also result in unjustified and unlawful exercise of prosecutorial discretion.

Corruption charges are levelled against opposition leaders (often without justification) to achieve a political end. Potential witnesses are often silenced, while corrupt officials use stolen wealth to buy access to political and economic opportunities. Witnesses are likely concerned about retaliation (from threats or harassment, to violent retribution) if they file a report. Corruption suspects continue to benefit from banking secrecy laws and the lack of whistle-blower protection laws that would encourage reporting. And financial documents, which are a primary source of evidence, are often protected by law, and therefore are difficult to obtain without resources and technical know-how that prosecutors may lack. Perpetrators have the influence and (stolen) wealth to hire the best lawyers, accountants, and so on, to help distort or hide evidence of their misconduct, take advantage of the holes in legal frameworks, and / or launder the proceeds of their crimes. Most perpetrators also often have unparalled access to the media, and some invest heavily in the industry, presumably to influence public opinion in particular directions.

Moreover, where prosecution of corruption does take place, it is an enormous expenditure of the resources of the criminal justice system. And regardless of the legal outcome, corrupt state officials are often allowed to keep their ill-gotten wealth (through for example, the questionable procedure of plea bargaining, because agreeing 'to bargain' suggests an admission of guilt and breach of public trust on the part of corrupt suspects, as people who truly work for their wealth will hardly agree to such a procedure). Presumably, apart from causing a minimal amount of disgrace, creating the inconvenience of legal battles, and occasionally imposing short jail sentences, criminal prosecution and punishment alone would seem unsatisfactory and ineffective ways of combating corruption and its effects on human rights. The level of prosecution and punishment for corruption involving high-ranking state officials is simply not commensurate with the gravity of the problem, particularly when combined with the lack of effective remedies for victims, and that corrupt officials can benefit from their crimes, including keeping the stolen assets.

Furthermore, cooperation among states in anticorruption matters, while

[21] Art 139 of the Angolan constitution, for example, is a good illustration of political control of the office of the attorney general. It provides that: 'The Vice-President, Ministers of State and Ministers [including the attorney general] shall be politically and institutionally responsible to the President of the Republic.' This is discussed in detail in Ch 3.

mandatory in criminal cases, is optional in civil and administrative matters,[22] and as such obligations relating to asset recovery, for example, imposed by anticorruption treaties, have not been fully embraced by states. A victim state can be awarded damages only if the requesting state recognises such damages, therefore it is a victimised government, not its victimised people and communities, that has the 'legal standing' to bring an action to recover damages. Recovered financial assets may be returned through civil recovery to a victim state that can prove ownership, but these assets are often quickly re-stolen and laundered by the senior officials of the corrupt state that encouraged or facilitated the acts in the first place.

In addition, although states have an obligation to respond to the consequences of corruption, this is limited to making it a relevant factor in legal proceedings: to rescind contracts and the contractual rights of third parties acquired in good faith. Similarly, while states are required to ensure the legal right to compensation for entities or persons who have suffered damage as a result of an act of corruption, this is limited to private sector corruption and to foreign states and governments. Any such obligation is also subject to the fundamental principles of states' domestic law.[23] In the case of African states, while there have been marginal improvements in cooperation to trace, freeze, seize, forfeit, or return stolen wealth, no consistent or coherent pattern has developed because much still depends on the vagaries of economic and political considerations and interests of the states. Sovereignty, technicalities, and a lack of adherence to the 'small details' are frequently put forward as justifications by both the victim state and the receiving state to refuse requests for mutual cooperation and assistance in cases of corruption involving high-ranking state officials.[24]

[22] See, eg, Arts 34, 43(1), and 53 of the UN Convention against Corruption, UN General Assembly, United Nations Convention against Corruption: Resolution adopted by the General Assembly, 21 November 2003, A/RES/58/4, www.unhcr.org/refworld/docid/3fdc4d3e7.html.

[23] The phrase 'where appropriate and in accordance with the fundamental principles of its legal system', appears 33 times in the UNCAC. This apparently was a compromise to allow many states to subscribe to the idea of the convention. Yet such provisions clearly fly in the face of Art 27 of the Vienna Convention on the Law of Treaties, which provides that: 'a party may not invoke the provisions of its internal law [not even its constitution] as justification for its failure to perform a treaty'. To allow states to breach this core international law principle would be to provide them with 'an escape route' from their voluntary obligations. See Vienna Convention on the Law of Treaties, 1155 UNTS 331.

[24] For example, Nigeria's former Attorney General of the Federation and Minister of Justice Michael Kaase Aodoakka refused, on the ground of sovereignty, to entertain the request of the UK Metropolitan Police (instead of the UK Home Office) and made under bilateral mutual assistance to Nigeria. The request was to question a former Nigerian governor involved in corruption and money laundering that had occurred in the United Kingdom. Aodoakka said: 'I think Nigeria, as a sovereign nation, deserves some respect. They [the Metropolitan Police] knew they were wrong, otherwise why did they now write through the Home Office requesting mutual assistance to quiz a prominent Nigerian . . . I cannot compromise the sovereignty of this country, if they make incompetent requests I will turn them down 20 times. Any request from Metropolitan Police would be refused by this office,

Whether or not a victim state will pursue stolen assets is entirely discretionary, and depends largely on political considerations and the closeness (or influence) of the corrupt suspects to political authorities. Importantly, if the victim state refuses to take action in this direction, individual victims of corruption cannot directly pursue the assets under existing criminal law instruments against corruption. Each state reserves the right to determine the circumstances under which it will make its courts available. Resorting to civil law, or administrative law – assuming they even exist – is difficult and costly in many parts of Africa.

The ability and performance of anticorruption mechanisms is often imperilled by a lack of independence and autonomy, and by undue influence. There is also the lack of effective enforcement mechanisms. The anticorruption treaties applicable within several African states establish only monitoring mechanisms with a limited and narrowed mandate, and there are no sanctions for non-compliance by states with their treaty obligations or domestic legislation. Foreign corporations which bribe high-ranking state officials pay settlements and compensation to the home government (that is, the state that serves as the headquarters of the corporation), but they rarely make payment to the victim state (that is, the state where the corporation operates and commits acts of corruption), and where they do it is significantly lower. This point is well illustrated by a recent report showing that only 3 per cent of government settlements in hundreds of bribery cases ($185m, out of $6.4bn in penalties) went to compensate states affected by the corruption, and in the majority of settlements, the states were neither directly or indirectly involved in the negotiations of the terms of the settlements.[25] Added to this, only a fraction of the hundreds of billions stolen in the past decades from African states has been identified and recovered, much less repatriated to the victim states.

A criminal law response to corruption is technical, onerous, and problematic, given the secrecy with which corruption is usually undertaken. No wonder then that the investment of resources to procure convictions for high-ranking officials has arguably not provided good value for the money. Strict adherence to the technical rules of evidence is necessary to achieve justice in individual cases, though this adherence can sometimes lead a corrupt state official to being 'let off the hook'. Also, as noted, corruption is still primarily treated only as a national crime, though it has regional and international consequences. However, without the cooperation, assistance, and support of other states in whose jurisdictions corrupt funds are stashed, corruption cannot be effectively prevented or combatted. Unfortunately, such cooperation is rarely forthcoming, in part

period'. 'Nigeria: UK Wants to Quiz Adenuga, Says AG', www.allafrica.com/stories/200712040005.html.

[25] See IACC, 'LEFT OUT OF THE BARGAIN – Settlements in foreign bribery cases and their effects on asset recovery', www.15iacc.org/agenda/agenda-day-2/left-out-of-the-bargain/.

because of lack of political will and especially given that states are generally not under any pressure from their citizens to offer such assistance to affected states. Adding corruption as a human rights issue might help to improve the level of cooperation, assistance and support a state gives, as citizens of Western countries, in particular, might be more sympathetic to efforts that address and bring to light the harmful consequences of corruption in poor states and regions. Public attitudes can change quickly, and have far-reaching effects; thus, the greater the public pressure, the more likely it is that states will find it difficult to justify not returning stolen assets to victim states. At any rate, exposing the effects of corruption on human rights might catch the public imagination in a way that a criminal law response alone has not been able to do.

Theoretically, corruption has implications for a state's human rights obligations in at least three ways. First, corruption, per se, is a human rights violation, insofar as it interferes with the right of the people to dispose of their natural wealth and resources, and thereby increases poverty and frustrates socio-economic development. Second, corruption can lead to a multitude of human rights violations. Third, corruption is a violation of the obligations to respect, protect, promote, and fulfil human and peoples' rights. These presumably will include a state's failure to create conditions to achieve human rights (and access to effective remedies in cases of violations) or to establish effective and independent anticorruption mechanisms to combat corruption.

There are many examples of corrupt practices that would directly or indirectly contravene human rights, but under current legal instruments against corruption the victims would not receive effective remedies. These practices include, for example, the siphoning-off of public funds (whether the funds are derived from illicit enrichment, embezzlement, abuse of office, trading in influence or even the proceeds of bribery) into private bank accounts of senior state officials. Understanding the effects of corruption on human rights, the theoretical and conceptual connections between the two issues, and how human rights law might apply as a complementary legal framework are therefore important not only as academic or philosophical matters but also as factual matters, in that it is individual victims who are injured when human rights violations stem from corruption, and it is rare for these individuals to obtain effective redress via the legal instruments against corruption for the harms done. It is the thrust of this book that as a matter of justice and fairness, victims of corruption should ideally be entitled to an effective remedy through the anticorruption legal framework or human rights law (or more appropriately, a combination of the two legal regimes) for the harms done. The book makes a strong case for reconceptualising corruption in order to better understand its ever-changing nature and its worsening effects – directly and indirectly – on human rights in African states.

Applying human rights law as a complementary legal framework is vital for improving the fight against corruption and for increasing international attention on its effects on human rights. Human rights norms and institutions that are established to implement them arguably offer well-established, robust, and independent verification processes. States in fact periodically appear before human rights treaties' bodies to defend their human rights record,[26] and nationally, courts and human rights commissions act as important watchdogs against abuse of human rights. Yet, the appropriateness of criminal law to fight corruption cannot be questioned. But as noted, while it remains a useful tool, a criminal law response, by itself, is unavoidably rigid, and limited to adequately address deep-seated human and social problems like corruption. As Susan Rose-Ackerman correctly put it, 'Corruption cannot be fought solely through criminal law. The criminal law can play a role as a backstop lying behind the needed structural changes.'[27] The utility value of criminal law is limited, in countries where the criminal justice system itself is overridden by corruption. A corruption-free judiciary for example may not be enough to make headway against corruption (or prevent a state's prosecutorial discretionary power from being politically, selectively, or unreasonably exercised) if the problem is (as it is often the case) enmeshed in other critical institutions of governance and the rule of law.

In sum, while criminal law can provide some short-term enforcement benefits, human rights law establishes both significant accountability mechanisms and normative standards for implementing long-term, durable, sustainable, and broad legal and institutional reforms against corruption. Human rights have long been recognised as 'the foundation of freedom, justice, and peace in the world.' Human rights 'reflect the value of inviolability',[28] and 'they hold that to violate a person's human rights is to fail to show them respect that they are owed'.[29] States also generally respect adverse judgments and decisions of human rights courts and institutions, and carry out important reforms under the terms of these judgments and decisions, as well as pay compensation to victims. This demonstrates that human rights law can be crucially effective in addressing some of the most sensitive areas previously considered to be within

[26] The process is part of the human rights enforcement structure: each of the major universal treaties is reviewed by an expert body that comments on the compliance reports that states must periodically submit.

[27] See Susan Rose-Ackerman, 'Corruption and the Criminal Law' (2002) 2 *Focus on Crime & Society*, UN Sales No E03IV2, 3. It has also been stated that, 'In order to effectively combat corruption, it is necessary to focus on the workings of institutions, not individuals. Penal law is therefore of less importance than one might think.' Claes Sandgren, 'Combating Corruption: The Misunderstood Role of Law' (2005) 39 *International Lawyer* 717, 728.

[28] See Simon Caney, 'Climate Change, Human Rights and Moral Threshold', in Stephen Humphreys (ed), *Human Rights and Climate Change* (Cambridge: Cambridge University Press, 2010), 74.

[29] ibid.

the exclusive domain of national sovereignty. Human rights thus represent 'moral thresholds below which people should not fall'.[30]

There may be exceptional circumstances when certain rights can be suspended; even so, any suspension of human rights must be temporary, and not lead to violations of other legal obligations. Characterising human rights as 'nonsense upon stilts ' seems a figment and off the mark. Sceptics about human rights law might also, for example, point to the fact that the carefully crafted norms of the UN Charter have not helped to prevent wars or threats to international peace and security despite several decades of existence of the charter. It is true that human rights law continues to face implementation and enforcement challenges across the globe, and there remain some differences of opinions in terms of its conceptual interpretation, scope or philosophical foundation. Yet to use these grounds as justifications to minimise the potential role for human rights law to combat corruption is to fail to recognise the significant improvements that have taken place in this field over the years, and the law's remarkable achievements. As noted, the fact that the world community has historically and consistently underscored the importance of human rights law shows the tremendous moral, legal, political, and institutional potential of this branch of international law for combating corruption. These include:

- providing legal and normative baseline for developing, strengthening, and improving the effective functioning of critical institutions of state, and increasing implementation of international obligations;
- enhancing the rule of law and reducing the impunity of perpetrators;
- ensuring that the legal responses against corruption keep pace with its changing nature and effects, and the public expectation to effectively address these problems;
- bringing a great moral force to the discussion about corruption, and arguably providing a better and more widely accepted language to capture the human consequences of corruption, and educating the public on this;
- establishing a 'human face' of corruption, and providing a powerful argument with potential to exert pressure on states to combat corruption and end violations of human rights;
- reducing the problems of selective application and enforcement of anticorruption laws and standards, and thus providing important safeguards against arbitrary treatment of those accused of corruption;
- empowering and placing the victims at the heart of the fight against corruption, in particular the economically and socially vulnerable; and ensuring their experience is not minimised or put aside; and

[30] ibid.

- allowing victims and civil society to demand accountability and seek effective remedies.[31]

Furthermore, the involvement of human rights defenders and groups potentially can ensure that valuable litigation and advocacy experiences gained over the last five decades are at the forefront of the fight against corruption, from a human rights perspective. At the same time, the anti-corruption movement and its mechanisms can benefit immensely from the rich experiences of the human rights law and movement, and its intrinsically empowering nature. As C Raj Kumar pointedly stated, 'Corruption being a law enforcement and public policy issue, and which only invites official response will start to receive a wider community and civil society response due to its human rights consequences.'[32] This complementary role for human rights law in the fight against corruption is consistent with the international community's oft-stated commitment to a comprehensive and multidisciplinary approach to corruption. Yet, human rights law on its own may not provide the whole solution to the corruption problem. Nonetheless, human rights law can ensure a measure of justice, fairness and effective remedies to victims of corruption and can serve as a strong deterrent, and incentive for action. The structural and sustainable reforms of a state's legal and political institutions to comprehensively tackle the root causes of corruption are brighter when built on a human rights law framework.

This book focuses on Africa, and it analyses the effects of corruption on the human rights and peoples' rights guaranteed under the African Charter on Human and Peoples' Rights. Specifically, the book evaluates the extent to which the AU Convention on Preventing and Combating Corruption, the Economic Community of West African States (ECOWAS) Protocol on the Fight against Corruption, the Southern African Development Community (SADC) Protocol against Corruption, and the UN Convention against Corruption can contribute to the fight against corruption in terms of their influence and ability to encourage states to prevent and combat corruption, and more importantly, provide effective remedies to victims. It argues that corruption cannot be effectively combated without a thorough and deeper understanding of its nature, and effects on human rights. Given the high costs of corruption on human rights, it is important to develop a comprehensive and complementary legal framework that addresses the criminal law dimension of

[31] In sum, 'A state that fails to protect fully individuals against human rights violations or that otherwise violates remedial rights commits an independent, further violation of internationally-recognized human rights.' Shelton, *Remedies* (n 11) 37.

[32] C Raj Kumar, 'Human Rights Approaches of Corruption Mechanisms – Enhancing the Hong Kong Experience of Corruption Prevention Strategies' (2004) 5 *San Diego International Law Journal* 349.

the problem and contributes to holding states accountable for the human rights violations that stem from corruption.

This book goes on to argue that a criminal law response alone is inadequate and insufficient if it includes institutional structures that facilitate or encourage corruption. Accordingly, the book argues for the deconstruction of a legal doctrine that allows only a state to be considered a victim of corruption, not its people. The book argues that allowing victims of human rights violations to bring cases against the state (or party or institution) for these violations would contribute significantly to the global efforts to combat the problem. While the emphasis of the book is to examine how human rights law can serve as a complementary framework to combat corruption, some consideration is given to both human rights and due process issues raised by the fight against corruption.

Chapter 1 details the context – historical and conceptual – of the arguments concerning the connections between corruption and human rights. Foundational issues include a discussion on the evolution and contested concepts of corruption and the fight for human rights, the 'justifications' (or excuses) often given for corruption, and the normative and moral stance against corruption, and whether there is even a human rights obligation to combat corruption. The chapter also discusses the Foreign Corrupt Practices Act (FCPA), the Organisation for Economic Cooperation and Development (OECD) Convention, and other relevant international and regional instruments in order to place the evaluation and assessment of the African-related treaties into the wider context of global anticorruption movements and developments. The chapter highlights the political and other difficulties that seem to have obstructed a firm, internationally accepted legal agreement on the meaning of corruption, and then makes the case for an expanded and unambiguous definition of corruption that incorporates human rights. A working definition of corruption that could plausibly remove the confusion surrounding the concept, minimise its opportunistic appropriation and ensure effective remedies for victims, is proposed.

Chapter 2 discusses the international dimensions of corruption and examines important contemporary issues, in particular the relationship between corruption, money laundering, and poverty. The chapter details the roles financial and other institutions play in the fight against money laundering, underscores the international and transnational nature of corruption, and explains why any effective response to corruption must necessarily combine strong actions (both domestically and internationally) built on human rights principles and criminal law.

Building on this, Chapter 3 assesses and analyses constitutional provisions and national legislation, and mechanisms for fighting corruption, and considers their adequacy and effectiveness in reducing or eliminating corruption, and its effects on human rights. It is clearly impracticable to discuss every legal system established to fight corruption occurring in many African states, especially given the multiplicity of anticorruption laws and institutions across these states. Also, many legal systems and approaches are quite similar substantively, and any variation depends to a large extent on whether it is a common law or civil law country. Therefore, in addition to the author's own country, Nigeria, the chapter discusses, through a thematic lens, the main legal instruments to fight corruption in Angola, and Equatorial Guinea. The major considerations that influenced the choice of countries are the comprehensive nature of the legal rules (substantive and procedural) and mechanisms that have been established to fight corruption in these countries, and their persistent low ranking in the TI's Corruption Perception Index. In addition, Angola, Equatorial Guinea, and Nigeria were chosen because many of the international investigations of corruption in African states have centred on these countries. The countries discussed also arguably best illustrate the integrated problems of corruption, money laundering, poverty and lack of respect for human rights in several African states. Similar considerations also justified the focus on these countries in Chapter 2.

Chapter 4 examines the international and regional legal frameworks against corruption, as well as the institutions and agencies that they establish. It discusses the four anticorruption conventions applicable to African states (that is, the AU Convention, the ECOWAS Protocol on the Fight against Corruption, the SADC Protocol against Corruption, and the UNCAC), and where necessary, their *travaux preparatoires*. The chapter also discusses whether these instruments add anything to domestic laws against corruption. A comparative approach is adopted using the UNCAC as the central instrument because of its comprehensive and international nature. The focus is on the four core components articulated in these instruments: prevention, criminalisation, international cooperation and assistance, and asset recovery. The chapter considers whether any of the provisions of these treaties can serve as useful framework for dealing with human rights violations caused by corruption, and then explores the potential of human rights law for addressing any deficiencies. Where appropriate, references are made as to how anticorruption institutions and other bodies have interpreted the provisions of the UNCAC (and other relevant anticorruption treaties and standards).

Chapter 5 considers the effects of corruption on human rights – civil, political, economic, social, and cultural, guaranteed by the African Charter and other similar treaties. Irrespective of the contested nature of the concepts of corruption, its contemporary effects on human rights can no longer be ignored as merely of academic interest. Concretely establishing the theoretical and conceptual connections between corruption and human rights requires a thorough understanding of the specific rights that might be affected by corruption, which in turn would help to develop a more effective legal response to corruption. In addition, while many of the cases discussed in detail here may at first blush appear to be only marginally relevant to an examination of the human rights dimensions of corruption, such jurisprudence (hardly fully explored in literature on human rights system), in fact provides important normative framework for the examination of effects of corruption on specific human rights, and helps to avoid a simplistic generalisation of issues. The cases elaborated can also provide important regional human rights jurisprudence upon which lawyers and activists alike might rely to make their claims on remedies for victims of corruption in the coming years.

Chapter 6 complements and builds on the extensive discussion of the substantive human and peoples' rights in Chapter 5, as it explores the potential contribution of human rights law to address the corruption that occurs in many African states, and makes the case for a comprehensive and complementary legal framework that includes human rights law. The chapter discusses the opportunities under human rights law for effective remedies for victims of corruption. It also highlights the procedural, substantive, and legal advantages for using human rights law to combat corruption. Specifically, the chapter evaluates article 21 of the African Charter, and explores the potential of this provision to provide a human rights basis for preventing and combating corruption. It should be pointed out that while the African Charter as a whole offers appropriate normative framework for addressing corruption, article 21 is more directly relevant to the issue. Crucially, article 21 underscores the reality that no human rights can be achieved without the availability of resources, and the transparent and accountable use of the resources, as well as development of the necessary societal structures to allow for the full and effective enjoyment of human rights. Similar provisions under Common Article 1 of the International Covenant on Economic, Social, and Cultural Rights and International Covenant on Civil and Political Rights are considered. The chapter then discusses the legal, procedural, and practical challenges that can arise when corruption is addressed through human rights law. Issues such as causation and legal standing, and the questions of whether remedies can be measureable, compensable, manageable, or reasonable, are discussed.

The concluding chapter provides an overview of the themes and central arguments canvassed throughout the book, and offers some recommendations.

For clarity, it is important to define the concept of 'corruption' as used in this book. Corruption is a generic term for a variety of misconduct of different but often overlapping forms, and it can be classified myriad ways, according to the type of power that is abused, and in relation to its nature, scale, effects, and further sub-classified according to its frequency, and spread. With respect to the first component – in relation to the type of power that may be abused – corruption can be classified as either public (governmental) sector corruption or private sector corruption. The definition of public corruption is much broader than private corruption, and it can be further sub-classified as 'large-scale' (so-called 'grand corruption') or 'petty'.[33] With respect to the second component – in relation to its frequency and spread – corruption (whether committed in the public or private sector) can also further be sub-classified as either 'systemic' or 'isolated'.

The primary focus of this book is public sector large-scale (also called political) corruption, which occurs when high-ranking state officials abuse their entrusted positions to convert public treasuries into private gain. As noted, this kind of corruption can be either systemic or isolated but experience has shown that whenever large-scale corruption occurs it is more often entrenched in the systems of governance, as high-ranking government officials take advantage of their state's weak and dysfunctional institutions of the rule of law to massively steal public funds (and often including international aid funds, either for themselves, their relations, or their friends or for all three), with impunity. Examples include outright embezzlement of public funds such as salaries (and pensions) of civil servants, or abusing entrusted position to negotiate and/or receive substantial bribes, in particular, from foreign companies.[34]

Petty (also called bureaucratic, street-level, or survival) corruption takes place nearly on a daily basis and is committed when junior or mid-level officials in agencies and parastatals meet the public directly. It usually involves the exchange of small amounts of money or favours. This level of corruption is virtually universal and can be found in all societies and nations. Examples include but are not limited to such actions as judicial or court clerk demanding bribes in return for adjournments, to 'facilitate' bail applications, or to make court files 'disappear'. It is important to point out that in this scenario, the court clerk may not be the only one involved, as others across the judiciary hierarchy may be indirectly implicated.[35] Reasons for petty corruption may include low salaries and poor conditions of service and lack of opportunity for professional growth and

[33] These classifications broadly mirror those used generally in anticorruption treaties, standards, and laws. In particular, the classifications used by the UN Convention against Corruption are: bribery, embezzlement, abuse of office, trading in influence, and illicit enrichment. Differences between these classifications are in general merely a matter of emphasis. For a discussion on this, see Ch 4.

[34] Other examples are abusing office to inflate procurement contracts and selling state's policy-making role to political supporters, relations, and friends in return for substantial cash.

[35] Other examples can include junior officials demanding payment of bribes from the economically and socially for routine government services, such as electricity, water, motor licence or driving licence; teachers demanding bribes (or other in-kind favours) from their students to write positive report cards; or tax office clerks pocketing cash in exchange for 'adjusting' the amount owed.

development (though these may not be compelling grounds for corruption), and more significantly, the corruptive influence of high-ranking public officials.

As noted, in contrast to 'isolated corruption', systemic corruption occurs when the whole machinery, all systems and institutions of a state, are enmeshed in corruption of all forms, but especially at the highest levels of government. This kind of corruption flourishes where the laws and institutions of government and accountability mechanisms are weak and dysfunctional, providing incentives for large-scale corruption to flourish, which in turn provides the environment for other forms of corruption to take place. Large-scale corruption is different from petty corruption in several respects not least in terms of the staggering amount of public funds involved, and the fact that much of the stolen funds are deposited in developed economies (often with complicated and secretive banking systems that tend to inhibit recovery of stolen assets) abroad. Corrupt senior state officials turn the public treasury into a more 'profitable business' for themselves probably than what they might be able to legitimately earn in any private business. Persistent incidents of large-scale corruption also precipitate systemic distortions of critical institutions of governance.

Furthermore, private sector corruption occurs when those with power in business (for instance, chief executive officials), abuse it by promoting their own interests over those of owners or workers. Corruption in the private sector can cause as much harm to the health of the economy as in the public sector. It must also be recognised that the distinction between public sector and private sector corruption is becoming increasingly blurred. Finally, while there may well be other ways to categorise corruption, the categories that have been discussed here probably provides the best analytical tools (especially because of the interrelationship and interconnection that is apparent from the classifications) for looking at the effects of corruption on human rights, and as such, will be relied upon and utilised throughout the book.

In this book, the terms 'large-scale corruption' or 'corruption' are used interchangeably to refer to the deliberate, intentional mass stealing of public wealth and resources by senior state officials entrusted with its fair and honest management for the common good and achievement of human rights, whether carried out individually or collectively, but with the support, encouragement, or acquiescence of the state, combined with a refusal to genuinely, thoroughly and transparently investigate and/or prosecute the mass stealing and recover stolen assets, which violates the human rights of the economically and socially vulnerable. If, as is argued in this book, corruption violates human rights, it seems sensible, reasonable, and appropriate to develop a definition that reflects this dimension. The proposed definition reflects the elements of a human rights law response to corruption canvassed throughout this book. The effects of corruption on human rights are considered in light of this definition, and also in relation to the 'chilling effects' of large-scale corruption on other forms of corruption. The definition would complement neatly the traditional criminal law instruments against corruption and ensure that the contemporary concepts of corruption, the accountability of states and the harms suffered by victims are appropriately and precisely captured. The rigorous and consistent application of this definition might also help to harmonise national legal responses, improve international cooperation and assistance, remove any political or ideological controversies surrounding the meaning of corruption, and ultimately enhance the effective implementation of human rights law and the legal instruments against corruption. While political consensus over the concept of corruption remains to be achieved, there is no technical or legal difficulty that would prevent an agreement to be reached on the proposed definition.

This book focuses on large-scale corruption for several reasons. In the first place, this kind of corruption fundamentally contrasts with even a minimal notion of the rule of law, and the ideal of government as a public trust. It is especially devastating to the rules of a law-based society, and leads to a loss of confidence by citizens. Large-scale corruption undermines the ability of states to carry out their good-faith human rights obligations and commitments as it diverts critical resources needed to achieve the full enjoyment of human rights. It is difficult to imagine a greater breach of trust than when senior public officials entrusted with the people's wealth and resources then turn around to use their public entrusted position to steal people's resources with impunity (basically turning public treasury into a private 'cashbox'). This creates a vicious cycle of corruption, because corrupt senior officials often use their stolen wealth to finance and sustain their political career and networks. Secondly, large-scale corruption also facilitates other forms of corruption (as it sends a devastating message to the rest of the society that corruption pays, and can taint the entire institutions of governance such as the police, military, schools, and health services), in particular, petty corruption of middle or lower-level public officials in positions of trust, and this is then copied and replicated by citizens who understand that this is how their society runs. Moral commitment compels most people to be law abiding, but large-scale corruption seriously compromises a society's belief in the force of its laws.

Finally, large-scale corruption encourages 'state capture', whereby a company influences the laws of a state, institution, or governmental policy in areas like the environment, taxation, or mining. Ultimately, the rule of law is imperilled because citizens in such circumstances tend to take the law into their hands. As David Bayley pointed out, 'If the elite is believed to be widely and thoroughly corrupt, the man-in-the-street will see little reason why he too should not gather what he can for himself and his loved ones.'[36] Thus, junior officials will often resort to seeking bribes from those in need of government services, especially the economically and socially vulnerable. This invariably weakens and jeopardises critical institutions, systems and structures of government, and the entire social fabric of a society. Because corruption in many African states generally begins at the highest level of political authority and survives on a chain of political and economic networks, there tends to be a conspiracy of silence among those involved. If the state and its resources are literally 'owned and controlled' by suspected perpetrators, they are less likely to be motivated to address corruption. The rule of law is thus inevitably substituted with the 'rule by the will' of high-ranking public officials.

As already noted, all categories of corruption are interconnected and have varying degrees of damaging effects especially on the economically and socially vulnerable. While petty corruption affects society less as compared to large-scale corruption, it is the latter that provides the fertile soil for the former to germinate. However, although the roots of petty corruption are not as deep, they are comparably corrosive, and can undermine long-term social order and cohesion. While the focus of this book is on large-scale corruption, it does not suggest that other forms of corruption should be ignored. On the contrary, the discussions throughout the book demonstrate how large-scale corruption can trigger other forms of corruption, and it is argued that effectively combating large-scale corruption will have a spin-off effect on the efforts to prevent and combat all forms of corruption.

[36] David Bayley, 'The Effects of Corruption in a Developing Nation' (1966) 19 *Western Political Quarterly* 719, 725.

# Part I

# Framework

# 1

# *Corruption and Human Rights Law: Historical and Conceptual Frameworks*

## INTRODUCTION

THE EFFECTS OF corruption on economic growth and development have long been recognised and are well documented in the literature,[1] but the idea of corruption as a violation of human rights entered international law discourse only relatively recently.[2] Whereas the effects of corruption on human rights may seem self-evident, this link is rarely seriously explored. Rarely does academic discussion on corruption and human rights contain either a conceptual or a theoretical foundation for a relationship between these two ideas. When it does, the discussion still overlooks the needed harmonisation and integration of these concepts to overcome the legal and other challenges that result when corruption is viewed from the perspective of human rights. Furthermore, despite its long history and existence, a truly satisfactory definition of corruption has not yet evolved. Corruption is still narrowly considered as 'ordinary crime' and 'victimless'. At the heart of the matter is the reliance on a restrictive notion of corruption to address the grave problem that it has become (and its effects on human rights). In addition, the definitions that do exist are usually vague, imprecise, sometime confusing, and limited to the criminal and law enforcement fields. They almost never include the *victim element* of corruption. Similarly, while there is international consensus and support for the fight against corruption, there is no universal agreement as to the definition of the word 'corruption'. This arguably has obstructed a better understanding of the problem and its effects on human rights and on legal and judicial institutions in developing regions like Africa. While a general concern is often raised in the literature about the lack of a universal definition, the concept remains undefined, and the possible ways to overcome this challenge have received little investigation.

[1] See, generally, Arnold J Heidenheimer (ed), *Political Corruption: Readings in Comparative Analysis* (New Brunswick, NJ: Transaction Publishers, 1978).

[2] See, W Michael Reisman, 'Harnessing International Law to Restrain and Recapture Indigenous Spoliations' (1989) 83 *American Journal of International Law* 56–57.

This chapter sets out the historical and conceptual contexts for the arguments that connect corruption with human rights. Foundational issues such as the meaning and evolution of both corruption and human rights and the 'justifications' given for corruption, are detailed. Included in this discussion are the rule of law, justice and fairness issues raised by the phenomenon of corruption; the reasons why the struggle for human rights and governance are so important, and the question of whether there is a human rights obligation to combat corruption, are also addressed. The chapter also discusses some of the theories of the rule of law and of victimisation, to provide a foundation for the connection between corruption and human rights. The concept of state (and its relationship with its people) and how it has been (re)defined over time – from the idea of state as the absolute and supreme authority to a representative one – is detailed. This chapter fills the void described above, as the reasons for an expanded definition of corruption that incorporate human rights elements are advanced.

## HISTORICAL OVERVIEW

As noted, corruption is as old as humanity (presumably starting with the 'apple scandal' in the Garden of Eden),[3] and its origins, and the efforts to combat it, can be traced back millennia and within several cultures and religions.[4] For example, Michael Levi and Monty Raphael stated that archaeologists in Syria unearthed an administrative centre of the Assyrian civilisation that contained evidence that bribery was prevalent as early as 3,400 years ago.[5] An interior minister's special archive listed data about

[3] See Genesis 3:1–13. For historical overview of corruption, see Henry H Rossbacher and Tracy W Young, 'The Foreign Corrupt Practices Act: An American Response to Corruption', in Barry Rider (ed), *Corruption: The Enemy Within* (The Hague: Kluwer Law International, 1997), 273.

[4] John T Noonan, Jr, *Bribes* (New York: Macmillan Publishing Company, 1984), xiii. There is a general paucity of literature on the evolution of corruption. According to Jacob van Klaveren, 'Corruption as a historical phenomenon is a problem that has never been dealt with systematically'. Jacob van Klaveren, 'Corruption as a Historical Phenomenon' in Arnold J Heidenheimer et al (ed), *Political Corruption: A Handbook* (New Brunswick, NJ: Transaction Publishers, 1999) 73. Nonetheless, available literature shows that corruption was widespread throughout Europe in the eighteenth century.

[5] Michael Levi and Monty Raphael, 'Anti-corruption – A Signpost for Transactional Lawyers' (1999) 1 *Business Law Journal* 80. Corruption was recognised as a problem among public officials in the ancient world. For instance, Indira Carr and Opi Outhwaite quote an Indian writer, Kautilya, who wrote on statecraft (*c* 250 BCE): 'Just as it is impossible not to taste the honey or the poison that finds itself at the tip of the tongue, so it is impossible for a government servant not to eat up, at least, a bit of the king's revenue. Just as fish moving under water cannot possibly be found out either as drinking or not drinking water, so government servants employed in the government work cannot be found out (while) taking money (for themselves)'. Indira Carr and Opi Outhwaite, 'The OECD Anti-Bribery Convention Ten Years On' (2008) 3 *Manchester Journal of International Economic Law* 4.

employees accepting bribes, the names of senior officials, and even the name of an Assyrian princess.[6] Maryvonne Génaux sees the development of corruption as analogous to that of the Christian–Western basis for modern law.[7] According to her, corruption fundamentally denotes injustice, as conceived in the Bible.[8] On this account, the 'apple scandal' in the Garden of Eden certainly denigrated divine commandment, corrupted the purity of Eden, breached the principles of justice that God obviously stands for, and ultimately separated man from divinity. This biblical perspective of corruption[9] largely reflects its evolutionary nature.

Furthermore, traditional African culture generally determines a person's place in society more by contributions to society's well-being than by birth or station in life.[10] Class-consciousness, which is a prevailing distinctive mark of Western culture, was considered to be prejudicial to the larger interests of society, and discouraged.[11] Thus, although a few African states, such as Ghana, 'probably experienced the reign of a corrupt dynasty between the sixth and eighth centuries',[12] corruption was not in general a common feature of the indigenous African system of government.[13] Decades of foreign rule following the Berlin Conference (1884–85) and the subsequent arbitrary and politically motivated division of Africa into different spheres of exploitation undermined African civil society.[14] Colonialism, slavery, and the resultant patrimonial African states, combined with the corrupt tendencies of some indigenous pioneers and 'activists' for Africa's independence, subverted hitherto traditional structures, institutions and values, or made them subservient to personal economic and political needs.[15]

By the time of their independence, not only were many African states left without valid structures for the future, but also corruption had already begun spreading its devastating effects across the continent. As former Senegalese President Abdoulaye Wade stressed at the United Nations Office on Drugs and Crime (UNODC) support seminar in Dakar in 2000, 'We have the will to fight corruption. We need to be uninhibited with those who make us think that our countries are corrupt. I reject that and I

[6] Levi and Raphael, 'Anti-corruption' (n 5), 80.

[7] Maryvonne Génaux, 'Social Sciences and the Evolving Concept of Corruption' (2004) 42 *Crime, Law and Social Change* 13–24.

[8] ibid.

[9] ibid. Several aspects of the Bible (King James Version) prohibit corruption. For example, in Exodus 23:8: 'You shall not take a bribe, for a bribe blinds the clear-sighted and subverts the cause of the just.'

[10] Nsongurua J Udombana, 'Fighting Corruption Seriously? Africa's Anti-corruption Convention' (2003) 7 *Singapore Journal of International & Comparative Law* 452.

[11] ibid.

[12] ibid.

[13] ibid.

[14] ibid.

[15] ibid.

cannot accept it. Africa is not corrupt, even if there are some corrupt individuals.'[16] Yet, this statement contrasts sharply with that of Mobutu Sese Seko Kuku Ngbendu wa Za Banga, former 'leader' of the Democratic Republic of Congo (DRC), who once admonished the citizens on how to 'cleverly' engage in corruption: 'If you steal, do not steal too much at a time. You may be arrested. Steal cleverly, little by little. And if you succeed in stealing, invest what you have stolen in the country itself. Those who export what they steal are the enemies of the Republic.'[17] He clearly did not fully practise what he preached, as most of his stolen wealth was stashed in foreign banks. After bleeding his country dry for 32 years, and being out of power, he boasted (rather arrogantly) that he could personally pay off his country's multi-billion dollar debt, but was unsure if he would ever get his money back.[18] In any case, the persistent low ranking of many African states on Transparency International's (TI) Corruption Perceptions Index (CPI) would seem to suggest the contrary. It may therefore be difficult to plausibly contest allegations of corruption involving indigenous African leaders.

Similarly, it is true that the existence of corruption in African states can correctly be traced in part to colonial domination and to a 'lasting colonial legacy' (for example, the practice of divide and rule, and colonial constitutions),[19] and that a proper understanding of the problem of corruption may not be possible without considering the 'colonialisation context'. However, while the excuses of 'colonial domination' and 'colonial legacy' might have been tenable during the early years of independence, these can no longer be properly relied upon to justify prevailing corruption by senior officials of many African states, especially since colonial rule ended over five decades ago, a period which should arguably have been enough time for 'African nationalists' to put right whatever may have gone wrong during colonisation. In any event, continued focus on the role of colonial rule in the 'corruption problem', rather than on the responsibility of African states and leaders, would remain a stumbling

[16] West Africa commits for implementation of the United Nations Convention against Corruption and validates a regional action plans a regional, www.unodc.org/westandcentralafrica/en/wssenegal1010.html.

[17] Quoted in JF Medard, 'Public Corruption in Africa: A Comparative Perspective' (1986) 1 *Corruption and Reform* 15.

[18] The Independent, 'Mobutu takes the money and runs to a safe haven', www.independent.co.uk/news/world/mobutu-takes-the-money-and-runs-to-a-safe-haven-1261945.html.

[19] Barbara Crutchfield George and Kathleen A Lacey, 'A Coalition of Industrialized Nations, Multilateral Development Banks, and Non-Governmental Organizations: A Pivotal Complement to Current Anti-Corruption Initiatives' (2000) 33 *Cornell International Law Journal* 555. Of particular note during the colonial period was the notorious use of official secret laws empowering governments to classify all their documents as top secret, secret, confidential, or restricted. It has been argued that the colonisation of the corruption discourse has had a profound and uneven impact on conceptual practices and developments. Also, during the Cold War, donors ignored corruption in Africa despite evidence of its widespread use. Ibid.

block to the efforts to address the problem. Relatedly, foreign corporations have frequently been accused of encouraging or facilitating corruption in Africa.[20] The 'explanations' why corporations from countries with less corruption engage in bribery in poor regions like Africa have included: competitive necessity, supposed respect for local 'cultural norms', extortion, and the inability or unwillingness to control rogue employees.[21] Nonetheless, on balance, these reasons alone are insufficient, especially in the face of the human consequences of such corruption in the continent. Also, while foreign corporations have for many years been complicit in corruption across the continent, African states and 'leaders' no doubt retain primary responsibility, insofar as 'it takes two to tango'.

Moreover, despite its longstanding history and effect on societies and civilisations, a conspiracy of silence about corruption was the norm. Prior to the 1990s, the word 'corruption' rarely featured in the lexicon of international relations, despite concerted efforts and initiatives started by the US government in the 1970s to influence the global agenda in this field.[22] Corruption was considered a national crime, so there was little international support for fighting it, or even concern about it. Notably in the West, governments (such as Germany's, where *bribes* were *tax-deductible* as an ordinary and necessary business expense) and international financial institutions (such as the World Bank and the International Monetary Fund, which acknowledged that 'corruption was endemic, [a] pervasive problem in the implementation of aid programs')[23] resisted attempts to internationalise corruption and its impact.[24] Such reluctance to condemn corruption (in all its forms, in particular bribery), despite its widespread occurrence in international business transactions, especially between developed and developing countries, seems unjustifiable but presumably was due in part to geopolitical or economic concerns and in part because it appeared to impinge on the 'sovereignty' or 'cultural sensitivity' of other states.

Nonetheless, the problem of corruption became a subject of international attention in the 1990s, when it became the most important policy issue in international economies.[25] As noted, this international attention was precipitated initially when the United States enacted its groundbreaking Foreign Corrupt Practices Act (FCPA) in 1977 following the Watergate scandal, which involved money laundering through foreign countries and the use of campaign funds to bribe foreign officials.

[20] David Hess and Thomas W Dunfee, 'Fighting Corruption: A Principled Approach; The C2 Principles (Combating Corruption)' (2000) 33 *Cornell International Law Journal* 594.

[21] ibid.

[22] ibid 595.

[23] See Alexander Jonathan Brown, 'What Are We Trying to Measure? Reviewing the Basics of Corruption Definition' in Charles Sampford et al (eds), *Measuring Corruption* (Aldershot: Ashgate, 2006): 57.

[24] Hess and Dunfee, 'Fighting Corruption' (n 20) 595.

[25] ibid 595.

Although enacted as national legislation, the FCPA inspired, among other activities, an international wave of anticorruption initiatives. Other factors that subsequently increased global attention to corrupt activities include a wave of scandals and severe economic crises (and the costs and uncertainties associated with foreign bribery); the defeat of Communism and the end of the Cold War; the process of globalisation; the emergence of democracy in many parts of the world; global acceptance of the regime of human rights; the increasing role of the media and advanced technology (such as the Internet, mobile phones and so on); the increased work of the International Chamber of Commerce on governance issues; and not least, the establishment of Transparency International in 1993.[26]

These factors took corruption out of the purely political or ethical realm by focusing attention on its economic impact nationally, regionally, and internationally, as failures of governance in one country reached beyond national boundaries to the capital markets, international institutions, individual consumers, or investors half-way around the world.[27] Furthermore, because Watergate gave impetus to this development and served as the precursor to the fight against corruption in international business transactions, the FCPA that came after the scandal deserves further discussion. Since the enactment of the FCPA in 1977,[28] the United States has, in fact, prioritised the fight against corruption, making it a key foreign policy objective and extending efforts to encourage other countries to adopt and implement similar legislation.[29] However, this effort by the United States

[26] It has also been stated that corruption became a matter of international concern in order 'to improve social and economic development of developing countries'. See Julio Bacio Terracino, *The International Legal Framework against Corruption: States' Obligations to Prevent and Repress Corruption* (Antwerp: Intersentia, 2012) 1.

[27] ibid.

[28] The FCPA has two key provisions: accounting and anti-bribery. The accounting provisions include the requirements of record-keeping and financial disclosure according to the 1934 Securities Exchange Act. The anti-bribery provisions criminalise the direct and indirect (that is, through intermediaries) bribery of foreign officials to obtain business or to secure an improper advantage. As noted, both provisions aim to remedy the problems that arose as a result of the Watergate investigation of improper payments by: ensuring proper recording-keeping of transactions; removing the opportunity for companies to falsify transactions or to hide improper transactions; ensuring that record-keeping captures the quantitative and qualitative elements of transactions; and requiring the establishment and maintenance of an internal accounting system. The US Department of Justice is responsible for the criminal enforcement of the FCPA by subjecting corrupt corporations and individuals to fines and/or imprisonment, while the US Securities and Exchange Commission is responsible for the enforcement of civil sanctions, including through fines. For a comprehensive discussion and analysis of the FCPA, see Andrea Goldbarg, 'The Foreign Corrupt Practices Act and Structural Corruption' (2000) 18 *Boston University International Law Journal* 273 and Kari Lynn Diersen, 'Foreign Corrupt Practices Act' (1999) 36 *American Criminal Law Review* 753.

[29] Goldbarg, 'The Foreign Corrupt Practices Act' (n 28). Nonetheless, scholars are divided as to the importance and utility of the FCPA in combating corruption. While the legislation is significant in the international fight, the concept has been rejected, as, for example, 'imperialist, ill-conceived, and imprudent because the needed element of extraterritoriality is paternalistic, intrusive and imposes foreign values'. Ibid 280.

to 'export' the fight against corruption has prompted many scholars to question what they call 'the morality' of the US approach. For example, David A Gantz has suggested that, 'The FCPA essentially reflects the view that corruption, and in particular its subset bribery, is so immoral that not even the loss of business by American companies could justify it.'[30]

Yet, while its application extends beyond the reach of US territory, the FCPA was not disguised as a 'shared international morality', as it was clearly designed to respond to a specific internal US problem: Watergate. In any case, such criticism would seem to ignore or minimise the pioneering and positive role the FCPA played in the global fight against corruption. Substantively, the FCPA is remarkably expansive and applies to both corporate entities and individuals (on the basis of nationality and territoriality principles). It applies to 'issuers', 'domestic concerns', and any 'other person'[31] who, while within a US territory, performs an act in furtherance of prohibited payment. But physical presence of the bribing party on US territory is not required, and the bribe itself does not have to take place within a US territory as long as some action leading to the eventual payment of the bribe occurred in the United States. This provision thus extends the FCPA's reach to any foreign conduct when, for example, a phone call or email can be traced back to a US territory. Payments made to a person who is not a foreign official are also illegal when such payments are made with knowledge that a portion of those payments will be offered, directly or indirectly, to a foreign official.[32] The FCPA also requires firms that are subject to reporting requirements under the US securities laws to keep books and records 'in reasonable detail' so as to adequately reflect corporate transactions and to improve internal accounting controls and to generally ensure that financial transactions can be properly accounted for. These accounting requirements are presumably designed to make it impossible, or at least difficult, for companies to maintain 'slush funds' for illegal purposes or otherwise conceal illicit payments in legitimate accounts.

The FCPA does not, however, effectively apply to foreign subsidiaries or affiliates of US firms, although it does apply to US citizens, employees, or executives who meet the knowledge requirements of circumstances

[30] David A Gantz, 'Globalizing Sanctions against Foreign Bribery: The Emergence of a New International Legal Consensus Citation' (1997–1998) 18 *Northwestern University Law Review* 457.

[31] The term 'issuers' is defined to include foreign and domestic corporations that issue securities registered in the United States or that are otherwise required to file periodic reports with the US Securities and Exchange Commission. The term 'domestic concern' is defined to include US citizens, nationals, and residents, as well as any incorporated or unincorporated business entities that have their principal place of business in the United States or are organised under US law. 'Other person' presumably applies to any foreign national and any business, such as sole proprietorships, organised under foreign law, as long as the act was committed to further prohibited conduct that occurred in a US territory.

[32] Gantz, 'Globalizing Sanctions' (n 30) 457.

that suggest illicit activities; that is, an awareness of a 'high probability of the existence of such circumstance'.[33] Nonetheless, while the FCPA offers broad coverage, there are issues with it. For example, it does not address bribery between entirely private entities.[34] The FCPA also excludes 'greasing' payments for 'routine government actions' by foreign officials, such as obtaining official documents, the provision of basic utilities, and so on. It also excludes the legality of payments under the law of the host country or reimbursement for allowed travel and lodging arising out of promotional activities aimed at obtaining or retaining new business. The legal payment exception is a narrow one, however. It applies only to actions expressly permitted under local laws: the failure of a foreign government to enforce local anti-bribery laws does not constitute a defence. Even so, as noted, the FCPA intervention aimed to repair the damaged reputation of US companies abroad, and for nearly two decades the United States remained the only country that criminalised the conduct of its citizens whether located domestically or internationally. This presumably placed US companies at a competitive disadvantage and undermined their ability to compete for business globally.[35]

In the face of such reality, the United States moved quickly to impose intense pressure on other countries to ensure parity of actions and to discourage foreign competitors from paying bribes (tax deductible or otherwise) to obtain business. This effort, initially unfruitful (because other countries had little incentive to agree a global anticorruption treaty that would presumably level the playing field), and considered 'premature',[36] ultimately succeeded, as it resulted in the adoption in 1997 of the Organisation for Economic Cooperation and Development's (OECD) Convention on Combating Bribery of Foreign Public Officials in International Business Transactions.[37] As the title suggests, the convention is limited only to a specific form of corruption – active bribery (that is, to promise, offer, or give a bribe) as it relates to business transactions. The convention requires states parties to criminalise the direct or indirect intentional offer, promise, or giving of any undue pecuniary or other advantage to a foreign public official to influence such official in the performance of his or her official duties, and with the aim of obtaining or retaining business or other improper advantage in the conduct of international business.[38] Combating corruption thus became a broader objective

[33] ibid.

[34] In contrast, the United Kingdom's Bribery Act 2010 prohibits bribery of both foreign officials and private companies and individuals.

[35] Gantz, 'Globalizing Sanctions' (n 30) 457.

[36] See Jan Wouters, Cedric Ryngaertt and Ann Sofie Cloots, 'The International Legal Framework Against Corruption: Achievements And Challenges' (2013) 14 *Melbourne Journal of International Law* 209.

[37] Gantz, 'Globalizing Sanctions' (n 30) 457.

[38] FCPA, Art 1.

of developed nations for economic growth and equitable development. Yet, as noted, only a restricted conception of corruption (in the form of bribery in business transactions) was recognised; and the convention applies only to 'foreign bribery'. Notwithstanding these limitations, the United States rather parochially (but admittedly consistent with the requirement of international law) amended the FCPA in 1998 to align it with the OECD Convention by enacting the International Anti-Bribery Act, designed to 'improve the competitiveness of American business and promote foreign commerce',[39] as well as to promote stronger local governments and to create a more reliable investment climate.

Since the adoption of the OECD Convention, international and regional treaties and standards against corruption have proliferated, and today around 14 such treaties and countless resolutions, declarations, and so on, exist on the issue. In 1994, the Organization of American States (OAS) recognised that corruption was undermining progress and preventing its members from establishing competitive markets, equitable development, and democratic reform.[40] The OAS did not have to wait for too long to augment its expressed political commitment with a legally binding instrument; two years later, in 1996, it successfully negotiated and adopted the Inter-American Convention against Corruption (hereafter, OAS Convention). The OAS Convention is a notable achievement both in terms of its rapid adoption and its scope. It requires mutual legal and judicial assistance, and more broadly criminalises transnational bribery and illicit enrichment.[41] In contrast with prevailing practice of narrowed prohibitions of corruption, the OAS Convention criminalises both sides of bribery (that is, the demand and supply sides). As another example of increased regulation, in 1998, leaders at the Santiago Summit called for broader ratification of the OAS Convention, and a symposium to promote its implementation was subsequently organised.

The OAS leaders renewed their commitment to codes of conduct for public officials, to legislation that requires disclosure of assets, and to increases in public participation. Similarly, the leaders endorsed the San

[39] See Goldbarg, 'The Foreign Corrupt Practices Act' (n 28) 279. Although important in several respects, the 1998 amendment did not fundamentally alter the foundation of the FCPA. It nonetheless introduced five key changes: (1) in relation to the criminalisation of payments, it amended 'inducing him to do or omit to do any act' to 'with any improper advantage'; (2) the FCPA only covered issuers with securities registered under the 1934 Securities and Exchange Act, but the 1998 amendment broadened that to 'any person', thus including foreign residents who commit corrupt acts while in the United States; (3) it incorporated the OECD Convention that includes officials of public international organisations; (4) it altered the definition of jurisdiction to incorporate 'acts of US businesses and nationals in furtherance of unlawful payments that take place wholly outside the United States'; and (5) it ensured that both US citizens and foreign nationals working in any capacity with US companies are subject to both civil and criminal penalties. Ibid, 280.

[40] ibid.

[41] ibid.

Jose Business Forum recommendation to launch negotiation of a Free Trade Area of the Americas (FTAA) agreement on transparency in procurement. The Santiago Summit also achieved agreement on other elements of a comprehensive attack on corruption. For example, it adopted a Plan of Action, which called for important complementary measures to increase transparency in campaign finance, to enhance the independence of the judiciary, to support a free press, and to promote educational programmes on integrity and ethics.

Furthermore, the various initiatives in the Americas were being considered and replicated in other regions. Thus, the Council of Europe adopted the Criminal Law Convention on Corruption and the Civil Law on Corruption in 1998 and 1999, respectively. These conventions well illustrate the several features that characterise the Council of Europe's approach to fighting corruption. For one, it is multidisciplinary, which underscores corruption as a complex, multi-faceted problem that requires different types of action at different levels. For another, it incorporates a monitoring mechanism, which shows the intention of the drafters and political leaders to ensure that the instruments that they adopt are credible. In contrast, the 'mechanism' established to monitor compliance with the OAS Convention seemed 'an afterthought'. As a further demonstration of its commitment to fight corruption comprehensively, the Council of Europe in 2008 established the Group of States against Corruption (GRECO) to monitor member states' efforts in promoting 'The Guiding Principles for the Fight against Corruption' resolution. It should be noted that all Council of Europe instruments are linked to the monitoring mechanism provided under the GRECO agreement.[42] This clearly is an important strategy for effective evaluation of states' compliance with their obligations arising from the instruments, and the efficacy, enforcement, and impact of any such initiative.

As other regions were developing and negotiating instruments to combat corruption, Africa's participation was rather sparse, and restricted to its role within the United Nations. Thus, the continent's noticeable initiatives only began at sub-regional levels in the 2000s with the negotiation and adoption of the Southern Africa Development Community (SADC) Protocol against Corruption in Blantyre, Malawi, in August 2001, and of the Economic Community of West African States (ECOWAS) Protocol on the Fight against Corruption in Accra, Ghana, in December of the same year. A continent-wide initiative occurred two years later, when the

[42] GRECO monitors states' implementation and compliance with the Criminal Law Convention on Corruption. GRECO aims to improve the capacity of its member states to fight corruption through a dynamic and flexible process of mutual evaluation and peer pressure, compliance with their undertakings in this field, and, in particular, with the 20 Guiding Principles resolution in the fight against corruption. GRECO is open to equal participation of member states and non-member states of the Council of Europe.

African Union (AU) Convention on Preventing and Combating Corruption was adopted in Maputo, Mozambique, in July 2003. It is useful to point out, though, that some important but isolated activities took place in Africa before the inception of binding criminal instruments against corruption. For example, there was a forum in 1999 in Kampala, Uganda (which was followed by a meeting in Washington DC) that discussed (albeit in generic terms, and within a non-binding framework) the relationship between corruption, human rights, and democracy, and called on African states to follow examples within the OECD and in the Americas to implement measures against corruption.

To cite other examples of non-binding initiatives across the continent during this time, in 1999 some African countries adopted the famous 'principles to address corruption' ('25 Principles to Combat Corruption in Africa'), specifically in international business and development programmes across the continent.[43] In addition, the 'Accra Declaration', adopted by ECOWAS ministers in June 2001, called on ECOWAS to create a comprehensive Protocol on Corruption.[44] According to the declaration, 'corruption is not only a criminal issue but also impacts the dynamics of national and international development that deserve collective solution'.[45]

Rather surprisingly, while anti-corruption initiatives were being embraced across the regions of the world, similar initiatives within the United Nations initially started rather slowly, bogged down by the politics, relations, and benefits of international business transactions and other national interests of states. According to Vito Tanzi, this lethargy was due in part to the advantage of being on the 'right side' in the Cold War, and therefore being able to turn the other cheek to corruption in one's state or one's inner circle.[46] Another explanation for the slowness was presumably that donor countries were not keen to advertise the fact that their expensive aid programmes were going into the pockets of 'petty dictators'.[47]

[43] For discussion on the principles, see Alhaji BM Marong, 'Toward a Normative Consensus against Corruption: Legal Effects of the Principles to Combat Corruption in Africa' (2002) 30 *Denver Journal of International Law and Policy* 100.

[44] ibid.

[45] ibid. See also Accra Declaration, West Africa, 'ECOWAS Justice Ministers Move against Corruption' (5 June 2001), www.allafrica.com/stories/200106050180.html.

[46] Vito Tanzi, 'Corruption Around the World: Causes, Consequences, Scope, and Cures, International Money Fund' (1998) 45 *Staff Papers* 56. The United Nations' initiatives against corruption grew very rapidly after the mid-1970s, when the General Assembly adopted the Code of Conduct for Law Enforcement Officials (in resolution 34/169). For detailed background on several resolutions, declarations, codes, and so on, adopted by the UN on corruption or corruption-related issues since the mid-70s, see UNODC, 'Travaux Préparatoires of the negotiations for the elaboration of the United Nations Convention against Corruption', www.unodc.org/unodc/en/treaties/CAC/travaux-preparatoires.html.

[47] Tanzi, 'Corruption Around the World' (n 46) 56.

As noted earlier, it was not until the mid-1970s that the media started to publicise occurrences of corruption and that international organisations subsequently began to take some action, basically following the United States' FCPA model of a criminal and law enforcement approach to corruption.[48] These 'media events' presumably prompted some developing[49] and Central European countries to pressure the UN General Assembly to pass a resolution[50] condemning corrupt practices in international commerce and calling for unilateral and multilateral action. Though clearly non-binding, the resolution requires states to take appropriate legal action, including prosecution, within their jurisdictions against transnational corporations. It also includes provisions on international cooperation, in particular in the area of information sharing. However, the resolution focused narrowly on the supply side of bribery, and had little substance.

More actions soon followed within the United Nations, when it mandated its Economic and Social Council (ECOSOC) to establish a specific policy on corruption, and in 1979 the council drafted an international agreement that could be used to prevent illicit payments. But due to a combination of factors, including lack of political will, the draft agreement was not made operative. Thereafter work in the UN on corruption progressed slowly though steadily with the Venice Economic Summit, which was organised in July 1980, again after intense pressure from the United States. It is worthwhile to point out that while this agreement was being drafted, the UN was also preparing a code of conduct for transnational corporations. The self-regulating document called on corporations to maintain accurate records of payments and to refrain from using subversive activities to interfere in the internal affairs of countries, including offering bribes to influence a public official's duties. However, despite its obvious potential, the code of conduct died prematurely and was never adopted.

Previously, in 1976, the UN had established an Ad Hoc Intergovernmental Working Group on Corrupt Practices to create a proposal for an international agreement to prevent and eliminate illicit payments in international financial transactions. In its report, submitted in 1978, the group proposed such a text and suggested a diplomatic conference to negotiate and adopt the agreement. However, another committee was instead established to continue this work. It did not matter, as the UN's priority had altered to transnational *corporations'* code of conduct. An initiative on an interna-

[48] For a comprehensive treatment on the evolution of the international fight against corruption, see Alejandro Posadas, 'Combating Corruption under International Law' (2000) 10 *Duke Journal of Comparative & International Law* 345.

[49] Eleven of these countries were from Africa: Algeria, Benin, Egypt, Gabon, Libya, Madagascar, Nigeria, Somalia, Togo, Tanzania, and Upper Volta.

[50] GA Res 3514 , UN GAOR, 2d Comm, 30th Sess, UN Doc A/10467 (1975).

tional agreement on illicit payments was however visited once again in 1979, following the introduction, yet again, by the United States of a draft resolution calling for an international conference to negotiate and conclude an international agreement. This proposal, however, was blocked by 77 member states, led by India, insisting rather flimsily that any such conference should wait until the transnational corporations' code of conduct was adopted. This proved influential, and as a consequence, the process of creating this code was again bogged down in the tensions and politics between the developed and developing nations at that time.[51]

It was not until the late 1980s and early 1990s that the UN was literally compelled to engage again with the issue of corruption, initially within the framework of its initiative against international organised crime. This included 'trans-nationalization of economic activity [and] the round of multilateral trade negotiations aimed at establishing an international regime on foreign direct investment measures'.[52] As stated in its 1989 resolution:

> [O]rganized crime has increased in many parts of the world and has become more transnational in character, leading, in particular, to the spread of such negative phenomena as violence, terrorism, corruption, illegal trade in narcotic drugs and, in general, *undermining the development process, impairing the quality of life and threatening human rights and fundamental freedoms.* [Emphasis added.][53]

A year later, in 1990, the UN published a manual elaborating national measures against corruption and proposed recommendations on how states could develop national anti-corruption programmes.[54] That same year the UN General Assembly adopted recommendations on international cooperation for crime prevention and criminal justice, including specific language calling on all nations to tackle corruption,[55] a recommendation that appeared to be rather utopian at the time. Other remarkable recommendations included requiring states to investigate and prosecute corruption, recover stolen funds, address corrupt practices by enterprises, review national criminal laws on corruption, develop non-criminal measures to combat corruption, and train law enforcement and

[51] The discussion on the code of conduct for transnational corporations stalled primarily because of disagreement – over the binding nature of the instrument, on whether international law or national law should govern the issue of compensation, on sovereignty and natural resources, but most importantly because of the political division and tensions. See Posadas, 'Combating Corruption' (n 48) 369.

[52] ibid.

[53] ESC Res 1989/70, UN ESCOR, 1st Sess, 50th mtg, 1; UN Doc E/RES/1989/70, E/1989/INF/7 (1989).

[54] *Manual Prepared by the Secretariat: Practical Measures Against Corruption, Eighth United Nations Congress on the Prevention of Crime and the Treatment of Offenders*, UN Doc A/CONF 144/8 (1990), revised by UN Doc A/CONF 144/8/Corr 1 (1990).

[55] GA Res 45/107, UN GAOR, 45th Sess, Agenda Item 100, UN Doc A/RES/45/107.

judicial officials.[56] More progress was made with the adoption in 1996 of the UN's International Code of Conduct for Public Officials.[57] This probably proved a turning point for anti-corruption initiatives within the UN, resulting in among other initiatives the development of a series of further recommendations for states to prevent and combat corruption, (for example, establishing independent anticorruption mechanisms to monitor the conduct of government officials, building national capacities and partnerships to fight corruption, and developing a framework for cooperation among nations). The UN also established several agencies to address corruption, the most important of them being the UNODC.

Yet, up until this point, many of the early efforts by the UN were sporadic and limited to bribery in international business transactions.[58] However, this restrictive approach to corruption was jettisoned when the UN Convention against Corruption was negotiated and adopted in Mexico on 9 December 2003, thus ending a rather long and tedious journey for a comprehensive, globally and legally acceptable criminal law instrument against corruption. More significantly, the convention contains important and ground-breaking provisions on asset recovery and international cooperation and assistance. It should be noted however that apart from specific treaties and declarations against corruption, other instruments of a general nature exist that may have implications for the fight against corruption.

In sum, corruption, initially treated only as a crime against the state and society, and then expanded as an economic crime and problem for international business transactions, is now increasingly considered a serious socio-economic threat to individuals and communities. Even so, as this chapter explains, the two major issues at present are that criminal law instruments against corruption remain focused on the prosecution and punishment of state officials (and not on the effects corruption has on people), and nearly all of the conventions and standards that have been adopted only describe corruption, but do not define it. So, despite the multiplicity of anti-corruption initiatives, at the moment, there is no single comprehensive list of acts that is universally accepted as constituting corruption. In addition, probably with the rare exception of the OECD

[56] ibid.

[57] GA Res 51/59, UN GAOR, 51st Sess, 82nd Plenary Mtg, Item 101, Annex, UN Doc A/RES/51/59 (1996).

[58] Other examples of standards-setting at the UN at the time included the Resolution on International Cooperation against Corruption and Bribery in International Commercial Transactions 1975, and the 1996 Declaration against Corruption and Bribery in International Commercial Transactions. The latter was broader than the one adopted in 1975 and captured both the active and passive elements of bribery, required states to end tax deductions on bribery payments, encouraged consideration of criminalising 'illicit enrichment' by government officials, and ended the practice of bank secrecy. It is useful to point out that the term 'illicit enrichment' appeared for the first time in the 1996 Inter-American Convention against Corruption.

mechanism, the treaties that have thus far been adopted and endorsed by states have not generally established any strong enforcement mechanisms to monitor or enforce states' compliance with their obligations. Whereas corruption is now universally condemned, any discussion of implementation and enforcement mechanisms has sadly become secondary to the overriding considerations of perceived national sovereignty and interests.

## MYRIAD DEFINITIONS OF CORRUPTION

The term 'corruption', probably the most used word (inevitably subjectively and controversially, but almost always habitually) in the whole vocabulary of politics, is derived from the Latin verb *curruptus*, which is translated as 'to break'.[59] Linguistically, the word is used rather pejoratively and censoriously to refer to any of the following: 'dishonest or illegal behaviour, especially of people in authority'; 'the act or effect of making someone or something change from moral to immoral standards of behaviour'.[60] Looked at closely, the definitions may not be as straightforward as they first appear. However, the definitions presuppose legal prohibition of some 'dishonest' conduct as 'corrupt', and also reflect some universal moral sensibilities, seeming to suggest that corrupt acts are those which do not agree with some moral and social norms presumably of universal application. Clearly, corruption would encompass dishonest and illegal acts. Together, they indicate abuse of entrusted position or misuse of authority for personal gain, which may not necessarily (or directly) be monetary. Yet, corruption can occur without the corrupt necessarily violating any duty.[61] Similarly, not every dishonest act may be corruption in the legal sense of the word, insofar as such act is not condemned, legally prohibited and censured.[62] Therefore, in addition to lacking specificity, the definitions would appear to invoke emotion about corruption, and potentially could act to prejudice an accused. As such, the definitions seem to be of limited legal value.

In addition, while it is true that 'corruption' is a phenomenon that is universally condemned, the word is overlaid with many meanings and connotations in several languages, cultures, and legal codes.[63] It is also often the case that a number of somewhat equivalent words, such as 'loot' and 'graft', are deployed as variants of corruption, but they are by no

[59] *Black's Law Dictionary*, 7th edn (St Paul, MN: West Group, 1999) 443.

[60] *Oxford Advanced Learner's Dictionary*, 6th edn (Oxford: Oxford University Press, 2000) 281.

[61] David Bayley, 'The Effects of Corruption in a Developing Nation' in Arnold J Heidenheimer (ed), *Political Corruption: Readings in Comparative Analysis* (New Brunswick, NJ: Transaction Publishers, 1978) 522.

[62] ibid.

[63] See Heidenheimer (ed), *Political Corruption: Readings in Comparative Analysis* (n 1) 3.

means entirely synonymous. Sometimes, too, individuals and groups ordinarily excluded from decision-making processes deploy the term, presumably to 'gain influence over the actions of the bureaucracy'.[64] Even so, the essential feature of the different meanings of corruption remains its emotive and 'ethical connotations'.[65] If it is true that knowledge comes from seeing, most people will probably 'know corruption when they see it'.[66] The use of such a phrase, however, offers little benefit in terms of clarifying corruption as a legal concept, and seems to short-circuit necessary attempts to define corruption. Nonetheless, it cannot be denied that corruption is at once a legal, moral, emotive, and ethical concept. Any accusation of corruption immediately carries with it popular moral indignation, and as such the moral and legal dimensions of the word can both actually serve to advance the idea of corruption as a breach of the public trust.

However, the historical ambiguities of 'corruption' have remained, and become apparent not only by the fact that scholars of different professional, academic, cultural, and theoretical backgrounds tend to use 'corruption' in different contexts, but also to describe (often subjectively) similar or overlapping conduct, for example, of public office-holders.[67] Furthermore, many treaties and declarations against corruption either do not define the concept (presumably to secure consensus on these instruments), or define it significantly narrowly and differently. The various definitions of corruption in these instruments are essentially contextual (basically reflecting its multi-faceted nature, and the multiplicity of its causes, consequences, and effects, which depend on the vastly different social, economic, political and historical contexts), and range from isolated acts of bribery based on quid pro quo, to corrupt acts in legal, judicial, economic, and political systems, invariably reflecting a society in decline and decay.[68]

[64] ibid.

[65] ibid.

[66] See Martine Boersma, *Corruption: A Violation of Human Rights and a Crime Under International Law?* (Antwerp: Intersentia Publishing Ltd, 2012) 25.

[67] Three basic categories of definitions of corruption can be identified: public-office centred definitions, market-centred definitions and public-interest centred definitions. The first two categories have been characterised as 'too narrowly conceived', while 'public interest' is considered a potentially useful tool to distil the word. Ibid, 4–6. There is also pressure to expand these categories to include public-opinion definitions of corruption. See Brown, 'What Are We Trying to Measure?' (n 23) 58. However, all the categories of definitions can play differing yet equally significant roles in clarifying difficult concepts like corruption.

[68] For a contemporary account of corruption as decay, see Laura Underkuffler, 'Captured by Evil: The Idea of Corruption In Law' (Duke Law School, Working Papers in Public Law, Durham, NC) www.scholarship.law.duke.edu/cgi/viewcontent.cgi?article=2030&context=faculty_scholarship: 'Corruption is one of the most powerful words in the English language. Charges of corruption have condemned men, destroyed the lives of women, and accelerated the decline and fall of governments. Corruption is something that humans instinctively loathe, and that we try to excise from our midst. The word itself conjures something that is

In many African states, this latter characterisation is more accurate, as corruption primarily comes from abuse of entrusted power (i.e., turning public office into a 'maximising unit' or 'business enterprise' to make money at the expense of the interest of the public), a lack of accountability and the rule of law, which takes root at the top of political and social systems (and quickly replicated by other members of the society); and inevitably affects individuals, communities, and virtually all aspects of society.[69] This notion of public office as a 'business enterprise' has been correctly admonished by Max Weber, when he pointed out that,

> Legally and actually, office-holding is not considered ownership of a source of income, to be exploited for rents or emoluments in exchange for the rendering of certain services, as was normally the case in the Middle Ages . . . It is decisive for the modern loyalty to an office that, in the pure type, it does not establish a relationship to a person, like the vassal's or disciple's faith under feudal or patrimonial authority, but rather is devoted to impersonal and functional purposes.[70]

Weber's idea pointedly shows that public offices are not 'private properties' to be appropriated for personal gain of the holders or their families and friends, but rather sacred institutionalised duties to be performed selflessly for the common good. This notion of 'public offices' suggests special responsibilities and duties upon both those who hold them, and the state that they work for, and is entirely compatible with the goals of modern states.

Furthermore, while it is true that the term 'corruption' historically has attracted myriad meanings and connotations (which, though frequently contested, have nonetheless shifted over time to suit changing times and circumstances), 'a core meaning readily emerges from an analysis of these different meanings'[71] that essentially reflects contemporary notions of corruption. Several (somewhat overlapping and repetitive) definitions have been suggested by a chorus of scholars from diverse academic and professional fields (such as anthropology, criminology, economics, political science and law). 'Corruption' has been widely used to describe any 'undesirable conduct'.[72] While a corrupt conduct would clearly be undesirable insofar as it breaches the public trust, this rather brief definition raises

powerful, insidious, and destructive of human lives and institutions.' Ibid 1. See generally, Susan Rose-Ackerman, *Corruption and Government: Causes, Consequences, and Reform* (Cambridge: Cambridge University Press, 1999).

[69] Reagan Demas, 'Moment of Truth: Development in Sub-Saharan Africa and Critical Alterations Needed in Application of the Foreign Corrupt Practices Act and other Anti-Corruption Initiatives' (2010–11) 26 *American University International Law Review* 315.

[70] See Max Weber, *Economy and Society* vol III (New York: Bedminster Press, 1968) 959.

[71] Carl Friedrich, 'Corruption Concepts in Historical Perspective', in Heidenheimer, *Political Corruption: A Handbook* (n 4) 15.

[72] Franklin A Gevurtz, 'Rethinking Corruption: An Introduction to a Symposium and a Few Additional Thoughts' (2007) 20 *Pacific McGeorge Global Business & Development Law Journal* 237.

numerous problems, among which are its broadness, subjectivity, and the fact that a conduct deemed 'undesirable' need not necessarily be 'corrupt'.

Although some scholars have contended that 'the question of formal legality is not the essence of the concept',[73] this author would argue that a conduct or behaviour is not corrupt unless prohibited as such by law. Yet, legal prescriptions are not static, and can change from time to time to establish and label conduct considered repugnant to the public interest, the rule of law (for example, as an arbitrary exercise of power for purposes other than the common good, and thus precipitating inequality), and human rights as 'corrupt'. Even so, '[n]ot all arbitrary power can be called corruption, since arbitrary power may also proceed from fancied patriotism or simply from a confused state of mind. Arbitrary power will sometimes result from corruption. But carelessness and inattention may also lead to it.'[74] However, while the term 'arbitrary power' might be subject to multiple meanings, the deliberate nature of large-scale corruption that is prevalent in many African states can hardly be characterised as a conduct arising from 'carelessness and inattention'. Thus, 'whereas today the venality of office is considered a form of political corruption, it was [in the feudal and patrimonial systems] perceived as a check on corruption'.[75]

As noted, the traditional and most common manifestation of corruption is bribery[76] (this notion of corruption has persisted for several years probably because it 'creates a very specific obligation on the part of the officeholder')[77] and it was initially permitted as a tax deduction,[78] though

[73] See Heidenheimer, *Political Corruption: Readings in Comparative Analysis* (n 1) 7, citing Joseph Senturia, who wrote 'Corruption, Political', in the *Encyclopaedia of the Social Sciences*.

[74] See HA Brasz, 'Sociology of Corruption', reproduced in Heidenheimer, *Political Corruption: Readings in Comparative Analysis* (n 1) 42.

[75] ibid 13. Charles-Louis de Secondat, Baron de La Brède et de Montesquieu and Jeremy Bentham were two of the early writers that supported the sale of public office, for example on the grounds that it would 'allow more of the wealthier and more moral middle-class types to have access to high government posts'. Ibid.

[76] Noonan, *Bribes* (n 4) xi.

[77] See Heidenheimer, *Political Corruption: Readings in Comparative Analysis* (n 1) 18.

[78] At one point, bribery to foreign countries was considered a tax-deductible expense for companies in some European countries. Beverly McLachlin, 'Horchelaga Lecture: Criminal Law: Towards an International Legal Order' (1999) 29 *Hong Kong Law Journal* 448, 450. Thomas Pogge criticised this practice, because it 'diverts the loyalties of officials in [developing regions like Africa] and also makes a great difference in terms of who is motivated to scramble for public office in the first place. Developing countries have suffered staggering losses as a result, most clearly in the awarding of public contracts. These losses arise in part from the fact that bribes are priced in: bidders on contracts must raise their price in order to get paid enough to pay the bribes. Additional losses arise as bidders can afford to be non-competitive, knowing that the success of their bid will depend on their bribes more than on the substance of their offer. Even greater losses arise from the fact that officials focused on bribes pay little attention to whether the goods and services they purchase on their country's behalf are of good quality or even needed at all.' Thomas Pogge, 'Recognized and Violated by International Law The Human Rights of the Global Poor' (2005) *Leiden Journal of International Law* 737.

it is now condemned and outlawed in every nation.[79] Bribery takes several forms, and its covert nature makes it very difficult to uncover.[80] Nonetheless, bribery, whether by public officials or private actors, often involves a cash payment, a deposit to a designated offshore account, or a consulting fee; and it can often buy access to public goods or inappropriate influence.[81] According to Judge John Noonan, 'The core of the concept of a bribe is an inducement improperly influencing the performance of a public function meant to be gratuitously exercised.'[82] Thus, one fundamental element of bribery is reciprocity (also known as quid pro quo), but 'there is uncertainty regarding the linkage required between the payment and the official act, and what intent the offeror and public official must have for the transaction to come within the criminal prohibition'.[83] Bribery has also been likened to auto-corruption, whereby a public official 'secures for himself the administrative privilege which would be secured by an outsider by bribery. He awards contracts to himself, perhaps using dummy corporations, which would go to reward a contractor in the organization'.[84]

However, the practice of defining corruption narrowly as 'bribery' also illustrates the confusion that has persisted over the years regarding the concept. Franklin A Gevurtz suggests that including bribes within the definition of corruption makes the task of defining corruption more problematic.[85] However, it is rather the interchangeable use of 'bribe' (a narrowed concept with corruption (a broad concept) than its inclusion within the broad notion of corruption that would seem to be a source of deep confusion. Defining corruption itself is problematic enough even without the inclusion of 'bribes'. The inclusion of bribes in the overall idea of corruption therefore does not necessarily bring with it an additional layer of difficulties in the definition exercise. Yet, while bribery is a key component of corruption, and, in fact the two are closely linked together, they are not at all inseparable. Thus, 'a person bribed is a person corrupt; but a man may be corrupt who does not take bribes'.[86] Similarly, although bribery is a traditional and important element of corruption, and many scholars and commentators often use the term interchangeably (and sometimes

[79] Philip M Nichols, 'Regulating Transnational Bribery in Times of Globalization and Fragmentation' (1999) 24 *Yale Journal of International Law* 257, 278.

[80] Crutchfield George and Lacey, 'A Coalition of Industrialized Nations' (n 19) 552.

[81] John G Peters and Susan Welch, 'Political Corruption in America: A Search for Definitions and a Theory' (1978) 72 *American Political Science Review* 974, 976.

[82] Noonan, *Bribes* (n 4) 4.

[83] Peter J Henning, 'Public Corruption: A Comparative Analysis of International Corruption Conventions and United States Law' (2001) 18 *Arizona Journal of International & Comparative Law* 801.

[84] VO Key Jr, 'Techniques of Political Graft' in Heidenheimer (ed), *Political Corruption*, (n 4), 46, 48.

[85] ibid.

[86] Bayley, 'The Effects of Corruption in a Developing Nation' (n 61) 522.

confusingly) with corruption, it is clear that in the case of Africa generally, corruption encompasses other potentially more devastating practices and breaches of public trust, such as large-scale theft of a state's wealth and natural resources by high-ranking state officials, which arguably is the source of many lesser forms of corruption.

Furthermore, most scholars and commentators treat all forms of corruption as equal, no matter the gravity, magnitude or effects. This prevailing conception of corruption is even used in the major criminal law instruments against corruption, such as the UN Convention against Corruption and the AU Convention on Preventing and Combating Corruption. For example, Joseph Nye defines corruption as:

> [B]ehaviour which deviates from the normal duties of a public role because of private-regarding (family, close private clique), pecuniary or status gains; or violates rules against the exercise of certain types of private-regarding influence. This includes such behaviour as bribery (use of reward to pervert the judgment of a person in a position of trust); nepotism (bestowal of patronage by reason of ascriptive relationship rather than merit); and misappropriation (illegal appropriation of public resources for private-regarding uses.[87]

Nye's broad definition articulates corruption in both the public and private sectors, which can be equally devastating and which is frequently missing in the anti-corruption discourse. His definition also encompasses corruption arising as a result of a conflict between the public and private spheres. Significantly, Nye's definition takes corruption beyond the narrowed conception of bribery to include 'illegal appropriation of public resources', and that this kind of corruption constitutes a breach of public trust. However, like most other definitions of corruption, Nye's ignores the element of 'harm' or 'effect'. Nye also discusses Robert Klitgaard's definition, which is similar to Nye's.[88] Klitgaard provides the widely cited formula: corruption = monopoly + discretion – accountability. Nye suggests that Klitgaard's definition contains the full range of plausibly corrupt behaviour: 'an official's act is corrupt when the motives for public action are excessively private-regarding, and a private individual's act is corrupt when the citizen attempts to incentivise an official to act in an excessively private-regarding manner.'[89] Klitgaard adds that to be useful in theory and practice, this definition must be further informed by:

- foundational political and ethical norms that identify motives that are excessively private-serving;
- the fact that some systems demand total disregard of self-interest in politics, while others permit some self-interest but constrain what types;

[87] Joseph Nye, 'Corruption and Political Development: A Cost-Benefit Analysis' (1967) 2 *American Political Science Review* 419.

[88] ibid.

[89] ibid 378.

- possible divergence between legal definitions and practices perceived as corrupt; and
- the understanding of 'the ethical appeal of politics',[90] of which there are several interpretations.

This author feels that another part of the definition must include what actions of officials qualify as public rather than private; the answer presumably is that an act is politically corrupt only when it falls within an actor's sphere of public duty. However, private motive and public status are ultimately informed by a system's ethical framework. Assessment of such corrupt motives raises the evidentiary problem of *mens rea*. Evidentiary concerns can be especially difficult when any official acts for unacceptable reasons – such as being bribed – but the action itself appears to be publicly acceptable. Without public vetting or formal supervision, the act may never come to light. Establishing appropriate standards for inferring corrupt intent thus requires striking a difficult balance. Harsher standards may identify more potential offenders, but it may also classify too many behaviours as presumptively corrupt.

Gevurtz (quoting Franklin Zimring) also makes a case for a more precise definition of corruption,[91] thus defining corruption as 'the illegal use of power for personal gain'.[92] This definition suggests that the use of power for personal gain, however reprehensible, may not amount to corruption unless criminalised in national law. It also suggests that a corrupt act be intentional. Yet, there are certain acts of corruption, such as illicit enrichment, which do not require proof of intention. Corrupt acts also often go beyond seeking personal gain, to seeking political power. Like Nye's definition, this definition also ignores the corrosive effects of corruption, especially when it is large-scale, on the economically and socially vulnerable. But unlike Nye's definition, Gervutz's seems to exclude corruption in the private sector.

The popular definition of corruption provided by the World Bank, and backed by Transparency International, is 'the abuse of public power for private benefit'.[93] The overriding consideration in this narrow definition is the reference to 'public power', and the fact that such entrusted power is used by state officials for personal gain.[94] The attention on public

[90] ibid.

[91] See Gevurtz, 'Rethinking Corruption' (n 72) 237.

[92] ibid.

[93] The World Bank, *Helping Countries Combat Corruption: The Role of the World Bank* (Washington, DC: World Bank, 1997) 8.

[94] It should be noted, however, that notwithstanding the World Bank's definition of corruption as a public-sector phenomenon, it acknowledges its existence in the private sector. Its *Helping Countries* report states that 'Fraud and bribery can and do take place in the private sector, often with costly results. Unregulated financial systems permeated with fraud can undermine savings and deter foreign investment. They also make a country vulnerable to financial crises and macroeconomic instability.' Despite this understanding, the World

officials, however, excludes corruption in the private sector,[95] such as those involving multinationals in developing countries who, for example, encourage or facilitate large-scale bribery (and other forms of corruption) or who promote the impunity of perpetrators by helping to hide stolen wealth abroad. Nevertheless, Transparency International's definition (as contained on its website) while largely similar in substance to the World Bank's, is significantly different in that it refers broadly to 'abuse of entrusted power for private gain',[96] suggesting that both public and private sector 'entrusted power' will be covered by the definition. Also, under Transparency International's definition, the 'private gain' will presumably include those accruing not only to corrupt state officials but to their families and relations, as well.

Furthermore, the World Bank's restrictive definition reflects a somewhat similar definition put forward by Joseph Senturia in his 'Corruption, Political', written in the 1930s: 'Corruption is the misuse of public power for private profit.'[97] But '[n]ot all acts which benefit the office-holder at the expense of the people are corrupt, else the term would include all taxation by an absolute monarch to provide accustomed luxuries for his family and court, all sacrifices and gifts given to the priestly class in theocracies.'[98] However, this exception would presumably only apply 'where a position of political power was regarded as the fruit of inheritance or property rights.'[99] At any rate, such feudal or patrimonial systems are largely outdated, and have since given way to the contemporary notions of democratic governance, the rule of law and respect for human rights, which at a minimum would implicitly empower citizens (in whom governmental legitimacy resides) to legitimately and justifiably challenge the state for any corrupt conduct of public office-holders.

Similarly, Senturia's definition, which clearly falls into the public-office centred category of definitions of corruption, may also be problematic because 'it virtually forecloses discussions of corruption in pre-bureaucratic systems'.[100] Even so, other categories of definitions, such as

Bank's view seems to be that public sector corruption is a 'more serious problem in developing countries' than private sector corruption. Ibid.

[95] Corruption in the private sector occurs when unscrupulous businessmen see the opportunity to gain advantage for themselves or their enterprises through illegal undertakings. This office-based concept of corruption evolved with the consolidation of the modern nation-states and the professionalisation of public administrations. This concept is by no means irrelevant, not least because of the enormous weight of political administrations within modern democracies.

[96] See Transparency International, www.transparency.org/whatwedo?gclid=CJW5pp-x-7sCFY_MtAodim8AUw.

[97] Joseph Senturia, 'Corruption, Political,' *Encyclopaedia of Social Sciences*, vol IV (New York: Crowell-Collier Macmillan, 1930–35) 448.

[98] ibid.

[99] See Heidenheimer, *Political Corruption: Readings in Comparative Analysis* (n 1) 9.

[100] ibid.

the market-centred definitions, might be utilised as a complementary tool to address any problems that may arise in the operationalisation of the public-office centred definitions. Furthermore, the World Bank's definition is also substantively similar to Franklin E Zimring and David T Johnson's definition, which is 'the criminal misuse of power [in] obtaining control over the property or person of another [through] the use of social and institutional power. When power granted to persons for restricted purposes is used instead for unauthorized personal aims, unlawful and socially wasteful exchanges take place.'[101]

A somewhat illuminating definition of corruption is that suggested by Colin Leys: 'Corruption = to change from good to bad; to debase; to pervert. It denotes patterns of action which derive their significance from role of value-systems in social behaviour.'[102] This shows that corruption is a 'bad thing'. Yet, those involved in corrupt acts may deem their action as a 'good thing', to achieve certain ends; and as shown below, there are scholars who actually strongly argue that corruption might be 'a good thing' on social, political, economic, and developmental grounds. However, looked at from the perspective of morality, few commentators would disagree that any such conduct would be considered wrongful, and against the contemporary concept of public office and public interest. Even so, Ley's definition is slightly problematic not least because of its broadness, subjectivity (although one would admit that it is almost impossible to achieve a value-free definition of corruption), and its limited legal value.

As is clear from the discussion thus far, corruption ultimately may be any conduct a society wishes to call 'corruption', but as previously argued, this will only be so if backed by legal prohibition. Also, early scholars and commentators seemed to be preoccupied with public sector corruption, although in most cases a rather narrowed conception of corruption actually emerged. Some scholars have raised concerns about the disproportionate focus on public sector corruption in academic literature and commentaries at the expense of corruption in the private sector. For example, Janet Dine, in Gevurtz's 'Rethinking Corruption', has shown that one such bias in the literature is corruption involving corporate officials. She explains that 'the identification of corruption with acts of public, rather than private, officials often comes as part of a normative agenda: If corruption is a problem with government, the facile answer is less government'.[103] Dine suggests that this biased focus does not necessarily indicate that governments are more corrupt than corporations, but it may be a crafty way to ensure that private power is consistently utilised for

[101] Franklin E Zimring and David T Johnson, 'On the Comparative Study of Corruption' (2007) 243(20) *Pacific McGeorge Global Business and Development Law Journal* 243.

[102] Colin Leys, 'What Is the Problem about Corruption' (1965) 3(2) *Journal of Modern African Studies* 215.

[103] Gevurtz, 'Rethinking Corruption' (n 72) 239.

public interest.[104] However, the focus on public sector corruption in developing regions like Africa may be justified, especially given the perpetual abuse of public office and the corresponding breach of public trust by many leaders who engage in corruption, and the negative effects of this on the legal and judicial institutions, as well as on individuals, communities, and virtually every aspect of society. In this context, focus on public sector may further be buttressed because large-scale corruption can have a devastating influence on the private sector, which has to 'play along' with corrupt state officials or risk losing vital business interests. Even so, the focus on public sector corruption, while it is fully justified in the case of Africa, may be problematic in other parts of the world where public sector corruption may not be the norm.

Another important point worthy of consideration (not least because it has also compounded efforts to precisely define corruption) is the relationship of the concept of corruption with certain cultural and traditional practices, in particular the notion of 'gift giving' prevalent in some developing countries. In many African cultures, gift-giving is an important aspect of hospitality and one important way that Africans show appreciation.[105] Gifts come in all sizes and may be given for a variety of reasons, obviously some of which will not be corrupt or suspect. For example, gift-giving without proof of influence in return or actual quid pro quo is not corruption.[106] Yet, the dividing line between gift-giving and corruption can be a blurry one. In Nigeria and other former British West African colonies, for instance, functionaries often expect or seek a tip, referred to as a 'dash', for services rendered to the public, and services may be denied if no dash is given.[107] As former Nigerian president Olusegun Obasanjo said (as is cited by Alhaji BM Marong):

> A gift is a token; it is not demanded; the value is in the spirit of the giving, not the material worth. The gift is made in the open for all to see, never in secret. Where a gift is excessive it becomes an embarrassment and is returned. If anything, corruption – as practiced by exporters from the north as well as by officials in the south – has perverted the positive aspects of this age-old tradition.[108]

[104] ibid.

[105] Transparency International has identified that 'the socialisation of gift-giving is a practical obstacle hampering the implementation of the UNCAC in Burundi'. Update on UNCAC implementation in Africa, www.u4.no/publications/uncac-and-africa/downloadasset/335.

[106] Tor Krevert said pointedly: 'The gods themselves are moved by gifts, wrote Euripides; experience shows, elected and appointed officials whose positions carry with them privilege or influence are often moved by gifts too.' Tor Krevert, 'Curbing Corruption? The Efficacy of the Foreign Corrupt Practices Act' (2007–2008) 33 *North Carolina Journal of International Law and Commercial Regulation* 83.

[107] Crutchfield George and Lacey, 'A Coalition of Industrialized Nations' (n 19) 554.

[108] Marong, 'Toward a Normative Consensus against Corruption: Legal Effects of the Principles to Combat Corruption in Africa' (n 43) 105.

On this account, a 'tip' need not per se be corruption but rather may be a voluntary gift, presumably prompted by some notion of kindness on the part of the 'giver', and to show appreciation for services rendered. However, tips, charity, and providing cheap holidays or sending gifts to opposition leaders during festive periods may well be corruption because 'the attitude of friendliness which accompanies a gift presupposes the same attitude being displayed by the receiving party. And corruption can fit into the framework of this friendly and sympathetic attitude.'[109]

Susan Rose-Ackerman distinguishes between bribes, gifts, prices, and tips in two ways.[110] The first is whether they are given in return as quid pro quo; the second is whether they are given to agents or principals. A bribe would be an informal offering to a principal where formally such an offering is not required in return for a benefit. A gift is an offering to a principal for no explicit reason. However, even if gifts lack an explicit quid pro quo arrangement, a subtle linkage may still exist,[111] because it is naive to claim that no favours are expected. One traditional method of differentiation between bribes and gifts (suggested in the Obasanjo quotation) is the size and the timing of the offering. Another is that a small gift may only signal politeness and appreciation; and gifts are usually given after a service is completed, whereas bribes are usually given beforehand. These distinctions, however, are easier to draw in theory than in practice. For instance, the differentiation of what is a small gift versus a large one can be highly subjective; one person's definition of 'small' may represent a significant proportion of another's person's monthly income. Rose-Ackerman correctly concludes that definitions are a cultural matter, and therefore are constantly changing.[112]

As noted, the distinguishing characteristic of bribery is the quid pro quo factor; that is, the evidence of giving valuables like large cash offerings to state officials in exchange for favourable exercise of public authority and trust. David Hess and Thomas W Dunfee have distinguished between harmful ('coarse') bribery, common practices involving social gifts, and payments that may constitute an authentic and accepted method of compensation.[113] Nonetheless, provincial bribery may be damaging, especially if it leads to coarse bribery.[114] Hess and Dunfee define coarse bribery specifically as 'the promise or payment of a benefit that induces a public official to breach a duty pertaining to a significant community

[109] See HA Brasz, 'Sociology of Corruption' in Arnold J Heidenheimer, (ed) *Political Corruption: Readings in Comparative Analysis* (n 1) 45.

[110] Rose-Ackerman, *Corruption and Government*' (n 68) 92–93.

[111] ibid.

[112] ibid.

[113] Hess and Dunfee, 'Fighting Corruption' (n 20) 595.

[114] ibid.

interest [most likely in investment projects, procurement spending, and extra-budgetary accounts]'.[115]

The manner in which the forerunners in the fight against corruption defined corruption is considered by some critics to be a form of Western cultural imperialism, because it condemns types of gift-giving historically acceptable in other societies.[116] The fact that the UN Convention against Corruption has been overwhelmingly ratified by a geographically and economically diverse group of states (numbering 169 as at February 2014), however, indicates that the fight against corruption is not simply a Western concept. The widespread acknowledgement of this historic document by civil society also implies that anti-corruption advocates are no longer in the minority amongst the global community.

Furthermore, given the range of reasons for giving gifts, some writers have cautioned against expansion of the concept of 'corruption' as a criminal offence, arguing that 'the greater the possibility that arguably acceptable conduct will come within the criminal provision and result in punishment for acts that are not morally blameworthy'.[117] Whereas an endless expansion of existing definitions of corruption can only lead to greater levels of incoherence or inconsistencies, a purposeful approach to the idea of corruption to reflect its human consequences is clearly not only warranted but also fully justified.

Notwithstanding the lack of clarity over the notion of corruption, it cannot be denied that the idea has expanded and broadened considerably over the years; covering other forms of lawlessness,[118] and hence prompting states to establish contemporary legal framework to address the changing nature of corruption. Indeed, since Judge Noonan's seminal book from 1984, *Bribe,* a criminal and law enforcement paradigm has incorporated a range of misconduct, such as embezzlement, and has characterised such misconduct as corruption, with varying penalties due. Also, as the experiences across African states have shown, corruption can range from seemingly inconsequential tokens, to systematic abuses of power combined with massive theft of state wealth and natural resources. The comprehensive nature and substantive content of the UNCAC (it has eight chapters and 71 articles) also shows how the focus of the anti-corruption movement has shifted from the traditional notion of bribery and embezzlement to other practices, including a range of preventive and criminalisation measures, asset recovery, and international cooperation provisions. This evolution reflects the growing scope and application of national and regional anti-corruption laws and standards. A broad range of actions against private and public sector corruption, foreign and

115 ibid.

116 Hess and Dunfee, 'Fighting Corruption' (n 20) 602–03.

117 Henning, 'Public Corruption' (n 83) 805.

118 ibid 801.

domestic bribery, trading in influence, political funding, and the liability of legal persons have all been covered by the myriad treaties, declarations, and laws on corruption.

Nonetheless, as noted above, all types of corruption, no matter the magnitude or effects, are still defined purely as legal crimes without victims. Moreover, as shown in what follows, despite the expansion over time of what constitutes corruption, its definition remains restrictive and unduly bogged down by international politics and relations. Yet, the deliberate and unacceptable invocation of 'cultures and tradition', 'sovereignty', or 'national interests' to justify some clear and serious cases of corruption or to unreasonably restrict its very concept, is harmful to everyone: citizens, society, and local and international communities. The long-standing restricted notion of corruption also means that the world nations have not deemed it necessary to reflect on the victims' loss in acts of corruption, especially when dealing with the large-scale official corruption such as is the case in several African states. The international politics of corruption has encouraged societies and regions to look the other way or to pay little to no attention to the victims' element of the problem. Luminita Ionescu suggests that the task of measuring and defining corruption has been avoided by what she called 'the global agenda'.[119] Because of this, the expectations that have been raised by international movements against corruption have largely remained unfulfilled. In addition, presenting corruption as a victimless phenomenon has arguably contributed to obscuring the effects and consequences of corruption on individual or groups of people. But the progressive, albeit slow, legal development on the concept of corruption proves that corruption can change according to time and circumstances.

## THE CAUSES AND CONSEQUENCES OF CORRUPTION

The causes and consequences of corruption – whether large-scale, or petty – vary from country to country, and the effects of corruption can depend on different political, legal, economic, and social variables. However, corruption is caused primarily by:

- the legacy of weak rule of law and ineffective governmental institutions;
- inadequate checks and balances within the executive branch;
- poverty;
- weak observance of human rights;
- non-democratic regimes;

[119] Luminita Ionescu, 'The Construction of Corruption as a Global Problem' (2011) 3 *Contemporary Readings in Law and Social Justice* 166–71.

- patronage systems that fill government posts;
- underdeveloped civil service and career systems;
- a lack of independent legal, judicial, and institutional mechanisms;
- impunity for perpetrators; and
- a lack of will on the part of political leaders.

But economic and statistical studies offer many other reasons for the development of corruption. For example, Kenny Feng tells of two researchers who, in seeking the causes of economic corruption, found that it is pervasive, in particular, in many African and Latin American countries with low levels of economic growth.[120] While the results of such studies often include subjective scales and opinions that can impair objectivity, the secretive nature of corruption limits the availability of hard empirical data. Consequently, researchers look to alternative approaches in attempting to establish the negative externalities of corruption.[121]

Furthermore, some scholars have debated the role and moral challenges of corruption, and whether it causes harm to the public. For example, Barbara Crutchfield George and Kathleen Lacey wrote that corruption was once viewed as expected and necessary.[122] So too did Colin Leys, who argued that, 'on occasion, bribes promoted efficiency and socially useful administration and served the persistent integrative needs of society'.[123] And James Wilson suggested that, 'honest graft brought profit to the office-holder and no harm to the public'.[124] Along these lines, Timothy L Fort and James J Noone stated that 'efficiency-based arguments against bribery unfortunately carry with them a new way of disorienting the world'.[125] In the same vein, some critics have suggested that corruption is an effective mechanism for evading inefficient bureaucratic red tape. Still others point to the supposed economic benefits of corruption, noting for example that bribery can prevent excessive wage inflation or that it may create a necessary price floor for certain goods and services in imperfect markets.

Joseph Nye argued that corruption in poor economies like in African states, was beneficial to the socio-political and socio-economic develop-

[120] Kenny Feng, 'The Human Rights Implications of Corruption: An Alien Tort Claims-Act Based Analysis' (2004) *Wharton Research Scholars Journal*, University of Pennsylvania, Philadelphia, PA, www.repository.upenn.edu/cgi/viewcontent.cgi?article=1005&context=wharton_research_scholars, 7.

[121] ibid.

[122] Crutchfield George and Lacey, 'A Coalition of Industrialized Nations,' (n 19) 558.

[123] Leys, 'What is the Problem about Corruption' (n 102) 215.

[124] James Q Wilson, 'Corruption Is Not Always Scandalous' in John A Gardiner and David J Olson (eds), *Theft of the City: Readings on Corruption in Urban America* (Bloomington, IN: Indiana University Press, 1974) 29–32.

[125] Timothy L Fort and James J Noone, 'Gifts, Bribes and Exchange: Relationships in Non-Market Economies and Lessons for Pax E-Commercial' (2000) 33 *Cornell International Law Journal* 515.

ment of those countries and necessary to prevent political instability and violent conflict, putting forward the cost-benefit analysis of corruption, or the 'grease the wheels' paradigm. According to Nye, corruption is necessary in transitional societies because of the lack of infrastructures of governance and because corruption helps to facilitate investment opportunities for entrepreneurs that, in turn, bring innovation and efficiency, contribute to economic development, and break down the wall of bureaucracy in those societies.[126] Other prominent social scientists, such as Samuel Huntington and Nathaniel Leff, have expressed similar views that corruption can be 'welfare enhancing'.[127]

However, this author considers these propositions to be seriously flawed and no longer tenable. Corruption is neither inevitable nor beneficial. To allow corruption to prevail over the rule of law and respect for human rights is to hand governments over to the highest bidder, which would result in the social and economic exclusion and marginalisation of the majority of the citizens, to the benefit of the few rich and politically connected people. The benefit-analysis of corruption can withstand neither a rigorous test of recent events, nor empirical evidence of the corrosive effects of large-scale corruption in regions like Africa. Scholars and anti-corruption advocates note that bribery can actually incentivise corrupt officials to develop more hurdles and more elaborate extortion schemes in order to solicit larger bribes. Thomas Dunfee, N Craig Smith, and William Ross state: 'bribery is wrong because it is an intentional violation of a binding moral duty', and forewarn us that it is harmful for a number of reasons: its corrosive effects on the social structure, diminished happiness of citizens, reduced credibility of the government, increased lawlessness, and even possible revolution.[128] For Thomas Donaldson and Thomas Dunfee, bribery violates the hyper-norm of necessary social efficiency[129] and it harms political participation because if a government

[126] Nye, 'Corruption and Political Development' (n 87) 419.

[127] See Samuel Huntington, *Political Order in Changing Societies* (New Haven, CT: Yale University Press, 1968); and Nathaniel H Leff, 'Economic Development through Bureaucratic Corruption' (1964) 8 *American Behavioral Scientist* 8–14. Huntington's and Leff's ideas resemble probably a more controversial (but equally disturbing) notion of 'honest graft' coined by Plunktt, and illustrated thus: 'There's an honest graft, and I am an example of how it works. I might sum up the whole thing by sayin: I seen my opportunities and I took em. Just let me explain by examples. My party's in power in the city and it's goin' to undertake a lot of public improvement. Well, I'm tipped off, say, that they're going to lay out a new part at a certain place. I see my opportunity and I take it. I go to that place and I buy up all the land I can in the neighbourhood. Then the board of this or that makes its plan public and there is a rush to get that land which nobody cared particular for before. Ain't it perfectly honest to charge a good profit and make a profit on my investment and foresight? Of course it is. Well, that's honest graft.' See William Riordan in Leys, 'What Is the Problem about Corruption?' (n 102) 217.

[128] Thomas W Dunfee et al, 'Social Contracts and Marketing Ethics' (1999) 63 *Journal of Marketing* 14.

[129] Thomas Donaldson and Thomas W Dunfee, *Ties That Bind: A Social Contracts Approach to Business Ethics* (Boston, MA: Harvard Business School Press, 1999) 129–30.

official makes a decision on the basis of a bribe, then public resources are allocated in a manner outside the control of the public, as the decision is not open to accountability mechanisms.[130]

As a hidden transaction, a bribe 'violates the societal norm designed to provide the least well-off the possibility of purchasing basic goods'.[131] Bribery also skews efficient distribution of resources.[132] Under Donaldson and Dunfee's analysis, the skewing of resources resulting from bribery may well hurt the weakest segments of society because, although a particular bribe may be relatively small relative to a country's gross domestic product, the distortions of the systems and diversion of funds that occurs may produce a profoundly negative cumulative effect on the economy. Moreover, some bribes are considerable, and these clearly would have a greater impact on the allocation of resources. Therefore, this economic-cum-moral argument is helpful in the analysis of bribery.

It is thus clear that corruption generally is bad for business because it increases risks and uncertainty, entails payments (pay-offs) that represent a kind of tax, and requires greater negotiation with state officials. Corruption that is government-sanctioned or acquiesced to sends a particularly damaging message to a society that corruption is acceptable, and it may encourage citizens to become corrupt because, like many other crimes, corruption can be contagious. There is another, perhaps greater, harm from corruption: the violation of the public trust, that leads to a denigration of society.[133] As noted earlier, not all abuses of office, however, are necessarily criminal offences, and many offences that might fit within a broad anti-corruption statute may be so trivial that they are not prosecuted with any degree of regularity. Therefore, a clear conceptualisation of corruption, in general, and of large-scale corruption, in particular, is crucial to the development of an effective response to address these issues.

Large-scale corruption has been described as the 'most devastating form of corruption in the developing countries, especially in Africa, as it accounts for hundreds of billions of dollars of stolen money stashed abroad by corrupt political and military leaders and officials',[134] not least because of its debilitating harm to citizens, in particular, the economically and socially vulnerable. Corruption invariably deprives the government and citizenry of the right of honest services owed by state officials, which is the foundation for the effective realisation of human rights. In his book, *Systemic Corruption: How Business Bribes Damage Developing Countries*,[135]

[130] ibid, 226–27.
[131] ibid.
[132] ibid.
[133] Daniel Hays Lowenstein, 'For God, For Country, or For Me?' (1986) 74 *California Law Review* 1479.
[134] ibid.
[135] George Moody Stuart, *Systemic Corruption: How Business Bribes Damage Developing Countries* (Oxford: WorldView Publishing, 1997).

George Moody Stuart argues that development initiatives motivated only by corruption lean towards large-scale, capital-intensive investment and away from those which maximise use of local labour and resources. Moody continues that it creates inadequate attention to long-term affordability and maintenance and inadequate environmental protections; and decisions are made secretly, outside normal government procedures, and with little or no consultation.[136]

It is the argument of this book that the fight against corruption can only succeed if it is comprehensive and multidisciplinary; and if it goes beyond the narrow criminal law response to address its manifestations and human consequences. Only such a multi-pronged approach can address and combat the root causes of corruption, and strengthen the critical institutions of the state. It can also build a merit-based system of governance, establish ethics regimes, and develop a framework that provides remedies to the victims of human rights violations that began as corruption. However, to reconceptualise the idea of corruption also invariably requires a reconsideration of the concept of states, and its relationship with its people. The next section discusses how notions of corruption and human rights can be connected through emerging theories of states, rule of law, justice, and participatory democracy.

## CORRUPTION AND HUMAN RIGHTS: THE RELATIONSHIP BETWEEN STATE AND CITIZEN

The concept of state historically reflected a supreme authority, whose words were law and which could do no wrong. As a corollary to this theory, the term sovereignty came to describe not only the relationship between a supreme authority and its subjects *within* a state, but also the relationship of that authority with other states. Simply put, sovereignty could be considered a form of absolute domestic jurisdiction; in other words, the exclusion of external actors from domestic authority structures within a given territory. Nonetheless, it should be noted that early theorists (for example, the renowned French lawyer Jean Bodin in the mid-sixteenth century) propounded the doctrine of unarguable absolute sovereignty to reflect the political and other realities of their time, which in turn informed their philosophies (such as that every conceivable right is an expression of divine will and real authority) and writings. The chaotic political events of those times, such as active or impending civil wars, the need to build strong governments, to secure political stability and security, and to prevent disorder and anarchy, probably helped to

[136] ibid.

advance and support the idea of the Divine Right of Kings, and absolute sovereignty.[137]

Furthermore, the prevailing political thoughts in the past were that only the existence of a supreme authority with 'absolute and perpetual' power to make incontestable decisions could serve as a panacea for sustainable peace, security, and orderly government.[138] The overriding considerations were then the preservation of the sovereign order, immunity from any wrongdoing, and the vesting of private privileges, not the interest of the citizens. The state was the sovereign and the sovereign was the state, and thus deemed above the law, invariably possessing 'indefinite law-making power'.[139] It is, therefore, understandable that it was in this context that the theory of absolute sovereignty and its corresponding immunities became widespread and subsequently accepted as the basis of international order and relations. However, those times are now long past, and the imperative for absolute power can no longer be conceivably sustained. Recent decades have witnessed fundamental changes, including weakening of strict doctrines of state sovereignty under international law. It follows that a state does not (and cannot) exist as an end in itself, but rather only as a means to further the purpose of governance and common good. Senior state officials are only agents to achieve these goals.

Other changes are developments in the field of human rights, with increasing concern for the common good, well-being, and dignity of individual citizens. Various national governmental changes include the entrenchment of representative democracies, the rule of law, and good governance. At the international level, changes have included the increasing role of intergovernmental organisations and the growth of international financial and multinational institutions.[140] These important

[137] Kofele-Kale offered some interesting and useful clarifications of the 'Bodinian State': 'Bodin did not conceive of sovereignty as unlimited right or as unconditioned or as involving a right to do anything. Sovereignty existed only to sub-serve the ends for which the State existed; and only in relation to those ends could it be conceived as existing at all. Thus, the clumsy attempts by some modern sovereign Presidents to appeal to Bodinian notions of absolutism to justify greed and avarice ignore the broad national interests that Bodin's doctrines were intended to serve. [In any case] the Bodinian Sovereign was restrained in three different ways. First, he was bound always by the constraints of natural and divine law; secondly, he was required to perform within the bounds of certain fundamental laws or *leges imperii* concerning the form and nature of government; and thirdly, he was bound always to respect the sanctity of property and of the family, which together form the foundations of the State . . . These legal and institutional constraints . . . are absent in the modern day sovereign Presidents.' Ndiva Kofele-Kale, *The International Law of Responsibility for Economic Crimes* (Hampshire: Ashgate Publishing Ltd, 2006) 277.

[138] ibid.

[139] Jeremy Bentham, *A Fragment On Government* (Cambridge: Cambridge University Press, 1776), xxiii.

[140] The absolutist doctrine of state has also been considerably altered by constitutional, ethical, class, and pluralist theories of state. There are, however, two important exceptions to the theory of sovereign immunity: the first is an act of state that is commercial in nature, and the second is when the state in question has no objection to being deprived of immunity for

developments have arguably altered almost beyond recognition the traditional concept of state sovereignty, rendering it out of date and irrelevant in this modern time of globalisation.

Yet, restrictions on state sovereignty might initially have been considered far-reaching and 'utopian' in the field of international law. Nonetheless, such restrictions, in the face of the oppression and tyranny faced by individuals, are proper and necessary to limit the exercise of absolute and arbitrary power by state, and crucially, to establish the normative framework for an 'international rule of law'. This idea of international rule of law and the corresponding human rights measures essential to protect individuals (in particular, the economically and socially vulnerable) against the state have since been championed globally. One notable element of these measures is the right to participate in government and democratic institutions, as well as the right to a law-based society, or what Thomas Franck has called the 'right to democratic governance' and 'a *sine qua non* for validating governance' as 'an immutable fact of life'.[141] According to Franck, the legal entitlement to democratic governance is based on custom and collective interpretation of treaties,[142] and this concept is gaining universal recognition. As he put it:

> The transformation of the democratic entitlement from moral prescription to international legal obligation has evolved gradually. In the past decade, however, the tendency has accelerated. Most remarkable is the extent to which an international law-based entitlement is now urged by governments themselves. This is a cosmic, but un-mysterious, change. For nations surfacing from long, tragic submergence beneath bogus people's democracy or outright dictatorship, the legitimation of power is a basic, but elusive move in the direction of reform.[143]

In Franck's view, open and free elections are one prerequisite for the enjoyment of the right to democratic governance and to validate the legitimate exercise of power,[144] but equally important is the existence of

sovereign acts. Other exceptions would be required in the light of the contemporary problem of large-scale corruption in developing countries, including in Africa; for example, by 'treating the problem as an extension of the commercial exception to sovereign immunity by placing it under the acts of a private nature category . . . or [carving out] a separate judicial exception [on the ground of] public interest.' Kofele-Kale, *The International Law of Responsibility for Economic Crimes* (n 137) 268–69.

141 Thomas M Franck, 'The Emerging *Right* to *Democratic* Governance' (1992) 86 *American Journal of International Law* 46, 48.

142 ibid.

143 ibid, 47.

144 Thomas Franck identified four indicators for measuring legitimacy: pedigree, determinacy, coherence, and adherence. Pedigree refers to the depth of the rule's roots in a historical process; determinacy refers to the rule's ability to communicate content; coherence refers to the rule's internal consistency and lateral connectedness to the principles underlying other rules; and adherence refers to the rule's vertical connectedness to a normative hierarchy, culminating in an ultimate rule of recognition, which embodies the principled purposes and values that define the community of states. Ibid, 51.

independent electoral bodies, an independent and impartial judiciary, a free press, and international election-monitoring mechanisms.[145] The existence of these processes and institutions presumably facilitate a consensual approach to governance, which is good for both the governing and the governed.[146] But the right to participate in the government of one's country is not just the right to free and fair elections. It embodies the totality of the right to participate in and influence the decision-making process of the government. Crucially, human rights law (such as the African Charter on Human and Peoples' Rights) provides the normative framework for the right to democratic governance and serves as 'internationally mandated restraints on governments'.[147] Franck adds:

> One can convincingly argue that states which deny their citizens the right to free and open elections are violating a rule that is fast becoming an integral part of the elaborately woven human rights fabric. Thus, the democratic entitlement has acquired a degree of legitimacy by its association with a far broader panoply of laws pertaining to the rights of persons vis-à-vis their governments.[148]

Conversely, the fundamental purpose of government as an institution that derives its powers from the consent of its people is to secure the inalienable rights of its citizens, and a government's legitimacy would depend on fulfilling these expectations. On this basis, it is possible to argue that states which condone or encourage corruption in essence undermine citizens' bona fide expectation that they will uphold human rights.[149] While there is at the moment no explicit legal right to a democratic governance entrenched in international law, (and the ideal of democracy itself may be a contested one), such right may however be implied from several already recognised legal rights, in particular, Article 13 of the African Charter (discussed fully in Chapter 5), which guarantees the right of every citizen to participate freely in the government of his country. The African Union itself has long established principles of democratic governance including in Article 4 of its Constitutive Act, which requires member states to refrain from interfering in the internal affairs of other states; to collectively intervene in another state 'in respect of grave circumstances, namely: war crimes, genocide and crimes against humanity'; to 'respect democratic

[145] ibid, 48.

[146] ibid.

[147] ibid, 79.

[148] ibid.

[149] For a comprehensive and excellent treatment of remedies under international human rights law, see Dinah Shelton, *Remedies in International Human Rights Law*, 2nd edn (Oxford: Oxford University Press, 2005). For an exhaustive list of international human rights treaties that include an 'effective remedy' provision, see Theo van Boven, 'Introduction to Basic Principles and Guidelines on the Right to a Remedy and Reparation for Victims of Violations of International Human Rights and Humanitarian Law' GA Res 1999/33, UN GAOR, 56th Session, Annex, Agenda Item 11(d), UN Doc E/CN 4/2000/62 (2000), 5.

principles, human rights, the rule of law and good governance'; and to condemn and reject any unconstitutional changes of governments.

Similarly, the AU adopted in 2007 the African Charter on Democracy, Elections, and Governance (also discussed in detail in Chapter 5), which explicitly guarantees the right to democratic governance.[150] It is arguable that these provisions support at a minimum a nascent right to democratic governance, which will be protected by addressing combating corruption as a human right issue. If the right to democratic governance means the right to a rule of law-based society, equality and participation, it is arguable that corruption attacks the fundamental values and directly undermines the legitimacy of government, and thus exacerbates a culture of impunity.[151]

In addition to the theoretical and normative arguments put forward by Franck, there is also a considerable body of interpretative law on the right to democratic governance.[152] For example, the conceptual links between a democratic government, the rule of law, and effective respect for human rights has been well stated by the Inter-American Court of Human Rights (IACtHR):

> The concept of rights and freedoms as well as that of their guarantees cannot be divorced from the system of values and principles that inspire it. In a democratic society, the rights and freedoms inherent in the human person, the guarantees applicable to them and the rule of law form a triad. Each component thereof defines itself, complements and depends on the others for its meaning.[153]

Furthermore, deliberative theorists suggest formal elections ought to be the denouement of a holistic political process.[154] Thus, deliberative

[150] Other similar international provisions include: Art 25 of the International Covenant on Civil and Political Rights (ICCPR) (guaranteeing the right of every citizen to take part in the conduct of public affairs, directly or through freely chosen representatives); Art 21 of the Universal Declaration on Human Rights (providing that the will of the people shall be the basis of the authority of government). See General Comment 25 adopted by the United Nations Human Rights Committee, established pursuant to the covenant. The General Comment clarifies the contours of the right contained in Art 25 to include: freedom of expression, assembly, association, and non-discrimination with respect to the citizen's right to vote.

[151] The IACtHR has defined impunity as 'the total lack of investigation, prosecution, capture, trial and conviction of those responsible for violations of the rights protected by the American Convention': *Case of Paniagua Morales et al* (8 March 1998) [173]. See also *Case of Loayza Tamayo* (27 November 1998) [170].

[152] See, eg, decisions of the European Court of Human Rights in *Mathieu-Mohin v Clerfayt* (1987) Series A no 113; *Socialist Party and Others v Turkey* ECHR 1998-III; and the decision of the African Commission on Human and Peoples' Rights in Communication 211/98: *Legal Resources Foundation v Zambia*, www.achpr.org/communications/.

[153] IACtHR, 'Habeas Corpus in Emergency Situations' (Arts 27(2), 25(1), and 7(6) of the American Convention on Human Rights). Advisory Opinion OC-8/87, 30 January 1987, paras 26, 41.

[154] Jacob Eisler, 'The Unspoken Institutional Battle Over Anticorruption: Citizens United, Honest Services, and the Legislative-Judicial Divide' (2010–11) 9 *First Amendment Law Review* 372.

democracies conceive of a process of debate and engagement as far more important than formal political outcomes.[155] As it increases participants' understanding of the reasonableness and legitimacy of others' positions, this deliberative process is an essential framework by which constituents gain an understanding of their own and others' goals.[156] It has been suggested that the deliberative approach takes 'a transformative view of human beings'.[157] Self-government 'means more than equal suffrage and frequent elections; it also means a partnership of equals, reasoning together about the common good'.[158] Theoretically, 'discourse' potentially can reconcile varied interests to reach a general agreement, but even if it does not, citizens that disagree and hold divergent views gain greater mutual understanding, allowing greater cooperation[159] and compromise. Deliberative democracy thus presumably aims to protect and achieve citizens' rights and to enhance the responsiveness of voters to their constituency.[160]

In sum, the notions of the 'right to democratic governance' and 'deliberative democracy' can operate as restraints on the exercise of governmental powers for the common good, and in the long run contribute to good governance, respect for the rule of law (which is the cornerstone and foundation for promotion and protection of human rights), and ultimately, better protection of human rights, and citizens' trust in institutions of governance. These human rights-cum-rule of law frameworks suggest that neither states nor their corrupt officials should be allowed to continue to benefit from or be allowed to hide behind or abuse doctrines such as 'sovereignty' to the detriment of the common good. This proposition is buttressed by scholars such as Wilfred Jenks, who has described international law as 'increasingly shifting from the formal structure of the relationships between States and the delimitation of their jurisdiction to the development of substantive rules on matters of common concern vital to the growth of an international community and to the individual well-being of the citizens of its member States'.[161] As W Michael Reisman eloquently added:

> Spoliation [large scale corruption] is not a legal problem if the supreme leader can plausibly say *'l'état, c'est moi'* ['the state that is me']. As long as the proprietary state was legitimate, there could be no question that the sovereign or his family was entitled to alienate or liquidate parts of the natural heritage of his fief and cache it in a convenient financial center elsewhere in the world. But the

[155] ibid.
[156] ibid.
[157] ibid, 372.
[158] ibid, 376.
[159] ibid, 379.
[160] ibid.
[161] See Wilfred Jenks, *The Common Law of Mankind* (New York: Frederick A Praeger, 1958) 17.

> incorporation of democratic ideals into international law and into transnational notions of political legitimacy, which has found its most authoritative expression in the United Nations Charter, changes, by necessary implication, the competence of national officials to dispose of the assets of a nation-state. The point of a declaration about the permanent sovereignty of peoples over their natural resources is not that the resources in question may not be mined and sold. Such a doctrine would render them valueless. The point is rather that the national community in which the resources are found is to be a significant beneficiary of their exploitation. By implication here, and explicitly in other international instruments, the nation-state is now expected to contribute to the welfare of *all* inhabitants, without even having the right to discriminate among them.[162]

The concept of human rights founded on the fundamental principle of human dignity, equality and respect, is thus inherent to the human condition, and as such has reduced the absolute content of the concept of sovereignty. Even the UN Charter balances the principles of sovereignty and non-interference with that of respect for human rights.[163] However, while the Charter has clearly been conceived as a mechanism to achieve basic needs and social justice, and the legitimacy of governments, in practice these norms are still mostly applied to favour states. Nonetheless, the growing body of human rights instruments[164] that have subsequently been adopted and ratified by several states have redefined what used to be exclusively within the domestic jurisdiction of individual states, and provided an ethical paradigm and benchmark to guide the contemporary international order, as well as to help individuals to create a defence of their autonomy against any oppressive governments.

In addition to the ideas of the right to democratic governance and deliberative democracy, the notion of the rule of law means that both governments and citizens are subject to the law,[165] and promote the

[162] Reisman, 'Harnessing International Law' (n 2) 83.

[163] Louis Henkin (ed), 'Introduction', in *The International Bill of Rights* (New York: Colombia University Press, 1981) 6; Thomas Buergenthal, 'The Normative and Institutional Evolution of International Human Rights' (1997) 19 *Human Rights Quarterly* 703–23.

[164] The 'seven core treaties' sponsored by the United Nations: the International Covenant on Civil and Political Rights (ICCPR); the International Covenant on Economic, Social and Cultural Rights (ICESCR); the International Convention on the Elimination of All Forms of Racial Discrimination (CERD); the Convention on the Elimination of All Forms of Discrimination against Women (CEDAW); the Convention against Torture and Other Cruel, Inhuman or Degrading Treatment or Punishment (CAT); the Convention on the Rights of the Child (CRC); and the International Convention on the Protection of the Rights of All Migrant Workers and Members of Their Families (CMW). See generally, Thomas Buergenthal, Dinah Shelton, and David Stewart, *International Human Rights in a Nutshell*, 3rd edn (St Paul, MN: West Group, 2002); and Bruno Simma and Philip Alston, 'The Sources of Human Rights Law: Custom, *Jus Cogens* and General Principles' (1992) 12 *Australian Yearbook of International Law* 82–108.

[165] The Magna Carta of 1215, in cl 39 provides: 'No free man shall be seized or imprisoned, or stripped of his rights or possessions, or outlawed or exiled, or deprived of his standing in any other way, nor will we [the King] proceed with force against him, or send others to do so, except by the lawful judgment of his equals or by the law of the land.'

legitimacy of government. There are essentially two ideals of the rule of law: the 'thin ideal' prohibits arbitrary exercise of power, and the 'thick ideal' requires the attainment of democratic values. The rule of law thus requires governance through the law. Predictability of rules, fairness, openness, transparency, and accountability are the hallmarks of any rule of law-based society. The rule of law is now universally recognised as a fundamental element in the 'virtuous trilogy' (together with human rights and democracy) upon which a legitimate, legal (national and international) order rests.[166] It has served as an extremely powerful and influential ideal for decades for those fighting authoritarianism, totalitarianism, and dictatorship, and it provides a robust normative framework for any serious representative and democratic government to flourish, to achieve sound political participation and engagement, and to meet the common good.[167]

Regardless of its forms, and differences in definitions, few would disagree that corruption fundamentally is exploitative of the public, leads to abuse of power, contributes to discrimination in the making and formulation of laws, and unquestionably creates uneven enforcement and application of the law, as the wealthy and politically connected can escape punishment for any wrongdoings. The extent to which people have resources often dictates the extent to which they access to, or are able to manipulate, the justice system. In an unequal society, the rich and powerful (and their friends and relations) often consider themselves as being above the law. Unequal distribution of resources among individuals and groups subverts institutions, including the work of those agencies with the responsibility to implement the law. Inequality enables the powerful to subvert local and national political, regulatory, and legal institutions for their own benefit. If a person is sufficiently richer than another, and the courts are corruptible, then the legal system is unlikely to favour justice, but rather what the rich can offer. Similarly, if political and regulatory institutions can be moved by wealth and influence, the chances are that they will favour the established, not the common citizen. Poverty and inequality, therefore, create disparity in the quality of justice. Amichai Magen stated:

> Social and economic exclusion, deriving from extreme and persistent levels of inequality, obliterates legal impartiality, causing the *invisibility* of the extreme poor, the *demonization* of those who challenge the system, and the *immunity* of the privileged, in the *eyes* of individuals and institutions. In synthesis, extreme and persistent social and economic inequality erodes reciprocity, both in the

[166] Amichai Magen, 'The Rule of Law and Its Promotion Abroad: Three Problems of Scope' (2009) 45 *Stanford Journal of International Law* 51.

[167] Oscar Vilhena Vieira, 'Inequality and the Subversion of the Rule of Law' (2007) 27 *Sur-International Journal on Human Rights* 6.

> moral and the mutual advantage sense, thus impairing the integrity of the Rule of Law.[168]

In a judgment delivered on 14 December 2012,[169] the ECOWAS Court of Justice held that states are to exercise their authority to enforce 'the law' that recognises human rights (such as economic, social, and cultural rights), and to 'prevent powerful entities (this presumably would include powerful corrupt state officials holding the state "hostage") from precluding the most vulnerable from enjoying the right granted to them'.[170] The Court frowned at the 'failure to use the State authority, in compliance with international obligations, to prevent the oil extraction industry from doing harm to the environment, livelihood and quality of life to the people of that region'.[171] While the court's ruling relates to the influence and excesses of powerful oil corporations and the need for the government to address this, it is possible to make a similar point in relation to state instrumentalities. On this account, a state would be required to exercise due diligence to prevent corruption, especially large-scale corruption that arises from the conduct of state organs, agents, or representatives, as determined by municipal or international law. If the state could hold due diligence duty to external and private actors, it seems fair and proper to impute at least the same level of responsibility to the state with respect to its own officials.

In general, human rights law can provide the framework for the sound operation of the rule of law and contribute to advancing justice, which in turn can produce good governance and a genuine representative state. If judges, legislators, auditors, and so on, are to be truly independent and are to entrench integrity in their work, a desire for the rule of law, and vigilance to protect these institutions against corruption, is essential. An incidental benefit may be a free press, which in turn can help to foster a well-informed and activist public, as well as well-paid, trained, and

[168] Magen, 'The Rule of Law' (n 166) 51.

[169] The case involved the Socio-Economic Rights and Accountability Project and the Federal Republic of Nigeria. The plaintiff's case concerned 'violation of the right to an adequate standard of living' – including adequate food – and the violation of the right to economic and social development. The plaintiff among others argued that the right to adequate food requires states to ensure the availability and accessibility of food; that 'availability' includes being able to feed oneself directly from productive land or other natural resources; that the Nigerian government clearly failed to protect the natural resource upon which people depend for food in the Niger Delta; and that as a result, the government contravened 'its obligation to ensure the availability of food in that thousands of oil spills and other environmental damage to fisheries, farmland and crops have occurred over decades without adequate clean-up'. This author helped to draft the legal brief that contributed to the positive outcome of the case. For details of the case, see www.courtecowas.org/site2012/pdf_files/decisions/judgements/2012/SERAP_V_FEDERAL_REPUBLIC_OF_NIGERIA.pdf.

[170] ibid [32].

[171] ibid [33].

competent civil servants who care about the public, rather than themselves. As Paul Farmer wrote:

> The concept of human rights may at times be brandished as an all-purpose and universal tonic, but it was developed to protect the vulnerable. The true value of the human rights movement's central documents is revealed only when they serve to protect the rights of those who are most likely to have their rights violated. The proper beneficiaries of the Universal Declaration of Human Rights... are the poor and otherwise disempowered.[172]

The idea of addressing corruption through the framework of human rights is not entirely without precedent. As early as 1992 the UN Human Rights Commission (now the Human Rights Council) came to the realisation that efforts to revitalise the implementation of economic and social rights would remain futile unless they addressed once and for all the question of corruption by high-ranking public officials. Thus, in Resolution 1992/50 it stressed that a link exists between acts of 'indigenous spoliation' (that is, large-scale corruption) and reduction of human rights, especially the economic and social rights of groups and individuals. The resolution recognised that this problem and its effects are global, especially in nations with vulnerable economies. In addition, the resolution indicated that the victims of corruption are entitled to some form of redress and compensation, and demanded an end to the transfer of stolen assets abroad. While this resolution may not be legally binding, it nonetheless firmly places the problem of large-scale corruption within the framework of human rights of the United Nations. Ironically, Nigeria, with its long history of corruption, was among the countries that voted in favour of the resolution.[173]

Similarly, the fact that the world nations symbolically mark International Anti-Corruption Day on 9 December each year, a day that immediately precedes Human Rights Day (10 December) is not a coincidence but would seem a deliberate and reasoned decision, suggesting that they recognise (at least in principle) the strong connection between corruption and human rights. This proposition is further buttressed by the explicit reference in the first paragraph of the Foreword to the UNCAC to this connection, to the effect that: '[Corruption] undermines democracy and the rule of law, leads to violations of human rights, distorts markets, erodes the quality of life and allows organized crime, terrorism and other threats to human security to flourish.'

Furthermore, the UNCAC, the Council of Europe's Criminal Law Convention on Corruption, the Civil Law Convention on Corruption, the

[172] Paul Farmer, *Pathologies of Power: Health, Human Rights and the New War on the Poor* (Berkeley, CA: University of California Press, 2003) 212.

[173] See Commission on Human Rights, Summary Record of the 52nd Meeting (First Part) E/CN 4/1992/SR 52.

Inter-American Convention against Corruption, and so on, all variously emphasise in their preambles the threat that corruption poses to the rule of law, democracy, human rights, good governance, fairness, justice, moral order, legitimacy of public institutions and sustainable development. Further, in June 2012 Morocco, on behalf of 132 states, addressed the UN Human Rights Council on how corruption undermined human rights and national initiatives to improve citizens' lives.[174] Similarly, in August 2013, Transparency International gave a presentation on the negative impact of corruption on human rights during the session of the UN Human Rights Council. The organisation made the following arguments. First, corruption violates human rights both directly and indirectly, perpetrating discrimination and widening inequality, for example by undermining due process and fair trial (through the bribing of judges), as well as the right to participation (through vote-buying), or when doctors demand payments for services that should be free. Second, corruption obstructs the right to development, undermines the rule of law and protection of human rights. Third, conceiving corruption as a human rights issue will 'strengthen the punishment against corruption.' Finally, TI suggested that 'there is ample cause for corruption to become a standing issue on the agenda of the Human Rights Council', and to effectively accomplish this, the Council should establish 'a mandate for a UN special rapporteur on corruption and human rights'.[175]

Earlier, on 13 March 2013, the Office of the High Commissioner for Human Rights organised a 'panel discussion on the negative impact of corruption on human rights' during the 22nd session of the Human Rights Council. Represented at the meeting were UN agencies specialised in human rights, anti-corruption and development, governmental institutions, as well as international and civil society organisations. The UN High Commissioner for Human Rights, Ms Navi Pillay, stated that:

[174] See 'Cross Regional Statement on Corruption and Human Rights', delivered by Morocco on behalf of a group of 132 states to the UN Human Rights Council, 26 June 2012.

[175] The special rapporteur would produce annual reports on the linkage between corruption and human rights, undertake country visits and make reports to the Council and General Assembly, receive individual communications alleging human rights violations as a result of corruption, and strengthen the connections between anti-corruption and human rights mechanisms internationally, regionally, and domestically. For similar arguments, see generally, Boersma, *Corruption* (n 66); Zoe Pearson, 'An International Human Rights Approach to Corruption' in Peter Larmour and Nick Wolanin (eds), *Corruption and Anti-Corruption* (Canberra: Asia Pacific Press, 2001); International Council on Human Rights Policy, *Corruption and Human Rights: Making the Connection* (Versoix: ICHRP, 2009); and Laurence Cockcroft, *Corruption and Human Rights: A Crucial Link*, available at http://resources.transparency.bg/download.html?id=229, 1–5. For earlier initiatives by the UN on the impact of corruption on human rights, see UN Docs E/CN.4/Sub.2/2003/18 14 -5 (2003) (where the Sub-Commission on Human Rights stated that 'those guilty of corruption should face international justice if they escaped national jurisdiction').

> Corruption is an enormous obstacle to the realization of all human rights – civil, political, economic, social and cultural, as well as the right to development. Corruption violates the core human rights principles of transparency, accountability, non-discrimination and meaningful participation in every aspect of life of the community. Conversely, these principles, when upheld and implemented, are the most effective means to fight corruption.[176]

Also emphasised was 'the need to protect [and "empower"] victims of corruption ["to claim their rights"], persons reporting crimes of corruption and experts dealing with such crimes, as well as the right to a fair trial for alleged perpetrators of corruption crimes.'[177]

Relatedly, the 2003 International Anti-Corruption Conference, which took place in Seoul, Korea, likened large-scale corruption to crimes such as torture and genocide, and suggested that it should be recognised as a crime against humanity, stressing that all people have a basic human right to live in a corruption-free society. For his part, Ndiva Kofele-Kale has proposed a similar concept of the right of individuals to live in a society free from corruption, elaborating what he called 'indigenous spoliation', which he argued should be considered a crime under international law.[178] According to Kofele-Kale, this concept supports the right of economic self-determination, and that life, dignity, and other vital human values depend upon this right.[179] As a universal human right, therefore, its contravention by corrupt officials is not only a violation of domestic law, but

[176] See www.ohchr.org/en/NewsE+vents/Pages/DisplayNews.aspx?NewsID=13131. According to Ms Pillay, 'A human rights-based approach to anti-corruption responds to the people's resounding call for a social, political and economic order that delivers on the promises of freedom from fear and want.' She disclosed that 'from 2000 to 2009 developing countries lost US$8.44 trillion to illicit financial flows, 10 times more than the foreign aid they received.'

[177] ibid. See also Jan Wouters, Cedric Ryngaertt and Ann Sofie Cloots, 'The International Legal Framework Against Corruption' (n 36); James Gathii, 'A Critical Appraisal of the NEPAD Agenda in Light of Africa's Place in the World Trade Regime in an Era of Market Centered Development' (2003) 13 *Transnational Law and Contemporary Problems*; Transparency International, Global Corruption Report 2004, www.archive.transparency.org/publications/gcr/gcr_2004; Davide Torsello, 'The Ethnography of Corruption: Research Themes in Political Anthropology' Working Paper Series 2, March 2011, The Quality Of Government Institute, www.pol.gu.se/digitalAssets/1357/1357836_2011_2_torsello.pdf, and Gauthier De Beco, 'Monitoring corruption from a human rights perspective' (2011) 15(7) *International Journal of Human Rights* 1107; and Michael, Bryane and Hajredini, Habit, 'What Does Kosovo Teach Us about Using Human Rights Law to Prosecute Corruption Offences?', www.papers.ssrn.com/sol3/papers.cfm?abstract_id=1549467.

[178] Kofele-Kale, *The International Law of Responsibility for Economic Crimes* (n 137). See also Brian C Harms, 'Note: Holding Public Officials Accountable in the International Realm: A New Multi-Layered Strategy to Combat Corruption' (2000) 33 *Cornell International Law Journal* 159.

[179] Kofele-Kale, *The International Law of Responsibility for Economic Crimes* (n 137) 163. See also Ndiva Kofele-Kale, 'Note: Holding Public Officials Accountable in the International Realm: A New Multi-Layered Strategy to Combat Corruption' (2000) 33 *Cornell International Law Journal* 159; and Kenneth Aceampong, 'Combating Grand Corruption: The Potential Impact of a United Nations Convention on Prevention and Punishment of the Crime of Economic Genocide' (1988) 7 *Revue Africaine des l'Homme*.

also a crime under international law.[180] While the proposition – by both the International Anti-Corruption Conference and Kofele-Kale – clearly has some appeal, its legal, normative and conceptual foundations would need to be further developed and clarified, to better contribute to the fight against corruption and protection of human rights. Similarly, at the moment the nature of obligation assumes by a corporation complicit in a state's corruption which causes human rights violations is unclear. As such, it might be useful to clarify the extent to which such corporations may be held accountable under human rights law.

## TOWARD A UNIVERSAL DEFINITION OF CORRUPTION

Two key questions to address here are, first, whether corruption is indefinable, and therefore unnecessary to strive to define it; and second, if the answer to this question is in the negative, whether corruption can be effectively combated without a universal agreement as to its meaning and its effects. In the first place, it has been suggested rather sceptically that 'the search for the definition of corruption is like the pursuit of the Holy Grail, endless, exhausting and ultimately futile'.[181] However, the fact that the term 'corruption' is complex, and plagued with so many meanings that make it very difficult to define, provides a compelling reason to come up with a more precise definition, if only to help distil a concept that has become mired in doctrinal, political and ideological controversies for decades.

Would additional types of definition of corruption contribute to solutions? Or would it simply compound an already complex concept? Alexander Brown has emphasised the need for 'more sound, reflexive and relatively clear conceptual frameworks in integrity and corruption research'.[182] It is argued that to strive for a better definition of corruption is to contribute to the efforts to address the conceptual confusion around 'corruption' (which easily leads to abuse or misapplication of the term for political or ideological purposes), and to advance the cause for a fair and just remedy for victims of corruption. Therefore, to casually dismiss attempts to define corruption as 'futile' would be unhelpful and counter-

[180] Kofele-Kale, *The International Law of Responsibility for Economic Crimes* (n 137) 166.

[181] Graeme Moodie, 'On Political Scandals and Corruption' (1980) 15 *Government and Opposition* 209. Martine Boersma has also suggested that 'For the purpose of international law, a single overall definition does not suffice to cover the multi-headed monster of corruption.' See Boersma, *Corruption* (n 66) 26. Nevertheless, she still went ahead to propose a 'working definition', which is basically the same as the World Bank's definition, except that 'political gain' is added to 'private gain'. In addition, Boersma's argument that a single definition would be insufficient for corruption is also not backed up by international practice of defining similarly complex concepts like 'enforced disappearances'.

[182] Brown, 'What Are We Trying to Measure?' (n 23) 58.

productive, not least because the full meaning of the very broad term has not yet been fully explored (whether from the perspective of law, political science or ethics, and so on) and the concept still lacks the precision and specificity required to combat the problem and its varying manifestations and consequences for human rights.

As for the second question, as already mentioned, so far no single definition of corruption has fully described the concept. Corruption from legal *and* human rights perspectives needs to be precise and clear, if it is to fully capture the problem and its consequences, and ensure effective remedies for victims. As already discussed in detail above, while the 'characterisations' of corruption constitute a good starting-point as adopted by anti-corruption treaties such as the UN Convention against Corruption and the AU Convention on Preventing and Combating Corruption, they fail to identify and define large-scale corruption as such, in part because they neither fully delineate the nature, gravity, or magnitude of the problem, nor properly align corruption to the harms caused to the economically and socially vulnerable.[183] Thus, despite several attempts[184] and the proliferation of anti-corruption instruments, there is as yet no universally accepted definition of corruption[185] because, as noted, the word is open to too many interpretations.[186]

It has proved difficult over the decades to determine what official misconduct should be designated as crimes. This is understandable, given the relatively recent history of the fight against corruption, the fact that corruption is a fluid concept, and that its causes and consequences vary from country to country and culture to culture. However, politics and claims of national sovereignty are additional stumbling blocks against international agreement on definition of corruption. Even so, these are insufficient reasons for the lack of international agreement on the definition of corruption. A universal definition of corruption that can break the barriers of politics, cultures, and religions is neither unrealistic nor unreasonable, and a universal agreement is certainly an essential precondition to curbing a transnational phenomenon like corruption. It is argued that it is precisely the lack of a consensus that has contributed to the often parochial

[183] Anti-corruption treaties such as the UN Convention against Corruption underscore the point that the level of sanctions for corruption should take into account the gravity of the offence, although these sanctions are not specified.

[184] The Inter-American Convention against Corruption, one of few anti-corruption treaties to attempt a definition of corruption, states that it includes 'Any act or omission in the discharge of his duties by a government official ... for the purpose of illicitly obtaining benefits for himself or for a third person.' Art 6(1)(c), Organization of American States, Inter-American Convention Against Corruption, March 29, 1996, 35 ILM 724, www.oas.org/juridico/english/treaties/b-58.html.

[185] Henning, 'Public Corruption' (n 83) 807; Peters and Welch, 'Political Corruption in America' (n 81) 974, 976.

[186] David Kennedy, 'The International Anti-Corruption Campaign' (1999 )14 *Connecticut Journal of International Law* 455 .

use or usurpation of the concept of corruption. History also suggests that it would be mistaken to assume that the concept of corruption is inherently incapable of precise legal definition. In any case, although there is no single definition, there is some broad consensus of which acts count as corruption, and these recognised acts are frequently included in international, regional and domestic instruments and laws. The normative and moral basis for this international consensus will constantly be challenged, until the world nations deem it imperative to agree on a definition of corruption.

As no nation, however corrupt, would declare that corruption is its peoples' way of life, cultural relativity cannot be used to justify corrupt practices, or to escape the consequences of such actions or their effects on victims.[187] Anti-corruption treaties that adopt a descriptive approach to the definition of corruption grant states some 'margin of appreciation',[188] and the flexibility to decide on the criminalisation of future acts of corruption. However, while the task of creating a universally accepted definition of corruption is necessary, it is very difficult. On the one hand, it is vital for a more profound understanding of corruption and its effects on individuals, communities and society that thus far have been minimised. This task is not technically impossible. Yet, on the other hand, it is difficult, because any such definition is certain to be disputed, especially given the remarkably complex nature of 'corruption', the political arena within which the fight against corruption arose, and the overriding considerations of national sovereignty and other interests that continue to drive this.

Arguably, if the fight against corruption in African states is to be meaningful and ensure accountability of states and effective remedies for victims, a clear and precise definition of corruption (normatively delineating all the fundamental elements and reflecting the serious harms suffered by victims) is imperative on the grounds of justice, fairness and the rule of law. It is simply not an academic matter, because the lack of clarity, objectivity, specificity, or precision would continue to obscure a better understanding of the problem, and consequently obstruct sustainable solutions, exacerbate the suffering of the economically and socially vulnerable, and circumvent the spirit of universal condemnation of corruption. This also

[187] Simon Coldham, 'Legal Responses to State Corruption in Commonwealth Africa' (1995) 39 *Journal of African Law* 116.

[188] Broadly speaking, a margin of appreciation is the latitude granted to member states of the Council of Europe in their implementation of the European Convention of Human Rights. It has been argued that the application of the margin of appreciation is a major threat to the rule of law. See, generally, Jeffrey A Brauch, 'The Margin of Appreciation and the Jurisprudence of the European Court of Human Rights: Threat to the Rule of Law' (2004) 11 *Columbia Journal of European Law* 113; Thomas A O'Donnell, 'The Margin of Appreciation Doctrine: Standards in the Jurisprudence of the European Court of Human Rights' (1982) 4 *Human Rights Quarterly* 474–75.

would presumably breach fundamental rule of law principles, such as proportionality and equality. As has been suggested (see Introduction and Chapter 2), there is a great deal of evidence to suggest connection between corruption and poverty. And many of the empirical reports that have been highlighted suggest that social and economic development will not occur without genuine commitments by African states to address governance, transparency and accountability issues.[189]

It is further argued that it is this corruption-cum-poverty (manifesting itself in the massive theft of states' resources, and consequently the weak institutions, inability to provide the most basic services to citizens, collapsed rule of law, and political and economic instability) that contributes significantly to the deaths of millions of children across the continent annually from entirely preventable diseases. In the case of Nigeria, for example, several reports by its Parliament, following investigations of allegations of corruption, ably illustrate the devastating nature and consequences of corruption in most parts of Africa and the need for a more precise legal and universal definition that effectively and coherently incorporates the victims' element.[190]

The US State Department country report for 2012 on Nigeria, for example, highlighted several cases of large-scale corruption, including alleged money laundering of close to five billion naira ($32m) of funds belonging to Bayelsa State by the former governor of Bayelsa State, Timipre Sylva; the alleged theft of 61.4 billion naira ($393m) by Ondo State Oil Producing Communities Development Commission Chair Debo Ajimuda; alleged theft from the Police Pension Fund of 32.8 billion naira ($210m) by a former director of the Police Pension Office; alleged theft of one billion naira ($6.4m) and 40 billion naira ($256m) by a former speaker of the House of Representatives and a deputy speaker, respectively; alleged theft of 58 billion naira ($372m), 25 billion naira ($160m), 18 billion naira ($115m), and 12.8 billion naira ($82m) by four former governors of Ogun State, Oyo State, Nasarawa State and Gombe State, respectively; and the guilty plea by a former Delta State governor to charges in Southwark Crown Court in London of money laundering and other financial crimes totalling 12.4 billion naira ($79m) he had committed during his eight years in office.[191]

[189] See eg, UNDP/Global Financial Integrity, 2011, 'Illicit Financial Flows from the Least Developed Countries: 1990-2008'.

[190] See, for example, 'US State Department Country Reports on Human Rights Practices, 2012', www.state.gov/j/drl/rls/hrrpt/humanrightsreport/#wrapper. The section on Nigeria stated that 'On April 18 a House of Representatives Committee led by Representative Farouk Lawan and charged with investigating the fuel subsidy program from 2009 to 2011 released a report showing massive fraud, corruption, and inefficiencies in the operation of the program. The report alleged misappropriation of nearly half the subsidy funds, with poor or non-existent oversight by government agencies. The report estimated government money lost to "endemic corruption and entrenched inefficiency" amounted to 1.067 trillion naira ($6.8 billion).' Ibid, 41–42.

[191] ibid, 42–43.

Even on this account alone, any ambiguity in the definition of corruption, especially within the framework of the UN Convention against Corruption, will continue to dilute the gravity and magnitude of corruption and the harms that it causes, as well as negating accountability of states and perpetrators alike and any global efforts to coordinate the complex legal rules against corruption. The absence of a universal definition also suggests that inconsistencies may arise in the implementation of treaty obligations, and this potentially can exacerbate politicisation of the fight against corruption, undermine international cooperation and assistance, and diminish the effectiveness of the fight against corruption. While the lack of international consensus on a definition might previously have been excusable, given the political and ideological divisions that surrounded the narrowed concept of corruption, things have since changed, as the world community has already condemned corruption (repeatedly since the mid-1970s, branding corruption a threat to progress, democracy, economic development and society as a whole) and now broadly agrees on the core acts that constitute corruption, and, significantly, has accepted responsibility for combatting the problem through, for example, globally accepted instruments such as the UN Convention against Corruption.

However, this responsibility would be fulfilled only when states cooperate with each other to concretely address the contemporary form of corruption and its effects on human rights that are now so apparent in many African states. The fact that the issue of the definition of corruption was discussed during the drafting of the convention also suggests the importance the world community has historically attached to it. Although sharp divisions among states (on issues such as national sovereignty) meant that attempts at definition were unsuccessful, nothing prevents the international community from revisiting the issue, especially because the ideal of corruption (as is international morality) is an evolving one, and changes over time. If the United Nations has now recognised that corruption infringes the fundamental values of human rights, justice and fairness, then it has to take the steps (in the face of changing circumstances) to establish the necessary normative framework to respond accordingly for the sake of the victims. When the FCPA was passed in the 1970s, 'corruption' was limited to prohibition of 'foreign bribery'; and several resolutions adopted by the United Nations (and OECD Convention) substantively followed this path. But the international community has now embraced a broader idea of corruption in major treaties such as UNCAC. If the international community has progressively expanded the notion of corruption over the years, it seems a natural progression to reach a global understanding and consensus on the legal and human rights meaning of corruption, especially large-scale corruption. This will no doubt help to remove the question marks that remain over the effectiveness of global and collaborative efforts against corruption.

Lack of agreement on the definition of corruption leaves considerable ambiguity and discretion – and thus unpredictability – in the enforcement process. The point is that global condemnation of corruption needs to be combined with a universal agreement of its nature, causes, and effects on the economically and socially vulnerable (as well as effective and coherent framework to provide victims of corruption effective remedies) if the political and legal commitments that have thus far been expressed are to be effectively and satisfactorily enforced. As noted, corruption is not only a national problem, but also a regional and global one, and it raises multi-jurisdictional issues because the perpetrators of corrupt acts often reside elsewhere from the parties who are hurt by such acts. For example, most of the public funds stolen from African states are stashed abroad in developed economies, while millions of poor citizens remain marginalised. A universal definition of corruption, therefore, would enhance the enforcement of the legal framework for corruption and widen the limited but oft-repeated view that corruption affects only a single party, tribe, or culture. Accordingly, re-conceptualising corruption must involve a more complete understanding of the problem and its concrete human consequences in order to unify the role of global and regional anticorruption treaties to combat corruption across borders.

While it is true that the concept of corruption may be open to political manipulation, this deficiency can certainly be addressed through the mechanisms of the rule of law and a transparent and participatory law-making process. The argument might be made that each jurisdiction should be able to define for itself what is (or is not) considered corruption. However, given that corruption has implications across national borders, any such 'margin of appreciation' is bound to undermine any possibility of a universal definition of corruption, and consequently, the international efforts to combat it. It has to be emphasised that corruption, while mostly a national phenomenon, has far-reaching regional and international consequences. As such, both the 'victim and complicit state' (the state committing an act of corruption) and the 'beneficiary state' (the state where corrupt funds are kept, indirectly benefiting or aiding their economy) should be able to exercise jurisdiction to enforce anti-corruption conventions, laws and standards.

Understanding the effect on the 'victim and complicit state' (in particular on the economically and socially vulnerable) is especially important for creating strong and effective enforcement, given the Catch-22 fact that in most cases the 'victim and complicit state' is unable to enforce and implement its own laws, because of its weak and dysfunctional institutions of governance (principally as a result of a lack of resources, caused to a large extent by large-scale corruption). Yet, the 'beneficiary state' can quickly acquire a complicit aspect if it aids and abets corruption in the 'victim and complicit state' by, for example, allowing its jurisdictional and legal systems to block asset recovery, or by declining to cooperate with the 'victim and complicit state.'

Furthermore, although the human rights and anti-corruption movements share many of the same goals, their legal and regulatory agendas have historically had little in common. Adopting a universal definition of corruption that is rooted in human rights norms would further help to overcome this divide and identify areas in which the two movements can collaborate on issues of corruption and human rights (and build on their respective strengths and commonalities) to find effective remedies for victims of corruption. Ultimately, the idea of a universal definition of corruption would serve to better harmonise the laws and legislation on corruption in order to develop a unified and consistent approach to the problem, eliminate differences among national legal systems that have in the past blocked mutual assistance efforts between countries, and translate global sentiment against corruption into concrete criminal prohibitions, defining misconduct as agreed upon by the international community.

## CONCLUSION

Corruption has primarily been considered a crime, and so a criminal law response has been the preferred strategy to combat it for decades. Despite the existence of several legal and other measures against corruption, it continued to exist, and in fact reappeared with devastating effect. Reports of corruption from many parts of Africa (and indeed, globally) are reported daily in the press. It is clear, though, that a one-size-fits-all response to corruption cannot satisfactorily or effectively address the problem, especially given its complexities, multidisciplinary and contemporary nature (and the fact that its causes vary widely), and its varying but devastating effects on human rights in regions like Africa. This invariably imposes new responsibilities on the part of the world nations to come up with innovative ideas, so that the inherent nature of corruption can be better understood, and a more effective legal response to the problem developed.

As this chapter has shown, there are many definitions of corruption, of varying normative content and significance. Even so, most of the definitions do not reflect elements of the accountability of states for the human rights violations faced by victims of large-scale corruption, most frequently the economically and socially vulnerable. The victims are largely neutralised (and virtually anonymous) in the criminal process, with no access to human rights remedies. Yet, focusing disproportionately on the prosecution of individuals will carry with it a moral accusation on the failings of individual character, and distract from routine patterns of corruption. Emphasising a human rights dimension to corruption would help correct the underlying structures precipitating it, not just its symptoms, ensuring that the victims are not left helpless and without effective remedies. While a comprehensive reform of the criminal justice system is one useful way to combat corruption, it has to be recognised that criminal law, by its very nature, is limited in terms of its ability to change human behaviour or to provide the kind of remedies available with the application of human rights law.

Furthermore, human rights law is distinguishable by its normative usefulness and comprehensiveness, for example requiring states to organise and structure their institutions of governance. Human rights have 'value because they protect interests that are constitutive of a decent life; they are necessary conditions for human flourishing'.[192] Human rights ascribe to human beings *qua* human beings, and do not depend on the vagaries, goodwill, or discretion of governments for their enjoyment. Thus, 'even all governments together cannot legislate such rights out of existence'.[193] Human rights actions against a state have a substantially greater chance for success than solely criminal prosecution of individuals because standards of proof are lower than the 'proof beyond a reasonable doubt' required in the prosecution of corruption *qua* corruption.[194] Nonetheless, for human rights law to be able to play this role satisfactorily, states will have to improve the capacity of national, regional, and international human rights institutions, mechanisms, and courts, and to make sure that the institutions themselves are not politicised or corrupt. Similarly, it will be desirable to consistently relax the requirement of exhaustion of domestic remedies before cases can be filed regionally or internationally against states with corrupt criminal justice systems.

Other significant legal and practical challenges such as causation, legal standing for victims, identification of victims, and evidence-gathering (a particularly daunting task, given the secretive nature of corruption), and so on, will need to be overcome if the potential of human rights law to combat corruption is to be realised and maximised. As will be argued throughout this book (see in particular Chapter 6), the challenges, while clearly daunting, are not politically, conceptually or legally insurmountable. Finally, while the international community does not yet share a uniform definition of corruption, it is essential on the grounds of fairness that states strive for greater specificity, and come to some agreement on the

[192] See Simon Caney, 'Climate Change, Human Rights and Moral Threshold', in Stephen Humphreys (ed), *Human Rights and Climate Change* (Cambridge: Cambridge University Press, 2010) 75.

[193] Pogge, 'Recognized and Violated by International Law' (n 78) 717.

[194] Human rights actions also increase the prospects that victims will receive an effective remedy for the damages and harms suffered as a result of corruption. Human rights litigation can result in judgments against a state or former high-ranking government officials that commit, support, or condone acts of official corruption, as immunity for acts of corruption will not be available in human rights actions.

definition of large-scale corruption, especially given its harsh human consequences regionally, nationally, and internationally. Yet, a legal definition (or any definition for that matter) may not be able to fully control the usurpation or manipulation of the concept of corruption. Nonetheless, the proposed definition outlined in the Introduction would provide the normative contours of corruption as a human rights issue, and might serve to limit the abuse of the concept of corruption for political, ideological and other reasons. It would also enhance the accountability of states for the acts of corruption by their officials. Variations in national legal systems in the application of the definition in practice will be warranted. Even so, such variations should not be allowed to dilute the normative contents (or criteria of reference) of the definition.

# 2

# *The International Dimensions of Corruption and Money Laundering*

## INTRODUCTION

THE TWIN PROBLEMS of corruption and money laundering, and their 'offspring' – poverty – have more in common than one might expect at the outset. This link is best captured by the second and third preambular paragraphs of the United Nations Convention against Corruption:

> Concerned also about the links between corruption and other forms of crime, in particular organized crime and economic crime, including money laundering . . .
>
> Concerned further about cases of corruption that involve vast quantities of assets, which may constitute a substantial proportion of the resources of States, and that threaten the political stability and sustainable development of those States.

Thus, 'corruption is a crime which relies significantly on the laundering process, which is essential for the corrupt to be able to enjoy the proceeds of crime'.[1] No wonder, then, that many anti-corruption instruments specifically contain measures to counter money laundering, while, conversely, money laundering instruments set out anti-corruption measures.

Evidently, the easier it is to launder corrupt public funds, the more likely it becomes for senior state officials to engage in corruption, and this cycle of corruption and money laundering naturally is a drain on the funds available to a government, and consequently burdens the institutions of governance as well as constraining the ability to implement basic human rights obligations and commitments. On this account (and because stolen public funds from Africa are more likely to end up in Europe and North America through the international financial system), the effects of corruption on human rights may not be fully understood without some grasp of how corruption is intrinsically linked to money laundering, and

[1] See Indira Carr and Miriam Goldby, 'The UN Anti-Corruption Convention and Money Laundering', http://idec.gr/iier/new/CORRUPTION%20CONFERENCE/The%20UN%20Anti-corruption%20convention%20and%20money%20laundering-INDIRA%20CARR.pdf.

how together they exacerbate poverty in African states, and consequently, adversely affect the economically and socially vulnerable.

In addition, while it is almost impossible to ascertain exactly the volume of money laundering (or 'dirty money') arising from corruption in African states (simply because of the very nature of the crime, but also because of modern means of electronic and other transfer techniques, and shell corporations), the African Union has estimated the amount to be $148bn annually. This figure may not be an exaggeration when it is considered that in Nigeria alone, over $400bn is estimated to have been lost to large-scale corruption since independence in 1960. However, the accuracy of such estimates has been questioned, on the grounds that were these estimates to be true, money laundering would have had more obvious and visible effects.[2] On top of this, there is also presumably a 'methodological difficulty' inherent in any measurement of the degree of money laundering.[3] Irrespective of the paucity of statistical evidence (or the near impracticability of attempting to estimate) on the extent of money laundering, it is clear that to steal an estimated $148bn annually from any economy and then stash the money in foreign banks is to leave significant holes in the system of finance, not least for a continent of limited resources. The implications however can be far-reaching in terms of not only constraining the ability of states to discharge important governmental services, but also to effectively carry out their international human rights obligations and commitments.

Moreover, a range of money laundering treaties, declarations and laws have been adopted and enacted. However, unlike other parts of the world such as Europe and North America, Africa as a whole has lagged behind in its efforts to develop and adopt anti-money laundering measures. For example, it was not until the adoption in 2003 of the AU Convention on Preventing and Combating Corruption[4] that there was a continent-wide initiative against money laundering. Current legal and other initiatives however are generally ineffective in practice, and the majority of money laundering activities linked to corruption remain undetected, uninvestigated or unpunished.

The first part of this chapter outlines the legal instruments that have been developed to address the problem of money laundering in Africa, and the extent to which financial institutions are able to detect and report (or 'police') money laundering activities (in light of access to their clients' financial operations and records). Also discussed is the relationship between corruption, money laundering and poverty. The emphasis here is

[2] P van Duyne, 'Money Laundering: Pavlov's Dog and beyond' (1998) 37 *Howard Journal of Criminal Justice* 359–74, 360.

[3] MM Gallant, *Money Laundering and the Proceeds of Crime* (Cheltenham: Edward Elgar, 2005) 11–12.

[4] The AU Convention is discussed extensively in Ch 4.

on international and regional initiatives and not national legislation, which will be considered in Chapter 3. Drawing on the outcomes of corruption and money laundering investigations, and published reports by, among others, the African Development Bank, Transparency International, the United Nations and US Congress, the second part of the chapter builds on earlier discussions and illustrates, through the examples of Angola, Equatorial Guinea and Nigeria, how corruption, money laundering and poverty are actually connected in practice. The chapter underscores the need for legal instruments against money laundering to place additional responsibilities on financial institutions in relation to money laundering activities. Such responsibilities will include implementing 'know your customer' (KYC) policies and procedures, so that they can identify any customers engaging in money laundering activities, and publishing and filing a currency transaction report with the authorities each time a 'politically exposed person' (or PEP[5]) from a developing region such as Africa executes a certain level of cash transactions. It is argued that without safe havens abroad where stolen public funds can be stashed, and the limited chances of detection, senior state officials are less likely to engage in corruption, because 'the ability to dispose of illegally obtained funds without being noticed gives [suspected] criminals an extra incentive to repeat their crimes'.[6]

Angola, Equatorial Guinea and Nigeria have been selected as examples because for many years they have been on the bottom rungs of Transparency International's Corruption Perception Index.[7] The countries were also chosen because many of the international investigations of corruption in Africa have centred on them. While the magnitude of corruption in these countries may differ (due primarily to the fact that different

[5] According to the 'Glossary of the FATF [Financial Action Task Force] Recommendations', foreign PEPs are 'individuals who are or have been entrusted with prominent public functions by a foreign country, for example Heads of State, or of government, senior politicians, senior government, judicial or military officials, senior executives of state owned corporations [and] important political party officials . . . *The definition of PEPs is not intended to cover middle ranking or more junior individuals in the foregoing categories*' (emphasis added). The definition of a domestic PEP is the same as for a foreign PEP, except that they have been entrusted with domestic public functions. See 'Glossary of the FATF Recommendations', available at www.fatf-gafi.org/pages/glossary/n-r/. The 2011 FATF Report, 'Laundering the Proceeds of Corruption', states that PEPs are 'the largest categories of high-risk customers for money laundering purposes. PEPs pose a high risk for money laundering by the very nature of their position; they have access to significant public funds and the knowledge and ability to control budgets, public companies and contracts': FATF, 'Laundering the Proceeds of Corruption', www.fatf-gafi.org/media/fatf/documents/reports/Laundering%20the%20Proceeds%20of%20Corruption.pdf.

[6] Steven Melnik, 'The Inadequate Utilization of the Accounting Profession in the United States Government's Fight Against Money Laundering' (2000–01) 4 *New York University Journal of Legislation & Public Policy* 143, 147.

[7] As noted in the Introduction, of the 177 countries ranked on 2013's CPI, the following countries ranked as follows: Angola 153 (scoring 23); Equatorial Guinea 163 (scoring 19); and Nigeria 144 (scoring 25).

corrupt senior officials capitalise on institutional weaknesses in different ways), the effects are substantively much the same across the countries: 'capital flight' that contributes to poverty and consequently denial of basic human rights for citizens, especially the economically and socially vulnerable.

Although this chapter only focuses on a limited number of African countries, it attempts to draw some broad conclusions on a number of issues raised in these countries in relation to corruption, money laundering and poverty. Finally, it is important to stress that the cases of corruption and reports highlighted in this chapter are only illustrative of the degrees of corruption in the countries covered (insofar as access to information on corruption is very limited, and allegations of corruption are a daily occurrence in those countries), and should not be considered exhaustive.

## MONEY LAUNDERING: LEGAL AND OTHER INITIATIVES

### Background

The international fight against money laundering[8] arose against the background of drugs trafficking and organised crime in the 1980s (and the establishment of the Financial Action Task Force (FATF) in 1989), and initially focused on twin legal instruments in the forms of confiscation of the proceeds from crime, and the incrimination of money laundering.[9] The primary aim was to increase the 'effective enforcement of the criminal law in relation to profit-oriented crime'.[10] However, the legal instruments to fight money laundering have evolved and expanded considerably over the years, to cover corruption and other financial crimes.

The past two decades have witnessed a steady and remarkable progress in the efforts of the international community to fight money flows related to criminal activities and, in particular, the financing of terrorism.[11] This renewed interest in money laundering by the world's nations is related to the terrorist attacks in the United States on 11 September 2001, and the activities of armed militias in Mali, Nigeria, and Somalia, and the links of growing capital flight to flourishing organised criminal or terrorist groups.

[8] Although a global phenomenon, the term 'money laundering' is derived from the early practice of criminal organisations in the United States, which used to operate launderettes as cash-intensive businesses to hide their criminal wealth. It later became connected with the Watergate scandal in the Unites States (see Ch 1). For a comprehensive treatment of the legal issues raised by the international fight against money laundering, see Guy Stessens, *Money Laundering* (Cambridge: Cambridge University Press, 2000).

[9] ibid, 3.

[10] ibid.

[11] ibid.

The link of large-scale corruption to terrorism is quite likely the most important incentive for the renewed interest of the United States and the European Union in the global fight against corruption and money laundering. Thus, in countries where incidents of terrorism are rampant, both the United States and the European Union have used a combination of political pressure, economic incentives, and technical assistance to address the problem at its source: preventing and combating corruption in developing countries.

## Meaning of Money Laundering

Money laundering (whether in traditional or non-traditional forms) is defined as the movement of 'secret deposits of illicit funds through a series of deceptive transactions designed to disguise the source of the funds and make them reappear in the market in a legitimate form, without a trace of their origin'.[12] For the purposes of this book, however, money laundering can be described as the process of concealing the true origin and ownership of public stolen funds with the twin aims of giving legitimacy to such funds (by 'laundering' or 'washing' them through the channels of financial institutions), and accessing and using the funds without detection that they were initially derived from corruption. This 'washing cycle' essentially helps to remove the 'stain' of criminality and disconnects corrupt officials from those funds.

Three phases of the washing cycle can be identified: placement, layering and integration of corrupt public funds (and other illegal funds). The placement phase occurs when corrupt funds are introduced for the first time to a financial institution. The layering phase involves a chain of transfers and movement of funds across financial institutions so as to make it extremely difficult for law enforcement agencies to detect or trace those funds to where they were originally deposited. The integration phase finally is the 'legitimisation phase', because it is at this stage that the corrupt funds (and so on) are actually transferred to legitimate business enterprises and thus given the appearance of being derived from those enterprises. 'Shell' companies, usually registered in offshore havens,

[12] Kathleen A Lacey and Barbara Crutchfield George, 'Crackdown on Money Laundering: A Comparative Analysis of the Feasibility and Effectiveness of Domestic and Multilateral Policy Reforms' (2002–03) 23 *Northwestern Journal of International Law and Business* 263. The International Monetary Fund (IMF) defines money laundering as 'the process in which assets obtained or generated by criminal activity, are moved or concealed to obscure their link with crime': 'The IMF and the Fight Against Money Laundering and the Financing of Terrorism', www.imf.org/external/np/exr/facts/aml.htm. The World Bank's definition is similar in substance: 'Ill-gotten Money and the Economy: The Experiences from Malawi and Namibia', http://siteresources.worldbank.org/EXTFINANCIALSECTOR/Resources/Ill_gotten_money_and_economy.pdf.

are often used at this level. It is useful to point out that the owners of shell companies keep their identities hidden beneath layers of bank secrecy laws and through their exercise of attorney–client privilege (and in the United States, for example, also through real estate agents and escrow agents, as both types of agent are exempted from the AML requirements of the Patriot Act). These outlined phases are the same routes for all illegal funds, and not just corrupt funds. But unless law enforcement and other relevant authorities have established an audit trail during the first two phases of the washing cycle, the funds' illicit origins will not be discovered.

However, it should be noted that, like corruption, there is no universal international definition of money laundering, and the differences of approach and perspectives are apparent from the various treaties standards and laws on the issue. Even so, the legal instruments against money laundering generally have a common four-layered strategy: (1) the criminalisation of money laundering; (2) strengthening the methods of tracing, freezing, and confiscating the proceeds of illegal activity; (3) implementing regulatory tools to prevent the use of financial systems for the purpose of money laundering; and (4) improving international cooperation.[13]

## Legal and Other Initiatives

There are several applicable international and regional anti-money laundering (AML) initiatives, in the form of treaties, resolutions, policies, and so on, which aim basically to 'take the dirty out of dirty money', and to obtain necessary evidence to prosecute anyone involved, whether directly or indirectly. Illegal removal of huge sum of public funds from the system will seriously threaten the political, social and economic institutions of states, and inevitably harm communities and individuals. Removing the financial incentive to steal public funds, and the financial ability to then use the funds to buy political, economic and other privileges, can play an important role in corruption prevention. Thus, even if this may not generally be understood as such, AML implicitly aims to serve a public interest objective by imposing important restraints and prescribing sanctions against those engaged in money laundering and predicate offences like corruption.

[13] See, for example, the Vienna Convention of 1988, which imposes on each party the duty to establish money laundering as a crime. See UNDOC 'Convention against Illicit Traffic in Narcotic Drugs and Psychotropic Substances', www.unodc.org/pdf/convention_1988_en.pdf. But the convention does not use the term 'money laundering' and only discusses property derived from drug-related offences. Nonetheless, it defines 'property' broadly to include any possible kind of asset, and such assets are to be considered proceeds of the specified offences, whether derived directly or indirectly. Since the Vienna Convention, criminalisation of money laundering has developed beyond the scope of drug-related proceeds, after it became obvious that the limitation was neither justified nor practical.

While some of these instruments impose specific AML obligations on states, others have more general provisions and constitute 'soft law' but may be equally crucial to combat money laundering. Among the legally binding instruments relevant to Africa are the UN Convention against Corruption and the AU Convention on Preventing and Combating Corruption. However, since the UN Convention provides the most comprehensive standards against money laundering, and has been more widely ratified than any other similar instrument, this section will focus primarily on its core provisions on the issue; first, in Article 23, which criminalises the laundering of the proceeds of corruption, and secondly, in Article 14 covering preventive issues with regard to proceeds of corruption. These provisions are very useful in the fight against corruption, especially considering the phenomenon of overwhelming corruption in many parts of Africa (and the subsequent depositing of proceeds in overseas financial institutions), and because they contain measures essentially aiming to prevent but also to identify and investigate money laundering, and as such, the information or evidence obtained can have a multiplier effect as it can be used to prosecute suspects for both money laundering and corruption. Effective money laundering regimes can also contribute to the efforts to retrieve and return stolen public money to victims. In addition to increasing the prospects of successful prosecution of corruption cases, they can also serve both deterrent and sanctioning purposes, and generally contribute to the effectiveness of the fight against corruption. Yet, like many of the provisions of the UNCAC, these provisions have significant weaknesses. The provisions of the UNCAC relating to money laundering will now be considered in turn, as will other initiatives and 'soft law' standards.

Article 23 requires the adoption of legislation to tackle the laundering of proceeds of crime. Subject to the open-ended 'fundamental principles of a State Party's domestic law', it requires states to punish the intentional acquisition, conversion, transfer, possession, use, concealment, or disguise of property in the knowledge that it is the proceeds of crime. Money laundering under these provisions is not confined to the laundering of cash, because of the very inclusive notion of 'property'.

In other permissive and discretionary language, the article also requires that, subject to the basic concepts of its legal system (or 'fundamental principles' of domestic law), a state must criminalise these actions, along with participation in, association with, conspiracy to commit, or attempts to aid, abet, facilitate, or counsel the commission of covered offences. Thus, the reach of Article 23 is insightful, as the provisions will presumably cover family members, friends, political associates (and party members), accountants, lawyers and other advisers (and charities and trusts) who while knowing the illicit source of the funds, nonetheless facilitate or allow such stolen public funds to be laundered, for example by facilitating or helping to open bank accounts or purchase property either in the corrupt official's name or their own names. The same will be true if any of these persons help to conceal the true nature, source, location, disposition or ownership of or rights with respect to illicit property, knowing full well that the properly is illegally obtained. In addition, anyone who 'knowingly' purchases the proceeds of crimes, such as the property of a senior corrupt official located for example in London or Berlin, can also be prosecuted pursuant to Article 23. This type of 'facilitative role' no doubt provides senior state corrupt officials with the incentive to engage in corruption at the expense of the citizens.

Furthermore, the predicate offences for money laundering must include a comprehensive range of criminal offences such as those established in Articles 15–22 of the UNCAC, discussed in Chapter 4 of this book. States must furnish the UN Secretary-General with copies of their laws giving effect to this article, and of any subsequent changes to their laws. Article 23 also imposes an international obligation on states to expand the reach of their laundering laws to predicate offences associated with corruption, largely mirroring Article 6 of the UN Convention against Transnational Organized Crime.[14] The UNCAC provides that each state shall 'consider' criminalising, when committed intentionally after the commission of any of the offences established in accordance with the convention, the concealment or continued retention of property by a person who knows that such property is the result of such offences.

There are also preventive measures relating to the prevention of money laundering in Article 14 of the UNCAC, and requiring some anti-money laundering measures in the realm of financial regulation rather than criminal law. Thus, state parties must impose customer identification, customer due diligence (the somewhat controversial 'know your customer' rule discussed more in detail below) and suspicious transaction reporting requirements, and should 'consider' the establishment of financial intelligence units. Article 14 closely follows the text of Article 7 of the UN Convention Against Transnational Organized Crime, although it contains some modifications. Importantly, Article 14 includes a clear extension of AML reporting obligations to alternative remittance systems, together with a requirement to identify beneficial owners when appropriate (those who have overseas accounts), and a stipulation that countries should 'consider' establishing wire originator information requirements. Like the Transnational Organized Crime Convention, Article 14 calls upon states, in establishing their domestic regulatory and supervisory regimes (and other bodies that may be susceptible to money laundering) both to impose

[14] It is useful to note that reference to the use of circumstantial evidence that is present in Art 6 of the Transnational Organized Crime Convention. These were not repeated in UNCAC's Art 14 because of the inclusion of Art 28, which is a broader article on the use of such evidence.

some thresholds of operation on the institutions, in particular regarding transfer of funds through traditional and non-traditional methods, and to be guided by existing international standards, such as the influential principles elaborated by the Financial Action Task Force and its regional counterparts.[15] States must also establish measures to detect and monitor movement of cash and negotiable instruments, and to ensure that accurate information is included on forms used to remit or transfer money electronically, presumably to trace the origins and final destination of the funds. Such information must be properly kept and maintained by banks and other financial institutions.

There are, however, other less detailed yet still useful instruments against money laundering. For example, the 2000 United Nations Convention against Transnational Organized Crime (the Palermo Convention) and its protocols essentially aim to establish uniform standards in the way states address transnational organised crimes such as money laundering.[16] Four crimes are established by the Palermo Convention: participation in organised criminal groups, money laundering, corruption, and obstruction of justice. The convention recognises the various forms of transnational organised crime and the threats they pose to security, democracy, rule of law, and political and financial stability. Additional crimes established under the protocols include, among others, trafficking in people, smuggling and illicit manufacture of firearms. States parties are to adopt legislation and policies to establish these crimes within the domestic legal systems, if the crimes do not already exist. More relevant to this book, the Palermo Convention requires states to combat money laundering by establishing a duty on their banks to keep accurate records and making sure that law enforcement agencies have access to those records.[17] Thus, both bank secrecy and anonymous bank accounts

[15] It should be noted that the *travaux préparatoires* indicate that references to 'relevant initiatives of regional, interregional and multilateral organizations' include the recent revisions of the FATF's 'Forty Recommendations on Money Laundering'.

[16] See also the websites of UNODC (www.unodc.org) and FATF (www.fatf-gafi.org). The United Nations' efforts to combat money laundering are coordinated by UNODC through its Global Program against Money Laundering (GPML). Through the GPML, UNODC assists member countries with policy development, legislation, technical assistance, problem-solving, and training in combating money laundering.

[17] Several other similar initiatives exist, including the United Nations Convention against Illicit Traffic in Narcotic Drugs and Psychotropic Substances (focusing mainly on money laundering of drug proceeds); the Council of European Communities' Convention on Laundering, Search, Seizure and Confiscation of the Proceeds from Crime of 1990 (containing both substantive law provisions to combat money laundering and mechanisms for international cooperation and mutual assistance in criminal matters (see Council of Europe Communities, www.conventions.coe.int/Treaty/EN/Treaties/Html/141.htm); the OAS Model Regulations Concerning Laundering Offences Connected to Illicit Drug Trafficking and Related Offences of 1999 (aiming to serve as a guide to OAS member countries in the adoption of national laws against money laundering); and the Wolfsberg Principles on Money Laundering (aiming among others to mitigate risks associated with transactions involving PEPs). In 2001, the US government passed the Uniting and Strengthening America

are disallowed. In this author's view, by consistently failing to implement these stringent measures to stop the flow of public funds into foreign banks, states are complicit in human rights violations caused by corruption.

Probably the most important AML instruments are those adopted by the FATF[18] (established by the Group of Seven (G7) in Paris 1989).[19] While the FATF initially started as a regional body, its impressive work and operations have extended to non-FATF members, and its influence and authority have grown to be global. Today, it is the only international body specialising in designing strategies to control money laundering. Thus, in February 1990, the FATF produced its renowned report, 'Forty Recommendations on Money Laundering',[20] (and revised in 1996 and 2003, to both keep up with changes in money laundering trends and to respond to September 11, 2001), which included an assessment of the scope of the problem and recommendations to establish a comprehensive strategy for dealing with it. These Recommendations against money laundering, lauded as 'the crown jewel of soft law',[21] have served as the international 'best practice' concerning AML measures in states' domestic laws.[22]

Although a 'soft law' (presumably to avoid a time-consuming and extensive ratification process), the 'Forty Recommendations on Money Laundering' provide a comprehensive strategy for action against money laundering, and are addressed to all institutions that affect or are affected

by Providing Appropriate Tools Required to Intercept and Obstruct Terrorism Act of 2001 (better known as the Patriot Act). Its primary aim is to follow the money trail of al-Qaeda and similar organisations. The Basel Committee on Banking Supervision (established by the central bank governors of the Group of Ten (G10) in 1974 (the G10 is actually made up of 11 industrial countries: Belgium, Canada, France, Germany, Italy, Japan, the Netherlands, Sweden, Switzerland, the United Kingdom, and the United States) in 1997 issued the Core Principles for Effective Banking Supervision, and in 2001 the Customer Due Diligence for Banks. Together, these documents among others require regulatory authorities to ensure that banks have internal policies, practices, and procedures, including 'Know Your Customer' procedures. Other intergovernmental organisations, such as the OECD, have also begun to focus their efforts on curbing and limiting opportunities for laundering the illicit proceeds of corruption from developing countries, including African states.

[18] The FATF consists of 31 member jurisdictions and two international organisations, the European Commission and the Gulf Cooperation Council. The FATF maintains a small secretariat at the offices of the OECD, which is assisted in its work by a number of regional FATF-style bodies, including the Asia/Pacific Group on Money Laundering, the Caribbean Financial Action Task Force, the Council of Europe Select Committee of Experts on the Evaluation of Anti-Money Laundering Measures, the Eurasian Group, the Financial Action Task Force of South America Against Money Laundering, Eastern and Southern Africa Anti-Money Laundering Group (ESAAMLG), and the Middle East and North Africa FATF.

[19] The Group of Seven comprises the US, Germany, the UK, Japan, Italy, France and Canada.

[20] FATF, 'Forty Recommendations on Money Laundering', www.accessbankplc.com/Library/Documents/Download%20Centre/FATF.pdf.

[21] Guy Stessens, *Money Laundering* (n 8) 17.

[22] ibid.

by money laundering, such as financial institutions, law enforcement and legislative bodies, and international institutions. They provide some level of flexibility in order to allow individual states some margin of appreciation to implement the guidelines within their domestic legal systems. However, most of the Forty Recommendations address regulatory changes and efforts that financial institutions should make to prevent money laundering. They are organised into four categories. The first deals with the issue of improving and strengthening national legal systems, including through legislative measures criminalising money laundering and punishing the crime. Among other recommendations under this category is the requirement that countries apply the crime of money laundering to all serious offences, with a view to including the widest range of predicate offences. The FATF has so far listed 20 categories of crimes for countries to consider as predicate offences, including extending such offences to conduct that occurs in another country, as long as it constitutes an offence in the country where it originated. Countries are also required to apply criminal, civil, or administrative liability to legal persons; to adopt provisions for the freezing, seizure, and confiscation of criminal assets; to ensure that financial institution secrecy laws do not inhibit the implementation of the FATF recommendations; to adopt 'safe harbour' rules to protect financial institutions, their directors, officers and employees from criminal and civil liability if they report suspicious transactions; and to establish effective, proportionate and dissuasive sanctions (criminal, civil, or administrative) for both natural and legal persons.

The second category of the FATF recommendations deals with the need to strengthen customer due diligence, such as reporting of suspicious transactions, together with regulations and supervision. The definition of financial institutions is very broad and covers any person or entity that conducts, as a business, at least one or more of 13 separate activities or operations for or on behalf of a customer. Any 'businesses providing a service of money or value transfer should be licensed or registered, and subject to effective systems for monitoring and ensuring compliance with national requirements to combat money laundering and terrorist financing'.[23] The recommendations have been extended to certain 'designated non-financial businesses and professions'[24] (that is, to casinos, real estate agents, dealers in precious metals and stones, lawyers, notaries, and other independent legal professionals and accountants, and trust and company service providers when they are involved with their clients or customers in preparing or executing financial or similar transactions). In addition, financial institutions are to implement enhanced customer diligence measures concerning PEPs, specifically to combat corruption, to

[23] FATF, 'Forty Recommendations on Money Laundering' (n 20).
[24] ibid.

address issues around correspondent banks, to maintain records for at least five years, and to establish appropriate training, compliance management and audit systems. Regulatory and supervisory bodies that oversee financial institutions are also to be improved and strengthened to ensure effective monitoring and oversight with respect to the implementation of the 'Forty Recommendations'. Criminals and their associates must be prevented from being the beneficiaries of a significant or controlling interest, or having management duties, in any financial institution, through the rigorous application of the fit and proper tests, or integrity standards, for financial institution officials.

The third category of the FATF recommendations deals with the issue of strengthening institutional and other measures on money laundering, specifically preventing and combating money laundering and effectively enforcing laws on the financing of terrorism. Countries are encouraged to: establish a financial intelligence unit to serve as a national centre for receiving, requesting, analysing and disseminating suspicious transaction reports for law enforcement purposes; equip their law enforcement authorities with the necessary powers of investigation, including the ability to obtain documents and information for their investigations, and furnish adequate financial, human and technical resources and effective mechanisms to these authorities to enable them to carry out their responsibilities effectively; prevent the unlawful use of legal persons by money launderers, military officials, senior executives of state owned-corporations and important political party officials by ensuring that there is adequate, accurate and timely information on the beneficial ownership and control of legal persons; and prevent the unlawful use of legal arrangements (such as express trusts) by money launderers, through information requirements.[25]

The fourth category of the FATF's 'Forty Recommendations' is concerned with the issue of international cooperation and mutual assistance. This category of recommendations requires countries to cooperate closely and effectively with, and extend mutual legal assistance to, other foreign judicial and law enforcement authorities in money laundering and terrorist financing investigations, including cooperation in the areas of requests by foreign countries to identify, freeze, seize and confiscate property

[25] To combat the problem of money laundering and improve citizens' right to know, in November 2013 the UK government established a publicly accessible register that contains details of who exactly owns and controls UK companies. The central registry of companies' beneficial owners (those holding more than 25% of shares or voting rights) is to be maintained by Companies House. This initiative followed decision in June by the leaders of the G8 group of the world's largest economies to establish registers of details of those who own and control companies within their territories, and to share this information upon request with other countries. This presumably will help to improve the problem of 'shell companies' and to improve public trust and confidence in companies and those that run them. Yet, exemptions on the ground of individual 'privacy safety' may be allowed. At any rate, whether an international consensus on the issue will emerge, and international agreements and standards will be effectively implemented, remains an open question.

laundered or proceeds from money laundering or predicate offences (or instrumentalities of offences), and to cooperate in the areas of extradition or prosecution of money laundering crimes.

Along these lines, the Stolen Asset Recovery (StAR) Initiative was published in November 2009, being a comprehensive report on how banks should handle PEP accounts. The report found a lack of effective implementation of international PEP standards, even including those issued by the FATF. The StAR report concluded that the international community lacks the political will and the enforceable legal and regulatory frameworks to address PEP issues. Other concerns raised by the report included limited due diligence requirements, inadequate PEP databases, and use of associates, intermediaries, and legal entities to hide PEP involvement. To reverse such trends, the report recommended the following: the strengthening of PEP identification systems by banks and the use of regulator-approved PEP databases; the elimination of artificial limits on the period during which an individual can be considered a PEP; the need for banks to obtain written beneficial ownership information for each account to detect PEPs using third parties to hide their activities; the requirement for public officials to provide information on their asset declarations lodged in their countries; and the need for regular (at least annual) reviews of PEP accounts to obtain full information about their relationships and to identify any suspicious transactions.

## ENHANCED PUBLIC INTEREST ROLE FOR BANKING AND OTHER FINANCIAL INSTITUTIONS

Banks, financial services, and other financial institutions have an important role to play in the global effort to prevent and combat large-scale corruption and money laundering. However, several concerns have been raised regarding the level of compliance by financial institutions with AML treaties, policies, and laws – one being the persistent use of bank secrecy, which has remained a significant obstacle in the effort to prevent money laundering. According to Kathleen A Lacey and Barbara Crutchfield George, the problem of bank secrecy can be traced as far back as the 1600s, when the Huguenots were fleeing religious persecution in France to a safe haven in Switzerland. A system of bank secrecy was thus developed to protect the Huguenots' assets; no wonder then that the use of the term 'bank secrecy' is so closely connected with Switzerland.[26]

[26] Lacey and Crutchfield George, 'Crackdown on Money Laundering' (n 12). In 1934, Switzerland passed its Federal Banking Law, rendering it a criminal offence punishable by imprisonment to violate bank secrecy. 'This shift was triggered by the need of Switzerland to maintain its neutrality as well as its national sovereignty against the intrusion of the Nazi government in Germany. In the 1920s, the Nazi government began its persecution of the

Other less-well known offshore banking havens now include the Bahamas, the Cayman Islands, Liechtenstein and Nauru. These locations are notorious for accepting deposits from corrupt senior state officials across Africa, primarily using nameless numbered bank accounts, making them attractive safe havens for stolen wealth by those officials.

Furthermore, one of the challenges that is raised by the elimination of bank secrecy and the adoption of a more transparent system (for example, the 'know your customer', or KYC rule) is that the KYC regulations may be constrained by the reality of limited knowledge of their PEP customers, and restricted access to information about them, which might in turn limit the possibility of verifying the accuracy of any information provided by PEPs. For example, limited resources and the incentive of profits may mean that financial institutions are not able to 'go all out' to verify the existence and validity of 'business interests' and addresses of PEPs, and as such may not know whether funds being deposited are derived from legitimate business interests or stolen public funds. A more serious challenge, however, is how to balance the depositor's right to privacy with the financial institution's duty of disclosure. There are concerns, for example, that the KYC rule may infringe a depositor's privacy, given that it allows banks to establish the identity of the depositor, and in some instances the identities of family members of depositors. On the other hand, it may be argued that this transparency process is justified on the grounds of 'public interests', necessity and reasonableness, especially if one balances this against the harm to millions of people victimised by corruption were the KYC rule to be ignored or not strictly enforced (as it is often the case).

As can be seen from the above outlined standards against money laundering, the UNCAC itemises a limited range of 'techniques' of money laundering: conversion, transfer, concealment, disguise, acquisition, possession and use. However, of these seven techniques, only conversion, transfer, concealment and disguise are mandatory, whereas the other three are optional, so the contracting parties can encode the criminalisation of these acts 'without violating their constitutional principles and basic concepts of their legal system'. Nonetheless, several other measures,

Jews and as a result money flooded out the country seeking refuge in neutral Switzerland. In an attempt to restore the fleeing capital, the Nazi government sought financial information in Switzerland and exerted pressure on employees of financial institutions, which resulted in the 1934 consolidation of the duty of confidentiality and the aggravation of penalties for any breach thereof.' Bank secrecy legislation also helped European Jews safeguard financial assets threatened by the Nazi regime in the 1930s and 1940s. Several rationales have been offered to justify bank secrecy. It has been argued that it serves as a personal right, in that financial privacy is analogous to client–lawyer or doctor–patient privileges, that it helps individuals against unfair tax systems, or that it gives financial refuge for those who are being persecuted on religious, political, or racial bases. Opponents of bank secrecy, however, have vigorously debated each of these arguments. The twin pillars of bank secrecy remain those that resulted in the Swiss Federal Banking Law: state sovereignty and individual rights.

like the FATF Recommendations, exist to combat money laundering, and banking and other financial institutions are heavily regulated. Even so, the effectiveness of the UNCAC, the FATF Recommendations and so on, and the regulatory and supervisory regimes they prescribe, are heavily reliant upon the existence of domestic criminal justice and financial systems that are effective, fair, credible and corruption-free. Unfortunately, the prevalence of large-scale corruption across African states creates an environment where other corrupt activities are replicated at various levels of society, and thus permeates a state's legal, political, social and economic systems. Largely because of this problem, the various measures, standards and policies are enforced either partially or not at all.

Since PEPs will always find it easier to manipulate a system already deep in corruption, questions will remain whether the proliferated AML measures and safeguards can ever be effective without first addressing the underlying factors precipitating corruption in those systems, and the corruption issue itself. Specifically, the enforcement of these far-reaching measures and standards with regards to financial institutions is often problematic, not least because of the immunity of corrupt senior public officials against investigation and/or prosecution for corruption while in office; and because of corruption in the criminal justice system or lack of independence and impartiality of the system. Law enforcement and other authorities may also under-use or abuse Suspicious Activity Reports (SARs), for political or pecuniary reasons. In addition, despite the negative consequences of money laundering on financial and economic systems and on society as a whole, as the case studies below show, many banking institutions consider the implementation of AML measures and standards to be too expensive and time-consuming, and therefore neglect their due diligence, reporting and record-keeping functions.

As will be shown shortly (through the case studies of Angola, Equatorial Guinea and Nigeria), one of the ways PEPs manipulate the rules and standards and avoid identification requirements is by using bank-to-bank transactions as a way to circumvent reporting requirements. Such transactions do not have identification requirements, so banks can develop relationships with offshore financial institutions and shell companies (for example, by means of correspondent accounts). Thus, at present there are too few restrictions on correspondent banks and shell companies. 'Going easy' on correspondent banks and shell companies invariably means 'going hard' on the public, in particular victims of human rights violations caused by corruption.

Furthermore, the AML measures and safeguards can also be easily sidetracked by, for example, separating larger sums of money into smaller amounts that can be deposited into several bank accounts, thereby sidetracking financial institutions' AML policies and procedures. This process, known as 'smurfing', will thus ensure that PEPs depositors can avoid completing a Suspicious Activity Report. There is also a lack of enforcement of AML rules and regulations, in particular, inadequate measures for the freezing or seizing of property suspected of being laundered. Failure to impose provisional rules that would prevent any further manipulation of the funds no doubt undermines money-laundering control, especially in an era of instantaneous global money transfers. With detection unlikely, and prosecution even more doubtful, money laundering remains a relatively low-risk, high-profit endeavour. Similarly, as noted, despite its prohibition by the UNCAC and the FATF, and so on, bank secrecy laws continue to exist in many safe haven jurisdictions like Cayman Islands and Luxembourg, which remain attractive for corrupt senior public officials from across Africa to keep their stolen funds.

The problem of safe haven jurisdictions is further exacerbated by the push for profits derived mostly from corrupt money from developing regions like Africa. This profit incentive also provides an explanation for the reluctance of many financial institutions to check, limit, or stop the laundering by PEPs, especially from Africa, of embezzled public funds. Thus, financial institutions may be unwilling to report their PEP clients' involvement in money laundering, presumably for fear of losing them to rival institutions. This will be the case, for example, with offshore banks, which are attractive and desirable tax havens because, in no small part, they are frequently located in countries that impose few taxes, offer depositors a guarantee of anonymity, and have strict bank secrecy laws. However, to continue to allow the highly lucrative and elaborate bank secrecy is to fail to effectively stop stolen public funds from across Africa from being deposited into safe haven jurisdictions, which among others can obstruct the gathering of important evidence on corruption and money laundering.

There are also the problems of proof and of the admissibility of vital evidence. For example, corrupt officials and safe haven jurisdictions can ensure that critical evidence cannot be accessed by law enforcement authorities in countries where such authorities are weak or not independent. Even where evidence is obtained, it may not be admissible if it is gained illegally; that is, if money laundering is not a crime in the foreign jurisdiction, as required by both the UNCAC and the FATF. However, this problem is unlikely to arise, given the wide ratification of the UNCAC, which requires states parties to criminalise money laundering.

Against this backdrop, it may seem unrealistic to expect corrupt criminal justice system to safeguard the public interest involved when senior state officials steal public funds; to stop the conversion of stolen funds/property; and to provide deterrence and sanctions through effective detection, investigation and prosecution of politically connected suspects, or those who are helping corrupt officials by for example, providing a method of hiding the true source of the stolen funds, and those who facilitate such activities. Yet, to allow PEPs and or their families and friends to benefit from their crime is to allow them to avoid responsibility for corruption or assistance in money laundering, and ultimately, to undermine the public good.

Accordingly, the above highlighted weaknesses of the AML regime demand the use of other approaches, in particular human rights law to complement existing instruments against corruption and money laundering. It has been stated that, 'while AML can be of great value in the fight against grand corruption . . . its limitations must be recognised and it should be viewed as only one of a number of tools which must be employed in the fight against corruption'.[27] Thus, one such 'tool' could be the reform of critical institutions of governance and the rule of law on the basis of human rights standards and values to contribute to corruption prevention and reduce the colossal costs and challenges often involved in responding to corruption and money laundering that have already taken place. While no reform may be able to completely stop corruption and money laundering *at source*, a reform based on human rights standards can at least contribute to promoting and establishing the rule of law, which in turn can make it difficult for corrupt senior state officials to manipulate the criminal justice systems for personal ends, and without the possibility of being caught or brought to justice.

In addition, the argument can be made that because of their access to PEPs' transactions, financial institutions are well placed to play a key watchdog role to detect and prevent money laundering by this category of clients. Thus, in relation to stolen public funds at least, this duty of due diligence would at the minimum demand complete fidelity to the public trust. If this is so, victims of corruption and public interest groups can rely on human rights law to ensure compliance with the duties of due diligence and KYC rules, thereby enhancing the effectiveness of the rules in practice.[28] This public trust function would be undermined, for example, if financial institutions were to unreasonably withhold information on transactions concerning PEPs from the public upon request. Allowing victims of human rights violations caused by corruption to access PEPs' records can act as a powerful dissuasive tool, as it can help to discourage potential corrupt senior state officials from engaging in corruption (and money laundering) in the first instance, knowing full well that the chances of being found out within the financial system are high.

[27] See Indira Carr and Miriam Goldby, 'The UN Anti-Corruption Convention and Money Laundering', http://idec.gr/iier/new/CORRUPTION%20CONFERENCE/The%20UN%20Anti-corruption%20convention%20and%20money%20laundering-INDIRA%20CARR.pdf.

[28] Such reporting will be consistent with the FATF's 'Forty Recommendations on Money Laundering' (n 20), which requires waiver of strict bank secrecy laws and provides safe harbour rules to protect reporting financial institutions and their officials from criminal or civil liability.

But it might be necessary to shield financial institutions from the risk of litigation or liability for disclosure of information on the ground of necessity and public interest if they are to be encouraged to play a more proactive role in detecting and preventing money laundering. While financial institutions have ethical duties in relation to their PEP clients, such duties should not be allowed to trump the overwhelming public interest considerations involved in detecting and preventing public funds derived from corruption (an illegal act) from being subject of money laundering. This enhanced public interest role for financial institutions may well help to reverse the perception about these institutions as being part of the money laundering conundrum (often considered to be carrying out the instructions of PEPs) and thus contribute to changing public attitudes to them, which in the long term may create an ethical (and profitable) business environment for the institutions. Financial institutions can recoup any potential fall in the profit margin that may result in the short term, by for instance establishing new areas of work and consultancy services in the field of anti-money laundering.

## MONEY LAUNDERING AND CORRUPTION IN AFRICA

Like large-scale corruption, money laundering has tremendous social, political and economic impacts on societies, especially in the developing world, including Africa. While corruption and money laundering can be considered as two sides of the same coin, the latter can form an important element of international criminal activities such as terrorism, arms smuggling, and drug trafficking.[29] It has been stated that:

> [The m]oney laundering process is traditionally thought of as taking place after funds have been received in some corrupt or criminal transaction. However, in the case of al Qaeda and other terrorist organizations, the money laundering occurs before the illegal act. In reverse order, 'clean money' is laundered in order to hide the sources of the money ultimately used to accomplish an illegal or destructive purpose. The series of deceptive laundering techniques prevent law enforcement officers from tracing the funds and determining the perpetrators and masterminds behind the vicious acts.[30]

However, while attention is focused on the corruption itself and the need to prosecute corrupt officials (a criminal law approach), there is less emphasis on the money-laundering element of the corruption process, including the effects on the economically and socially vulnerable. However, as already noted, without the opportunity and ability to

[29] Lacey and Crutchfield George, 'Crackdown on Money Laundering' (n 12).
[30] ibid.

launder corruptly acquired funds, it is less likely that the corruption would have occurred. As Lacey and Crutchfield George pointedly stated,

> The underlying harmful nature of money laundering is the corruption associated with it. Less apparent is a multiplicity of other negative consequences, which result from the money laundering process. There is an insidious core affecting society and the global economic welfare. The core tends to be largely ignored because the concentration is on the criminal activity in the initial stages, e.g., the bribe, and apprehending the wrongdoer on the other end, e.g., the punishment. Meanwhile, irreparable damage is done during the interim process of deviously legitimizing fruits of corrupt activity by shifting the funds through a series of complex financial transactions. Some of these negative consequences are: undermining public trust in the integrity of financial institutions; posing a challenge to the legitimate authority of national governments; corrupting officials and professionals; facilitating the looting of national treasuries, and the International Monetary Fund (IMF) and World Bank funds of capital-poor developing countries . . . causing a routine violation of legal norms, property rights, and human rights; facilitating other crimes such as drug trafficking, tax evasion, bribery, and terrorism.[31]

Further, the Africa Economic Outlook 2012,[32] published by the African Development Bank, shows that African states as a whole lost $18.4bn *annually* between 1970 and 2008 as a result of capital flight, most of it from large-scale corruption, thus putting 'strain on human development'.[33] The report suggested that if the capital had been reinvested in Africa with the same level of productivity, poverty levels would have been cut by 4 to 6 per cent every year between 2000 and 2008. The report also stated that 'capital flight also deepens inequality. The people benefiting from capital flight are the elites who . . . have the power to *unlawfully appropriate and transfer resources abroad.* Almost all those engaging in capital flight in Africa are among the 10% richest segment of the population.' (Emphasis added.)[34] According to the report, 'African countries could as a group have reached the Millennium Development Goal of halving the 1990 level of poverty by 2015, an objective they will not achieve on the current rate of poverty reduction.'[35] The report recommended 'improved domestic governance and elimination of the practices that foster capital flight'[36] as two solutions to the problem. It

[31] ibid. In addition, the FATF suggested in 2011 that there is a strong inverse correlation between corruption and income (GDP per capita): richer countries have lower levels of corruption, while developing and transitioning countries, such as those across Africa, have the highest levels. See FATF report 'Laundering the Proceeds of Corruption', www.fatfgafi.org/media/fatf/documents/reports/Laundering%20the%20Proceeds%20of%20Corruption.pdf.

[32] Africa Economic Outlook 2012, www.africaneconomicoutlook.org/fileadmin/uploads/PAGES-%20Pocket%20Edition%20AEO2012-EN.pdf, 21.

[33] ibid.

[34] ibid.

[35] ibid.

[36] ibid.

called on the international community to assist African states in identifying and repatriating stolen wealth, in particular through international mechanisms like StAR.[37] However, the report sees this as unlikely to happen any time soon, especially given the reality of the significant financial interest that accrues in safe haven bank accounts in developed economies from the proceeds of corruption across Africa, or, as the report put it, 'the reticence of some countries benefiting from these practices'.[38]

Moreover, Léonce Ndikumana and James K Boyce, in their seminal book, *Africa's Odious Debts: How Foreign Loans and Capital Flight Bled a Continent*,[39] show the deeply intertwined links between foreign loans and capital flight, and explore the human cost of fund transfers and mechanisms, to appeal for more responsible international financial systems. According to Ndikumana and Boyce, more than half of the money borrowed by African states in recent decades was misdirected within a year, transferred in many cases to private accounts in offshore tax secrecy jurisdictions. Given the important issues that they raise and their sensible and important recommendations, the following passage deserves to be quoted *in extenso*:

> Resource-starved African nations are subsidizing developed countries' industries and social services [through the] exodus of human capital [and] the illicit export of financial capital from African countries – or capital flight. This is not a new phenomenon, and it shows no signs of abating. Over the past four decades, sub-Saharan Africa has lost a staggering $700 billion due to capital flight. In addition to trade mis-invoicing, smuggling, and embezzlement of revenues from natural resource exports, a substantial part of the capital flight was financed by external borrowing. We estimate that every year 40 to 60 cents of each borrowed dollar spins out of the revolving door as capital flight, often returning to the same banks that issued the loans. On net basis, Africa is transferring more money to the rest of the world than it is receiving in terms of borrowing and aid . . . Capital flight, and the burden of servicing the debts that financed it, are partly to blame for the conditions that create the other economic problems faced by the continent ... Illicit financial flows drain scarce public resources that could have been used to finance public services including education and health. It partly explains why there are not enough schools, clinics, and medical equipment; it also explains the poor working conditions for doctors, teachers, and other professionals that force them to seek greener pastures abroad . . . Obviously African countries have the primary responsibility to devise and implement strategies to keep capital onshore. But the international community also has an equally important responsibility to root out the perverse incentives and opacity in the financial system that enable and perpetuate the financial haemorrhage faced by the continent.[40]

[37] ibid.
[38] ibid.
[39] Léonce Ndikumana and James K Boyce, *Africa's Odious Debts: How Foreign Loans and Capital Flight Bled a Continent* (London: Zed Books, 2011).
[40] ibid, 74–80.

Also, following an investigation, the US Congressional Permanent Subcommittee on Investigations (hereafter, the subcommittee) in 2010 issued a report disclosing how PEPs abused their public trust and stole public funds from Angola, Equatorial Guinea, and Nigeria, and then laundered and deposited the money in banks across the United States by taking advantage of attorney–client privileges and estate agent and escrow agent exemptions.[41] Regarding Equatorial Guinea[42] – which is one of the wealthier nations in the world yet whose citizens live in absolute poverty – it was discovered that for four years, between 2004 and 2008, the son of President Teodoro Nguema Obiang Mangue[43] laundered and transferred some $110m of public funds into the United States. Such an amount of money is extraordinary, given Mr Obiang's reported modest official salary of the equivalent of $60,000 per year as Equatorial Guinea's Minister of Agriculture and Forestry. Among the methods used to side-step US money laundering standards and regulations were attorney–client privilege and shell-company accounts (with such names as Beautiful Vision, Inc; Unlimited Horizon, Inc; Sweetwater Malibu, LLC; Sweetwater Management, Inc; and Sweet Pink, Inc). Mr Obiang transferred large amounts of stolen public funds to the United States, including to Citibank, some of which he used to buy a residence in Malibu, California, worth approximately $30m, and a Gulfstream jet reportedly worth $38.5m, both sales aided by escrow agents.

According to the subcommittee, Citibank refused to take any action, on the flimsy pretext that identifying, freezing, and investigating the wire transfers would 'generate too much work'[44] for its AML staff. As previously noted, both real estate agents and escrow agents are exempted from

[41] 'Keeping Foreign Corruption Out Of the United States: Four Case Histories': Hearing before the Senate Committee On Homeland Security & Government Affairs, Permanent Subcommittee On Investigations, 111th Congress 75–83 (2010), available at www.hsgac.senate.gov/subcommittees/investigations/hearings/-keeping-foreign-corruption-out-of-the-united-states-four-case-histories. For this report, the subcommittee carried out more than 100 interviews with lawyers, real estate agents, escrow agents, lobbyists, bankers, university professors, and government officials. Millions of pages of documents, including bank records, correspondence, contracts, emails, property records, flight records, news articles and court pleadings, were reviewed. Consultations were also held with foreign officials, international organisations, financial regulators and anti-corruption experts.

[42] ibid. A small West African country with a population of about 1 million, Equatorial Guinea is flanked by Cameroon and Gabon. The country obtained its independence from Spain in 1968, and its official languages are Spanish and French. Like Angola and Nigeria, Equatorial Guinea is blessed with abundant natural resources, including timber, hydrocarbon deposits, and oil (the latter is about 90 per cent of its economy), and is in fact the third-largest oil producer in sub-Saharan Africa. Despite its massive resources and its impressive gross domestic product per capita (largely because of its revenue), the majority of its citizens live in poverty.

[43] It should be noted that the president of Equitorial Guinea and his son share the same name. For clarity, in this chapter the son is referred to as either Mr Obiang ,or Obiang Jr. The father is referred to as President Obiang.

[44] 'Keeping Foreign Corruption Out Of the United States' (n 41).

the AML requirements of the Patriot Act. The 2004 investigation of Riggs Bank by the subcommittee also showed that, between 1997 and 2003, Mr Obiang had more than a dozen bank accounts, which, at times, held millions of dollars in deposits. After extensive investigations and hearings, the subcommittee concluded that the total value of assets held by Riggs Bank amounted to nearly $700m, making 'Equatorial Guinea' the bank's single largest depositor. There were also more than 60 accounts held by government entities, senior officials, and family members. The report found that for years Riggs Bank had disregarded its AML obligations with regard to Equatorial Guinea and had turned a blind eye to evidence that the bank was handling the proceeds of foreign corruption. The bank had allowed, and sometimes actively facilitated, suspicious financial activity. One of the suspicious transactions documented in the report showed that approximately $26.5m was transferred in 16 payments over a three-and-a-half year period between 2000 and 2003, directly from the official Equatoguinean governmental oil revenues account into a private account maintained at Banco Santander in Spain. These deposits were made by 'Kalunga Company SA', a company the subcommittee found reason to believe might be owned in whole or in part by Mr Obiang. The basis for this might be that the authorised signatories for the governmental oil revenues account were the president and either his nephew or Obiang Jr himself. The subcommittee report summed up these accounts thus:

> While the E.G. President's eldest son, Teodoro Nguema Obiang, the E.G. Minister of Forestry, did not have any personal accounts at Riggs, he was the beneficial owner of three accounts opened in the name of companies he controlled. Two of these accounts were opened in the name of his California entertainment company, TNO Entertainment LLC. The first, Account No. 76-889-555, was opened in 2000 and closed in 2001, and the funds were transferred to Account 76-923-450, which was opened in 2001 and remained open in early 2004. From 2001 to 2003, the second account had balances that fluctuated between about $17,000 and $11.6 million. The third account, Account No. 25-380-038, was opened in the name of Awake Ltd., a Bahamian offshore shell company that Riggs helped to establish. This money market account, opened in 2002, saw virtually no account activity.[45]

Several other accounts associated with Mr Obiang, including those with JPMorgan Chase and Citigroup, were traced and identified by the subcommittee.

Another related case is that of *APDHE v Obiang Family*,[46] in which a Canary Islands court also admitted a criminal complaint against President

[45] ibid.

[46] Open Society Institute and Soros Foundations Network, 'APDHE v Obiang Family', http://www.opensocietyfoundations.org/litigation/apdhe-v-obiang-family.

Obiang and his family, alleging the crime of money laundering for illegally diverting large sums of public funds to purchase real estate in Spain. The case was based essentially on the US subcommittee's 2004 report, discussed above. Further investigations carried out by Asociación Pro Derechos Humanos de España (APDHE) showed strong correlations in timing between at least five money transfers and nine real estate purchases in Madrid, Gijon, and Las Palmas de Gran Canaria on behalf of the President, members of his family, and close associates. The case was made possible by the provision of the Spanish Penal Code, which makes it a crime for anyone to acquire, convert, or transfer property knowing that such property was purchased by the proceeds from a serious crime, or for anyone to perform any other act to conceal or disguise its unlawful origin or to aid another person who has participated in the crime in evading the legal consequence of the crime. The plaintiff, who claimed 'a lawful and direct interest'[47] in the matter, argued that the defendants regularly diverted funds from the Equatoguinean Treasury by ordering Riggs Bank to make the various transfers to private accounts held by a shell company controlled by the defendants. It was argued that it was irrelevant that the acts of corruption were committed abroad because the Spanish Penal Code grants jurisdiction to Spanish courts over money laundering cases occurring in Spain, regardless of where the underlying crime occurred. According to the plaintiff's complaint:

> This 'laundered' money was apparently used by Equatorial Guinean personalities and their families for their own benefit, for the acquisition of properties in various Spanish provinces. Extensive corruption, induced by multinational companies, through the direct or indirect bribing of a large number of Equatorial Guinean officials, government members and their relatives, thus facilitating a systematic embezzlement of funds from the national budget.[48]

The plaintiff also argued that:

> [T]he system is supported by the fact that the gas and oil companies or their subsidiaries have participated from the outset in the exploitation of the vast resources of the country as partners or associates of President Obiang or of companies controlled by him, with the result that most of such companies' revenues are diverted for the personal benefit of the President and of other persons close to him. Some financial corporations have played a key role in the management of this structure.[49]

The plaintiff stated that the system operated within a 'framework of the dictatorship'[50] by violating human rights, persecuting political opponents,

[47] Open Society Justice Initiative partner organisation *Asociación Pro Derechos Humanos de España* (APDHE), www.opensocietyfoundations.org/litigation/apdhe-v-obiang-family.
[48] ibid.
[49] ibid.
[50] ibid.

creating political instability, and non-enforcement of the law, all with near absolute impunity. The plaintiff identified three main justifications as to why the case should be heard. The first was large-scale corruption, through which the government of Equatorial Guinea plundered the country's wealth with the acquiescence and cooperation of its partners (multinational oil companies and financial corporations). The plaintiff argued that this practice was large-scale and depleted the much-needed resources of the country. It explained that bribes were customary among Equatorial Guinean authorities, leaving President Obiang and the Mongomo clan (his family) in control of nearly all of the country's wealth. The second justification was oppression. The plaintiff argued that 'Equatorial Guinea is one of the worst dictatorships. It is subject to a merciless rule and to constant violations of Human Rights. The president and his clan concentrate in themselves all the political power, controlling the Government and Institutions.'[51] The third justification was extreme poverty. The plaintiff asserted that most of the population live in extreme poverty, arguing that 'the child and female death rates are alarmingly high'.[52] The plaintiff framed its written argument thus:

> Life expectancy at birth is 50.4 years, when, in view of the country's wealth, it should be 78 years. The three aspects [that is, large-scale corruption, oppression and the corresponding extreme poverty] are not independent, but are rather related to each other. Corruption with a capital 'C' is the word that defines Equatorial Guinea, but oppression is no separate issue. In fact, in Equatorial Guinea, oppression is an instrument for corruption. The extensive corruption framework through which the country is governed can only be maintained by means of a system of suppression of the population and of political opponents. Poverty is also no isolated issue: it is the necessary consequence of the amazingly high corruption level, which places Equatorial Guinea in the ninth position among the countries with the highest levels of corruption in the world.[53]

In January 2009, the *Fiscalía* (Office of the Prosecutor) concluded that there was a legitimate case and opened an official investigation in the *Juzgado de Instrucción* (Pre-Trial Investigative Court). The prosecutor concluded that the investigation should not commence in Madrid but rather in the Canary Islands, because the 'Kalunga Company SA' account was located there.

The TI France and SHERPA suit was the result of a 2007 French police investigation, which found that these three leaders (Denis Sassou Nguesso (Congo-Brazzaville), Omar Bongo Ondimba (Gabon, now deceased) and Téodoro Obiang (Equatorial Guinea) and their relatives owned homes in exclusive areas in Paris and on the Riviera, as well as luxury cars

[51] ibid.
[52] ibid.
[53] ibid.

(including not only Bugatti Veyrons but also Ferraris and Maseratis). Both TI France and SHERPA argued that it was not possible that the men and their entourages could have bought these assets with their legitimate salaries. They also claimed that President Téodoro Obiang owned vehicles worth more than EUR 4m (around $6m) and that his relations owned a combined 39 homes, and that Denis Sassou Nguesso and his relations held a combined 112 bank accounts. The Court of Appeal decision overturned an earlier ruling by a French magistrate who had ruled the case, known as the 'Ill-gotten Gains case', was admissible in a French court. The three leaders had appealed the first ruling, and the two organisations had appealed the second decision, calling it a 'legally questionable decision'.[54] William Bourdon, a lawyer for TI France, stated:

> Those in France and Africa who organise and take advantage of the looting of African public money will be celebrating with champagne. The ruling showed that French law still needs to evolve to allow groups [such as ours] to take legal action. Without that, we will continue to deprive victims of corruption of an indispensable means to guarantee their rights.

TI France and SHERPA were successful on appeal. Overruling the Court of Appeal, the French Supreme Court in 2010 declared that, for the first time in France regarding corruption cases, the TI France and SHERPA case was admissible. This decision allowed the appointment of an investigating judge and the opening of a judicial inquiry to determine the conditions under which the assets in question were acquired, how the numerous bank accounts identified by the police were accumulated, and how the various intermediaries identified as suspect by the French police might have facilitated operations. First among those were the banking institutions.

This case illustrates the fundamental weakness present in asset recovery efforts, not only in France but globally, because states' national legislations do not grant legal standing (see Chapter 6 for detailed discussion on legal standing, causation, etc) to victims of corruption and civil society groups. However, it also illustrates the important role courts can play in remedying the lacuna and holding African states and leaders accountable for the sake of the victims of human rights violations caused by corruption. Furthermore, the politics of corruption played itself out, as Western states normally do not pursue corrupt high-ranking officials while they were still in power. The difficulties encountered by TI France and SHERPA, despite strong police evidence, highlight how much need there is for legal clarity, political will (considering that the French government appealled against the initial ruling by the magistrate), and greater transparency in the implementation of anti-corruption standards on asset recovery.

[54] 'Keeping Foreign Corruption Out Of the United States' (n 41).

The French admissibility ruling would seem to be an isolated case of judicial bravery, and it is unlikely to have any major impact in key Western countries where many corrupt African leaders place their ill-gotten cash because these countries have complex legal rules on real estate agents, escrow agents, PEPs, and assets recovery, and generally do not allow court cases to be brought by victims or NGOs. Therefore, accountability for corruption and money laundering including such issues as the recovery of assets would continue to be dependent on the authorities in developed countries, something that fluctuates with political, economic, and other matters of national interest. This highlights the argument in Chapter 1 of this book on why a human rights approach can play a complementary role to the traditional criminal law approach.

Angola[55] is another country investigated by the US subcommittee, which in 2004 examined three Angolan PEP accounts. The first was that of Angolan arms dealer Pierre Falcone (a very close friend of Angolan President Jose Eduardo Dos Santos), who supplied weapons during the prolonged Angolan civil war. Through personal, family, and US shell company accounts in Arizona, Falcone transferred millions of dollars of Angolan public funds into the United States and freely moved funds across a global network of accounts, maintaining nearly 30 accounts with the Bank of America between 1989 and 2007. Despite being an arms dealer and the fact that in 2000 he was jailed in France following a prolonged criminal investigation, he was not considered a PEP; so his accounts were not treated as high-risk. He was also convicted and sentenced in 2007 to a six-year prison sentence in France on charges related to illegal arms dealing, tax fraud, and money laundering.

The second PEP account related to Dr Aguinaldo Jaime, a senior Angolan government official who headed Banco Nacional de Angola (BNA), the Angolan Central Bank. In 2002, he attempted unsuccessfully to transfer $50m of Angolan public funds into a private account in the United States or to purchase US Treasury bills for transfer into a private securities account in California. Following its suspicions, in 2003 Citibank (rather

[55] Angola is on the coast of western Africa, and is known for ongoing corruption problems, weak AML controls, and a cash-intensive banking system. Its official language is Portuguese, and it has a population of roughly 13 million. Angola gained its independence from Portugal on 11 November 1975. The country was immediately engulfed in civil war, initially among three factions: the Popular Movement for the Liberation of Angola (MPLA), the National Front for the Liberation of Angola (FNLA), and the National Union for the Total Independence of Angola (UNITA). Under the 1991 Biscesse Accord, the MPLA and UNITA agreed to a ceasefire and to hold elections in 1992. Jose Eduardo dos Santos of the MPLA won a plurality of the vote and assumed the presidency. UNITA rejected the results and the country returned to war, while MPLA, by default, became the recognised government. The 1994 Lusaka Protocol brought another ceasefire, but localised fighting spread and war continued until 2002. The civil war resulted in the death of as many as 1.5 million Angolans and the displacement of 4 million others. Angola is currently one of Africa's largest oil producers, with oil accounting for more than 90 per cent of its exports.

belatedly) not only closed BNA's accounts and all other accounts belonging to Angolan government entities, but it also closed its offices in Angola. It is unclear how much of the stolen funds were returned to Angola. However, HSBC continued to provide banking services to BNA in the United States and elsewhere. HSBC has a history of accepting stolen funds from Angola, as seen in the next case the subcommittee investigated.

The third PEP account involved Banco Africano de Investimentos (BAI), a $7bn Angolan private bank that serves, ironically, PEP clients. Its largest shareholder is Sonangol, the Angolan state-owned oil company. For more than a decade, despite the presence of PEPs in its management and as clients, and its failure to send a copy of its AML procedures to HSBC, BAI freely operated accounts at HSBC in New York and frequently used HSBC wire transfer services, foreign currency exchange, and credit card services.

In just these three investigations, it is clear that Angola's citizens were deprived of billions upon billions of dollars from their government treasury, which means this money was not spent on their betterment, such as education, health, or jobs, but rather in lining the pockets of a privileged few. Yet, as previously noted, other cases of corruption abound. For example, according to the 2004 Diamond Industry Annual Review,[56] Angola Selling Corporation (ASCorp) was established in 2000 to enhance compliance with UN sanctions by providing a system that would tighten Angola's diamond certificate of origin system and ensure the exclusion of UNITA diamonds. But the procedures were never fully implemented. According to a study conducted by the Institute for Security Studies:

> [The] Angola Diamond Corporation (ADC) has the lowest profile of any mining company in Angola. The opaque nature of the company results from the fact that it is not known to have mined diamonds in considerable quantities and is allegedly linked to Isabelle dos Santos, daughter of President dos Santos and former Endiama chief Noe Baltazar. The company allegedly has multiple alluvial concessions in Lunda Norte.[57]

The third country investigated by the US subcommittee is Nigeria.[58] The subcommittee found that between 2000 and 2008, former Nigerian vice

[56] Partnership Africa Canada, 'Diamond Industry Annual Review' 2004, www.pacweb.org/en/publications/diamond-archive.

[57] Institute for Security Studies, 'Inventory of Formal Diamond Mining in Angola', www.iss.org.za/Pubs/Books/Angola/8Dietrich.pdf.

[58] Nigeria is located on the west coast of Africa on the Gulf of Guinea. With more than 160 million citizens, it is the eighth most populous country in the world and the most populous nation on the African continent. Nigeria has a diverse ethnic make-up, with three major ethnic groups – the Hausa, Ibo and Yoruba – comprising nearly 40 per cent of the population. The official language of Nigeria is English. Nigeria gained its independence from the United Kingdom on 1 October 1960, and now operates as a federal republic of 36 states. Following years of military rule, Nigeria elected its first president, Olusegun Obasanjo, in 1999; he was re-elected in 2003. Nigeria ranks among the top 10 nations in the world for oil reserves, is the second largest oil producer in Africa, and is one of the world's largest exporters of oil. Oil revenues make up about 95 per cent of the country's generated revenues. Its oil

president Atiku Abubakar and his fourth wife Jennifer Douglas, a US citizen, transferred into US banks (through offshore corporations) more than $40m of Nigerian public funds. A civil complaint was filed in 2008 by the US Securities and Exchange Commission on alleged bribery of more than $2m received by Ms Douglas between 2001 and 2002 from Siemens AG.[59] The US banks were apparently unaware of Ms Douglas's PEP status. Upon questioning, Ms Douglas said that all of the funds came from her husband and she claimed lack of knowledge of the offshore corporations that deposited the money into her accounts. However, after one bank closed her accounts because of the offshore wire transfers, she opened new accounts at another bank.

Apart from the subcommittee investigation, numerous other reports of corruption in regard to Nigeria exist. A few of these reports may suffice for our purposes. In the case of *Attorney-General of Delta State & Ors v EFCC & Ors* (2007),[60] the Economic and Financial Crime Commission (EFCC) stated by affidavit that the investigations it carried out revealed massive corruption involving, among others, former governor Chief James Ibori. The investigation showed the diversion of N5 billion[61] (around $300m) from the accounts of the Delta State government at Nigerian-based Oceanic Bank and Zenith Bank, to purchase Afribank shares for Mr Ibori. According to the EFCC, 'the fraudulent transactions were perpetrated through the use of 14 fictitious companies'.[62] The EFCC subsequently claimed that it recovered the funds from Mr Ibori's accounts, with some capital gain on the investment, and that the funds were returned to the coffers of the Delta State government 'to enable the Government [to] carry out valuable projects for the people of Delta State'.[63] It is unclear, though, exactly how much was actually recovered and for what purposes these returned funds were spent. It should be noted that the citizens of Delta State, who suffered as a result of the illegal diversion, received no effective remedy.

production facilities are concentrated in the Niger Delta region, which, nonetheless, is an impoverished area.

[59] Siemens AG is a 'global powerhouse in electronics and electrical engineering, operating in the industry, energy and healthcare sectors'. Siemens is headquartered in Munich and Berlin. See www.siemens.com/entry/cc/en/.

[60] The details of this case, and other cases involving Nigeria, are drawn from the StAR website, http://star.worldbank.org/star/. StAR is a partnership between the World Bank Group and the UNODC, and it financially supports international efforts to end safe havens for corrupt funds. StAR works with developing countries and financial centres to prevent the laundering of the proceeds of corruption and to facilitate more systematic and timely return of stolen assets.

[61] The official currency of Nigeria is the naira.

[62] StAR, http://star.worldbank.org/corruption-cases/node/18620.

[63] ibid.

In another case – The *Federal Republic of Nigeria v Dariye and Dariye*[64] – filed in London on 16 December 1999, former governor Joshua Dariye applied to the Abuja branch of All-states Trust Bank PLC to open an account in the name of 'Ebenezer Retnan Ventures'. He signed the application form as Ebenezer Retnan, this name clearly being an alias. When he was questioned by the Metropolitan Police on 2 September 2004, he admitted that the Ebenezer Retnan account was his, though he had not registered Ebenezer Retnan Ventures with the Nigerian Corporate Affairs Commission and he had requested (and apparently manipulated) the bank management to waive all requirements for opening accounts beyond completion of the application form. The Ebenezer Retnan account was accordingly opened on 22 December 1999, with the first transaction on 1 March 2000. Former governor Dariye used this account to receive large sums from Plateau State, of which he was then governor. His abuse of office involved, among others, the diversion of approximately £2.6m (over $4m) in public funds from Plateau State to this account. He transferred nearly £762,000 (around $1.1m) from the same account to his London bank accounts. It was argued for the Nigerian government that Mr Dariye's actions amounted to 'misappropriation of public funds or secret profits obtained through the abuse of position as governor, and a public officer'. It was also argued that he violated the constitutional provisions prohibiting public officers from maintaining overseas bank accounts, and that there were huge discrepancies between his income, declared assets, and undeclared assets. The government also argued that it was impossible for Mr Dariye to have acquired his assets legitimately, given his income as a governor; the EFCC was able to prove this by showing that the assets investigated were derived from the theft of public funds. As is the norm with many cases involving large-scale corruption, there is no information as to what happened to the recovered stolen wealth, which included foreign properties, bank accounts, investments, and cash exceeding £10m (over $15m) in value. The total amount that has been recovered is also unclear. What is clear, however, is that Mr Dariye remains a free man in Nigeria, enjoying his alleged stolen wealth without being held accountable.

Probably the most famous case of corruption in Nigeria is that involving former Nigerian dictator General Sani Abacha.[65] When General

[64] ibid. *The Federal Republic of Nigeria v Joshua Chibi Dariye and another* [2007] EWHC 708 (Ch).

[65] It is difficult to estimate exactly how much Abacha stole, as most of the funds were taken away in cash from the Central Bank of Nigeria (CBN) through instructions from Abacha to his National Security Adviser. For example, the Adviser would seek and obtain authorisation from Abacha for funds for alleged 'desperate and imminent' security problems, which are in 'bad taste and not in our national interest', and requiring 'immediate solution and implementation'. This authorisation was then presented to the CBN for payment. The funds were released and stashed abroad. See Julio Bacio Terracino, *The International*

Abacha died unexpectedly in June 1998, the Nigerian government began looking into his family's wealth and the billions of dollars missing from Nigeria's treasury. According to bank records, at the same time that the corruption inquiry was going on, Citibank received a request from one of the general's sons, saying that he urgently needed $39m from one of their London accounts. However, the son may not have known that the money was in a 'time deposit' and could not be redeemed without a financial penalty. As clients of Citibank's Private Bank, bank officials had long accommodated the Abacha family by setting up accounts under secret names and a shell entity to hold the proceeds. Unsurprisingly the bank found a way to immediately transfer the amount and still not ask for the hefty penalty. One month later, Citibank records showed the transfer was intended to be only the first step in closing the account.

Before the account could be officially closed, however, a London court issued an order in a civil suit that froze all accounts related to the Abacha family. During investigation, it was found that between 1988 and 1999, Abacha's three sons had channelled more than $110m of public funds to Citibank accounts in London, the funds later frozen by the British government. Some of the stolen wealth was recovered and repatriated, but based on information obtained from parliamentary records of the Nigerian National Assembly, it would seem that the wealth may have been re-stolen. But while the victims of corruption are denied access to basic services and human rights, corrupt officials benefit from their corrupt acts.

## CORRUPTION AND POVERTY

A report by the World Bank confirmed that the number of people living in poverty across Africa has risen in recent times, despite the increasing prevalence of wealth and the abundance of natural resources in many African states.[66] While the report noted a marginal decline in the overall number of people living in extreme poverty, it also showed that 'Africa [still] has the highest poverty rate in the world, with 47.5 percent of the population living on $1.25 a day. They account for 30 percent of the world's poor.'[67]

*Legal Framework against Corruption: States' obligations to prevent and repress corruption* (Cambridge: Intersentia Publishing, 2012) 277. This example probably best illustrates how public funds are often stolen and diverted in several African states, including Angola and Equatorial Guinea.

[66] ibid, vii.

[67] ibid.

However, the meaning of 'poverty' (whether extreme or absolute), and how to measure it, remain somewhat controversial,[68] insofar as the 'man or woman in the street', lawyers, economists, political scientists and so on, naturally see 'poverty' in varying ways. It is arguable though that the definition and measurement of poverty ought to vary and be determined according to how it is actually experienced by a particular society and region. Generalisation of indicators and measurement tools may therefore be unhelpful and can be counterproductive. A particularly useful 'multi-dimensional meaning of poverty' has been suggested by the UN Committee on Economic, Social and Cultural Rights. According to the Committee, poverty is 'a human condition characterised by sustained or chronic deprivation of the resources, capabilities, choices, security and power necessary for the enjoyment of an adequate standard of living',[69] and one might add, indispensable to achieving the dignity and well-being of the human person and enjoyment of all human rights, insofar as human rights are universal, indivisible and interrelated. Similarly, 'whether measured in relative or absolute terms or in terms of capabilities, the problem of global poverty is staggering'.[70] While poverty affects all nations in some ways, it is more entrenched in developing regions like Africa. In addition, irrespective of the theoretical or academic postulations on poverty or the hierarchy of human rights, 'there seems to be little doubt that political freedoms are positively related to economic growth and that rising living standards foster democratic freedoms, while declining living standards subvert them'.[71]

[68] See Stephen Marks, 'Poverty' in Daniel Moeckli, Sangeeta Shah, and Sandesh Sivakumaran (eds), *International Human Rights Law* (Oxford: Oxford University Press, 2010).

[69] General Comment No 8, 'Substantive Issues Arising in the Implementation of the International Covenant on Economic, Social and Cultural Rights: Poverty and the International Covenant on Economic, Social and Cultural Rights', statement adopted by the Committee on Economic, Social and Cultural Rights on 4 May 2001, UN Doc E/C 12/2001/10, para 12. See generally, Declaration on the Right to Development, adopted by General Assembly Resolution 41/128 of 4 December 1986; Jeffrey D Sachs, with John W McArthur et al, 'Ending Africa's Poverty Trap', UN Millennium Project, Brookings Papers on Economic Activity (Washington, DC, 2004). The Committee on Economic, Social and Cultural Rights has also highlighted the negative effects of corruption on the full implementation of human rights, in particular, economic, social and cultural rights. See, for example, UN Committee on Economic, Social and Cultural Rights (CESCR), 'Concluding Observations: Nigeria', 16 June 1998, UN Doc E/C 12/1/Add 23, www.refworld.org/docid/3ae6ae690.html.

[70] Stephen Marks, 'Poverty' in *International Human Rights Law* (n 68) 605.

[71] ibid, 610. Thus, 'from the capability perspective, both human development and human rights increase freedom. From the utilitarian perspective, both enhance human well-being . . . [But] the greatest obstacle to those choices is poverty, which is both capability deprivation and a measure of the denial of human rights.' Ibid, 619–20. See also, Vienna Declaration and Programme of Action, A/CONF 157/23 (25 June 1993) paras 14–25; UNESCO, 'Education for Sustainable Development (ESD)', www.unesco.org/new/en/education/themes/leading-the-international-agenda/education-for-sustainable-development/ and OHCHR, *Claiming the MDGs: A Human Rights Approach* (New York and Geneva: United Nations, 2008).

Several questions have also arisen as to whether there is a right to development,[72] and what might actually be responsible for poverty in Africa. Is the present global institutional order the root cause of poverty in Africa? Are human rights 'inherently' the preserve of the rich and wealthy? Or are human rights indifferent to the plight of those who live in poverty? However, more important from the perspective of this book is the question of whether a state's obligation to protect human rights naturally implies a duty to eliminate poverty,[73] and indirectly, prevent and combat corruption, insofar as corruption creates a 'negative and hostile environment' for human rights. As previously noted and as discussed in subsequent chapters, irrespective of 'the deep political and even ideological issues involved in the relationship between poverty and human rights',[74] or the disagreement that may exist over the measurement of 'poverty' and the causal links between corruption and poverty, the majority of people who truly 'know the region' and who have lived and have families across Africa can hardly disagree that poverty is the continent's major, even though not fully recognised killer or sufficiently treated as such in antipoverty initiatives and programmes. Corruption, especially large-scale, is arguably both a cause and consequence of poverty.[75] The basis for this proposition may not be too far-fetched. On the one hand, corruption enriches a select few, while invariably subjecting many to poverty, especially the economically and socially vulnerable groups of society. Clearly, the enrichment of the few at the expense of the many, especially in a continent of limited resources, can hardly help the cause of those who live in poverty. And, as noted, the theft and stashing abroad of public funds, where such funds are then invested to improve the economies of developed countries,[76] is unfair as it undermines developing countries' foreign investment, long term growth, development and prosperity.

Thus, from a societal standpoint, corruption ultimately breeds poverty, weakens or destroys critical institutions of governance, erodes the operation of democracy, the rule of law and moral fabric of society, obstructs justice, and retards social and economic development. From a government standpoint, it promotes impunity and arbitrariness, and encourages both money laundering and illicit money transfers ('dirty money'). On this account, corruption violates human and people's rights

[72] See United Nations, 'Development on the Right to Development (1986)', www.un.org/documents/ga/res/41/a41r128.htm.

[73] See generally, Thomas Pogge (ed), *Freedom from Poverty as a Human Rights: Who Owes What to the Very Poor?* (Oxford: Oxford University Press, 2007) and Jeffrey Sachs, *The End of Poverty: Economic Possibilities for Our Time* (London: Penguin Press, 2005).

[74] See Stephen Marks, 'Poverty' in *International Human Rights Law* (n 68) 602.

[75] Claes Sandgren, 'Combating Corruption: The Misunderstood Role of Law. A New View of Corruption, Development and Culture' (2005) 39 *International Law* 717.

[76] Much of Africa's looted funds has ended up in countries with strong traditions of coded secret bank accounts, such as Switzerland and Liechtenstein.

– civil, political, economic, social, and cultural – disproportionately affecting the economically and socially vulnerable. Former President of the Inter-American Court of Human Rights, Professor Antonio A Cançado Trindade, has pointedly stated that:

> The denial or violation of economic, social, and cultural rights, materialized, for example, in extreme poverty, affects human beings in all aspects of their lives (including civil and political rights), clearly revealing the interrelation or indivisibility of human rights. Extreme poverty constitutes, ultimately, the denial of all human rights. How can one speak of freedom of expression without the right to education? How can one conceive of the right to enter and leave the country (freedom of circulation) without the right to housing? How can one consider the right to free participation in public life, without the right to adequate food? How can one speak of the right to legal assistance without also taking into account the right to health? And the examples multiply. Clearly, we all experience the indivisibility of human rights in our everyday experience, and that is a reality that cannot be left aside. There is no place for compartmentalization, an integrated vision is needed of all human rights.[77]

Accordingly, the idea of corruption as a human right issue is intrinsically linked with the relationship between poverty, under-development and lack of respect for human rights. This proposition is buttressed by the consensus reached at the World Conference on Human Rights in Vienna in 1993, that extreme poverty and social exclusion should be regarded as violations of human dignity and human rights. This viewpoint was reinforced by the 1996 report on the question of the impunity of perpetrators of human rights violations, by El Hadji Guisse.[78] The report identified corruption as one of the practices impeding the fulfilment of economic and social rights (and one would say that the same goes also for civil and political rights). Mr Guisse speaks of corruption as 'the abuse of public trust for private purposes. A public office is used for the benefit of one or more individuals, rather than in the national interest.'[79] The report also identified both the corrupter and the corrupted as including civil servants, state agents, private individuals and elected officials.[80] More significantly, the report called for attention to be paid to the harm suffered by victims of corruption, adding that 'corruption can engage the responsibility of the state if the latter is organising it through the operation of its

[77] IACHR, 'Second Report on the Situation of Human Rights in Peru' (2000) ch VI, para 4, citing Antonio A Cançado Trindade, 'La Justiciabilidad de los derechos económicos, sociales y culturales en el plano internacional' in *Revista Lecciones y Ensayos, 1997–98* (Buenos Aires: Universidad de Buenos Aires, School of Law and Social Sciences/Abeledo-Perrot, 1998) 80.

[78] El Hadji Guisse, Special Rapporteur, 'Second Interim Report on the Question of the Impunity of Perpetrators of Human Rights', www.unhchr.ch/Huridocda/Huridoca.nsf/(Symbol)/E.CN.4.Sub.2.1996.15.En?Opendocument.

[79] ibid, para 73.

[80] ibid.

agents or when, by a permissive attitude, it accepts the fact that private entities or private individuals are practising it'.[81]

Similarly, the United Nations declared in 2003 that corruption is the primary reason behind dictatorships or lack of democracy, poor law enforcement, cultural backwardness and moral decay,[82] thus undermining social justice and public trust in critical institutions of state. The report concluded that:

> Economically, corruption leads to the inefficient allocation of resources, raises the cost of investment, decreases investors' confidence, promotes inequalities and inefficiencies in the private sector and raises the cost, and decreases the quality of, public-sector projects and services. Diversions of public funds into private pockets or bank accounts (whether foreign or local) by corrupt officials lead to the denial of rights.[83]

The UN continued its examination of the normative elements of the relationship between poverty, corruption and human rights when its former Commission on Human Rights and Sub-Commission on the Promotion and Protection of Human Rights initiated a series of work on the issues.[84] In the final report commissioned by the sub-commission, titled 'Human Rights and Extreme Poverty', Leandro Despouy concluded that poverty perpetuates itself and creates a vertical vicious circle of poverty.[85] The report's broad definition of poverty is substantively similar to the one provided by the UN Committee on Economic, Social and Cultural Rights, and noted earlier. According to the report, poverty is:

> [A] string of misfortunes: poor living conditions, unhealthy housing, homelessness, failure – often – to appear on the welfare rolls, unemployment, ill-health, inadequate education, marginalization, and an inability to enter into the life of society and assume responsibilities. The distinguishing feature is that these deprivations – hunger, overcrowding, disease, and illiteracy – are cumulative, each of them exacerbating the others to form a horizontal vicious circle of abject poverty.[86]

The report speaks of extreme poverty as a state of 'severe deprivation of basic human needs, including food, safe drinking water, sanitation facili-

[81] ibid, para 77.

[82] UN Doc E/CN 4/Sub.2/2003/18 14-5 (2003).

[83] ibid.

[84] See, eg, Asbjørn Eide's study of the right to adequate food as a human right (United Nations Human Rights Study Series, No 1); and Danilo Türk's final report of the Study on the Realisation of Economic, Social, and Cultural Rights (United Nations Human Rights Study, E/CN.4/Sub.2/1992/16). In 1992, the General Assembly passed Resolution 47/196, which declared October 17 'International Day for the Eradication of Poverty'. With Resolution 48/183, the General Assembly proclaimed 1996 the 'International Year for the Eradication of Poverty', and in its Resolution 50/107 it proclaimed the first 'United Nations Decade for the Eradication of Poverty (1997–2006)'.

[85] Leandro Despouy, 'Final Report on Human Rights and Extreme Poverty', www.unhchr.ch/huridocda/huridoca.nsf/(Symbol)/E.CN.4.Sub.2.1996.13.en?Opendocument, para 8.

[86] ibid, para 7.

ties, health, shelter, education and information', adding that it 'depended not only on income but also on access to social services'.[87] The report underscored that poverty strips people of any real opportunity to exercise their human rights and to take responsibility for themselves.[88]

These various initiatives influenced the recent work of the UN Human Rights Council considering the effects of poverty on human rights.[89] In July 2012, the special rapporteur on human rights and extreme poverty, Magdalena Sepulveda Carmona, submitted her final report on 'the guiding principles on extreme poverty and human rights'[90] to the Human Rights Council. This document was delayed for more than a decade, having been started in 2001. Nonetheless, the guiding principles was adopted by the Human Rights Council at its 21st session in September 2012. Significantly, the guiding principles underscore the idea that poverty is not just an economic or development issue, but also an important human rights issue,[91] and that poverty is not a natural problem but something 'created, enabled and perpetuated by acts and omissions of States and other economic actors'.[92]

However, while the norms and statements thus far outlined are clearly remarkable, and capable of providing the fundamental building blocks for a comprehensive human rights framework to corruption, their impact has been noticeably modest because there has not, as yet, been a concerted, consistent and coherent effort to develop these ideas further, and to harmonise the two fields. As such, the vision of 'a social and international order' (canvassed by the UN Universal Declaration of Human Rights and later reinforced in numerous instruments), in which human rights can flourish, remains largely unfulfilled dream.

## MONEY LAUNDERING AND ASSET RECOVERY INITIATIVES

Barely three years after its adoption, the UNCAC Conference of States Parties, held in Amman, Jordan in December 2006, reaffirmed that com-

[87] ibid, para 55.

[88] ibid.

[89] See, eg, Commission on Human Rights Resolution 2001/31, adopted 23 April 2001; Sub-Commission on the Promotion and Protection of Human Rights: Resolution 2001/8, adopted 15 August 2001; and Resolution 2006/9, adopted 24 August 2006. See also, Human Rights Council: Resolution 2/2, adopted 27 November 2006; Resolution 7/27, adopted 28 March 2008; Resolution 12/19, adopted 2 October 2009; and Resolution 15/19, adopted 30 September 2010.

[90] See A/HRC/21/39 agenda item 3, the guiding principles on extreme poverty and human rights: http://daccess-ods.un.org/TMP/6578931.80847168.html.

[91] ibid.

[92] ibid.

mitment to the detailed asset recovery provisions of the convention[93] by establishing an open-ended intergovernmental working group to 'continue global cooperation in asset recovery with a view to tracing financial flows linked to corruption, seizing assets derived from corruption and returning such assets'.[94] However, while the international community has repeatedly lauded the asset recovery framework contained in the UN Convention against Corruption,[95] the framework has been only a marginal success at least for Africa (as noted in the country case studies just discussed, and as discussed throughout the book). The current framework does not go far enough because it is still tied to the political apron strings of states parties; so very little may ultimately be achieved without the requisite political will on the part of the victim states to pursue stolen assets and for the receiving states in whose jurisdictions the assets are stashed to repatriate such assets.

Nonetheless, as noted in Chapter 4 of this book, if genuinely and fairly implemented across borders, the UNCAC potentially can serve as an effective asset recovery mechanism to ensure that cash-starved victim states have access to critical resources for development and other programmes, while also having a powerful deterrent effect and making sure that corrupt officials do not benefit or profit from their crimes, as there will be no safe haven for looted public funds. Further, although this point will be amplified in Chapter 4, it is important to note briefly that asset recovery can occur through international cooperation and mutual assistance, or through civil action in any jurisdiction of states parties. Civil actions do not require a criminal conviction, have far less rigorous standards and burdens of proof, sidestep immunity clauses prevalent in the constitutions of many African states (as action may be brought against friends and family of corrupt public officials), and may be brought even if the corrupt official is exiled or deceased. There is even a specific requirement for states parties to recognise judgments from jurisdictions of other state parties. In addition to civil actions, opportunities for direct recovery of stolen public funds exist, a particularly significant development against the backdrop of protracted delays in which litigations across national and international borders are often bogged down. States in whose jurisdictions stolen public funds are deposited can even take action *suo moto*, without prompting from the victim state. The victim states too can

[93] For a general discussion on developments regarding asset recovery in practice, see Mark V Vlasic and Jenae N Noel, 'Fighting Corruption to Improve Global Security: An Analysis of International Asset Recovery Systems' (2010) 5 *Yale Journal of International Affairs* 106.

[94] UN Conference of States Parties, www.unodc.org/unodc/en/treaties/CAC/CAC-COSP.html.

[95] With the exception of the SADC Protocol, all the African-focused anti-corruption treaties contain varying provisions on assets recovery.

benefit from access to multiple jurisdictions and venues where cases of corruption and money laundering can be heard.

Even so, while it is true that the UNCAC has global consensus on the important need to both recover and return stolen assets from poor countries, the current asset recovery framework only empowers the states to recover assets, but not necessarily enforce their return. Recovery provisions within UNCAC are only optional and can be ignored at will by states parties. As previously noted, corrupt public officials have access to large amounts of wealth and to the best available legal and other experts to resist prosecution or to hide and benefit from their stolen wealth. This latter issue is particularly true because of weak law enforcement systems (and the rule of law in general), and the general lack of coordination among international, regional, and national anti-corruption mechanisms in the area of asset recovery. Even in cases where recovered funds are returned, there is no guarantee that they will not be re-stolen or mismanaged in countries where corruption is the norm. Enormous resources are required to trace, locate, seize, recover and repatriate stolen assets.[96] Moreover, political, national and economic interests of states in whose jurisdictions the stolen funds are deposited remain overriding considerations, and as the case studies discussed have shown, powerful financial institutions within these countries have few incentives to cooperate, and may even work to block any repatriation exercise.

In addition, the current complex asset recovery procedures also raise some questions about the rights to privacy or a fair trial of public officials accused of corruption. The right to privacy, for example, may be violated through the investigative tools and mechanisms employed in the asset recovery process. It is also important to balance the right of the victims to an effective remedy for the return of stolen public funds with the right of the suspects to a fair trial. For example, in order to preserve the presumption of innocence, confiscation may only take place after conviction, though under Article 54 of the UNCAC, confiscation can take place even without conviction in cases where the suspects have died, are on the run, or cannot be otherwise prosecuted for any other reasons. While the provision on non-conviction confiscation is clearly important, if it is considered against the backdrop of the legal obstacle of immunity for high-ranking corrupt officials against prosecution in African states, reasonable care should be taken to ensure at all times the right to fair trials for alleged suspects, as well as to promote the rights of witnesses, whistle-blowers, experts and victims.

[96] As the StAR Initiative puts it, 'Many developing countries lack the capacity to prepare indictments, collect, preserve, and present evidence, properly adjudicate cases, and obtain convictions, as well as trace the proceeds of corruption and obtain valid freezing and confiscation orders.'

Further, the UNCAC asset recovery provisions have, for the most part, not affected how states behave, although as already noted, some successful asset recovery stories exist. For example, there has been the recovery from bank accounts in Switzerland, Luxembourg, and Liechtenstein of nearly $505.5m of Nigerian public funds stolen by the late General Abacha. However, the asset recovery process, in practice, is bogged down by the legal, political, and logistical challenges highlighted above. Most state parties to the UNCAC have not domesticated or fully internalised their international obligations and commitments (despite some important, though isolated and limited, reforms of banking institutions, as in Switzerland),[97] due in part to differing legal systems and, crucially, to an absence of political, national or economic incentives. It is doubtful if the government of Nigeria would have made requests for mutual legal cooperation when General Abacha was still alive, given his influence and ability to buy patronage within the political and economic communities. While the 'Abacha requests' are clearly encouraging, the selective approach by the government in its fight against corruption and money laundering is apparent, given that the government ignored the clamour for it to pursue other public officials and retired generals (who probably stole even more than Abacha stole), in part because of the huge political costs of taking any such initiatives. Even with the Abacha case, it was still very difficult to pursue prosecution within Nigeria's legal system, and success came only after the Swiss authorities accepted certain acts as sufficient proof and corroboration of criminal origin. It should be noted, too, that the settlement reached was questionable and unfair, because the Abacha family was allowed to retain nearly $100m of the money repatriated to the government of Nigeria.

Moreover, while some financial assets may have been returned without strings to states whose officials were responsible for the theft of public funds, some countries, including Switzerland, often attach conditions or specify the projects on which returned funds can be spent. Before returning Abacha's stolen funds, for example, the Swiss government imposed conditions on the Nigerian government to spend the returned funds on poverty alleviation programmes, to create employment, to promote health, education, and agriculture, to build roads, and to generally improve living conditions for the economically and socially vulnerable.[98]

[97] For example, while some significant progress has been made by the government of Switzerland in terms of lifting the veil of banking secrecy and making it more difficult for corrupt public officials to make deposits of stolen funds, many legal obstacles, such as statutes of limitation on asset restitution, remain. This was the situation when the Swiss Federal Supreme Court overturned the decision of the lower Federal Office of Justice to return to the people of Haiti approximately $6m stolen by former dictator Jean-Claude 'Baby Doc' Duvalier.

[98] There are other examples from outside Africa. For example, the Swiss authorities set clear conditions for the spending of the Marcos stolen funds in Philippines: some of the

Similarly, before returning funds to Angola, the Swiss conditions were to spend recovered funds for the benefit of the economically and socially vulnerable, in particular to construct medical infrastructure, to buy equipment, to provide basic professional training and to promote local capacities. Presumably, the overriding goals in setting such conditions are to ensure transparency in the spending of returned funds and to make sure that the funds are not re-stolen or mismanaged. But available evidence suggests that these conditions are rarely complied with. For example, in the case of Abacha, although the returned public funds were to be used to improve infrastructure and social programmes in Nigeria, the Swiss government and the World Bank soon raised concerns about the use to which the funds had been put. Relatedly, the practice of requested states setting conditions on the use of recovered funds may however be challenged on the ground of violating the 'sovereignty' of the requesting states. However, the practice may well be justified, especially given that recovered funds are frequently re-stolen, and if only to ensure that returned stolen funds are spent transparently and accountably.

Apart from these cases, encouraging national and regional legal initiatives involving civil society groups are now taking place, such as the Open Society Justice Initiative before the African Commission in the case of *APDHE v Equatorial Guinea*,[99] which alleges the theft of national oil revenue by the Equatorial Guinea government and the consequent violation of the right of the Equatorial Guinean people to freely dispose of their natural wealth and resources, as recognised in Article 21 of the African Charter.[100] However, as there is still no specific reference to corruption in the charter, much more is needed in the areas of legal and human rights reforms to increase victims' participation (and give them a voice), enhance the legal standing of the citizens, and encourage public interest litigation in this field.

In sum, the provisions of treaties, in particular the UNCAC, on asset recovery are clear acknowledgement by the international community of the need to address challenges often associated with money laundering and effective repatriation of stolen public funds for the growth and devel-

funds were to be spent to finance agricultural reform that would benefit the economically and socially vulnerable. Significantly, the Swiss government also required compensation measures for the sole benefit of the victims of human rights violations under Marcos's brutal regime.

[99] Communication 347/07 – Association Pro Decheros Humanos De Espana (APDHE) v Equatorial Guinea, http://www.achpr.org/files/activity-reports/32-and-33/achpr5152_actrep32and33_eng.pdf.

[100] Art 21 provisions are extensively discussed in Ch 6. Another development of note is the ongoing Socio-Economic Rights and Accountability Project's request for advisory opinion before the African Court on Human and Peoples' Rights, seeking the court's interpretation of Art 21, corruption, and poverty in Africa. The Centre for Human Rights of the University of Pretoria, Amnesty International, and the Human Rights Implementation Centre at the University of Bristol have filed an amicus brief in support of this case.

opment of the countries affected by large-scale corruption. Asset recovery is important for making resources available to states to fulfil their human rights obligations and commitments, and to be able to provide essential public services for society, in general, and the economically and socially vulnerable, in particular. Identifying, tracing, seizing, freezing, recovering, and repatriating stolen public funds is vitally important, not least because it sends a strong message to corrupt officials that they will not be allowed to keep their pilfered wealth and (if properly utilised) the returned funds can pay for the needed services that ultimately lift people out of poverty.

## CONCLUSION

This chapter has demonstrated a strong link between organised crime, terrorism, large-scale corruption, money laundering, poverty and violations of human rights. Large-scale corruption weakens the state, in part because those who commit these crimes have the resources to finance their corruption and to distort the rule of law and manipulate already corrupt criminal justice systems; corruption in the criminal justice system discriminates against those who live in poverty and exacerbates the arbitrariness of the system. Money laundering is directly associated with corruption and is a criminal activity that can trigger concealment of the underlying crime. As has been observed, corruption precipitates poverty because it undermines economic growth, drives away foreign investment, and diverts critical resources needed for infrastructure, public services and poverty prevention programmes.

The corrosive effects of corruption are far-reaching, permeating the critical institutions of governance and endangering the rule of law. As a result, the effective enjoyment and implementation of human rights is seriously compromised. The extent and effects of the problem are well illustrated by the fact that more than $148bn of public funds are stolen annually, and secretly deposited in developed economies in Europe and North America. Clearly, such activities can jeopardise any economy, but even more so African states with already limited resources and fragile economies.

The case studies ably illustrate the destructive, large-scale corruption prevalent in many African states. But they also show that the various legal and other initiatives against money laundering have not been very effective in terms of preventing the volume of money laundering that has been investigated and discovered in countries like the United States. The case studies also show the lack of transparency and due diligence regarding deposits from PEPs from across African states into financial institutions in developed countries. This lack of transparency and due diligence is what allowed, for example, President Ali Bongo of Gabon to launder $50m of illicit funds through France's Citibank Private Bank, and this, according to the US sub-committee, was done with the knowledge and complicity of bank officials. There are other challenges raised by these selected cases, including law enforcement and jurisdictional problems; for example, the challenge of obtaining evidence from foreign financial records, and the difficulty of stopping significant laundering when attorneys, estate agents, and escrow agents are involved. But the cases mentioned seem to be merely the tip of the iceberg of money laundering in these countries and elsewhere in Africa.

Part of the problems is that nearly 50 of the world's largest banks and financial institutions are licensed to operate in offshore locations. This practice negates the UN Convention against Corruption, to which some 168 states have subscribed; thus, a review of standards and policies (that currently allow for the anonymity of depositors of stolen wealth from developing countries), to meet the requirements of the convention and other standards, is warranted. Some incorporation of human rights principles (such as the expanded and more legally binding notion of international cooperation and assistance) might also help to secure greater transparency in bank transactions and promote more accountability on the part of financial institutions. These principles may assist in accelerating the pace of reforms regarding the application of bank secrecy laws and policies, which in turn will contribute to the development of better asset recovery mechanism.

The discussion thus far clearly shows, as discussed in Chapter 1, why the criminal law approach is insufficient to prevent and combat the problems of corruption and money laundering, and why a complementary framework built around human rights law will increase the effectiveness of existing money laundering regimes, as is the accountability of states for stopping capital flight due to corruption at source. The application of human rights law in particular would ensure that less emphasis is placed on national sovereignty and economic interests when developed economies are dealing with corruption and money laundering problems from developing regions such as Africa.

# Part II

# National and International Laws against Corruption

# 3

# *National Legal Frameworks for Fighting Corruption in Africa*

## INTRODUCTION

ALTHOUGH THE SCOPE, nature, and application may vary, it is rare to find any country in Africa without legal frameworks or institutions to prevent and combat corruption. The variation depends not only on whether the frameworks are common law or civil law, but also whether the government has ratified (and domesticated or directly incorporated) any of the African-focused treaties (discussed in Chapter 4) in their legal systems. In addition, each national legal framework for fighting corruption is piecemeal, scattered, diffused, and cannot be found in a single instrument in any country. Nonetheless, these frameworks can be broadly classified into two categories: constitutional and legislative. All the countries (Angola, Equatorial Guinea, and Nigeria) discussed in Chapter 2 in relation to PEPs, banking secrecy, money laundering, asset recovery, poverty, and so on, have established some forms of constitutional and legislative frameworks to combat corruption. There are also countless laws which, though not specific to corruption, by their enforcement may have implications for tackling the problem.

In Angola, Equatorial Guinea, and Nigeria (as in many other African states), a constitution is the primary source of law to fight corruption.[1] The constitutions of these countries elaborate, in varying degrees, the limits of the exercise of governmental powers and other functions conferred on all institutions of government, and – significantly – entrench and guarantee some fundamental human rights. There is a plethora of specific and general legislation on corruption, and some forms of institutional mechanisms have been established in these countries. Sometimes laws complement one another, but more often they conflict, suggesting that a proliferation of laws on corruption can be counter-productive. It is useful to note that before the introduction of specific anti-corruption legislation in the three countries being discussed, criminal codes served as the

[1] See eg, Art 6 of the Angolan Constitution of 2010, s 2 of the Nigerian Constitution of 1999 (as amended) and Pt 1, item 2 of the 1996 Constitution of Equatorial Guinea (as amended).

primary legal instruments for combating corruption. However, for a number of reasons they were deemed inadequate: outdated provisions; limited number of corruption-related offences (and corresponding evidentiary, investigatory and enforcement gaps); narrowed and limited definitions (for bribery, extortion, and other related areas of abuse of public office); and inability to deal effectively and proportionately with contemporary forms of corruption and their effects. This prompted legal reforms that resulted in the enactment of laws to specifically address these problems.

Furthermore, the case studies discussed in Chapter 2 suggest that the legal response to corruption in Angola, Equatorial Guinea and Nigeria is often motivated by public pressure on these governments to take action to combat corruption against the backdrop of recurring public scandals in which governments are enmeshed. The legal rules also generally aim to improve the efficiency and transparency of public (and private) entities and to ensure that public trust and functions are exercised on the basis of defined ethical principles and values. In general, national legal frameworks against corruption mirror international standards that are contained in the African-focused treaties: the UN Convention against Corruption, the AU Convention on Preventing and Combating Corruption, the SADC Protocol against Corruption, and the ECOWAS Protocol on the Fight against Corruption. Each of the three countries has ratified the UN Convention against Corruption. Both Equatorial Guinea and Nigeria have ratified the ECOWAS Protocol, while Angola has ratified the SADC Protocol. However, of these countries, only Angola has incorporated all three anti-corruption instruments to which it is a state party into its domestic law.

This chapter discusses some core constitutional provisions and national legislation against corruption, and considers their effectiveness in eliminating or reducing large-scale corruption as well as its effects on human rights across African states. The chapter examines the contours and features of the national legal frameworks against corruption across Africa through the lens of Angola, Equatorial Guinea and, most frequently, Nigeria (because of its detailed laws, both substantive and procedural, against corruption – of the countries studied, Nigeria's anti-corruption laws and case law are the most comprehensive and accessible). It would obviously be impracticable to analyse all the myriad national laws that exist in the three countries to combat corruption. Several such laws exist in Angola (where many laws against corruption were enacted in 1990 alone) and Nigeria (where there are constitutional provisions, two major anti-corruption laws, criminal codes and dozens of other laws against corruption). Finally, given the wide variety of national laws and institutions against corruption, this chapter neither provides a detailed discussion of the laws covered, nor a comprehensive appraisal of the anti-corruption institutions in those countries. The central concern is with the overall objectives of such legal and institutional mechanisms, and the extent of their effectiveness in light of human rights law and anti-corruption instruments, discussed in detail in Chapter 4.

While the choice of countries is necessarily selective, their core legal responses to corruption (constitutional and legislative approaches) are representative of the legal frameworks against corruption across countries in Africa. The discussion of the legal frameworks found in the selected countries aims to highlight the general legal issues and challenges that often undermine the fight against corruption in African states. Furthermore, as there are significant similarities in the substance of the laws against corruption in the countries studied, discussion on Angola and Equatorial Guinea will focus on those provisions which differ from their counterparts in Nigeria, so as to avoid repetition. As previously noted, these countries have a great deal in common politically, economically, and culturally; arguably they best highlight the legal issues examined in this chapter; and all are member states of the African Union and states parties to the African Charter. They also ranked very poorly in Transparency International's Corruption Perception Index and in the US State Department Country Report for 2012.

## LEGAL FRAMEWORKS AGAINST CORRUPTION ACROSS AFRICA

### Constitutions

Like elsewhere in the world, countries in Africa have developed constitutions which, in one form or another, prohibit corruption and set ethical standards for public officials. Several features of constitutional prohibitions against corruption common to Angola, Equatorial Guinea, and Nigeria can be identified: requirements regarding the taking of oath of office by senior public officials; establishment of codes of conduct; asset declarations; specific 'anti-corruption-related objectives' (as related to the duties of the executive, legislative and judicial branches); and transparency and accountability provisions for breach of constitutional prohibitions against corruption. Each of these features will now be discussed in turn.

#### *Oaths of Office*

All constitutions of African states require public office holders to take an oath of office at the beginning of their term of office, thus implicitly binding them to abstain from all acts, including corrupt acts, that are inconsistent with their entrusted positions and the overall objectives of the constitutions. While the form of the oath statement may vary from country to country, the substance remains essentially the same.[2] It has been stated that, 'as regards the point to be confirmed by oath, that it be neither false, nor unlawful, and this requires both truth . . . and justice, so that one confirm what is lawful. A rash oath lacks judgement, a false oath lacks truth, and a wicked or unlawful oath lacks justice.'[3] In addition, the taking of an oath is a 'natural and universal custom that has been found virtually everywhere human society exists.'[4] This universality of oaths can be traced to two important human but conflicting responses: an inclination for truth, and misdirected (venal) self-interest.[5] In general, the oath statement requires the oath taker to commit to uphold and defend the constitution, and it is customary for them to add 'so help me God' as their closing words.

The countries discussed in this chapter have constitutions that require their presidents to take oaths, though Angola prefers the term 'swearing in'. In section 150 of the Angolan Constitution of 2010, for example, the presidential oath includes that the president 'do swear on my honour [to] faithfully perform the office with which I am invested; to observe [the] Constitution of the Republic of Angola and the laws of the country and cause them to be observed'.[6] In the case of Nigeria, the president takes an oath to 'be faithful [and to] discharge my duties to the best of my ability, faithfully and in accordance with the Constitution of the Federal Republic of Nigeria and the law, and always in the interest of the sovereignty, integrity, solidarity and well-being of Nigeria'.[7] Of the countries discussed here, the Nigerian Constitution of 1999 has the most comprehensive provision on oath-taking. To illustrate, the president also commits to 'strive to preserve the Fundamental Objectives and Directive Principles of State Policy contained in the Constitution, [and not to] allow my personal interest to influence my official conduct or my official decisions'. The president also commits to abide by the constitutional code of conduct (in the Seventh

[2] An 'oath' refers to any attestation by public officials signifying a commitment to discharge a public duty truthfully and faithfully. See Eugene Milhizer, 'So Help Me Allah: An Historical and Prudential Analysis of Oaths as Applied to the Current Controversy of the Bible and Quran in Oath Practices in America' (2009) 70 *Ohio State Law Journal* 1, 5.

[3] ibid.

[4] ibid.

[5] ibid.

[6] See also Item 35 of the 1996 Constitution of Equatorial Guinea: 'The President of the Republic shall . . . take the oath of office before the August presence of members of parliament and the Supreme Court meeting in solemn session.'

[7] The Seventh Schedule to the Constitution contains the oaths of allegiance and oaths of office of the president and vice president of the Federal Republic of Nigeria and also those of the state governors, deputy governors, ministers, commissioners, and special advisers. Nigeria also has a judicial oath and oaths for the members of the National Assembly and States Houses of Assembly. See ss 52, 94, 135, 140, 142, 180, 185, 187, 194 and 290 of the 1999 Nigerian Constitution (as amended), which make it mandatory for the class of persons named therein to take an oath.

Schedule to the Constitution), protect and defend the constitution, and to 'do right to all manner of people according to law [and to] devote myself to the service and well-being of the people of Nigeria'.

It is clear that the oath statement is a solemn reminder to senior state officials to act consistently and faithfully for the common interest of the public. This suggests that such officials and the states that they represent should desist from corruption, establish the mechanisms to prevent and combat it, and allow such mechanisms to function independently, effectively and fairly. Interpreted broadly, oath statements can thus play an important role in the fight against corruption because they command and require state officials to observe the limits of their authority and not to abuse their constitutionally delegated and entrusted powers for gain. A state would implicitly be required to exercise due diligence to ensure that such commitments by their officials are not breached or otherwise undermine international obligations and commitments. In general, then, the constitution is sacrosanct, and any senior state officials directly or indirectly engaging in or encouraging corruption through for example decisions or policies or even inactions, clearly will be contravening the requirements of the constitution.

For example, in Nigeria, President Goodluck Jonathan exercised his power of pardon under section 175(1)(a) of the constitution, which deals with the prerogative of mercy, to pardon (former governor) Chief Dipreye Alamieyeisegha, a convicted state public official.[8] The phrase 'any person' and 'any offence' in section 175 may be broadly read to include 'corrupt officials' and 'corrupt offences' established under the Independent Corrupt Practices Act. On the basis of the pardon, therefore, Alamieyeisegha might be entitled, for example, to the return of the stolen assets confiscated by the government.[9] This exercise of the prerogative of mercy, while it is perfectly within the discretion of the Nigerian president, nonetheless raises serious questions about its consistency with the president's oath statement and the overall objectives of the constitution. In the first place, section 175 does not stipulate the conditions under which such power should be exercised. However, section 15(5) may provide some

[8] This decision was backed by the Council of State pursuant to its advisory role under s 153(1)(b) of the Constitution. The relevant part of s 175(1)(a) reads: 'The President may grant any person concerned with or convicted of any offence created by an Act of the National Assembly pardon, either free or subject to lawful conditions.'

[9] There is a precedent for this possibility. In the case of *Falae v Obasanjo (No 2)* 1999 4 NWLR 599, 476, the Court of Appeal of Nigeria held that: 'Under the Nigerian law, a "pardon" and "full pardon" have no distinction. A pardon is an act of grace by the appropriate authority which mitigates or obliterates the punishment the law demands for the offence, and restores the rights and the privileges forfeited on account of the offence . . . The effect of a pardon is to make the offender, a new man (novus homo), to acquit him of all corporal penalties and forfeiture annexed to the offence pardoned . . . by virtue of the pardon . . . the disqualification the 1st Respondent was to suffer because of his conviction, has been wiped out. His full civil rights and liberties are fully restored.' (Ibid, 495.)

guidance in regard to the minimum thresholds required for the exercise of any such power, as it provides that 'the State shall abolish all corrupt practices and abuse of power'. Thus, sections 175 and 15(5), read in conjunction with the oath provision, would appear to impose some ethical conditions on the president to ensure that the exercise of the discretionary power of prerogative of mercy is not such that it will encourage corruption or provide an escape route for perpetrators.

Two more examples may suffice to underscore the fundamental importance of the oath provisions. In Equatorial Guinea, the president commits to promote 'the economic development of the nation [and to] support the principles of social justice',[10] while also guaranteeing 'the strict implementation of the constitution, the functioning of state institutions'.[11] However,

> the broader population – just above half a million people – enjoys little of the benefit [of valuable natural resources] and has not been lifted from poverty, while the elite directs the country's newfound wealth into its own pockets: the president's son spent more than US$42 million between 2004 and 2006 on luxury houses and cars in South Africa and California, nearly a third of the total amount the government spent on social programs – including health, education, and housing – in 2005.[12]

Similarly, in Angola, whereas the government within a space of 10 years enacted some 10 items of legislation to combat corruption,[13] presumably in fulfilment of the president's oath commitment, at the same time it passed anti-media and other repressive laws to suppress civil society protests against corruption.[14] The operation of these laws is exacerbated by the wide discretionary constitutional powers of the president combined with limited safeguards against any abuse of the oath statement (or other constitutional provisions), suggesting that 'Angola law rarely serves as a check on power, but instead is used as a tool to enable an environment of

[10] See Item 5 and 5th preambular para respectively of the 1996 Constitution.

[11] See Item 39 of the 1996 Constitution. It is instructive to note that Item 33 also describes the president as 'capable of interpreting the constitution'.

[12] Human Rights Watch, 'Well Oiled Oil and Human Rights in Equatorial Guinea' (2009), www.hrw.org/sites/default/files/reports/bhr0709web_0.pdf.

[13] See for example, the Law on Public Sector Discipline (Law 22/90), the Statutory Law on Remuneration of Members of Government (Law 23/90), Decree on the Patrimonial Benefits of Senior Public Officials (Law 24/90), and Decree on Small Gifts to Members of Government (25/90). Increasing concerns about large scale corruption prompted the enactment in 1996 of the Law on High Authority against Corruption. Also, in 1989, the government passed three major (but largely repetitive) anti-corruption laws: the Law on Crimes against the Economy, the Law on the Crimes Committed by Public Office Bearers, and the Law on Economic Crimes. All of these laws were harmonised in 2010 through the enactment of the Law on Administrative Probity (although this legislation fails to use the word 'corruption' throughout its 45 articles).

[14] See for example, Law to Combat Crime in the Area of Information Technologies and Communication. For overview on this and other similar legislation, see Rafael Marques de Morais, 'Corruption in Angola: An Impediment to Democracy', http://allafrica.com/download/resource/main/main/idatcs/00021715:000c02d3f1b90033585c6d991ec1546a.pdf.

high-level corruption and impunity.'[15] Thus, Angola's Constitution has been likened to the 1933 Constitution of its former colonial power, Portugal, as drafted by the authoritarian Salazar regime, and called 'hyper presidentialist'.[16]

### *Codes of Conduct*

Another common constitutional tool to address corruption is the code of conduct for public officials. Codes of conduct generally aim to influence attitudes, not prescribe behaviour. Essentially, their ultimate purpose is to achieve the highest standards of propriety in public life. Such codes are thus preventive mechanisms to address corruption. Thus, 'they propound the official morality. They are the mirror against which communities are to be educated towards an anti-corruption consciousness'.[17] The Constitution of Nigeria, for example, elaborates code of conduct (in its 5th Schedule). The code prohibits public officers[18] from placing their personal interests over and above their official duties. Significantly, the code also prohibits any of these public officers from maintaining or operating a foreign bank account, accepting property or benefits of any kind in the discharge of their duties,[19] or engaging or participating in the management or running of any private business, profession, or trade (except when employed on a part-time basis).

The code also prohibits bribery of public officers, public officials from holding two paid posts, pensioners from drawing remuneration from public funds in addition to their pensions, and certain retired senior public officials from serving in the employment of foreign companies.[20] While

[15] ibid, 3.

[16] See 'Angola: Origins and Historical Development of the Constitution', http://web.up.ac.za/sitefiles/file/47/15338/Angola%20final.pdf.

[17] Mark Findlay, 'Implementing Corruption Prevention Strategies Through Codes Of Conduct' 3 (1991–92) *Current Issues in Criminal Justice* 252.

[18] For the purposes of the Nigerian code of conduct, public officers include: the president, vice president, attorney-general, ministers of government; chief of defence staff, chief of army staff, chief of naval staff, chief of air staff and all members of the armed forces; the secretary to the government, head of civil service, permanent secretaries, directors-general, and all other persons in the civil service of the Federation or of the state; the president and deputy-president of the Senate, the speaker and deputy-speaker of the House of Representatives, and speakers and deputy-speakers of Houses of Assembly of states and all members of legislative houses, governors and deputy-governors of states. For other categories, see paras 1–9, Pt II, 5th Schedule to the 1999 Nigerian Constitution.

[19] Under para 6(2) of the 5th Schedule, 'the receipt by a public officer of any gifts or benefits from commercial firms, business enterprises, or persons who have contracts with the government shall be presumed to have been received in contravention [of para 6(1)] unless the contrary is proved.' Under para 7(b), no public official should accept 'any benefit of whatever nature from any company, contractor, or businessman, or the nominee or agent of such person'.

[20] The officials are those that have held office as president, vice president, chief justice or as governors or deputy governors of a state.

the prohibition against employment by foreign companies may be necessary to safeguard national security and reduce any potential foreign influence, a life ban in the circumstances would seem unfair, and may actually put pressure on public officials to engage in corruption while in office, knowing that opportunities for employment will be limited once out of office. The code however does not forbid a public official from farming or entering a partnership business, provided the official does not hold a managerial position and is not involved in the daily running of the farm or partnership. But the code controversially allows some gift-giving from relatives and personal friends 'to such an extent and [on] such occasions as are recognised by custom'. However, the lack of a definition for 'custom' suggests that public officials may use this as a 'cover' to engage in corruption.

In *Okoye v Santilli*,[21] the Nigerian Supreme Court held that a public officer is precluded by the code of conduct from engaging in any other business, consistent with section 20(1) of the Code of Conduct Bureau Act.[22] The Court ruled illegal a contract entered into by one of the defendants while still a public officer. Similarly, in *Nwankwo v Nwankwo*,[23] the Supreme Court shed some light on the meaning of 'engaging in business' when it held that the provision of para 2(b) of Part 1 of the Fifth Schedule to the 1979 Constitution (similar to the Fifth Schedule to the 1999 Constitution) is not intended to prevent any public officer from acquiring an interest in a business (such as in a partnership). However, the Court also declared that the provision does prohibit a public officer from holding a managerial or other similar position.

Relatedly, in *Ogbuagu v Ogbuagu*, the Supreme Court, in a majority decision, overruled an earlier case in which it was held that only the Code of Conduct Bureau and the Code of Conduct Tribunal could entertain allegations of breach of the code of conduct.[24] Regrettably, the Court also held that the Nigerian code of conduct does not create a private right or interest for which a person could claim relief. Although the Court admitted that the purpose of the code of conduct is to protect public interest, it rejected the idea of granting legal standing to a private citizen to challenge or prosecute a violation of the code. Even more worrying is the ruling in the case involving former Governor of Plateau State, Joshua Dariye, that the interpretation of the code of conduct must be subject to section 308, which protects the president, vice president, governor and deputy governors from arrest, prosecution, imprisonment, and civil and criminal proceedings while they are in office (section 308 is discussed below, under 'Immunity clauses'). Dariye, arrested in London in 2004 by the

[21] *Okoye v Santilli* [1994] 4 NWLR (pt 338) 256, 289.
[22] Code of Conduct Bureau and Tribunal Act (1990) c 56 s 20(1).
[23] *Nwankwo v Nwankwo* [1995] 5 NWLR (pt 394) 153.
[24] *Ogbuagu v Ogbuagu* [1981] 2 NCLR 680.

Metropolitan Police for money laundering (see Chapter 2 for details of the case), was prosecuted by the Code of Conduct Tribunal on charges of concealing a foreign account. But an Abuja Federal High Court declared his prosecution to be unconstitutional, on the basis that the tribunal breached section 308. However, in another case,[25] the Court of Appeal held that the police have the discretion to decide whether to investigate a state official while still in office.

Unlike the Nigerian constitution, no specific code of conduct provisions are found in the constitution of Equatorial Guinea. However, some items of the constitution arguably imply a 'code of behaviour' that is expected of a high-ranking officials. For example, Item 2 provides that 'the duties of the authorities [such as the president] responsible for the management of the state shall be determined by the supreme law and others. No section of the people or any individual [such as the president] shall arrogate to itself or to himself the exercise thereof.' Similarly, analogous conducts are criminalised under the Penal Code of Equatorial Guinea, discussed below. As for Angola, Article 226 of the constitution broadly provides that 'The validity of laws and the various acts of the state, the public administration and the local authorities shall depend on their compliance with the Constitution. Laws or acts which violate the principles and norms enshrined in this Constitution shall be unconstitutional.' There is however a limited provision in Article 138 which prohibits a minister of state, minister, secretary of state or vice minister from engaging in any 'paid employment in any public or private institution except those dedicated to teaching or academic research'. They must not engage in 'any administrative, managerial or any other corporate position' or 'profit-making pursuit', or in 'liberal professions.'

### *Assets Declarations*

As a way of tackling corruption, many constitutions in Africa require senior public officials to declare their wealth and assets. Ideally, the asset declaration of material worth at the time of taking office is compared to that person's material worth upon leaving office. Both the constitutions of Equatorial Guinea and Angola are silent on the requirements of assets declarations, though there are other laws which deal with or have implications for declarations of assets by state officials. In contrast, Part I of the

[25] *IMB Securities PLC v Bola Tinubu* (2001) 45 WRN 1. But whereas it was held in this case that the defendant, then a state governor, was immune from legal proceedings, it has also been held that s 308 does not stop public officials such as the President from suing other people. See *Jonathan v Jones Abiri & Anor* Suit No FCT/CU/505/07. See also the following cases upholding the constitutional immunity clause to stop corruption cases: *Attorney-General of the Federation, Code of Conduct Bureau, and Code of Conduct Tribunal v Alh Atiku Abubakar* [2007] 8 NWLR (Pt 1035) 117, 155; *Atiku Abubakar v Attorney-General of the Federation* [2007] 3 NWLR (Pt 1022) 546, 648.

Fifth Schedule to the Nigerian constitution contains detailed provisions on asset declaration. The Nigerian code of conduct requires that every public officer submit a written declaration of their assets (and those of their minor children) to the Code of Conduct Bureau immediately after taking their oath of office, every four years thereafter, and at the end of their term of office (paragraph 11(1)). Technically, public officials may not be able to perform their entrusted functions until they have declared their assets. In addition, the Code of Conduct Bureau, established under the Third Schedule of the Constitution, is charged with the responsibility of enforcing compliance with the constitutional requirements. A Code of Conduct Tribunal is also established in paragraph 15(1) of Part 1 of the Fifth Schedule, with the power to try cases of alleged breaches of the code of conduct and to impose appropriate sanctions upon conviction.

However, while constitutional directives on asset declaration are important, and suggest the value a society places on transparency, integrity and accountability of senior public officials, it is clear that the existence of a mechanism of asset declaration alone is insufficient to combat large-scale corruption, as there is some evidence through the work of the (largely ineffective) Code of Conduct Bureau to suggest that some public officials failed to make any declarations, or made incomplete, false, or anticipated asset declarations (that is, officials manipulating their asset declarations to reflect not their current assets but what they would have earned at the end of their terms of office). Any false or anticipated declaration amounts to a breach of the code, but constitutional sanctions are rarely applied.[26]

Nonetheless, while declaration by the president and so on is not by law required to be made public, some public officials have voluntarily published their declarations as a gesture to promote transparency and to prevent corruption and abuse of office, albeit they are by far in the minority. Thus, whether an asset declaration list will be made public depends on the individual involved. For example, former president Shehu Yar'Adua released his asset declaration publicly (despite advice against this by the Code of Conduct Bureau), while President Jonathan resisted all pleas to make his asset declaration available to the public.

Furthermore, under the Nigerian constitution, the Code of Conduct Bureau can make asset declarations available for inspection by any citizen of Nigeria 'on such terms and conditions as the National Assembly [Nigeria's legislature] may prescribe'. Regrettably, the National Assembly has not, as yet, made any such laws to prescribe the 'terms and conditions' for making this information available. Obviously, it is nearly impos-

[26] Sanctions for any breach of the code of conduct include: loss of office or seat in any legislative house, disqualification from membership of a legislative house and from holding any public office for a period not exceeding 10 years, and forfeiture to the state of any property acquired by abuse or corruption of office. Additional penalties may be imposed where the conduct is also a criminal offence.

sible to detect any false declarations if citizens lack access to this information. Perhaps the Nigerian Freedom of Information Act might help to address this problem, though given the supremacy clause of the constitution, it is doubtful whether any headway will be made in this respect without the National Assembly making a law that defines these terms and conditions or amending the constitution to make asset declarations available to the citizens unconditionally.

### *Anti-corruption-related Objectives*

Nearly every country in Africa elaborates some anti-corruption-related objectives in their constitutions, mostly in the form of 'fundamental objectives and directive principles of state policy'.[27] For example, the Angolan Constitution provides in Article 1 that the primary objective of the government is to achieve 'human dignity [and to build] a free, just, democratic, solidary society of peace, equality and social progress'.[28] The constitution also elaborates several other provisions on the fundamental objectives of the government, including in Article 2 to the effect that Angola will be guided by the rule of law, the primacy of the constitution, the separation of powers, and promotion and defence of human rights.[29] In addition, Article 12 requires the government to abolish all forms of exploitation of the people; and significantly, Article 21 (on the 'fundamental tasks of the state') provides that the government will: establish conditions for the effective implementation of economic, social, and cultural rights of its citizens; promote their well-being, social solidarity, and improved quality of life for citizens (in particular for the 'most deprived groups of the population'); eradicate poverty; promote primary free health care, access to compulsory free education, equal rights and opportunities for citizens, and sustainable development; and protect the environment and natural resources for the benefit of its citizens.

Article 90 of the Angolan constitution further requires the state to promote social development and social justice, and to prioritise citizens, especially 'the more vulnerable and needy sectors of society'. Similarly, Article 198 provides that public administration shall pursue the public interest, and be governed by the principles of equality, legality, justice, proportionality, impartiality, accountability, administrative probity, and respect for public assets.

[27] De Villiers offered the concept that a constitutionally entrenched chapter on directive principles for state policy was borrowed from the Irish Constitution. See Bertus De Villiers, 'Directive Principles of State Policy and Fundamental Rights: The Indian Experience' (2011–2012) 10 *Northwestern Journal of International Human Rights* 26.

[28] See Item 1 of the Constitution of Equatorial Guinea for a similar provision.

[29] See Items 2 and 5 of the Constitution of Equatorial Guinea for similar provision.

The constitutions of Equatorial Guinea[30] and Nigeria contain nearly identical provisions. It is noteworthy to mention that Item 25 of the constitution of Equatorial Guinea provides that 'Work shall be a right and social obligation. The state shall recognize its role in improving on the well-being and development of its national resources conditions to eradicate poverty, misery and ensure the equal occupation of its national territory and shield its citizens from need.' However, unlike the Nigerian constitution, the constitutions of both Angola and Equatorial Guinea utterly omit any specific reference to corruption, although the Angolan constitution does require 'abolition of all forms of exploitation' and 'protection of natural resources', both of which can imply prohibition of corruption.

Apart from this, the Nigerian constitution contains the most comprehensive provisions on fundamental objectives. In its Chapter II, the constitution's objectives and directive principles are broadly categorised as, among others: fundamental obligations of government; political, economic, social, and foreign policy objectives; and obligations of the mass media. The constitution also provides that the government shall be guided by: the principles of democracy and social justice; the desires and interests of its people (as 'sovereignty' belongs to them); and the preservation of the security, welfare, and participation of its people, as well as their freedom and happiness (on the basis of social justice and equality of status and opportunity). Significantly, the Nigerian government shall also 'abolish corrupt practices and abuse of power', prevent exploitation of natural resources, ensure human dignity and the sanctity of the human person, and guarantee the independence, impartiality and integrity of and accessibility to their courts of law. The Nigerian state should ensure the treatment of all citizens without discrimination; secure opportunities for citizens to enhance their means of livelihood, including suitable employment with just, safe, and humane work conditions; provide adequate facilities for leisure and for social, religious, and cultural life; protect children, young persons, and the aged against any exploitation whatsoever and against moral and material neglect; and ensure equal and adequate educational opportunities at all levels.

It should be noted, however, that while the various constitutional provisions that have been outlined are particularly important in terms of their potential to serve as a code of behaviour to fight corruption, they are deemed 'programmatic and aspirational goals' and therefore are mostly not justiciable, in the sense that citizens have no legal standing to challenge the government for non-compliance. The enforcement of these goals, however, requires financial (and political) will, but the presence of corruption in the countries means that such resources remain lacking. One might argue that given the inclusion of these objectives in the 'funda-

[30] See in particular Items 1–29 of the Constitution of Equatorial Guinea.

mental law of the land', they possess some binding character, and therefore the failure to enforce them may amount to a breach of public trust and oaths of office. In any case, governments will do well to strive to increase the legal enforcement of their constitutional objectives and principles in practice. The judiciary in countries across Africa, and particularly in the countries under discussion in this chapter, can play a crucial role in ensuring the legal enforcement of these objectives and principles.

### *Other Transparency and Accountability Provisions*

Many constitutions across Africa also contain other important transparency and accountability principles. For example, an important anti-corruption provision in the Nigerian constitution is section 125, which establishes the public account process to ensure that expenditure on projects and programmes of the executive branch complies fully with the sums and projects as appropriated by the legislature; in other words, the expenditure on projects is in accordance with what the legislature has voted upon. Other provisions are in sections 225 and 226, which both relate to transparency in the financing of political parties. In addition, the Nigerian constitution in section 88 empowers the legislature to investigate, inter alia, the conduct of any person, authority, ministry, or government department charged with the responsibility of executing or administering laws, or disbursing or administering money as appropriated or to be appropriated by the legislature.

More significantly, section 88(2) states that this power shall be exercised not only for the purpose of law-making and amending any defective laws, but also to 'expose corruption, inefficiency, or waste in the execution or administration of laws within its legislative competence and in the disbursement or administration of funds appropriated by it'. However, the limited democratic experiment in Nigeria has shown that its legislature lacks the necessary independence and desire to discharge its fundamental constitutional mandate to combat corruption. The National Assembly itself has been bogged down by several allegations of corruption. Although the body has undertaken some important investigations of corruption, most if not all of its reports remain unpublished and unimplemented. The situation with Nigeria's state House of Assemblies is not dissimilar, and shows that many of the provincial legal bodies are tied to the apron strings of the governors of their states, being little more than paper tigers.

In contrast with the Nigerian constitution, the constitutions of both Angola and Equatorial Guinea contain insufficient provisions on the separation of powers and checks and balances necessary to curtail excesses and potential abuse of executive powers. For instance, the Angolan constitution does not establish separation of power as such, nor are there any checks and balances among the executive, legislative, and judicial branches. On the contrary, it establishes wide-ranging powers for the Angolan president, as for example being responsible for appointing the Vice President of the Republic from amongst the individuals on the respective election list, and discharging them from office; calling general and local elections; appointing the Presiding Judge of the Constitutional Court and the other judges of the Court; appointing and discharging from office the Attorney General, the Deputy Attorneys General and, the Public Prosecutor's Office, the Assistant Attorneys General, as well as the Military Prosecutors of the Supreme Military Court (Article 119); defining the political orientation of the country and directing national policy (Article 120); issuing provisional presidential legislative decrees which will have the force of law (Article 126); and enjoying immunity against criminal prosecution 'for actions practised in the exercise of his functions', and can only be prosecuted after five years out of office for crimes committed after leaving office (Article 127). However, the provision on immunity for senior state officials is substantively similar to those contained in the constitutions of Equatorial Guinea and Nigeria.

Like the Angolan constitution, the constitution of Equatorial Guinea in Item 31 describes the president as 'the symbol' of the nation, and hands the president virtually all powers of appointment contained in the constitution, including those of the prime minister. Under Item 103, the president can also 'summon a referendum to revise the constitution'; only the difficult requirement of 'absolute majority of members of Parliament' can exercise similar power. Item 34 provides no time-limit for election of the president, which is made 'renewable' every seven years, and the date of election is decided by a ministerial council, which the president heads. Item 36 even grants the president the power to 'determine the politics of the nation, arbitrate and model the normal functioning of all institutions of the state', and his authority 'shall extend over the national territory'. Item 18 controversially requires that all citizens are to 'respect the Head of State'. Probably the most far-reaching and excessive constitutional powers of the president are contained in Items 39 and 41. Item 39 provides that the president 'shall ratify the decision of Parliament on its elections', granting the president the 'right to dissolve the parliament'. According to Item 41, the president can unilaterally suspend the constitution on open-ended grounds, 'where circumstances so warrant'. While the suspension may be for an initial period of three months, the president can continuously extend this where he considers that 'the situation remains dangerous'.

Despite (or even because of) these far-reaching and clearly excessive powers with potential for abuse, the president in 2011 instigated further constitutional changes to further tighten executive powers and control over governance, including legislative and judicial branches of government. Among significant changes to the new constitution are provisions allowing the president: to singlehandedly pick his successor and retain significant political influence even after he leaves office; to chair the body called 'the Supreme Council on Judicial Power' (which oversees judges); to appoint an unspecified number of members of a newly created Senate, and of a new 'independent' agency on government finances. The president would also approve the selection of a new ombudsman tasked with considering citizen complaints. And after leaving office, the president would enjoy the 'status of senator', with the rights and immunity accorded that office, as well as chair a new high-level council to advise his successor on national security and other sensitive issues. These constitutional changes were adopted and approved, having been 'voted' on in a referendum in November 2011, although the voting was manipulated and probably not a true reflection of the people's wishes.

## Legislation

Another important source of national legal rules against corruption in Africa is legislation. As previously noted, a multiplicity of (largely ineffective and sometimes conflicting) laws exists in Angola, Equatorial Guinea and Nigeria to prevent and punish corruption. The primary legislation in Angola is the Law on Administrative Probity, which contains 45 articles, while Equatorial Guinea's Penal Code contains less than 20 articles. It should be noted that Equatorial Guinea has neither specific legislation against corruption, nor anti-corruption commission or agency.[31] Apart from isolated cases of corruption involving low-level civil servants working in telecommunications and finance, it is rare to find cases of large-scale corruption filed in court.[32]

Nigeria's primary legislation is the most detailed, with the Independent Corrupt Practices and Other Related Offences Act 2000, containing 71 articles. As such, the central point of discussion will be the Independent Corrupt Practices and Other Related Offences Commission (ICPC). In addition, five components of the legislative framework can be identified: preventive measures, criminalisation, asset recovery, and institutional mechanisms. These will be discussed individually.

### *Preventive Measures*

Similar to international and regional anti-corruption treaties, national anti-corruption laws incorporate important preventive measures, such as

[31] See 'Interview Notes with *Marise Castro'*, Amnesty International Researcher on Equatorial Guinea for over two decades, on file with the author. The interview was conducted on 10 February 2014.

[32] ibid.

the requirement of anti-corruption policies and anti-corruption bodies, awareness-raising and training of criminal justice officials, and the establishment of codes of conduct for public officials (discussed above). The anti-corruption legislation in many of the countries under discussion in this chapter contain preventive provisions. For example, Angola has enacted the Law on Crimes against the Economy and the Law on High Authority against Corruption to prevent and combat corruption. Both laws were passed in 2010, but have now been replaced by a new legislation called the Law on Administrative Probity.[33] This legislation harmonised the previously scattered laws that had existed since the 1990s.[34]

In addition, like the Nigeria's constitutional provisions on asset declaration, the law establishing the National Commission on Public Ethics requires public officials, to declare their assets (and those of their spouses and minor children) to the commission. However, the provisions of the law are far limited, and there are no penalties for non-compliance. But like the constitution of Nigeria, declarations made are not released to the public. As under the constitutional requirements in Nigeria, government officials are also prohibited from conducting business while in office. However, unlike Angola and Nigeria, Equatorial Guinea has no genuine and independent anti-corruption commission, as 'the Presidency and Prime Minister's Office are the lead agencies for anti-corruption efforts'.[35]

In Angola, the Public Probity Law requires all government officials to declare their wealth, including revenues, bonds and shares, or any other property and valuables, domestic or abroad. But the law does not establish any effective review mechanism to monitor compliance, and is rarely implemented. Similarly, while on the one hand the 2002 Law on Access to Administrative Documents grants citizens the right to information and access to public documents, on the other hand the consistent application of the State Secrets Law of the same year makes nonsense of the right, as it empowers the government to classify information with high discretion.

In contrast, section 64 of Nigeria's ICPC Act[36] provides for protection of whistle-blowers and that informers' identities shall not be disclosed to the

[33] See Rafael Marques De Morais, 'Corruption in Africa and The Impact On Human Rights: Angola: A Case Study', Workshop on Corruption and Human Rights in Third Countries, http://knjiznica.sabor.hr/pdf/E_publikacije/Corruption_and_human_rights_in_third_countries.pdf, 12.

[34] ibid.

[35] See US State Department, 'Human Rights Report' (2012), www.state.gov/documents/organization/204327.pdf, 16.

[36] See Independent Corrupt Practices and Other Related Offences Act 2000. Other related legislation enacted during Nigeria's military era included: the Recovery of Public Property (Special Military Tribunals) Act 1984; Failed Banks (Recovery of Debts and Financial Malpractices) Decree No 18 of 1994; the Bank Employees (Declaration of Assets) Decree 1986; the Civil Service Commissions and Other Statutory Bodies (Removal of Certain Persons from Office) Decree No 16 of 1976, under which any corrupt person can be summarily dismissed or removed from office; the Special Tribunal (Miscellaneous Offences) Decree

public except as it relates to disclosure to a trial judge and defence lawyer in any civil, criminal, or other proceedings in any court or tribunal. In addition, section 39 protects privileged information or communication (in the course of pending proceedings) between solicitor and client, though a court can grant an order for disclosure of information relating to any transaction which is under investigation, or any property which is liable to seizure. This is similar to the rule under common law. It remains unclear, however, what kind of information will be protected in cases involving the investigation of and prosecution for corruption. Nonetheless, section 39 requires the order of a court before any disclosure can occur, and as such, provides some safeguards against any unreasonable or inappropriate infraction of the common law privilege. It should be noted that section 64(3) states that 'Any person who gives information [leading to the investigation of a suspect for corruption] knowing the information to be false shall be guilty of an offence and shall on conviction be liable to imprisonment for a term not exceeding ten years, and shall also be liable to a fine not exceeding one hundred thousand naira.'

*Criminalisation*

As a matter of substantive reach, Angola's and Equatorial Guinea's legislation against corruption, much like Nigeria's comprehensive ICPC Act, prohibit active and passive bribery and varying forms of corruption. Angola's Law on Administrative Probity criminalises both public-sector and private-sector corruption, and contains a detailed definition of 'public servant'. Strangely, though, the legislation fails to use the term 'corruption' in its entire 45 articles, and the definition of corruption is found in the mostly outdated Penal Code (Articles 318–22). Furthermore, the Law on Probity in Articles 18 and 25 prohibits public officials from receiving (directly or indirectly) gifts, money, assets or other economic benefits (such as a commission, a percentage or gratification in a business deal over which he/she has decision powers or influence). Yet, the law allows the receipt of certain gifts in specific circumstances. Under Article 25, a public official while in office cannot purchase assets 'disproportionate to official earnings, and its patrimonial applications', and cannot pursue another job or 'consulting arrangements that might be a source of conflict of interest.' This seems similar to the offence of 'unexplained wealth' under the ICPC Act.

No 24 of 1984, which prescribes harsh penalties for corruption and other related offences. Other interesting initiatives introduced in the 1980s, but with limited success (largely due to their selective application) included the 'War Against Indiscipline' (by the military government of Muhammadu Buhari), and the 'Ethical Revolution' (by the civilian government of Shehu Shagari).

Section 2 of Nigeria's ICPC Act, which deals with 'interpretation', defines corruption rather broadly and vaguely to include bribery, fraud, secret or unjustified profit, abuse of office,[37] conflict of interest,[38] and procedural breaches in private or public property by the suspects, and 'other related offences [such as] gratification'.[39] As noted elsewhere in this book, defining corruption precisely is a universal challenge, and not one particular to Africa.[40] Nonetheless, the ICPC Act details circumstances under which an offence may be committed. The Act does not consider motive as a defence, and ascribes criminal responsibility to anyone involved in corruption, no matter their part in the act. Further, the Act elaborates on various forms of corruption in sections 8–25; and to increase deterrence, these corruption offences carry significantly high penalties.[41] For example, the ICPC Act prescribes, upon conviction, punishment of up to seven years imprisonment for 'corruptly offering' any property or benefit to a public official in the performance of his or her duties.[42] The same punishment applies in cases where a public official demands or receives any such property or benefit in the course of performing official duties.[43] Other categories of offences covered under the Act include fraudulent acquisition of property or interest (such as contracts, agreements, or investments) by public officials as a result of their positions and in circumstances that suggest a conflict of interest (carrying seven years' imprisonment);[44] and accepting or obtaining (or attempting to do either) any gift or consideration as inducement or reward in the course of official duties.[45] It is irrelevant if any such public official does not personally benefit from the gift. Article 385 of Equatorial Guinea's Penal Code prescribes 'short-term imprisonment and a fine equal to or up to three times the value of the gift'.

[37] See similar provision in Art 131 of the Penal Code of Equatorial Guinea to the effect that, 'Any public official who, abusing his position, compromises the dignity or the interests of the Spanish Nation in a manner not included in this chapter shall be punished with long term imprisonment and debarment.'

[38] See similar provision in Art 198 of the Penal Code of Equatorial Guinea prohibiting any 'authority' or public official from 'taking advantage of his position, practices any profession directly related to the sphere of his official authority' or involvement in private associations or companies to make profit. The punishment is 'debarment and a fine of 5,000 to 250,000 pesetas'.

[39] Others include: counselling offences relating to corruption; criminal receipt of property; postal fraud; obstructing an investigation; offering bribes to public officers; providing advantages as a measure of appreciation or to secure future reward; and attempt, preparation and conspiracy to commit offences.

[40] For detailed discussion, see Ch 1.

[41] See similar provisions in Arts 196, 200, 202, 385, 386, 387, 390, 394, 400, 401, 404, 493, 496, 503, 528, and 533, of the Penal Code of Equatorial Guinea.

[42] ICPC Act, s 9.

[43] ibid s 10.

[44] ibid s 12.

[45] ibid s 17(a).

In addition, the ICPC Act also makes it an offence (carrying five years' imprisonment upon conviction) for a public officer to solicit or accept, or to be given, 'any gratification' to induce or reward such an officer to perform a public duty (which should be performed as a matter of employment) or to gain corrupt or unfair advantage, whether personally or for associates or relations.[46] Unwisely, however, the Act does not cover the public officials' relations or friends who might benefit from these corrupt acts. This omission is problematic, especially given that family members, such as wives and children, often perform important public or quasi-public duties and may have nearly unlimited access to corrupt public funds, as demonstrated in the country studies discussed in Chapter 2.

Other issues commonly addressed by anti-corruption laws include presumption of innocence, burden of proof and evidential burden in relation to the offences they establish, and often controversially entrench the principle of presumption of corruption (not innocence) of senior state officials. This principle is found, for example, in Nigeria's ICPC Act.[47] The offence of 'illicit enrichment' or 'unexplained lifestyle' creates a 'presumption of corruption' and shifts the traditional burden of proof in criminal cases, as the suspect is required to explain the source of the investigated wealth and to show that it is not linked to corruption. While this provision may be prompted by the challenges often encountered in proving and successfully prosecuting corruption, its enforcement will most likely offend the right of protection against self-incrimination and the presumption of innocence. Similarly, the ICPC Act also shifts evidential burden to suspects to give information that may eventually be used against them in a criminal trial,[48] though it is unclear what kind of information a suspect is required to provide to an investigation officer under section 40 of the Act. This provision would seem to suggest that if the suspect fails to answer any specific questions during questioning, an offence would have been committed under the Act, for which a fine of 10,000 naira (around $100) or six months' imprisonment is prescribed upon conviction. As will be discussed in Chapter 4, the establishment of such offences has serious implications for the human rights of suspects to the presumption of innocence and the right of protection against self-incrimination. While one can understand the public interest and evidentiary considerations involved here, a fair balance must be struck to ensure that human rights are not unreasonably, inappropriately or unnecessarily compromised in the fight against corruption.

[46] ibid ss 18 and 19.

[47] See s 44, which confers the duty on the chairman of the Commission to decide whether or not an offence has been committed under the Act, and then to decide whether to bring any charges of corruption. The chairman is tasked with the responsibility of determining ownership and control of any property, the origin of which a suspect cannot explain given present or past emoluments, and other relevant circumstances.

[48] See s 53.

Relatedly, section 60 of the ICPC Act covers the somewhat controversial issue of culture and corruption, in particular the notion of gift-giving, even though this is a common tradition throughout African states (see Chapter 1). Suffice it to say here, that the Act explicitly outlaws the defence of 'custom'. Section 60 declares that, 'In any proceedings under this Act, evidence shall not be admissible to show that any such gratification mentioned in this Act is customary in any profession, trade, vocation or calling or on a social occasion'. However, under section 71, anyone convicted of an offence under the Act, or other relevant laws, shall enjoy the right to appeal. This fundamental human right is not only within Nigeria's constitution, but is also internationally recognised, including under the African Charter (see Chapter 5 for detailed discussion on this).

*Other Provisions*

As with the international and regional anti-corruption treaties that are discussed in Chapter 4, national anti-corruption legislation generally also provides for asset recovery. For example, section 20 of the ICPC Act permits confiscation of the proceeds and instruments of corruption. However, these provisions are limited in scope and application in some important respects, not least given that most stolen assets are stashed in developed economies in Europe and North America (see Chapter 2), mostly beyond the reach and mandate of national anti-corruption agencies.

In addition, anti-corruption legislation in general also establishes implementation or institutional mechanisms, such as anti-corruption commissions, agencies or ombudsmen. However, while Nigeria has special agencies for corruption, Equatorial Guinea does not. As for Angola, although the Financial Court handles corruption cases, as the US State Department Country Report for 2012 shows, Angola 'does not have a special entity mandated with the responsibility of combating corruption'.[49] Accordingly, the remainder of this section will focus on the Nigeria's ICPC Act, which establishes an anti-corruption commission with a comprehensive mandate.

Section 3 of the ICPC Act established the Independent Corrupt Practices and Other Related Offences Commission.[50] The Act maintains that the commission's independence is sacrosanct, and that its operation will be free of 'direction or control of any other person or authority'. The commission is composed of one chairperson and 12 members, and it must include

[49] See Country Reports on Human Rights Practices for 2012, www.state.gov/documents/organization/204298.pdf, 23.

[50] Previous anti-corruption bodies include the Public Complaints Bureau (PCB) and the Corrupt Practices Investigation Bureau (CPIB), but both institutions soon disappeared and were replaced with the Code of Conduct Bureau and the Code of Conduct Tribunal, whose effectiveness and relevance continue to be questioned.

a retired police officer not below the rank of commissioner of police, a legal practitioner with no less than 10 years' post-call experience, a retired judge of a superior court of record, a retired public servant not below the rank of director, a woman, a chartered accountant, and a young person between 21 and 30 years of age.[51] Moreover, the chairman must be either a retired judge or someone who is qualified to hold office as a judge of a superior court of record in Nigeria.[52] In addition to detailed investigatory,[53] administrative, and educational functions, the commission also performs important duties such as promoting public support for the fight against corruption, and periodic reviews of the practices, systems, and procedures of public bodies so as to remove scope for corruption, and, as the ICPC Act indicates, 'other related offences'.[54]

Under section 5 of the ICPC Act, officers of the commission have the powers and immunities of a police officer.[55] Accordingly, they thus can, in the course of an investigation, obtain a court order to enter any premises and, where reasonable grounds exist, carry out a personal search of persons and seize any property that is either the subject or evidence of an offence covered by the Act.[56] They can also stop, search, and seize any vehicle or conveyance, remove by force any obstruction preventing entry to any premises for purposes of an investigation, and detain any persons found in the premises or conveyances until the search is completed.[57] Similarly, the Act also grants extensive powers to the chairman to obtain information[58] from persons suspected, on reasonable grounds, of having committed an offence covered by the Act.[59] However, the extensive powers of the commission may be abused if its officials are over-zealous or if they are used for politically motivated reasons. Nonetheless, any potential abuse may be remedied by recourse to legal action.

[51] ICPC Act, s 3(3)(a)–(f).

[52] ibid, s 3(4).

[53] This refers to the powers to receive complaints – based on reasonable grounds that suggest commission of an offence under the act – to investigate them, and to bring suspects to justice.

[54] ICPC Act, s 6.

[55] ibid, s 5(1): 'Subject to the provisions of this Act, an officer of the Commission when investigating or prosecuting a case of corruption, shall have all the powers and immunities of a police officer under the Police Act and any other laws conferring power on the Police, or empowering and protecting law enforcement agents.'

[56] ibid, s 37.

[57] ibid, s 36.

[58] ibid, s 23. Such information includes background on properties (whether within or outside Nigeria), bank accounts, documents and records relating to the business, travel, sources of income, and gifts or other assets. While the commission can obtain this information through its investigatory tools or by volunteer staff, the public officer has a duty to report to the commission cases of bribery or other related offences. Any breach of this duty carries a fine of 100,000 naira ($750), two years' imprisonment, or both.

[59] ibid, s 44.

## CONSTITUTIONAL AND LEGISLATIVE OBSTACLES IN THE FIGHT AGAINST CORRUPTION

### Immunity Clauses

One major obstacle to the successful fight against corruption in many countries is the inclusion in constitutions and legislation[60] of so-called immunity clauses, which protect high-ranking state officials from prosecution while in office. For example, section 308 of the constitution of Nigeria provides:

> (1) Notwithstanding anything to the contrary in this Constitution, but subject to subsection (2) of this section –
>
> (a) no civil or criminal proceedings shall be instituted or continued against a person to whom this section applies during his period of office;
> (b) a person to whom this section applies shall not be arrested or imprisoned during that period either in pursuance of the process of any court or otherwise; and
> (c) no process of any court requiring or compelling the appearance of a person to whom this section applies, shall be applied for or issued:
>
> Provided that in ascertaining whether any period of limitation has expired for the purposes of any proceedings against a person to whom this section applies, no account shall be taken of his period of office.
> (2) The provisions of subsection (1) of this section shall not apply to civil proceedings against a person to whom this section applies in his official capacity or to civil or criminal proceedings in which such a person is only a nominal party.
> (3) This section applies to a person holding the office of President or Vice-President, Governor or Deputy Governor; and the reference in this section to "period of office" is a reference to the period during which the person holding such office is required to perform the functions of the office.

Simply put, section 308 protects the president, vice president, governors and their deputies against civil and criminal proceedings while they are in office.[61] Sub-section 1 appears to suggest that section 308 is 'absolute', by the use of 'notwithstanding'. Thus, not even the fundamental human rights provisions contained in Chapter IV of the constitution may be used

[60] The rare exception is Art 140 of the Angolan constitution, which provides that: 'Ministers of State, Ministers, Secretaries of State and Vice Ministers shall be answerable to the Supreme Court for any crimes committed either during the exercise of their duties or outside them. [They] may only be imprisoned after being charged when the infraction is punishable by a prison sentence of more than two years, except in the case of *flagrante delicto*, for a serious crime punishable with a prison sentence of more than two years.' However, as a subsection to the article provides, such public officials will only be sent to prison if the offence is punishable by more than two years' imprisonment.

[61] Criminal or civil proceedings can also be brought against them if they are impeached by the National Assembly or their State House of Assembly (see s 143 for the president and vice president; and s 188 for governors and deputy-governors).

to challenge the 'immunity clause'. However, section 308 does not prohibit investigation of cases of corruption against the officials mentioned during their tenure of office. Such investigation is rarely undertaken, and where it is carried out, has limited deterrence value because no civil or criminal proceedings may be taken against any such officials. Similarly, by sub-section 2, section 308 'shall not apply [where the president, vice president, governor or deputy governor] is only a nominal party.'

As previously noted, the constitutions of both Angola and Equatorial Guinea contain substantially similar immunity clauses. Thus, for example, under Article 127 of the constitution of Angola, high-ranking government officials, including the president, enjoy immunity against criminal prosecution 'for actions practised in the exercise of his functions', and can only be prosecuted after five years out of office for crimes committed after leaving office. The 'immunity clause' under the constitution of Equatorial Guinea is provided by a combination of Items 32, 48 and 49, and under new changes to the constitution, the president will continue to enjoy immunity even after leaving the office. Ironically, Item 84 provides that, 'judges and magistrates shall not enjoy any form of immunity in the exercise of their duties'.

On the one hand, the argument may be made that to allow the investigation and prosecution of high-ranking government officials for corruption while they are in office may diminish the powers and authorities of those offices, disrupt democratic governments, and expose these officials to litigation, which may distract them from their public functions. Thus, instead of removing immunity clauses from the constitutions, the best solution to fight corruption would be to promote effective leadership and to improve institutions of governance so as to increase the chances of preventing corruption in the first place. On the other hand, the doctrine of official immunity can shield particular public officials from the power of the judiciary and deepen the longstanding principles of the separation of powers and checks and balances.

The case against the entrenchment of the notion of absolute immunity in constitutions is buttressed by the fact that such immunity is the most significant impediment to the successful fight against corruption in many countries. While immunity clauses may be understood to serve some general public purpose in the way of running a government, absolute immunity is counterproductive, and as experienced in many African countries, can encourage senior public officials to engage in corruption with near absolute impunity, knowing that they are effectively shielded from the law even when they leave office, as the case of the constitutional amendment in Equatorial Guinea demonstrates. Often, state officials refuse to leave office because they know that they are protected against prosecution only for as long as they remain in office, thereby contributing to a violation of the right of the citizens to a democratic governance, including the right to participate in their own government. It is therefore difficult to sustain the argument of 'good for the government' in cases where there is strong evidence of or perception that a public official's (and most likely multiple officials') actions have, in fact, clearly violated established constitutional or statutory standards. It would seem reasonable to remove immunity clauses, especially given the corrosive effects of corruption involving high-ranking state officials. As it stands, immunity clauses in many countries are used by high-ranking officials as 'protection or assurance' to commit corruption and then used to prevent their prosecution.

While immunity for senior public officials generally may not be harmful, unleashing a defence of official immunity in the face of clear allegations of corruption cannot be defended on the basis of the rule of law (or even on the minimal notions of equality, fairness and justice), and would obviously run counter to the goal of a fair and just legal system to remedy egregious official misconduct and other crimes or to establish an environment conducive to the enjoyment of basic human rights. It should be the case that a public official, regardless of title or office, will receive the immunity that corresponds only to lawful official actions, and not serious crimes like corruption. At any rate, public officials who are genuinely committed to the well-being of the state and its people, and to the establishment of an effective and functioning system of administration of justice, should have absolutely nothing to fear from establishing an exception that would ensure that immunity is removed in special circumstances, such as when officials are engaged in corruption. Several examples, including from Israel, the United Kingdom, and the United States, in which senior state officials have been forced to resign and/or are prosecuted for corruption, show that providing exceptions in corruption cases in African states would not lead to the collapse of government. Rather, it would strengthen transparency and accountability of governments, and considerably improve the rule of law, the fight against corruption, and respect for human rights.

## Prosecutorial Discretion and Political Appointees

The exercise of discretionary powers in the investigation and prosecution of corruption cases raises at least two important questions. The first is the degree to which the official making any determinations is objective, impartial, rational, and independent of political authorities. The second, which is intertwined with the first, concerns the considerations that inform the decision to prosecute. Investigating and prosecuting corruption allegations eventually involve the police, anti-corruption agencies, and government lawyers, all deciding the most effective use of scarce resources; whether there is sufficient admissible evidence to justify investigation and prosecution; and, most crucially, whether any prosecution will meet the interests of justice or the 'public interest', produce conviction, and bring about the recovery of stolen assets. Such exercises invariably require enormous discretion and are essential elements of all criminal investigations and prosecutorial decisions, not just those involving allegations of corruption.

National laws across African states, as elsewhere around the globe, emphasise and entrench the notion of independence and impartiality of prosecutorial authorities in all instances. As noted, in many countries, the investigation and prosecution of corruption cases, including those involving high-ranking state officials, generally require the consent of the government's chief law officer, commonly known as the attorney general or minister of justice. In Angola,[62] Equatorial Guinea[63] and Nigeria[64] (as in many other African jurisdictions), the position of the attorney general or minister of justice is vested in a single person appointed by the head of government, and that person is directly accountable to the appointing authorities. It should be noted that chief law officers often belong to the ruling party. Not that this legal-cum-political arrangement is peculiar to Africa (the same arrangement exists, for example, in the United Kingdom and the United States), but as will be shown shortly, the operation of this arrangement is especially problematic in several African states (where the rule of law is very weak) when the chief law officer is called upon to exercise discretion in both investigation and prosecution of large-scale corruption.

The perception of a conflict of interest frequently exists, as such chief law officers are often accused of lacking independence, objectivity, and impartiality in the exercise of their constitutionally and legally sanctioned discretionary powers and responsibilities in corruption cases involving high-ranking state officials. Even where the constitutional and legal provisions vest prosecutorial responsibility in anti-corruption agencies or commissions, as is the case in Nigeria, such provisions usually provide that the chief law officer must exercise final responsibility over the exercise of the prosecutorial discretion. Officials exercising legal but not personal discretion often use constitutional and legal loopholes to halt or undermine investigations and prosecutions of high-profile corruption

[62] Art 139 of the Angolan constitution, for example, is a good illustration of political control of the office of the attorney general. It provides that: 'The Vice-President, Ministers of State and Ministers [including the attorney general] shall be politically and institutionally responsible to the President of the Republic.'

[63] Several provisions of the constitution of Equatorial Guinea show the near absolute powers of the president, including in Item 93 the appointment of the Attorney General 'and his deputies'. Under Item 91, the president shall single-handedly appoint the president of the Supreme Court.

[64] See for example s 5 of the constitution of Nigeria dealing with the executive powers of the president.

cases, even when there is a compelling 'public interest case' for such matters to proceed. This controversial exercise of discretionary powers is apparent, for instance, in the abuse of *nolle prosequi* in several countries.

In many countries, the decision of a minister of justice or attorney general to enter *nolle prosequi* is constitutionally endorsed and cannot be questioned by a court, not even where there is compelling evidence of bias, malice, or political or extraneous considerations. In the Nigerian case of *State v SO Ilori & Ors*,[65] for instance, the Supreme Court described the attorney general as a 'master unto himself and under no control whatsoever, judicial or otherwise, vis-a-vis his powers of instituting or discontinuing criminal proceedings'.[66] The Court, though, was affirming the decision of the lower court that 'there cannot be any doubt about' the right of the attorney general to discontinue the criminal proceedings instituted by him or any other person at any stage before judgment.[67] The Supreme Court also held that the expression 'shall have regard to', contained in section 191(3) of the constitution, meant: 'only enable something to be done'. Such an expression is what is known in the interpretation of statutes as a permissive language: 'A language, which imports a discretion but certainly does not create a condition.'[68] The Court then concluded: '[T]he only sanction, where there is an abuse of his powers by an Attorney-General, is this reaction of his appointor or adverse public opinion which may force him to resign'.[69]

Another case, involving a former Permanent Secretary in the Ministry of Defence, Dr Julius Makanjuola and four others, for allegedly stealing N420m (around $3m) of public funds, clearly illustrates how the application of *nolle prosequi* can stifle the fight against corruption. In that case, former attorney general Kanu Agabi entered a *nolle prosequi*.

These cases are illustrative of the legal obstacles that exist but should be addressed if the fight against corruption is to be meaningful. To hold that the exercise of the constitutional powers and discretion conferred on the attorney general is unquestionable under any circumstances is antithetical to the overall objectives of the rule of law, and detrimental to the fight against corruption. This lack of independence of the office of the attorney general as an appointee of the president provides an explanation why the office has historically played a limited role in the fight against corruption. While it may be argued that democracy grants elected representatives the authority to establish policies and legal frameworks against corruption

[65] *SO Ilori* & 4 *Ors*, (1983) 1 SCNLR 94; (1984) 2 SC 155.

[66] In this case, the *nolle prosequi* was entered pursuant to s 191 of the Nigerian 1979 Constitution, which deals with the constitutional authority of the commissioners for justice of the states. This is similar to s 160, which deals with constitutional authority of the minister of justice and attorney general of the Federation.

[67] ibid, para 8.

[68] ibid.

[69] ibid.

and to diligently prosecute cases of corruption involving high-ranking government officials, such entrusted and delegated powers should meet the expectation that it would be exercised fairly, objectively, and in the overall best interest of the public. Furthermore, granting political appointees the power and discretion to make decisions on the investigation and prosecution of corruption cases or to exercise oversight and approval control over such decisions without independent and politically neutral authority can be counterproductive in the fight against corruption, in part because of the high possibility that such decisions will be made on the basis of inappropriate, unfair or irrational considerations, such as partisan interests.

In addition, prosecutorial discretion often encourages the frequent use of pre-trial negotiation, or plea bargaining, in corruption cases. The use of this procedure is often justified on the grounds of 'efficiency of administration of justice' and cost effectiveness, but questions remain as to the consistency, fairness or usefulness of this practice in the fight against corruption. The deterrence of criminal prosecution is lost during plea bargaining because material and financial proceeds of corruption are frequently shared, as corrupt officials are often allowed to keep some of their ill-gotten wealth. In general, then, if states genuinely seek to tackle corruption, they should review the constitutional and legal roles of an attorney general or minister of justice, and put in place independent oversight mechanism that would ensure the most effective exercise of discretionary powers in cases of corruption involving high-ranking state officials.

## Existing Anti-corruption Mechanisms: Questions on Independence and Effectiveness

As previously noted, independent anti-corruption bodies are virtually non-existent in Angola and Equatorial Guinea. In contrast, Nigerian anti-corruption legislation contains provisions safeguarding the independence of the main anti-corruption bodies. Even so, these safeguards are rarely effective in practice. This section will now consider the main anti-corruption agencies in Nigeria and underscore the need for greater legal protection to achieve independence of anti-corruption agencies.

The chairman and members of the Code of Conduct Bureau are appointed by the Nigerian president, though their appointment is subject to confirmation by the Senate, a branch of the parliament.[70] Furthermore, the chairman and bureau members can only be removed from office by

[70] The Nigerian Senate (with a term of four years, subject to renewal) and House of Representatives (also with a term of four years, subject to renewal) comprise the Nigerian National Assembly (discussed earlier in this chapter).

the president pursuant to an address seeking removal on the grounds of misconduct (among other reasons), and which is supported by a two-thirds majority of the Senate. Even so, the majority members of the parliament share the same political party as the president, and as such, the parliament is not always proactive in taking action in this respect. In addition, any prosecution before the Code of Conduct Bureau or the Code of Conduct Tribunal is subject to the powers of the attorney general, who, as noted earlier, is a political appointee of the president, and who thus also belongs to the same political party.[71]

Similarly, whereas section 3(14) of the ICPC Act provides that the commission in the discharge of its functions will not be subject to the direction or control of any other person or authority, section 26(2) provides that prosecution for an offence under the Act 'shall be initiated by the Attorney-General of the Federation, or any person or authority to whom he delegates his authority'. The way the commission has portrayed itself over the years would suggest that these provisions have had debilitating effects on its work. In practice the ICPC has focused more on petty corruption, and ignores allegations of corruption among high-ranking government officials. A special adviser to the attorney general has described the performance of the ICPC as 'somewhat disappointing'.[72] In addition, the provision of section 52 of the ICPC Act is very weak. It provides for the appointment of an independent counsel (a legal practitioner of no less than 15 years' post-call to the Bar; to investigate high-ranking elected public officials protected under the immunity clause of the constitution (section 308). However, more than a decade after its enactment, this provision has never been used in practice. While on one occasion the ICPC reportedly sent requests to the chief justice of Nigeria to appoint an independent counsel to investigate cases of corrupt former governors, a lack of resources was cited as the reason for refusing to do so.

Further, when section 52 is applied, it is doubtful whether it will be effective because the concept has not been fully embraced, as the law merely empowers the chief justice of Nigeria's Supreme Court to appoint an independent counsel whose only task is to carry out an investigation and report back to the National Assembly (or to state Houses of Assembly, in the case of a governor). In other words, the independent counsel has no powers to carry out any prosecution, leaving some commentators like

[71] S 3(2) of the Code of Conduct Bureau and Tribunal Act 1990, c 15 Laws of Federation of Nigeria (2004) provides that: 'Prosecutions for all offences referred to in this Act shall be instituted in the name of the Federal Republic of Nigeria by the Attorney-General of the Federation or such officers in the Federal Ministry of Justice as the Attorney-General of the Federation may authorize so to do.'

[72] Deji Adekunle, 'Independent Prosecution Systems in Nigeria: Challenges and Prospects', presented at African Network of Constitutional Law Conference on Fostering Constitutionalism, 2007, www.ancl-radc.org.za/sites/default/files/Independent%20Prosecution%20Systems%20by%20Deji%20Adekunle.pdf, 12.

Deji Adekunle to question the necessity of creating such a paper-tiger mechanism, especially given that the Nigerian parliament is already empowered under section 88 of the constitution to conduct 'an investigation inter alia into the conduct of affairs of any person, authority Ministry or government department charged or intended to be charged with the duty of disbursing or administering public funds'.[73] The constitution prescribes that such powers shall be exercised to enable Parliament to 'expose corruption, inefficiency or waste in the disbursement of funds'. Yet, while section 88 powers have been exercised several times and have led to a plethora of reports issued by the Parliament, these reports are rarely officially published, let alone implemented.[74]

The ICPC also has no independent power to initiate investigations, though it can act on complaints submitted to it in writing. In countries where there is illiteracy, suspicion of government, widespread ignorance of legal rights, or situations in which there is a need for urgent action, there is a limit to the potential usefulness of such commissions. Yet, by consistently denying these institutions the necessary independence and freedom of action, governments invariably fail in their good faith obligations to establish and ensure an effective framework to combat corruption. In general, then, such an attitude would breach states' human rights obligations and commitments, such as the obligations to afford effective remedies for victims, to align their national laws and practices with international obligations and to establish an environment conducive to the effective implementation of human rights. (See Chapters 5 and 6 for detailed discussion on this.)

## CONCLUSION

It is clear that while several laws exist to fight corruption, such laws are generally weak or 'empty', as they merely exist on paper. Thus, enforcement of anti-corruption legislation and policies has lessened steadily,

[73] ibid. Adekunle writes that s 52 has also been described as 'unwarranted delegation of powers vested by the Constitution in the legislature to the Chief Justice, since it provides that appointment of the Independent Counsel is at the initiative of the Chief Justice'. Ibid, 14–15.

[74] Similarly, weakness is also seen in Nigeria's Economic and Financial Crimes Commission (EFCC). The chairman and members of the EFCC are also appointed by the president and subject to the confirmation of the Senate. The president may, under s 3, remove any member of the EFCC (presumably also the chairman, although this is not explicit) for inability to discharge the functions of the office, for several reasons, including misconduct. While the EFCC recorded some impressive successes early on in its establishment (due largely to the personality of former chairman Mallam Nuhu Ribadu), it soon became largely a political tool to target political opposition leaders and others who opposed (former) President Olusegun Obasanjo's alleged plan to run for a third term in office.

See generally, Richard Akinnola, *The Politics of Corruption and Corruption of Politics* (Lagos, Rich Konsult, 2008) v–vi.

resulting in few or even no prosecutions of high-ranking state officials for corruption. The absence of independent anti-corruption commissions and agencies (whether in terms of appointment, budget control or investigative powers), coupled with the existence of immunity clauses, means that the institutions rarely take potent measures against those accused of corruption. The susceptibility of such bodies to executive pressure also presents huge moral, legal, and political challenges to any effort to trace, recover, and repatriate stolen assets, and suggests that these laws are public relations exercise to give the impression of addressing corruption. The inevitable result of immunity clauses for example, is that high-ranking officials who steal their state's wealth and natural resources are shielded from prosecution and punishment.

Furthermore, judicial apathy (in most cases due to the lack of adequate legal rules safeguarding the independence and integrity of the judiciary) in corruption cases further limits the ability of the legal and institutional mechanisms to tackle corruption. Similarly, mechanisms for asset recovery and repatriation are weak, and in some African states virtually non-existent.[75] The current criminal law instruments against corruption allow for indicted corrupt officials to retain some of the recovered stolen wealth by agreement, including through so-called 'pre-bargaining agreement'. This legal arrangement allows corrupt officials to negotiate their way out of their crimes.

In addition, the legal rules and cases that have been highlighted in this chapter raise some serious questions about the independence, objectivity, and impartiality of prosecutorial authorities. This is particularly true of chief law officers of governments that fail to exercise their discretionary powers in a manner that meets the basic interests of justice and public interest in cases of large-scale corruption. Broad official discretion without necessary oversight mechanisms can make the criminal justice system less fair as it may promote the unfair exercise of prosecutorial charging discretion for improper reasons. Leaving decisions to investigate and prosecute large-scale corruption exclusively in the hands of government-appointed lawyers risk undermining the global aim of combating corruption. Excessively vigorous prosecution of petty corruption or corruption involving opposition leaders may be politically expedient for a prosecutor who covets greater political influence and security. Given the inherent limitations of such offices, chief law officers may not always act independently, objectively, impartially, and in the best interests of justice and the public.

Increased safeguards through constitutional or legal amendments are needed, but these may also count for little if those appointed as chief law

[75] For example, the Nigerian government's attempts to repatriate the late General Abacha's frozen assets of approximately $1bn were impeded.

officers lack the required fortitude and personal integrity to function appropriately, and in the absence of strong, independent, and impartial institutions of governance (and public accountability mechanisms) established to prevent and combat corruption. The rule of law is key to the impartial enforcement of anti-corruption laws because 'without adequate enforcement, any anti-corruption program becomes a comedy of errors at best and a farce at worst'[76]

Moreover, the problems associated with abuses of prosecutorial discretion provide additional justification for granting legal standing to victims of corruption to sue for violations of their human rights caused by corruption. The fear of 'judicialisation' and the complexity, expense, and time-consuming nature of litigation appears to be imperfectly founded. Far from resulting in victims 'taking over' corruption cases, prosecutorial functions would still rest with state authorities, the only difference being greater oversight control and independent options by victims in cases where states are either unwilling or unable to effectively implement their anti-corruption and human rights obligations and commitments. The judiciary can also play a part in the effort to limit prosecutorial discretion by, for example, refusing to validate expansive interpretations of constitutions and legislation that promote policies that the drafters may not have intended. Parliaments should be more proactive in carrying out their legislative responsibilities to make laws for the prosperity of their countries and for the greatest happiness of the greatest number. They will also need to provide standards and benchmarks for the independent, objective, and impartial exercise of prosecutorial discretion in cases of corruption, and for entrenching transparency and accountability generally. The establishment of constitutionally sanctioned review commissions and citizens' oversight mechanisms that would challenge prosecutorial decisions to suspend prosecution where strong evidence of criminal conduct exists might help to balance the interest of powerful public prosecutors (with the overall public interests) by ensuring that discretion is fairly, reasonably, accountably and consistently applied.

Apart from the African Charter on Human and Peoples' Rights, inspiration for developing the necessary legal and policy framework to implement the proposal for a human rights approach to corruption can be found, rather surprisingly, in the abandoned 1995 draft Constitution of Nigeria (proposed, ironically, while Abacha, regarded as one of the most corrupt leaders of Nigeria, was in power), which explicitly grants legal standing to the citizens to sue for violations of their human rights occasioned by corruption. The draft constitution provided in section 35 that

[76] Sam Jacobson and Maria Slavova, *Democracy Against Corruption: A New Way of Thinking About Public Administration* (Sofia, Bulgaria: Institute of Public Administration and European Integration 2006) 101.

'Every person shall have the right to: (a) ensure the eradication of corrupt practices, and abuse of power; (b) protect and preserve public property; (c) fight against misappropriation and squandering of public funds.'[77]

[77] See also Art 74 of the Angolan constitution guaranteeing that: 'Every citizen, either individually or through associations representing specific interests, shall have the right to take legal action in the cases and under the terms established by law, with the aim of annulling acts which are harmful to public health, the public, historic and cultural heritage, the environment, quality of life, consumer rights, the legality of administrative acts and any other collective interests.' Art 75 adds: 'The state and other public corporate bodies shall be jointly and civilly liable for any actions and omissions committed by their organs, their respective officeholders, agents and staff in the exercise of their legislative, judicial and administrative duties or as a result of the said duties which result in the violation of rights, freedoms and guarantees or in losses to those entitled to them or third parties. The individuals responsible for these acts or omissions shall be held liable for them, in criminal and disciplinary terms, under the terms of the law.'

# 4

# *International Legal Frameworks for Fighting Corruption across Africa*

## INTRODUCTION

AS PREVIOUSLY NOTED, the history of the fight against corruption in Africa,[1] as in many other regions, is in several respects traceable to the US Foreign Corrupt Practices Act. While the Organization of American States was the first intergovernmental organisation to adopt a legally binding instrument to fight corruption, the genesis of international developments and initiatives lies in early discussions within the United Nations. These developments consisted of different phases: first was the tolerance of corruption in international business transactions, with some countries (such as Germany) treating bribery as a tax-deductible expense; second was the twofold denial of the negative effects of corruption, and political resistance to adopting strong instruments to address the problem; and third was the engagement and discussions around development and governance concerns in developing countries. Discussions at this stage focused mainly on the most effective way of combating corruption. The third phase coincided with the end of the Cold War, globalisation, increased technology, and the establishment of Transparency International. The developments within the United Nations prompted regional discussions and initiatives, including in Africa. Even so, the influence of the US Foreign Corrupt Practices Act was apparent throughout this period.

Two of the four anti-corruption treaties and protocols discussed in this chapter are sub-regional and applicable to Africa: the SADC Protocol against Corruption, and the ECOWAS Protocol on the Fight against Corruption. The former was adopted in Blantyre, Malawi, on 14 August 2001 by the SADC Heads of State and Government. It entered into force on 6 July 2005. The ECOWAS Protocol was adopted in Dakar, Senegal, on 21 December 2001 by the ECOWAS Heads of State and Government and entered into force on 14 December 2005. The other two are global and regional anti-corruption instruments: the UN Convention against

[1] For detailed discussion on historical and conceptual backgrounds on corruption, see Ch 1.

Corruption (UNCAC), which was adopted in New York by the UN General Assembly on 31 October 2003, and entered into force on 14 December 2005. As of February 2014, 44 of the 54 African Union member states had ratified the convention. The other document is the continent-wide instrument AU Convention on Preventing and Combating Corruption, which was adopted on 11 July 2003 in Maputo, Mozambique, just three months before the adoption of the UNCAC. The AU Convention entered into force on 5 August 2006. As of February 2014, 43 of the 54 AU member states had ratified the convention.

Nonetheless, in terms of scope and application, the UNCAC (with 71 articles – the AU convention has 28 articles, the ECOWAS protocol has 27 articles and the SADC protocol has 21 articles) is the most comprehensive of the instruments, and all member states of the UN are expected to ratify it.[2] Although all these instruments have virtually similar objectives and features, they nonetheless differ significantly not only in terms of scope and application but also in substance, procedures, and enforcement mechanisms, as will be shown shortly. This chapter examines and compares the four instruments, and the institutions that have been set up under them. The chapter also discusses whether these instruments add anything to individual national legislation against corruption. This approach uses the UNCAC as the central comparative instrument because of its comprehensive and international nature.

The remainder of this chapter is devoted to an analysis of the effectiveness and sufficiency of these treaties in combating corruption and its manifestations from a human rights standpoint. The four major areas of the criminal law instruments analysed are: prevention, criminalisation, international cooperation and assistance, and asset recovery. As noted in Chapter 3, these elements of the fight against corruption were already an integral part of many national legal initiatives against corruption before the development of international law in this field. The four elements are discussed in order, after an explanation of the object and purpose of the instruments and the definitions of terms across the instruments are clarified.

[2] The UNCAC is to the anti-corruption movement what the Universal Declaration of Human Rights is to the human rights movement. It is thus unsurprising that International Anti-Corruption Day, celebrated globally on 9 December each year, is immediately followed by International Human Rights Day, celebrated globally on 10 December. On discussion of international anti-corruption treaties and standards, see generally, Julio Bacio Terracino, *The International Legal Framework against Corruption: States' obligations to prevent and repress corruption* (Cambridge: Intersentia, 2012).

## COMPARATIVE ANALYSIS

### Object and Purpose

The objects and purposes of the four anti-corruption instruments are essentially the same, although there are some important differences. The UNCAC, the AU Convention, the SADC Protocol, and the ECOWAS Protocol all aim to develop measures and mechanisms to tackle corruption, establish a framework for cooperation among the states parties, and harmonise national laws and policies with the treaties. However, unlike the AU Convention, the SADC Protocol, and the ECOWAS Protocol (which each contain some good though limited references to human rights and good governance),[3] the UNCAC omits any explicit reference to human rights. Although attempts were made during the drafting of the convention to include reference to 'good governance', such attempts were roundly rejected on the rather untenable ground that it would offend 'national sovereignty'. Nonetheless, the UNCAC contains some reference to the rule of law (which carries with it some notions of good governance and human rights) in its preamble.

In contrast to the UNCAC's restrained approach to the important principles of good governance, development and human rights, the African-initiated instruments unsurprisingly embraced these ideas. Thus, the ECOWAS protocol underscores the importance of the fight against corruption in the ECOWAS initiative to promote integration and to achieve other important objectives of ECOWAS, such as good governance and democracy. The protocol acknowledges 'the grave consequences of corruption on investment, economic growth and democracy; and the need for improved transparency and good governance to strengthen democratic and other institutions'.[4] Member states therefore commit themselves 'to take all necessary measures to harmonize their strategies and policies and to refrain from any action that may hinder the attainment of the aims and objectives of the Community [which is] to achieve the integration of its members'.[5]

However, unlike the UNCAC, the SADC Protocol, or the ECOWAS Protocol, the objectives of the AU Convention are stated explicitly as being

[3] With regard to the AU Convention, Adama Dieng's report provided the foundational document that resulted in the drafting of the convention, and indeed emphasised this, when he observed: 'Corruption and impunity are antithetical to the enjoyment of economic, social and cultural rights and the enemy of the principle of good governance . . . [It is] an infringement on human rights by virtue of the fact that it increases the debt of states.' It is noteworthy to mention that the Constitutive Act of the African Union recognised the need to promote good governance, rule of law, and human rights.

[4] ECOWAS Protocol on the Fight against Corruption, http://archive.transparency.org/global_priorities/international_conventions/conventions_instruments/ecowas_protocol.

[5] ibid.

to 'promote and strengthen development and good governance',[6] thus significantly recognising the developmental challenges that corruption poses across Africa. It has been stated that the AU Convention 'takes a rights and good governance approach to the problem of corruption'.[7] Even so, this fundamental feature of the AU Convention has not been fully and coherently developed.[8]

Further, while both the AU Convention and the SADC Protocol merely refer to the fight against 'public and private sectors corruption' in their statements, the UNCAC emphasises the need to take efficient and effective measures to combat corruption in the management of 'public affairs and public property'. Similarly, the AU Convention refers to public affairs, which presumably includes public property. In general, the ECOWAS Protocol, the SADC Protocol, and the AU Convention contain a virtually similar statement of principles including:

- respect for democratic principles and institutions, popular participation, the rule of law, and good governance;
- respect for human and peoples' rights;
- transparency and accountability in the management of public affairs;
- promotion of social justice to ensure balanced socioeconomic development; and
- condemnation and rejection of acts of corruption, related offences, and impunity.

Implicit in the elaboration of these principles is the recognition of the critical roles they play in developing a comprehensive and effective response to corruption. However, this strong tendency to recognise the connection between corruption, development, good governance and human rights is not reflected in the normative contents of the instruments as, for example, the AU Convention excludes from its enumerated objectives the issue of assets recovery. Nonetheless, Article 16 of the convention contains some important, albeit limited, provisions on the 'Confiscation and Seizure of the Proceeds and Instrumentalities of Corruption'.

Of the four instruments, the UNCAC is the only treaty whose stated objectives include the promotion of international cooperation for the primary purpose of asset recovery, which is essential for securing the return of stolen funds stashed abroad, and if returned funds are well spent, would help to contribute to development, good governance and respect human rights in Africa.

[6] See third preambular para and Art 2(1).

[7] Thomas R Snider and Won Kidane, 'Combating Corruption through International Law in Africa: A Comparative Analysis' (2007) 40 *Cornell International Law Journal* 691.

[8] ibid, 692.

## Definitions and Use of Terms

The four instruments, while similar in some respects in relation to their use of terms and definitions of concepts, nonetheless differ in terms of their contents, sometimes significantly. Thus, under Article 2 of the UNCAC, only nine terms are specifically defined: public official;[9] foreign public official;[10] official of a public international organisation;[11] property;[12]

[9] In the UNCAC, a public official 'shall mean: (i) any person holding a legislative, executive, administrative or judicial office of a State Party, whether appointed or elected, whether permanent or temporary, whether paid or unpaid, irrespective of that person's seniority; (ii) any other person who performs a public function, including for a public agency or public enterprise, or provides a public service, as defined in the domestic law of the State Party and as applied in the pertinent area of law of that State Party; (iii) any other person defined as a "public official" in the domestic law of a State Party. However, for the purpose of some specific measures contained in chapter II of the Convention, "public official" may mean any person who performs a public function or provides a public service as defined and applied in the domestic law of the State Party.' The *travaux priparatoires* indicate that the word 'executive' is understood to encompass the military branch, where appropriate. The definitions under the AU Convention, the SADC Protocol, and the ECOWAS Protocol, although along the same lines, are less comprehensive. Both the AU Convention and the ECOWAS Protocol use 'selected to perform functions in the name of the state', which presumably would mean the same thing as 'appointed'. The ECOWAS Protocol defines the term 'state' to comprise the national, provincial, regional, local, and municipal levels and other public agencies. The SADC Protocol uses 'any person exercising a public function or duty'. In general, 'public office' imposes duties to be carried out for the benefit of the public. An interesting question is whether the wife/husband of a senior public officer such as the president is considered a 'public officer'? The fact of marriage does not *ipso facto* grant the spouse of a public officer any such status, unless they are exercising some forms of delegated government functions, so that the purpose of government is achieved.

[10] In the UNCAC, a foreign public official 'shall mean any person holding a legislative, executive, administrative or judicial office of a foreign country, whether appointed or elected; and any person exercising a public function for a foreign country, including for a public agency or public enterprise'. The ECOWAS Protocol also defines foreign public official to mean 'any person exercising a public function in enterprises or a public establishment in another Member State'. Neither the AU Convention nor the SADC Protocol contains any definition of foreign public official.

[11] In the UNCAC, official of a public international organisation 'shall mean an international civil servant or any person who is authorized by such an organization to act on behalf of that organization'. The AU Convention, the SADC Protocol, and the ECOWAS Protocol do not contain any reference to this phrase.

[12] In the UNCAC, property 'shall mean assets of every kind, whether corporeal or incorporeal, movable or immovable, tangible or intangible, and legal documents or instruments evidencing title to or interest in such assets'. The *travaux preparatoires* indicate that the phrase 'assets of every kind' is understood to include funds and legal rights to assets. The SADC Protocol also uses the word 'property'; the AU Convention uses 'proceeds of corruption'; and the ECOWAS Protocol uses 'assets'. Th UNCAC, the SADC Protocol, and the AU Convention contain nearly identical words on this subject, although the AU Convention adds emphasis, with 'assets acquired as a result of act of corruption'. Further, the ECOWAS Protocol uses the words 'legal instrument demonstrating or purporting to demonstrate, or relating to ownership or other rights pertaining to such assets'.

proceeds of crime;[13] freezing or seizure;[14] confiscation;[15] predicate offence;[16] and controlled delivery.[17] The *travaux préparatoires* indicate that for countries with subnational units of a self-governing nature, it is up to each state to decide whether the term 'office' is considered to apply to positions at the subnational level. This definition is important in part because it clarifies the UNCAC's provisions requiring criminalisation of bribery of foreign public officials, and provides some guidance to states in terms of the categories of foreign officials that should be covered under their criminal laws.

In addition, unlike the AU Convention, the SADC Protocol, or the ECOWAS Protocol, the UNCAC's definition of 'public official' defers significantly to domestic law and practice to determine which group of persons must be covered by certain preventive measures and criminalisation provisions. Similarly, the UNCAC's definition section is shorter than those contained in the AU Convention (which has 12 defined terms, with additional clarifications on the use of singular and plural), the SADC Protocol (which also has 12 defined terms) and the ECOWAS Protocol (with 13 defined terms). It should be noted, however, that some of the definitions in these instruments are less substantive than those contained in the UNCAC. Nonetheless, although the definition of the terms used should have been more detailed and used across all of the provisions of the UNCAC, especially given the complexities of the issues addressed and the diversity of the societies that are required to implement it, the terms

[13] In the UNCAC, proceeds of crime 'shall mean any property derived from or obtained, directly or indirectly, through the commission of an offence'. This is similar to the definitions of 'assets' used in the ECOWAS Protocol; 'proceeds of corruption' used in the AU Convention; and 'property' in the SADC Protocol.

[14] In the UNCAC, freezing or seizure 'shall mean temporarily prohibiting the transfer, conversion, disposition or movement of property or temporarily assuming custody or control of property on the basis of an order issued by a court or other competent authority'. The AU Convention, the ECOWAS Protocol, and the SADC Protocol do not contain any definition of freezing or seizure.

[15] In the UNCAC, confiscation, which includes forfeiture where applicable, 'shall mean the permanent deprivation of property by order of a court or other competent authority'. Both the AU Convention and the SADC Protocol define confiscation in identical manners, to mean 'any penalty or measure resulting in a final deprivation of property, proceeds or instrumentalities ordered by a court of law following proceedings in relation to a criminal offence or offences connected with or related to corruption'. The ECOWAS Protocol contains no definition of confiscation.

[16] In the UNCAC, predicate offence 'shall mean any offence as a result of which proceeds have been generated that may become the subject of an offence as defined in article 23 of this Convention'. The ECOWAS Protocol contains an identical definition of predicate offence. But neither the AU Convention nor the SADC Protocol define the term.

[17] In the UNCAC, controlled delivery 'shall mean the technique of allowing illicit or suspect consignments to pass out of, through or into the territory of one or more States, with the knowledge and under the supervision of their competent authorities, with a view to the investigation of an offence and the identification of persons involved in the commission of the offence'. Neither the AU Convention, the SADC Protocol, nor the ECOWAS Protocol define controlled delivery.

defined are still useful as they can contribute to a better understanding of the convention and its effective implementation.

## Preventive Measures

The World Bank has described prevention as the 'preferred method'[18] to address the problem of corruption, and the four instruments reinforce that without effective preventive measures, states cannot achieve the objective of combating corruption in all its forms and manifestations. Article 3 of the ECOWAS Protocol underlines the broader push towards recognition of 'prevention' as an indispensable anti-corruption tool when it provides in part that, 'This Protocol shall also be applicable whenever a national institutional system fails to provide the most basic preventive measures enumerated in Article 5.' In addition, as will be shown below, the UNCAC establishes detailed preventive measures which states can adopt to tackle corruption at source. However, despite their formal recognition as an important dimension of the fight against corruption, 'preventive measures' are generally rarely accorded prominence, or effectively implemented in practice.

Further, as has been argued throughout this book, the complex and diverse nature of corruption demands a comprehensive and multi-layered response in the short, medium and long terms. Preventive strategy is thus crucial to the viability and success of any such response, and should in fact be prioritised in practice, and not just on paper. Prevention has the added benefit of removing opportunities and incentives for corruption, and therefore reducing the reliance on criminalisation and sanctions to fight corruption, which as this book has demonstrated, has not proved to be a sufficient deterrent to corruption.

All the four instruments contain provisions on provisional measures, though in varying degrees. For instance, in contrast to the AU Convention, the ECOWAS Protocol, or the SADC Protocol, the UNCAC's provisions on preventive measures are quite detailed, taking up the entire chapter 2 of the treaty (Articles 5–14). Further, the UNCAC balances its coverage of both public-sector and private-sector corruption, thus recognising the increasingly blurred lines between the public and private sectors, which are brought about largely by privatisation, the growth of the private sector and the growing influence of multinational corporations. In contrast, the provisions of the AU Convention, ECOWAS Protocol and SADC Protocol on preventive measures focus somewhat disproportionately on public-sector corruption. Further, unlike the UNCAC, which requires states to establish mechanisms to enforce some of its preventive provisions, neither

[18] Richard Mesick and Rachel Kleinfeld, 'Writing an Effective Anti-Corruption Law', World Bank PREM Note 58, October 2001.

the AU Convention, the ECOWAS Protocol, nor the SADC Protocol prescribe penalties for non-compliance.[19] As such, the discussion below will focus on the UNCAC's preventive measures.

Broadly, the UNCAC preventive measures underscore the need for states to adopt and implement important public administration and public-focused principles and policies. Thus, the UNCAC in Article 6 requires states parties to establish independent and fully resourced anti-corruption commissions or agencies (and with specialised staff that receive regular training) to implement, coordinate and oversee their anti-corruption policies elaborated in Article 5 of the convention and discussed below. Under Article 6(3), states are also expected to share information with the Secretary-General of the United Nations about bodies or agencies that 'may assist other States Parties in developing and implementing specific measures for the prevention of corruption.

Among others, such commissions or agencies are expected to carry out activities that would increase and disseminate knowledge about corruption prevention. This is a crucial function that would improve civil society's participation in the fight against corruption. However, such functions require in law and practice the existence of competent, independent, transparent, and accountable anti-corruption institutions that can act boldly, fairly and freely of political or economic influence, something which, as noted in Chapter 3, is lacking in many African states.

The 'anti-corruption policies and practices' under Article 5 which states are expected to promote and advance include: the participation of society, the rule of law, proper management of public affairs and public property, integrity, transparency and accountability. In particular, states are to periodically evaluate relevant legal instruments and administrative measures to ensure that they are adequate to prevent and fight corruption. Finally, states are to collaborate with each other and with relevant international and regional organisations (for example, through international programmes and projects) in their efforts to fight corruption. However, like many of the preventive provisions discussed here, both Articles 5 and 6 are prefaced with the very limiting phrase 'in accordance with the fundamental principles of its legal system'.

By Article 13, states are to promote public awareness and education in the fight against corruption, promoting participation of the civil society (such as NGOs and community-based organisations), but 'within its means and in accordance with fundamental principles of domestic law'. This article provides general examples of how a state could strengthen the participation of civil society, including promoting the contribution of the

[19] This is also in contrast with the Inter-American Convention, whose preventive provisions cover both private and public-sector corruption and which requires the establishment of an enforcement mechanism for preventive measures.

public to decision-making and ensuring that the public has effective access to information.

The UNCAC also includes in its Article 8 principles relating to a code of conduct for public officials. Of particular importance is that each state must endeavour to apply a code or standard of conduct to its public officials and, where appropriate, require public officials to declare to appropriate authorities their outside activities, employment, and investments. States should also 'consider' establishing systems to facilitate reporting by public officials of acts of corruption and to take measures against public officials who violate codes or standards of conduct.

The UNCAC in Article 7 also requires states to establish a strong public service through an open, fair, merit-based and transparent system of recruitment, promotion and retirement, and the establishment of a transparent public procurement system. In addition, states should prevent conflicts of interest. They are also to ensure that individuals who are exposed to corruption should be rotated to other positions, and promote adequate remuneration and equitable pay scales, and training. In addition, each state is 'to consider' whether to prescribe criteria for candidatures up for election and whether to enhance transparency in the funding of candidatures and of political parties. However, while the inclusion of this provision reflects the value attached to a transparent and accountable political party system, the use of the rather unhelpful phrase 'to consider' indicates the discretionary nature of this formal commitment. As such, it leaves room for states to determine whether, and to what extent, transparency and accountability in political funding is necessary. The provision on campaign finance was 'a substantial compromise',[20] due mainly to pressure from the United States, whose delegates wanted watered-down and voluntary clauses on the issue. This was unexpected, especially given the US position on similar issues during negotiations on the OECD Foreign Bribery Convention and the country's strong domestic laws on transparency in political funding.[21]

The UNCAC also covers important criminal justice issues, such as the very challenging issue of corruption in law enforcement agencies and processes; and in the judiciary (such as strengthening judicial independence, integrity and reducing opportunities for corruption among judges) in Article 11; and with money laundering in Article 14, discussed in Chapter 2. It requires states to 'take measures to strengthen integrity and

[20] Philippa Webb, 'The United Nations Convention against Corruption: Global Achievement or Missed Opportunity?' (2005) 8 *Journal of International Economic Law* 191–229. See generally, Indira Carr, 'Fighting Corruption through Regional and International Conventions: A Satisfactory Solution?' (2007) 15 *European Journal of Crime, Criminal Law and Criminal Justice* 121; Alejandro Posadas, 'Combating Corruption under International Law' (2000) 10 *Duke Journal of Comparative & International Law* 345.

[21] ibid, 212.

to prevent opportunities for corruption among members of the judiciary'. However, all of these articles are also prefaced with the phrase 'in accordance with the fundamental principles of its legal system'.

Public procurement and management of public finances are covered in Article 9, which includes that each state is required to establish transparent and fair government procurement systems based on competition and objective criteria for decision-making, in particular, the advance publication of participation in procurements. It also requires each state to take appropriate measures to promote accountability and transparency in the management of public finances, such as timely reporting of revenue and expenditures. These measures are taken further in Article 10, which requires states to implement freedom of information laws, and to proactively and periodically publish information in relation to public administration generally.

Yet, as noted, the convention's focus is not just on the public sector, as it also establishes important principles of compliance, transparency, and accountability in the private sector, as in Article 12. This article requires states parties to take measures to prevent corruption and to enhance accounting and auditing standards in the private sector, and it sets forth a list of possible measures to achieve these objectives, including prescribing civil, administrative, and criminal penalties for failure to comply with these standards. Of particular note, states are required to take measures to prohibit acts such as conflict of interest and 'off-the-books' recordkeeping and the recording of non-existent expenditures. In addition, states parties are required to disallow the tax deductibility of bribes, a welcome development given the widespread practice in the past of developed countries allowing tax deductions for foreign bribery.

In general, not only are most of the UNCAC preventive provisions voluntary, some are downright permissive, suggesting that states enjoy a wide margin in picking and choosing which of the provisions to implement in their domestic laws. Of the 10 articles on preventive measures, the only provision with some sort of binding language is Article 12(4), relating to prohibition of tax deductibility of expenses that constitute bribes. It is regrettable that the otherwise progressive preventive provisions of the UNCAC are severally diluted with broad and non-legally binding language such as 'in accordance with the fundamental principles of its domestic law'. This wording presumably aims to accommodate the 'constitutional requirements' of each state, but it can inadvertently provide an 'escape route' that potentially can undermine the authority or influence of the convention, making it a less effective tool for the fight against corruption domestically, with uneven implementation among states. It should be noted that the AU Convention, the ECOWAS Protocol, and the SADC Protocol suffer from similar weaknesses.

## Criminalisation and Law Enforcement

In addition to preventive measures, the four instruments, in varying degrees, devote provisions on criminalisation of specific corrupt acts and omissions and on law enforcement matters. All of them address both the supply and demand sides of corruption, although, again, with some significant differences in emphasis and details. For example, they contain nearly identical provisions on corrupt practices such as bribery, but as will be shown below, they differ in some important details on the definitions of particular corrupt acts. Overall, the focus of the fight against corruption has been on criminalisation and prosecution of suspects, but states across Africa have generally fallen short of consistently bringing high-ranking corrupt officials to justice.

The AU Convention, the ECOWAS Protocol, and the SADC Protocol criminalise far fewer corrupt practices than the UNCAC. In particular, the AU Convention does not criminalise embezzlement, and the SADC Protocol only focuses on the supply and demand sides of bribery; so, for example, it does not criminalise other important corrupt practices like illicit enrichment. While the ECOWAS Protocol does criminalise illicit enrichment, it does not specifically elaborate on embezzlement, yet in Article 6 it criminalises the 'creating or using [of] an invoice or any other accounting document or record containing false or incomplete information'.

In addition, the AU Convention also criminalises the diversion or improper use of state property by a public official, though this provision is terse and not mandatory.[22] The UNCAC's provisions on diversion, on the other hand, are mandatory, a rare departure from its mostly discretionary provisions on preventive measures. Further, all four instruments criminalise the use and concealment of proceeds of corruption independently of and in addition to the underlying offences, and both the UNCAC and AU Convention in particular adopt similar wording to criminalise the

[22] Among the issues that proved the most difficult and controversial was whether Art 4(1)(d), concerning diversion of funds, should be removed, given that this was not yet a corrupt act in some jurisdictions. The argument was that there exist significant differences between the French and English legal systems in terms of the characterisation of certain offences. For example, Senegal objected to the inclusion of the offence of embezzlement, on the ground that there would be problems of interpretation from the perspective of the French Penal Code. After some debate, it was agreed that the article should be reformulated to take into account the different meaning in Francophone and Anglophone countries. On the same basis, Art 8, concerning illicit enrichment, was redrafted to achieve a consensus that now gives greater flexibility to states. If their domestic laws have established illicit enrichment as an offence, they may consider it as an act of corruption or 'a related offence' for the purposes of the convention. The Republic of Benin even proposed that the title of the convention be changed to the Convention on Preventing and Combating Corruption and Other Related Offences. Although the initial reasoning was to adopt a title that embraced both the prevention and combating dimensions of the corruption problem, this proposal was never enacted. The proposal by Benin is actually quite dissimilar to the convention's final title, although it was accommodated under the convention's key substantive provisions.

'conversion, transfer or disposal of property, knowing that such property is the proceeds of corruption or related offences for the purpose of concealing or disguising the illicit origin'. However, unlike the UNCAC and the ECOWAS Protocol, the AU Convention and the SADC Protocol do not criminalise participation and related inchoate offences in their provisions on money laundering. Furthermore, the UNCAC is the only instrument that addresses in detail corruption relating to the judiciary and prosecutorial services. Since it is the most comprehensive of the instruments discussed here, this next section also emphasises this treaty.

The UNCAC, apart from encouraging member states to criminalise corruption such as bribery, embezzlement, trading in influence, abuse of functions, and illicit enrichment,[23] also elaborates provisions on related offences, such as concealment of proceeds of corruption and obstruction of justice. Three types of provisions dealing with criminalisation can be identified in chapter 3 of the UNCAC. First are the substantive provisions requiring each state to criminalise certain corrupt practices. Second are what are called the 'permissive provisions' under which state parties are merely 'to consider' criminalising certain corrupt practices. Third are those provisions concerning participation, attempt, and procedural issues, such as jurisdiction and statutes of limitations. Unfortunately, like the preventive measures in chapter 2 of the UNCAC, most of the provisions on criminalisation and law enforcement are deemed optional. It has been suggested that 'the use of permissive and non-mandatory language in the various provisions is apparently the result of the negotiation process and suggests a realistic compromise'.[24] Nonetheless, a few of the provisions of the UNCAC are mandatory. One example of its mandatory provisions is Article 15 (on what is probably the best-known form of corruption – bribery) criminalising bribery of national public officials. It provides:

> Each State Party shall adopt such legislative and other measures as may be necessary to establish as criminal offences, when committed intentionally:
>
> *(a)* The promise, offering or giving, to a public official, directly or indirectly, of an undue advantage, for the official himself or herself or another person or entity, in order that the official act or refrain from acting in the exercise of his or her official duties;
> *(b)* The solicitation or acceptance by a public official, directly or indirectly, of an undue advantage, for the official himself or herself or another person or entity,

[23] The provision of 'illicit enrichment', modelled after similar provisions in the Inter-American Convention and the AU Corruption Convention, initially drew objections from the Russian Federation and the member states of the European Union, which expressed a strong wish to have it deleted from the final text.

[24] Thomas T Snider and Won Kidanett, 'Combating Corruption through International Law in Africa' (n 7) 691–704.

> in order that the official act or refrain from acting in the exercise of his or her official duties.[25]

This provision contains both the 'active' and 'passive' elements of bribery (ie, the promising, offering or giving; and the soliciting or accepting). Relatedly, Article 16 requires states to prohibit bribery of foreign public officials and officials of public international organisations (by domestic public officials), though partially mandatory as it merely requires states in sub-section 2 to 'consider' the adoption of legislation to criminalise the 'solicitation or acceptance' of bribes. The major difference between sub-sections 1 and 2 is that the former deals with the so-called 'supply or active side' of bribery, while the latter is on the 'demand or passive side'. But all the elements of 'intention', 'promise', 'offering' or 'giving'; and 'soliciting' or 'accepting' are also required for Article 16 prohibition. However, in contrast to Article 15, Article 16 provides that the bribery must be for 'the purpose of obtaining or retaining business or other undue advantage in relation to the conduct of international business'.

In addition, as Articles 15 and 16 indicate, bribery can take many shapes and forms, and it is fairly easy to recognise, for example, illegal payments to government officials. Essentially both the giver and the recipient of bribes can be prosecuted under these provisions. Further, although the UNCAC does not define 'undue advantage', it is presumably broader than purely pecuniary benefits, gifts, or favours, because all the offences listed in the UNCAC incorporate an 'intent requirement'. This is clear for example, in the quote from Article 15 on the anti-bribery provision.

Although the UNCAC uses the phrase 'when intentionally committed' consistently in all the provisions that define crimes, it does not define the exact status of *mens rea* required. Nonetheless, while it can be presumed that knowledge and purpose are anticipated, given the complexities of corrupt transactions, the lack of clear definition of these requirements might be problematic in practice. It is noteworthy to mention that the AU Convention, the ECOWAS Protocol, and the SADC Protocol do not include any specific reference to a criminal intent requirement. This may have serious implications as to the interpretations of the obligations of any state under these instruments, and can potentially produce inconsistency in the application of their criminalisation provisions, as states may need to decide this within their domestic jurisdictions. It is therefore suggested that states that are domesticating the AU Convention, the ECOWAS

[25] But Art 16(2) of the UNCAC, which concerns bribery by foreign public officials, is an example of the many voluntary and permissive provisions contained in the convention. It provides, 'Each State Party *shall consider* adopting such legislative and other measures as may be necessary to establish as a criminal offence, when committed intentionally, the solicitation or acceptance by a foreign public official or an official of a public international organisation, directly or indirectly, of an undue advantage, for the official himself or herself or another person or entity, in order that the official act or refrain from acting in the exercise of his or her official duties.'

Protocol and the SADC Protocol through national legislation should adopt the best practices on *mens rea*, including from the UN Convention and the Foreign Corrupt Practices Act (and its case law).

As noted, the UNCAC covers embezzlement, misappropriation, and other diversion of property by a public official. Article 17 requires states to criminalise, when committed intentionally, the embezzlement by a public official of any property entrusted to him or her, and by virtue of his or her position. There are also provisions, albeit permissive in wording, covering trading in influence. This wording characterises the convention's conceptualisation of corruption. For example, Article 18 suggests that states 'should consider' whether to criminalise the provision of an undue advantage to or acceptance by a third party to induce that person to use his or her real or supposed influence to obtain, from a public authority of the state party, an undue advantage for the original instigator of the act. In Article 19, states are also 'to consider' criminalising a public official's abuse of his or her function in order to obtain an undue advantage personally or for another person.

Furthermore, the UNCAC addresses corruption in the private sector from a criminalisation perspective. Its Article 21 requires states to consider criminalising the measures described therein – in particular, the receipt of bribes when committed in the course of economic or business activities, so that a person either acts or refrains from acting in breach of his or her duties. Article 22 focuses on embezzlement of property in the private sector, and it requires states 'to consider' criminalising embezzlement of property by anyone who works in the private sector who has taken property during the course of economic or commercial activities entrusted to him or her by virtue of the job position. The criminalisation obligation established by the convention in Article 25 relates to obstruction of justice in criminal proceedings on corrupt practices. The offence under Article 25 has two principal elements. The first is the 'intentional use of force, threats, or intimidation, or the promise, offering, or giving of an undue advantage, in order to induce false testimony or to interfere in the giving of testimony or the production of evidence'. The second is 'the intentional use of force, threats, or intimidation to interfere with the exercise of official duties by a justice or law enforcement official'.

The UNCAC's Article 26 takes on the vexing issue of the liability of legal persons, requiring states to fill what historically had been a loophole in the ability of many states to prevent and combat corruption: their inability to hold not only natural persons but also legal ones liable for illegal conduct. This provision requires the creation of criminal, civil, or administrative liability, and accompanying sanctions, for corporations that participate in the offences established in the convention. Such corporate liability is without prejudice to the criminal liability of the natural persons who committed the offences. Along the lines of the UNCAC, the AU

Convention, the ECOWAS Protocol, and the SADC Protocol allow for states, if they agree, to establish and criminalise other acts of corruption not described in their respective instruments.

While the bribery provisions of the AU Convention on public officials do not require proof of a breach of duty, those relating to the private sector do. It should be noted here that the AU Convention defines the private sector as exclusively private, and thus outside government control. The AU Convention also criminalises 'the offering or granting, directly or indirectly, to a public official or any other person, of any goods of monetary value, or other benefits, such as a gift, favour, promise or advantage' (Article 4(1)(b)). The UN Convention, however, provides in sub-section 21(b), 'The solicitation or acceptance, directly or indirectly, of an undue advantage [includes] any person who directs or works, in any capacity, for a private sector entity', whereas the AU Convention provision omits those who authorise the 'offers, promises or payments'. The significance of 'authorisation responsibility' relates to the chain of command in multilateral enterprises, which often operate through agents and subsidiaries. Unlike the other three, however, the AU Convention does not prohibit corruption by foreign officials or officials of international organisations. Yet, as one scholar has pointed out, '[T]the offering of bribes to foreign public officials, including officials of public international organisations, is at the root of many corrupt administrations in Africa.'[26]

In addition, in contrast to the ECOWAS Protocol, both the AU Convention and the SADC Protocol criminalise breach of duty for the purpose of obtaining illicit benefit. For example, the AU convention provides that 'any act or omission in the discharge of his or her duties by a public official or any other person for the purpose of illicitly obtaining benefits for himself or herself or for a third party' (Article 4(1)(c)). This prohibition presumably applies in addition to or irrespective of the underlying corrupt act of solicitation or acceptance. However, the provision is problematic for several reasons. First, its wording embraces a single preparatory act done with the requisite 'purpose' of profiting illicitly at some future time, even though the course of conduct is neither pursued, nor in any sense consummated. Second, because breach of duty is an essential component of the main solicitation or acceptance provision without which no responsibility could attach, it may raise some substantive due process and double jeopardy issues.

The solicitation-or-acceptance and the breach-of-duty provisions essentially punish the same conduct. A distinction may be made, however, that the solicitation provision could apply where there is no conduct or omission but a promise to breach a lawful duty. This definition, which includes

[26] Nsongurua J Udombana, 'Fighting Corruption Seriously? Africa's Anti-corruption Convention' (2003) 7(2) *Singapore Journal of International and Comparative Law* 464.

promises regardless of whether the act or omission materialises, is indeed a liberal interpretation of the 'in exchange for' language contained in the AU convention's subparagraph 4(1)(b). The UNCAC includes a better formulation, which addresses some of the concerns noted with the AU convention. It provides that 'the solicitation or acceptance by a public official, directly or indirectly, of an undue advantage, for the official himself or herself for another person or entity, in order that the official act or refrain in the exercise of his or her official duties'. The discharge-of-duty provision states: 'The abuse of functions or position, that is, the performance of or failure to perform an act, in violation of laws, by a public official in the discharge of his or her functions, for the purpose of obtaining an undue advantage for himself or herself or another person or entity.'

Of the four instruments discussed here, only the UNCAC explicitly contains the controversial provision protecting sovereignty of states parties. In this vein, Article 4 provides that states respect each other's sovereign equality and territorial integrity. It also states that the UNCAC 'does not authorize a state party to undertake in another state's territory the exercise of jurisdiction and performance of functions reserved for the authorities of that other State by its domestic law'. However, the *travaux préparatoires* indicate that the principle of non-intervention is to be understood in the light of Article 2 of the Charter of the United Nations, which could potentially further undermine the effectiveness of the UNCAC.

Probably the most controversial provision of the UNCAC is Article 20, which, despite strong opposition from some Western nations, including the United States, was approved with powerful backing and, in fact, at the instigation of many developing nations. Article 20 covers illicit enrichment and asks states 'to consider' establishing the offense of 'illicit enrichment', which is defined as a significant increase in the assets of a public official who cannot reasonably or justifiably explain this in relation to his or her lawful income. The support for the inclusion of this article in the UNCAC by developing nations, including African countries, is perhaps not surprising, as both the AU Convention and the ECOWAS Protocol contain similar provisions. The SADC Protocol, however, does not.

One problem associated with these provisions is that the offence of illicit enrichment could require a defendant to bear the burden of establishing the legitimate source of the income in question, thus raising serious human rights questions such as the internationally guaranteed right of presumption of innocence. However, the inclusion of this corrupt practice in several anti-corruption treaties, despite the human rights concerns that have been raised, suggests that it has become an accepted concept in the global fight against corruption. One reason may be put down to the difficulty in detecting corruption and the corresponding challenges in obtaining sufficient evidence to meet the universal standard of proof beyond reasonable doubt for a criminal prosecution. The use of the offence of illicit enrichment may also be one reason Hong Kong has been hailed as one of the few success stories in the fight against corruption.[27]

Nonetheless, while holding officials criminally liable for unexplained increases in their wealth has considerable appeal, particularly in systems where the courts are weak, as is the case in many parts of Africa, the human rights concerns against it are understandable. It has been stated that the whole concept of illicit enrichment is 'fundamentally flawed as a matter of recognised principles of criminal justice'.[28] Given that the implementation of the provisions on illicit enrichment offence in anti-corruption conventions is subject to states' fundamental laws, such as constitutions, it is doubtful whether the provisions on illicit enrichment will ever pass the test of rationality, reasonableness, and proportionality. Related to this issue, it should be pointed out here that except for the AU Convention, the other instruments pay scant attention to the issue of fair trial. Nevertheless, due consideration to guarantees of fair trial is absolutely necessary to prevent the possibility of anti-corruption laws and treaties being abused and used as a political tool to target opposition, civil society, and human rights activists.

As for the AU convention, the offence of illicit enrichment may offend its Article 14 provision, which guarantees to anyone accused of acts of corruption 'a fair trial in criminal proceedings in accordance with the minimum guarantees contained in the African Charter on Human and Peoples' Rights and any other relevant international human rights instrument recognised by the concerned States Parties'. Included among these minimum guarantees is the unqualified 'right to be presumed innocent until proved guilty by a competent court or tribunal', as found in Article 7(1) of the African Charter. Restrictions on the presumption of innocence are usually justified on the grounds that the rights granted in human rights instruments are qualified, subject to a rational limitation, and require some balancing between two competing sets of public interests. These are the wider interests of society (such as national security, public order, and public safety) and the rights of particular individuals. Any restrictions on guaranteed individual rights must be a proportional response to the social problem being addressed: restricting no more than is reasonably necessary to safeguard the relevant public interest. The establishment of the offence of illicit enrichment 'might mean prescribing

[27] See s 10(1) of the Prevention of Bribery Ordinance in Hong Kong, which provides that: 'Any person who, being or having been a Crown servant (a) maintains a standard of living above that which is commensurate with his present or past official emoluments or (b) is in control of pecuniary resources or property disproportionate to his present or pass official emoluments shall, unless he gives a satisfactory explanation to the court as to how he was able to maintain such a standard of living or how such pecuniary resources or property came under his control, be guilty of an offence.'

[28] Snider and Kidane, 'Combating Corruption through International Law in Africa' (n 7) 691.

a remedy that is worse than the ailment'. One would, however, suggest that there is at least a need to incorporate some fair trial safeguards and to ensure strict adherence to those safeguards in the application of the crime of illicit enrichment. While the accused should not be allowed to use human rights as a 'trump card' to frustrate prosecution or defeat the course of justice, the need for an effective fight against corruption (and money laundering) must constantly be balanced against legitimate concerns to safeguard human rights of the accused.

Furthermore, all four instruments address as criminal the attempt to participate, or actual participation, in any capacity in any corrupt practices established in their respective instruments, although the UNCAC, once again, is the most detailed. Article 27 of the UNCAC, for example, allows that states may decide to criminalise the attempt to commit or the preparation to commit corrupt practices. In addition, Article 28 recognises that 'knowledge, intent, or purpose', when a requisite element of a crime, may be inferred from objective factual circumstances. The UNCAC criminalises this attempt or preparation to commit a corrupt act as underlying offences, as does the AU Convention. For example, the AU Convention covers 'participation as a principal, co-principal, agent, instigator, accomplice or accessory after the fact, or any other manner in the commission or attempted commission of, in any collaboration or *conspiracy* to commit, any of the acts referred to in this article' [emphasis added]. The ECOWAS Protocol and the SADC Protocol do not include the offence of conspiracy.

In addition, of crucial importance to preventing and combating the prevailing culture of impunity of perpetrators of large-scale corruption is UNCAC's Article 29, which requires each state (where appropriate) to establish a statute of limitations in which to commence proceedings for any of the corrupt practices established under the convention. Equally important is that Article 23 provides for a longer statute of limitations (or its suspension) where the accused has evaded the administration of justice. In Article 29 the UNCAC accounts for prosecutions, adjudications, and sanctions, and identifies a series of important considerations for states in pursuing prosecutions concerning corrupt practices the UNCAC establishes. Provisions range from ensuring that criminal law sanctions are sufficiently serious to minimising defendants' risk of flight. These provisions are missing from the other three instruments.

Moreover, sub-paragraph 30(2) of the UNCAC requires each state to establish or maintain, subject to the usual limitation of state's 'legal system and constitutional principles', balance between any immunities it affords to its public officials and the ability to prosecute offences established in the convention. Sub-paragraph 30(9) makes clear, however, that each state has the prerogative to determine (again, under its domestic law) the extent or scope of immunities it wishes to accord to its officials.

Thus, it states that 'nothing in the Convention shall affect the principle that the description of the offenses established in accordance with the Convention and of the applicable legal defences or other legal principles controlling the lawfulness of conduct is reserved to the domestic law of a State Party'. In a rather more positive formulation, the AU Convention provides that any immunity granted to public officials shall not be an obstacle to the investigation of allegations against and the prosecution of such officials but neither the SADC Protocol nor the ECOWAS Protocol contain similar provisions. Nonetheless, the UNCAC and AU Convention provisions fall short of complete elimination of immunity for corruption, and it is unclear how the AU convention's formulation will be operationalised in practice.

In addition, all four instruments cover in varying detail the freezing, seizing, and confiscation of proceeds of corrupt practices. For example, Article 31 in the UNCAC requires a state to adopt measures to the greatest extent possible, within its legal system which enable confiscation of proceeds, property of equivalent value, or property used in or detained for use in offences established in the convention. Each state party's courts or other competent authorities are to be empowered to order that bank and other records be made available to enable confiscation proceedings to go forward, and bank secrecy may not be invoked in this context.

Both the UNCAC and the ECOWAS Protocol go a step further than the other two instruments by elaborating provisions for protection of victims of corruption. For example, the UNCAC, in large part, requires states to take appropriate measures within their means to protect witnesses, experts and victims (but to the extent that they are witnesses), and their relatives and other persons close to them, from retaliation or intimidation when they testify in corruption cases. Among the measures a state may implement are witness protection programmes and evidence-taking techniques that ensure the safety of witnesses, for example, videotaping from a remote location. Article 32 of the UNCAC encourages states 'to consider' assisting one another in providing witness protection, and requires a state, subject to its domestic laws and in a manner not prejudicial to the rights of the defence, to enable victims' views to be considered during criminal proceedings. However, victims' views will only count if they are witnesses (Article 32(4)). Similarly, many provisions of Article 32 are clearly permissive or voluntary (non-mandatory) as they allow for the exercise of discretion in particular cases. Relatedly, Article 33 of the UNCAC requires states to incorporate into their domestic law protections against unjustified treatment for persons reporting in good faith and on reasonable grounds any facts relating to the convention offences.

Clearly, it is important to recognise that corruption, especially large-scale corruption, is not a victimless crime (contrary to some widely held but erroneous views). In this regard, Article 34 of the UNCAC would seem to incorporate this important issue by requiring states to take measures (but again, subject to the 'fundamental principles' of their domestic laws), to address the consequences of corruption.

Similarly, Article 9 of the ECOWAS Protocol also provides for assistance and protection of victims and requires states to take appropriate measures 'within [their] means' to provide assistance and protection to victims of corruption, in particular in cases of threat, retaliation, or intimidation. Most significantly, the protocol requires states to establish procedures to provide access to compensation and restitution for victims of corruption. It also requires states to permit the views and concerns of victims to be presented and considered at stages of criminal proceedings, but this must not be done in a way that prejudices the rights of the defence. The UNCAC contains similar provisions in its Article 35, which provides for compensation for damage for victims of corruption, but as with its Article 34 (discussed above), what could have been a remarkable step in the fight against global corruption, especially large-scale corruption that is prevalent across many African states, has been turned into a limited, vague and confusing (and thus controversial) idea, and is arguably one of the weakest provisions of the convention. To put things in their proper context, the provisions of Article 35 are such that:

> Each State Party shall take such measures as may be necessary, in accordance with principles of its domestic law, to ensure that entities or persons who have suffered damage as a result of an act of corruption have the right to initiate legal proceedings against those responsible for that damage in order to obtain compensation.

Literally, Article 35 would seem to establish the principle that states parties should put in place mechanisms that would permit persons or entities suffering damage because of corruption to initiate legal proceedings against those responsible for such damage in order to obtain compensation. While it would seem, on the one hand, that Article 35 (much like Article 9 of the ECOWAS Protocol) can be interpreted as providing a private cause of action[29] (and this author strongly supports that interpretation), there are others who reject it. Of particular note is the US government, which has rejected any such notion of the private right of action in Article 35, or indeed in any provision of the UNCAC. The position of the US was made clear during presentation of the UNCAC to the Congress for endorsement:

> According to the *travaux préparatoires*, Article 35 was intended to address only legal proceedings against those who commit acts of corruption, rather than those who may be associated with others who commit acts of corruption. The

[29] Two provisions of the private remedies in Art 35 are that it provides a private cause of action to seek compensation for damages as a result of corrupt practices, and it provides the right to invalidate contracts or other relations vitiated by corruption. Snider and Kidanett, 'Combating Corruption through International Law in Africa' (n 7) 704.

> article intentionally provides the States Parties significant flexibility in its implementation. The article does not restrict the right of a State Party to decide the precise circumstances under which it will make its courts available, nor does it require or endorse a particular choice made by a State Party in determining how it will meet its obligations under this article. . .. *None of the provisions of the Convention creates a private right of action* [emphasis added].[30]

It has also been stated that this provision stemmed from concerns expressed by US businesses that a private sector provision in the convention 'could create a private right of action that would open the door to lawsuits in foreign courts over contract and procurement irregularities'.[31] This omission has, however, been criticised as a parity of anti-corruption laws to both the private and the public sectors, and that both would have benefited 'national economies and international development by eliminating loopholes and recognising the increasing convergence between the sectors in many areas of economic life'.[32] Furthermore, although it would seem that the drafters of Article [33] (and Article 9 of the ECOWAS Protocol) intended the provision to mirror similar standards already established by the Council of Europe Civil Law Convention against Corruption, it does not go as far as the Civil Law Convention, not least because of its permissive and voluntary nature.[34] National legislation and practices across Africa also fall short of the requirements of Article 35.

In general, the provisions on the protection of witnesses, experts, and victims reflect a concern that those accused of corruption, especially the powerful and the well-connected in developing countries such as those across Africa, should not be allowed to undermine judicial processes. However, as noted, the provisions on protection of victims of corruption contained in both the UNCAC and the ECOWAS Protocol fail woefully to include any specifically mandated implementation measures, and do not

[30] 'US Senate Treaty Document 109-6', 109th Congress (2005) http://www.gpo.gov/fdsys/pkg/CDOC-109tdoc6/html/CDOC-109tdoc6.htm.

[31] Concerns were also raised that including a private right of action in the convention would place 'undue and unwanted restraints on trade and the ability of private sector entities to pursue their activities for the benefit of national economies and international development'. Webb, 'The United Nations Convention against Corruption' (n 20).

[32] ibid, 205.

[33] See the *travaux préparatoires* to the UNCAC, which provide that 'this article is intended to establish the principle that States Parties should ensure that they have mechanisms permitting persons or entities suffering damage to initiate legal proceedings, in appropriate circumstances, against those who commit acts of corruption (for example, where the acts have a legitimate relationship to the State Party where the proceedings are to be brought). While article 35 does not restrict the right of each State Party to determine the circumstances under which it will make its courts available in such cases, it is also not intended to require or endorse the particular choice made by a State Party in doing so.'

[34] See 'Report of the Ad Hoc Committee for the Negotiation of a Convention against Corruption on the Work of Its First to Seventh Sessions, Addendum: Interpretative Notes for the Official Records (Travaux Preparatoires) of the Negotiation of the United Nations Convention against Corruption' UN Doc A/58/422/Add 1 (2003), 635.

go far enough in establishing concrete state accountability. There are no serious consequences to a state's support of or encouragement of large-scale corruption, its failure to establish appropriate legal and judicial mechanisms to effectively investigate and prosecute it, or, crucially, its avoidance of addressing the consequences to the victims – whether individuals or communities – in terms of providing effective remedies. Articles 34 and 35 of the UNCAC, and indeed all the instruments,[35] would need to be strengthened to address these gaps and to grant right of action against states themselves (through a comprehensive and multidisciplinary approach that includes the application of human rights law), if the benefits that they ought or purport to give victims are not to remain more academic than real. The repeated articulated vision by the international community of a comprehensive and multidisciplinary approach to corruption can be achieved through the application of human rights law, and is especially needed to address the magnitude, gravity, and debilitating consequences of corruption for human rights.

Apart from the above issues, the four instruments also address the important issue of cooperation with law enforcement authorities, but the UNCAC contains significant variations. For example, its Article 37 requires each state to take appropriate measures to assist law enforcement investigations into the corrupt practices under the convention. In so doing, states are broadly 'to consider' reducing criminal penalties or granting immunity from prosecution for those who cooperate substantially. This provision also envisages that states will 'consider' working with one another to apply these inducements to persons located in one state who can assist an investigation into corrupt practices in another. However, given its broad and discretionary nature, it is unclear whether this provision would have any serious effect on serial perpetrators of large-scale corruption in Africa. It may, in fact, be counter-productive, as these would-be perpetrators may still view corruption as a risk worth taking, considering that they may be able to evade justice, escape punishment, and keep any stolen wealth.

The importance of cooperation between different elements of a state's domestic system is highlighted in another provision of the UNCAC: Article 38. Under this provision, a state must encourage cooperation between its public authorities and its prosecuting authorities that investi-

[35] It should be pointed out that neither the AU Convention nor the SADC Protocol expressly provide for a private right of action. However, the AU Convention provides that, 'State Parties undertake to establish mechanisms to encourage participation by the private sector in the fight against unfair competition, respect for the tender procedures and property rights'. This provision will mean little unless states grant private legal standing to anyone who suffers harms as a result of corruption, especially large-scale corruption, to obtain effective remedies. The omission by the AU Convention is especially disappointing given the clear references to human rights and good governance in particular the African Charter on Human and Peoples' Rights.

gate and prosecute criminal offences. Similarly, a state is to take measures to encourage cooperation between national investigating and prosecuting authorities and private sector entities on matters relating to the commission of corrupt practices under the convention, and to 'consider' encouraging its nationals and others who habitually reside in its territory to report to those authorities regarding the commission of such offences.

All four instruments address the longstanding and problematic issue of bank secrecy, but as with other issues, the UNCAC is the most comprehensive in this area. The importance of fighting bank secrecy is highlighted by the fact that most of the stolen wealth from Africa is located in developed countries, as detailed in Chapter 2. The UNCAC's Article 40 provision on bank secrecy – in the context of freezing and confiscation – supplements the treatment of bank secrecy in Article 31 by more broadly requiring each state to ensure that its domestic laws contain appropriate mechanisms to avoid obstacles in domestic criminal prosecutions that may arise out of bank secrecy laws. Previously, efforts to trace and recover the proceeds of corruption were thwarted by the wall of silence that private banks erected to shield their clients from investigations. However, a banker's instinct to value a client's confidentiality over society's interest and the reflexive respect for secrecy has proven to be valuable tools for money laundering.

In addition, the UNCAC, the AU Convention, the ECOWAS Protocol, and the SADC Protocol all contain generally important jurisdictional principles, which govern their respective mandatory criminalisation provisions. But under the AU Convention, anyone who commits the crime of corruption anywhere can be brought within the jurisdiction of each state if, in the view of the state concerned, the crime affects its vital interests, or if the deleterious, harmful consequences or effects of such offences impact the state. However, again, the UNCAC contains the most comprehensive provisions on jurisdictional issues. In Article 42, each state is required to establish jurisdiction in respect of any corrupt practices when committed in its territory, on board a vessel flying its flag, or an aircraft registered under its laws. Each state may, in its discretion, establish jurisdiction over the five corrupt practices[36] when committed by one of its nationals or residents against another of its nationals or residents or against the state itself. Under the UNCAC, only permissive and voluntary jurisdiction is contemplated in the offence of money laundering when it is committed outside a state territory with a view to establishing certain offences within its territory. The provision also requires a state to establish its jurisdiction when it refuses to extradite an offender for corrupt practices under the UNCAC because the person is one of its nationals.

[36] These are: bribery, embezzlement, abuse of office, trading in influence, and illicit enrichment.

**International Cooperation**

In addition to establishing preventive measures and criminalisation provisions, all the four instruments contain varying and far-reaching provisions on international assistance and cooperation. Being a universal problem, no state can fight corruption effectively or successfully on its own, hence the need for collaboration and cooperation, either bilaterally or multilaterally. The critical areas are sharing information, studies, research, and expertise, and offering assistance in prevention, detection, investigation and punishment. Of particular note, the ECOWAS Protocol requires states to periodically review their legislation to ascertain its effectiveness, including in the area of jurisdiction related to the prosecution of the bribery of foreign public officials. If the state finds any weaknesses, it is to take appropriate remedial measures. However, states are encouraged to consult and agree upon which ECOWAS jurisdiction is able to prosecute such practices. This provision would provide states parties some flexibility in their fight against corruption in the sub-regions. This is significant, especially given the fact that the AU Convention does not include the prosecution of foreign bribery.

Article 15 of the AU convention covers extradition issues. Discussions during drafting of Article 15 focused on how to clarify the proposed draft to ensure that extradition proceedings are fair and accountable, and to exclude any possibility of politically motivated extradition or refusal to extradite on flimsy grounds. Sub-paragraph 6 that finally emerged requires states that refuse extradition on the grounds of having jurisdiction over the offence covered under the convention to submit, without delay, the case to its competent authorities for prosecution. Another point of debate was sub-paragraph 5 which requires states to extradite any person charged with or convicted of corruption and 'related offences'. It was suggested that this clause should be deleted, given that in some jurisdictions persons charged but not convicted might not be legally extradited. States argued, though, that the clause would not pose any problem within such jurisdictions, and thus the clause should be left intact. The clause was retained without any major amendment.

Nonetheless, since most of the wealth stolen from Africa is located in Western economies, only the provisions of the UNCAC are of any practical value for combating money laundering in Africa. Article 43 of the UNCAC covers international cooperation, providing an overview of the requirements in the other articles, and suggests that states work together in criminal matters and but only 'to consider' cooperating with each other in civil and administrative matters relating to corruption. Article 43 also clarifies how the issue of dual criminality, which arises in the context of extradition and mutual legal assistance, is to be analysed and resolved.

Furthermore, Article 44 addresses the issue of extradition and elaborates a plan for extradition of persons for any convention offences, as long as the corrupt practice is criminal under the laws of both the requesting and the requested states. Additionally, states may make extradition conditional on a bilateral extradition treaty, and the prevailing practice today is for states to increasingly rely on these treaties. For states that do not make extradition conditional, however, the convention can afford that international legal basis *inter se*. Thus, a state that does not extradite its nationals is required, if requested by another state seeking extradition for any of the convention offences, to submit the case for domestic prosecution and to conduct the proceedings in the same manner as it would for purely domestic offences of similar gravity.

A state may satisfy this requirement by, for example, temporarily surrendering its national for trial in the state seeking extradition, on the condition that he or she will be returned to serve any resulting sentence. However, Article 44 also contains voluntary provisions aimed at facilitating extradition, including, for example, a mechanism for provisional arrest in urgent circumstances. These include an exemption from the obligation to extradite in a case where the requested state has substantial grounds to believe that the request has been made in order to prosecute or punish a person on account of sex, race, religion, nationality, ethnic origin, or political opinions. Another exemption is if the request would cause prejudice to that person's position for any of these reasons. In addition, in Article 45, a state may consider entering into bilateral or multilateral agreements or arrangements to enable the transfer of incarcerated persons who have been convicted abroad for any of the convention offences, so that they may complete their prison sentences in their country of nationality. States are also required, in Article 46, to render to each other the widest measure of mutual legal assistance in investigations, prosecutions, and judicial proceedings in relation to the corrupt practices the convention establishes. However, as is noted in paragraph 46(6), if other international agreements governing mutual legal assistance exist between states, those agreements will apply.

Essentially, all of Article 46, and in particular paragraphs 9 to 29, provide a framework for mutual legal assistance to states that do not have a separate mutual legal assistance treaty. This article deserves a detailed look. It identifies the range of purposes for which mutual assistance may be requested and the requirements for the content of such requests. It allows that, on the one hand, even in the absence of a request, a state may transmit information concerning criminal matters that it believes could assist inquiries or proceedings in another state. Also, it should be noted that in paragraph 46(9), detained persons may be transferred voluntarily for the purpose of providing evidence in another state. States may, on the other hand, decline to offer mutual legal assistance in certain cases on the grounds of an absence of dual criminality. They are, however, encouraged to make this the exception rather than the rule. Where a request involves coercive action, matters of a *de minimis* nature, or matters for which the cooperation sought is available under other provisions of the UNCAC (such as law enforcement cooperation pursuant to Article 48), states may decline to offer assistance in the absence of dual criminality.

However, where a request involves non-coercive action, states are to provide mutual legal assistance, unless to do so would be inconsistent with the basic concepts of its legal system. In addition, states are encouraged to use video-conferencing as an alternative to taking of evidence in person (paragraph 18). In paragraph 20, a requested state may also be obliged to keep confidential the fact and substance of a request, except to the extent necessary to execute it, or where the information or evidence provided is exculpatory to an accused person. Under paragraph 21, there are four grounds for refusing mutual legal assistance:

(1) if the request does not conform to the requirements of the UNCAC;
(2) if the requested state party considers that execution is likely to prejudice its sovereignty, security, *ordre public*, or other essential interests;
(3) if domestic law in the requested state prohibits the action requested under its own jurisdiction; and
(4) if granting the request would be contrary to the 'legal system' of the requested state party concerning mutual legal assistance.

In sub-paragraph (8), assistance may not be refused on the ground of bank secrecy or on the sole ground that the offence involves a fiscal matter. Moreover, if a request cannot be refused on any of the general grounds just highlighted, or postponed on the ground that it interferes with an ongoing domestic investigation, prosecution, and so on, the states involved will 'consider' whether it may be conditionally granted. If the requesting state accepts such assistance, it is bound to comply with any conditions that are attached to it. In the absence of another mutual legal assistance treaty (MLAT) in force between the states concerned, paragraph 27 establishes a procedure for providing safe conduct guarantees to a person who travels to a requesting state in order to give evidence. The rule in paragraph 28 is that the ordinary costs of executing mutual assistance requests are to be borne by the requested state. However, if the expenses are substantial, the requesting and requested states shall consult on their allocation and what is called a 'sharing formula'.

In addition, the state may also make use of mutual legal assistance mechanisms to obtain documents from another state, such as government records, or information on the same terms as they are available to the general public under domestic law. However, if not available to the general public, a requesting state's access to them is basically at the discretion of the requested state. It is also possible, under Article 47, to transfer criminal proceedings between states, in recognition of the fact that the transfer can be efficient in cases where several jurisdictions are involved and all are with different aspects of acts related to corruption.

Moreover, apart from formal mutual legal assistance, the UNCAC allows for police-to-police cooperation. Thus, Article 48 requires states to cooperate, in line with their 'domestic legal and administrative systems', to improve and enhance effective action among their law enforcement authorities, inter alia, by sharing information on persons, groups, and property involved in convention offences.

Addressing the serious issues raised by the cross-border nature of corruption and organised crimes, UNCAC's Article 49 encourages states to reach agreements or arrangements to conduct joint investigations. Taking this further, Article 50 provides that, subject to the 'basic principles of a state's domestic legal system', law enforcement authorities may be allowed to use controlled delivery, electronic surveillance, and undercover operations, and were these to be used internationally, the states involved would be able to provide some regulatory agreements or arrangement for the use of such techniques. However, while the use of these special investigative techniques are not per se violations of Article 7 provisions (on fair trial) of the African Charter on Human and Peoples' Rights, and indeed may be necessary for gathering evidence in corruption cases (especially given the secretive nature of corruption), they should be subject to safeguards, and utmost care must be taken to ensure that human rights of the citizens are not thereby adversely affected.[37]

Finally, there is an interesting provision in Article 17 of the ECOWAS Protocol that deserves mention here. It requires the application of the protocol even to 'acts of corruption committed before the entry into force of this Protocol', as long as this is requested by a state party. This would then 'form the basis of judicial cooperation', insofar as national and international standards in the area of extradition are respected. Even so, it states in a rather contradictory formulation that, 'This provision shall in no way affect the non-retroactive nature of criminal law'.

## Asset Recovery

Although all four instruments contain asset recovery provisions in some form,[38] unarguably the most important and detailed provisions, once again, are in the UNCAC. It treats asset recovery as 'a fundamental principle of this Convention', and requires states to 'afford one another the

[37] See eg, *Ramanauskas v Lithuania* App no 74420/01 (ECtHR, 5 February 2008).

[38] For example, sub-s 15(1)(c) of the AU Convention covers the repatriation of proceeds of corruption. This provision was advocated by TI, and later added to Art 16 to grant states greater powers in terms of what to do with the proceeds, or 'instrumentalities', of corruption.

widest measure of cooperation and assistance in this regard'. Its provisions elaborate obligations of states on preventive measures and on recovery itself. The UNCAC provisions are also crucial from the perspective of Africa, not least because vast amounts of stolen public wealth from the continent end up in developed countries, as shown throughout this book, and recovering and repatriating that wealth has been a particularly difficult task for a victim state already weakened by years of corruption.

As previously noted, the equivalent of nearly $148bn annually is lost to corruption across Africa, and much of this money is deposited in private accounts in foreign banks. Stolen wealth from African states has been flaunted in countries in Europe and North America, including the United Kingdom and the United States, where indicted African senior government officials have used as favourable destination to spend their people's resources to buy expensive homes and other luxuries. While stolen wealth from Africa is used to develop economies abroad, the continent's own economies and development remain stagnant or even arguably in decline, because largely unrecovered stolen wealth takes precious resources away from projects that could otherwise improve the lives of African states and their people, and thus contribute to their socioeconomic expansion, growth, and development. It has been stated that,

> The AU Corruption Convention is a profound step by its own accord, but as a regional instrument, its scope, including its degree of international cooperation, is limited to combating corruption in Africa. In reality, however, international corrupt practices, particularly the movement of illicitly obtained assets that have a significant impact on Africa's economy, involve States on the other continents that the AU Corruption Convention cannot bind. The full benefits of the AU Corruption Convention can materialize only if there is a corresponding obligation on the part of the destination countries. The only legal instrument of a universal nature that could bind all states to the same standard is the UNCAC. In relation to the corruption that involves other continents, therefore, to avoid clapping with one hand, States Parties to the AU Corruption Convention and all other nations who wish to fight corruption through international law must accede to the UNCAC. That is the best way of addressing issues involved in the cross-continent corruption that is seriously affecting Africa's development today.[39]

The effective enforcement of the provisions on assets recovery, therefore, has the potential to limit opportunities to hide such stolen funds, as well as to discourage corrupt practices, since senior state officials may be less likely to engage in corruption if they know there will be no place to hide their plundered national wealth. This, in turn, could make available the required resources for governments to provide basic necessities of life and

[39] Snider and Kidanett, 'Combating Corruption through International Law in Africa' (n 7) 747.

other human rights for millions of their economically and socially vulnerable citizens.[40]

Before further discussion about the UNCAC's asset recovery provisions, a brief background on the inclusion of the provisions in the instrument is warranted for context, especially given its overall significance. In the preparation of the UNCAC, existing legal instruments against corruption were analysed.[41] The UNCAC is thus considered a robust response to the corruption problem,[42] although the issue of protection of sovereignty championed by many developing countries proved to be controversial. This issue was raised in the context of the specific provisions on the confiscation and seizure of funds of illicit origin, money laundering, and the return of funds to their country of origin.[43] Western countries in particular seemed less than enthusiastic about the prospect of including provisions on asset recovery, with some recommending that any such provisions should be voluntary. For example, the Swiss representative stated that the principle was good, but that any provisions on freezing, confiscation, and returning of illicit funds should complement other preventive measures, and that the UNCAC's purpose should be limited to encouraging states to implement the necessary national legislation, legal bases for international cooperation, and mutual legal assistance in the recovery and return of illicit assets.[44]

Given the division on the issue of asset recovery between the Commission on Crime Prevention and Criminal Justice, the Group of 77, and the Group of African States, on the one hand, and China and Western economies, on the other hand, Peru sought and obtained the approval of the Ad Hoc Committee to organise a technical workshop on asset recovery to improve members' understanding of the issue.[45] Peru's initiative

[40] ibid. See also, Ad Hoc Committee for the Negotiation of a Convention Against Corruption, 'Global Study on the Transfer of Funds of Illicit Origin, Especially Funds Derived from Acts of Corruption' 4th Sess, Agenda Item 3, UN Doc A/AC 261/12 (2002), 3.

[41] General Assembly Resolution 55/61, para 3.

[42] Report of the Ad Hoc Committee Negotiating the UN Convention against Transnational Organized Crime, at its eighth session, A/AC 254/25.

[43] The main concern was the hiding of large amounts of stolen wealth by corrupt leaders in developing countries in overseas bank accounts. For example, the UN's Group of 77, plus China, agreed that particular attention should be paid to the provisions on: exchange of information, removing bank secrecy in corruption investigations; criteria emphasising determining the country of origin of illicit assets; tracing the transfer of such funds; forfeiture and confiscation of the proceeds of corruption; and shifting the burden of proof when such activities were reasonably suspected. The Group of African States raised similar concerns, including the need to prevent and combat money laundering and the transfer of funds of illicit origin, as well as the return of illicit funds to their countries of origin. See Report of the Ad Hoc Committee, second session, 17–28 June 2002, A/AC 261/4, paras 26–28.

[44] Preparatory Meeting of the Ad Hoc Committee, A/AC 261/IMP/2, paras 11(a) and (c).

[45] The workshop discussed mechanisms for preventing the transfer of illicit funds, including through an early warning system, stronger implementation of existing national and international financial institution regulations, and capacity-building for law enforcement and judicial agencies. It also looked at the identification of funds as the proceeds of corruption; tracing; the possibility of criminal proceedings in the country of origin; freezing and

went ahead with the initial agreement that the workshop would not result in any formal conclusions or positions on the issue.[46] Nonetheless, after six sessions of intense negotiation, some compromise (considered by former UN Secretary General Kofi Annan as a 'breakthrough') was reached on the convention's provisions on money laundering, asset recovery, and mutual legal assistance. As with every international legal agreement, the UNCAC struggled with the tension between domestic sovereignty and international obligations. During the third session, the chairman of the Ad Hoc Committee expressed his concern about the repeated references in the text of the convention to its conformity with domestic law. The issue was that such references should be the exception rather than the norm, because international law was not meant to be a mere reflection of national laws. According to the chairman, '[These] negotiations . . . [offer] an opportunity to codify innovative approaches to common problems, to which national laws [can] aspire. Such an opportunity should not be missed.'[47] However, such wise counsel from these negotiations and discussions was ignored in the final form of the UNCAC.

The UNCAC provision on asset recovery is in its chapter 5, and on technical assistance and exchange of information, in chapter 6. It cannot be stressed enough that the effective implementation and enforcement of these chapters would go a long way in addressing the consequences of corruption and the debilitating conditions of victims in countries across Africa. It is therefore a welcome development that the UNCAC requires states to take certain preventive measures specifically focused on the detection of transactions or deposits involving politically exposed persons, as discussed in Chapter 2. In this respect, the first, and probably the most important, obligation of states as a matter of prevention is to require financial institutions to follow the 'know your customer' rule (see Chapter 2): to take reasonable steps to determine the identity of beneficial owners of funds deposited into high-value accounts and to conduct enhanced scrutiny of accounts held by individuals who are or have been in prominent public positions. These provisions can be found in UNCAC's Articles 51 and 52. According to the *travaux préparatoires,* these requirements are to be implemented on a national basis with due regard to particular risks of

seizures abroad; obligations of financial institutions; and establishment of the legal framework necessary for effective mutual legal assistance in this field. The workshop also considered the return of stolen funds to its country of origin, including identification of the legal beneficiaries; the use of asset-sharing mechanisms; competing claims between the country of origin and other natural or legal persons; legal remedies available to affected third parties in the recipient country and the country of origin; and the division of costs and taxation.

[46] First session of the Ad Hoc Committee, 21 January–2 February 2001, A/AC 261/2, para 23.

[47] Report of the Ad Hoc Committee for the Negotiation of a Convention Against Corruption On Its Third Session, Vienna, 30 September–11 October 2002, UN Doc A/AC 261/9 (2002), 7.

money laundering. For example, some countries will apply the enhanced scrutiny standards only to foreign officials, while other countries apply them to their domestic officials as well.

In addition, states are required to put mechanisms into place to ensure adequate record-keeping by financial institutions and to prohibit the establishment of banks that have no physical locations. They may therefore consider taking such measures to establish financial disclosure systems for public officials and mechanisms for sharing information obtained through these systems, as covered in paragraph 52(5); and paragraph 52(6) provides that states parties may 'consider' establishing measures to require reporting by appropriate public officials of foreign financial accounts. There are similar provisions in most constitutions of countries in Africa, but as discussed in Chapter 3, these are also some of the most breached by corrupt senior state officials. This author hopes that enforcement mechanisms and sanctions will be established in the future to prevent and deter this type of practice, which is patently inconsistent with the principles of public trust and public interest. These could serve as preventive steps to stop corrupt state officials from stealing and laundering their ill-gotten wealth.

In terms of the actual recovery of stolen assets, two types can be identified under the UNCAC: direct and indirect recovery measures. The convention covers measures for direct recovery of property by requiring each state to have three basic methods for allowing another country to make a direct claim: as any other private litigant, on property located in its territory, and where that property is acquired through the acts of corruption that states must criminalise under the UNCAC. Such direct recovery, as spelled out in Article 53, is to take place without recourse to mutual legal assistance procedures. In the first basic method, states that have had such property stolen must allow the states holding this property to initiate court civil actions to establish title or ownership of the property in question. The second is that states must have a mechanism in place by which their courts can order that another state be compensated or paid damages, such as through court-ordered restitution following a criminal conviction. The third is that states are also required to establish a mechanism for confiscation proceedings to allow for the recognition of another state's claim as a legitimate owner of the property.

The UNCAC also covers indirect recovery of property through international cooperation on confiscation in its Article 54.[48] Thus, states are required to establish a legal framework to enable them to provide assistance to other states in the recovery of assets acquired through corrupt

[48] To assist states in the assets recovery process, states are to 'consider' establishing a financial intelligence unit. According to the *travaux préparatoires*, these units, contemplated in UNCAC's Art 58, may be the same as mentioned in its Art 14.

practices recognised under the convention. Specific mechanisms required are authority to give effect to foreign confiscation judgments, and domestic procedures to confiscate property of foreign origin involved in offences over which it may have jurisdiction. However, states are also required 'to consider' establishing mechanisms for confiscation in the absence of a criminal conviction. Among other things, states are to establish certain mechanisms for freezing or seizing property, including on the basis of a freeze or seizure order by another state party, or upon a request by another state that provides sufficient grounds for taking such action. Furthermore, states are to 'consider' establishing additional measures for freezing or seizing property, for example, on the basis of a foreign arrest or charge. In practice, states responding to a request from another state to use the mechanisms in Articles 31 and 54[49] in order to seek either an order of confiscation or the execution of a foreign judgment would be required to utilise the freeze or seizure mechanisms established under the UNCAC.

Additionally, in implementing this provision, states are to use mutual legal assistance procedures including the provisions of Article 46, as well as the exceptions to the obligation to provide assistance.[50] It is useful to note that Article 46 also elaborates on the type of information that must be provided by the requesting state in its request for assistance. However, these provisions would apply alongside relevant domestic law and other bilateral and multilateral agreements. Given the role of effective information exchange in any successful asset recovery case, states are encouraged, in Article 56, to engage in spontaneous information-sharing with each other where such sharing would assist in an asset recovery case.

Another issue of importance is how to dispose of confiscated property. On this, Article 57 requires that this take place under the domestic law of the state party executing the confiscation. Each state is to establish mechanisms that permit, at the request of another state, the return of the confiscated property to its rightful owners, taking into account the rights of bona fide third parties. Of course, all the exceptions to mutual legal assistance will also apply to the process of disposing of confiscated property. In cases involving the proceeds of corruption, the enforcement of a confiscation judgment of one state over another would require that the said property be returned to the requesting state.[51] Yet it is unclear whether

[49] To assist states in the assets recovery process states are 'to consider' establishing a financial intelligence unit. According to the *travaux préparatoires*, these units contemplated in UNACs' article 58, may be the same as mentioned in its article 14.

[50] In addition to reasons previously discussed, assistance may also be refused if the requesting state fails to provide sufficient and timely evidence or if the value of the property in question is of a *de minimis* value. It should also be noted that any provisional measures cannot be lifted without the requested state first consulting with the requesting state, and it is expected that the rights of bona fide third parties will be protected.

[51] The requested state may deduct reasonable costs before disposition of the property. According to the *travaux préparatoires*, these costs are intended to be actual expenses, rather than finders' fees or other unspecified charges.

international asset-sharing, procedures to compensate victims, or other mechanisms must be enforced to complete such a return. Similarly, the provision on asset-sharing may seem unfair, on the simple ground that the jurisdiction of the requested states may have already benefited economically from the stolen assets. To deduct 'reasonable expenses' or share assets in this circumstance may amount to double jeopardy for the citizens of the victimised states.

Nonetheless, requested states are required to give priority consideration to returning the property to the requesting state or to the prior legitimate owners, or compensating victims of crime. One would hope that the interests of the victims of corruption – individuals and communities, rather than of the 'victim-state' (whose officials often mismanage or even re-steal returned public funds) – would receive serious consideration in the implementation of this provision. However, as it has been shown throughout the book, the effectiveness of the asset recovery provisions depends to a large extent on the measures for mutual legal assistance. It has been argued that despite repeated statements to the contrary, UNCAC's chapter 5 on asset recovery 'is not as revolutionary as some people say. The impact of the asset recovery provisions should therefore not be exaggerated; they focus attention on a certain aspect of corruption that afflicts developing countries, but do not supply a panacea to their problems.'[52] It is nonetheless, 'a significant step forward in dealing with a complex problem in international affairs'.[53]

Furthermore, to ensure effective international cooperation in the fight against corruption and money laundering, in Article 60, states are required to train domestic law enforcement personnel on matters relating to the prevention and detection of corruption, including in the area of the preparation of mutual legal assistance requests. States are also 'to consider' various potential methods to provide technical assistance to each other in their plans and programmes to prevent and combat corruption. Additionally, states are to work with their scientific and academic communities in undertaking analytical studies relating to corruption and to share the results with each other, as outlined in Articles 48 and 61. Of particular importance is the fact that, in order to facilitate the effective implementation of the UNCAC, developed countries are required to work towards strengthening the ability of developing countries such as those across Africa to fight corruption.

In general, then, given the challenges (such as the lack of know-how and resources) frequently faced by countries in Africa that have attempted to trace, identify, recover, and repatriate stolen public funds, it is crucial for developed economies that have benefited from these deposits to

[52] Webb, 'The United Nations Convention against Corruption' (n 20).

[53] ibid.

make greater efforts to assist the victim states and, importantly, the economically and socially vulnerable of those states. In this respect, effective realisation of the notion of international cooperation and assistance will require assistance not just in the repatriation of such wealth and in the provision of training and technical assistance to victim states, but also in direct developmental and other support (on a consistent and institutional basis) to individuals and communities that suffer as a result of corruption and money laundering. This can happen through, for instance, multilateral agencies such as the Office of the High Commissioner for Human Rights and citizens' supervised initiatives, which can have a direct and real impact on the lives and conditions of the economically and socially vulnerable. Even so, the framework of international cooperation and assistance will only be able to achieve its full potential for curbing corruption and money laundering if states are able to muster the necessary political will to dismantle traditional stumbling blocks like bank secrecy (in offshore havens), bank–customer confidentiality, immunity, and other legal obstacles that limit victims' legal standing and access to ill-gotten wealth.

One way of dealing with the cases of unwilling or uncooperative offshore havens is to consider, first, the possibility of judicial intervention through the mechanism of the International Court of Justice (already contemplated as a means of resolving disputes among states parties to the UNCAC). Second, in cases of jurisdictions that persistently violate international rules against money laundering, the international community should consider imposing heavy political and economic sanctions against those jurisdictions, and, as Guy Stessens has suggested, the imposition of 'punitive taxes and especially the prospect of exclusion from the global financial community [to] persuade these jurisdictions to accept the fundamentals of the international anti-money laundering regime'.[54] Thus, recalcitrant offshore havens can be blacklisted or 'named and shamed'; while similar sanctions can be considered against so-called victim states and high-ranking public officials who continue to take advantage of the laxity of offshore jurisdictions to launder their plundered wealth and, thereby, benefit from their crime (while the economically and socially vulnerable continue to face debilitating conditions).

## Implementation Mechanisms

Among the fundamental weaknesses of the UNCAC, the AU Convention, the ECOWAS Protocol, and the SADC Protocol is the absence of any serious implementation or enforcement mechanisms. With respect to the

[54] , Guy Stessens, *Money Laundering: A New International Law Enforcement Model* (Cambridge: Cambridge University Press, 2000) 430.

UNCAC, for example, only Article 63 moves in that direction. Even so, this article merely establishes a conference of the States Parties, whose work is to be supported through voluntary contributions by the states. Under this article, the conference would have the responsibility for 'promoting and reviewing the implementation of the Convention', including through information exchange, periodic review of implementation by states, and facilitating technical assistance among states. However, a grave weakness is that the implementation and enforcement of the requirements and provisions of the UNCAC are solely left open to the states.

Nonetheless, the UNCAC permits the conference to develop other supplemental review mechanisms. The UN Secretary-General is to provide the secretariat for the conference, which, as designated by the UN General Assembly resolution, is the Vienna-based UN Office on Drugs and Crime.[55] Although the Conference of States Parties at their meeting in Doha, Qatar in November 2009 set up a review mechanism for the UNCAC (a completely desk-based review that excludes the possibility of a country visit), this was considered largely unsatisfactory by civil society groups lead by Transparency International. Among the mechanism's shortcomings are its voluntary provisions for civil society involvement and the fact that the mechanism established does not properly qualify as an 'effective review body', since the mechanism is limited to 'self-assessment checklists by states parties' and covered just 15 articles of the UNCAC.[56] However, while a self-assessment checklist is not an adequate implementation mechanism in itself, it can serve as a means of not only exerting public and peer pressure (through for example potential publication of reports and rounds of mutual evaluation) but also in assessing the effectiveness of the measures states are taking to implement their obligations under the UNCAC, and might hopefully encourage them to improve their fight against corruption.

The UNCAC nonetheless underscores in Article 65 the need for states to ensure the proper implementation of the convention, such as through legislative and administrative measures. In addition to this, the application of the UNCAC does not preclude the adoption of stricter measures to prevent and combat corruption. As previously noted, the UNCAC establishes, under Article 66, a mechanism for states to settle disputes concerning the interpretation or application of the convention. However, if a dispute cannot be settled within a reasonable amount of time through negotiation, a state may refer it to arbitration, or if the parties are unable to

[55] It should be noted also that the United Nations has established a Global Programme Against Corruption to assist in implementation of the UNCAC. UN Office on Drugs & Crime, 'UNODC and Corruption', www.unodc.org/unodc/en /corruption/index.html.

[56] The UNCAC only has self-assessment checklists for states' parties and pilot review projects, while the process to establish a mutual evaluation mechanism has not yet been completed.

agree on the organisation of the arbitration, it may, as noted, refer it to the International Court of Justice. A state may opt out of dispute settlement mechanisms, other than negotiation, by making a declaration to that effect.

Given the various provisions of the UNCAC allowing states to implement the convention subject to domestic laws, and the voluntary and discretionary nature of many of its provisions, it is unlikely that any implementation mechanism, if it were to ever be established, would be effective. Nonetheless, the experience of the OECD monitoring mechanism suggests that the UNCAC might benefit from the existence of a mechanism if states were able to exercise the required political will to implement their obligations under the convention. Options to consider might include harmonising any implementation initiatives with other similar commitments by states, coordinating with regional and national anti-corruption mechanisms where they exist, and encouraging a greater level of involvement and participation by civil society groups, including anti-corruption and human rights NGOs. Whether states will be able to pull together the resources needed to establish a credible monitoring mechanism, however, remains an open question. As Philippa Webb stated:

> The [UNCAC] can be seen as a blueprint for policy reform on a global level, and as with any reform proposal, there is a need to consider not just the formal provisions, but how they will impact on societies. 'Law', in the sense of a set of formal written documents, will be largely irrelevant if the rules are not embedded in an institutional and organizational structure that favours compliance.[57]

Also, like any other provisions of the UNCAC, the effective implementation of these provisions will depend largely on the willingness of states to prioritise the interest of the victims of corruption over national, political, or economic interests. However, it is rare to find states – developed or developing – that request extradition solely on the grounds of corruption. Without the requisite political will, it is difficult to expect states to make extradition requests to prosecute corrupt suspects. Simeon Aisabor Igbinedion has argued that:

> Even where the political will to request fugitives' extradition exists, the *extradite or prosecute* rule is weakened by the hortatory language of the *UNCAC's Article 42(4)* which, unlike *Article 42(3)*, does not *obligate* the requested State to prosecute the fugitive offender . . . [also] the mechanism of extradition may even be redundant since most offenders are not necessarily fugitives.[58]

Similarly, with respect to the AU Convention, while most of its articles commence with a mandatory general principle, the manner of implementation is left to the discretion of each state. However, the AU Convention in

[57] Webb, 'The United Nations Convention against Corruption' (n 20), 221.

[58] Simeon Aisabor Igbinedion, 'A Critical Appraisal of the Mechanism for Prosecuting Systemic Corruption Offenders under the United Nations Convention against Corruption' (2003) 6 *Manchester Journal of International Economic Law* 56.

article 22 establishes an advisory board of 11 members elected by the AU Executive Council, who each serve for a period of two years, renewable once.[59] The advisory board is responsible for promoting anti-corruption work; collecting information on corruption and on the behaviour of multinational corporations operating across Africa; developing methodologies; advising governments; developing codes of conduct for public officials; and establishing partnerships with stakeholders and partners. The board has the responsibility of submitting a report to the executive council on a regular basis on the progress made by each state in complying with the provisions of the AU Convention. The board also receives reports from states on the progress they are making in their implementation of the convention, initially within a year after the coming into force of the AU Convention and then subsequently on an annual basis from national anti-corruption authorities. As with other enforcement issues, the advisory board lacks any real power because its advice may be rejected by the states. The advisory board does not even have a structure of its own, but is housed within a small department in the Secretariat of the AU Commission in Addis Ababa.

With respect to the ECOWAS Protocol, its implementation mechanism is the Technical Commission, whose responsibilities are to: monitor the implementation of the protocol on domestic levels; gather and disseminate information among states; regularly organise relevant training programmes; and provide states with appropriate additional assistance. The Technical Commission is comprised of experts from states' ministries of finance, justice, and internal affairs and from security. It is designated to meet at least twice each year to establish transparent procedures (which must be balanced against the need for confidentiality in certain cases) and to submit its reports to the Council of Ministers. The protocol also contains mechanisms for dispute settlement so that disputes between states that arise over the interpretation or application of the protocol can be amicably settled through direct agreement. In the event of failure of amicable settlement, the matter may be referred by a party to the dispute (or another state) to the Community Court of Justice. The decision of the Community Court of Justice is final. It is clear that this mechanism, like the ones discussed in this chapter, faces similar challenges to its enforcement.

With respect to the SADC Protocol, the Southern African Development Community in 2000 established the implementing mechanism known as

[59] Discussions on this during the drafting phase of the convention centred mainly on 'bracketed' substantive provisions, leaving aside any serious negotiations on the institutional part of the convention. The basis for this decision was that states preferred implementing individual mechanisms within their own countries that were then complemented by peer pressure, but did not want a strong regional implementation mechanism. The only exception was South Africa, which took the view that all AU member states should ensure that Art 22, established under the convention, has the capacity to move forward the efforts at preventing and combating corruption.

the Southern African Forum against Corruption (SAFAC). SAFAC's main functions are to: strengthen networking among member organisations; update members on appropriate legislation and relevant international instruments on corruption; facilitate the upgrading of skills relevant to fighting corruption through training; cooperate and facilitate transboundary investigations and prosecution of corruption cases; identify and share experiences on best practices for combating corruption; share relevant information on corruption and intelligence; and implement the provisions of the SADC Protocol against Corruption. In general, it is necessary that the SAFAC be transformed from an informal institution to a formal organ of the SADC, with responsibilities of implementing the protocol because all anti-corruption agencies in the region are members of SAFAC and because its constitution allows for participation of civil society, particularly at the national level. The SADC itself should draw up an implementation plan of action for the protocol. While the protocol is clearly an important step for the SADC region, it is nonetheless only the beginning of a long journey. Political will, citizens' education and empowerment, and providing effective *legal standing* and remedies for victims of corruption will be necessary for advancing the fight against corruption.

## CONCLUSION

One of the major weaknesses of anti-corruption conventions and standards is the implicit assumption that all forms of corruption are the same, regardless of scope, magnitude, or effect. This lacuna in the legal framework against corruption may be due in part to the poor understanding of large-scale corruption, its many manifestations, and its effects on developing regions like Africa by members of the international community.

Regionally and internationally, existing implementation mechanisms for anti-corruption instruments applicable to Africa have limited mandates, and are often too close to the intergovernmental bodies that establish them. Additionally, although it has its weaknesses (which will need to be addressed), the role that the UNCAC can play as a mechanism to deter, prevent, and combat lodgement of stolen public funds in the jurisdictions of developed countries, is buttressed by the reality of the rather limited coverage of the SADC Protocol against Corruption, the ECOWAS Protocol on the Fight against Corruption, and the AU Convention on Preventing and Combating Corruption as these regional initiated treaties are inapplicable to several developed countries that continue to provide safe havens for stolen funds from across Africa.

Nonetheless, as noted, given the many optional and 'get-out' clauses contained in the UNCAC, and its over-emphasis on 'national sovereignty', it remains to be seen whether corrupt states and high-ranking officials will muster the appropriate political will to effectively implement the convention, including by aligning their national laws and institutions along the lines of any potential recommendations from the process. In any event, the possibility that the mutual evaluation mechanism will significantly enhance the effectiveness of the UNCAC in terms of its ability to combat large-scale corruption is immediately undermined by the fact that the conference of states parties underlined that such a review mechanism should be non-intrusive and should not produce any form of ranking. This raises concerns as to whether this mechanism will be simply a paper exercise or whether states are prepared to remove political considerations and empower the conference to develop a more critical role. Yet, it may well be that 'the most fundamental weakness of mutual evaluation mechanisms as a means of heightening the effective implementation of international measures [against corruption] is that these self-and mutual evaluation rounds result more in procedural than substantive compliance'.[60] This may be the case as such mechanisms seem to aim only at 'attaining harmonization of legislation than gauging the effectiveness'[61] of any measures to combat corruption.

However, states should not use the absence of a strong, independent and effective implementation mechanisms as an excuse not to implement these treaties in their relations *inter se*, and individually and must strive to realise the promises of the treaties domestically for their citizens.

Whatever the potential contribution of any mutual evaluation system, ultimately, states will still have to take responsibility to enforce critical legislation and reforms on the domestic level, but this can only realistically occur by increasing the direct accountability of states and empowering victims of corruption through the framework of human rights. Michael Reisman has stated that, 'To date, the international efforts that have been mounted [against corruption] seem more on the order of a crusade than reform. Their major contribution appears to be a feeling that something laudable is being done.'[62] Rose-Ackerman also suggests that tribunals in the fields of human rights, international labour standards, and nuclear energy might be models for victims of corruption to lodge a complaint.[63] It is therefore time to realise that 'soft diplomatic measures, such as mutual evaluations and public condemnations [and prosecution] which have been used hitherto will by themselves not suffice to make the global fight against money laundering [and corruption] effective'.[64] It is the argument of this book that the continuing serious implications of large-scale corruption for

[60] Stessens, *Money Laundering* (n 53) 426–27.

[61] ibid.

[62] W Michael Reisman, *Folded Lies: Bribery, Crusades and Reforms* (New York: Free Press, 1979) 157.

[63] Susan Rose-Ackerman, *Corruption and Government: Causes, Consequences and Reform* (Cambridge: Cambridge University Press, 1999) 196.

[64] ibid, 431.

development, good governance, democracy, rule of law, institutional building and reform, and ultimately respect for human rights, create a special and justificatory circumstance that should compel the application of human rights as a complementary legal framework to address the problem.

The application of human rights law, in particular the African Charter on Human and Peoples' Rights, would help to address some of the shortcomings that have been identified in the current legal frameworks against corruption; help to establish an effective and functioning legal and judicial system with which to fight corruption and money laundering, and, more significantly, to afford victims legal standing and effective remedies. In general, while the problem of corruption (and human rights violations) will not and cannot be combated overnight, even with the invocation of human rights law, it does not mean that the international community's vision of curbing all forms of corruption is unattainable in the long run. The experience and achievements of the antislavery and antiapartheid movements suggest that, with the appropriate strategy and requisite political will, the phenomenon of corruption can be ultimately surmounted. Or at least considerably minimised and made negligible in that it does not constitute much danger to individuals and communities in particular, the economically and socially vulnerable.

# Part III

# Human Rights Law and Corruption

# 5

# *Effects of Corruption on Human and Peoples' Rights*

## INTRODUCTION

NEARLY 30 YEARS ago, on 21 October 1986, the African Charter on Human and Peoples' Rights came into force. It had been adopted five years earlier, on 27 June 1981, by the then Organization of African Unity (OAU), now known as the African Union (AU).[1] It introduced striking innovations, by the normal canons of human rights law, in that it embedded the concept of peoples' rights with civil, political, economic, social, and cultural rights, all in one document. Like most human rights treaties, the African Charter imposes positive obligations on states to take specific legal and other measures to give effect to the rights and freedoms it guarantees and to provide remedies in the event of violations. But the charter also imposes negative obligations on states parties to abstain from all violations or restrictions of their citizens' human rights. The AU adopted its Constitutive Act in 2000, which affirmed member states' commitments to the human and peoples' rights guaranteed by the African Charter. The African Charter has been ratified by 53 of the 54 member states of the African Union.[2]

The text of the African Charter comprises a preamble and 68 articles divided into two parts: the first part contains a list of substantive human

[1] The OAU was founded on 25 May 1963, when its charter was adopted by the Heads of State and Government of 32 countries in Africa. Following the adoption of the Constitutive Act of the African Union on 11 July 2000, and its entry into force on 26 May 2001, the AU was established to replace the OAU. The AU's main mandates are to address issues of political and economic nature, but its constitution proclaims commitment to the promotion and protection of human rights on the basis of the African Charter and other relevant treaties and standards. See, generally, Frans Viljoen, *International Human Rights Law in Africa*, 2nd edn (Oxford: Oxford University Press, 2012); Malcolm Evans and Rachel Murray (eds), *The African Charter on Human and Peoples' Rights: The System in Practice, 1986-2006*, 2nd edn (Cambridge: Cambridge University Press, 2008); Rachel Murray, *Human Rights in Africa: From the OAU to the African Union* (Cambridge: Cambridge University Press, 2004).

[2] On this point, see for example, the *Sarah H Longwe v International Hotels (Zambia)* 1993 4 LRC 221, in which Justice Musumali of the Zambian High Court observed that 'ratification of such [instruments] by a nation state without reservations is a clear testimony of the willingness by the state to be bound by the provisions of such [instruments]'.

and peoples' rights guarantees as well as duties; the second establishes the African Commission on Human and Peoples' Rights and its mandates. The human rights recognised by the charter are covered by Articles 3–17; peoples' rights are covered by Articles 18–24; and individual duties are covered by Articles 27–29. The African Commission's tasks, mandates, and procedures are elaborated in subsequent provisions of the charter. Further work in the AU has led to the adoption of additional important human rights instruments, such as the Protocol to the African Charter on Human and Peoples' Rights on the Establishment of the African Court on Human and Peoples' Rights,[3] the Protocol to the African Charter on Human and Peoples' Rights on the Rights of Women in Africa (hereafter African Women's Rights Protocol), the African Charter on the Rights and Welfare of the Child (hereafter African Children Rights Charter); and the African Charter on Democracy, Elections, and Governance (hereafter African Governance Charter).[4]

This chapter examines the effects of corruption on the full and effective enjoyment of human and peoples' rights – civil, political, economic, and social rights – guaranteed by the African Charter and other relevant instruments, such as the African Women's Rights Protocol, the African Children Rights Charter, and the African Governance Charter. The aim is to show the immense human consequences of corruption and to demonstrate the need for human rights law to serve as a complementary framework to combat corruption. The chapter analyses individual substantive rights guaranteed by the African Charter, and although the focus clearly is on the charter, other relevant instruments are also considered. The discussion throws light on these rights through the instructive case law of the African Commission, and where it exists, the African Court on Human and Peoples' Rights, and other relevant comparable jurisprudence. While

[3] The Protocol on the Statute of the African Court of Justice and Human Rights was adopted in Sharm El Sheikh, Egypt, on 1 July 2008. As of April 2014, only seven states had ratified the protocol: Benin, Burkina Faso, DR Congo, Libya, and Mali. 29 states have signed the protocol. The court merges the AU Court of Justice and the African Court on Human and Peoples' Rights, and will replace the two courts once the protocol establishing it enters into force. However, cases before the Court of Human Rights will be transferred to the new court if they have not been completed by the time the protocol establishing the Court of Justice and Human Rights enters into force. There will also be a one-year transitional period for the Court of Human Rights to complete its work. The jurisdiction is the same as the Court of Human Rights, and the court will be able to enter cases on the interpretation of the AU Constitutive Act, the African Charter, the African Charter on the Rights and Welfare of the Child, the Protocol to the African Charter on the Rights of Women in Africa, and any 'any other legal instrument relating to human rights, ratified by the States Parties': www.au.int/en/treaties.

[4] Other relevant African human rights' related treaties include the Protocol on the Statute of the African Court of Justice and Human Rights, the Protocol to the Treaty Establishing the African Economic Community Relating to the Pan-African Parliament, the African Union Convention on Preventing and Combating Corruption the Protocol of the Court of Justice of the African Union, and the African Charter on Values and Principles of Public Service and Administration.

the commission and the court have regrettably not done much to consider directly the effects of corruption on the human rights under the charter, it is arguable that their jurisprudence provides a helpful guidance and analytical framework to throw some light on the contents, contours, and conceptions of human rights guaranteed by the charter (and their corresponding obligations), and the potential human rights obligations of states to prevent and combat corruption. The discussion here is based on the assumption that if the charter's full potential for combating corruption is to be effectively grasped and maximised, the interpretations of its various contents (and normative value and utility) have to be thoroughly analysed and fully understood. The idea is to show the potential of the charter (and other relevant instruments) for overcoming the challenges raised by the criminal law instruments against corruption discussed in preceding chapters.

Furthermore, where appropriate, references are made to the jurisprudence of other relevant human rights treaty bodies, in particular to explore the usefulness and importance of the limited (and even generalised) references by UN human rights mechanisms to the connection between corruption and human rights.[5] While in some cases there may be several explanations for human rights violations, which may (admittedly) make it difficult to establish a link between corruption and specific violations, as will be argued here and more fully in Chapter 6, to deny that when a government is overrun by corruption, human rights and the rule of law are directly or indirectly seriously affected is to fail to recognise its corrosive effects on human beings (and dignity), and on all the institutions of governance.[6]

## THE OBJECT AND PURPOSE OF THE AFRICAN CHARTER

The starting point for interpreting the African Charter in light of corruption is the 1969 Vienna Convention on the Law of Treaties, Article 31 of which states that treaties are to be interpreted according to their ordinary meaning in their context (including preambles and annexes) and in the

[5] African governments have subscribed to several UN human rights treaties, including the International Covenant on Civil and Political Rights and the International Covenant on Economic, Social and Cultural Rights. It should be noted that the Economic and Social Council (ECOSOC) of the United Nations and the Office of the High Commissioner for Human Rights have developed an elaborate system for implementing rights in the two main covenants, as well as in other UN human rights treaties. These include the appointment of independent experts to the human rights treaty committees; increasing the use of special rapporteurs by the Human Rights Council; various channels for bringing individual petitions to United Nations bodies; and the so-called mainstreaming of human rights in various international organisations.

[6] For detailed discussion on proving the causal link between corruption and human rights, see Ch 6.

light of their object and purpose. Moreover, Article 31(1) provides that subsequent practice or agreement of parties to a treaty may establish an agreed interpretation, even if it is at variance with its original meaning. This suggests that any serious interpretation of the provisions of the charter (being a constitutive instrument and not 'a static formula') should take into account the object and purpose of the charter, so that its progressive provisions are favourably advanced, and conditions that allow corruption to flourish redressed. Yet, while the charter can be an important tool to combat corruption and its effects on human rights through creative interpretations of the ordinary, contextual and purposive meanings of its provisions, it cannot act as a 'blank cheque'. It would be desirable to adjust the charter to increase its ability to specifically address corruption if the charter is not to be textually overstretched.

It has been observed that 'the object and purpose serves a parameter of interpretation that prevents the destruction of the essence of the substantive provisions of a treaty'.[7] In other words, the object and purpose provide a treaty's mission statement in terms of providing a framework of legally binding human rights and corresponding obligations. The central object and purpose of the African Charter are to promote and achieve the substantive human and peoples' rights that the charter guarantees to make a difference in the lives of individuals (and 'all peoples') across Africa, in particular the economically and socially vulnerable.[8] 'Vulnerability' conceivably could be construed to impose a corresponding obligation on states to take 'reasonable precautions' (such as efficient, transparent, and accountable management of already limited available resources, and the establishment of appropriate legal and institutional order) to protect individuals for example, against abuse of entrusted public positions that inevitably lead to corruption. One might add that this component of 'vulnerability' is indispensable for the effective realisation of the human and peoples' rights guaranteed, and arguably imposes a duty on states to provide an environment in which such legal order and institutions may flourish.

This principle has been somewhat affirmed by the African Commission on Human and Peoples' Rights, the principal body established to oversee

[7] Mashood Baderin, *International Human Rights and Islamic Law* (Oxford: Oxford University Press, 2003) 50.

[8] See also the preamble of the African Charter, which, among others, articulates the object and purpose of the charter to promote 'freedom, equality, justice and dignity', 'achieve a better life for the peoples of Africa', 'promote international cooperation' and 'promote the universality and interdependence of all human rights'. See, for example, the case of *Legal Resources Foundation v Zambia*, Communication No 211/98 (2001), in which the African Commission stated that 'the African Charter must be interpreted holistically and all clauses must reinforce each other. The African Charter must also be interpreted, in light of international norms and consistently with the approach of the other regional and international human rights bodies.' See Communication 211/98 *Legal Resources Foundation v Zambia* (2001), para 70.

the effective implementation of the African Charter on the domestic level. In *Amnesty International v Zambia*,[9] for instance, the commission held that Article 2 (which together with Article 1 articulates the object and purpose of the charter) imposes 'an obligation on the . . . Government to secure the right protected in the African Charter to all persons within its jurisdiction irrespective of political or any other opinion'.[10]

The argument can thus be made that the charter, being a treaty regulated by the rules of international law, can (and should) be interpreted in conformity with these principles so that it can provide a powerful framework to complement the criminal law response to corruption, which clearly flies in the face of the object and purpose of the charter, and undermines the obligations imposed on states parties, which as noted include abstaining from all violations or unauthorised restriction of the charter's rights, and taking positive measures to guarantee the widest possible protection of the individuals under their jurisdiction. Without establishing the necessary conditions and infrastructure, states obviously cannot fulfil these obligations. On this basis, it is arguable that the failure or lack of due diligence to for example establish effective and independent mechanisms to prevent corruption or to provide effective remedies to victims would be entirely inconsistent and incompatible with the object and purpose of the African Charter, which has been further buttressed by both the AU in its Constitutive Act, and subsequently the Convention on Preventing and Combating Corruption (discussed in Chapter 4 of this book).

These clear affirmations of voluntary commitments in the convention would seem to suggest that AU member states understand the theoretical and practical relationship between corruption and the human rights guaranteed by the charter, and reaffirmed in their own Constitutive Act. Yet, it needs to be admitted that the convention's provisions linking corruption to human rights are preambular statements, and not substantive provisions. Even so, it has long been recognised that preambular provisions set the tone for the remainder of a treaty, and can serve as an important legal tool to clarify the intentions of those who created it. Indeed, courts and

[9] Communication No 212/98 (1999).

[10] Communication 212/98, *Amnesty International v Zambia* (1998). Also, in its seminal case, *Association of Victims of Post Electoral Violence & INTERIGHTS v Cameroon* Communication No 272/03 (2003), (on the post-electoral violence and destruction of property that followed the victory of candidate Paul Biya of the Cameroon Peoples' Democratic Party in the 1992 presidential election), the commission clarified the nature of states' obligations and the object and purpose of the African Charter thus: 'All obligations contained in a Treaty . . . seek to attain an objective, a purpose or a result . . . Article 1 of the African Charter imposes on the States Parties the obligation of using the necessary diligence to implement the provisions prescribed by the Charter since the said diligence has to evolve in relation to the time, space and circumstances, and has to be followed by practical action on the ground in order to produce concrete results.' See Communication 272/2003, *Association of Victims of Post Electoral Violence & INTERIGHTS v Cameroon* (2003), paras 106 and 107. This decision was reiterated most recently in Communication 313/05, *Kenneth Good v Botswana* (2010).

other institutions regularly refer to preambles for guidance. As the International Court of Justice stated in the *Sovereignty over Frontier Land* case:

> This statement [preamble] represents the common intention of the two States. Any interpretation under which the Boundary Convention is regarded as leaving in suspense and abandoning for a subsequent appreciation of the status quo the determination of the right of one State or the other would be incompatible with that common intention.[11]

## OBLIGATIONS OF STATES PARTIES UNDER THE AFRICAN CHARTER

Both Articles 1 and 2 of the African Charter require states parties to recognise the rights and freedoms set out in the document:

> Article 1: The Member States of the Organization of African Unity parties to the present Charter shall recognize the rights, duties and freedoms enshrined in this Chapter and shall undertake to adopt legislative or other measures to give effect to them.
>
> Article 2: Every individual shall be entitled to the enjoyment of the rights and freedoms recognized and guaranteed in the present Charter without distinction of any kind such as race, ethnic group, color, sex, language, religion, political or any other opinion, national and social origin, fortune, birth or other status.

The consideration of Articles 1 and 2 is warranted not least because the effective realisation and enjoyment of the human and peoples' guaranteed by the charter is closely tied to their meaningful implementation. As an example, it is apparent from the ordinary reading of both provisions that a combined reading of their operative clauses will impute states' obligations to respect, protect, promote, and fulfil human and peoples' rights without exception. The concept of equal and non-discriminatory enjoyment of the rights articulated in the two articles also cuts across other provisions of the charter and, in particular, are found in Article 3 of the charter, which provides:

> 1. Every individual shall be equal before the law.
> 2. Every individual shall be entitled to equal protection of the law.

While Article 2 does not explicitly mention discrimination, it nonetheless prohibits it where it affects the enjoyment of a right or freedom guaran-

[11] *Belgium v Netherlands*, ICJ Reports 1959, 221–22. Similarly, the International Court of Arbitration in the *Beagle Channel* case stated: 'Although Preambles to treaties do not usually – nor are they intended to contain provisions on dispositions of substance – (in short they are not operative clauses) it is nevertheless generally accepted that they may be relevant and important as guides to the manner in which the Treaty should be interpreted, and in order, as it were, to "situate" it in respect of its object and purpose'. *Beagle Channel* 52 ILR 132 [19].

teed by the charter. As the commission has stated: 'Article 2 of the Charter [prohibits] discrimination on the basis of any of the grounds set out, among them "language . . . national or social origin, birth or other status" . . . The right to equality is very important.'[12]

Similarly, Article 3 contains a general guarantee of equality that supplements the ban on discrimination.[13] This right implies, first, that citizens will receive fair and just treatment within the legal system, and second, that without the enjoyment of the right to equality, the realisation of other human rights invariably suffers. The commission has found a violation of Articles 2 and 3 of the charter where the guarantee of legal remedies is 'only available to the wealthy and those that can afford the services of private counsel.'[14] In the *Kenneth Good* case, the commission stated more elaborately that the principle of non-discrimination is violated if: (a) equal cases are treated in a different manner; (b) a difference in treatment does not have an objective and reasonable justification; and (c) there is no proportionality between the aim sought and the means employed.[15] These requirements have been expressly set out by other human rights supervisory bodies, including the European Court of Human Rights, the Inter-American Court of Human Rights, and the Human Rights Committee.[16]

All of these provisions are important because they underline the fundamental principle upon which the charter is rooted: human dignity and security, equality of every individual before the law, and equal protection under the law; a state cannot invoke its domestic laws to avoid them,

[12] Communication 211/98, *Legal Resources Foundation vs Zambia*, para 63.

[13] See, eg, Communication 253/02, *Antonie Bissangou v Congo* (2006), para 70. As the commission stated in Communication 241/01, *Purohit and Moore v Gambia (The)* (2003), para 49, 'Articles 2 and 3 of the African Charter basically form the anti-discrimination and equal protection provisions of the African Charter. These provisions are non-derogable.'

[14] Communication 241/01 *Purohit and Moore v Gambia*, paras 53–54.

[15] Communication 313/05 *Kenneth Good v Republic of Botswana* (2010), paras 218 and 219.

[16] For example, human rights treaties, such as the International Covenant on Economic, Social and Cultural Rights, also explicitly emphasise the principle of non-discrimination and equality. See International Covenant on Economic, Social and Cultural Rights, Art 2, which is much broader than the provisions of Arts 2 and 3 of the charter in that it incorporates elements such as 'property'. The Committee on Economic, Social and Cultural Rights has asserted that Art 2 should be interpreted, to the greatest extent possible, in ways which facilitate the full protection of economic, social and cultural rights. See General Comment No 9, para 15. In addition, in its General Comment on Non-Discrimination, the UN Human Rights Committee reaffirmed the special nature of Art 26 of the International Covenant on Civil and Political Covenant, when it stated that 'the application of the principle of non-discrimination contained in Art 26 is not limited to those rights which are provided for in the Covenant [on Civil and Political Rights]'. See General Comment No 18: Non-Discrimination, in Report of the Human Rights Committee, UN GAOR, 45th Sess, Supp No 40, Annex VI, UN Doc A/45/40 (1990), 173–75. The committee also states in para 10 that 'the principle of equality sometimes requires States parties to take affirmative action in order to diminish or eliminate conditions which cause or help to perpetuate discrimination prohibited by the Covenant. For example, in a State where the general conditions of a certain part of the population prevent or impair their enjoyment of human rights, the State should take specific action to correct those conditions.'

without violating the charter. In *Legal Resource Foundation v Zambia,*[17] the commission reiterated this point when it stated pointedly that 'international treaties which are not part of domestic law and which may not be directly enforceable in the national courts nonetheless impose obligations on States Parties'. The commission has consistently underscored the centrality of the obligations assumed under the charter, and has asserted its own authority to hold states accountable even in the face of strong resistance by some states. Such was the case in *Kenneth Good v Botswana,* when the commission, citing its earlier precedent on the same matter, stated unequivocally:

> The Commission was established to make sure that the acts of the executive, legislative and judicial branches of States Parties are compatible with the provisions of the Charter. Therefore, the fact that the provisions of the Charter are not domesticated into the laws of Botswana does not bar the Commission from assessing the compatibility of Botswana laws and executive actions with the provisions of the Charter . . . If a State Party fails to recognise the provisions of the African Charter, there is no doubt that it is in violation of Article 1.[18]

However, while discrimination is prohibited in human rights law, poverty induced by large-scale corruption is not, even though poverty results in the unfair and discriminatory treatment of the economically and socially vulnerable. Poverty therefore ought to be included under the open-ended phrase 'other status'.[19] This idea will naturally follow the path of recent emergence of new international norms against discrimination on grounds of 'disability', 'sexual orientation' and 'age'. The Inter-American Court of Human Rights has already stated that the guarantee against discrimination would include grounds like 'economic situation',[20] which conceivably will include 'poverty'. It is possible to suggest that corruption has precipitated the growing inequality and discrimination in several African states. Just to cite one example, those who are rich and politically connected are insulated from the negative of effects of corruption, whereas the economically and socially vulnerable suffer the most. On this basis alone, a distinct economic and social status such as dispossession, hunger,

[17] *Legal Resource Foundation v Zambia,* Communication No 211/98 (2001), para 60.

[18] Communication 313/05, *Kenneth Good, v Botswana* (2010), paras 240 and 241.

[19] The broad interpretation of 'other status' contained in Art 2 of the African Charter was adopted by the African Commission when, in *Zimbabwe Lawyers for Human Rights,* it added 'property' to the list of grounds for discrimination and went on to define discrimination as 'any act which aims at distinction, exclusion, restriction or preference which is based *on any ground* such as race, colour, sex, language, religion, political or other opinion, national or social origin, property, birth or other status, and which has the purpose or effect of nullifying or impairing the recognition, enjoyment or exercise by all persons, on equal footing, of all rights and freedoms' [emphasis added]. *Zimbabwe Lawyers for Human Rights and Institute for Human Rights and Development in Africa (on behalf of Andrew Barclay Meldrum) v Zimbabwe,* Communication No 294/04 (2004), para 91.

[20] OC/18, *Juridical Condition and Rights of the Undocumented Migrants,* IACtHR Series A No 18 (2003) paras 100–01 and 173–74.

disease, illiteracy, insecurity and neglect – brought about by corruption – can be implied or made more explicit within the definition of 'other status'. Such an interpretative approach can help to contribute to the enjoyment of the charter's provisions by those who live in poverty (and in turn they can attain a minimum threshold of well-being that is necessary to preserve human dignity, integrity, and freedom).

The commission has gone further to identify four core elements of the obligations assumed by states parties under Article 1 of the charter.[21] The first element is for states to respect the human and peoples' rights guarantee; that is, states should do nothing to undermine or violate those rights, and the actions of states must be consistent and compatible with the provisions of the charter.[22] The second element, the obligation to protect, is more of a positive nature; that is, states must guarantee that private individuals do not violate these rights. For example, any failure to exercise due diligence to effectively achieve the rights under the charter would violate this obligation. States will still be held accountable for failing or neglecting to guarantee and protect the rights under the charter, regardless of whether such violations are directly or indirectly attributable to the state or its officials (or perpetrated by private individuals).[23]

The third element is the obligation to promote rights, including as already noted, by creating an appropriate environment for building the infrastructure necessary for their enjoyment.[24] The fourth element is the obligation to fulfil human rights; that is, states must achieve the rights and freedoms they freely undertake under the charter by moving their legal and institutional machinery towards the actual realisation of these rights.[25] Any stagnation or retrogressive steps or actions would clearly be inconsistent or incompatible with the effective implementation of this obligation.[26] For example, in *Association of Victims of Post Electoral Violence & INTERIGHTS v Cameroon*, the commission stated that failure to 'take adequate measures to prevent the violence which led to the physical harm and material damage suffered by the victims' violated Article 2, even if, as alleged by Cameroon, 'the post-election events are [an] act of God'. It then ruled that, 'the State of Cameroon failed to fulfill its obligation to protect which [is] incumbent upon the State'.[27]

[21] *Zimbabwe Human Rights NGO Forum v Zimbabwe*, Communication No 245/02 (2002) paras 151–56.

[22] ibid.

[23] ibid.

[24] ibid.

[25] ibid. The African Commission has also held that the rights guaranteed under Art 2 'are an important entitlement as the availability or lack of them affects the capacity of one to enjoy many other rights': Communication 245/02, *Zimbabwe Human Rights NGO Forum v Zimbabwe* (2002), para 81.

[26] Communication 245/02, *Zimbabwe Human Rights NGO Forum v Zimbabwe* (2002), para 81.

[27] Communication 272/03, *Association of Victims of Post Electoral Violence & INTERIGHTS v Cameroon*, paras 124–26.

Along the same lines, in the case of *Institute for Human Rights and Development in Africa, and Association Mauritanienne des Droits de l'Homme v Mauritania,* the commission stated that victims of human rights violations legitimately expected that they would receive effective remedies to restore their rights, and that the state would be held to account, including, for example, being warned to prevent similar violations in the future.[28] As one scholar put it, human rights obligations 'entail a responsibility on the state to avoid depriving, to protect from deprivation and to aid the deprived respectively'.[29] The charter, therefore, is not indifferent to the plight of the economically and socially vulnerable who have suffered human rights violations as a result of corruption in many parts of Africa.[30]

Finally, the provisions of Articles 1, 2 and 3 of the African Charter as well as the preamble have to be read in conjunction with each of the human and peoples' rights guaranteed by the charter, discussed below. It is arguable that states' obligations to remedy human rights violations caused by corruption will arise where authorities fail to do all that might reasonably be expected of them to prevent their officials from stealing public funds that would expose the citizens to real and immediate risk of violation of their rights (of which states have or ought to have knowledge) under the charter.

## HUMAN AND PEOPLES' RIGHTS AFFECTED BY CORRUPTION

### The Right to Life and Integrity of Person

Article 4 of the African Charter provides: 'Human beings are inviolable. Every human being shall be entitled to respect for his life and the integrity of his person. No one may be arbitrarily deprived of this right.' This provision is comparatively short but normatively rich as it makes clear the inviolability of the right to life, which is to be enjoyed by 'every human being'. Yet, the last paragraph of Article 4 suggests that the right to life is not absolute, being protected only against *arbitrary deprivation*. Even so, the right to life can appropriately be described as the 'mother of all human rights', given that other rights depends on the existence of life, which has been said to be 'mankind's most valuable asset from which all other

[28] *Institute for Human Rights and Development in Africa, and Association Mauritanienne des Droits de l'Homme v Mauritania,* Communication No 373/09 (2009), paras 28 and 29.

[29] Paul Arnell, 'Extraterritorial human rights: a tool for poverty reduction?' (2005) 38 *Comparative & International Law Journal of South Africa* 400.

[30] See for example, Dinah Shelton, *Remedies in International Human Rights Law* (Oxford: Oxford University Press, 1999) 358: 'Remedies not only provide redress for the individual victim, but they serve the community interest in sanctioning the perpetrator and deterring future violations by the same or other wrongdoers. They thus serve the rule of law at all levels of society . . . The nature of remedial justice, of wiping out the consequences of the wrong, is a general principle of law on which there is broad consensus.'

human possibilities arise'.[31] The commission itself has described the right to life as 'the supreme right of the human being. It is basic to all human beings and without it all other rights are without meaning.'[32]

The right to life imposes in equal measure both positive obligations to respect, promote and ensure conditions that are conducive to the exercise of the right to life, and negative obligations on states or their agents not to take life away *arbitrarily* or *unlawfully*. The correct interpretation of the Article 4 provision will be determined by discovering the appropriate meaning of the word 'arbitrarily'. The charter does not define the word, but it presumably means illegally or unjustly.[33] In *Article 19 v Eritrea*, the commission for instance noted, '[A]rbitrariness is not to be equated with against the law but must be interpreted more broadly to include elements of inappropriateness, injustice, lack of predictability and due process'.[34] The commission has consistently followed this path in its broad interpretation of this provision. The fact that the commission is able to document over 30 cases on the right to life shows the constant engagement of the commission with this provision, as well as its importance to the citizens of countries across Africa.[35] States are to take preventive measures to protect citizens' life, to ensure that the right to life is not undermined by expropriation, and to take actions through legislation and other measures to prevent loss of life.

In several cases, the commission has found that the failure of states to investigate and prosecute allegations of arbitrary and unlawful killings or to provide compensation and redress to victims has amounted to a violation of the Article 4 provisions.[36] The decision of the commission in the

[31] Baderin, *International Human Rights and Islamic Law* (n 7) 66.

[32] Communications 279/03–296/05, *Sudan Human Rights Organisation & Centre on Housing Rights and Evictions (COHRE) v Sudan* (2009), para 146.

[33] The *Oxford Advanced Learner's Dictionary* has several definitions, including: 'of an action, a decision, a rule, etc, not seeming to be based on a reason, system or plan and sometimes seeming unfair . . . Using power without restriction'. See *Oxford Advanced Learning's Dictionary*, 6th edn (Oxford: Oxford University Press, 2000) 52. *Black's Law Dictionary* defines arbitrary to include 'irrational or capricious', 'depending on individual discretion', and 'founded on prejudice or preference rather than on reason or fact'. For an interesting discussion of the word in human rights law, see, generally, Parvez Hassan, 'The Word "Arbitrary" As Used in the Universal Declaration of Human Rights Illegal Or Unjust?' (1969) 10 *Harvard International Law Journal* 225.

[34] Communication 275 (2003), *Article 19 v Eritrea*, para 93. The International Court of Justice in the case of *Elettronica Sicula SpA (ELSI) (United States of America v Italy)* Judgement 20 July 1989, ICJ Reports 1989, 128 also stated that 'arbitrariness is not so much something opposed to a rule of law, as something opposed to the rule of law . . . It is a wilful disregard of due process of law, an act which shocks or at least surprises, a sense of judicial propriety'.

[35] It should be noted that the commission has adopted several resolutions on the right to life, and has been influenced by the jurisprudence of other human rights bodies such the Human Rights Committee.

[36] See, eg, Communication 266/03, *Kevin Mgwanga Gunme et al v Cameroon* (2009), para 112; Communication 272/03, *Association of Victims of Post Electoral Violence & INTERIGHTS v Cameroon* (2009), para 115.

case of *Association of Victims of Post Electoral Violence & INTERIGHTS* is illustrative of its approach to the interpretation of Article 4. Here, the commission ruled that states must use their 'legal, technical, human and material resources' to produce the expected result of guaranteeing the protection of the right to life.[37] Thus, 'the post-electoral events which gave rise to serious violations against the lives and property of the citizens would not have taken place if the State which, through its investigations knew or should have known about the planning of the said events, had taken (within reasonable time) the necessary measures to prevent their happening'.[38] This, according to the commission, exacerbated the violence and accompanying human rights violations and destruction of property.[39]

However, despite its expansive jurisprudence on the right to life, the commission has not, regrettably, directly considered the causal relationship between corruption and the right to life. Yet, while the cases highlighted above may not be specifically related to the issue of corruption, the fundamental principles that they espoused can be read in ways that make them relevant for combating corruption. For instance, the principle of due diligence and the obligations to respect, protect, promote, and fulfil can serve as a framework to combat corruption. On this basis, large-scale corruption in society, in general, and corruption in the criminal justice system, in particular, directly violates a fundamental duty imposed by Article 4 (read together with Articles 1 and 21). It would undermine the ability and capacity of the state and its institutions to 'promote and ensure' a proper and fair administration of justice, which is necessary to guarantee and secure the right to life in its broadest sense.[40] In such an environment, it is virtually impossible for any state to fulfil either its 'positive or negative obligations' relating to the right to life, as the state is too corrupt and thus weak to ensure that life is not arbitrarily and unlawfully taken away; and when life is threatened or taken away (for example through corruption in the justice process), it cannot, for the same reasons, secure victims or their families the right to an effective remedy; that is, to investigate the violation, to punish the perpetrators, and to provide *legal standing* and effective remedies to victims.

[37] Communication 272/03, *Association of Victims of Post Electoral Violence & INTERIGHTS v Cameroon* (2009), para 115.

[38] ibid.

[39] ibid, paras 115–21.

[40] For additional support for this proposition, see, eg, Communications 279/03–296/05, *Sudan Human Rights Organisation & Centre on Housing Rights and Evictions (COHRE) v Sudan* (2009), para 147. The African Commission stated that it is the duty of the state to protect human life against unwarranted or arbitrary actions by public authorities as well as by private persons, including by taking preventive measures, establishing effective provisions in criminal law (and strong, independent and fully resourced law enforcement machinery that is able to prevent, suppress, investigate, and penalise breaches of criminal law).

The consequences of corruption on the fair administration of justice are many, but vary from country to country. They can include: inadequate training of personnel due to the stealing of budget for training (which would seriously undermine the ability of personnel to ensure safety and security of citizens); arbitrary exercise of discretion or political interference in the prosecution of politically sensitive cases (which would tilt justice in favour of the powerful and politically connected); restricted access to justice for the economically and socially vulnerable (which exacerbates their vulnerability and denies them access to justice and effective remedies); a culture of impunity that would encourage more violations of rights, leading to ineffective investigations and prosecutions; imposition and execution of the death penalty based on denial of due process of law (for example, the lack of means to afford adequate legal representation that may lead to irreparable damage);[41] deaths in custody due to torture or neglect; attacks and deaths caused by gangs tolerated by the state; or unreasonable, unnecessary, and disproportionate use of force.

The commission has interpreted the right to life innovatively to include not only civil, political rights but also economic, social, and cultural rights. This approach provides an additional norm that can plausibly serve to combat corruption. For instance, in *Social and Economic Rights Action Center v Nigeria*, the commission held that the rights to food and health were violated (even though the charter does not expressly provide for the right to food) as a result of environmental pollution that prevented people from accessing sources of existing food and caused hazardous conditions for the communities.[42] Although it was not explicitly stated, the commission's decision in this case may, by extension, be read to suggest that large-scale corruption that has corrosive effects on the quality of life of citizens may constitute a violation of Article 4 provisions. In this case, the commission indeed found a violation of Article 21, which guarantees the right of the people to wealth and natural resources, although it did not specifically use the word 'corruption'.

Yet, a broad and extensive reading of the decision would imply corruption. Even though corruption has not been specifically recognised by the commission as such, its ruling in a separate case that the term 'life [itself

[41] While the imposition of the death penalty under Art 4 of the African Charter is not, per se, unlawful, a judicial and sentencing process (such as the application of legislation that fails to meet the requirements of a fair trial as set out in Art 7 of the African Charter) induced by corruption (by preventing compliance with the minimum threshold of the rule of law and fair trial) will render it a breach of the right to life.

[42] Thus, the commission has stated that all human rights (civil, political, economic, social, and cultural) generate at least four levels of duties for a state: the obligation to respect, to protect, to promote, and to fulfil. Similarly, as noted, the obligations are both positive and negative in nature. See Communication 155/96, *Social and Economic Rights Action Center (SERAC) and Center for Economic and Social Rights (CESR) v Nigeria*, paras 44–47.

includes] the right to dignity and the right to livelihood'[43] further suggests that poverty induced by corruption may constitute a failure of a state to respect the natural resources and wealth belonging to the people, or in the commission's own words, 'to use the same resources to satisfy [citizens'] basic needs'.[44] It is obvious that the basic needs of the citizens, which the African Commission eloquently spoke of in *Social and Economic Rights Action Center (SERAC) and Center for Economic and Social Rights (CESR) v Nigeria*, cannot be met when the resources to provide those needs are stolen, diverted into private pockets, and then stashed abroad. A combined (and evolutionary) interpretation of Articles 4 and 21 would indicate that the right to life is violated when a state fails to prevent or punish corruption that results in extreme poverty, which inevitably deprives the people of their 'right to dignity and livelihood'. This progressive and logical interpretation is entirely consistent and compatible with the broad vision of the drafters of the charter.

Moreover, the ruling by the commission in *COHRE v Sudan* that 'African people are entitled to the right to dignity and livelihood' merits further discussion. As noted, despite its acknowledgement that the term life itself includes 'the right to dignity and the right to livelihood', again the commission, regrettably, has not developed an analysis of the relationship between extreme poverty caused by corruption and the denial of the rights to life, dignity and livelihood. While the concept of dignity may be difficult to capture in precise terms,[45] extreme poverty (measured, for example, through the concept of 'minimum core obligation'),[46] unarguably denies citizens the right to dignity and livelihood. Human rights derive from the inherent dignity of the human person.[47] The influential and widely respected Indian Supreme Court held that:

[43] Communications 279/03-296/05, *Sudan Human Rights Organisation & Centre on Housing Rights and Evictions (COHRE) v Sudan* (2009), para 146.

[44] Communication 155/96, *Social and Economic Rights Action Center (SERAC) and Center for Economic and Social Rights (CESR) v Nigeria*, para 45.

[45] 'Even where there is not a ... consensus on some aspect of the minimum requirements of human dignity, there may be good reason to affirm its validity'. Paolo G Carozza, 'Human Dignity and Judicial Interpretation of Human Rights: A Reply' (2008) 19 *European Journal of International Law* 937.

[46] For example, in the context of the International Covenant on Economic, Social and Cultural Rights, the UN Committee on Economic, Social and Cultural Rights has developed the concept of 'minimum core obligation'. Essentially this means that states, regardless of their level of resources (or even at times of economic downturn or other emergencies), are required to ensure that 'a significant number of individuals' within their jurisdiction enjoy at least essential levels of protection for each of the rights guaranteed by the covenant. Among others, states are required to protect their citizens from starvation, and ensure that they live a dignified life. General Comment 3, *Nature of State Obligations* (1990), para 10. Thus, 'If the Covenant were to be read in such a way as not to establish such a minimum core obligation, it would be largely deprived of its raison d'être.' Ibid.

[47] See, for example, the case of the South African Constitutional Court, *State v Makwanyane* 1995 (3) SA 391 (CC), para 328, 179 (O'Regan, J, concurring): 'The importance of dignity as a founding value of the new Constitution [and human rights treaties] cannot be overempha-

> The right to life includes the right to live with human dignity and all that goes along with it, namely, the bare necessaries of life such as adequate nutrition, clothing and shelter and facilities for reading, writing and expressing oneself in diverse forms, freely moving about and mixing and commingling with fellow human beings. The magnitude and content of the components of this right would depend upon the extent of the economic development of the country, but it must, in any view of the matter, include the right to the basic necessities of life and also the right to carry on such functions and activities constitute the bare minimum expression of the human self. Every act which offends against or impairs human dignity would constitute deprivation *pro tanto* of this right to live and it would have to be in accordance with reasonable, fair and just procedure established by law which stands the test of other fundamental rights.[48]

The jurisprudence of the Supreme Court of India might inspire both the commission and the court in advancing and elaborating on the content of the right to dignity and to livelihood alluded to by the commission in *COHRE v Sudan* so that peoples' wealth and resources are used to ensure their right to dignity and livelihood, and not stolen for the private benefit of corrupt officials. This approach can be achieved for example through the use of the precautionary principle, which has been consistently applied in several cases heard by the Indian Supreme Court. For example, in *MC Mehta v Kamal Nath,* the Court stated:

> Our legal system – based on English common law – includes the public trust doctrine as part of its jurisprudence. The State is the trustee of all natural resources which are by nature meant for public use and enjoyment. Public at large is the beneficiary of the seashore, running waters, airs, forests and ecologically fragile lands. The State as a trustee is under a legal duty to protect the natural resources. These resources meant for public use cannot be converted into private ownership.[49]

Corruption also clearly affects the right to life in cases where medications and other essentials are not made available in public hospitals because they have been diverted for the private use of senior government officials and their friends, thus putting low-income patients in unnecessary danger (as they lack the means to seek alternative or apparently more expensive medical care elsewhere), and making it very difficult for doctors and other practitioners to carry out their professions. Implicitly violated in these instances are not only the rights to life, health, and dignity for patients, but also the right to livelihood for the medical staff. The underlying effects of corruption in the violations of these rights are part of a continuum of behaviour. The argument may be extended further that the theft and diversion of critical resources to offshore accounts and the

sised. Recognising a right to dignity is an acknowledgement of the intrinsic worth of human beings: human beings are entitled to be treated as worthy of respect and concern.'

[48] *Francis Coralie Mullin v Adm'r, Union Territory of Delhi* (1981) 2 SCR 516, 529.

[49] *MC Mehta v Kamal Nath* (1997) 1 SCC 388, 34.

failure of states to effectively bring suspected perpetrators to justice may satisfy the requirement of 'arbitrary deprivation' of life. These activities contribute significantly to a culture of impunity and a lack of accountability of states and their officials, and deny victims the protections of due process established under the African Charter. The inherent nature of the right to life, specifically, and the special nature of human rights generally, demand holistic and comprehensive interpretations, if only to ensure that these rights are made practical, effective, and concrete in individual situations. Is it not then now the time for the underlying effects of large-scale corruption to be considered a direct or indirect detriment to the human rights to life, dignity, and livelihood?

### The Right against all Forms of Slavery, Slave Trade, Torture and Inhumane or Degrading Treatment

Article 5 of the African Charter provides that:

> Every individual shall have the right to the respect of the dignity inherent in a human being and to the recognition of his legal status. All forms of exploitation and degradation of man particularly slavery, slave trade, torture, cruel, inhuman or degrading punishment and treatment shall be prohibited.

Article 5 is clearly very broad in its scope and application,[50] presumably to avoid an overtly narrow approach. This provision allows neither restrictions nor derogation, even in time of public emergencies. According to the commission, Article 5 is 'aimed at the protection of both the dignity of the human person, and the physical and mental integrity of the individual'.[51] The contents of this right and the obligations of states have been further elaborated by the commission through the drafting and adoption of the Robben Island Guidelines.[52] Similarly, the commission has interpreted Article 5 in some 60 cases that have come before it. The commission has found that 'cruel, inhuman, or degrading treatment' includes not only

[50] Not many cases have come before the commission involving slavery, the few that have been heard mostly coming from Mauritania, where the commission has found 'practices analogous to slavery' in violation of Art 5. The commission has also used the ground of 'consequences of slavery in Mauritania' to find violation of Art 14 on the right to property. See, for example, Communications 54/91, 61/91, and 210/98.

[51] Communications 279/03–296/05, *Sudan Human Rights Organisation & Centre on Housing Rights and Evictions (COHRE) v Sudan* (2009), para 155. Since the African Charter does not define the meaning of the phrase 'torture or inhuman or degrading treatment or punishment', the African Commission (in this and other cases) relied on the meanings provided under Art 1, para 156 of the United Nations Convention against Torture.

[52] Resolution on Guidelines and Measures for the Prohibition and Prevention of Torture, Cruel, Inhuman or Degrading Treatment or Punishment in Africa, ACHPR/Res 61 (XXXII) 02. The guidelines were adopted in 2002 at the 32nd Ordinary Session of the African Commission. The commission established a follow-up committee in 2004, at its 35th Ordinary Session.

actions that caused serious physical or psychological suffering, but also that humiliated individuals or forced him or her against his or her will or conscience,[53] and that the phrase includes the widest possible protection against abuses, including physical or mental.[54]

The commission has also found violation of Article 5 in several cases of 'widespread utilization of torture, and of cruel, inhuman and degrading forms of treatment' involving Mauritania and concerning abuses against prisoners, including beating, burning, electrical shocks, rape of women, leaving prisoners to 'die slow deaths',[55] denying detainees' visitations (inhumane treatment of both the detainee and the family concerned);[56] deplorable prison conditions;[57] denial of bathroom facilities;[58] detention in dirty, hidden, and underground cells;[59] soaking detainees in cold water; destruction of homes of human rights defenders;[60] lack of access to medicine;[61] the use in court of evidence obtained through torture;[62] and personal suffering and indignity occasioned by forcing individuals to live as stateless persons under degrading conditions.[63] Torture and ill-treatment are thus a tool for discriminatory treatment of persons who are subjected by the state or by non-state actors exercising control over such persons.

It is, however, the peculiar circumstances of each case that determine whether an act constitutes inhuman, degrading treatment, or punishment.[64] Even so, the validity of the aim of Article 5 to protect the dignity of the person, as well as their physical integrity, can hardly be contested. As the commission put it, '[T]here is no right for individuals, and particularly the government of a country to apply physical violence to individuals for offences. Such a right would be tantamount to sanctioning State

[53] Communication 334/06, *Egyptian Initiative for Personal Rights and Interights v Arab Republic of Egypt* (2011), para 190.

[54] Communication 224/98, *Media Rights Agenda v Nigeria*, para 71. See also Communications 25/89, 47/90, 56/91, and 100/93, *Free Legal Assistance Group, Lawyers' Committee for Human Rights, Union Interafricaine des Droits de lHomme, les Temoins de Jehovah v Zaire*; and Communication 232/99, *John D Ouko v Kenya*.

[55] Consolidated Communications 54/91, 61/91, 98/93, 164/97–196/97, and 210/98.

[56] Communications 48/90, 50/91, and 83/93.

[57] The African Commission has adopted many standards on the improvement of prison conditions in Africa. These include Resolution on Prisons in Africa, ACHPR/Res 19 (XVII) 95 and Resolution on the Adoption of the Ouagadougou Declaration and Plan of Action on Accelerating Prison and Penal Reform in Africa, ACHPR/Res 64 (XXXIV) 03. The commission has also appointed a Special Rapporteur on Prisons and Conditions of Detention.

[58] Communication 232/99.

[59] Communications 143/95, 150/96.

[60] Communications 140/94, 141/94.

[61] Communication 151/96: *Civil Liberties Organisation v Nigeria*, para 27.

[62] Communication 334/06, *Egyptian Initiative for Personal Rights and Interights v Arab Republic of Egypt* (2011), para 156.

[63] Communication 97/97, *John K Modise v Botswana* (2000); and Communication 212/98, *Amnesty International v Zambia* (1998).

[64] ibid, para 37.

sponsored torture under the [African] Charter and contrary to the very nature of this human rights treaty.'[65] Furthermore, human dignity is an inherent basic right to which all human beings are entitled without discrimination, regardless of their mental capabilities or disabilities, and which every state is obliged to respect and to protect by all means possible.[66] In *John Modise v Botswana*, the commission elaborated further, noting 'exposing victims to personal sufferings and indignity violates the right to human dignity'.[67]

The commission has also recognised the right to a lawyer as part of the prohibition against torture and procedural safeguards for victims.[68] It has stressed that 'the right to be brought promptly before a judicial authority constitutes an essential safeguard against torture and ill-treatment'.[69] Through a combined reading of Articles 7 and 26, the commission has also held that 'having access to appropriate justice and the independence of a justice system [are] the bedrock of a sound justice delivery system'.[70] This is fully consonant with the respect for human dignity contained in Article 5 of the African Charter, which is 'the central concept and value and serves as a touchstone for the assessment of state conduct'.[71] Among the ways in which a state can fulfil its obligation are a transparent, independent and efficient legal system, with effective investigations and prosecution of allegations of torture or ill-treatment, and by providing compensation to the victims. Unfortunately, non-compliance grants wide discretion to states in the administration of their justice processes, thereby ultimately undermining the fairness, impartiality, and independence of criminal justice and law enforcement systems. There is thus a strong causal link between a state's obligation to prevent torture or ill-treatment and to ensure full and effective access to justice and procedural guarantees.

Yet, despite its detailed and impressive jurisprudence on Article 5, the commission has not considered the link between corruption and the persistent practice of torture or ill-treatment. As noted, the commission's lack of effort in this regard cuts across all the provisions of the charter, and not just Article 5. Nonetheless, as the above exposition of the jurisprudence of

[65] ibid, para 42.

[66] Communications 279/03–296/05, *Sudan Human Rights Organisation*, para 156.

[67] Communication 97/93, *John Modise v Botswana* (2000).

[68] Robben Island Guidelines, para 20. See also Resolution 61/153 of 2007, reaffirming the UN Body of Principles for the Protection of All Persons under Any Form of Detention or Imprisonment, in which the General Assembly underscored that permitting prompt and regular access to legal counsel constitutes an 'effective measure for the prevention of torture and other cruel, inhuman or degrading treatment and punishment'.

[69] Robben Island Guidelines, para 20. See also Communication 334/06, *Egyptian Initiative for Personal Rights and Interights*, para 185.

[70] ibid, para 195.

[71] Chidi Anselm Odinkalu, 'Analysis of Paralysis or Paralysis by Analysis? Implementing Economic, Social and Cultural Rights under the African Charter on Human and Peoples' Rights' (2001) 23 *Human Rights Quarterly* 366.

the commission suggests, one connection of the effects of corruption on the prohibition of torture and ill-treatment contained in Article 5 is through the relationship between torture and poverty. Although most of the cases of torture that are in the media have involved political opposition and human rights activists, there is evidence to suggest that the majority of people subjected to torture and ill-treatment are the economically and socially vulnerable,[72] since they do not have access to good lawyers (and legal aid remains unavailable or very limited for most) and are frequently denied access to their families. Poor women also face gender-specific forms of torture, including rape, sexual abuse and harassment, virginity testing, and forced abortions or miscarriage.[73]

Moreover, it is often the case that where there is corruption and resultant extreme poverty, poor children are in prisons, institutions, or refugee camps, and they face severe conditions, including overcrowding, insanitary conditions, and inadequate and/or insufficient food and clothing. Children's lack of access to medical, emotional, educational, rehabilitative, and recreational support can be exceedingly traumatising, and may constitute cruel or inhuman treatment. Criminal suspects who are economically and socially vulnerable may not know that they have the right not to be tortured, or if tortured or ill-treated, to seek redress and effective remedies.[74] These categories of people and their families are rarely accorded any respect by the police, prosecutors, or judges. For instance, while in detention, the economically and socially vulnerable are often denied access to life-saving health care or nutritious food, because medicine and food are frequently stolen and diverted to prison personnel, who are often underpaid and undertrained. The criminal justice systems in several countries in Africa are perhaps the most exposed sector of governance to corruption. The reality and perception of corruption in the law enforcement and criminal justice systems is especially damaging because it affects public trust and confidence in the systems, and ultimately undermines citizens' access to justice, which is a fundamental element of a proper and efficient administration of justice. Thus, corruption in this sector would invariably threaten people's access to fair trial, contribute to discrimination (as it would allow only those with means to purchase

[72] The UN Special Rapporteur on Torture stated in his report: 'It is true that many of the more high-profile cases of torture that come to international attention concern people involved in political activities of various sorts. Such victims of torture may well be of a class or connected with organizations that have international contacts. The experience of missions in several parts of the world has led the Special Rapporteur to observe, however, that the overwhelming majority of those subjected to torture and ill-treatment are ordinary common criminals from the lowest strata of society.' UN E/CN 4/1995/34 and E/CN 4/1996/35.

[73] ibid.

[74] As the UN Special Rapporteur on Torture noted, '[T]hey are often members of the lowest level of an underclass that is disconnected from all opportunity of leading decent lives as productive economic citizens.' Ibid.

access to the justice system), and victimise the economically and socially vulnerable.

Additionally, as is the case with the other provisions of the charter, states' obligations under Article 1 apply to Article 5. When read together, therefore, an obligation of states to ensure due process of law in their respective criminal justice system becomes clear. Thus, states are not only to refrain from using their criminal justice systems to perpetrate torture, inhuman and degrading treatment, or punishment, but must also enact necessary policies and legislation and to put in place administrative measures against the practices prohibited under Article 5. Any discriminatory or non-implementation of such policies, legislation, or administrative measures as a result of corruption not only exposes innocent citizens to torture or inhuman and degrading treatment, but also denies them their right to an effective remedy. Obviously, a criminal justice system that is weakened by corruption will provide a fertile ground for such actions and encourage a culture of impunity, since such violations will neither be truly investigated nor prosecuted. A further legal proposition needs to be put forward: by failing to prevent and combat corruption in its criminal justice system, a state also may be failing in its due diligence, which requires it to organise its governmental apparatus to prevent torture and inhuman and degrading treatment and to punish suspected perpetrators where this occurs.[75] Yet, in most cases, victims of human rights violations cannot access international accountability mechanisms without first seeking remedies through their local justice system.[76]

## The Right to Liberty and Security of Person

Article 6 of the African Charter provides:

> Every individual shall have the right to liberty and to the security of his person. No one may be deprived of his freedom except for reasons and conditions previously laid down by law. In particular, no one may be arbitrarily arrested or detained.

[75] See, for example, No 16 of the Robben Island Guidelines, which states that 'in order to combat impunity States should: a) ensure that those responsible for acts of torture or ill-treatment are subject to legal process; and b) ensure that there is no immunity from prosecution for nationals suspected of torture, and that the scope of immunities for foreign nationals who are entitled to such immunities be as restrictive as is possible under international law'.

[76] The rationale of the Exhaustion of Local Remedies rule in the African Charter and other international instruments is to ensure that before proceedings are brought before an international body, the state has had the opportunity to remedy matters through its own local system. However, the African Commission has stated on several occasions that the condition of exhaustion of local remedies cannot act as an unjustifiable impediment to access international remedies.

Article 6 guarantees the right to liberty and security of the person and aims to protect those in detention who are unable to help themselves because their protection, welfare, and security depend on the decisions of prison and police authorities. The ultimate aim is to ensure the security, safety, and freedom of individuals, whether or not they are in detention. Thus, Article 6 requires states to protect persons within their jurisdiction from non-state actors. The commission underscored the importance of this right in several cases, and defined personal liberty as:

> [A] fundamental condition, which everyone should generally enjoy. Its deprivation is something that is likely to have a direct and adverse effect on the enjoyment of other rights, ranging from the right to family and private life, through the right to freedom of assembly, association and expression, to the right to freedom of movement.[77]

Simply put, the right to liberty is the 'right to be free',[78] that is, freedom from restraint and the ability to do as one pleases as long as it is lawful and does not affect the rights of others. So far, the commission has heard nearly 60 cases on Article 6 provisions. In *Amnesty International v Sudan*,[79] the commission stated: 'Article 6 must be interpreted in such a way as to permit arrests only in the exercise of powers normally granted to the security forces in a democratic society.'[80] Similarly, in *Purohit and Moore v The Gambia*, the commission held that prohibitions against arbitrariness require that deprivation of liberty 'shall be under the authority and supervision of persons procedurally and substantively competent to certify it'.[81] Nonetheless, arbitrariness is not synonymous with *against the law*, 'but must be interpreted more broadly to include elements of inappropriateness, injustice, lack of predictability and due process of law'.[82] On this account, while an arrest or detention may be legal under national law, it may nonetheless be illegal due to its unpredictable nature or from being inappropriate or unjust.[83]

As noted, Article 6 also guarantees the right to security of the person. The commission has stated that although the right to liberty and to security are closely linked, they are nonetheless different.[84] According to the commission, 'security of the person can be seen as an expansion of rights based on prohibitions of torture and cruel and unusual punishment . . .

[77] Communications 279/03–296/05, *Sudan Human Rights Organisation & Centre on Housing Rights and Evictions (COHRE) v Sudan* (2009), para 171.

[78] ibid, 172.

[79] Communications 48/90, 50/91, 52/91 and 89/93, *Amnesty International v Sudan*, para 59.

[80] ibid.

[81] Communication 241/01, *Purohit and Moore v Gambia (The)* (2003).

[82] Communication 275/03, *Article 19 v Eritrea*, para 93.

[83] ibid.

[84] Communications 279/03–296/05, *Sudan Human Rights Organisation & Centre on Housing Rights and Evictions (COHRE) v Sudan* (2009), para 173.

The right to security of the person includes, *inter alia*, national and individual security.'[85] However, the enjoyment of the right to liberty and security of person is subject to the law. Even so, governments cannot justify violations of the charter by relying on the limitations under Article 6;[86] they must, in fact, convince the commission that the measures or conditions they are taking are in compliance with Article 6.[87]

The commission has found that the following violate Article 6: failure of a state to take appropriate measures to protect the physical integrity of its citizens from abuse either by official authorities or other citizens/third parties;[88] arbitrary arrest;[89] indefinite detention;[90] prolonged detention without charge;[91] arrests without reasons;[92] and mass arrests and round-ups of political or human rights defenders and journalists.[93] As with other rights guaranteed by the charter, the obligations regarding Article 6 are both positive and negative in nature.

Corruption affects the enjoyment of the right guaranteed under Article 6 in several ways. In the first place, it seriously weakens the institutions of the state, including the infrastructure of prisons (contributing to the phenomenon of 'decent prison cells' for the wealthy while the disadvantaged are accommodated in dirty and unhygienic cells) and police stations, by taking away the resources that would normally be available for the establishment and maintenance of such infrastructure and the training programmes for prison and police officers, and creates arbitrariness in the exercise of law enforcement and criminal justice functions. This frequently contributes to arbitrary arrests and prolonged detentions (which can put detainees at risk of ill-treatment and other violations of human rights) without any legal justification. The end result of collapsed prison infrastructure and detention facilities clearly would be unnecessary suffering for prisoners and detainees who often face exceedingly harsh treatment in overcrowded cells, often without food, water, or other basic necessities of

[85] ibid, paras 174 and 175.

[86] Communication 266/03, *Kevin Mgwanga Gunme et al v Cameroon*, para 118. With this case the commission reaffirmed its jurisprudence that 'no State Party to the Charter should avoid its responsibility by recourse to the limitations and "claw back" clauses in the Charter . . . The Charter must be interpreted holistically and all clauses must reinforce each other.'

[87] ibid.

[88] Communications 279/03–296/05, *Sudan Human Rights Organisation & Centre on Housing Rights and Evictions (COHRE) v Sudan* (2009), para 179.

[89] Communication 292/04, *Institute for Human Rights and Development in Africa v Angola* (2008), para 54. In its Resolution on the Right to Recourse Procedure and Fair Trial, the African Commission further states that 'persons who are arrested shall be informed at the time of arrest, in a language which they understand of the reason for their arrest and shall be informed promptly of any charges against them'. Ibid.

[90] Communications 25/89, 47/90, 56/91 and 100/93.

[91] Communications 137/94, 139/94, 154/96.

[92] Communications 222/98–229/99, *Law Office of Ghazi Suleiman v Sudan* (2002).

[93] Communications 54/91, 61/91, 98/93, and 164/97–196/97.

life (presumably because they have been stolen, or the budget for this purpose simply disappeared). One would consider these conditions distressing, as they exceed the unavoidable level of suffering inherent in detention, and in any case, incompatible with respect for human dignity. Yet, it is common for citizens who are economically and socially vulnerable to be detained for non-criminal matters, such as disputes with relatives or neighbours, or for civil debts. These groups of citizens are often the targets for police roadblocks or during police raids, and only those that can pay bribes avoid arbitrary detention.

In other instances, arbitrary arrests and detentions are justified on the basis of 'orders from above'. This is often the case with human rights defenders, anti-corruption activists, and opposition leaders who are arrested for exposing corruption of high-ranking official or for simply criticising the government. These politically motivated arrests lead to violations of other human rights, such as the freedoms of opinion and expression, association, assembly, and political participation. Occasionally, arrests are made by those without the legal powers to do so and without any repercussions for their actions. Similarly, applications and the legal process for securing the release of anyone wrongly detained are often ineffective and, again, compromised by corruption, leading to a further violation of the right to effective remedies. Detainees who are too poor to afford a lawyer often are asked to defend themselves because of a state's lack of resources to establish an effective legal aid system. Where legal representation is provided, it is often weak and ineffective.

In several countries, families cannot even visit their loved ones in detention without paying bribes. Officials who engage in arbitrary arrests and detentions are rarely punished, contributing further to a climate of impunity. Where corruption is the norm, the judiciary is often affected, as judges' appointments, and any promotions, are frequently based on political and pecuniary considerations, rather than on merit. Even where there are established constitutional and legal frameworks regulating the criminal justice system, they are less likely to be implemented if there is corruption, as constitutions and laws are often selectively applied. Where the constitutional and legal frameworks are already weak, senior public officials are unlikely to embark on any serious legal and judicial reforms, without sustained pressure and legal (and other advocacy) interventions from the citizens.

Overall, without strong, transparent, and corruption-free institutions, it is impossible to achieve an effective and functional administration of justice, which is the basic foundation for the meaningful enjoyment of Article 6 guarantees. As the UN Working Group on Arbitrary Detention observed: '[T]he corruption [which the Working Group] has observed in some countries [including Africa] makes the whole system of guarantees devoid of any content and reduces the credibility of the entire administration of justice system.'[94] The Working Group also noted that 'during the various visits [it] conducted, the devastating effects caused by corruption on the effective fulfilment of human rights, including the right to be free from arbitrary detention', were clear, and so urged states to ratify the UN Convention against Corruption.[95] According to the Working Group,

> [O]ne main cause for [the] discrepancy between theory and practice [of human rights] [is] the issue of corruption, which it observed to continue to exist among some officials in the police, the judicial, legislative and other State institutions. When police officers, prison administration staff, judicial civil servants, judges, public prosecutors and lawyers approach individuals deprived of their liberty varyingly, depending on whether or not bribes or other irregular payments or favours have been received, then the whole system of guarantees becomes devoid of any content, empty and meaningless; it renders defenceless all those who cannot or refuse to pay the amounts that are asked from them and in turn further reduces the credibility of the entire system of administration of justice. . . . From the viewpoint of the mandate of the Working Group, it is considered that corruption can have an enormous consequence on any legal system in that corruption prevents such legal systems from being effective instruments for its eradication. If there is a legal system perceived to be generally corrupt, it is essential to analyse in the first place the underlying root causes facilitating corrupt conduct . . . However, the Working Group considers it important, among other things, to highlight the following: the absence of a system of information for citizens with respect to their rights and a lack of awareness resulting from it; the lack of transparency in judicial proceedings due to their obscurity and complexity; and the absence of effective instruments to investigate into and redress allegations of corruption which can be approached anonymously.[96]

Corruption can also undermine the stability and security of societies, institutions, values of governance and democracy, ethical values and justice, sustainable development, and the rule of law. The breakdown of the rule of law, the lack of public trust and confidence in the administration of justice, and the denial of access to justice often contribute to insecurity in many parts of Africa, and consequently lead to self-regulation, whereby vigilante groups, armed gangs, militants and similar groups spring up, engaging in kidnapping and abduction for ransom. In such an environment, the government, already weakened by corruption, would be helpless as it is often unable to provide the much-needed protection for its citizens, as it is too unstable to put into place credible measures that prevent such gangs from attacking citizens, mostly the economically and socially vulnerable. The inadequacy of a state's approach to security is evident at several stages: shortcomings in the prevention of violence, a lack of adequate victim support or access to remedies, and a serious

[94] UN Working Group, A/HRC/10/21 16 February 2009.
[95] ibid, para 56.
[96] ibid, paras 59–63.

dearth of resources (primarily due to corruption) and political will to investigate incidents of violence. Equally disturbing, corruption is usually present and widespread in law enforcement, eroding the citizenry's trust in the rule of law and contributing to a sense of lawlessness that further leads to more violence and abuse. This invariably would undermine the primary duty of a state to guarantee the security of its population, and the absence of concrete measures contributes to the continuation of violence.

## The Right to a Fair Trial

Article 7 of the African Charter provides:

> 1. Every individual shall have the right to have his cause heard. This comprises:
>
> (a) the right to an appeal to competent national organs against acts of violating his fundamental rights as recognized and guaranteed by conventions, laws, regulations and customs in force;
> (b) the right to be presumed innocent until proved guilty by a competent court or tribunal;
> (c) the right to defence, including the right to be defended by counsel of his choice;
> (d) the right to be tried within a reasonable time by an impartial court or tribunal.
>
> 2. No one may be condemned for an act or omission which did not constitute a legally punishable offence at the time it was committed. No penalty may be inflicted for an offence for which no provision was made at the time it was committed. Punishment is personal and can be imposed only on the offender.

Article 7 is one of the few detailed provisions of the charter.[97] It is, therefore, the provision with which the commission is most engaged, having decided close to 80 cases on it. Article 7 provisions grant protection to those arrested and detained, but it also guarantees the right of access of any citizens to independent and impartial judicial bodies to obtain effective remedies. This article complements Article 26, which provides that: 'States Parties to the present Charter shall have the duty to guarantee the independence of the courts and shall allow the establishment and improvement of appropriate national institutions entrusted with the promotion and protection of the rights and freedoms guaranteed by the

[97] However, unlike Art 14 of the International Covenant on Civil and Political Rights, Art 7 of the African Charter does not explicitly provide for the right to a public hearing, to interpretation, or the right against self-incrimination and double jeopardy. Nonetheless, the jurisprudence of the commission indicates that it has interpreted Art 7 to include these rights. The commission has developed detailed standards to expand the content of Art 7, including its adoption of a 1992 Resolution on the Right to a Fair Trial and the 2003 Principles and Guidelines on the Right to Fair Trial and Legal Aid in Africa.

present Charter.' The guarantees contained in Article 7 aim to ensure citizens' access to a fair and efficient administration of justice in order to enjoy the rights to an effective remedy. As the commission stated,

> A combined reading of Articles 7 and 26 brings to the fore two core issues – having access to appropriate justice and the other relating to the independence of justice system. These two issues constitute the bedrock of a sound justice delivery system. The African Commission believes that the right to a fair trial is analogous with the concept of access to appropriate justice and requires that one's cause be heard by efficient and impartial courts.[98]

Article 7(1)(d) provides for a trial within a reasonable time and by an impartial court, and it builds on Article 26, which requires states to 'guarantee the independence of the Courts' in their respective countries. Similarly, in its Principles and Guidelines on Fair Trial the commission stated:

> [J]udicial bodies shall be established by law to have adjudicative functions to determine matters within their competence on the basis of the rule of law and in accordance with proceedings conducted in the prescribed manner; there should not be any inappropriate or unwarranted interference with the judicial process nor shall decisions be subject to revision except through judicial review.[99]

Article 7 is also directly linked with Article 4 on the right to life; Article 5 on torture and ill-treatment; and Article 6 on liberty and security of person. For example, in the case of *International Pen and Others (on behalf of Saro-Wiwa) v Nigeria* the commission found that the execution and implementation of a death sentence emanating from a trial that did not conform to Article 7 amounted to an arbitrary deprivation of life.[100] The commission stated that Article 7 provisions include the right 'to the execution of a judgment'.[101] Even procedural rules cannot be allowed to frustrate the obligations of states parties relating to the application of Article 7, or any other provisions of the charter for that matter.[102] Furthermore, under Article 7, anyone who feels that his or her rights have been violated is entitled to take the case before appropriate national organs, including the courts. Another layer of the right to a fair trial is that it must be enjoyed without discrimination of any kind, and be accessible to all.[103] Non-nationals are entitled to the enjoyment of this right, just as are nationals.[104]

[98] Communication 334/06, *Egyptian Initiative for Personal Rights and Interights*, para 195.

[99] Principles and Guidelines on Fair Trial, ss A(4)(b); A(4)(f); A(4)(g); A(4)(a); and A(4)(h).

[100] Communications 137/94, 139/94, 154/96, and 161/97, *International Pen and Others (on behalf of Saro-Wiwa) v Nigeria* (2000), para 103.

[101] Communication 253/2002, para 75.

[102] Communication 243/2001, *Women's Legal Aid Center (on behalf of Sophia Moto v Tanzania* (2004).

[103] Communication 313/05, *Kenneth Good v Republic of Botswana* (2010), para 162.

[104] ibid, para 163.

As the commission stated, 'Can a victim's right to have his cause heard be limited or derogated upon for "public interest"? The answer to this is NO.'[105]

In terms of the content of the right and obligations contained in this provision, the commission has found violations of Article 7 to include: failure to allow right of appeal to a higher tribunal in deportations and denial of citizenships cases;[106] nullification of court decisions by executive decrees;[107] absence of the right of mental health detainees to challenge the lawfulness of their detention;[108] laws preventing national courts from examining the constitutionality of an executive act;[109] ousting the jurisdiction of national courts from granting bail;[110] requiring an accused person to defend himself and using a confessions obtained by force in reaching a verdict;[111] public officials openly asserting the guilt of individuals facing trial;[112] use of national security grounds to prevent a public trial;[113] judicial bodies not established by law;[114] inappropriate or unwarranted interference with the judicial process;[115] and non-independence of judicial bodies from the Executive branch.[116]

Overall, the notion of fair hearing requires that the procedures of a trial should not prejudice the accused, the general public or the victims. The scales of justice must be held so as to maintain an even balance. On the other hand, a perception of unfairness and injustice or miscarriage of justice is created when the judiciary in particular and the justice system in general is susceptible to corruption and political influence. This in turn contributes to the loss of public trust and confidence in the judicial process. In such an environment, citizens are less likely to approach the courts to seek justice in cases of violations of their human and peoples' rights; and 'self-justice' or 'self-help' naturally becomes the norm. In addition, corruption inevitably has adverse effects on the fair and predictable administration of criminal justice; and on law enforcement's ability to prevent, detect, investigate and prosecute criminals and to apprehend malefactors. Corruption among law enforcement agencies can also threaten transnational initiatives to promote and assure security and

105 ibid, para 175.

106 Communication 156/96, Communication 97/93.

107 Communications 140/94, 141/94 and 145/95.

108 Communication 241/2001.

109 Communication 129/94, *Civil Liberties Organization (in respect of the Nigerian Bar Association) v Nigeria*.

110 Communication 251/2002, *Lawyers for Human Rights v Swaziland*.

111 Communication 54/91, *Malawi African Association and others v Mauritania*.

112 Communications 222/98 and 229/99.

113 Communication 224/98.

114 Communication 334/06, *Egyptian Initiative for Personal Rights and Interights*, paras 123, 124 and 131.

115 ibid.

116 ibid.

safety of African citizens. Lack of judicial independence and impartiality (and uncertain tenure of judges) when combined with the failure to prevent corruption or properly investigate allegations of corruption in the justice system and punish offenders contributes to a culture of impunity, and consequently, a system that is unable to provide either a fair trial or equality of arms. Specifically, it compromises equal access to justice, and hands over the temple of justice to the highest bidders, while conversely, the economically and socially vulnerable suffer discrimination, judicial abuses, are denied the right to an independent and impartial court, [117] to counsel, and to be tried within a reasonable time. At the same time, the outright theft of budgeted resources creates a dysfunctional system of administration of justice, thus contributing to a slow pace of justice. Yet justice delayed is justice denied.

Although it is clear from the preceding discussion regarding Articles 4, 5 and 6 that corruption undermines the right to a fair trial, the commission has, again, not as yet specifically considered this issue. While it has spoken about 'a process that denied [the suspects] due process', it has not explicitly used the word corruption in cases where corruption had apparently contributed to undermining the right to a fair trial.[118] Yet, corruption in the judiciary involves not only mass theft of funds budgeted for the judicial branch of government, but also bribe-taking by the judiciary and support staff, or simply trading in influence through, for example, political or judicial patronage. Even the power over appointments, nominations, and selection of judges for training may be tainted with corruption to achieve undue private advantage (in some cases, candidates are asked to pay for the appointment). Yet, there is hardly a public trust more imperative than the exercise of the constitutional power to recruit and select members of the judiciary on the basis of merit, integrity, quality, competence and equality.

Even in countries where the judiciary may be independent, corruption in other agencies of the criminal justice system, such as police departments, can undermine people's access to justice and jeopardise their right to a fair trial. Allowing citizens to sue in order to challenge these violations brought about by corruption would arguably serve the best interest of justice, help to reduce corruption, and contribute to better protection of human rights. Furthermore, corruption in the judicial and criminal justice

[117] Communication 334/06, *Egyptian Initiative for Personal Rights and Interights v Arab Republic of Egypt* (2011), para 204. The African Commission noted that 'in all cases, the independence of a court must be judged in relation to the degree of independence of the judiciary vis-à-vis the executive. This implies the consideration of the manner in which its members are appointed, the duration of their mandate, the existence of protection against external pressures and the issue of real or perceived independence: as the saying goes, justice must not only be done: it must be seen to be done.' Ibid, para 206.

[118] ibid. See eg, Communication 334/06, *Egyptian Initiative for Personal Rights and Interights v Arab Republic of Egypt* (2011), para 232.

systems, and the corresponding breakdown of the rule of law, would provide a fertile environment and incentives for the following serious human rights violations to occur:[119] mass arrests and detentions of citizens asserting their right to freedom of assembly and association; torture and ill-treatment of suspects during their detention by law enforcement and security agencies during their 'confession' of involvement in a particular crime; held incommunicado without access to a lawyer; denial of necessary medical attention or examination during interrogation sessions; and imposing the death sentence (even, in some cases, execution) following a seriously flawed process.[120]

As noted, corruption will have similar effects on the law enforcement processes, such as altering or manipulating evidence at the level of investigation. As Susan Rose-Ackerman eloquently stated, 'A corrupt or politically dependent judiciary can facilitate high-level corruption, undermine reforms, and override legal norms. When the judiciary is part of the corrupt system, the wealthy and the corrupt operate with impunity, confident that a well-placed pay-off will deal with any legal problems.'[121]

Another area where the right to a fair trial is frequently violated is in the unjust or unfair prosecution of corruption cases, where suspects are immediately presumed guilty rather than innocent until found guilty. The fight against corruption may also be characterised by selectivity. Yet, fair trial standards are to apply in all situations, to all persons, and to all cases, even to those involving corrupt senior officials or opposition leaders. Using anti-corruption measures (or allegations of corruption) to deliberately violate or contribute to undermining the human rights of suspects to the presumption of innocence, no matter their antecedents or previous records, will contradict Article 7 provisions. Even so, any abuse of due process and the lack of fairness by defence counsel, through the use of legal techniques to delay or frustrate the legal process or to target judges with integrity, should be avoided at all times.

The UN Special Rapporteur on the Independence of Lawyers and Judges has summed the impact of corruption on the effective administration of justice thus:

[119] See eg, the Robben Island Guidelines, para 20, which requires states to make sure that 'all persons who are deprived of their liberty by public order or authority should have that detention controlled by properly and legally constituted regulations. Such regulations should provide a number of basic safeguards, all of which shall apply from the moment when they are first deprived of their liberty'.

[120] The African Commission, in the case of *International Pen and Others (on behalf of Wiwa) v Nigeria*, took the view that the execution and implementation of a death sentence emanating from a trial that did not conform to Art 7 of the African Charter amounts to an arbitrary deprivation of life.

[121] Susan Rose-Ackerman, *Corruption and Government: Causes, Consequences, and Reform* (Cambridge: Cambridge University Press, 1999) 151.

> Corruption of the judiciary is one of the most pernicious threats to the rule of law and one of the most difficult to eradicate. There are many contributing factors. High levels of corruption and judicial apathy are often attributed to the poor remuneration of judges and lawyers and the judiciary's lack of financial independence; however, the Special Rapporteur would stress the significance of other factors such as judges' ideological or political allegiances. The Special Rapporteur's experience shows that such factors have a decisive impact on judges' ability to act in an effective, independent and impartial manner, in accordance with their professional ethics, particularly when several contributing factors coincide with a weak institutional framework and a culture of corruption. These situations often arise in countries where the principles of judicial independence and international fair trial standards are not well established. The Special Rapporteur has therefore strongly urged States to adopt and subscribe to the Bangalore Principles of Judicial Conduct.[122]

On this basis, victims of corruption ought to be able to avail themselves of Article 7 protection if they can for example show that due process has been violated and that the judicial proceedings are far from being impartial because the judge is corrupt.

## The Right to Information and Freedom of Expression

Under Article 9 of the African Charter:

1. Every individual shall have the right to receive information.
2. Every individual shall have the right to express and disseminate his opinions within the law.

Article 9(1) and (2) are substantively similar because the right 'to receive information' is derived from the 'right to express and disseminate' one's opinions. Perhaps the guarantee under Article 9 is the most universally recognised, though probably the least respected, human right. This is especially true in developing countries, including across African states, where seeking and attaining the truth is seen generally as inherently injurious to the existence or survival of governments. Yet, there is no doubt that the right to receive information and the freedom to express one's opinion is of paramount importance, not only because it oils the engine of a representative democracy but also because it creates a free and open environment, or what Justice Oliver Wendell Holmes has described as the 'marketplace of ideas' – a *sine qua non* to the full development and self-fulfilment of society. The commission has so far heard nearly 40 cases on Article 9 provisions and has stated: 'the right to freedom of expression is a fundamental individual human right which is also a cornerstone of democracy and a means of ensuring the respect for all human rights and

[122] UN Doc A/HRC/4/25, 18 January 2007, para 19.

freedoms'.[123] According to the commission, freedom of expression under the charter has two primary elements: the right to receive information and the right to express and disseminate opinion.

In *Amnesty International v Zambia*, the commission stated that freedom of expression is a fundamental human right, essential to individual personal development, political consciousness, and participation in the public affairs of a country. In addition, the commission found that 'a higher degree of tolerance is expected when it is a political speech and an even higher threshold is required when it is directed towards the government and government officials'.[124] There are caveats to this, though, as the right may be restricted to protect the rights or reputation of others or for national security, public order, health, or morals.[125] Even so, 'any restrictions on freedom of expression shall be provided by law, serve a legitimate interest and be necessary in a democratic society'.[126] The commission has interpreted the phrase 'within the law',[127] contained in sub-paragraph (2), to mean that any restrictions on the freedom of expression have to be 'provided by law'.[128] The phrase according to the commission 'does not, however, mean that national law can set aside the right to express and disseminate one's opinions guaranteed at the international level; this would make the protection of the right to express one's opinion ineffective'.[129] This seemingly mirrors 'prescribed by law', contained in the European Convention on Human Rights, and 'established by law', contained in the Inter-American Convention on Human Rights. The clause is exactly the same as that contained in sub-paragraph 19(3) of the International Covenant on Civil and Political Rights.

Moreover, freedom of expression is closely related to freedom of conscience, as guaranteed by Article 8, which is frequently considered with Article 9,[130] that no one should suffer any consequences from the state for

[123] Preamble to the Resolution on the Adoption of the Declaration of Principles on Freedom of Expression in Africa, adopted by the African Commission at its 32nd Ordinary Session, held 17–23 October 2003 in Banjul, the Gambia.

[124] See, eg, Communication 313/05, *Kenneth Good v Republic of Botswana* (2010), para 198.

[125] ibid, para 187.

[126] ibid. It should also be pointed out that the commission has consistently stated that 'the only legitimate reasons for limitations of the rights and freedoms recognised in the African Charter are found in Article 27(2), that is, that the rights of the Charter shall be exercised with due regard to the rights of others, collective security, morality and common interest'. Ibid.

[127] ACHPR Res 62 (XXXII) 02: Resolution on the Adoption of the Declaration of Principles on Freedom of Expression in Africa (2002), para 11.

[128] ibid.

[129] Communications 140/94, 141/94, and 145/95, *Constitutional Rights Project, Civil Liberties Organization and Media Rights Agenda v Nigeria*, 13th Activity Report 1999–2000, Annex V, para 40.

[130] See, eg, Communication 212/98, *Amnesty International v Zambia*, 12th Activity Report 1998–99, Annex V (Documents of the African Commission p 745), where it was stated that 'the Commission has to determine whether the deportations, being politically motivated, violate the provisions of Article 9(2) of the African Charter as the two victims were denied the right to freedom of conscience as stipulated in Article 8 of the Charter.'

exercising freedom of expression.[131] Further, in Articles 60 and 61, the charter allows the commission to give consideration to other relevant human rights instruments in its work. The commission has helped to advance and develop the contours of Article 9 provisions through its case law,[132] the adoption of the Resolution on the Right to Freedom of Expression in Africa,[133] the Declaration of Principles on Freedom of Expression in Africa, and the appointment of a Special Rapporteur on Freedom of Expression in Africa.[134]

Additionally, the provisions of Article 9 are subject to paragraph 27(2) of the charter. As the commission has explained, 'the right to freedom of expression carries with it certain duties and responsibilities and it is for this reason that certain restrictions on freedom of expression are allowed'.[135] Although the limitations contained in paragraphs 9(2) and 27(2) omit important requirements (for example, that any limitation must be necessary in a democratic society) when compared with other international or regional instruments, the commission has attempted to bring the provisions in line with other instruments. In the case of *Constitutional Rights Project and others v Nigeria*, the commission emphasised: '[I]t is a well settled principle of the African Commission that any laws restricting freedom of expression must conform to international human rights norms and standards relating to freedom of expression and should not jeopardise the right itself.'[136] Consequently, 'if any person expresses or disseminates opinions that are contrary to laws that meet the [above criteria],

[131] See, eg, Communications 140/94, 141/94, and 145/95, *Constitutional Rights Project, Civil Liberties Organization and Media Rights Agenda v Nigeria*, 13th Activity Report 1999–2000, Annex V. But see *Kosiek v Germany* (1986) Series A no 105, (1987) 9 EHRR 328, where the European Court of Human Rights suggested that while the right remains, the person espousing the particular views must live with the consequences of those views, where the views are not regulated by the convention.

[132] See, eg, Communications 48/90, 50/90, and 89/93, *Amnesty International, Comite Loosli Bachelard, Lawyers Committee for Human Rights, Association of Members of the Episcopal Conference of East Africa v Sudan*, 13th Activity Report 1999–2000, Annex V. Although Art 9 is silent on what is commonly referred to as freedom of the press, many of the cases that have come before the commission illustrate that the press is well covered under that provision.

[133] Resolution on the Right to Freedom of Expression in Africa, adopted at the 11th Ordinary Session of the African Commission, 2–9 March 1992.

[134] Declaration of Principles on Freedom of Expression in Africa, adopted at the 32nd Ordinary Session of the African Commission, 17–23 March 2002. The commission appointed a Special Rapporteur on Freedom of Expression in Africa during its 36th Ordinary Session in December 2004 in Dakar.

[135] See para 19(3). However, the Human Rights Committee has not expanded much on the requirement that Art 19 restrictions be 'provided by law', and it is likely that the provisions would be 'interpreted in the context of other ICCPR guarantees, i.e., that the limitation must be sufficiently delineated in a State's Law'. Sarah Joseph, Jenny Schultz and Melissa Caston (eds), *The International Covenant on Civil and Political Rights, Cases, Materials and Commentary*, 2nd edn (Oxford: Oxford University Press, 2004) 525.

[136] Communication 297/05, *Scanlen & Holderness v Zimbabwe* (2009), para 108.

there should be due process and all affected persons should be allowed to seek redress in a court of law'.[137]

Following on this path, the African Commission has, in a series of cases,[138] adopted a somewhat robust approach in its interpretation and application of Article 9, in a way that has ensured that the restraints imposed on the freedom of expression do not go beyond the limits necessary for the purposes set out in paragraphs 9(2) and 27(2), along with those that have been subsequently articulated by the commission. In the case of *The Law Offices of Ghazi Suleiman v Sudan*,[139] for example, the complainant alleged that he had been stopped by state security officials from travelling to Sinnar, Blue Nile State in the Sudan, to honour an invitation to deliver a public lecture on human rights on 3 January 1999. The complainant, Ghazi Suleiman, also alleged that state security officials had threatened to arrest him if he honoured that invitation, and argued that his rights, including under Article 9, had been violated. The commission upheld the complaint, stating: 'When an individual's freedom of expression is unlawfully restricted, it is not only the right of that individual that is being violated, but also the right of all others to "receive" information and ideas.'[140]

According to the commission, 'the charges levelled against Mr Ghazi Suleiman by the government of Sudan indicate that the government believed that his speech threatened national security and public order',[141] but given that his speech 'was directed towards the promotion and protection of human rights, it is of special value to society and deserving of special protection'.[142] This case indicates that the commission is reluctant to allow restrictions on freedom of expression on the basis of a ready-made excuse of 'national security and public order'. In *Open Society Justice Initiative (on behalf of Pius Njawe Noumeni) v Cameroon*,[143] the complainant, Messager Group, alleged that despite its application for a licence in 2003 with the Ministry of Communications of Cameroon, 'an illegal decision'

[137] Communication 232/99, *John D Ouko v Kenya*, 14th Activity Report 2000–01, Annex V. The more recent Declaration of Principles on Freedom of Expression in Africa, in Principle II(2) provides that 'any restrictions on freedom of expression shall be provided for by law, serve a legitimate interest and be necessary and in a democratic society'.

[138] See, eg, Communications 140/94, 141/94, and 145/95, *Constitutional Rights Project, Civil Liberties Organization and Media Rights Agenda v Nigeria*, 13th Activity Report 1999–2000, Annex V (Documents of the African Commission).

[139] Communication 228/99, *The Law Office of Ghazi Suleiman v Sudan*, 16th Activity Report 2002–03, Annex VII.

[140] ibid, paras 46 and 50.

[141] Ibid, para. 51.

[142] Communications 48/90, 50/90 and 89/93, *Amnesty International, Comite Loosli Bachelard, Lawyers Committee for Human Rights, Association of Members of the Episcopal Conference of East Africa v Sudan*, 13th Activity Report 1999–2000, Annex V (Documents of the African Commission).

[143] Communication 290/2004, *Open Society Justice Initiative (on behalf of Pius Njawe Noumeni) v Cameroon*, 20th Activity Report 2006, Annex IV (Documents of the African Commission).

had banned their operation of private radio in Douala. When Messager Group announced that it would begin broadcasting programmes, the ministry banned the operation and then sealed the premises of the radio station.[144] The commission ultimately did not need to decide the merits of the case, because the parties agreed on a settlement. However, the commission should have at least considered the compatibility of the operations of the Ministry of Communication with the provisions of the African Charter, especially given that the allegations appeared to indicate widespread discrimination in the granting of operational licences to operators of radio stations in Cameroon (which suggests an abuse of entrusted position).

The rights to freedom of expression and information can be affected by corruption in several ways. While not explicitly using the term corruption, the commission seems to imply that one's right to hold opinions and to seek, receive, and impart information and ideas should not be arbitrarily or unduly restricted. As noted, poverty, which is frequently precipitated by corruption in many African states, restricts and undermines the enjoyment of human and peoples' rights, including the rights to freedom of expression and information. The economically and socially vulnerable have no access to modern communication technologies, and often cannot make their voices heard on issues that directly affect them. This invariably results in disempowerment, marginalisation, discrimination, and entrenched vulnerability. Limited enjoyment of the right to freedom of expression seriously undermines the rule of law, good governance, and democratic societies. It also denies citizens the enjoyment of other human rights, such as the right to participate in the government of one's country, contribute to public policies, or demand transparency. Lack of access to information by citizens also affects the transparency of public services and the management of a state's wealth and resources, which in turn undermines public confidence and trust in the government. Thus, the Independent Expert on the Question of Human Rights and Extreme Poverty stated:

> [E]ffective and meaningful participation by people living in poverty requires that a broad set of rights are respected, protected and fulfilled, including freedom of expression . . . In practice, this requires the establishment of specific mechanisms and arrangements at different levels to ensure that there are ways in which those living in poverty have a voice and play an effective part in the life of the community.[145]

Additionally, the right to freedom of expression facilitates citizens' right to participate in their own government, and it is an important tool for preventing and combating corruption, because it allows and encourages

[144] ibid.
[145] United Nations, Report of the Independent Expert, A/63/274, para 22.

information-sharing concerning corruption cases and empowers investigative journalists to educate the public about such cases. Yet, violations and restrictions of the right to freedom of expression through the use of defamation and sedition laws make it difficult for the media to perform its important role of exposing corruption. Corruption will also imperil the right of citizens to receive this information when investigative journalists are prevented from reporting cases of corruption. While investigative journalism can identify weaknesses in laws and regulations that provide incentives for corruption, corruption and a climate of impunity would mean journalists face real danger in the discharge of their important role. Where journalists and others blow the whistle and publish cases of police abuse, unlawful killings, or breach of public trusts (or any information considered too sensitive or embarrassing by a government), corruption (and the consequent breakdown of the rule of law) leads to targeting the media and journalists with threats, attacks, assaults, arbitrary arrests, detentions, torture and ill-treatment, unlawful seizure of materials and resources (such as research and video and audio equipment), closure of publications, and, in extreme cases, assassination. Worse still, such cases are then rarely effectively investigated, allowing perpetrators to enjoy nearly absolute impunity.

In addition, because corruption thrives in secrecy, without transparency and accountability of government there can be no enjoyment of the right to the freedom of expression and the right to information. A corrupt government is simply not tolerant of these rights, especially when critical issues against it are publicly discussed. Punitive legislation such as sedition and defamation laws shield high-ranking officials from scrutiny and accountability, and may make the media self-censor their reporting of public affairs, thus contributing to further violations of freedom of the press. A clear illustration is the August 2013 imprisonment of Rodney Sieh, editor-in-chief of the Liberian investigative newspaper *FrontPage Africa*, because he could not pay a $1.5m civil libel judgment. The judgment arose from a lawsuit brought in 2010 by a former government minister, Dr J Chris Toe, against the newspaper and Sieh for allegedly falsely linking Toe to corruption scandals. The Supreme Court dismissed Sieh's appeal because he failed to post a huge bond, required under Liberian law to file an appeal.

Article 9 was presumably violated because Sieh's harsh treatment seemed to relate to his activities as a journalist. The penalty can neither be said to serve 'a legitimate interest' nor to be 'necessary in a democratic society'. Even if a defamation case was warranted, imprisonment would still not be an appropriate penalty under human rights law. The clearly excessive penalty imposed on the journalist makes imprisonment the only likely outcome of the judicial process, as it is obvious that many journalists in Sieh's position will not be able to pay such fines. While this procedure seemed permissible under Liberia's law, as noted, it certainly offends the letter and spirit of Article 9 provision, suggesting the need for the law to be changed and brought into line with the charter. There was no 'pressing social need' at stake, and Sieh's article in any case should have been considered fair comment on such a matter of great public importance as corruption, even if it had exaggerated the extent of Toe's involvement in the corruption scandals. Publicising cases of corruption (being matters of public interest), especially those involving high-ranking state officials, ought to be the rule rather than the exception. Sieh's disproportionately severe (and unjustified) penalty may have a 'chilling effect' on other journalists or whistleblowers who may wish to expose high-level corruption in the country.

Furthermore, as the above examples illustrate, the denial of the rights to freedom of expression and information can also negatively affect the enjoyment of other human rights – for example, the right to participate in one's government, because effective participation requires citizens to know and understand issues of critical governance in order to partake in discussions in a meaningful manner. When the press, which performs the important role of informing public opinion, is restricted or curtailed or is itself affected by corruption, citizens' access to information is further limited, thus impeding their participation in government.

Corruption, and a state's failure to seriously combat it, also directly impacts the media as it amounts to 'paid news', because the information being communicated to the general public may not be the result of independent and impartial reporting but of bribery; or, in the case of government-owned newspapers, political interference and patronage. Corrupt governments find it 'normal' to pay bribes to secure favourable news coverage and to hide information on large-scale theft of a state's wealth and resources. Such corruption further weakens the independence, objectivity, and impartiality of the media, contrary to the well-established jurisprudence of the commission, highlighted above.

A similar tactic is that substantial government advertisements may be withdrawn from media organisations in response to harsh or unfavourable editorials on government policies, or because of coverage of corruption by senior public officials or party leaders. This inevitably puts pressure on the affected media organisations to consider their economic survival and sustainability at the expense of publishing the truth. In such an environment, it becomes unrealistic to expect the media to effectively perform its critical watchdog role against corruption, to act as the repository of the public trust, or to hold the government to account. Overall, the perception of corruption in the media potentially would allow for rumour-mongering to flourish; the consequences of such a scenario in any country can be devastating for its peace and development, and ultimately, respect for human rights.

## The Freedom of Association and the Freedom of Assembly

Article 10 of the African Charter guarantees the right to freedom of association:

> 1. Every individual shall have the right to free association provided that he abides by the law.
> 2. Subject to the obligation of solidarity provided for in Article 29, no one may be compelled to join an association.

Article 11 provides that:

> Every individual shall have the right to assemble freely with others. The exercise of this right shall be subject only to necessary restrictions provided for by law in particular those enacted in the interest of national security, the safety, health, ethics and rights and freedoms of others.

Although both the freedom of association and the freedom of assembly are of paramount importance to one's participation and contribution to society, neither has generated much charter jurisprudence. By the commission's own account, fewer than 40 cases have been heard on these two human and peoples' rights. Moreover, the bulk of the commission's jurisprudence on Articles 10 and 11 has involved cases related to political participation and political parties. Furthermore, while both freedoms are covered under separate articles of the charter, they are nonetheless closely related. In fact, the approach by the commission is often to emphasise this close relationship. The commission has stated in a case that, 'there is a close relationship between the right to freedom of expression and the rights to association and assembly. Because of that relationship, the actions of the government not only violated the rights to freedom of assembly and association, but also implicitly violated the right to freedom of expression.'[146] Because of the close connection between these freedoms, both are discussed consecutively.

### *The Freedom of Association*

The freedom of association 'permits persons formally to join together in groups to pursue common interests'.[147] Such groups may include bar associations, student unions, medical associations, political parties and trade unions. Freedom to associate with others in common pursuits or for certain lawful purposes is essential to the proper functioning of a representative

[146] Communications 137/94, 139/94, 154/96 and 161/97, *International Pen, Constitutional Rights Project, INTERIGHTS on behalf of Ken Saro-Wiwa Jr. and Civil Liberties Organisation v Nigeria*, 12th Activity Report 1998–99, Annex V (Documents of the African Commission) 729.

[147] Joseph et al, *The International Covenant on Civil and Political Rights* (n 136) 575.

democracy.[148] A review of the commission's jurisprudence on Article 10 suggests that the commission is sympathetic to a broad interpretation of the right to freedom of association.[149] In one case, the African Commission, quoting paragraph 3 of its Resolution on the Right to Freedom of Association, held that the regulation of the exercise of the freedom of association should be consistent with states' obligations under the African Charter. The commission also stated that governments should not 'enact provisions which would limit the exercise of this freedom [or] override constitutional provisions or undermine fundamental rights guaranteed by the constitution and international standard'.[150]

In *Sir Dawda Jawara v The Gambia*, the commission held that the ban on political parties 'is a violation of the complainants rights to freedom of association guaranteed under Article 10(1) of the charter'.[151] In a case against Swaziland, the commission found that the king's proclamation outlawing the formation of political parties or any similar structures violated Articles 1, 7, 10, 11, 13, and 26 of the charter, thereby undermining 'the ability of the Swaziland people to participate in the government of their country'.[152] In *Amnesty International v Zambia*,[153] the commission found that the deportation of two businessmen, William Banda and John Chinula, had been politically motivated, and ruled that because they were prevented from joining a political party, the government of Zambia had denied them the exercise of their right to freedom of association. In *Civil Liberties Organization v Nigeria*,[154] the complainant protested against the Legal Practitioners' Decree, which vested control of the body (called the Body of Benchers) responsible for the bar association in the government. The commission decided that the decree violated Article 10 of the African Charter.[155]

There are at least three permissible limitations to the right to freedom of association under the African Charter: the first and second are contained in paragraphs 10(1) and 10(2), respectively, and the third is in paragraph

[148] However, compared to both Art 11 of the European Convention on Human Rights and Art 22 of the International Covenant on Civil and Political Rights, which each expressly mention trade unions as a form of association, Art 10 of the African Charter is silent on the forms of association that may be allowed.

[149] Communication 225/98, *Huri-Laws v Nigeria, African Commission on Human and Peoples' Rights* (2000).

[150] ibid.

[151] Communications 147/95 and 149/96, *Sir Dawda K Jawara v The Gambia*, 13th Activity Report, 1999–2000, Annex V (Documents of the African Commission).

[152] Communication 251/2002, *Lawyers for Human Rights v Swaziland*, 18th Activity Report 2004–05, Annex III (Documents of the African Commission).

[153] Communication 212/98, *Amnesty International v Zambia, African Commission on Human and Peoples' Rights* (1999).

[154] Communication 101/93, *Civil Liberties Organisation in Respect of the Nigerian Bar Association v Nigeria*, 8th Activity Report 1994–95, Annex VI (Documents of the African Commission) 394.

[155] ibid.

27(2). Paragraph 10(1) guarantees freedom of association to all people, provided that they abide by the law. This expression is somewhat different from many of the so-called clawback clauses, or limitations, contained in the African Charter, but the commission's approach to Article 10 appears to underline their substantive similarities, between the limitation imposed by paragraph 10(1) and clawback clauses. As such, the interpretation of paragraph 10(1) has been consistent with what the commission has said with regard to the clawback clauses found in other provisions of the charter. Also, paragraph 10(2) says that no one may be compelled to join an association, suggesting a positive obligation to protect individuals from coerced association. This may, for example, entail some right to refuse to associate with groups with which one disagrees.

However, the first sentence of paragraph 10(2) would seem to negate this right, as far as it concerns obligations of solidarity. This restriction is also contained in paragraph 29(4), which, inter alia, imposes a duty on every individual to preserve or strengthen national solidarity if it is threatened. The commission has not yet interpreted the phrase 'obligation of solidarity', but it is likely that its approach will mirror its interpretation of clawback clauses that help underline the essence, objective, and purpose of the human rights and freedoms guaranteed under the African Charter. Otherwise, paragraph 10(2) would hardly serve its purposes or offer adequate protection. Indeed, the commission's view of paragraph 27(2), which requires the right to collective security, morality, and common interest, subject to the rights of others, is indicative of how the commission might interpret this phrase in the future: '[For] the African Commission the only legitimate reasons for restricting the rights and freedoms contained in the Charter are those stipulated in Article 27(2), namely that the rights shall be exercised with due regard to the rights of others, collective security, morality and common interest'. Additionally, 'the restrictions should be based on legitimate public interest and the inconvenience caused by these restrictions should be strictly proportional and absolutely necessary for the benefits to be realised'.[156]

### *Freedom of Assembly*

Freedom of assembly guarantees the right of persons to gather intentionally and temporarily for a specific purpose. Article 11 guarantees the right to 'assembly freely with others'. Although it is not explicit, it is fair to conclude that the drafters of the charter intended peaceful assembly, as inferred from the second sentence of the article, which subjects the right to assembly to 'necessary restrictions provided for by law'. Such laws may aim to promote national security or the safety, health, ethics, and rights of

[156] ibid, paras 68 and 69.

others. Nonetheless, although reflecting some differences of forms, this limitation mirrors (in substance) those found in many of the provisions of the charter, and it is likely that the commission's interpretation of the limitations in Article 11 will be consistent with its general approach to limitations under the charter.

As is the case with many of the provisions of the charter, the commission's jurisprudence on Articles 10 and 11 have not yet been fully developed, and the commission has not looked at the issue of how corruption may affect these articles' provisions. One way that corruption can violate the rights to association and assembly is that it can contribute to the political exclusion of the economically and socially vulnerable from electoral systems and can consequently lead to outright political or electoral malpractice and manipulation. Denial of the rights to freedom of association and assembly as a result of corruption would also lead to violations of other human rights, including the right to equality and non-discrimination. In particular, women and the disabled are disproportionately affected, as they are afforded limited opportunities to participate in government primarily due to the lack of access to and control of economic resources. However, it should be pointed out that these categories of people, and other similar vulnerable sectors of the population, suffer discrimination by a combination of social and cultural beliefs which also limit their rights to association and assembly.

Additionally, because corruption leads to the breakdown of the rule of law it is plausible to argue that it contributes to an arbitrary exercise of political powers and authority, which in turn would create a climate for human rights violations (including freedoms of association and assembly) to flourish. In terms of Articles 10 and 11, corruption may lead to underrepresentation of the economically and socially vulnerable in critical institutions of government because it creates an uneven political playing field and seriously undermines the rights to freedom of association and assembly. This is mostly due to the fact that political party structures are sold to the highest bidders, and mostly to former senior government officials, some of whom may already be indicted for corruption yet still have access to huge wealth. When honest politicians are prevented from participating in the political process because they do not possess enough wealth to match the 'moneybags' or connected politicians, or because the corrupt former government officials who have bought influence and patronage can afford to distribute 'free cash' to unsuspecting would-be voters and community leaders, the citizens' right to partake in the conduct of public affairs, through freely chosen representatives, is thereby grossly compromised and violated. Furthermore, corrupt governments tend to be oppressive and arbitrary, and as such are more likely to stifle fair political competition, or at the very least prevent citizens from freely expressing their political views or enjoying the freedom to vote out their leaders.

Many governments in Africa target, intimidate, threaten, harass, imprison, and even occasionally kill political opposition leaders, human rights activists, anti-corruption defenders and labour leaders, often to satisfy personal, political, or economic interests. Such targets are critical of a government's policies or are exposing corruption. Civil society organisations, including human rights NGOs, are prevented from freely carrying out their legitimate public duties. Relying on questionable national security laws or other corruption-induced laws, governments ironically often level bogus and unsubstantiated corruption allegations and charges against opposition defenders and leaders. Bogus laws may also be enacted to stop the registration of civil society organisations or to limit their sources of finance, including banning them from accepting international funding.

Unsubstantiated allegations of corruption can be used to prevent or exclude prominent and popular opposition leaders from contesting elections. Such situations are compounded by public pressure, which corrupt governments, law enforcement, and judicial agencies often use, ironically, as an excuse to pursue these leaders, even when there is no clear evidence to obtain a prosecution. Yet, unsubstantiated allegations not only often lead to violations of human rights (such as the rights to life, liberty and security of person, a fair trial, privacy, freedoms of expression, association and assembly, and to seek and receive information) but also contribute to reduced transparency, accountability, and public trust and confidence in government.

Political parties' funding is opaque, and it is the norm that the party with the highest number of corrupt senior government officials has an unfair advantage, and that it tends to stay in power even when it is obvious that it is unpopular. Such senior officials and political elites can perpetuate their power (through, for example, constitutional amendment), and continue to accumulate wealth and economic power. In many respects, a corrupt political party is one and the same as a corrupt government. Corrupt funds are therefore often spent to buy political influence, thereby keeping unpopular and corrupt governments in power, as shown in some of the country studies discussed in Chapter 2. Such funds can buy election rigging and votes, violating citizens' right to participate in their own government, and undermining their freedom to freely elect their representatives. Elections campaigns are one-sided if opposition leaders are barred from the media while the ruling party's messages are freely aired. State resources are channelled to finance the ruling party, thus granting to the party in charge an unfair advantage. As shown in Chapter 3, in some countries laws do exist to address most of the issues highlighted here, but these laws are rarely implemented or enforced by governments already weakened by or complicit in corruption. To enforce such laws would mean that government and party officials would need to probe each other, a near impossibility in most African states.

In addition, the right to join and form trade unions and the right to strike often are similarly suppressed by a corrupt government, for example through harassment, intimidation, or collective dismissal of workers for simply joining a union or participating in a strike. The workers, then, hardly have access to effective remedies. Peaceful protesters, and journalists covering such events, are often violently treated with excessive force, are dispersed, or are arbitrarily arrested and detained, with nearly absolute impunity. In such a hostile environment, citizens are likely to be too afraid to exercise their legitimate human rights through peaceful association and assembly that have been robustly interpreted by the commission, as shown above. Since the rights to freedom of association and assembly (including collective bargaining) depend largely on other human rights – such as the right to freedom of expression and information, liberty, human dignity, and security – they are invariably compromised when these other human rights are violated as a result of corruption.

### The Freedom of Movement

Article 12 of the African Charter provides that:

> 1. Every individual shall have the right to freedom of movement and residence within the borders of a State provided he abides by the law.
> 2. Every individual shall have the right to leave any country including his own, and to return to his country. This right may only be subject to restrictions, provided for by law for the protection of national security, law and order, public health or morality.
> 3. Every individual shall have the right, when persecuted, to seek and obtain asylum in other countries in accordance with laws of those countries and international conventions.
> 4. A non-national legally admitted in a territory of a State Party to the present Charter, may only be expelled from it by virtue of a decision taken in accordance with the law.
> 5. The mass expulsion of non-nationals shall be prohibited. Mass expulsion shall be that which is aimed at national, racial, ethnic or religious groups.

The commission has described the right to freedom of movement as 'a fundamental human right to all individuals within States'.[157] According to the commission, 'Free movement is crucial for the protection and promotion of human rights and fundamental freedoms. Freedom of movement and residence are two sides of the same coin.'[158] Thus, the right to freedom of movement grants citizens the right to reside in or work in any state they wish, and the right to leave and return at any time to their state of

[157] Communications 279/03-296/05, *Sudan Human Rights Organisation & Centre on Housing Rights and Evictions (COHRE) v Sudan* (2009), para 187.
[158] ibid.

origin.[159] Under the charter provisions, citizens have a right to obtain travel documents from their state. Article 12 of the charter guarantees freedom of movement in the broadest sense, and also expressly prohibits mass expulsion, a recurring problem in many parts of Africa. As stated by Joseph and colleagues, '[T]he right to liberty of movement constitutes the right to move unhindered throughout the territory of the State'.[160] However, like most of the rights already discussed, the enjoyment of this right is subject to restrictions provided by law (and limitations contained in Article 27 of the charter),[161] also explained above. On the basis of the earlier discussion of the issues, the exercise of sovereign power by a state to expel non-nationals who are legally admitted into its territory must follow due process, and be manifestly legal and comply with international standards.[162]

The commission to date has heard approximately 27 cases on Article 12 provisions, with most relating to the rights of non-citizens. Moreover, the commission's jurisprudence on this article has frequently referred to the principle of non-discrimination in Article 2. Regarding paragraph 12(5), the commission stated in *Rencontre africaine pour la Défense des Droits de l'Homme v Zambia* that, 'those who drafted the Charter considered large scale expulsion as a special threat to human rights'. It concluded: '[I]n consequence, the action of a State targeting specific national, racial, ethnic or religious groups is generally qualified as discriminatory in this sense as it has no legal basis'.[163]

Similarly, in *DRC v Burundi, Rwanda and Uganda*,[164] the allegation of mass transfer of persons from the eastern provinces of the Democratic Republic of the Congo to camps in Rwanda was found by the commission

[159] ibid.

[160] Joseph et al, *The International Covenant on Civil and Political Rights* (n 136) 349.

[161] In general, Art 12 of the charter, which is similar to wording in Arts 13 and 14 of the Universal Declaration of Human Rights (UDHR), guarantees freedom of movement and freedom to choose one's residence. However, it is considerably more detailed than the provisions of the UDHR. Art 12 mirrors both Art 12 of the International Covenant on Civil and Political Rights and Art 22 of the American Convention on Human Rights. With respect to Art 12 of the International Covenant on Civil and Political Rights, the Human Rights Committee has stated that the right to reside in a place of one's choice within a territory includes protection against all forms of forced internal displacement. See General Comment 27, para 5.

[162] Communication 97/93, *John K Modise v Botswana* (2000), para 205, where the commission held: '[W]hile the decision as to who is permitted to remain in a country is a function of the competent authorities of that country, this decision should always be made according to careful and just legal procedures, and with due regard to the acceptable international norms and standards.'

[163] Communication 71/92, *Rencontre Africaine pour la Défense des Droits de l'Homme v Zambia*, 11th Annual Activity Report of the African Commission on Human and Peoples' Rights, 1997/98, 22nd and 23rd Ordinary Sessions, 2–11 November 1997 and 20–29 April 1998, Banjul, Gambia: Annex II, para 15.

[164] Communication 227/99, *DRC v Burundi, Rwanda and Uganda*, 20th Activity Report, Annex IV (Documents of the African Commission).

to violate the rights to freedom of movement, to leave and to return to one's country under paragraphs 12(1) and 12(2). In *Rencountre Africaine pour la Defense des Droits de l'Homme v Zambia*, involving the expulsion of nearly 517 West Africans by the government of Zambia on the grounds of residing in Zambia unlawfully, the commission stressed that 'Article 12 imposes an obligation on the contracting states to secure the rights protected in the Charter to all persons within their jurisdiction, nationals and non-nationals'.[165] The commission found a violation of paragraph 12(5), stating that the deportees were expelled because of their nationality.[166] States are required to 'take all measures to avoid conditions which might lead to displacement and thus impact the enjoyment of freedom of movement and residence'.[167] Violation of the right to movement often leads to other violations of human rights guaranteed by the charter, including Articles 7, 9, 10, 11 and 18.[168] Article 12 provisions can also be violated when victims are denied the opportunity to be heard regarding the decision to expel them, either prior to or after their expulsion.

However, the commission has not yet looked at how corruption might violate Article 12 provisions. But it is undeniable that corrupt governments often arbitrarily and unjustly restrict freedom of movement of human rights activists, anti-corruption defenders, and political opposition leaders.[169] While in theory the laws of these states may provide for judicial or administrative remedies for violations, in practice such remedies are often ineffective and inaccessible to victims because of corruption. Resorting to any such local remedies may also sometimes expose victims to additional threats to life, security, and other freedoms. In *Law Offices of Ghazi Suleiman v Sudan*, the commission held that restriction of

[165] Communication 71/92, *Rencountre Africaine pour la Defense des Droits de l'Homme v Zambia* (n 162), para 22.

[166] Communication 159/96, *Union Interafricaine des Droits de l'Homme, Féderation International des Ligues des Droits de l'Homme, Rencontre Africaine des Droits de l'Homme, Organisation Nationale des Droits de l'Homme au Sénégal and Association Malienne des Droits de l'Homme v Angola*, 11th Activity Report 1997–98, Annex II, para 17 (Documents of the African Commission) 615. This also involved a violation of Art 14 as the commission found that the expulsion of the West Africans resulted in some of them losing property they owned in Angola. See also Communication 73/92, *Mohammed Lamine Diakité v Gabon*, 13th Activity Report 1999–2000, Annex V (Documents of the African Commission).

[167] Communications 279/03–296/05, *Sudan Human Rights Organisation & Centre on Housing Rights and Evictions (COHRE) v Sudan* (2009), para 189. See also Principle 5 of the Guiding Principles on Internal Displacement, which requires states to adhere to international law so as to prevent or avoid situations that might lead to displacement. Thus, displacement by force and without legitimate or legal basis amounts to a denial of the right to freedom of movement and choice of residence.

[168] See, for example, Communication 313/05, *Kenneth Good v Republic of Botswana* (2010); Communications 279/03–296/05, *Sudan Human Rights Organisation & Centre on Housing Rights and Evictions (COHRE) v Sudan* (2009).

[169] See, for example, Communication 228/99, *Law Offices of Ghazi Suleiman v Sudan*. As described earlier in this chapter, Suleiman was invited by a group of human rights defenders to deliver a public lecture, but was prohibited from travelling by security officials.

the complainant's movement also resulted in the violation of his right to freedom of expression and information and freedom of association.[170] The commission probably implied corruption in this case when it stated: 'The Complainant had difficulty to obtain justice and exhaust existing local remedies *due to the political situation of the country*' [emphasis added].[171] Arguably, the use of the phrase 'political situation' seems to be diplomatic code for corruption. The political situation to which the commission alluded was brought about primarily as a result of years of corruption and lack of access to resources, causing prolonged armed conflict, unnecessary deaths, and human suffering. The commission held that domestic remedies would 'yield no results' and admitted the case, though there was no analysis of the corruption context. Had the commission undertaken a comprehensive and holistic analysis, it might have possibly led to the commission making concrete recommendations on reparation and on the need to combat one of the root causes of the violations; that is, corruption leading to the breakdown of the rule of law and consequently to violations of human rights, such as arbitrary restriction of the right to freedom of movement.

In addition, the right to freedom of movement is also violated when corruption and any resultant armed conflict causes people to flee their homes.[172] It is also violated when governments either arbitrarily restrict the movement of internally displaced persons within their territories, or force them from their chosen and established places of residence as a result of the state's lack of security or denial of access to basic necessities of life, such as water and health care. Relatedly, a culture of bribery by police and immigration authorities often leads to the violation of the right to freedom of movement, as, for example, when citizens are refused free passage from one area of their country to another or across borders in the African region, even when the victims are in possession of valid travel documentation. It is their inability to pay bribes that prevents their movement. Such practices, apart from causing distress and unnecessary delays in journeys, increase the cost of movement and travel (and the cost of doing business), which ultimately is then passed on to to the economically and socially vulnerable in the form of higher prices for goods and commodities.

This practice indirectly contributes to violations of other human rights, because the refusal or inability to pay bribes can lead to threats, intimidation, harassment, arbitrary arrest and detention, torture, or ill-treatment.

[170] ibid, paras 47–56.

[171] ibid, para 36.

[172] Communications 279/03–296/05, *Sudan Human Rights Organisation & Centre on Housing Rights and Evictions (COHRE) v Sudan* (2009). Although the commission once again did not use the word corruption in this case, it is beyond doubt that years of corruption by the government are primarily responsible for the serious and widespread violations of human rights in that country.

Detainees are frequently asked to pay bribes before being set free, and are rarely afforded any fair trial guarantees. In sum, corruption across the borders of Africa violates the rights of refugees, undermines the effectiveness of states' asylum processes, and contributes to the trafficking of asylum-seekers, in particular women and children, thus exacerbating their vulnerability.

Unlawful restriction of movement as a result of corruption (and resultant arbitrary exercise of power) may also lead to stagnation in economic development and opportunities, especially in countries that are dependent on cross-border trade and exchange. It may also contribute to extreme poverty, which itself amounts to the denial of the security and dignity of the person. In such circumstances, women, children and people living with disabilities are the most deeply affected. While citizens with legitimate reasons and papers to travel within and outside a state are often prevented from doing do, corruption may actually facilitate easy passage for illegal immigrants or traffickers in human beings and drugs, and thus contribute to terrorist activities that result in the mass killing of innocent citizens. Whereas citizens of countries in African sub-regions (including refugees and internally displaced persons) are entitled to travel freely, bribery of underpaid immigration and custom officials at border posts is commonplace. According to the website modernghana.com:

> There is no way you can cross any of the West African borders today without paying money to the security agents. Between the Aflao (Ghana) and Lome (Togo) border posts, a traveller must have at least CFA 5,000 (GH₵25)[173] to be able to cross to either side. Between Elubo and Noe, border posts between Ghana and Ivory Coast, a traveller with a single piece of luggage needs about CFA 4,500 to cross to either side. The same thing applies to the Ghana–Burkina Faso border between Paga and Dakola. When crossing from Aflao in Ghana to Lome in Togo the traveller with a Ghanaian passport pays CFA 1,000 at each of five different points in the Togo section of the border. A traveller with a Francophone passport pays the same amount at about three different points at the Ghanaian section of the border just to be able to cross over. Only heads of state, Presidents, diplomats and other high ranking state officials are exempted from such extortion when crossing the borders of West Africa.[174]

## The Right to Participate in the Government of One's Country

Article 13 provides:

> 1. Every citizen shall have the right to participate freely in the government of his country, either directly or through freely chosen representatives in accordance with the provisions of the law.

[173] The equivalent of $100.

[174] Kwabena Adu Koranteng and Ouamar Abdulai, *Deadly Borders of West Africa*, http://www.modernghana.com/news/415420/1/deadly-borders-of-west-africa.html.

> 2. Every citizen shall have the right of equal access to the public service of his country.
> 3. Every individual shall have the right of access to public property and services in strict equality of all persons before the law.

The right to participate in the government of one's country is important not only to involve citizens in the decisions that affect them, but also to allow them to monitor and assess the performance of government officials in the discharge of their official duties. The commission has thus far heard approximately 15 cases on Article 13 provisions. The right to participation empowers citizens and ensures that they are involved in important decision-making processes. Whereas this right is traditionally conceived as the freedom to vote and stand for elections (which must be transparent, corruption-free, and open to any individual without any discrimination whatsoever), Article 13 is much broader and includes other human and peoples' rights, such as the right to freedoms of association and assembly, as elaborated on earlier in this chapter.

Given the impracticality of direct participation of all citizens, Article 13 provides that a citizen shall exercise political power either directly or through freely chosen representatives. Free elections are thus a condition of an effective political participation process referred to in the first sentence of Article 13.[175] This article should be closely read with Article 20, which provides that 'all peoples shall have the right to existence. They shall have the unquestionable and inalienable right to self-determination. They shall freely determine their political status and shall pursue their economic and social development according to the policy they have freely chosen'.

The commission has found the following to violate Article 13 provisions: the dissolution of political parties,[176] banning of ministers and

[175] In contrast to Art 25 of the International Covenant on Civil and Political Rights, which expressly mentions 'periodic elections' as the means of choosing one's representatives, the charter does not indicate how the representatives will be chosen. The commission's adoption of Resolution on Electoral Process and Participatory Governance during its 19th Ordinary Session seems to rectify the problem. It states that 'elections are the only means by which people can elect democratically the government of their choice in conformity with the African Charter on Human and Peoples' Rights', and requires governments to take measures to ensure the credibility of electoral processes. ACHPR/Res 23 (XIX) 96, Resolution on Electoral Process and Participatory Governance (1996), para 1. Unfortunately, it is unclear if Art 13 applies only to nationals of a state or also to non-nationals, and the commission's jurisprudence has not helped to clarify this. In view of the use of the term 'every individual' in para 13(3) – in contrast to 'every citizen' in paras 13(1) and 13(2) – the commission needs to resolve whether para 13(3) confers only to a citizen of the state the 'right of access to public property and services' or to all people within a state's territory or jurisdiction. Given the practice of human rights bodies, it appears that the provision in para 13(3), that is, the right to participation, is conferred only to state citizens.

[176] Communication 242/2001, *Interights, Institute for Human Rights and Development in Africa, and Association Mauritanienne des Droits de l'Homme v Islamic Republic of Mauritania*, 17th Activity Report 2003–04, Annex VII (Documents of the African Commission).

members of Parliament from taking part in any political activities after a military coup,[177] and deportation of an immigrant soon after founding an opposition political party.[178] The commission has also found legislation that excludes Zambians from being able to contest the office of president, because they cannot prove that both their parents are Zambians by either birth or descent, contrary to Article 13.[179] In *Lawyers for Human Rights v Swaziland*, the commission also found that the king's proclamation in 1973, which restricted participation of citizens in governance, 'clearly outlaws the formation of political parties or any similar structure', and thus violated Article 13, citizens' ability to participate in their own government having been seriously undermined.[180] The commission has suggested that representation of a section of a country in government would satisfy the requirement of paragraph 13(2) of participation in public affairs and the right to access public positions.[181]

Article 13 guarantees remain critical to achieving transparent and accountable governance in Africa states, where citizens generally do not count in the political arrangements and running of their own countries. However, despite encouraging decisions on the Article 13 cases mentioned here, the commission has not yet considered the effect of corruption on the enjoyment of the guarantees provided by Article 13, even though it undermines the right to participation in several ways. Basically, corruption violates the ground rules of democracy and participatory government, such as free elections, legitimacy of government, constitutionalism, a fair political process, equal access to power, and the rule of law. The absence of accountable democratic process also suggests that those 'elected' are less likely to prioritise or commit to human rights of the citizens. And the perception that a government is illegitimate can seriously undermine citizens' trust and confidence in government.

Perhaps the gravest effect of corruption on Article 13 is that persons living in poverty are denied the chance to be involved in the political decisions that affect them. As mentioned above, persons living in poverty – the economically and socially vulnerable – suffer discrimination in access to basic public services and public property because of their inability to pay for such services or to pay bribes. Poverty, in this sense, means lack of choices, capabilities, and power, not only income. The right to participation provides avenues for the poor and other disadvantaged segments of the population to lift themselves out of poverty and to fight their disem-

[177] Communications 147/95 and 149/96, *Sir Dawda K Jawara v The Gambia*, 13th Activity Report, 1999–2000, Annex V, para 67.

[178] Communication 97/93, *John K Modise v Botswana* (2000), 7th Activity Report 1996–97, Annex IX (Documents of the African Commission) 349.

[179] Communication 211/98, *Legal Resources Foundation v Zambia* (2001).

[180] Communication 251/2002, *Lawyers for Human Rights v Swaziland*, 18th Activity Report 2004–05, Annex III (Documents of the African Commission).

[181] Communication 266/03, *Kevin Mgwanga Gunme et al v Cameroon*, paras 143 and 144.

powerment and marginalisation. Joseph and colleagues have written that '[u]nder-participation in public life causes substantial and continuing disadvantage for the under-represented group; the political interests of under-represented groups are often marginalized and ignored'.[182]

As the Special Rapporteur on Extreme Poverty and Human Rights, Magdalena Sepúlveda, aptly put it,

> Poverty is not solely a lack of income, but rather is characterized by a vicious cycle of powerlessness, stigmatization, discrimination, exclusion and material deprivation, which all mutually reinforce each other. Powerlessness manifests itself in many ways, but at its core is an inability to participate in or influence decisions that profoundly affect one's life, while decisions are made by more powerful actors who neither understand the situation of people living in poverty, nor necessarily have their interests at heart[183]

Similarly, the economically and socially vulnerable are permanently denied a fair opportunity to run for office, because of the unreasonable costs of running an election. In some cases, corruption and abuse of power displace merit, integrity, or competence, by allowing a government to make critical public service appointments (whether within the executive, judiciary, or legislature branches) on subjective grounds, such as on personal, political or ethnic bases. Poor people have little hope of being placed in government jobs, and even so, public servants often lack the necessary independence, as they are largely part and parcel of the ruling party,

There are frequent cases of undemocratic and unaccountable exercises of governmental power; that is, leaders who seek to perpetuate their power through constitutional amendments, political manipulation, or election-rigging, as is currently the case in many African states. In such circumstances, citizens are rarely afforded access to judicial or administrative remedies. Corruption thus renders nugatory the whole concept of a representative government, as a corrupt government will not hold itself accountable to its citizens. Clearly, corruption allows the exercise of governmental power for the personal benefits of senior public officials rather than the common good. On top of this, the failure of states to establish politically neutral electoral commissions with the integrity to prevent or to punish anyone, including state officials, from engaging in corrupt practices with registration or voting processes, whether by intimidation, harassment, coercion or other means, leaves victims without effective remedies and redress.

In addition, the right to participate in one's government is frequently compromised when those with money and power run the process (mostly

[182] Joseph et al, *The International Covenant on Civil and Political Rights* (n 136) 675.

[183] Report of the Special Rapporteur on extreme poverty and human rights, Magdalena Sepúlveda Carmona, A/HRC/23/36 11 March 2013, paras 12.

by corrupt former senior officials who continue to enjoy impunity from prosecution); election results are falsified; or economically and socially vulnerable voters are manipulated or bribed to vote for a particular candidate. When the electoral process is weakened by corruption, other human rights violations can and, in fact, do frequently occur, such as when a corrupt government uses the machinery of the state to kill political opponents and opposition leaders, thus denying them the very right to life.

Citizens expect that individuals entrusted with positions of power and authority will exercise such power for the public interest and for the common good. However, when senior government officials abuse their trust by engaging in corruption, they deny citizens the right to an honest government. This is not a new right, but an implicit element of the fundamental right to participation. Corruption thus not only undermines support for democracy and participatory government, but also undermines the ability of a government to ensure and provide conditions conductive to the genuine exercise of participatory rights. Corruption in the political and electoral process also means that a government is unable to fully and transparently investigate allegations of corrupt practice, let alone bring perpetrators to justice. Often, a ruling party refuses to announce unfavourable election results. As mentioned earlier, corrupt governments can abuse the power of incumbency to unleash police and security agents against opposition leaders and to intimidate voters, election monitors, and journalists. There are also instances of governments failing to provide adequate security for electoral officials and at election centres.

Although in many countries laws exist to regulate party funding (including campaign funding), such laws are more honoured in the breach than in the observance. This situation is hardly surprising, given that state institutions are compromised by corruption. Indeed, party corruption is a major violation of the right to political participation and democratic governance, as a political party with a corrupt structure that wins an election can hardly be expected to commit to the institutionalisation of the rule of law, democracy or respect for human rights. There is a continuum of corruption and impunity of perpetrators, thus not only decreasing the legitimacy and representational value of parties, but also jeopardising trust in democracy, in all institutions of governance, and in the rule of law. In sum, corruption limits a state's ability to achieve and consolidate democratic goals, to establish neutral and impartial mechanisms for managing elections, and to ensure the integrity of the ballot through appropriate security and other measures that realise the will of the people and the integrity of the process for counting and collating votes and preventing electoral violence.

**The Right to Property**

Article 14 provides:

> The right to property shall be guaranteed. It may only be encroached upon in the interest of public need or in the general interest of the community and in accordance with the provisions of appropriate laws.

Article 14, in guaranteeing the right to property, reinforces the notion of the universality, indivisibility, and interrelatedness of human rights, encompassing civil, political, economic, social and cultural rights. The commission so far has heard nearly 30 cases on this article. The commission has described the right to property as 'a traditional fundamental right in democratic and liberal societies'.[184] According to the commission, 'The role of the State is to respect and protect this right against any form of encroachment, and to regulate the exercise of this right in order for it to be accessible to everyone, taking public interest into due consideration.'[185] Two primary principles relating to the right to property can be identified: the first relates to ownership and peaceful enjoyment of property, the second provides for the possibility and conditions of deprivation of the right to property.[186]

Simply put, Article 14 requires states to refrain from arbitrarily interfering in one's possession of property and to prevent such interference by third parties. But the right to property can be denied in the 'interest of public or the community'; any denial must comply with the 'provisions of appropriate laws'. These limitations appear to be sweeping inroads into the enjoyment of the right to property, especially in the absence of an express reference to adequate compensation. However, reading Article 14 in conjunction with Article 21 seems to address this problem, as Article 21 guarantees the right of peoples to freely dispose of their wealth and natural resources and, as noted, provides that 'in case of spoliation the dispossessed people shall have the right to the lawful recovery of its property as well as to an adequate compensation'.[187]

The commission's jurisprudence has shown a willingness to strike a fair balance between the demands of the 'general interest of the community' and the requirements of the protection offered in Article 14. A combined reading of the two articles also raises the question of whether the right to property is only an individual right or is also a peoples' right. One would

[184] Communication 373/09, *INTERIGHTS, Institute for Human Rights and Development in Africa, and Association Mauritanienne des Droits de l'Homme v Mauritania*, para 45.

[185] ibid.

[186] ibid, para 46.

[187] However, in contrast to Art 14, Art 23 of the American Convention on Human Rights not only requires the payment of 'just compensation' in case of deprivation of the right to property, but also prohibits 'usury and other forms of exploitation of man by man'.

argue that in its broadest sense, the right to property is one that can be enjoyed either individually or collectively. Though there have been few cases involving Article 14, the commission has frequently found violations in those that have come before it. In *DRC v Burundi, Rwanda and Uganda*,[188] for example, the commission stated:

> The looting, killing, mass and indiscriminate transfers of civilian population, the besiege and damage of the hydro-dam, stopping of essential services in the hospital, leading to deaths of patients and the general disruption of life and state of war that took place while the forces of the Respondent States were occupying and in control of the eastern provinces of the Complainant State are in violation of Article 14 guaranteeing the right to property.[189]

In the case against Nigeria,[190] the commission found violations of Article 14, stating that: 'The right to property necessarily includes a right to have access to one's property and the right not to have one's property invaded or encroached upon.'[191] Similarly, the commission held that 'Article 14 implies that owners have the right to undisturbed possession, use and control of their property however they deem fit.'[192] Corruption would constitute, to use the commission's own words, 'an invasion and encroachment upon property.' The commission takes a seemly broad view of the term property in this article, judging from the cases that have come before it.[193] However it is unclear whether Article 14, *per se*, gives rise to compensation, since this is not expressly mentioned under the provision. Nonetheless, there can be no expropriation without adequate compensation. This approach would be entirely consistent with the objective of a provision in Article 21 which is designed to protect, in some forms, a right to property: 'the right to adequate compensation [in cases of] spoliation of resources of a dispossessed people'. As C Krause wrote:

> [A] perception of human rights as an interdependent and indivisible whole calls for a wider interpretation of the right to property. If the realization of property rights only entails a right to own property for those who are in a position to acquire property and a protection against arbitrary interference in these existing property rights, it can hardly be claimed that the entire right to property is effectively realized.[194]

[188] Communication 227/99, *DRC v Burundi, Rwanda and Uganda*, 20th Activity Report, Annex IV (Documents of the African Commission).

[189] ibid, para 88.

[190] Communications 140/94, 141/94 and 145/95, *Constitutional Rights Project, Civil Liberties Organization and Media Rights Agenda v Nigeria*, 13th Activity Report 1999–2000, Annex V, para 54.

[191] ibid, para 77.

[192] ibid, para 52.

[193] See, eg, Communication 227/99, *DRC v Burundi, Rwanda and Uganda*, 20th Activity Report, Annex IV (Documents of the African Commission).

[194] C Krause, 'The Right to Property' in A Eide (ed), *Economic, Social and Cultural Rights* (The Hague: Martinus Nijhoff, 1995) 156–57.

Clearly, the more corrupt a state, the more likely it is to violate and infringe on the right to property. While this right and other rights may also be violated by a non-corrupt state, the nature of violation by corrupt states is more entrenched, persistent, and often characterised by a culture of impunity of perpetrators and a lack of effective remedies and redress for victims. Although often used to describe the right to privately owned property, there is no legal or moral reason why the right to property in Article 14 cannot be conceptualised and widely interpreted to include publicly and state-owned property, especially because such property is held in trust for the citizens. The right to state-owned property may be violated by corruption when such property, for example public service providers of electricity, water or natural gas, is sold to political allies as a bribe (or for undue advantage) during a privatisation process.

While privatisation can be good for the economy in terms of private investment opportunities and efficient service delivery that may come with it, it also provides additional avenues for corrupt governments to give patronage to supporters and to steal funds derived from privatisation. In such circumstances, the citizens and the general public (that is, the taxpayers) rarely receive value for the property sold. The gross earnings from government privatisation are huge, but usually mismanaged or stolen. Public properties are frequently undervalued, and then sold for a fraction of their true worth. Yet, lack of compliance with the basic standards of transparency, fairness, participation, and accountability in the sale and privatisation of public properties leads to violations of other human rights, such as the right to work and adequate standards of living, as many citizens can lose their jobs during or after a privatisation process. Moreover, allegations of corruption in this process are rarely transparently or satisfactorily investigated, and suspected perpetrators enjoy impunity because of their closeness to the highest political authorities. Although corruption in the privatisation process amounts to a squandering of public funds, victims lack legal standing and thus rarely have access to effective remedies and redress.

Additionally, corruption violates an individual's or a community's right to own property. Government officials' authorisation of planning or construction permits, based on bribery or political patronage – and the laws and processes relating to access and ownership of property – are often applied and enforced discriminatorily. The vulnerable are disproportionately affected by a corrupt government's decisions on access, ownership, and control of property. Denial of access to property as a result of corruption also contributes to additional violations, such as to the right to livelihood for those who use and work on land. In that vein, corruption also affects the integrity of the management of natural resources and jeopardises irrigation and agricultural output. Consequently, that creates food insecurity within the population and has serious implications for economic, social, and cultural rights (such as the right to health), and invariably some civil and political rights, as well.

Such corruption leads to distortions in policies and decisions in land allocation that benefit only a handful of wealthy high-ranking officials and politically and economically connected citizens. This means housing rights – ownership and access to property – by the economically and socially vulnerable is restricted or very limited, as they cannot afford to pay the bribes needed to register property ownership, title deeds and certificates, obtain land information, rent government's properties or afford the excessive private rents (which are also excessively taxed). The wealthy and those close to government leaders enjoy better services and information, so it is no surprise that a 2009 Transparency International survey found that land ministries and departments are some of the most corrupt public entities, closely trailing the police and the judiciary in TI's ranking of most corrupt institutions.

## The Right to Equitable and Satisfactory Conditions of Work

Article 15 provides:

> Every individual shall have the right to work under equitable and satisfactory conditions, and shall receive equal pay for equal work. [195]

The commission has heard fewer than 10 cases on this article's provisions. The right to work is a core fundamental human right because it constitutes a means for self-realisation and development of human personality.[196] However, the right to work can only serve as a basis of independence if work is available, if individuals can freely choose the work, and if sufficient income is obtained from it. States are obligated to implement policies and measures to combat unemployment, and to address vulnerable and disadvantaged groups.[197] An essential precondition to the formulation of policies is an accurate evaluation of the situation.[198]

The right to work requires states to ensure, establish, and consistently pursue non-discriminatory and non-arbitrary policies that have as their main objectives the achievement of full employment. To be considered discriminatory, a distinction must have the effect of nullifying or impairing the recognition, enjoyment, or exercise of equality of opportunity or

[195] Unlike the ICESCR, the charter does not identify trade union rights as an important component of the right to work.

[196] For a comprehensive discussion on the right to work, see, generally, Matthew Craven, *The International Covenant on Economic, Social and Cultural Rights (A Perspective On Its Development)* (Oxford: Oxford University Press, 1998).

[197] ibid, 206.

[198] ibid.

treatment in employment or occupation.[199] Any distinctions made with respect to particular or inherent requirements of a job should not promote discrimination, but rather equality, among other factors.

The right to work encompasses the cardinal elements of equal access to employment, such as: freedom from arbitrary dismissal, freedom from forced labour,[200] and the right not to be arbitrarily deprived of work,[201] which can be implied from the recognition of an obligation to respect, protect and fulfil the right to work.[202] States must strive to ensure that there is work for all who seek employment. Without a guarantee against arbitrary dismissal, the right to work would remain hollow.[203]

Like many other human rights, in particular economic, social and cultural rights, insufficient available resources due to corruption will invariably breach the requirement of human rights law for states to take steps progressively to implement human rights (and to ensure, at the very least, minimum essential levels of each of these rights). Similarly, given universality, indivisibility and interrelationship between all human rights, judicial corruption will also presumably undermine the enjoyment of economic, social and cultural rights as victims may be denied access to judicial remedies in countries that have recognised these rights as justiciable in their laws.

Corruption would violate the right to work when states arbitrarily deny or undermine access to work, or to satisfactory work conditions, to the economically and socially vulnerable, such as women, youth, older or disabled workers, and migrant workers. Corruption allows these categories of people to be discriminated against by denying them access to vocational guidance and training, freely chosen employment, and tenure of employment. Corruption creates discrimination on the basis of poverty, as poor people are mostly unemployed, underemployed, or work as low-paid casual labourers in unsafe, inhuman, or degrading conditions. They tend to work long hours and lack social security amenities such as sick or vacation leave, pensions, and other related benefits. In a corrupt state, the poor and other vulnerable groups are more likely to face enforced labour or arbitrary dismissal.

Corruption also affects the right to work when the recruitment process for public service and government positions is tainted with bias and favouritism, rather than being based on merit, knowledge, integrity, competence, equity or aptitude. Ultimately, by allowing recruitment to be closed to the public, the effectiveness of government to deliver basic social services and human rights is seriously compromised. In such instances,

[199] ibid.
[200] ibid, 224.
[201] ibid, 221.
[202] ibid.
[203] ibid.

the right to work is affected, as such recruitment leads to an incompetent and unprofessional workforce. With broken public services, a government cannot deliver on their human rights obligations and commitments. Further, corruption affects the right to work by deterring genuine investments by the government, creating political and economic instability, and purposely increasing the time, cost, and uncertainty of doing business. The absence of investments means there will be less money, and thus fewer opportunities for work in the public sector. Similarly, the right to just and favourable work conditions may be violated when a government allows a climate of failure or impedes the right to work enumerated in this section. Labour laws are rarely enforced, because the agencies responsible for ensuring equitable work conditions are often bribed and compromised. Finally, the right to work can be violated when a government cannot pay living wages to its civil servants because its resources have been diverted into the private pockets of senior state officials.

## The Right to Health

Article 16 of the African Charter provides that:

> Every individual shall have the right to enjoy the best attainable state of physical and mental health. States Parties to the present Charter shall take the necessary measures to protect the health of their people and to ensure that they receive medical attention when they are sick.[204]

Article 16 requires states to provide access to both satisfactory and quality health care and health conditions.[205] Even though it is not explicitly mentioned in Article 16, the right will conceivably cover social health, access to health-related education, information, and generally the enjoyment of an enhanced quality of human life. The broad obligation to 'take the necessary measures' grants wide latitude to states, and the 'measures' to be taken will naturally vary from state to state, but may sometimes require international cooperation and assistance. When read together with Articles 1, 2, 3, and 21 of the charter, it seems proper and reasonable (if states are not to adversely impact upon the right to health) to include among the 'necessary measures' critical components and systems such as

[204] The African Charter does not define the term 'health'. Nonetheless, the Constitution of the World Health Organization defines it as 'a state of complete physical, mental and social well-being and not merely the absence of disease or infirmity'. This definition indicates that health is a state of affirmative well-being. See World Health Organization, WHO Constitution, Basic Documents of the World Health Organization, 37th edn (1992). See also UN Doc A/CONF 32/8.

[205] Communications 279/03–296/05, *Sudan Human Rights Organisation*, para 208. In this case, the commission held that the destruction of homes, livestock, and farms, as well as the poisoning of water sources, exposed the victims to serious health risks that amounted to a violation of Art 16.

the establishment of the rule of law, effective judicial remedies and other mechanisms of protection against actions by both states and non-state actors, and efficient management of available resources, so that a certain level of development can be attained, which in turn can provide the underlying conditions for the full and effective realisation of the right.

The commission has heard approximately 20 cases on this provision. The right to health is part of the clusters of human rights necessary to achieve an adequate standard of living for the individuals, and a life in dignity. Thus, the commission has stated that the right to health is 'vital to all aspects of a person's life and well-being, and is crucial to the realisation of all the other fundamental human rights and freedoms. This right includes the right to health facilities, access to goods and services to be guaranteed to all without discrimination of any kind'.[206] Article 16 requires states to take the necessary measures to protect the health of its people and to ensure that they receive medical attention when they are sick. States are to ensure that health systems are designed to achieve sufficient availability, accessibility, and quality of health care and services in an equal and non-discriminatory manner.

The commission has elaborated on the precise individual entitlements and scope of obligations with respect to this right. According to the commission, violations of the right to health can occur through the direct action of a state or entities insufficiently regulated by a state.[207] The commission has also stated that 'the right to health contains four elements: availability, accessibility, acceptability and quality, and imposes three types of obligations on States – to respect, fulfil and protect the right. In terms of the duty to protect, the State must ensure that third parties (non-state actors) do not infringe upon the enjoyment of the right to health'.[208] The commission has stated that the right to health requires states to identify specific vulnerable groups, such as children, women, the poor, detainees and prisoners, and to afford them access to health protection that addresses specific health problems.[209] Indeed, some vulnerable members of society, such as mothers and children, may require additional health services. However, the availability of health care to these groups may not be enough to guarantee their right to health in the absence of other measures to safeguard their human dignity, integrity, and freedom.

To demonstrate that individual physical, mental and social well-being and a generally satisfactory (and healthy) environment are essential to a fulfilled life, the commission has held the failure of a government to provide basic services, such as safe drinking water, electricity, and sufficient

[206] Communication 241/01, *Purohit and Moore v Gambia (The)* (2003), para 80.
[207] ibid, para 210.
[208] ibid, para 209.
[209] 'II.17. Article 16. 2, Right to Social Security', Guidelines for National Periodic Reports.

levels of medicine, to be a violation of Article 16.[210] In *Social and Economic Rights Action Centre*,[211] the commission found that the Nigerian government violated Article 16. While emphasising the connection between the right to health and the right to a 'clean and safe environment' guaranteed in Article 24, the commission stated that Article 24 requires a state to take reasonable measures to prevent pollution and ecological degradation, to promote conservation, and to secure an ecologically sustainable development and use of natural resources.[212] For example, while the Nigerian government has a right to produce oil, it must do so in a manner that does not violate the provisions of Articles 16 and 24.[213]

Additionally, by reading Articles 16 and 18 together, the commission has held that mental health patients must be accorded special treatment to enable them to attain and sustain their optimum level of independence and performance.[214] The enjoyment of the right to health by these categories of people is important for their survival. [215] The commission stated: '[I]t is aware that millions of people in Africa are not enjoying the right to health maximally because African countries are generally faced with the problem of poverty which renders them incapable to provide the necessary amenities, infrastructure and resources that facilitate the full enjoyment of this right', insisting that governments take 'full advantage of its available resources, to ensure that the right to health is fully realised in all its aspects without discrimination of any kind'.[216]

Corruption can lead to violations of the right to health in several ways, such as when governments fail and/or neglect to improve conditions and the quality of service and facilities in public hospitals because of the stealing of critical funding for achieving individual physical and mental well-being. Similarly, the lack of performance-based budgeting in several countries is the greatest incentive for corruption in social services. The realisation that a government's budget for basic public services – including the right to health – is being diverted into private pockets means a state is unable to use its 'maximum available resources' to fulfil the mini-

[210] Communication 100/93, *Union Inter-africaines des Deroits de lHomme v Zaire.*

[211] Communication 155/96, *The Social and Economic Rights Action Centre (SERAC) and the Center for Economic and Social Rights (CESR) v Nigeria*, 27 October 2001. For an excellent commentary on the decision, see Dinah Shelton, 'Decision Regarding Communication 155/96 (*Social and Economic Rights Action Center/Center for Economic and Social Rights v Nigeria*)' (2002) 96 *American Journal of International Law* 937.

[212] Communication 155/96, *The Social and Economic Rights Action Centre (SERAC) and the Center for Economic and Social Rights (CESR) v Nigeria*, 27 October 2001, para 52.

[213] ibid, para 53.

[214] Communication 241/01, *Purohit and Moore v Gambia (The)* (2003), para 81. In the case, the commission stated that 'mental health care' includes analysis and diagnosis of mental conditions and treatment, care and rehabilitation for a mental illness or suspected mental illness.

[215] ibi, para 85.

[216] ibid, para 84.

mum thresholds of these rights. Diversion of critical spending away from the health sector can also lead to the denial of access to adequate health and can create an incentive for corruption among health professionals and practitioners.

According to the UN Special Rapporteur on the Right of Everyone to the Enjoyment of the Highest Attainable Standard of Physical and Mental Health, the obligation to respect, protect, and fulfil the right to health is violated when, because of corruption in the health sector, a state makes no progress to achieve the right.[217] Although the General Comment on the right to health does not specifically discuss corruption,[218] UN mechanisms in several areas of human rights, such as the right to health, have looked at the issue of corruption in relation to their specific mandates.

Apart from undermining the quality of conditions and infrastructure of health care, corruption also impedes citizens' access to basic care and deprives the health sector of much-needed resources to establish an environment to carry out a government's obligations regarding the right to health. It is obvious that a dysfunctional health care system can hardly fulfil the physical and health needs of citizens. Consequently, such a system denies people access to the highest attainable standard of health care and simultaneously undermines their ability to pursue personal development and prosperity.

Aside from having devastating effects on health expenditure, corruption contributes to worst-case population health outcomes, resulting in health goods and services becoming unaffordable or unavailable. This lack of services substantially and disproportionately affects the economically and socially vulnerable. For example, pregnant women who are poor are disproportionately affected during both prenatal and postnatal periods. Corruption exacerbates inequality in already unequal and unfair political, social, and economic environments, and it produces a 'cash and carry' health care system based on one's ability to pay for care. In addition to being subjected to long waiting periods, the vulnerable are more likely to be seen not by a doctor, but by a nurse, physician's assistant, or other health care professional who may not necessarily possess the requisite expertise or experience.

Additionally, while middle- and upper-class citizens can access health care services from private clinics, the vulnerable cannot afford such clinics and must often seek services and treatment in unsafe and unregulated environments, leaving them susceptible to avoidable injuries and death. Even in cases where a state attempts to prevent and remedy, for example, through legislation, the effects of harmful traditional practices that

[217] UN E/CN 4/2006/48, para 40.

[218] However, the General Comment on the Right to Health suggests in its para 18 that inappropriate health resource allocation (implicitly referring to systemic corruption) can lead to discrimination that may not be overt.

generate stigma and discrimination against women, corruption means such a state will be unable to enforce or implement any such legislation.

Despite the availability of considerable funding, including from bilateral and international donors, corruption in health care delivery systems suggests that the economically and socially vulnerable are more likely to be denied access to appropriate treatment, such as to HIV anti-retroviral treatment, cancer treatment, rehabilitation, organ transplants, surgeries, or even orthopaedics. Such an environment invariably undermines and limits, in particular, women's choices regarding their sexual and reproductive health, contraceptives, and family-planning services.

A corrupt government's inability to regulate or properly monitor private health care delivery systems often contributes to poor sanitation and hygiene, dirty water, and other problems that lead to or exacerbate disease. Reduced health funding, in turn, affects the sustainability of health by weakening international confidence in, and assistance and support for, the sector. Similarly, a lack of physical and human resources to provide the necessary care, a lack of training opportunities for young doctors, and poor conditions of service (leading to a failure to recruit or retrain competent professionals) means governments are unable to adequately address health or mental health concerns.

As noted with other rights, a failure in one area affects other areas. For example, where Article 24 is neglected, a polluted environment can cause water and food contamination, thus the right to health is affected. Continuing on, a state's failure to fulfil obligations relating to the right to health can lead to other human rights violations, such as the right to life. Citizens who cannot exercise the right to information in relation to the right to health are unable to make informed choices on where to seek health care, or to determine how much such services cost or whether they are provided free of charge. Therefore, where corruption directly or indirectly reduces the funds meant for health care, and a state is unable or unwilling to provide this care to its people in a non-discriminatory manner, this amounts to multiple violations of the right to health and a state's corresponding obligations and commitments assumed under the charter.

### The Right to Education

Article 17 of the African Charter provides that:

> Every individual shall have the right to education. Every individual may freely take part in the cultural life of his community. The promotion and protection of morals and traditional values recognized by the community shall be the duty of the State.

Notably, unlike many other provisions of the Charter, Article 17 has no 'claw-back clause'. Among many aims, education is essential not only to achieve the full development of the human personality but also to strengthen respect for human rights. Presumably, Article 17's brief and generally worded provisions cover primary, secondary, and tertiary education. The commission has identified the contents of the right to education to include the right of access without discrimination to public educational institutions and programmes, and the right to free primary education to all. The commission has recognised in its resolution, adopted in 1993, the importance of education 'as an active vehicle of inculcating the values and corresponding behaviours in a civil society based on full respect for human and peoples' rights, democracy, tolerance and justice'.[219] The resolution acknowledged the importance of the right to education for the effective realisation of the charter.[220] Significantly, the commission underscored the importance of education to meet the needs of specific groups, including women, children, refugees, internally displaced persons, victims of armed conflicts, and other disadvantaged groups.[221]

In a case involving Zaire (Democratic Republic of Congo),[222] the commission held that a two-year long closure of universities and secondary schools in Zaire violated the right to education as provided for under Article 17. The commission held that this was such a grave and massive violation of human rights that it referred the matter to the AU's Assembly of the Heads of State, and requested to visit Zaire so that it could investigate the extent and cause of the violations. Zaire refused to respond to the request, but the commission nonetheless held that Zaire had a legal duty to respect, protect, promote, and fulfil the human and peoples' rights guaranteed under the charter.[223] The commission determined that Zaire had also failed to provide other basic services, such as safe drinking water, electricity, and medicine, and that this too affected the enjoyment of Article 17 provisions.[224] Although the complainant alleged that public

[219] ACHPR/Res 6 (XIV) 93, Resolution on Human Rights Education (1993), adopted at its 14th Ordinary Session, in Addis Ababa, 1–10 December 1993. Before this, the commission adopted resolution AHG/Res 227 (XXIX), published in the commission's Sixth Annual Activity Report, 1992–93, in which it called on states to 'ensure among other things (a) that human rights are included in the curriculum at all levels of public and private education and in the training of all law enforcement officials, and (b) that education for human rights and democracy should involve every organ of the society as well as the media'.

[220] ibid, para 1.

[221] ibid, para 4.

[222] Communications 25/89, 47/90, 56/91, 100/93 (joined), *Free Legal Assistance Group, Lawyers Committee for Human Rights, Union Interafricaine des Droits de l Homme, Les Temoins de Jehovah v Zaire.*

[223] ibid. This approach followed other African Commission's decisions that set the principle that where allegations of human rights abuse go uncontested by the government concerned, the commission must decide on the facts provided by the complainant and treat those facts as given.

[224] ibid, para 45.

finances were mismanaged and that the government failed to provide basic services as a result, the commission failed to rule on this aspect of the communication, thus missing an important opportunity to clearly connect the effects of corruption on the enjoyment of the human and peoples' rights guaranteed by the charter.

In a case involving Kenya,[225] the complainants alleged that the government's decision to turn the Endorois' traditional lands into a game reserve denied the Endorois access to the area, jeopardised the community's pastoral enterprise, and imperilled its cultural integrity. The complainants also claimed that 30 years after evictions had begun, the Endorois had still not received full and fair compensation for the loss of their land and their rights to it. The complainants alleged that the Endorois' cultural rights were violated because the community's access to its cultural sites had been restricted and the Kenyan authorities had violated their cultural rights and pastoral way of life. The commission found violations of Article 17, and stated that the provision is 'of a dual dimension in both its individual and collective nature, protecting, on the one hand, individuals' participation in the cultural life of their community and, on the other hand, obliging the state to promote and protect traditional values recognised by a community'.[226]

The right to education means it must be physically accessible, financially affordable, adaptable, and non-discriminatory. States are required to provide free and compulsory education, consistent with their available resources and duties. However, corruption can deny this right by the theft of funds meant for building institutions, or improper construction of school buildings that may contribute to the collapse of such buildings, sometimes leading to deaths and physical injuries to children. It can also occur where bribery is used in awarding contracts and procurements, in stealing and diverting education materials for the private use of government officials, in appointing teachers based on political considerations, or even in securing admission to government schools. In such circumstances, the economically and socially vulnerable who lack the means to send their children to private schools suffer disproportionately.

Education is central to every country's sustainability. But corruption in the education sector deprives millions of school-aged children of the opportunity to learn, thus severely crippling a country's future social and economic growth and development. As noted, corruption clearly implicates violation of the right to education when, for example, a state fails to take positive measures to construct suitable schools or to recruit qualified teachers because the needed resources have been mismanaged or stolen.

225 Communication 276/03, *Centre for Minority Rights Development (Kenya) and Minority Rights Group (on behalf of Endorois Welfare Council) v Kenya* (2003).

226 ibid, para 241.

Similarly, the right to education can also be violated when a government fails and/or neglects to stop public officials from diverting social welfare or education funds meant to be used for children's education, especially needy, vulnerable, and marginalised children, and where the distribution and allocation of national funds are influenced by political considerations. In such circumstances, it is the students from poor and disadvantaged backgrounds, particularly girls, who are most often denied access to needed quality education.

The persistent absence of a suitable environment and conditions needed for education, including school buildings, textbooks, and teachers, unquestionably undermines access to quality education. Corruption in the education sector also often takes the form of rigged tenders and bids, outright theft of funds, illegal registration fees, and examination fraud. In many countries, parents are asked to pay for their children's primary education, but the quality of that education is low in developing countries, because of inadequate funding exacerbated by corruption. The diversion of education funds into private pockets can result in teachers not being paid their salaries and the absence of books, important educational materials, and resources.

The lack of access of millions of poor children, especially girls, to quality education exposes them to hazards that include child labour and sexual exploitation, which invariably leads to violations of other human rights and exacerbates a cycle of poverty and discrimination for these children. Education is invaluable, allowing people to pursue personal development and prosperity. Thus, apart from being a human right, the right to education possesses instrumental values. Consequently, the denial of access to quality education (and the resultant low enrolment and high illiteracy and drop-out rates among the economically and socially vulnerable) exacerbates and compounds the effects of poverty. Education is the surest way for vulnerable groups to lift themselves out of poverty. By denying children access to education, corruption thus denies them the right to effectively participate in society. The right to education is further violated when a state fails to establish effective regulatory and institutional mechanisms that prevent and combat large-scale corruption.

In the case filed by the Registered Trustees of the Socio-Economic Rights and Accountability Project (SERAP) (a Nigerian-based human rights and anti-corruption NGO)[227] the Court of Justice of the Economic Community of West African States (ECOWAS) ordered the government of Nigeria to replenish a shortage of funds in its education sector due to corruption, so that it could fulfil its obligation relating to the right to education under the

[227] *SERAP v Nigeria*, ECW/CCJ/APP/0808 (ECOWAS, 27 October 2009) www.right-to-education.org/node/719. This author helped to draft the legal arguments that aided the court to reach its conclusion.

African Charter. Briefly, the facts of the case are that SERAP sued the Federal Republic of Nigeria and the Universal Basic Education Commission (UBEC), alleging that Nigeria had violated its obligations under the charter to realise the rights to education (Article 17). SERAP argued that corruption and theft by high-ranking officials within the ranks of the UBEC had left the education sector woefully underfinanced and, therefore, unable to provide free, basic, and compulsory education to all Nigerian children. The organisation also alleged that the Nigerian government was complicit by its failure to satisfactorily investigate these allegations of corruption. Further, it argued that Nigeria had, in effect, denied its citizens the right to freely dispose of their wealth and natural resources, which are the bases for realising the right to education and other human rights.

SERAP's suit before the ECOWAS Court was based on the report of the Independent Corrupt Practices and other Related Offences Commission (ICPC), published in 2007, which was written following a petition it had received from SERAP. The report detailed the mismanagement of funds allocated for basic education in 10 states of the Federation of Nigeria. According to SERAP, more than five million Nigerian children lacked access to primary education as a direct consequence of the corruption and theft. The organisation thus sought from the court a declaration that every Nigerian child be entitled to free and compulsory education pursuant to Nigeria's own domestic legislation and the African Charter, an order compelling the government to replenish the stolen funds to the education sector, and an order asking Nigeria to prosecute those responsible for the theft or corruption and to monitor the recovery of stolen funds.

Before deciding the merits of the case, the court first had to hear several preliminary objections that challenged the court's jurisdiction, the justiciability of the right to education, and SERAP's legal standing as an NGO to bring cases before the court. These challenges were dismissed.

In its final judgment, the court held that the ICPC report provided only prima facie evidence of incidents of corruption. Although the court accepted the report's contents as true, it felt it could not rule on it, since it was not a criminal court and the innocence or guilt of those indicted in the report had not yet been established. Nonetheless, the court ordered the government to make adequate provisions for the compulsory and free education of every child forthwith. Significantly, the court asked the government to ensure that the right to education not be undermined by corruption. The court also held that the UBEC was responsible for making sure that the funds were to be properly disbursed for basic education and used for this purpose. It stated further that while steps are to be taken to recover the funds and/or prosecute the suspects, the Nigerian government should, in the meantime, provide the funds necessary to cover the shortfall in order to avoid denying any of its people the right to education.

While the judgment has been widely lauded as a victory for education advocates throughout Nigeria, as well as the African and international communities, it also represents a noteworthy development for better realisation of human rights in the sub-region in particular and the continent as a whole. By requiring the government of Nigeria to invest additional resources in its education sector, the court effectively recognised the harsh consequences of corruption and general neglect, forcing the government to root out detrimental conduct within its ranks or risk compensating from other parts of its budget. The court's decision makes clear that corruption and mismanagement of education funds did not excuse Nigeria from reaching a baseline standard in accordance with its obligations.

Whereas both paragraph 15(4) of the ECOWAS Treaty and paragraph 19(2) of the 1991 Protocol make the judgment of the court binding and final, and immediately enforceable, respectively, the judgment has not been implemented in Nigeria.[228] Because of this, it has had little impact,[229] and has not translated into justice for the Nigerian children, who continue to lose their right to education. Poor implementation of judgments invariably undermines the work of the court, discourages citizens from pursuing their cases before it, diminishes public confidence in its authority, impact and effectiveness, and continues to deny victims the fruits of the judgments (and ultimately their right to effective remedies). It should be pointed out, however, that the lack of implementation of decisions and judgments of international and regional courts and institutions is a universal problem, and is not peculiar to the ECOWAS court.

Even though the judgment may not have been implemented, the finding nonetheless provides important jurisprudence on the legal obligations of states to use maximum available resources (and regarding the right to wealth and resources in Article 21, discussed extensively in Chapter 6) to realise and achieve human rights. The case itself has helped to draw greater level of attention to the problem of corruption in the education

[228] Art 24 of that Supplementary Protocol sets out the procedures to be followed in respect to the enforcement of decisions. Each member state is to appoint a national authority responsible for the enforcements of its decisions in accordance with their national rules of civil procedure (in this case, Nigeria has appointed the Attorney General of the Federation and Minister of Justice). Under ECOWAS protocols and rules, economic or political sanctions may be imposed on member states by the political body of the ECOWAS (the Authority of Heads of State and Government), including, for example, the withdrawal of voting rights or suspension from the subregional bloc. In cases where judgments are not voluntarily implemented by member states, this can be referred to a political body, such as the Council of Ministers or the Authority of Heads of State.

[229] According to information on SERAP's website, since the judgment was delivered in November 2010, SERAP has sent approximately four letters to the Nigerian government demanding implementation of the judgment, to which there have been no replies. In fact, the government has not publicly acknowledged the judgment, despite the enormous publicity about it. Along with others, SERAP has asked for a legal and constitutional review to guarantee the right to education domestically, and for 'structural or general deficiencies in national law or practice' to be addressed: www.serap-nigeria.org.

sector and to show that corruption is a crime with victims. Public pressure has also contributed to portraying Nigeria as not taking seriously its legal obligations and commitments assumed under the ECOWAS treaties and protocols. Increasing the impact of judgments such as this ultimately depends on the political will of governments and the level of pressure that the court itself, and civil society, can bring to bear to persuade or encourage governments to comply with judgments and decisions against them.

## Protection of the Family and Related Rights

Article 18 of the African Charter provides:

> 1. The family shall be the natural unit and basis of society. It shall be protected by the state which shall take care of its physical health and moral.
> 2. The state shall have the duty to assist the family which is the custodian of morals and traditional values recognised by the community.
> 3. The state shall ensure the elimination of every discrimination against women and ensure the protection of the rights of the woman and the child, as stipulated in international declarations and conventions.
> 4. The aged and the disabled shall have the right to special measures of protection in keeping with their physical or moral needs.

As noted throughout this book, the African Charter is unique in its scope and comprehensive recognition of not only individual rights, but also peoples' (collective) rights.[230] Significantly, the charter recognises the independence and interrelationship between individual and peoples' rights, and even asserts that the effective realisation and enjoyment of peoples' rights is necessary to achieve individual human rights.[231] This is, however, not surprising given the traditions and values of African societies that recognise that a person 'is not an isolated and abstract individual, but an integral member of a community'.[232]

[230] See, generally, Clive Baldwin and Cynthia Morel, 'Group Rights' in Malcolm Evans and Rachel Murray (eds), *The African Charter on Human Rights And Peoples' Rights: The System in Practice, 1986–2006* (Cambridge: Cambridge University Press, 2008) 244–88. Although 'peoples' is also used in para 2 of the Preamble to the UN Charter and in Art 1 of both the International Covenant on Civil and Political Rights and the International Covenant on Civil and Political Rights, these treaties are very limited in scope and application when compared with the provisions of the African Charter relating to 'peoples' rights'. In addition, the Optional Protocol to the International Covenant on Civil and Political Rights allowing for individual complaints excludes the application of Art 1.

[231] ibid, 244. See also para 5 of the preamble of the African Charter, to the effect that, 'Recognizing, on the one hand, that fundamental human rights stem from the attributes of human beings which justifies their national and international protection and, on the other hand, that the reality and respect of peoples rights should necessarily guarantee human rights.'

[232] ibid. As the African Commission's jurisprudence has established, the concept of peoples' rights is not just a mere aspiration: these are justiciable and enforceable rights. Thus, the commission has stated: 'The African Charter in its Article 20 through 24, clearly provides

Article 18 is the charter's core provision on peoples' rights, in that it imposes both positive and negative obligations on states to assist families towards meeting their needs and interests, to protect the institution of the family from abuse of any kind by their own officials and organs or by third parties, and, equally significantly, to refrain from violating the rights and interests of the family.[233] Article 18 also specifically recognises the rights of the child, the aged, people with disabilities, and women. Despite its undoubted importance, however, the jurisprudence of the commission on Article 18 provisions is scant, and most of the cases that have come before it relating to Article 18 have either been withdrawn or ruled inadmissible.

Nonetheless, in the few cases that have been heard, the commission has found violation of this Article in deportation cases, and has criticised the forcible break-up of family units.[234] The commission has suggested that states' failure to make available the required resources 'and programmes of treatment of persons with mental disabilities . . . falls short of satisfying the requirements laid down in Articles 16 and 18(4) of the African Charter'.[235] Reading Articles 16 and 18 together, the African Commission has stated:

> [A]ware that millions of people in Africa are not enjoying the right to health maximally because African countries are generally faced with the problem of poverty which renders them incapable to provide the necessary amenities, infrastructure and resources that facilitate the full enjoyment of this right. Therefore, having due regard to this depressing but real state of affairs, the African Commission would like to read into Article 16 the obligation on part of States party to the African Charter to take concrete and targeted steps, while taking full advantage of its available resources, to ensure that the right to health is fully realised in all its aspects without discrimination of any kind.[236]

Along with the right to health, Article 18 is also closely linked to several other rights in the charter: Article 2 (equality and non-discrimination),[237] Article 19 (equality),[238] Article 20 (existence),[239] Article 21 (wealth and

for peoples to retain rights as peoples, that is, as collective. The importance of Community and collective identity in African culture is recognized throughout the African Charter.' See Communication 155/96, *The Social and Economic Rights Action Center and the Center for Economic, and Social Rights v Nigeria*, para 40.

[233] Communication 313/05, *Kenneth Good v Republic of Botswana* (2010), para 212.

[234] ibid, para 214.

[235] Communication 241/01, *Purohit and Moore v Gambia (The)* (2003), para 83.

[236] ibid, para 84.

[237] Art 2 is similar to Art 19 in that it guarantees to 'every individual' the rights under the charter 'without any discrimination whatsoever'.

[238] Art 19 guarantees the right to equality of 'all peoples' and equal respect and enjoyment of rights.

[239] Art 20 guarantees the right to existence of 'all peoples'; in particular the right to self-determination whether of political or economic nature and the 'right to assistance in liberation struggle against foreign domination'.

natural resources),[240] Article 22 (economic, social, and cultural development),[241] Article 23 (peace and security),[242] and, uniquely, Article 24 (environment for development).[243] Regarding this last right, Dinah Shelton has suggested that the term 'environmental rights' means 'any proclamation of a human right to environmental conditions of a specified quality'.[244] This is because the primacy of human rights texts specifies the protection of the rights of the individual. As such, rights must be interpreted in a dynamic manner.[245] Similarly, ensuring the true well-being and dignity of people, and their enjoyment of human rights, generally depends on a satisfactory and enabling environment, insofar as a degraded and polluted environment is destructive to both individuals and communities.

In its interpretation of Article 20, the commission has generally refrained from questioning the 'sovereignty and territorial integrity of states parties'.[246] Nonetheless, the commission believed that 'self-determination may be exercised in any of the following ways: independence, self-government, local government, federalism, confederalism, unitarism or any other form of relations that accords with the wishes of the people but fully cognisant of other recognised principles such as sovereignty and territorial integrity'.[247] In a case involving Cameroon, the commission underscored: '[States are] under an obligation to invest [their] resources in the best way possible to attain the progressive realisation of the right to development, and other economic, social and cultural rights.'[248]

240 Art 21, which is discussed in detail in Ch 6, essentially guarantees the right of 'all peoples . . . to freely dispose of their wealth and natural resources in the exclusive interest of the people'.

241 Art 22 guarantees the right of 'all peoples . . . to economic, social and cultural development', and imposes a duty on states individually or collectively to achieve this.

242 Art 23 guarantees the right of 'all of peoples . . . to national and international peace and security'.

243 Art 24 guarantees the 'right [of all people] to a general satisfactory environment favorable to their development'.

244 Dinah Shelton, 'Developing Substantive Environmental Rights' (2010) 1 *Journal of Human Rights and Environment* 1. See also Dinah Shelton, 'Human Rights and the Environment: What Specific Environmental Rights Have Been Recognized?' (2006) 35 *Denver Journal of International Law and Policy* 129.

245 Shelton, 'Developing Substantive Environmental Rights' (n 244) 1.

246 The commission suggests that if there were evidence of violations of human rights, such as the right to political participation, it could question states' 'sovereignty' and territorial integrity. Thus the commission stated: 'In the absence of concrete evidence of violations of human rights to the point that the territorial integrity of Zaire should be called to question and in the absence of evidence that the people of Katanga are denied the right to participate in government as guaranteed by article 13 of the charter, the Commission holds the view that Katanga is obliged to exercise a variant of self-determination that is compatible with the sovereignty and territorial integrity of Zaire.'

247 Communication 75/92, *Congrès du peuple katangais v DRC*, para 4.

248 Communication 266/03, *Kevin Mgwanga Gunme et al v Cameroon*, para 206.

It can be argued that by undermining economic development,[249] corruption violates the right to economic, social and cultural development, and seriously imperils the fundamental principle of social justice. Corruption destroys the institutions of the family and trust in state institutions, too. There is no question that a lack of equality and opportunities, precipitated by corruption in several African states, clearly prevents people from living a worthy existence, obstructs their inherent right to live in dignity and to pursue economic and social development, and prevents positive contributions to the development and growth (political, social or economic) of society. In such circumstances, underprivileged families in particular will be unable to meet their basic needs, and discrimination against the most vulnerable groups of society, whose rights are recognised throughout the charter, in particular Article 18, are exacerbated.

The right to protection of the family guaranteed under Article 18, and also under Articles 20 to 24, may be destroyed when corrupt officials allow toxic waste to be dumped into areas designated as residential, invariably resulting in serious health problems for families and communities. This clearly will violate the right to life and the right to health and well-being. A 1996 UN report found that environmental degradation following the dumping of toxic waste would adversely affect human rights, in particular, to life and to a clean, safe and healthy environment.[250] These violations are exacerbated when spending is focused on facilitating corruption and the hiding of stolen funds, rather than improving public facilities, such as government hospitals. Moreover, corruption also undermines the effective enjoyment of the right to peace and security as stated in Article 23 of the charter. Indeed, the situation of persistent and long-standing armed conflict and the fight over natural resources (the so-called 'resource curse', or the paradox of lack amidst plenty) across several parts of Africa, such as in Angola, the DRC, and Somalia, illustrate the close link between corruption and lack of security, inordinate ambition to hold on to power even against constitutional arrangement, and popular demands, political instability, and prolonged violence and suffering. Even in countries such as Nigeria, which has relative peace, corruption and the absence of the rule of law have continued to undermine national security and have provided an unstable environment in which extremist groups such as Boko Haram can spring up, flourish, and kill thousands of

[249] See, eg, Transparency International, 'The Anti-Corruption Catalyst: Realising The MDGs by 2015' (2010) 2: 'Corruption exacts a high cost on development. Abuses in one sector do not spare the others from collateral damage [and can] undermine public trust in government and the services it provides.' See generally, Philip Alston and Mary Robinson (eds), *Human Rights and Development: Towards Mutual Reinforcement* (Oxford: Oxford University Press, 2005).

[250] See Preliminary Report of the Special Rapporteur on the Adverse Effects of the Illicit Movement of Toxic and Dangerous Products and Wastes on the Enjoyment of Human Rights, E/CN 4/1996/17 (22 February 1996).

innocent citizens with absolute impunity, because the government is unable or unwilling to effectively investigate the killings or bring the perpetrators to justice. Yet other factors such as political grievances, and perceived domination of one ethic group over another are potential sources of violence and conflict. However, corruption can exacerbate these tensions and thus breed cycles of poverty that together can deny the economically and socially vulnerable the right to peace and, consequently, the rights to freedom of personal development and prosperity.

## Women's Human Rights Contained in the Protocol to the African Charter on Human and Peoples' Rights on the Rights of Women in Africa

As noted above, the African Charter contains provisions relating to women's rights that prohibit discrimination, including on the grounds of sex, as in Articles 2, 18 and 19. It should be pointed out that the peoples' rights guaranteed in the charter apply equally to both men and women. In fact, states are required to guarantee equal protection for all their citizens without any distinction of any kind. Yet, given the vulnerability and disadvantages experienced by women, and the disproportionate burdens of poverty that they carry, it was thought that a separate protocol specifically to expand women's rights was necessary to advance and increase protection for African women. As the African Commission itself stated, 'the provisions of the Charter do not ensure an effective protection of the fundamental rights of women'.[251] Thus, in July 2003 in Maputo, African Union member states adopted the Protocol to the African Charter on Human and Peoples' Rights on the Rights of Women in Africa, which came into force on 25 November 2005.[252]

The protocol has 32 Articles, and aims to draw greater attention to issues of women's rights, to increase the legal protections for African

[251] Draft Terms of Reference for the Special Rapporteur on the Rights of Women in Africa, DOC/OS/34c (XXIII, Annex 2, Art 1). Mary Robinson, former United Nations High Commissioner for Human Rights (1997–2001), was thus correct when she stated: 'Fighting for women's rights is a positive struggle which recognizes the quality of women's contribution to every aspect of the community . . . I therefore invite all to renew their energies in undertaking practical and creative initiatives to achieve full respect of the human rights of women.' Mary Robinson, 'Foreword' in John Braithwaite (ed), *Yearbook of Women's Rights* (Den Bosch: BookWorld Publications, 2002) 1–2.

[252] For discussion on early African standard-setting initiatives that contain important provisions on women's human rights, the drafting history of the protocol, and analysis and perceived shortcomings in terms of inconsistency in the standards the protocol establishes, see Fareda Banda, 'Protocol to the African Charter on the Rights of Women in Africa' in Malcolm Evans and Rachel Murray (eds), *The African Charter on Human Rights and Peoples' Rights: The System In Practice, 1986-2006* (Cambridge: Cambridge University Press, 2008) 441–74.

woman (and children),[253] and to ensure that 'human rights really do begin to be seen as women's rights'.[254] The protocol contains a comprehensive list of not only civil, political, economic, social, and cultural rights, but also development rights. States are required to ensure access to justice for women (including widows, elderly women, and women with disabilities) through the provision of legal aid, and to strive to achieve gender balance in the judiciary. States must, through legislation, public education, information, and communication strategies, prevent and combat harmful practices that affect the rights of women, such as their right to life, health, dignity, physical integrity, and education.

Similarly, to ensure that women are able to enjoy the full benefits of all human rights befitting of human dignity, security, freedom, independence and development, states must ensure rights to education, clean drinking water, food, housing, sustainable development, participation in policy-making processes, access to resources, and women's economic activities (including in the informal sector).[255] The protocol in Article 10(3) requires states to prioritise 'spending on social development in general and the promotion of women in particular' over military expenditure.

The protocol specifically recognises women's economic vulnerability by characterising 'economic harm' as constituting violence against women. The protocol requires states to integrate the principles of equality between men and women in their national constitutions and laws (Article 2). States must identify the causes and consequences of violence (Article 4(2)(c)), promote peace education in schools (Article 4(2)(d)), and take steps to eradicate elements in traditional and cultural beliefs, practices, and stereotypes that legitimise and exacerbate the persistence and tolerance of violence against women (Article 4(2)(d)). Moreover, states are to take corrective and positive action in those areas, such as law, where discrimination against women continues to exist (Article 2). States are required to offer rehabilitation and counselling and are to make available adequate budgetary and other resources to achieve this (Article 4(2)(i)). Largely following the path of CEDAW, paragraph 1(f) of the protocol defines discrimination against women as:

> [A]ny distinction, exclusion or restriction or any differential treatment based on sex and whose objectives or effects compromise or destroy the recognition, enjoyment or the exercise by women, regardless of their marital status, of human rights and fundamental freedoms in all spheres of life.

The protocol prohibits all forms of violence against women, including trafficking and sexual harassment within the employment and education

[253] ibid. See also Art 1(k) of the African Women's Rights Protocol, which provides that *women* 'mean persons of female gender, including girls'.

[254] Banda, 'Protocol to the African Charter on the Rights of Women in Africa' (n 252) 444.

[255] For the range of economic, social, and cultural rights of women contained in the protocol, see Arts 12–19.

sectors. It also requires states to protect women with disabilities, refugee women, and women who are asylum-seekers and internally displaced. Any such violence should be considered a crime under international law, and states must ensure that perpetrators are brought to justice swiftly. According to paragraph 1(j), violence means:

> [A]ll acts perpetrated against women which cause or could cause them physical, sexual, psychological, and economic harm, including the threat to take such acts; or to undertake the imposition of arbitrary restrictions on or deprivation of fundamental freedoms in private or public life in peace time and during situations of armed conflict or of war.

Despite these impressive provisions, women and children are disproportionately affected by the poverty primarily caused by corruption. Corruption contributes to the violence and discrimination against women, and denies them access to resources (such as property) and to participation in the government of their own countries. Overall, corruption worsens gender inequality, which is a major human rights problem in several parts of Africa. Lack of political participation and opportunities for women means fewer positions in government, which can lead to a vicious cycle of marginalisation, discrimination, and neglect, as they are excluded from the decision-making processes of their government. Corruption can also lead to cross-border trafficking of women and girls through the bribery of immigration and custom officials, as noted earlier.

In addition to safeguarding the safety, privacy, and lives of women, Article 14 of the protocol reads that states must allow women to exercise their reproductive rights, such as the right to control their fertility (para (1)(a)) to choose any method of contraception (para (1)(c)); to know their own and their partners' HIV status (para (2)(c)); and to have an abortion in cases of sexual assault, rape, incest, and where the continued pregnancy endangers the mental and physical health or life of the mother or the life the foetus (para (2)(c)). However, primarily because of the debilitating effects of corruption and the resulting breakdown of the rule of law and good governance, women remain at risk and continue to face violence, socioeconomic and political inequality, and discrimination in many African countries.

## Children's Human Rights Contained in the African Charter on the Rights and Welfare of the Child

The African Charter on the Rights and Welfare of the Child was adopted by the AU Assembly of Heads of State and Government in July 1990,[256]

[256] It is useful to point out that the African Charter's provisions cover the rights of 'every individual' including children, and prohibit discrimination on the basis of age. Therefore,

and entered into force in November 1999. A committee was established to monitor states' compliance with the charter and to interpret its provisions. The charter[257] aims to promote and ensure respect for the rights and welfare of children in the light of the peculiar sociocultural and economic challenges faced by children in many African states. The charter requires states to prevent discrimination against children (Article 2), promote participation of children in the decisions that affect them (Article 12), ensure that states prioritise the best interests of the child through legal, policy, and other appropriate measures (Article 3), and ensure the right to life, survival, and development of the child, including children with disabilities (Article 6).

To promote the development and welfare of the child, the charter elaborates a range of civil, political, economic, social, and cultural rights for the African child. These include the rights to a fair trial; protection from all forms of torture, inhuman and degrading treatment; due process in the administration of justice; freedom of expression, thought, conscience and education; social security; adequate standards of living, leisure, recreation and cultural activities; health and health services; care and support of handicapped children; and protection from economic exploitation. States are also required to ensure that children are protected from all forms of physical or mental violence, injury or abuse, neglect or negligent treatment, and maltreatment or exploitation (including sexual abuse while in the care of parents or guardians). Furthermore, the charter prohibits the recruitment of children into armed conflicts, and requires states to ensure the protection of internally displaced children. Parents are also to be guaranteed the right to provide guidance and direction to their children with the right to freedom of religion. The charter provides in Article 3 that:

> Every child shall be entitled to the enjoyment of the rights and freedoms recognized and guaranteed in this Charter irrespective of the child's or his/her parents' or legal guardians' race, ethnic group, colour, sex, language, religion, political or other opinion, national and social origin, fortune, birth or other status.[258]

States thus have a responsibility to justify the difference in treatment of children, indicating how such treatment falls within the notion of fair discrimination.[259] Unlike adults, children are susceptible to human rights violations and abuses because of their vulnerability, disadvantages, and dependence on adults. Children also disproportionately suffer the effects

the human and peoples' rights already discussed have equal application for African children.

[257] The charter defines a child as a human being under the age of 18 years.

[258] See Institute For Human Rights And Development In Africa And The Open Society Justice Initiative (On Behalf Of Children Of Nubian Descent In Kenya) V The Government Of Kenya, Communication: No Com/002/2009, para 56.

[259] ibid.

of extreme poverty. Poverty caused by large-scale corruption across many African states constitutes an affront to the dignity and best interests of children, as elaborated in the charter.The committee has stated: '[T]he reasons for possible limitations must be founded in a legitimate state interest and . . . limitations of rights must be strictly proportionate with and absolutely necessary for the advantages which are to be obtained.'[260]

The committee also stated that the obligations contained in the charter to respect, protect, promote and fulfil human rights must be enacted. It is considered a violation of the charter when corruption leads to, for example, minimal access to health facilities or medical assistance, or to basic needs like electricity, drinking water, and medicines.[261] The committee stated that : 'It is incumbent upon States Parties to the African Children's Rights Charter to ensure that Article 14(2)(g) is given full implementation, within available resources.'[262]

The failure to provide access to institutions of learning is a violation of the right to education.[263]. Clearly, children affected by poverty have less access than wealthy children to educational facilities, services, and resources for the fulfilment of their right to free and compulsory primary education. This is de facto inequality. When corruption is the norm and it is rampant at the highest levels of government, states invariably have fewer available resources in the spheres of education and health care, exacerbating the vulnerability, marginalisation, and discrimination of poor children, and undermining the key idea of the 'best interest of the child'. Indeed, corruption undermines and restricts states' ability to achieve the best interests of children, to ensure equality and non-discrimination, and to protect the survival and development of children. Corruption also significantly violates other rights of children, including the right to protection in the course of adoption (such as arbitrary decisions that do not take into consideration the best interest of the child but are induced by bribes), to dignity and security (such as from sexual exploitation), and protection from inhuman or degrading treatment or punishment (such as child labour).

The UN Committee on the Rights of the Child, established pursuant to the Convention on the Rights of the Child, has expressed concern 'at the negative impact corruption may have on the allocation of already limited resources to effectively improve the promotion and protection of children's rights, including their right to education and health'.[264] The committee has also stated that states experiencing corruption cannot comply with their obligations to implement the economic, social, and cultural

[260] ibid, para 57.
[261] ibid, paras 58 and 59.
[262] ibid, paras 60 and 61.
[263] ibid, para 64.
[264] UN CRC/C/COG/CO/1 para 14.

rights of children guaranteed under Article 4 of the convention.[265] The rights to which the committee alluded are very similar to those guaranteed under the African Children's Right Charter, and as such, it is clear that corruption will have similar negative effects on the enjoyment of children's civil and political rights contained in the Charter (for example through corruption in the legal and law enforcement systems that permit or facilitate abuses, such as the trafficking of children).

## The Right to Good Governance Contained in the African Charter on Democracy, Elections and Governance

In a move to recognise the interconnection and interrelationship between bad governance, unrepresentative government, corruption and the lack of respect for human rights, the African Union adopted, during its Eighth Ordinary Session of the Assembly of the Heads of State and Government (convened in Addis Ababa, Ethiopia, on 30 January 2007), the African Charter on Democracy, Elections and Governance (hereafter, governance charter).[266] The governance charter is unique in its human rights approach to important issues of governance, transparency, and accountability in Africa. The governance charter has 53 articles, and entered into force on 15 February 2012.[267] While the governance charter was motivated by the need to combat the frequent change of governments through unconstitutional means, its scope and application are far-reaching, in that it also aims to promote peace, stability, and political, social, and economic development throughout Africa.

Indeed, the desire of the AU to improve the rule of law, security, human rights, and development – holistically and comprehensively – is underscored in the first preambular paragraph of the governance charter, which underlines 'the significance of good governance, popular participation, the rule of law and human rights'. The governance charter elaborates

[265] UN CRC/C/15/Add 136, para 5; CRC/C/15/Add 160, para 9; and CRC/C/15/Add 124, paras 18 and 19.

[266] For background discussion on this charter, see Nsongurua J Udombana,, 'Articulating the Right to Democratic Governance in Africa', (2002–2003) 24 *Michigan Journal of International Law* 1209 and Solomon T Ebobrah, 'Is Democracy Now an Issue In Africa? An Evaluation of the African Charter on Democracy, Elections and Governance' (2007) 1 *Malawi Law Jounal* 131.

It is useful to point out that similar initiatives at the subregional levels exist. They include the Protocol on Democracy and Good Governance Supplementary to the Protocol relating to the Mechanism for Conflict Prevention, Management, Resolution, Peacekeeping and Security of the (ECOWAS Protocol), adopted by the Economic Community of West African States (ECOWAS), and the Protocol on Politics, Defence and Security Cooperation (SPDS), adopted by the Southern Africa Development Community (SADC).

[267] As of December 2013, 17 countries had ratified the charter and 41 countries had signed it.

broad democratic and development objectives, principles, and rights and imposes corresponding obligations on states to respect, protect, promote, and fulfil those rights. The governance charter has a detailed list of 13 objectives and 11 principles. It aims to: promote adherence to the universal values of democracy and human rights (para 2(1)); promote and enhance the application of the rule of law, sustainable development, human security, popular participation, and the fight against corruption (para 2(2), (3), (8) and (9)); promote the independence of the judiciary (para 2(5)); prevent unconstitutional change of government (para 2(4)); encourage effective coordination and harmonisation of governance policies (para 2(7)); promote transparency, access to information, freedom of the press, and accountability in the management of public affairs (para 2(10)); promote gender balance and equality in the governance and development processes (para 2(11)); and best practices in the management of elections (para 2(13)).

Understanding that these clearly ambitious – but achievable – objectives can only be met when rooted in a sound foundation, states set out some principles to guide them in their effort to ensure the effective realisation of these objectives. Thus, states commit to implement the charter with due regard for:

- human rights (para 3(1));
- the rule of law, including separation of law (para 3(2) and (5));
- a representative and participatory government including through free and fair elections (para 3(3), (4) and (7));
- gender equality in public and private institutions (para 3(6));
- transparency and fairness in the management of public affairs (para 3(8);
- political pluralism (para 3(11)); and
- condemnation and rejection of corruption and the impunity of perpetrators (para 3(10)).
- ensuring equality and eliminating discrimination (Article 8);
- establishing democratic institutions (Articles 14 and 15);
- holding transparent, free, and fair elections (Article 17); and
- establishing independent national electoral commissions (Article 20).

States are also required to adopt legislation and other measures to ensure the effective implementation and enforcement of the governance charter. Regionally, the AU Commission is the central coordinating body for implementation of the governance charter overall, and specifically for coordinating the implementation and evaluations of the key bodies named in Article 45. The important role of the African Commission on Human and Peoples' Rights in the enforcement of the governance charter is well articulated and recognised by states. Yet, the only regional obligation for states is reporting to appropriate AU institutions.

Overall, the governance charter underscores that, without respect for the rule of law, human rights, transparency, and accountability, the right to democratic and good governance is illusory. This recognition of the relationship between democracy, the rule of law and human rights is important, as their holistic and effective implementation provides the framework for combating and preventing corruption across African states. Under Article 5 of the governance charter, states are required to ensure constitutional rule and transfer of power, and any such constitution must be the supreme law of the land (Article 10). Justifying further its human rights character, Article 8 recognises the rights of minorities. Article 6 reaffirms the universality, interdependence, and indivisibility of all human rights. In Article 7, states are committed to improving the resources for the operation and work of African human rights mechanisms and to end impunity. The sum of these articles is that the right to democratic entitlement constrains the exercise of government power for the sake of human dignity and security.

As noted previously, the concept of human rights has expanded over the years, and today it is widely seen to include the right to democratic and good governance. Thomas Franck has stated that democratic entitlement is a recognised right[268] because the power to govern is derived from the consent of the people.[269] Similarly, the African Commission has stated that the right to free political participation entails, inter alia, the right to vote for the representative of one's choice and a duty to respect the results of that choice, since a breach of that duty renders the right of free expression of the will of the voters meaningless. The commission has also stated: '[T]he best government is one elected by, and accountable to, the people.'[270]

Poor governance and the absence of the rule of law provide incentives for honest high-level government officials to turn to corruption. Clearly,

[268] Thomas M Franck, 'The Emerging Right to Democratic Governance' (1992) 46 *American Journal of International Law* 56. Some scholars, however, disagree with the idea of a right to democratic entitlement, arguing that such a right can legitimise a neo-imperialist agenda. This is not a new argument, as it is similar to that put forward by the critics of the global fight against corruption. However, the peculiar experience of Africa justifies the elaboration of the right to democratic governance and the need for an effective fight against corruption in order to promote and respect human rights and to advance the rule of law.

[269] ibid. The UN Human Rights Commission in 1999 adopted a resolution on the Promotion of the Right to Democracy. This resolution recognises the right to a democratic entitlement. It views the right as a value deserving of international protection, and underlines the interdependence of this concept with human rights. The UN Human Rights Commission identified the elements of the right to democratic governance to include the rights to freedom of opinion and expression; to freedom of thought, conscience and religion; to peaceful association and assembly; to seek, receive and impart information and ideas through any media; to the rule of law, including legal protection of citizens' rights, interests and personal security, and fairness in the administration of justice and independence of the judiciary; to universal and equal suffrage; and to free voting procedures and periodic and free elections.

[270] Communication 266/03, *Kevin Mgwanga Gunme et al v Cameroon*.

large-scale corruption impedes the effective realisation of human rights and institutionalisation of the right to democratic governance. Corruption also jeopardises the very ideal of representative and participatory government by allowing the politically connected and the wealthy to manipulate and distort the electoral and political processes to the disadvantage of the poor and the vulnerable sectors of the population. Corruption thrives on weak and dysfunctional institutions, and lack of political accountability and the near secrecy of governmental activities mean that regulatory and legislative measures against corruption are less effective, as those governments have little incentive to implement or enforce any such measures.

The problem is not that national and international resources have not been committed to improving the rule of law and governance across Africa. Rather, corruption is the major factor why billions of dollars in national resources and in foreign aid have not made much difference in improving the quality of governance in many African countries, and why only a tiny number of public officials have been prosecuted. Whatever way it is viewed, corruption generally jeopardises, undermines, and contradicts the right to democratic governance. As Juliet Sorensen wrote,

> An election is meaningless if the outcome is fixed; a trial does not dispense justice if the judge is bribed; an official who acts to line his own pockets does not act in the best interests of the community he serves. In other words, a functioning democracy is undermined by a lack of public integrity.[271]

## The Right to Adequate Food, as Implied in the African Charter

It is often said that human beings do not live by bread alone. Yet, access to adequate food (physical and economic) and to food security is indispensable for the realisation of other human rights, in particular the right to life, to quality health care, to water, and to the dignity of the human person. Although the African Charter does not explicitly provide for the right to food,[272] or to be free from hunger, the African Commission has used the charter's provisions (including Articles 60 and 61) to elaborate on the content and obligations relating to this right. Thus, in a case involving Nigeria, the commission read the right to food into the charter's provisions on the right to life, as guaranteed in Article 4, and the right to health, in Article 16.[273] According to the commission, the right to food is 'inseparably linked

[271] Juliet Sorensen, 'Ideals without Illusions: Corruption and the Future of a Democratic North Africa' (202) 10 *Northwestern University Journal of International Human Rights* 19.

[272] But see Art 11 of the International Covenant on Economic, Social and Cultural Rights, which guarantees the right to food. Many countries in Africa have subscribed to the covenant.

[273] Communication 155/96, *The Social and Economic Rights Action Centre (SERAC) and the Center for Economic and Social Rights (CESR) v Nigeria*.

to the dignity of human beings and is therefore essential for the enjoyment and fulfilment of such other rights such as health, education, work and political participation'.[274] The commission therefore held that the treatment of the Ogoni people by the Nigerian government violated the minimum duties of the state towards ensuring the right to food, because it allowed private oil companies to destroy food sources, thus creating significant obstacles for the Ogoni to feed themselves.[275]

Corruption violates or undermines the right to food in several ways. Poor government regulations can affect the quality, safety, and distribution of food produce; can lead to stealing or diversion of funds budgeted for food programmes; and can restrict access to land and other natural resources. These acts violate the right to food and disproportionately affect the economically and socially vulnerable. In fact, the UN Special Rapporteur on the Right to Food has stated that corruption hinders or prevents the effective realisation of the right to food.[276]

### The Right to Adequate Housing, as Implied in the African Charter

Like the right to food, the right to housing is not expressly mentioned in the African Charter. Nonetheless, the African Commission has held that a state's failure to prevent forced evictions, or to take urgent steps to ensure displaced persons can return to their homes, violates paragraph 12(1) of the charter guaranteeing the right to freedom of movement and residence.[277] In addition, the commission has interpreted housing needs, in particular in relation to women, as involving an obligation upon states to provide the right to equal access to housing and to acceptable living conditions in a healthy environment. In the Ogoni case mentioned earlier, the commission underscored two fundamental elements in the realisation of the right to housing: the duty on states not to destroy housing, and not to obstruct efforts by individuals and communities to rebuild lost homes. Accordingly, 'the right to housing goes beyond having a roof over one's head. It extends to embody the individual's right to be let alone and live in peace – whether under a roof or not.'[278] States and their agents must therefore not engage in any act that obstructs the enjoyment of the core contents of the right to housing.[279] As the commission emphasised, 'the

[274] ibid, para 64.

[275] ibid, para 66.

[276] UN Special Rapporteur on the Right to Food. The 1996 Declaration of the World Food Summit also identified corruption as a major cause of food insecurity.

[277] Communications 279/03–296/05, *Sudan Human Rights Organisation & Centre on Housing Rights and Evictions (COHRE) v Sudan* (2009), para 190.

[278] Communication 155/96, *The Social and Economic Rights Action Centre (SERAC) and the Center for Economic and Social Rights (CESR) v Nigeria*, para 61.

[279] ibid.

corollary of the combination of the provisions protecting the right to enjoy the best attainable state of mental and physical health [and] the right to property, and the protection accorded to the family forbids the wanton destruction of shelter because when housing is destroyed, property, health, and family life are adversely affected'.[280]

The right to housing guarantees everyone a degree of legal security of tenure and protection against forced eviction, and requires states to make sure that the price of housing is reasonable, affordable, and culturally suited. Similarly, states must ensure availability and accessibility of housing, especially for the vulnerable segments of society, and with the basic facilities to meet the security, health, comfort and nutrition of the citizens. This includes heating, safe drinking water, electricity and sanitation.

Corruption within the land sector, and stealing and diversion of states' resources into private pockets, reduces investments in housing (that is, low-cost housing for the poor) and allocation of lands. This causes artificial scarcity of lands and allows only the wealthy and the influential to bribe or rely on patronage for access to land and to enjoy the full protection of law. This situation further exacerbates poverty, inequality, marginalisation, underdevelopment, poor governance and abuses of power. Poor regulation of the land sector because of corruption leads to other violations of human rights, including the right to life when substandard buildings imperil habitability and security. As is often the case with respect to other economic, social, and cultural rights affected by corruption, it is the disadvantaged and vulnerable groups that are disproportionately affected.

## CONCLUSION

The myth that corruption is a victimless crime has prevailed for many years, in part because of the narrowed conception of corruption, and the perceived legal and practical challenges, such as causation, legal standing, and evidence-gathering. It is often said that corruption is a 'collective crime' (because it affects everyone), and as such difficult to identify a clear and direct victim. However, this chapter has attempted to rebut this assumption and has demonstrated the strong causal relationship between corruption and the human and peoples' rights contained in the African Charter. While it is true that certain legal and practical challenges do exist that might obstruct the application of human rights law to corruption, as noted, (and as will be argued in Chapter 6), the challenges are not insurmountable and cannot (and should not) stand in the way of establishing a comprehensive and multidisciplinary approach that is victim-focused.

[280] ibid, para 60.

Furthermore, despite initial pessimism about its potential and relevance, the African Commission has over the years contributed significantly to the development of human rights law through its expansive case law and jurisprudence, as shown throughout this chapter. In some respects, such as those involving economic and social rights, the commission's jurisprudence has been ground-breaking, leading to some effective remedies for victims of violations of human and peoples' rights covered by the charter. Additionally, other instruments have been developed to elaborate further the substantive contents and contours of the charter, while institutions such as the African Court on Human and Peoples' Rights (and the African Court of Justice and Human Rights that has been established to replace it) have been established to make more legally binding pronouncements on the charter.

However, despite its impressive jurisprudence, the commission has not directly considered the effects of corruption on the effective realisation of any of the human and peoples' rights guaranteed by the charter, although a few cases are pending before the commission. NGOs and other representatives of victims of human rights violations caused by corruption appearing before the commission also share some responsibility for the lack of attention to the effects of corruption on the African Charter. Furthermore, while the court has become operational, its jurisprudence is still evolving, as witnessed by the fact that the court has declined jurisdiction in many of the cases that have come before it, due primarily to the limited access of victims of human rights violations to the court.[281] The court's potential and relevance as a forum to engage the charter, its own protocols, and 'other instruments ratified by the state concerned' as a complementary framework for combating corruption have therefore not been fully explored or fulfilled. This is perhaps understandable, given the court's relatively short period of existence. Of the more than 30 cases that have been filed before it, the court has assumed jurisdiction in just a few. Among the cases that have been accepted by the court are those filed before it by the commission against Kenya (threats of forced eviction of the Ogiek community of the Mau Forest) and Libya (arbitrary detention of Saif Al-Islam Gaddafi since 2011, without charge or trial, and without

[281] Victims of human right violations cannot approach the court directly unless states parties to its protocol make a declaration pursuant to para 34(6) to recognise the competence of the court. Regrettably, not many African Union (AU) member states have embraced the court as only 27 states have as at April 2014 ratified the protocol, and just seven of them (Burkina Faso, Côte d'Ivoire, Ghana, Malawi, Mali, Rwanda, and Tanzania) have made declarations that would allow direct access for individuals and non-governmental organizations (NGOs) to the court. Similarly, only 5 AU member states have ratified the Protocol on the Statute of the African Court of Justice and Human Rights that will eventually replace the African Court on Human and Peoples' Rights once 15 AU member states have ratified the protocol. No state has yet made a declaration under the protocol that would allow NGOs and victims of human rights violations direct access to the court.

access to legal representation, family or friends).[282] The court is also currently hearing requests for advisory opinion including one on the relationship between the charter, poverty, and corruption.

For the sake of victims of human rights violations, the commission should increase its interventions before the court, and states parties to the court's protocol that have not yet done so should move swiftly to make declarations that will allow direct access for individuals and NGOs to the court. Only then can both the commission and the court optimise their mandates and become more relevant institutions for litigating violations of human rights caused by corruption. To accomplish these important human rights and judicial tasks, it is suggested that both the commission and the court should adopt progressive legal concepts and principles, such as the precautionary principles and the public trust doctrine (see Chapter 6) in their interpretation of the charter and other similar treaties.

Both the commission and the court should follow the path of other highly respected judicial and human rights bodies, such as the South African Constitutional Court and UN mechanisms (in particular the UN Committee on the Rights of the Child), that have recognised the causal relationship between corruption and human rights. Adapting the principles articulated in the case of *Glenister v President of the Republic of South Africa and Others*,[283] for example, could help to provide the encouragement and inspiration for the commission, the court, and AU member states to take the matter further through a creative interpretation of the charter, and to develop and draft an appropriate text to specifically recognise the connection and grant legal standing to victims.

In the *Glenister case*, it was argued for the applicant among others that in enacting anti-corruption laws, the government had a responsibility to act reasonably and accountably, to cultivate good human resource management, to respect international treaty obligations and the values enshrined in the Bill of Rights (virtually similar to those just discussed under the African Charter), and to maintain an independent anti-corruption unit and allow its proper functioning. The respondents maintained that the scheme of the laws served a legitimate governmental purpose to pursue

[282] In each of the cases, the court issued 'provisional measures . . . in view of the urgency and gravity of the matter'. In the Kenyan case, the government was restrained from evicting the Ogiek community from their land pending the hearing of the substantive application. In the Libyan case, the court asked the government to observe 'the principles of justice that requires every accused person to be accorded a fair and just trial, including access to family and legal representation of his own choosing', and to refrain from 'taking any measures that may affect the Detainee's physical and mental integrity as well as his health'. For details on these and its other cases, see African Court on Human and Peoples' Rights, www.african-court.org/en/.

[283] *Glenister v President of the Republic of South Africa and Others* (CCT 48/10) [2011] ZACC 6; 2011 (3) SA 347 (CC); 2011 (7) BCLR 651 (CC). See also, *Doctors for Life International v The Speaker of the National Assembly and Others* (CCT12/05) [2006] ZACC 11; 2006 (12) BCLR 1399 (CC); 2006 (6) SA 416 (CC).

corruption, and that the means sought to achieve this end were logical, rational, and consistent with the constitution. The court held that the Hawks, a unit charged with investigating corruption, were not sufficiently independent and that the state had therefore failed in its obligations to respect, protect, promote, and fulfil the rights in the Bill of Rights as required by section 7(2) of the constitution,[284] and thereby infringed the rights to equality, human dignity, freedom, security of the person, administrative justice, and socioeconomic rights – including the rights to education, housing, and health.[285]

Even so, the extent to which the commission and the court can address corruption and human rights along the lines outlined by the constitutional court will ultimately depend on the ability of victims and NGOs to specifically submit complaints before these bodies (and on the domestic level, before human rights commissions, the judiciary and other appropriate fora). Also, while more specific standards will need to be developed and agreed upon by AU member states to better achieve the potential of the African Charter to combat corruption, in the meantime, the charter can be used creatively to interpret and to open the door for a better enforcement of anticorruption instruments and protection of human rights. Both the commission and the court must act as the spur to encourage such actions, because human rights law is at a development stage and if it is constantly compromised by corruption, it will be helpless to respond to violations. Yet, as has been consistently noted, combating corruption may not in itself prompt a well-spring of human rights. There are countries where human rights have increased, yet with an increase in corruption. Conversely, there are countries where corruption is quite low but their human rights record is poor. However, while addressing corruption may not be the only step needed to foster respect of human rights, it is unarguably a significant one, especially in countries (with weak legal and judicial institutions) where corruption is large-scale and where it precipitates human rights violations. It has been the central argument of this book that corruption cannot be effectively combated by reliance only on

[284] However, the minority decision considered that the Hawks unit was sufficiently protected from such interference.

[285] On the implications of s 7(2) of the constitution, the court stated eloquently: 'I accept that corruption has a deleterious impact on a number of rights in the Bill of Rights and that the state has a positive duty under section 7(2) to prevent and combat corruption and organized crime. I also accept that, in giving content to the obligations of the state in section 7(2), a court must consider international law as an interpretive tool as required by section 39(1)(b). Under section 7(2), there are a number of ways in which the state can fulfill its obligations to protect the rights in the Bill of Rights. The Constitution leaves the choice of the means to the state. How this obligation is fulfilled and the rate at which it must be fulfilled must necessarily depend upon the nature of the right involved, the availability of government resources and whether there are other provisions of the Constitution that spell out how the right in question must be protected or given effect.' *Glenister v President of the Republic of South Africa and Others* (n 277) 175–76.

the criminal and law enforcement approach, and a comprehensive and multidisciplinary approach which incorporates human rights law will be required to adequately and effectively deal with the problem and its effects on human rights.

The following chapter complements and builds on the discussions here, specifically focusing on Article 21 of the charter. While Article 21 is part and parcel of the substantive provisions of the charter, the provisions possess some special character not least because it is the closest point in the charter that is directly relevant to any discussion on corruption from a human right perspective. It is to that discussion we now turn.

# 6

# *The Potential of Human Rights Law in Combating Corruption in Africa*

## INTRODUCTION

THIS CHAPTER EXPLORES the potential contribution of human rights law to address corruption across African states; it makes the case for a comprehensive and complementary legal framework that includes human rights law. The chapter considers the effective remedies that exist under human rights law for victims of corruption (who are mostly the economically and socially vulnerable). The chapter first discusses (and attempts to clarify) the concept of the right to wealth and natural resources under international law. While acknowledging the different meanings and characteristics of this concept and its uncertainties, the chapter then highlights some basic principles upon which there is a general agreement. It specifically examines and evaluates Article 21 of the African Charter on Human and Peoples' Rights in the context of corruption and explores the potential of this provision to provide a human rights basis for preventing and combating the problem. It will be argued that Article 21 is crucial to the effective enjoyment of many other substantive human and peoples' rights in the charter, discussed earlier in Chapter 5.

The chapter also looks at the relationship between Article 21 and other substantive provisions of the charter, as well as the approach of the African Commission on Human and Peoples' Rights to these provisions as a whole. Where appropriate, comparative jurisprudence, including provisions under Common Article 1 of the International Covenant on Economic, Social and Cultural Rights (ICESCR) and International Covenant on Civil and Political Rights (ICCPR), are considered.

The chapter also considers the procedural, substantive and practical challenges that might arise when corruption is combated through human rights law, and it looks at the legal tools, as well as regional and international 'best practices', that might be utilised to overcome these challenges. Key concepts such as 'victims of corruption', 'economically and socially vulnerable', 'legal standing', 'causation', and the whole issue of how to measure the harm that corruption causes are discussed as important principles – such as 'precautionary principle', 'public trust doctrine', and the 'reasonableness test' – and their potential for operationalising Article 21 to combat corruption. The chapter also discusses the relationships between human rights law and criminal law approaches to corruption, and underscores the advantages of the former over the latter.

## THE CONCEPT OF RIGHT TO WEALTH AND NATURAL RESOURCES

The idea of the right to wealth and natural resources, commonly known as the doctrine of permanent sovereignty over natural resources (or PSNR, but hereafter, right to resources) is a longstanding, though generally controversial one.[1] The concept has existed since the colonial period, and the controversy around it was generated in part because of the fusion of the right over resources with the right to self-determination.[2] Nonetheless, since the United Nations General Assembly adopted Resolution 626 (VII) in 1952, declaring that 'the right of peoples freely to use and exploit their natural wealth and resources is inherent in their sovereignty', several more statements and resolutions have subsequently followed, reaffirming the right.

One of the factors behind the adoption of the 1952 resolution was presumably to protect the interests of emerging and newly independent governments against foreign investors and others who might effectuate expropriations, such as wealth and resources, without compensation. Thus, the resolution was adopted against the background of unequal distribution of wealth and resources brought about by colonialism. It essentially aimed to safeguard and promote the national economy of developing states, and served as a mechanism for resolving interstate disputes between colonising states and newly independent colonies (that is, foreign claims of entitlement to continued rights over natural resources acquired during the colonial period).[3] It was thought at the time that the exercise of human rights to self-determination would be impossible without providing peoples of the state with a right to permanent sovereignty over natural resources.4 Accordingly, the resolution recognises the rela-

[1] See, eg, Lillian Aponte Miranda, 'The Role of International Law in Intrastate Natural Resource Allocation: Sovereignty, Human Rights, and Peoples-Based Development' (2012) 45 *Vanderbilt Journal of Transnational Law* 785. The origin of the concept of the right to resources is traceable to the General Assembly Resolution 626 (VII) of 21 December 1952. In 1954, the Commission on Human Rights recommended that the General Assembly, through the ECOSOC, should establish a commission with a mandate to further elaborate upon the substantive contours of the right of peoples and nations to 'permanent sovereignty over their natural wealth and resources', which they deemed a 'basic constituent of the right to self-determination'; however, it was not until 1958 that the General Assembly actually established the Commission on Permanent Sovereignty over Natural Resources.

[2] Miranda, 'The Role of International Law' (n 1) 785.

[3] ibid, 786.

[4] ibid, 793.

tionship between economic development and international peace and security, and affirms the importance of the right to wealth and natural resources of developing regions. But the resolution also states that this right should not be exercised in a manner that would impede the free flow of capital or undermine economic cooperation among states.

A decade later, in 1962, the General Assembly adopted Resolution 1803 (XVII), building on the 1952 resolution and reaffirming that both peoples and nations have a right to exercise sovereignty over natural resources.[5] Elaboration of the right took place, notably in the form of the Charter of Economic Rights and Duties of States,[6] which expanded on the applicability of the principle beyond the physical natural resource wealth of the state, to include economic activities. The right thus includes the sovereign right of states to pursue economic activities commensurate with national development goals.

The articulation of the two rights together has led to suggestions that the right to self-determination is intimately linked with the notion of permanent sovereignty over natural resources. However, as will be shown in this chapter, while Article 21 of the African Charter guarantees the right to resources, it omits any explicit reference to the right to self-determination. Similarly, unlike the right to self-determination, which is recognised as a right of peoples, the scope of the right to resources, and who may be entitled to claim that right, remains relatively unclear and controversial. According to Ian Brownlie, self-determination is 'the right of cohesive national groups (for example, "peoples") to choose for themselves a form of political organization and their relation to other groups. The choice may be independence as a State, association with other groups in a federal State, or autonomy or assimilation in a unitary State.'[7] This definition, however, only puts forward the internal notion of self-determination.

Progressively, therefore, the right has been developed primarily as a shield used by developing states to presumably control the goals and means of their economic development.[8] Nonetheless, concepts like 'sovereignty' and 'states' 'have only that significance and meaning which a particular international society at a particular time chooses to give them; they may change as social attitudes, circumstances, and purposes change'.[9] In addition, these concepts have meaning only in the context of the broader

[5] See, also, Permanent Sovereignty over Natural Resources, GA Res 1803 (XVII), UN Doc A/5217 (14 December 1962).

[6] GA Res 1803 (XVII) of 1962; GA Res 2158 (XXI) of 1966; UNCTAD Res 88 (XII) of 1972; and resolutions on the Declaration on the Establishment of a New International Economic Order (A/Res/321-S-VI) and the Programme of Action on the Establishment of a New International Economic Order (A/Res/3202 S-Vi) 7.

[7] Ian Brownlie, *Principles of Public International Law*, 6th edn (Oxford: Oxford University Press, 2003) 553.

[8] ibid.

[9] ibid.

international legal system, which may condition or limit these rights.[10] As discussed earlier in Chapter 1, the idea of an absolute sovereign is outmoded and has been replaced with the notion of representative government. Furthermore, the inclusion of the right to resources in human rights treaties indicates a progressive development under international law to ensure that the exercise of the right by states is not abused, and that states use their resources solely for the benefit and welfare of their citizens.

In a general sense, natural resources[11] are 'the individual elements of the natural environment that provide economic and social services to human society'.[12] Traditionally, natural resources include those that provide quantifiable economic products, such as industrial minerals, energy sources, timber, or agricultural land.[13] More recently, however, the concept of natural resources has expanded considerably, to include things like 'ecological elements and the services derived from ecosystem processes'.[14] Additionally, resources located in a nation's territory, including its natural resources and territorial waters, are subject to its sovereignty. This rule is now 'so strongly established that territorial sovereignty and sovereignty over resources present within a nation's territory usually are linked inseparably in peoples' minds'.[15] The sovereignty of states over resources is analogous to the domestic law notion of the right of ownership over property (which grants broad control over the use of property or resources), and presumably extends to 'the seas adjacent [within the exclusive economic zone] to but not legally within national territory'.[16] As noted, while the right to resources has traditionally been featured as a framework for claims between colonial powers and newly independent states, it has regrettably played a less prominent role 'in current struggles between local elites controlling the state apparatus and the local population'.[17]

Even so, while a plethora of declarations and resolutions on the right to resources have existed for many years, and the formulation of the right may seem straightforward to understand, conceptual uncertainties remain as to the parameters of the right. For example, opinions are divided

[10] ibid.

[11] Natural resources are actual or potential forms of wealth supplied by nature, such as coal, oil, water power, arable land. *Black's Law Dictionary* defines a natural resource as 'any material in its native state which when extracted has economic value ... The term includes not only timber, gas, oil, coal, minerals, lakes, and submerged lands, but, also, features which supply a human need and contribute to the health, welfare, and benefit of a community, and are essential to the well-being thereof.' *Black's Law Dictionary,* 6th edn (St Paul, MN: West Publishing, 1996) 1027.

[12] James Peck, 'Measuring Justice For Nature: Issues In Evaluating And Litigating Natural Resources Damages' (1998–99) 14 *Journal of Land Use & Environmental Law* 277.

[13] ibid.

[14] ibid.

[15] ibid.

[16] ibid.

[17] ibid.

as to who exactly is entitled to the enjoyment of this right[18] (that is, whether the right 'inheres' in states or peoples, or whether both states and peoples enjoy the right jointly).[19] It is generally accepted that the notion of permanent sovereignty grants to a state the right to expropriate or nationalise foreign and national property rights found within its jurisdiction.[20] This right in turn allows a state to make rules and regulations over wealth and resources within its territory, and to enforce them without any external interference. Those who argue that the right belongs to each state justify this on the grounds that the concept emerged initially from relations between multinational resource extraction corporations and their host states, as well as from the right of the state to make laws for the common good in the area of natural resources.[21] As James Crawford observed, '[W]hat was originally treated as a right of peoples is here treated as a right of States, thus casting doubt upon the legitimacy of the assertion that peoples have a right to permanent sovereignty over their natural resources.'[22]

Nonetheless, whereas Articles 1(2), 13, and 55 of the UN Charter suggest that a state controls their wealth and natural resources, the development and evolution of human rights law has constituted a limitation to state's 'sovereignty' and control, and today the notion of a sovereign people (both politically and economically) is now a widely accepted norm. In this respect, other commentators have stated that while the right may have belonged solely to the state in the past, the right to resources (and to self-determination of these resources) belongs jointly to the state and to the peoples within the state.[23] When exercising the right to resources, a state acts as 'a temporary guardian, custodian, agent, or trustee charged with the responsibility of managing the natural resources for the benefit

[18] Emeka Duruigbo, 'Realizing the People's Right to Natural Resources' (2011) 111 *Whitehead Journal of Diplomacy & International Relations* 12; Hurst Hannum, 'Rethinking Self-Determination' (1993) 1 *Virginia Journal of International Law* 34; Hurst Hannum, 'The Right to Determination in the Twenty-First Century' (1998) 55 *Washington & Lee Law Review* 773; Richard N Kiwanuka, 'The Meaning of "People" in the African Charter on Human and Peoples' Rights' (1988) 80 *American Journal of International Law* 82; Rachel Murray and Steven Wheatley, 'Groups and the African Charter on Human and Peoples' Rights' (2003) 25 *Human Rights Quarterly* 213–236; Joseph Oloka-Onyango, 'Reinforcing Marginalized Rights in an Age of Globalization: International Mechanisms, Non-State Actors, and the Struggle for Peoples' Rights in Africa' (2003) 18 *American University International Review* 851; Theo van Boven, 'The Relations Between Peoples' Rights and Human Rights in the African Charter' (1986) 7 *Human Rights Law Journal* 186.

[19] Emeka Duruigbo, 'Realizing the People's Right to Natural Resources' (n 18).

[20] John Barolo, 'Some International Legal Problems Arising from the Definition and Application of the Concept of "Permanent Sovereignty Over Wealth and Natural Resources" of States' (1987) 20 *Comparative & Intellectual Law Journal of South Africa* 335.

[21] ibid.

[22] James Crawford (ed), 'The Rights of Peoples: Some Conclusions' in *The Rights of Peoples* (Oxford: Clarendon Press, 1995) 170.

[23] ibid.

of all the people in the country'.[24] According to Theo van Boven, the world community decided deliberately to develop the right of peoples to resources, which stemmed from the experiences of World War II.[25] Judge Antonio Cassese agreed that while every state has the right over its natural resources, the right clearly belongs to its people.[26] In the same vein, Makau Wa Mutua suggested that the inclusion of the right in human rights treaties shows that human rights attach not only to individuals but also to peoples.[27]

Apart from the controversies over who may claim the right to resources, there is also some conceptual confusion in relation to the terms found in the formulation of the right. Perhaps the most important is the meaning and characteristics of the term 'peoples', which has been variously defined. During the process of decolonisation, it originally referred to those peoples who had not yet been able to exercise their right to political self-determination. Mutua has described the right to resources as 'a legal by-product of decolonization, that expresses the sovereignty and proprietary entitlements of states and their people over the resources found on their territory'.[28] Yet, according to *Black's Law Dictionary*, it means: 'A state; a nation in its collective and political capacity.'[29] As used in constitutional law, however, the word peoples generally means 'the entire body of those citizens of a state or nation who are invested with political power for political purposes, that is, the qualified voters or electors'.[30] In the context of the 'rights of the people, or of the government of the people by law, or of the people as a non-political aggregate',[31] the word can also mean 'all the inhabitants of the state or nation, without distinction as to sex, age, or otherwise'.[32]

In this respect, some commentators agree that the term 'peoples' can be used to refer to an entire population of a state.[33] On the one hand, peoples may serve as a 'proxy for state'.[34] This conception of peoples suggests that the right to resources can also be enjoyed by 'states'. On the other hand,

[24] ibid.

[25] Theo van Boven, 'Human Rights and Rights of Peoples' (1995) 6 *European Journal of International Law* 470.

[26] Antonio Cassese, 'The Self-Determination of Peoples' in Louis Henkin (ed), *The International Bill of Human Rights: The Covenant on Civil and Political Rights* (New York: Columbia University Press, 1981) 103.

[27] Makau wa Mutua, 'The Banjul Charter and the African Cultural Fingerprint: An Evaluation of the Language of Duties' (1995) 35 *Virginia Journal of International Law* 376.

[28] ibid.

[29] *Black's Law Dictionary*.

[30] See, for example, *Koeliler v Hill* 00 Iowa, 543, 15 NW 009; *Dred Scott v Sandford* 60 US 393 (1857); ; *Boyd v Nebraska* 143 US 135, 12 S Ct 375, 30 Law Ed 103; and *Rogers v Jacob* 88 Ky 502, 11 SW 513, among others.

[31] *Black's Law Dictionary*.

[32] ibid.

[33] Duruigbo, 'Realizing the People's Right' (n 18).

[34] ibid.

even though peoples and state are often used interchangeably, they are not generally synonymous. Peoples are 'discrete communities within the national polity'.[35] The term 'peoples' has also been used to include those under colonial occupation; a portion of the population, such as indigenous peoples, or as noted, the whole of the population.[36]

Emeka Duruigbo has argued that the right to resources is, in fact, 'a right of peoples, not states'. [37] One would add that it is important to recognise peoples' right to resources if they are to be able to hold states accountable under international law (including the African Charter) for corruption by high-ranking officials. It has been stated that, 'while there may be legitimate scholarly, political, and judicial disputes as to the right repository of the sovereign right over natural resources – between the state and the people – there is hardly any question that the people have a right to the proper management of natural resources to their benefit'.[38] There is indeed a broad consensus that the right to wealth and natural resources must be exercised in the interest of national development and the well-being of the people of a state. This proposition is buttressed further by the inclusion of the right in Article 21 of the African Charter, and before that, common Article 1 of the International Covenant on Civil and Political Rights and International Covenant on Economic, Social and Cultural Rights.[39]

Although initially developed as a political concept aimed to protect equality and sovereignty of states over their resources against abuses by other states, the right to resources has evolved rapidly over the years under international law, to cover states' duties to ensure that wealth and natural resources are used for the sole benefit of a state's people. As Kamal Hossain has written, 'permanent sovereignty reflects the inherent and overriding right of a state to control the exploitation and the use of its natural resources. However, a state has to exercise this right for the benefit of its citizens'.

In the context of the ICESCR, for example, Richard Falk contends that the term 'peoples' in the covenant implies 'that governments are the authoritative representatives of people, that they act in international institutions in a fundamental representational role, and that it is ultimately the legitimacy of the peoples that they represent, not their own expression of State interests, that is the underlying ground of their validity'.[40] He goes on to argue that it is the legitimacy of the peoples, not the transient and potentially dubious legitimacy of governments, which constitutes the

[35] Miranda, 'The Role of International Law' (n 1) 802.

[36] ibid.

[37] Duruigbo, 'Realizing the People's Right' (n 18).

[38] ibid, 112.

[39] However, unlike Art 21 of the African Charter which only covers the right to wealth and natural resources, Common Art 1 also articulates the right to self-determination.

[40] Richard Falk, 'The Rights of Peoples (In Particular Indigenous Peoples)' in James Crawford (ed), *The Rights of Peoples* (Oxford: Clarendon Press, 1995) 25.

purpose and rationale for the instruments protecting human rights and for the whole idea of international solidarity.[41] Thus, 'states in this sense are an artificial and derivative political reality as compared to peoples'.[42] And according to James Crawford, given its entrenchment in human rights treaties such as the ICESCR, 'the precedent for treating questions of permanent sovereignty over natural resources as rights of peoples, rather than as rights of States, is an established one'.[43] He argues that the principle of permanent sovereignty over natural resources has the capacity of operating as a guarantee of peoples against their own government, thus limiting the capacity of governments in the interests of the community.[44] In his view, Article 21 makes a state's natural resources policy justiciable in the African Commission.

On Richard N Kiwanuka's account, the term 'peoples' in the African Charter was not defined by its drafters, 'so as not to end up in [a] difficult discussion'.[45] But he defined it to mean 'the state and the people as synonymous and all persons within a state'.[46] Nonetheless, the drafting history of the charter would seem to provide some clues as to the rationale for the inclusion of peoples' rights. For example, the Organization of African Unity (OAU) rapporteur responsible for the drafting process reported that, 'Noting that in Africa, Man is part and parcel of the group, some delegations concluded that individual rights could be explained and justified only by the rights of the community. Consequently, they wished that the draft charter made room for the peoples' rights.'[47] However, others have questioned the appropriateness of including a right of peoples in the context of a human rights treaty concerned primarily with the position of individuals. But as Kiwanuka put it in the context of the African Charter, 'peoples' rights are ultimately destined for individuals, they are *ipso facto* human rights'.[48] Peoples' rights can 'serve as tools of liberation for the deprived, the oppressed, the have-nots and victims of discrimination'.[49] This would seem to resonate very well with Kiwanuka's notion of peoples' rights, and the 'mission statement' of human rights

[41] ibid.
[42] ibid.
[43] James Crawford (ed), 'The Rights of Peoples: "Peoples" or Governments?' in *The Rights of Peoples* (Oxford: Clarendon Press, 1995) 63.
[44] ibid, 64.
[45] Kiwanuka, 'The Meaning of "People" in the African Charter on Human and Peoples' Rights' (n 18) 82. The Charter of the United Nations refers copiously to the rights of peoples, as does the Universal Declaration of the Rights of Peoples, adopted in 1976 during a conference in Algiers.
[46] Kiwanuka, 'The Meaning of "People" in the African Charter on Human and Peoples' Rights,' (n 18) 101.
[47] Rapporteur's Report, OAU Doc CM/1149 (XXXVII), Annex 1: 4(14) (1981).
[48] ibid, 85.
[49] van Boven, 'The Relations between Peoples' Rights and Human Rights in the African Charter' (n 18) 192.

law, which is exactly to improve the welfare of populations (both individually and collectively) and to enhance the dignity of the human person. Ultimately, the effectiveness of human rights treaties such as the African Charter will be measured by the extent to which governments and indeed the international community accord equal priority attention to all rights.

At any rate, regardless of the conceptual uncertainties and controversies as to the legal nature of peoples' rights,[50] these rights remain legally enforceable by virtue of their inclusion in the African Charter. Article 1 of the charter makes it clear that states parties are bound to recognise all the rights and freedoms it enshrines. It is also clear from the provisions of the charter that human and peoples' rights are closely intertwined, as individual rights can only be realised within the context of a community. Accordingly, the charter 'places individual human rights in the contextual setting of peoples' rights, with due respect for the human person as the central subject of development'.[51] Theo van Boven stated convincingly that, 'the notion of peoples' right itself is not destructive of human rights; rather, it places peoples' rights and human rights in a positive and dialectical relationship as mutually supportive and complementary concepts. Both . . . inherently reflect the quest for justice.'[52]

The African Commission on Human and Peoples' Rights has considered the issue of who constitutes peoples within the context of the charter, though with less clarity and perhaps, inconsistency. It has used the term 'people' to variously refer to the entire population of a state, to the entire population of the continent, and to a segment of the population of a state. The commission's approach suggests peoples' rights are collective rights to be enjoyed by those sharing some common identity. For example, in the case of *Centre for Minority Rights Development v Kenya*,[53] the African Commission had to address the state of Kenya's argument that the Endorois did not constitute an indigenous people entitled to the collective

[50] Theo van Boven captured the controversy surrounding peoples' rights succinctly when he stated, 'the notion of peoples' rights is controversial and contentious in the minds of politicians and diplomats who defend the interests of governments and States. Likewise, many legal experts do not feel at ease at this notion. They question the legal nature of peoples' rights'. Ibid. For example, Ebow Bobdzie-Simpson has described peoples' rights in the charter, rather erroneously, as 'aspirational and exhortatory'. Ebow Bobdzie-Simpson, 'A Critique of the African Charter on Human and Peoples' Rights' (1988) 31 *Howard Law Journal* 654. See also Philip Alston, to the effect that, 'there is no reason to expect that the African Charter will prove in the years ahead to be a force for the progressive development of peoples' rights, despite the occasional invocation of the concept for rhetorical purposes'. Philip Alston, 'Peoples' Rights: Their Rise and Fall, in *Peoples' Rights* (Oxford: Oxford University Press, 2001) 287.

[51] van Boven, 'The Relations between Peoples' Rights and Human Rights in the African Charter,' (n 18) 194.

[52] ibid.

[53] *Centre for Minority Rights Dev v Kenya*, African Commission on Human & Peoples' Rights, Communication No 276/2003, 145 (2009).

rights granted by the African Charter. The commission recognised the challenge of defining peoples: 'What is clear is that all attempts to define the concept of indigenous peoples recognize the linkages between peoples, their land, and culture and that such group expresses its desire to be identified as a people or have the consciousness that they are a people.' However, while the term 'peoples' is generally a social entity with a unique identity and characteristics and a special relationship with a territory, it is not synonymous only with ethnic, religious, or linguistic minorities.[54] In *Saramaka People v Suriname*,[55] for example, the Inter-American Court of Human Rights ruled that a tribal group which shares the characteristics that make indigenous peoples unique – a spiritual relationship with the land and a distinct culture, language, and traditions – is entitled to the same spectrum of land and resource rights.

For the first time, the International Court of Justice (ICJ) had the chance in *Armed Activities on the Territory of the Congo* (*Democratic Republic of the Congo v Uganda*)[56] to rule on the nature of the right to resources. The facts of the case briefly are as follows. The case, filed before the ICJ on 23 June 1999 by the Democratic Republic of the Congo (DRC) against Uganda had its genesis in the military assistance provided by both Uganda and Rwanda, which aided the coming to power in May 1997 of former President Laurent Desire Kabila. The DRC claimed that Ugandan armed forces had invaded its towns and territory in August 1998 and that the Ugandan government had defied all requests to remove its troops from Congolese territory. It was also claimed that Uganda had actively recruited, funded, trained and equipped armed Congolese groups attempting to overthrow the Kabila government. The DRC therefore wanted the ICJ to hold Uganda responsible for violation of (1) principles of conventional and customary law by its military and paramilitary activities against the DRC; (2) human rights obligations, by failing to prevent human rights abuses perpetrated by persons under Uganda's control, and (3) conventional and customary law, by exploiting and pillaging Congolese resources. But Uganda on its part claimed that it was the DRC which had violated (1) Article 2(4) of the UN Charter and customary international law by acting inconsistently with the prohibition on the use of force, and (2) the Vienna Convention on Diplomatic Relations for attacks on its diplomatic personnel, premises, and Ugandan nationals.

[54] ECOSOC, Sub-Commission on Prevention of Discrimination and Protection of Minorities, 'The Right to Self-Determination' 71, UN Doc E/CN 4/Sub 2/404/R 1, 39–41.

[55] *Case of the Saramaka People v Suriname*, Inter-Am Ct HR (ser C) No 172 (28 November 2007).

[56] *Armed Activities on the Territory of the Congo (Dem Rep Congo v Uganda)* 2005 ICJ 116, 222–50.

The court held that Uganda had gravely violated the prohibition on the use of force, and also its international humanitarian and human rights obligations, during its occupation of the territory of DRC. However, the court also held DRC to be in violation of Article 2(4) of the UN Charter, by acting inconsistently in relation to the prohibition on the use of force, and Vienna Convention on Diplomatic Relations by attacking Ugandan diplomatic personnel, premises and Ugandan nationals. Regrettably, the ICJ, apart from simply reaffirming the existence of the right to wealth and natural resources in customary international law, bluntly refused to consider this right in the specific circumstances of the case. This refusal was in part due to the court's 'policy considerations' and the fact that the court had other, more precise (and presumably less controversial) sources of international law on which to draw to establish the international legal obligations of the various actors involved.[57] The basis for the court's decision to reject the DRC's argument on the basis of the right to resources has been explained thus:

> The PSNR doctrine has certainly been useful in formulating redistributive claims in situations of patent imbalance of the division of wealth between local actors and foreign investors. But this use of the principle has itself led to questionable patterns of distribution. Because PSNR is operationalized through government authorities, it has produced a concentration of the resource-based wealth in the hands of the political elites controlling state apparatuses, obscuring any assessment of the internal sharing among different groups.[58]

Nonetheless, it is noteworthy to mention that both the DRC and Uganda agreed upon the idea that resource exploitation must be exercised in the interest of the people, although their approaches to the issue were slightly different – whereas the DRC took 'a more statist approach', Uganda took 'a localist one'. Uganda also repeatedly underscored in its argument the notion of the right to resources that stressed the connection of people with the resources and their ability to freely dispose of any such resources. Arguably, the court's rejection meant that it did not want to either sanction or adopt a statist approach to the interpretation of the right to resources, or extend its application in a situation of armed conflict.[59] Even so, the ICJ held that some of the resource exploitation that took place during the conflict in the DRC was illegal. The court's decision rested on the prohibition of pillage in Article 47 of the Hague Regulations of 1907, Article 33 of the Fourth Geneva Convention of 1949, and, of relevance to this book, Article 21(2) of the African Charter to address the issue

[57] Robert Deferens, 'Reflections and Extrapolation on the ICJ's Approach to Illegal Resource Exploitation' in *The Armed Activities Case*, http://nyujilp.org/wp-content/uploads/2013/02/40.S-Dufresne.pdf, 171, 214.
[58] ibid.
[59] ibid.

of recovery and compensation in the case of spoliation. But the court missed a rare opportunity to articulate its position on the right to resources – the court simply said that the right could not apply in conflict situations. It has been observed that, '[T]he Court's reasoning is characterized by an attitude of doctrinal traditionalism and restraint'.[60] This criticism of the ICJ's decision would seem well justified, being based on the grounds that the court ignored the 'doctrinal innovations and novel arguments that the parties, as well as other institutional actors who have examined the question, put forward to assess the resource exploitation dimension of the conflict'. [61]

It is noteworthy though that while the court failed to deal with the question of resource exploitation by non-state actors and non-occupying states, its decision has nonetheless somewhat helped to resolve some theoretical confusion on the meaning and scope of the right to resources, and who may be able to claim it.[62] Robert Dufresne identified four important dimensions of the ICJ's approach to the issue of the right to resources.[63] First, the court's approach was rooted in classic categories found in international humanitarian law to identify the forms of misappropriation that were unlawful.[64] The court also treated the legal categories of misappropriation mostly as an ensemble of equivalent, interchangeable, or aggregate forms of acquisition, thereby restraining itself from distinguishing between the various categories.[65] Second, the court deferred significantly to the law of occupation to flesh out the multilayered state obligations, in its appraisal of the illegality of the resource exploitation that took place in eastern DRC.[66] Third, the ICJ applied these two classical branches of international law (humanitarian law and the law of occupation) through the framework of state responsibility, which in Dufresne's view, 'primarily leaves the conduct of private economic actors in the field of international law's blind spots'.[67] Fourth, the ICJ rejected 'novel arguments anchored in the notion of permanent sovereignty over natural resources, deeming the notion irrelevant to conflict situations'.[68] Similarly, the ICJ refused to uphold 'a stretched and state-centric interpretation of the PSNR principle: one which claims that Congolese governmental authorities have the authority to order, and benefit from, the exploitation of the country's nat-

[60] Robert Dufresne, 'Reflections and Extrapolation on the ICJ's Approach to Illegal Resource Exploitation' (n 57) 205.

[61] ibid.

[62] ibid.

[63] ibid.

[64] ibid.

[65] ibid.

[66] ibid.

[67] ibid.

[68] ibid.

ural resources'.[69] Thus, 'the decision invites a reconstruction of the notion of PSNR that would be less attached to central governments and, hopefully, less prone to abuse'.[70]

One would contend that the application of Article 21 (and other substantive provisions) of the African Charter to combat corruption would contribute to this process of 'reconstruction' of the right to resources. Dufresne wrote that, 'the [court's] decision does not discard PSNR, but it rather opens the door to its rejuvenation and to a better dovetailing with today's social reality'.[71] A reconstruction of the notion of the right to resources to achieve 'a better consideration of the interests of the peoples, notably of affected populations, potentially through a relaxation of governmental privileges',[72] would therefore be a worthwhile exercise, not only in terms of improving the effective enjoyment of all of the rights contained in the African Charter, but also in sustaining the credibility and legitimacy of the regional human rights protection mechanism in particular and global system of human rights in general.

It would be a travesty to sustain the notion of the right to resources as that solely belonging to a state, not least because of the human consequences that inevitably occur when the resources are stolen by high-ranking officials without accountability and without the possibility for peoples (in particular the economically and socially vulnerable) to challenge this theft through the due process of law that the African Charter provides, and to receive effective remedies. Further, as noted, the inclusion of the concept in human rights treaties suggests that the exercise of the right by states cannot be absolute and has to be subject to some transparency and accountability requirements. As Lillian Aponte Miranda put it, 'if the phrase "rights of peoples" has any independent meaning, it must confer rights on peoples against their own governments'.[73]

This next section specifically discusses Article 21 and its relationship with other similarly formulated rights.

## RIGHT TO WEALTH AND NATURAL RESOURCES IN THE AFRICAN CHARTER

Article 21 of the African Charter provides that:

> 1. All peoples shall freely dispose of their wealth and natural resources. This right shall be exercised in the exclusive interest of the people. In no case shall a people be deprived of it.

[69] ibid.
[70] ibid.
[71] ibid.
[72] ibid.
[73] Miranda, 'The Role of International Law' (n 1) 790.

> 2. In case of spoliation the dispossessed people shall have the right to the lawful recovery of its property as well as to an adequate compensation.
> 3. The free disposal of wealth and natural resources shall be exercised without prejudice to the obligation of promoting international economic cooperation based on mutual respect, equitable exchange and the principles of international law.
> 4. States parties to the present Charter shall individually and collectively exercise the right to free disposal of their wealth and natural resources with a view to strengthening African unity and solidarity.
> 5. States parties to the present Charter shall undertake to eliminate all forms of foreign economic exploitation particularly that practiced by international monopolies so as to enable their peoples to fully benefit from the advantages derived from their national resources.

Before addressing the specific contents of Article 21, a number of important points should be highlighted at the outset. Article 21 provisions would seem broad in nature, and general, thus leaving the way open to a variety of interpretations in a manner that presumably would not restrict the scope of the protection it offers, and consistent with the object and purpose of the charter. Crucially, the broad nature of Article 21 might also provide scope for a dynamic and evolutionary interpretation of the provisions. This broadness also provides both interesting challenge and opportunities for the African Commission and the African Court to engage in the normative development and clarification of Article 21 in relation to its potential for addressing corruption.

Furthermore, Article 21 is absolutely important in itself as a right, but also equally at the heart of the entire substantive human and peoples' rights in the charter, as discussed in Chapter 5 of this book. Both the text of the charter and the intentions of its drafters would seem to support such a conclusion. Clearly, human and peoples' rights cannot be realised without efficient and effective use of the resources available to states. The full and effective enjoyment of the rights in the charter invariably assumes the existence and maintenance of legal and institutional orders. Because establishing and maintaining these orders requires not only that states have the necessary resources available, but also the use and application of any such resources to achieve the result sought by the charter. Accordingly, not only are resource issues relevant to the effective and meaningful implementation of all the human and peoples' rights in the charter, but the right to resources itself provides an important framework for addressing the human rights dimension of corruption.

Whereas the clear purpose of the African Charter, as a human rights treaty, is to protect human and peoples' rights,[74] the wording of Article 21

[74] As the preamble underscores, the charter recognises that 'fundamental human rights stem from the attributes of human beings which justifies their national and international protection and [that] the reality and respect of peoples' rights should necessarily guarantee human rights'.

indicates that the right it guarantees is to be enjoyed not only by all peoples but also by all states. As discussed generally above, this might be interpreted as saying that both the peoples and their state are entitled to the enjoyment of the guarantees in Article 21 in equal measures. However, as noted, by its inclusion in a human rights treaty, Article 21 provisions only apply in relation to people, and a state has a 'duty of care' (or what the ECOWAS Court has called 'vigilance' and 'due diligence') to ensure the enjoyment of the right by peoples. As explained in Chapter 1 of this book, the power and authority of a state is no longer absolute. Within the context of Article 21, therefore, people plausibly should be able to exercise the right through their representative (that is, the state). The corollary is that obligations implicit in Article 21, of 'attitude' and 'result', for example, thus provide a preventive framework against corruption and place on states the expectation to use and manage their wealth and resources maximally for the sole benefit of the peoples.

Arguably, Article 21 not only serves to prohibit corruption by high-ranking officials but also requires them to take proactive and progressive steps to use the wealth and resources for peoples' benefit and development. Accordingly, implicit in Article 21 are the guarantees to the right of citizens to demand better management by states of wealth and natural resources in order to ensure that the resources benefit the people to the maximum extent, and not a few high-ranking officials. This proposition can be extended further by arguing that the application of Article 21 is to empower citizens to hold their states accountable for corruption. This stems not only from the fact that human rights are aimed at regulating the domestic relationship between governments and their nationals, but also at the interpretation of the charter's provisions to advance, rather than undermine or impair, the rights guaranteed. Article 21 also strengthens states' obligations towards the effective realisation of those rights as recognised by the charter.

Additionally, the effective enjoyment and realisation of Article 21 provisions can contribute to enhancing economic development and growth which, in turn, might provide an environment for the development and prosperity of individuals and communities, especially the economically and socially vulnerable. Given the nature and negative effects of corruption across African states, any other interpretation of the concept of right to resources would be hollow, and indeed allow corrupt officials to continue to arrogate resources for personal benefit rather than the common good. In this respect, it is crucial for some transparency and accountability requirements and benchmarks to be developed in the context of Article 21, so as to make sure that states' discretion over peoples' wealth and resources are not abused; but if that happens, that the victims are granted legal standing and afforded effective remedies. Moreover, while Article 21 guarantees the right of peoples, it is also absolutely essential for the effective enjoyment of the rights of individuals. Thus, the Human Rights Committee, established pursuant to the International Covenant on Civil and Political Rights, stated:

> [Common article 1 to the two covenants] is of particular importance because its realization is an essential condition for the effective guarantee and observance of individual human rights and for the promotion and strengthening of those rights. It is for that reason that States set forth the right to self-determination in a provision of positive law in both Covenants and placed this provision as article 1 apart from and before all of the other rights in the two Covenants.[75]

Nonetheless, as previously noted, the inclusion of the word 'peoples' in a human rights treaty has not, regrettably, made its definition less controversial or conceptually less ambiguous. The evolutionary interpretation of Article 21, as with other substantive provisions of the charter on peoples' rights, would help to overcome these conceptual difficulties, and ensure that the protection offered by the African Charter and the rights that it recognises are effectively realised. It would also serve as the foundation upon which the realisation of all the other rights recognised under the charter, are to be based.

## The Approach of the African Commission and the Court

Despite its clear importance, however, only a limited number of cases specifically on Article 21 have come before the commission. A chairperson of the commission indeed recently suggested that the commission has so far heard just three cases on Article 21. The paucity of cases directly based on Article 21 probably explains why the commission has not begun to make headway in developing and clarifying the normative contents of that essential right, but it may seem surprising, especially given the well-documented problem of corruption in many African states. One can however understand this conundrum because the idea of combating corruption through human rights law is one that is gaining global attention and scrutiny. It is pertinent to examine how the commission as a body has dealt with the issues of corruption and human rights, specifically with respect to Article 21, and then to contrast this with the views that have been expressed by some commissioners interviewed by this author.

Perhaps the most prominent of the commission's 'jurisprudence' on Article 21 is the case involving devastation of the environment and communities in Ogoniland in Nigeria.[76] This case has been discussed in Chapter 5 but it is useful to note here that the commission found viola-

[75] General Comment 12, para 1.

[76] *The Social and Economic Rights Action Centre (SERAC) and the Center for Economic and Social Rights (CESR) v Nigeria*, Communication 155/96.

tions of Article 21, and several other provisions of the charter, by the Nigerian government.[77] The commission found that Nigeria had violated its charter-based obligations to respect, protect, promote, and fulfil these rights.[78] It stated further that these obligations 'universally apply to all rights and entail a combination of negative and positive duties'[79]; and that 'there is no right in the African Charter that cannot be made effective'.[80] The commission ruled that Nigeria had an obligation to respect the free use of resources of people, individually or collectively, for 'the purpose of rights-related needs',[81] and that Nigeria should ensure adequate compensation for victims of violations.

This was the first time the commission would address substantively issues relating to alleged violations of economic, social and cultural rights. The commission indirectly found violation of Article 21 stating that the Ogonis were denied the right to freely dispose of their wealth and natural resources because the Nigerian government facilitated the destruction of Ogoniland by failing to protect its inhabitants from the devastating activities of the oil companies. The commission found this neglect to '[fall] short of the minimum conduct expected of governments, and therefore, is in violation of Article 21 of the African Charter'.[82] This presumably means that the Nigerian government failed to exercise due diligence with respect to the activities of the oil companies and their effects upon the population of Ogoniland. As has been argued throughout this book, this point by the commission can be extended to suggest that states parties to the charter that fail to exercise due diligence to prevent corruption by their officials will violate the right to resources. If the commission could impute a duty of diligence on the part of states with respect to the operation of oil companies (mainly private companies, with some involvement from a state corporation, NNPC), then nothing stops the commission from reaching similar conclusion with respect to states' own officials that engage in corruption, which arguably has the same effects as with the operation of the oil companies in this case.

However, while the petitioners raised a number of alleged serious human rights violations of the Ogoni people, and the decision of the commission was quite ground-breaking, the commission did not consider the corruption dimension of the case. The commission probably was right not

[77] These include freedoms without discrimination (Art 2); the right to life (Art 4); the right to property (Art 14); the right to health (Art 16); the right to housing, as read into para 18(1) on the duty to protect family; the right to food, as read into Arts 4, 16, and 22; and the right of peoples to a general satisfactory environment (Art 24).

[78] Communication 155/96, *The Social and Economic Rights Action Centre (SERAC) and the Centre for Economic and Social Rights (CESR) v Nigeria*, paras 55–58.

[79] ibid, para 44.

[80] ibid, para 68.

[81] ibid, para 45.

[82] ibid, para 58.

to delve into this area, as the petitioners did not specifically plead corruption in their communication but instead merely referred to a general violation of Article 21. Even so, while the issue of corruption was not raised in this case, the principles that the commission advanced, in particular the notion of the obligations to respect, to protect and to fulfil human rights (which encompass the obligation of prevention of harm to human rights), can be expanded and interpreted to elaborate a human right obligation to combat corruption.

The commission adopted the approach in the *Ogoni case* in a case involving Kenya,[83] by refusing to use the word 'corruption', again, probably because this issue was not raised by the petitioners. This case also has been discussed in Chapter 5 but it is useful to note that the petitioners alleged that the government's decision to turn the Endorois' traditional lands into a game reserve denied the Endorois access to the area, jeopardised the community's pastoral enterprise, and imperilled its cultural integrity. The petitioners also claimed that 30 years after evictions had began, the Endorois had still not had full and fair compensation for the loss of their land and their rights to it. They claimed, inter alia, violation of their Article 21 right to resources. Specifically, the petitioners argued that the Endorois community were unable to access the vital resources in the Lake Bogoria region since their eviction from the game reserve, and that 'the medicinal salt licks and fertile soil that kept the community's cattle healthy are now out of the community's reach. Mining concessions to Endorois land have been granted without giving the Endorois a share in these resources.'[84]

The commission stated that Article 21 imposes a duty on the state to consult with the people and ensure the 'reasonable participation' of people in the benefits derived from the use of resources.[85] Thus, 'a people inhabiting a specific region within a state can claim the protection of Article 21'.[86] Crucially, the commission stated that 'the Endorois have the right to freely dispose of their wealth and natural resources in consultation with the Respondent State'.[87] According to the commission, Article 21(2) 'also concerns the obligations of a State Party to the African Charter in cases of a violation by spoliation, through provision for restitution and compensation. The Endorois have never received adequate compensation or restitution of their land. Accordingly, the Respondent State is found to have violated Article 21 of the Charter.'[88] Like the SERAC case discussed

[83] Communication 276/03, *Centre for Minority Rights Development (Kenya) and Minority Rights Group (on behalf of Endorois Welfare Council) v Kenya* (2003), paras 1–21.
[84] ibid, paras 120–24.
[85] ibid, para 265.
[86] ibid, para 267.
[87] ibid, para 268.
[88] ibid.

above, these principles potentially can be further elaborated and clarified to impute a human rights obligation on states to combat corruption. It is also important to note that the commission elaborated on the notion of 'peoples' and interpreted this to mean not only 'a collective of individuals' bound by a common history tradition, racial or ethnic identity but also significantly, by 'a common economic life'.[89] This presumably would include economically and socially vulnerable.

In a slightly different case,[90] the commission used the word 'looting', thus suggesting that it sees Article 14 as complementary to Article 21, and as such to be read together and interpreted holistically. In this case, involving DRC, Burundi, Rwanda and Uganda, the commission stated,

> The looting, killing, mass and indiscriminate transfers of civilian population, the besiege and damage of the hydro-dam, stopping of essential services in the hospital, leading to deaths of patients and the general disruption of life and state of war that took place while the forces of the Respondent States were occupying and in control of the eastern provinces of the Complainant State are in violation of Article 14 guaranteeing the right to property.[91]

Whereas the commission once again did not specifically use the word corruption, the reference to looting is one of the rare occasions where the commission has come close to addressing the problem of stealing from a government's treasury. As Stuart Green wrote, 'Looting is viewed as a species of the genus of theft, which is typically characterized by unauthorized entry, misappropriation of property, and, often, concerted action. What distinguishes looting from other forms of theft is a lack of normal security brought on by emergency circumstances, resulting in the unusual vulnerability of its victims and a general loss of social order.'[92] Nonetheless, although it is a word commonly used during armed conflicts to refer to stealing by victorious forces, looting in the sense of large-scale corruption by high-ranking officials occupying a position of trust could also arguably be used interchangeably with corruption during peacetime.

Probably the only known case before the commission directly seeking to enforce Article 21 provisions in relation to corruption is the case involving Equatorial Guinea. This case is still pending before the commission. Briefly, the case was filed on behalf of an NGO by the Open Society Justice Initiative and supported through an amicus brief by the Lowenstein International Human Rights Clinic of the Yale Law School. In *APDHE v*

[89] ibid, para 151.

[90] Communication 227/99, *DRC v Burundi, Rwanda and Uganda*, 20th Activity Report, Annex IV (Documents of the African Commission).

[91] ibid, para 88.

[92] Stuart Green, *Law, Looting and Lawlessness* (Berkeley Electronic Press, 2006), www.johnpauliihs.org/johnpaul/community/pattiweinbrenner/files/2011/11/lootingandlawlessness.pdf.

*Equatorial Guinea*,[93] the petitioner claimed that corruption – the alleged stealing of national oil revenues – by Equatorial Guinea government officials violated the right of the Equatorial Guinean people.[94] Although the communication was filed before the commission in 2007, it has suffered several adjournments, and decisions on admissibility have been repeatedly deferred. But the commission decided to be seized of the communication despite a preliminary objection by the government. The petitioner claimed a violation of Article 21 guarantees because 'a small clique of ruling families reaps huge profits through corruption and monopoly control of the national petro-carbon industry, while leaving the ordinary people to live in poverty'.[95] The petitioner seeks the following remedies: oversight by the people of generated government revenue; full implementation of the Extractive Industries Transparency Initiative; periodic and full financial disclosure; and provision of adequate resources in the budget to meet the basic human rights obligations and commitments assumed by the government of Equatorial Guinea.[96]

The amici said that it intervened in the matter because of the 'massive and pervasive resource spoliation in the country',[97] which it considered to be so grave that the commission should admit the petition and hear the claims on the merits. The amici also claimed that the government breached Article 21 because it engaged in 'spoliation of natural resources and corrupt extraction practices [resulting in] denying the people the benefits and revenue derived from their natural resources'. The amici further alleged violation of other charter rights, stressing that, 'as a result of this spoliation, the government also violates the African Charter rights to education, health, development and lawfully acquired property'. The amici concluded:

> Corruption and spoliation of natural resources present a serious challenge to the successful development of Equatorial Guinea and violates collective and individual rights of the people guaranteed in the African Charter . . . Protection from spoliation is also necessary in order to enable people to fully enjoy other human rights . . . [A duty to protect is thus] violated. Preventing spoliation and corruption is critical to ensuring that states meet their human rights obligations.[98]

As the above cases show, the commission's approach (in relation to Article 21 and its potential to address corruption) has been rather less than satis-

[93] For details, see Communication 347/07, *APDHE v Equatorial Guinea*, www.opensocietyfoundations.org/litigation/apdhe-v-equatorial-guinea.

[94] ibid. See sections A–D of the communication detailing the alleged violations of Art 21, 1–8.

[95] ibid, 4.

[96] ibid, 10.

[97] See Communication 347/07, *APDHE v Equatorial Guinea* 'Amicus Brief', www.opensocietyfoundations.org/sites/default/files/c_amicus_20090313.pdf, 3.

[98] ibid 23–26.

factory because its decisions have lacked specificity, incisiveness, and depth in relation to the legal analyses required to achieve the potential and full effect of Article 21. While this problem may not be peculiar to the commission's interpretation of Article 21 and, indeed, is a general and longstanding problem in the interpretative work of the commission as a whole, Article 21 provisions are unquestionably the least enunciated and developed body of work in relation to other substantive provisions of the charter. Although the commission continues to be concerned with matters such as poverty, and has on many occasions pointed out situations – in communication procedures, reporting processes, or promotional and other mechanisms – that are inconsistent and incompatible with the charter, it rarely refers to or uses the term corruption in its work on Article 21, or generally in relation to other substantive provisions of the charter. Clearly, Article 21 does not refer explicitly to corruption. Nonetheless, as this study argues, when read in conjunction with the charter's Article 1, which the ECOWAS Court of Justice has interpreted as imposing the obligations of attitude and results on states, it implicitly prohibits corruption in some ways and can potentially be used to combat it.

In this respect, given the widely recognised close link between corruption and human rights, the vulnerability of those most affected, the impunity of perpetrators, and the potential of the charter to identify the victims and provide them effective remedies, the paucity of the commission's jurisprudence on Article 21 in relation to corruption is unfortunate. In addition to the newness of the issues raised by the relationship between corruption and human rights, the limited engagement of the commission with the idea may also be attributed to other factors, not least of which is the general failure of NGOs (both human rights and anti-corruption NGOs) participating in the work of the commission and thus limited communications that directly raise the issue of corruption within the context of the charter. Other factors include, inter alia, the commission's strict reading of its mandate and, perhaps significantly, the lack of knowledge and expertise of members of the commission in anti-corruption areas. The lack of expertise of members also probably explained the rather limited role played by the commission in the consultations leading to the development, drafting and eventual adoption of the AU Convention on Preventing and Combating Corruption, discussed in Chapter 4.

As suggested by the members of the commission interviewed by the author (interview notes on file), that specific reference was made in the convention to the African Charter was due to a large extent to the contribution of the commission. But while the participation of the commission in the process leading to the drafting and adoption of the convention is not in doubt, the extent of the commission's contribution to the process remains unclear. And the drafting history of the convention does not indicate clearly the degree to which the commission influenced the final document. However, it should be noted that the initial study (carried out by Adama Dieng) commissioned by the AU on the possibility of a regional convention against corruption specifically (and elaborately) mentioned the rights contained in the charter. If anything, most of these seem to have been dropped, as the very limited reference to human rights in the document that was eventually adopted would seem to suggest. This fact perhaps indicates that whatever role the commission might have played was minimal.

Remarkably, in contrast to the commission's limited institutional approach to its work in relation to corruption, interviews conducted by this author with some former and current members of the commission revealed that, as one interviewee admitted, '[They] would carefully consider such a case [that raises corruption issues in relation to the charter] if it is brought before us'. Indeed, all of the commissioners interviewed, past and present, believe that corruption is a violation of the African Charter, though only a few directly linked it to Article 21. This author believes this is correct, as corruption not only affects Article 21, but also other substantive provisions of the charter. In all, this author interviewed three former and two present commissioners, of whom two had served as chairperson. Interviews were conducted between April 2012 and June 2012. Responses received were mostly similar in substance, but two were quite detailed and engaging.

One chairperson of the commission made some important and revealing points. First, she recognised that 'corruption is a big challenge in Africa . . . despite numerous policy diagnoses, public campaigns to raise awareness, and institutional and legal reforms to improve public administration'. Importantly, she hinted that this view was widely, though privately, shared among commissioners. Second, she underscored the links between corruption and human rights. While acknowledging the recent global focus on the issues as 'a good thing', she regretted the fact that 'often times such assertions fail to show in a detailed manner the ways in which the rights are infringed on by different corrupt practices'. She offered some illustrations to back up her position that corruption directly violates the African Charter:

> When such claims are made [that corruption violates human rights] a range of issues are in play. It may mean that, when corruption is widespread, people do not have access to justice, are not secure and cannot protect their livelihoods. Court officials and the police pay more heed to bribes than to law. Hospitals do not heal people because the medical staff gives better treatment to patients who pay backhanders or because clinics lack supplies due to corrupt public contracting procedures. Poor families cannot feed themselves because social security programmes are corrupt or distorted to support a patronage network. Schools cannot offer their students a sound education because the education budget has been looted and as a result teachers cannot be paid and books cannot be pur-

> chased. In numerous ways like these, corruption encourages discrimination, deprives vulnerable people of income, and prevents the enjoyment of all human rights.[99]

She concluded, however: 'I am not able to consider corruption generally or large-scale corruption as a direct violation of the African Charter on Human and Peoples' Rights', though she seemed to contradict herself when she argued (in response to another question[100]):

> The answer should be yes but on an extended interpretation of their obligation. It is now commonly understood that states have three levels of obligation in relation to human rights: the obligations to respect, to protect and to fulfil . . . The obligation to protect is normally taken to be a central function of states, which have to prevent irreparable harm from being inflicted upon members of society. This requires states: (a) to prevent violations of rights by individuals or other non-state actors; (b) to avoid and eliminate incentives to violate rights by third parties; and (c) to provide access to legal remedies when violations have occurred, in order to prevent further deprivations. Noncompliance with this level of obligation may be a vital determinant of state responsibility in corruption cases. By failing to act, states may infringe rights. If they do not criminalize particular practices or fail to enforce certain criminal provisions, for example, they may not prevent, suppress, or punish forms of corruption that cause or lead to violations of rights. A violation of a human right therefore occurs when a state's acts, or failure to act, do not conform with that state's obligation to respect, protect or fulfill recognized human rights of persons under its jurisdiction.

Her follow-up responses seemed to provide further clues as to where she stands on the relationship between corruption and human rights, and specifically in relation to the charter. She differentiated between two approaches in dealing with corruption in what she termed as 'the criminal law enforcement approach to recognizing criminal culpability and the human rights approach to seeking accountability for corruption'. She argued strongly:

> Corruption in Africa has become a growing and pervasive concern. It undermines not only the democratic institutions, but also the social fabric, political and bureaucratic structure of our society. Corruption should be examined from a human rights perspective. [On this] we can analyse corrupt practices that lead to violation of constitutional rights of individuals.[101]

She acknowledged that the commission had the chance to interpret and, indeed, had found violations of Article 21 in at least three cases,[102] and

[99] See Ch 5 of this book for details on how corruption affects the rights to health care, education, housing, etc.

[100] The question was whether the obligations of states to respect and ensure human rights under the African Charter automatically encompass a duty to combat corruption

[101] She recommended that, 'in order to address the systemic inefficiencies in dealing with the problem, key legislative and institutional reforms should be undertaken'.

[102] The three communications she mentioned are: *Democratic Republic of Congo v Burundi, Rwanda, and Uganda; Social and Economic Rights Actions Centre (SERAC) v NIGERIA;* and the

held that the states concerned did not use the resources referred to in the article to the exclusive benefit or interest of the citizens. She conceded – rather regrettably – that 'there is no jurisprudence in the African Commission where Article 21 has been used to combat large scale corruption'. She pointed out that, 'the cause may very well be due to corruption, but the Commission has not so found. It would be interesting for a Complainant to bring a case under this rubric and see how the Commission interprets large-scale corruption'. Yet, whereas the commission may not have used the term corruption in its communication procedure, the chairperson revealed that the commission does in fact use it 'occasionally in Concluding Observations', in relation to state reporting mechanism. She cited as an example the recent concluding observations regarding Nigeria's Fourth Periodic Report, in which the Commission stated: 'Despite Nigeria's fight against corruption, it still remains a challenge and is proving to be a major impediment to development and securing the rights of all Nigerians.'[103] This kind of approach is welcomed, but needs to be further coherently and consistently developed, and not just sporadically in the soft process of constructive dialogue but also in the communication procedures and in other mechanisms of the commission.

Additionally, any conclusions that corruption violates the charter's substantive provisions must automatically translate into concrete remedies and redress available in the African Charter for victims of corruption – individuals and communities – especially the economically and socially vulnerable that are most affected. As argued, while there may not be any explicit reference to remedies for victims of corruption, such remedies can be inferred from the various provisions of the charter through evolutionary and dynamic interpretation. As a former member and chairperson of the commission (now a judge and vice president at the International Criminal Court) wrote pointedly in response to the questionnaire prepared by this author:

> An ingenious and extended interpretation is worth the try. Take the principle of nondiscrimination and equal treatment. It is asserted in regional instruments, including the African Charter [in Articles 2 and 3]. The principles of equality and nondiscrimination are fundamental principles of human rights. The principle that every individual is equal before the law and has the right to be protected by law on an equal basis is affirmed in all the main human rights treaties. The point being made is that, in the case of unequal corrupt treatment lead to unequal and discriminatory outcomes. If corruption restricts a person's access to adequate housing, for instance, it is discriminatory. Housing should be accessible to all, and disadvantaged groups in particular should be granted some degree of priority. After eviction, people are often promised alternative hous-

*Centre for Minority Rights Development (Kenya) and Minority Rights Group International (on behalf of Endorois Welfare Council) v Kenya* (the *Endorois* case).

[103] Nigeria's Fourth Periodic Report.

> ing, but they may subsequently be denied effective access because the officials in charge require bribes. Well-intentioned low-cost housing programmes, designed to benefit disadvantaged groups, may be exploited to the economic advantage of officials in the same way.

Overall, she made important points that are substantially similar to those raised by another former chairperson of the commission, discussed above. First, she agreed that 'corruption violates all provisions that deal with economic and political rights that are provided for in the Charter', but also significantly concurred that 'corruption is a governance issue, [and] most times government officials are involved and complicit'. Second, she suggested that the effective implementation of the charter's rights on the domestic arena would be difficult unless corruption is tackled. As she puts it, '[without addressing corruption] these men and women who are entrusted with the protection and promotion of human rights in a country cannot and will not do it'. Beyond this, she cited several others instances of the negative effects of corruption on the rights guaranteed in the charter, including lack of sound healthcare and education systems because 'corruption reduces the level of government social expenditure on these facilities'; inequality in education; increased costs of governance; an increase in child and infant mortality rates and in school dropouts and teenage pregnancies; inequality in wealth and poverty; impunity of perpetrators; and the culture of 'blame games'. She concluded that, 'the skewed policies and behaviour [resulting from corruption] often lead to violations of all the rights in the Charter, eg property rights.'

On the question of how frequently she used the word corruption when she was on the commission, she wrote: 'Never. Perhaps because complainants do not raise issues of corruption. I think the Commissioners, if they investigated and encouraged shadow reports, could focus on corruption when they interrogate human rights reports. They could also follow [up] on corruption when they undertake promotional missions'. She seemed to suggest that the commission had missed an important opportunity to consider corruption in relation to the charter, in the SERAC, where according to her, 'there were obvious indications of corruption'. This was because the 'issue had not been pleaded with concrete evidence', and that therefore relief was not sought in relation to corruption. But she concluded on a more positive and encouraging note: 'I think the Charter is a proper tool which only needs sophistication and creativity in how it is applied.'

These views by the commissioners interviewed by the author, while not reflecting the position of the commission as a whole, might gain the concurrence of other members. The views also offer some good insights into the thinking of many commissioners on the issues of corruption and human rights, and appear to suggest the direction in which the commission might be moving in the future regarding its normative development and clarification of Article 21 in a manner to achieve the full effect of that provision to address corruption and its effects on other substantive provisions of the charter. As far as the African Court on Human and Peoples' Rights is concerned, however, it has had little to no engagement with Article 21. Although there is a request for advisory opinion pending before the African Court, it has not yet ruled on Article 21 in relation to corruption. The court's lack of jurisprudence may be due to its relative newness and limited access by individual victims and NGOs. The African Court has not been fully functional as regards the interpretation of the African Charter because it has had to turn down many cases on the ground of lack of jurisdiction when the state concerned has not made a declaration pursuant to paragraph 34(6) of the protocol establishing the court.

To be relevant, both the African Commission on Human and Peoples' Rights and the African Court on Human and Peoples' Rights (and the African Court of Justice and Human Rights that will ultimately replace it) must improve their interpretive ability of the charter to ensure that it provides effective remedies for victims of corruption. As noted, this is especially important given the unique provisions of Article 21, which recognises and guarantees the right to wealth and natural resources. It is also important given the status of the charter as a living instrument requiring a dynamic interpretation to be applied in context and in the light of present-day conditions and the human rights challenges posed by corruption. Because Article 21 invariably imposes public interest duties (that is, those interests common to the general public) upon states, it should be exercised for the benefit of the peoples, especially the economically and socially vulnerable. Probably the best way to protect the resources to which Article 21 alludes is for the commission and the court to take a broad approach by imputing a progressive notion of 'public office'. The commission and the court should avoid any interpretation of the charter's provisions (including Article 21) that would give the human and peoples' rights in the charter a narrower construction than that contemplated by the drafters or which are contained in other similar treaties. It would be wrong to approach Article 21 with a hands-off attitude, on the theory that the resources belong to states, especially because of the possibility (even the reality) that such resources are frequently stolen and hard to trace.

In their interpretive functions, the African Commission and the African Court can look to Common Article 1 of the International Covenant on Civil and Political Rights and the International Covenant on Economic, Social and Cultural Rights, as well as comparative jurisprudence, for guidance. While the jurisprudence of both the Human Rights Committee (established to oversee the implementation of the civil and political rights covenant) and the Committee on Economic, Social, and Cultural Rights (established to oversee the economic, social and cultural rights covenant) may have been less than satisfactory, other human rights mechanisms such as the Inter-American Court of Human Rights, have contributed to clarifying the concept contained in common Article 1. As Michael Reisman wrote:

> The point about the permanent sovereignty of peoples over their natural resources is not that the resources in question may not be mined and sold. Such doctrine would render them valueless. The point is rather that the national community in which the resources are found is to be a significant beneficiary of their exploitation. The nation-state is now expected to contribute to the welfare of all inhabitants, without even having the right to discriminate among them.[104]

## OPERATIONALISING ARTICLE 21: INTERPRETATIVE TOOLS, LEGAL DOCTRINES AND THEORIES

Article 60 of the charter allows the commission and the court to 'draw inspiration from international law [including] the Charter of the United Nations . . . the Universal Declaration of Human Rights, [and] other instruments adopted by the United Nations'. Similarly, Article 61 of the charter also allows both the commission and the court:

> [To] take into consideration, as subsidiary measures to determine the principles of law, other general or special international conventions . . . African practices consistent with international norms on human and people's rights, customs generally accepted as law, general principles of law recognized by African states as well as legal precedents and doctrine.

Thus, interpretative tools such as the Vienna Convention on the Laws of Treaties, and common law theories such as proprietary interest can be operationalised through the mechanism of Article 21 to enhance its legal value so that it is able to effectively serve as a basis to empower victims of corruption, and to secure for them effective remedies. Further, proprietary interest of peoples' is clearly recognised in the wording of Article 21.

Words – written or spoken – are a central element of any language, and their usage often convey different meanings and connotations, depending on which particular words are used, where they are used, and who is using them. In a legal and human rights document such as the African Charter, the need arises for an explanation or interpretation of the words and phrases used, in order to elicit the exact intention of the drafters, and the circumstances prompting their choice of words. This is especially important because what at first appear to be concise words and phrases may turn out to be ambiguous. It is thus the work of legal and judicial experts and human rights bodies to clarify the words used in treaties or statutes. It should be noted that these experts are practitioners and

[104] W Michael Reisman, 'Harnessing International Law to Restrain and Recapture Indigenous Spoliations' (1989) 83 *American Journal of International Law* 56–57.

academics with different regional, theoretical, and professional backgrounds. Because of any particular word's complexities, these experts may not always agree about its meaning or the meaning it conveys.

The relationship between law's language and the English language is a close and important one. Ibrahim Imam and Abdulraheem Mustapha stated that, 'Words in their proper order are the raw materials of law and having a magic of their own, color, sound, meaning and associations.'[105] The Supreme Court of Nigeria, in *Attorney General Bendel State v Attorney General of the Federation*, declared: '[W]ords are the common signs that mankind make use of to declare their intention to one another and when the words of a man express his meaning plainly, there is no occasion to have recourse to any other means of interpretation.'[106] Similarly, as Sims Cecil wrote, quoting the novel *Guy Mannering* by Walter Scott, 'these are my tool of trade, a lawyer without history or literature is a mechanic, a mere working if he possesses some knowledge of these he may venture to call himself an architect'.[107]

Human rights, whether contained in a treaty, constitution, or bill of rights, are inevitably imprecise and vague. The interpretative role of judges and human rights bodies, along with others, is of particular importance in clarifying the meanings and the intentions of the drafters in order to ensure the goal of protecting those human rights. In the field of human rights, the rules for engaging in the interpretative exercise, in the context of a treaty like the African Charter, are clearly set out in the Vienna Convention on the Law of Treaties, which is recognised as reflecting customary international law. It is important to interpret Article 21 in the context of the text of the charter and its preamble, and in its object and purpose as a human rights treaty, discussed extensively in Chapter 5. As the European Court of Human Rights declared, regarding the European Convention on Human Rights: 'The Convention is to be read as a whole.'[108] The African Commission itself has stated clearly that, 'The [African] Charter must be interpreted holistically and all clauses must reinforce each other.'[109]

Part of unravelling the holistic interpretation of human rights treaties, in this instance the African Charter, is how to construe phrases such as 'in light of the object and purpose', and in 'good faith'. Clarifying these phrases will assist in identifying the intention of the drafters of the charter and in achieving a practical and effective interpretation of Article 21, ulti-

[105] Ibrahim Imam and Abdulraheem Mustapha, 'An Over1view of Judicial Attitude to Semantic and Grammatical Ambiguities in Law', www.unilorin.edu.ng/publications/imami/SEMANTIC.pdf.

[106] *Attorney General Bendel State v Attorney General of the Federation* (1981) 10 SC 1.

[107] Sims Cecil, 'The Lawyer and the Classics' (1953–54) 8 *Arkansas Law Review* 345.

[108] *Soering v UK* 161 Eur Ct HR (ser A) (1989), 103.

[109] Communication 211/98, *Legal Resources Foundation v Zambia* (2001).

mately leading to a cohesive implementation of the charter's provisions. Both Articles 1 and 2 of the African Charter, (on the object and purpose of the charter), which are necessary to clarify the provisions of Article 21, have been discussed in Chapter 5, but it is worth stressing that any serious interpretation of Article 21 must seek to achieve and safeguard its practical and effective meanings and interpretations in order to secure the reason and purpose for adopting the charter. Also worthy of emphasis are pronouncements by other human rights institutions and courts in relation to the terms 'practical and effective.' For example, the European Court of Human Rights, as stated in *Papamichalopoulos et al v Greece,* that 'The Convention is intended to safeguard rights that are practical and effective.'[110] In several cases, the European Court of Human Rights has affirmed this objective and the special nature of obligations assumed by the states to the European Convention on Human Rights. Thus, in *Ireland v UK,* the court stated:

> Unlike international treaties of classic kind, the Convention comprises more than mere reciprocal engagements between contracting states. It creates, over and above a network of mutual, bilateral undertakings, objective obligations which in the words of the Preamble benefit from a collective enforcement.[111]

Similarly, the purpose of human rights law is to protect rights, not the states. This has been the position of the Inter-American Court of Human Rights in several of its cases, as human rights are said to be inspired by higher shared values (focusing on protection of the human being), they have specific oversight mechanisms, they are applied according to the concept of collective guarantees, they embody obligations that are essentially objective, and their nature is special vis-à-vis other treaties that regulate reciprocal interests among the states parties.[112] Thus, the International Court of Justice, in its Advisory Opinion on the 1948 Genocide Convention, held that:

> In such convention, the contracting states do not have any interests of their own; they merely have, one and all, a common interest, namely, the accomplishment of those high purposes which are the *raison-d'etre* of the convention. Consequently, in a convention of this type one cannot speak of individual advantages or disadvantages to states or of the maintenance of perfect contractual balance between rights and duties.[113]

[110] *Papamichalopoulos et al v Greece* App no 14556/89 (24 June 1993).

[111] *Ireland v UK* (1980) 58 ILR 188, 291.

[112] *Mapiripán Massacre v Colombia,* Judgment of September 15, 2005. Series C No 134 , 104.

[113] International Court of Justice Reports (1951): 23. Also, in the context of the International Covenant on Civil and Political Rights, the Human Rights Committee, which was established to monitor implementation of the covenant by states, observed: 'In an instrument which articulates very many civil and political rights, each of the many articles, and indeed their interplay, secures the objectives of the Covenant. The object and purpose of the Covenant is to create legally binding standards for human rights by defining certain civil and political rights and placing them in a framework of obligations which are legally bind-

Because it directly and arbitrarily deprives peoples of their wealth and natural resources, it is difficult to deny that corruption breaches the content, intent, object, and purpose of Article 21, and indeed all the provisions of the African Charter. The effects of corruption are that it not only deprives peoples of their right to freely dispose of their wealth and natural resources for their own benefit, but it also causes serious injuries and harms to the people – individuals and communities – especially the economically and socially vulnerable, and reflects violations of other human and peoples' rights guaranteed by the charter. The application of the object and purpose test to Article 21 in light of corruption by states parties to the African Charter raises additional human rights and legal issues. The charter not only guarantees the right of people to their natural resources and wealth, but also to important complementary rights. As argued previously, when interpreted together with the concept of object and purpose, this provides a legal framework for implementing states' obligations and for securing the right to resources and wealth and to the other rights guaranteed in the charter.

Another rule of interpretation that might be useful to clarify the contents of Article 21 is the Subsequent Practice Rule. This rule, provided for under Article 31(3)(a) and (b) of the Vienna Convention on the Law of Treaties, covers the interpretation of treaties using subsequent agreements and practices as the main tools for determining the consent of parties to evolving interpretations of treaty obligations. Relying on the preparatory works of the Vienna Convention, Martin Scheinin has pointed out that 'subsequent practice' within the context of Article 31(3)(a) and (b) of the Vienna Convention does not just 'refer to explicit acceptance by all State Parties to a multilateral treaty', but also covers 'the tacit approval of a practice engaging only some of the Parties'.[114] He thus argues that,

> [I]t would be legitimate to treat the outcomes of the human rights treaty monitoring procedures, such as final views on individual complaints, concluding observations on State Party reports, and general comments as codifications of earlier practice, as various forms of 'subsequent practice' in the meaning of VCLT Article 31(3)(b) – at least in the vast majority of instances where no formal objection is made by State Parties. [115]

This suggestion is appealing, and would indicate that the practice of human rights bodies (to which states have subscribed) and states' practice regarding adoption or subsequent endorsement (by states parties to the

ing for those States which ratify; and to provide efficacious supervisory machinery for the obligations undertaken. Human rights treaties . . . are for the benefit of persons within their jurisdiction.' See UN Doc CCPR/C/21/R 1/Add 6 (1994), para 7.

[114] See Martin Scheinin, 'Impact on the Law of Treaties' in Menno Kamminga and Martin Scheinin (eds), *The Impact of Human Rights Law on General International Law* (Oxford: Oxford University Press, 2009) 33.

[115] ibid.

African Charter) of treaties such as the UN Convention against Corruption and the AU Convention arguably reflect the contemporary interpretation of Article 21. This proposition is buttressed by the specific reference to the African Charter in the AU corruption convention. Therefore, when read together, the argument can be made that the failures to investigate, prosecute, and provide effective remedies for victims violate Article 21, and obligations embodied in Articles 1 and 2 of the charter.

Two additional points on rules of interpretation are pertinent here. First, in addition to the above, the Vienna Convention also provides in its Article 32 that *travaux preparatoires* may be used as a supplementary means of interpretation in cases where the initial interpretation is ambiguous or 'manifestly absurd'. This is relevant to human rights treaties, not only because of the imprecise and vague nature of human rights, but also because of the added uniqueness, peculiarities, and significance of the charter's Article 21. Secondly, the importance of using dictionaries to find out the meanings of treaties like the African Charter is well illustrated by the practice of the International Court of Justice to turn to dictionaries such as *Black's Law Dictionary* and the *Oxford English Dictionary* in the exercise of its judicial functions. This approach to legal interpretation suggests that Article 21 ought to be interpreted in its ordinary meaning, consistent with the object and purpose of the charter as a human rights treaty and, as such, the interpretation must be done favourably to advance human and peoples' rights.

Therefore, a preliminary analysis of the terms used in Article 21, how they are linked, and their implications in relation to other provisions in the African Charter would seem necessary against the background of the discussion thus far. First, it should be stated that all the previous analysis in relation to 'peoples' applies with equal force to Article 21 provisions as far as the interpretation of the term 'peoples' is concerned. One would stress however that the conclusion that the right to resources guaranteed in Article 21 is meant to be enjoyed by the peoples and not the state. In fact, the remainder of Article 21 – 'This right shall be exercised in the exclusive interest of the people' – supports the conclusion of the existence of a trustee–beneficiary relationship, with the state or government being the trustee and the individuals and communities being the beneficiaries.

This additional layer of interpretation is buttressed by the next sentence of Article 21: 'In no case shall a people be deprived of it.' The question that immediately arises is: by whom? As noted, answering this is of particular importance because the peoples cannot logically deprive themselves of their own resources, as it already belongs to them. The phrase 'deprived of it' thus means the taking of it. When it is understood that the right is held by individuals and communities – the peoples – against the state, it is easy to know who is doing the taking: the state. Nonetheless, the concept of deprivation is much more complex. For example: what is the deprivation of natural wealth and resources, the use of which Article 21 seeks to protect?

Perhaps, some initial answers can be found in the wording of the article itself: 'In case of spoliation the dispossessed people shall have the right to the lawful recovery of its property as well as to an adequate compensation.' Deprivation presumably relates to taking away or stealing the resources by what the charter characterises as spoliation, which can be variously defined. It is argued that spoliation in the context of the charter literally means large-scale corruption, but its meanings could potentially include, according to *Black's Law Dictionary*: 'the act of despoiling or plundering'; 'the process of robbing or plundering, especially on a large scale'; 'destruction of a thing by the act of a stranger; as, the erasure or alteration of a writing by the act of a stranger'; and 'the total destruction of a thing'.[116] *Black's Law Dictionary* also defines spoliation as 'an injury done by one clerk or incumbent to another, in taking the fruits of his benefice without any right to them, but under a pretended title'.[117] Against these various meanings, spoliation in the context of Article 21 may indicate two things. First, the wealth and natural resources stolen by those entrusted with it is on a large scale, but other forms of corruption may be contemplated as well.[118] Additionally, Article 21 provides that 'the dispossessed shall have the right to the lawful recovery of it as well as to an adequate compensation'. As has been suggested throughout this book, the dispossessed would be considered as victims of corruption who are mostly the economically and socially vulnerable. Second, and it has been argued, stealing, especially on a large-scale, not only deprives people of their wealth and natural resources but also causes an injury, which in the context of the African Charter suggests serious and systematic violations of the human and peoples' rights guaranteed under the charter.

The third element of Article 21 suggests that the exercise of authority over the resources should comply with principles of international law, which, for our purposes, would include international human rights law. Further, Article 21(4) provides that, 'States parties to the present Charter shall individually and collectively exercise the right to free disposal of their wealth and natural resources with a view to strengthening African unity and solidarity.' This would presumably impose specific obligations on states in terms of the objective of using the resources to strengthen African unity and solidarity. This would appear to be consistent with earlier interpretations offered by commentators, and suggests that, as a way of solidarity, the peoples would share the resources with their African brothers and sisters who may be in need.

[116] *Black's Law Dictionary*.

[117] ibid.

[118] For detailed discussion on the categories of corruption, see the Introduction of this book.

Finally, sub-paragraph 5 requires states parties to eliminate all foreign economic exploitation (for example, by multinational corporations) so that the peoples can effectively and meaningfully enjoy their right to resources. In relation to this, the ECOWAS Court in the *SERAP* 'oil pollution case' against Nigeria (discussed below) has indicated the attitude required of states parties is that of 'vigilance and diligence'. As the court stated, 'it is incumbent upon the Federal Republic of Nigeria to prevent or tackle the situation [of oil pollution by multinationals] by holding accountable those who caused the situation and to ensure that adequate reparation is provided for the victims'.[119] In this case, it was 'precisely this omission to act, to prevent damage to the environment and to make accountable the offenders, who feel free to carry on their harmful activities, with clear expectation of impunity, that characterises the violation'[120] (of Articles 1 and 24) by the government. Accordingly, states must take responsibility and be proactive by not only preventing any exploitation by multinationals but also taking steps to ensure full accountability whenever exploitation occurs. The ECOWAS Court also held that:

> Contrary to the assumption of the Federal Republic of Nigeria in its attempt to shift the responsibility on the holders of a licence of oil exploitation, the damage caused by the oil industry to a vital resource of such importance to all mankind, such as the environment, cannot be left to the mere discretion of oil companies and possible agreements on compensation they may establish with the people affected by the devastating effects of this polluting industry.[121]

Several theories and interpretive tools might help to facilitate an evolutionary interpretation of the charter's substantive provisions (including Article 21), and to achieve their full effect. One such of these is the public trust doctrine. The application of the public trust doctrine to Article 21 provisions would enhance the enjoyment of the right to resources, as it would be made clear that the right of states contemplated under Article 21 is held in trust for the benefit of the peoples referred to therein. As noted, the wealth and resources cannot be expropriated by states except to promote their public interest. The public benefits the state is to protect will presumably include ensuring that its officials do not engage in corruption; effectively investigating and punishing perpetrators and providing redress to victims; using resources to establish effective and functioning institutions; and generally putting in place the legal and institutional infrastructure that will enhance the promotion and protection of the human and peoples' rights recognised and guaranteed by the African Charter.

[119] *Socoio-Economic Rights and Accountability Project v Federal Republic of Nigeria*, Judgment No ECW/CCJ/JUD/18/12 http://www.courtecowas.org/site2012/pdf_files/decisions/judgements/2012/SERAP_V_FEDERAL_REPUBLIC_OF_NIGERIA.pdf, para 97.

[120] ibid, para 111.

[121] ibid, para 109.

Although the issues of causation and *locus standi* (and how to identify victims of corruption) are discussed in detail later in this chapter, a few words on them here is appropriate. The victim bringing a case should only be required to show by evidence that a state's lack of due diligence to prevent corruption and avoid punishing those who caused the harm, and that the harm was not the result of an independent cause. Sophisticated sampling and modelling techniques may be necessary to demonstrate injury (or harm) causation. The application of *res ipsa loquitur* to Article 21 provisions, for example, might help to infer negligence from circumstantial evidence that may not normally be sufficient to establish causation. Against the background of the secrecy behind the corruption, and the well-known difficulties in accessing primary evidence, *res ipsa loquiter* will operate to shift the burden to a state to come forward with evidence that corruption by its officials and the consequent human rights harms is not due to its failure to exercise due diligence. The ECOWAS Court in the *SERAP* oil pollution case cited above appeared to have adopted a similar approach.

In the case, the Nigerian government denied the allegation that oil spill led to poverty in the Niger Delta area (describing this as 'speculative'),[122] but admitted that most of the oil spillage was 'caused by errant youths,'[123] who made it 'difficult' for the government to function effectively in the region. The government also denied that it was negligent or complicit in the violations of the charter's rights in the area. Finally, the government argued that the allegations against it had not been sufficiently proved or established by SERAP, insisting that 'the existence of pollution needs to be proved by expert evidence or at least evidence of people affected supported by medical report.'[124] But the court dismissed these arguments. In rejecting the government's arguments, the court established some important legal principles, which are relevant to buttress its general approach to 'causes and liability'. First, the court considered that 'the [Amnesty International] report, *as well as other well-known facts*, constitutes for the Court a kaleidoscope of elements and indices that may specifically help enlighten it on the actual existence and scope of the problem' [emphasis added].[125] This suggests that to establish violations of the charter's rights, the court will consider 'well-known facts', which will presumably include information widely in the public domain, ie, reports by NGOs, media, victims, etc.

However, the fact that the government did concede that pollution had occurred was also, in the court's view, 'decisive'.[126] Nonetheless, the court

[122] ibid, para 74.
[123] ibid, para 75.
[124] ibid, para 88
[125] ibid, para 94
[126] ibid, para 94

stated that, 'though the Defendant's contention is that the Plaintiff allegations are mere conjectures, this Court highlights and takes into account the fact that it is public knowledge that oil spills pollute water, destroy aquatic life and soil fertility with resultant adverse effect on the health and means of livelihood of people in its vicinity'.[127] Thus the court presumed that, 'in the normal cause of events in such a situation, to wit, consequential environmental pollution exist there'.[128] Second, the court stated that, 'the question as to the causes or liability of the spills is not in issue in the instant case. What is being canvassed is the attitude or behaviour of the Defendant, as ECOWAS Member State and party to the African Charter.'[129] It went on to rule that it was incumbent upon the government 'to prevent or tackle the situation by holding accountable those who caused the situation and to ensure that adequate reparation is provided for the victims'.[130]

One way both the African Commission and the African Court could advance the promise of the African Charter generally, and of Article 21 particularly, is through the use of the reasonableness test and public interest test. Implicit in the positive obligations to respect, protect, promote, and fulfil human rights is the requirement that the steps a state takes must be reasonable and effective, and that any such steps must serve the public interest. Although there are many ways in which a state can take positive measures to fulfil internationally human rights, it must strive to take progressive measures to achieve these obligations. Such measures are set out, in part, in the anti-corruption laws and treaties to which many African states are parties. However, to sign, ratify, and domesticate the anti-corruption treaties but then fail to rigorously implement and enforce them would invariably fail the tests of reasonableness and progressiveness.

Against the background of the preceding discussion, the remainder of this section explores further the nature of a state's right to dispose of its wealth and natural resources for the benefit of its people, in terms of whether it implies a fiduciary relationship between the state or its agents and its citizens. According to *Black's Law Dictionary*:

> [A fiduciary relationship is] [f]ounded on trust or confidence reposed by one person in the integrity and fidelity of another. Such relationship arises whenever confidence is reposed on one side, and domination and influence result on the other . . . Out of such a relation, the law raises the rule that neither party may exert influence or pressure upon the other, take selfish advantage of his trust, or deal with the subject-matter of the trust in such a way as to benefit

[127] ibid, para 96
[128] ibid, para 97
[129] ibid, para 97
[130] ibid, para 97.

> himself or prejudice the other except in the exercise of the utmost good faith and with the full knowledge and consent of that other.[131]

Commentators have attempted to describe those aspects of relationships that justify imposition of fiduciary relationships, or what Deborah DeMott has called 'fiduciary constraints'.[132] In general terms, the law governing fiduciary obligation addresses two questions: first, in what circumstances do fiduciary obligations apply? Second, what do the obligations require a person to do?[133] If a person in a particular relationship with another is subject to a fiduciary obligation, that person (the fiduciary) must be loyal to the interests of the other person (the beneficiary).[134] However, the fiduciary's duties go beyond mere fairness and honesty; they oblige him or her to act to further the beneficiary's best interests.[135]

Although one can identify common core principles of a fiduciary's obligations, these principles apply with greater or lesser force in different contexts involving different types of parties and relationships.[136] Recognition that the law of a fiduciary obligation is situation-specific should therefore be the starting point for any further analysis.[137] Accordingly, a fiduciary relationship can be presumed or inferred from the factual circumstances of any given relationship.[138] Although traditionally applied to prototypical fiduciary relationships such as agency and trust, fiduciary obligations have been frequently imposed in novel situations that go beyond these conventional categories.[139]

As DeMott explains:

> [F]iduciary constraint on a party's discretion to pursue self-interest resists tidy categorisation . . . fiduciary obligation is [thus] a device that enables the law to respond to a range of situations in which, for a variety of reasons, one person's discretion ought to be controlled because of characteristics of that person's relationship with another. This instrumental description is the only general assertion about fiduciary obligation that can be sustained.[140]

[131] *Black's Law Dictionary*, 626. The Restatement of Trusts captures the scope of the doctrine of trusts vividly when it defines a trust as 'a fiduciary relationship with respect to property, subjecting the person by whom the title to the property is held to equitable duties to deal with the property for the benefit of another person, which arises as a result of a manifestation of an intention to create it'. Similarly, it defines a fiduciary as one with a duty to act for the benefit of the other as to matters within the scope of the relation. See Restatement (Second) of Trusts 2 (1959).

[132] Deborah A DeMott, 'Beyond Metaphor: An Analysis of Fiduciary Obligation' (1988) *Duke Law Journal* 879.

[133] ibid, 882.

[134] ibid.

[135] ibid.

[136] ibid, 879.

[137] ibid.

[138] ibid.

[139] Ndiva Kofele-Kale, *The International Law of Responsibility for Economic Crimes* (Hampshire: Ashgate Publishing, 2006) 113–14.

[140] DeMott, 'Beyond Metaphor: An Analysis of Fiduciary Obligation' (n 132) 915.

Relating these important principles to preceding discussion on Article 21 provisions, the following additional points may be made to establish whether or not Article 21 establishes a fiduciary relationship between a state and the peoples in the enjoyment of the right to resources. It may be plausibly argued that Article 21 imposes on states an obligation of fidelity and suggests a fiduciary relationship or a trust-like relationship between the state and the peoples. This relationship would further ensure that the right to resources is exercised solely for the benefit of the peoples, and that states' attitudes would not be such that would impair the enjoyment of the right. Though not explicitly mentioned, the application of this principle seemed to be behind the ECOWAS Court's doctrine of 'vigilance and diligence' articulated in the *SERAP* case highlighted above. It would be fair, just, and reasonable to impose a duty of care in relation to Article 21 of the charter, and to the obligation to prevent human rights violations generally.

## ARTICLE 21, HUMAN RIGHTS AND CORRUPTION: COMPARATIVE JURISPRUDENCE

To advance the practical value of Article 21, achieve its full effect, and create sound precedents, the African Commission, and indeed the African Court, might profit from other human rights mechanisms and comparative national jurisprudence that are already conceptualising corruption as a violation of human rights. This section highlights some of the practices of human rights mechanisms and national courts in relation to corruption and human rights.

Among prominent human rights institutions that have considered corruption in relation to human rights is the Committee on the Rights of the Child, which has said that corruption has a negative effect on the implementation of the Convention on the Rights of the Child. For example, in a case involving Kenya, the committee stated that 'depleted resources' would have been available (had they not been stolen) for essential public functions and an array of services, including health, education, and welfare. This, the committee noted, was essential for the realisation of economic, social and cultural rights of all Kenyans, and one would say, civil and political rights too. Similarly, some courts in Africa have also acknowledged the threat that corruption poses to human rights and other associated values. For example, the South African Constitutional Court, in *S v Shaik and Others*, warned that corruption is 'antithetical to the founding values of [South African] constitutional order'.[141] In the same case, the Supreme Court of Appeal stated:

[141] *S v Shaik and Others* [2008] ZACC 7, 2008 (5) SA 354 (CC), 2008 (8) BCLR 834 (CC) [72].

> The seriousness of the offence of corruption cannot be overemphasised. It offends against the rule of law and the principles of good governance. It lowers the moral tone of a nation and *negatively affects development and the promotion of human rights* . . . Corruption threatens our constitutional order. We must make every effort to ensure that corruption with its putrefying effects is halted. Courts must send out an unequivocal message that corruption will not be tolerated and that punishment will be appropriately severe. [Emphasis added.][142]

The Constitutional Court in *Hugh Glenister v President of the Republic of South Africa & Ors* also emphasised:

> Endemic corruption threatens the injunction that government must be accountable, responsive and open; that public administration must not only be held to account but must also be governed by high standards of ethics, efficiency and must use public resources in an economic and effective manner. As it serves the public, it must seek to advance development and service to the public . . . It is incontestable that corruption undermines the rights in the Bill of Rights, and imperils democracy. To combat it requires an integrated and comprehensive response. The state's obligation to 'respect, protect, promote and fulfil' the rights in the Bill of Rights thus inevitably, in the modern state, creates a duty to create efficient anti-corruption mechanisms.[143]

As these cases reveal, the Constitutional Court has established some fundamental principles in relation to the connection between corruption and human rights. First, corruption undermines the very foundation of a representative government, the rule of law, good governance, and the tenets of human rights law. As such, it incapacitates states from effectively discharging their voluntary human rights obligations and commitments. Of particular importance to the court is the obligation to respect, protect, promote and fulfil human rights, also extensively discussed in Chapter 5 of this book. The court also made clear that this layer of obligations would require a 'modern state' to establish effective anti-corruption mechanisms and ensure full accountability for perpetrators. This will be true of the provisions of Article 21 (and indeed other substantive provisions of the African Charter) to the extent that the persistent failure of many African states to adopt and implement legal frameworks and institutions to fight corruption invariably constitutes a violation of obligations within the charter.

[142] *S v Shaik and Others* 2007 (1) SA 240 (SCA) [223]. See also *S v Kwatsha* 2004 (2) SACR 564 (ECD), 569–70; *S v Salcedo* 2003 (1) SACR 324 (SCA) [3]; and *S v Sadler* 2000 (1) SACR 331 (SCA) [13]. See also the case of *South African Association of Personal Injury Lawyers v Heath and Others* [2000] ZACC 22, 2001 (1) SA 883 (CC), 2001 (1) BCLR 77 (CC) [4], where the Constitutional Court of South Africa held: 'Corruption and maladministration are inconsistent with the rule of law and the fundamental values of our Constitution. They undermine the constitutional commitment to *human dignity, the achievement of equality and the advancement of human rights and freedoms*. They are the antithesis of the open, accountable, democratic government required by the Constitution' [emphasis added].

[143] *Hugh Glenister v President of the Republic of South Africa & Ors* (CCT 48/10) [2011] ZACC 6, 176–77.

Second, the court recognises that corruption hinders the ability of states to combat poverty, which in turn effectively constrains them to deliver on their human rights commitments. Thirdly, the court also underscores judiciary's role in the efforts to combat corruption and to deter wrongdoers. However, the judiciary will not be able to discharge this sacred duty if it is itself corrupt. Further, the court emphasises the benefits of 'an integrated and comprehensive approach' to corruption, the view which this author has advanced throughout this book. Overall, given the negative impact of corruption on the human rights guaranteed under the charter, a positive human rights obligation may be imputed on states to combat corruption, as strongly articulated by the Constitutional Court of South Africa. States' obligations under anti-corruption treaties, laws, and standards, such as the UN Convention against Corruption, the AU Convention, the SADC Protocol, and the ECOWAS Protocol (discussed in Chapter 4 of this book), presumably give content to a state's duty to protect and fulfil their obligations. While it is true that these obligations can be implemented in several ways, and that international law grants some margins of appreciation to states on the choice of means to do this, the level of implementation is dependent on the nature of the human rights, the extent of the resources available to governments, and the specific provisions of treaties, laws, and standards. It is the argument of this book that the positive obligations to guard rights must be interpreted in the light of the object and purpose of human rights treaties, and must be consistent with international law.

## POTENTIAL LEGAL, PROCEDURAL, SUBSTANTIVE AND PRACTICAL CHALLENGES

Whereas it is unquestionable that corruption results in violations of human and peoples' rights in the charter, it is less straightforward to identify victims, establish legal standing and causation. It may also be difficult to establish causation for the human rights violations caused by corruption, especially given the secrecy within which corrupt acts are carried out, and the multiplicity of factors that might be at play in any given situation. While it may be less cumbersome to measure the indirect harm that corruption causes, especially to economically and socially vulnerable, the same may not be true of direct harm. These challenges have created the perception that corruption is a victimless crime. This section discusses potential legal, procedural, substantive, and practical challenges that may arise when corruption is addressed from a human rights law dimension. Important issues of sovereign immunity, legal standing, and causation are discussed, as is the measurement of damages for victims of corruption and the meaning of the term victims of corruption.

Also addressed in this section is the question of whether remedies for human rights violations caused by corruption can ever be measureable, compensable, manageable, or risk-free (that is, the cost and burden of protracted litigation to victims and the public at large, fear of frivolous suits, and reprisal to victims and the public. Ways are then suggested in which the African Commission on Human and Peoples' Rights and the African Court on Human and Peoples' Rights might each address these legal issues in the light of Article 21 and other substantive rights in the charter, and advance the object and purpose of the charter in order to contribute to the efforts to combat corruption. It should be stressed at once that under international law, the fact that the provisions of Article 21 are contained in a human and peoples' rights treaty, whose primary purpose is to secure the rights for individuals and peoples of the states to the treaty, serve as a formidable defence in knocking down some of these challenges.

## State Immunity

The law of state immunity 'relates to the grant in conformity with international law of immunities to States to enable them carry out their public functions effectively and to the representatives of States to secure the orderly conduct of international relations'.[144] However, this 'state immunity' is one of the potential legal challenges that may obstruct the application of human rights law to corruption cases abroad. This problem arises when foreign courts are called upon to assess the validity of an official act of a foreign state. Under current legal principles, 'a successful assertion of the act of state doctrine precludes a litigant from bringing action against a foreign state, regardless of the litigant's jurisdictional arguments'.[145] Thus, sovereign states generally are required to respect each other's independence, and a state is not expected to allow its courts to sit in judgment on the acts of the government of other states. However, 'while the act of state doctrine has remained essentially the same [over the years] it has been narrowed in recent years beginning with the exception created based on the separation of powers doctrine'.[146] A 'commercial exception' has also been created to limit the operation of the act of state doctrine. Thus, 'an essential element of the application of the act of state doctrine is the characterisation of the action as the public, not private or commercial, act of a sovereign'.[147]

[144] See Hazel Fox, *The Law of State Immunity* (Oxford: Oxford University Press, 2008) 1.
[145] Kofele-Kale, *The International Law of Responsibility for Economic Crimes* (n 139) 286.
[146] ibid.
[147] ibid, 287.

In addition, *Keller v Central Bank of Nigeria*[148] was filed in the United States Sixth Circuit Court of Appeals, on an appeal from the United States District Court for the Northern District of Ohio at Cleveland. The facts of the case are that Henry Keller, of HK Enterprises, Inc, filed suit against the Central Bank of Nigeria (CBN), its governor, and six employees, claiming that he had been the victim of an illegal financial scam. The defendants[149] sought dismissal from the allegations under protection of the Foreign Sovereign Immunities Act (FSIA), and disputed Keller's civil claim that they had engaged in criminal activity under the Racketeer Influenced and Corrupt Organizations Act (RICO). The district court ruled that FSIA did not grant immunity to the defendant from the alleged RICO violations and that the financial transaction that had occurred was an exception of FSIA under its commercial activity clause.

The Sixth Circuit Court overturned this decision on appeal in favour of the defendant, holding that foreign sovereigns (states) are immune from civil RICO claims under FSIA. Keller asserted 'civil claims for violation of RICO, common law fraud, intentional misrepresentation, negligent misrepresentation, breach of contract, quantum merit, and fraud of $40,000 [as a result of entering into a] questionable and most probably illegal' scheme with the defendant.[150] Keller alleged that the defendants had engaged in 'racketeering activities', which, according to the RICO statute, are 'indictable, punishable, and chargeable'.[151] The defendant, alleging having acted for the CBN, claimed immunity from the charges under the FSIA.

The key legal issues were:

1. Did the alleged financial scam fall under the commercial activities exception of FSIA?
2. Were the activities of the individuals of the CBN commercial in nature, and therefore illegal in this context?
3. Was the CBN considered a sovereign entity in the eyes of the court, and therefore immune from civil RICO claims??
4. Did the defendant engage in activities that are by RICO statute definition indictable?
6. Does the FSIA provide immunity from criminal prosecution as well as civil prosecution?

Addressing these issues, the Sixth Circuit Court ruled that as a collective, the defendant was acting as a sovereign and therefore was potentially protected by FSIA. The court also overturned the decision of the lower court, which characterised the financial transaction as commercial activity

[148] *Keller v Central Bank of Nigeria* 277 F 3d 811, 815 (6th Cir 2002).
[149] The defendants were Paul Ogwuma, Alhaji MR Rasheed, and Alhaji MA Sadiq.
[150] *Keller v Central Bank of Nigeria* (n 148).
[151] ibid.

and therefore an exception to FISA. The district court had held that this motion would allow civil claims under RICO to be brought against the defendant for criminal racketeering activities. The final decision of the court of appeals, however, held that the FSIA granted foreign sovereigns immunity from civil RICO claims.

It should be noted that this case established the principle that a non-individual sovereign (that is, individuals acting as agents on behalf of the sovereign) enjoy immunity under FSIA. The fact that the collective faced criminal persecution for racketeering, from which they were ultimately granted immunity, supersedes the fact that their initial activities were deemed commercial and not protected under FSIA. However, the Court of Appeal's decision to dismiss the RICO claims is the opposite of the decision reached by the Tenth Circuit in *South Way v Central Bank of Nigeria*.[152] By holding that foreign sovereigns are immune from civil RICO claims, the Sixth Circuit expressly rejected the *South Way* decision in this regard.

Many of these court decisions may have been influenced by theories of an unlimited, supreme, and absolute state and its immunity. Nonetheless, it should be noted that, as highlighted in Chapter 1 of this book, the theorists who propounded the doctrine of absolute sovereignty (such as Jean Bodin) unarguably reflected the political and other realities of their time: the need for a sovereign government for political stability to prevent disorder and anarchy. The preservation of the immune sovereign over the interest of the individuals kept the state safe. But the strict doctrines of state sovereignty under international law have changed with time and with globalisation, though corruption remains rampant. Furthermore, the legal experts who drafted the African Charter endorsed the inclusion of Article 21; they certainly would not have done so if they were not prepared to ensure its full enforcement and effect in cases of victimisation of economically and socially vulnerable from corruption. Sadly, however, the continued marginalisation of Article 21 to address this victimisation continues to deny peoples legal standing and access to remedies, and reduces the accountability of states for massive theft of public resources. Attacking the strict adherence to the traditional and old-fashioned legal doctrine of state and sovereign immunity, Ndiva Kofele-Kale eloquently stated:

> The concept of state and [its] corresponding immunity has become the instrument through which corrupt oligarchies justify the plunder of natural wealth and resources. The concept operates as a sword for cutting loose the purse strings to the State confers so that looters can go in and remove however much they can without any hindrance . . . [The] idea of sovereignty [has also] made it difficult for courts to exercise jurisdiction over top state officials involved in

[152] *South Way v Central Bank of Nigeria* 198 F 3d 1210 (10th Cir 1999).

> [corruption while also keeping] perpetrators beyond the jurisdictional reach of domestic as well as foreign courts. In both formulations, victims of spoliation are rendered helpless, unable to rely on the legal order for vindication of the rights promised to them in international human rights treaties [such as the African Charter on Human and Peoples' Rights]. The concept of state sovereignty is inconsistent with the doctrine of leadership responsibility and the time has come [to reassess its] viability in light of the contemporary problem of indigenous spoliation [large-scale corruption].[153]

## Legal Standing and Causation

The concepts of standing and causation are closely intertwined. However, the nature, application, and relevance of causation vary significantly between international law and domestic legal orders. Whereas international law attributes responsibility to states for the acts or conduct of its agents or officials (through, for example, the agency theory), domestic legal orders demand establishment of causal links between damage and breach. These two concepts are now discussed in turn.

### *Legal Standing*

Basically, legal standing, or *locus standi,* meaning a place of standing or a right of audience in court, indicates whether or not a litigant seeking a court's intervention has a personal interest to challenge a particular state's action, or to invoke judicial determination of the rights of parties to a dispute. This doctrine is derived from the theory that remedies and rights are correlative and therefore only a person whose own rights have been violated is entitled to seek remedy. According to *Black's Law Dictionary, locus standi* is: 'A place of standing; standing in court. A right appearance in a court of justice, or before a legislative body, on a given question.'[154] This principle is a major element of the legal system of any common law country. Thus, only a person whose rights have been violated or are in danger of being violated by the act complained of can approach a court for redress. The term 'legal standing' is also used to determine whether anyone has suffered human rights violations over and above other members of a society (distinct and palpable injury to oneself or a group) in order to qualify them as a 'proper party' to present issues for judicial adjudication. Courts all over the world have always insisted on the rights and duties of persons 'properly before them.' The idea is based on two important considerations: first, the effective and efficient functioning of a

[153] Kofele-Kale, *The International Law of Responsibility for Economic Crimes* (n 139) 261.
[154] *Black's Law Dictionary*, 941.

court system and a just and fair administration of justice; and second, the longstanding principle of separation of powers.

Proper judicial adjudication of cases relies on the presentation of adequate and admissible evidence and legal arguments before a court, something which is the responsibility of any potential litigant to discharge. Therefore, in part because of a longstanding fear of opening a floodgate of cases and frivolous applications, courts will not normally entertain actions of abstract or academic concerns or of a general, undifferentiated, and common interest problem that does not satisfy the requirement of specificity of issues to produce just and fair judicial interpretations and decisions. It is also often argued that public-focused legal actions can be particularly strenuous for a court system, as they can overstress judicial function and authority. Common law courts have until now adopted strict interpretation of the principle of legal standing to exclude even well-merited cases. In the Nigerian case of *Amusa Momoh v Jimoh Olotu*, for example, the Supreme Court of Nigeria stated:

> The Plaintiff says that he is a member of the Olukare family. The question may be asked: Is it enough for the Plaintiff to state that he is a member of the family? Has he not got to state that he has interest in the Chieftaincy? Surely not every member of a Chieftaincy family as such has interested in the Chieftaincy title.[155]

This case would appear to suggest that an applicant seeking to enforce his or her rights in court will be refused an audience if they do not show a sufficient interest to sustain any such claim. In the more recent case of *Owodunni v Celestial Church of Christ*, the Supreme Court, again, adopted a strict application of legal standing when it held that,

> At common law, the position is that, in the realm of public right, for a person to invoke judicial power to determine the constitutionality of legislative or executive action, he must show that either his personal interest will immediately be or has been adversely affected by the action or that he has sustained or is in immediate danger of sustaining an injury to himself, and which interest or injury is over and above that of the general public.[156]

However, in some of the cases that have come before it, the Supreme Court appeared to have jettisoned the idea of 'sufficient interest or injury test', although the practice of the court in this respect would seem to be inconsistent at best and contradictory at worst. For example, in *Attorney-General of Bendel State v Attorney-General of the Federation*, the Supreme Court held that 'The Constitution has opened the gates to the Courts by its provision and there can be no justifiable reasons for closing the gates against those who do not want to be governed by a law enacted NOT in

[155] *Amusa Momoh v Jimoh Olotu* (1970) 1 All NLR 117.

[156] *Owodunni v Celestial Church of Christ* (2001) 1 WRN 1 45.

accordance with the provision of the Constitution.'[157] Thus, 'On constitutional issues, if this is what it imports, let there be a floodgate. The Constitution can only be tested in the courts and it is access to the courts for such test that will give satisfaction to the people for whom the Constitution is made.'[158] Yet, in many other cases the Supreme Court appeared to jettison this progressive statement. For example, in *Thomas v Olufosoye* it was stated that, 'This court already laid guidelines as to when a party could be deemed to have a locus standi in a litigation while condemning interlopers and professional litigants.'[159] But then, again, the Court decided to relax the rigid application of the doctrine of *locus standi* in *Fawehinmi v Akilu*, when it held:

> *Adesanya v President of Nigeria* and *Irene Thomas v Olufosoye* are both in respect of civil cause or matter and provide sound and solid authority for the locus standi of the Appellant. The narrow confines to which section 6(6)(b) restricts the class of persons entitled to locus standi in civil matters have been broadened by the criminal code, the Criminal Procedure Law and the Constitution of the Federal Republic of Nigeria, 1979 . . . *The peace of the society is the responsibility of all persons in the country and as far as protection against crimes is concerned, every person in the society is each other's keeper.* Since we are all brothers in the society, we are our brother's keeper . . . The Criminal Code and the Criminal Procedure Law of Lagos State in so far as prevention of crime and punishment of those who commit crimes are concerned, have made every one of us, nay, all Nigerians, our brother's keeper. [Emphasis added.][160]

It would seem, at least on the strength of this case, that the Supreme Court has finally embraced the trend in many jurisdictions to adopt a liberal and progressive interpretation of legal standing. This might be due in part to the fact that rigid application of *locus standi*, especially in public interest-related cases (such as those relating to enforcement of human rights), has resulted in substantial miscarriages of justice. These lacunas may also

[157] *Attorney-General of Bendel State v Attorney-General of the Federation* (1982) 3 NCLR 1.

[158] ibid. See also *Adediran v Interland Transport Limited* (1991) 9 NWLR (PT 214) 155, in which the Supreme Court upheld the *locus standi* of private persons to institute actions in respect of public nuisance.

[159] *Thomas v Olufosoye* (1986) 1 NWLR (PT 18) 699.

[160] *Fawehinmi v Akilu* (1987) 4 NWLR (PT 67) 797. The Court concluded: 'So interlined with the criminal law, our interpretation of Section 6(6)(b) of the Constitution must be approached with a true liberal spirit in the interest of society at large'. See also *Attorney-General, Ondo State v Attorney-General of the Federation* (2001) 27 WRN 1, (2002) 9 NWLR (PT 772) 222: 'Unlike previous constitutions the 1999 Constitution has imposed a duty on every citizen to abide by the Constitution, respect its ideals and institutions, respect the dignity of other citizens and the legitimate interests of others, live in the spirit of common brotherhood and make positive and useful contribution to the advancement progress and well-being of the society. While it may be said that the provision of Section 24 of the 1999 Constitution is not justiciable it cannot be denied that it has conferred a binding duty on every citizen to promote the legitimate interests of the society "in the spirit of common brotherhood".' For contrast and early practice of the Supreme Court on the subject, see *Adesanya v The President of Nigeria* (1981) 1 All NLR (PT 1).

explain the development of another doctrine, *actio popularis* (of Roman law), which allows any citizen to challenge the breach of a public right in court. The African Commission for example has long indicated that *actio popularis* is allowed under the African Charter.[161] In fact, in the past decades, courts have shown willingness, especially in cases involving human rights, to entertain private citizens' and public interest litigation where otherwise such actions would be precluded on grounds of lack of economic or other personal interests. Further, the existence and operation of freedom of information laws in many African countries already allows anyone whose request for information has been denied to seek public disclosure and release of government documents through judicial intervention. The *legal standing* afforded to victims or concerned public through freedom of information laws is not in any way restricted or affected even though the interest of the person seeking information and judicial remedy is often of a general, undifferentiated, and common nature.

The concern about a floodgate of cases therefore seems unwarranted also given the experience of other countries like India, where the standing to file complaints before the Supreme Court is relaxed; or as with the recent case law of the ECOWAS Court of Justice and national jurisprudence and practices (discussed below). The acceptance of standing for public-initiated actions in these jurisdictions has clearly not resulted in a flood of litigation or overwhelmed the court systems. On this account, it can be stated that to allow legal actions against violations of human rights caused by corruption is not to produce or open a floodgate of cases. Human rights litigation against corruption will surely contribute to reducing the problem, which in turn will enhance the effectiveness of government's institutions because greater public participation and oversight is likely to ensure better recovery of stolen assets, and thus, increase resources to the treasuries for states to discharge their human rights and other obligations and commitments.[162] This can be seen in the Supreme Court of India's ruling in *Fertilizer Corporation Kamager Union v Union of India*:

> Restrictive rules about standing are in general inimical to a healthy system of growth of administrative law. If a Plaintiff with a good cause is turned away merely because he is not sufficiently affected personally that could mean that some government agency is left free to violate the law. Such a situation would be extremely unhealthy and contrary to the public interest. Litigants are unlikely to spend their time and money unless they have some real interest at stake and in some cases where they wish to sue merely out of public spirit, to

[161] Communication 155/96, *The Social and Economic Rights Action Centre (SERAC) and the Centre for Economic and Social Rights (CESR) v Nigeria*, paras 55–58.

[162] See, eg, Comment, 'Defending the Public Interest: Citizen Suits for Restitution Against Bribed Officials' (1981) 48 *Tennessee Law Review* 347, 348. See also 'Garnishing Graft: A Strategy for Recovering the Proceeds of Bribery' (1982) 128 *Yale Law Journal* 92.

> discourage them and thwart their good intentions would be most frustrating and completely demoralizing.[163]

Litigants have accordingly taken advantage of the Indian Constitution's framework of public interest litigation for actions involving corruption. Thus, in *SP Gupta v Union of India*, the court stated:

> Where a legal wrong or a legal injury is caused to a person or to a determinate class of persons by reason of violation of any constitutional or legal right or any burden is imposed in contravention of any constitutional or legal provision or without authority of law or any such legal wrong or legal injury or illegal burden is threatened and such person or determinate class of persons is by reason of poverty, helplessness or disability or socially or economically disadvantaged position, unable to approach the court for relief any member of the public can maintain an application for an appropriate direction, order or writ in the High Court under Article 226 and in case of breach of any fundamental right of such person or determinate class of persons, in this Court under Article 32 seeking judicial redress for the legal wrong or injury caused to such person or determinate class of persons.[164]

This trend has continued, and many other common law jurisdictions and indeed regional human rights mechanisms have embraced the liberal and progressive approach in order to reverse the traditional rule of legal standing that judicial remedy is available only to a person who is personally aggrieved.[165] From a plethora of Commonwealth and other jurisdictions' pronouncements, several considerations can thus be identified upon which courts today will most likely rely in their approach to legal standing. First, courts will uphold legal standing in public interest litigation in order to promote the public good;[166] this presumably will include citizens' (especially the economically and socially vulnerable) fight against corruption, as there is probably no greater public good than to promote a clean, transparent, accountable and truly representative government. Thus, it will be enough if anyone discloses 'a personal interest in the performance of the legal duty which if not performed or performed in a manner not permitted by law would result in the loss of some personal

[163] *Fertilizer Corporation Kamager Union v Union of India* (1981) AIR (SC) 344.

[164] *SP Gupta v Union of India* (1982) 2 SCR 365, 377.

[165] The strict application of the doctrine of legal standing to public law (like human rights law) has been said to be outdated. See *Inland Revenue Commissioner v National Federation of Self-Employed and Small Businesses Ltd* (1981) 2 WLR 723, 740 in which the court said: 'It would, in my view, be a grave lacuna in our system of public law if a pressure group, like the federation, or even a single public-spirited tax payer, were prevented by outdated technical rules of *locus standi* from bringing the matter to the attention of the court to vindicate the rule of law and get the unlawful conduct stopped.'

[166] See, eg, jurisdictions such as India, Pakistan, and Bangladesh, where legal standing is usually granted to public-spirited individuals and groups where the petition is bona fide. See also *SP Gupta & Others v Union of India & Others* (1981) AIR (SC) 344; *British American Tobacco Ltd v Environmental Action Network Ltd* (2003) 2 EA 377; and *Fazal Din v Lahore Improvement Trust* 21 DLR (SC) 225.

benefit or advantage or the curtailment of a privilege or liberty of franchise'.[167] Second, courts will hear any interested person raising issues of grave public importance (this, also presumably, includes corruption, as one can hardly identify any other public issue that would have more compelling public importance) that endangers the rule of law and human rights law.[168] It has been stated that 'every member of the public has an interest in ensuring that the fundamental law of the State is not defeated'.[169] It is not necessary for any concerned citizen to show that the unlawful acts affect them personally.[170] As the US Supreme Court in *NAACP v Button* correctly stated:

> [L]itigation is a means for achieving the lawful objectives of equality of treatment . . . for the members of the Negro community in this country . . . Groups which find themselves unable to achieve their objectives through the ballot frequently turn to the courts . . . litigation may well be the sole practicable avenue open to a minority to petition for redress of grievances.[171]

Third, in regions such as Africa, with high levels of poverty, difficult socioeconomic conditions and illiteracy (with the consequence that a majority of the population is unaware of their rights, let alone how those rights can be realised), it is even more compelling to allow concerned citizens access to the court systems in cases of abuse of governmental powers, the rule of law, and general breach of human rights law. In a case challenging corruption in the education sector, the ECOWAS Court of Justice stated pointedly:

> The authorities citied by both the government and SERAP support the viewpoints canvassed by them. However, we think that the arguments presented by SERAP are more persuasive for the following reasons: first, the doctrine of 'Actio Popularis' developed under Roman law to allow any citizen to challenge a breach of public right in Court was a way of ensuring that the restrictive

[167] *Fazal Din v Lahore Improvement Trust* (n 166) 225.

[168] See, eg, *Benazir Butto v Federation of Pakistan,* (*PLD* 1998 SC 161), 416. See also *East African Law Society & Others v Attorney-General and Others* (2007) Jurisprudence on Regional and International Tribunal Digest 367: 'The Applicants herein are Bar Associations in their respective Partner States and have a duty to promote adherence to the rule of law. We are therefore satisfied that the Applicants are genuinely interested in the matter complained of, that is, the alleged non-observance of the Treaty by the Respondents.'

[169] *The Society for the Protection of Unborn Children (Ireland) Ltd v Coogan* (1989) IR 734. For similar pronouncements from common law countries across Africa, see, for example, *Greenwatch v Attorney-General and Others* (2003) 1 EA 87, where it was held: 'I have studied the application and the two affidavits filed in support and I found them pointing a finger at the State that it has failed or neglected its duty towards the promotion or preservation of the environment. The State owes this duty to all Ugandans. By so failing or neglecting the government is in breach of its duty towards the citizens of Uganda.'

[170] *Tuffuor v Attorney-General* (1980) GLR 637.

[171] *NAACP v Button* 371 US 415 (1963) 429–30. See also the constitutional cases where the Supreme Court of Canada developed the concept of public interest standing: *Thorson v Canada (Attorney-General)* (1975) 1 SCR 138; *Nora Scotia Board of Censons v McNeil* (1976) 2 SCR 265 and *Minister of Justice v Borowski* (1981) 2 SCR 575.

> approach to the issue of standing would not prevent public spirited individuals from challenging a breach of a public right in Court. Second, SERAP citied authorities from around the globe which all concur in the view that in a human rights violation the plaintiff need not be personally affected or have any special interest worthy of protection.[172]

Similarly, in another case involving SERAP and the Federal Republic of Nigeria, also before the ECOWAS Court,[173] the government maintained that SERAP 'has no *locus standi* because its Application was filed without the prior information, accord and interest of the People of Niger Delta, and that SERAP acts in its own name, with no proof that it is acting on behalf of the people of Niger Delta.' However, the court, citing its earlier decision in the *SERAP Right to Education* case, held that, 'SERAP, in the instant case, has *locus standi*'.[174] In sum, courts will not turn away an applicant if the issues raised have merit. It is sufficient if an applicant can show some substantial default or abuse, even if his or her personal rights or interests were not directly affected. Clearly, challenging a breach of public trust implicit in Article 1 of the African Charter (as eloquently articulated by the ECOWAS Court) will clearly have merit. As it has been argued throughout this book, apart from directly violating human rights, corruption also retards development and undermines the fair operation of the rule of law upon which human rights rely for their efficacy and effectiveness. These are obviously matters of grave human rights and public concern in which, apart from the individuals and communities (mostly economically and socially vulnerable) that are directly affected, every citizen has an interest. Therefore, the economically and socially vulnerable whose human rights suffer the most as a result of corruption should be granted the legal standing to challenge any such violations and to seek effective remedies, and if as it is often the case, they are unable to do this because of their conditions, to allow 'public spirited citizens' to do this on their behalf. As the ECOWAS Court has reasoned, 'this is a healthy development in the promotion of human rights', which would help 'to satisfy the aspirations of citizens of the sub-region [in particular and Africa as a

[172] The ECOWAS Court of Justice concluded on this point thus: 'Public international law in general is in favour of promoting human rights and limiting the impediments against such a promotion, lends credence to the view that in public interest litigation, the plaintiff need not show that he has suffered any personal injury or has a special interest that needs to be protected to have standing. Plaintiff must establish that there is a public right which is worthy of protection which has been allegedly breached and that the matter in question is justiciable. This is a healthy development in the promotion of human rights and this court must lend its weight to it, in order to satisfy the aspirations of citizens of the sub-region in their quest for a pervasive human rights regime.' *SERAP v Federal Republic of Nigeria*: www.courtecowas.org/site2012/pdf_files/decisions/judgements/2012/SERAP_V_FEDERAL_REPUBLIC_OF_NIGERIA.pdf, para 33.

[173] *Serap v Federal Republic of Nigeria*: www.courtecowas.org/site2012/pdf_files/decisions/judgements/2012/SERAP_V_FEDERAL_REPUBLIC_OF_NIGERIA.pdf.

[174] ibid, para 45.

whole] in their quest for a pervasive human rights regime'. Otherwise, the public good and well-being of citizens, for whom human rights law exists, will continue to be undermined.

Along the lines of the jurisprudence discussed above, the establishment of a complaint mechanism within a human rights treaty, whether regionally or internationally, allows an individual or the individual's representative, or, in some circumstances a group of individuals, to complain to a treaty body regarding alleged violations of the human rights contained within the terms of a treaty, and perhaps provides some additional best practices on the ways the international community has attempted to address the challenges of legal standing, causation, and justiciability in circumstances similar to those relating to the fight against corruption and protection of human rights. At the international level, there are opportunities for victims of human rights violations to approach accountability mechanisms established to hear cases of violations of civil, political, economic, social and cultural rights;[175] torture; violations of the rights of the child; arbitrary detention; racial discrimination and discrimination against women; and violations of freedom of speech or religion.[176]

The protocol to the International Covenant on Economic, Social and Cultural Rights,[177] for example, clearly addresses poverty and poverty-related issues from economic and social rights viewpoint (and also presumably from civil and political rights viewpoints given the notion of universality and indivisibility of all human rights). Under the protocol, victims that have suffered from, for example, chronic malnutrition, on-going inadequate health care, continuing lack of educational opportu-

[175] See, eg, the Optional Protocol to the International Covenant on Economic, Social and Cultural Rights. The protocol was adopted by consensus of the United Nations General Assembly on 10 December 2008, and barely a year later, 29 states signed the document in New York. While the discussions on the protocol took several years to complete, it took less than a year to draft the document. Optional Protocol to the International Covenant on Economic, Social and Cultural Rights, adopted 10 December 2008, UN GAOR, 63d Sess, UN Doc A/63/435 (2008). See Catarina de Albuquerque, 'Chronicle of an Announced Birth: The Coming into Life of the Optional Protocol to the International Covenant on Economic, Social and Cultural Rights – The Missing Piece of the International Bill of Human Rights' (2010) 144 *Human Rights Quarterly* 32.

[176] Other core treaties with individual complaint mechanisms are: the International Covenant on Civil and Political Rights; International Convention on the Elimination of All Forms of Racial Discrimination; the Convention on the Elimination of All Forms of Discrimination Against Women; the Convention against Torture and Other Cruel, Inhuman or Degrading Treatment or Punishment; the International Convention on the Protection of the Rights of Migrant Workers and Members of Their Families; and the Convention on the Rights of Persons with Disabilities. See, generally, Alexandra R Harrington, 'Don't Mind The Gap: The Rise of Individual Complaint Mechanisms Within International Human Rights Treaties' (2011–12) 153 *Duke Journal of Comparative & International Law* 2.

[177] The protocol has been seen as an important mechanism to expose visible economic, social, and cultural rights abuses that are usually linked to poverty, discrimination, and neglect. For example, in a press release of 2008 titled 'Human Rights Made Whole,' http://www.escr-net.org/docs/i/431553 former UN High Commissioner for Human Rights Louise Arbour congratulated the HRC on its adoption of OP-ICESCR.

nities, or a combination of all these, will now have the right to access international accountability mechanisms for redress.[178] Specifically, under the protocol, communications can be received from individuals or groups that have suffered violations of the covenant's rights.[179] Crucially, the protocol establishes several rules on the admissibility conditions for the presentation of communications, as well as provisions on inquiry procedures and interstate complaints. Both the covenant and the protocol seek to enhance the legal protection of the economic, social, and cultural rights of individuals and groups.

The protocol applies to all the rights contained in Articles 1 to 15 of the covenant. Therefore, if the international community could disprove the notion that economic and social rights are imprecise (or non-justiciable), and that such rights may depend on factors external to the states and that such rights were thus non-existent, the community could plausibly adopt legal instruments that would specifically clarify the conceptual and legal relationship between human rights and corruption, thus providing unambiguous legal standing and remedies to victims. It has to be stressed that the protocol allows individuals or groups that have suffered violations of the human rights recognised by the covenant to approach the Committee on Economic, Social and Cultural Rights for redress.[180] In terms of admissibility criteria, the protocol requires exhaustion of 'available domestic remedies', but this 'shall not be the rule where the application of such remedies is unreasonably prolonged'. Other criteria include: that communication can only submitted within one year after the exhaustion of domestic remedies, unless it is shown that this is an impossibility, and the communication must either 'reveal that the author has suffered a clear disadvantage' or that the communication raises 'a serious issue of general

[178] de Albuquerque, 'Chronicle of an Announced Birth' (n 175).

[179] Under the protocol, an individual complaint is not admissible if among others: the complaint was submitted more than a year after the final exhaustion of appropriate domestic remedies (unless the complainant was demonstrably unable to comply with this limitation); the facts upon which the complaint is based occurred before the relevant state party became legally bound by the terms of the ICESCR Protocol (unless the acts continued after the state party became bound by the ICESCR Protocol); the subject of the complaint is pending before another international body or there was an examination of the subject of the complaint by another international body; the terms of the complaint are 'incompatible with the provisions of the Covenant', so there is insufficient evidence presented to substantiate the complaint; or the complaint is 'exclusively based on reports disseminated by mass media'; or it is an abuse of the right to submit a communication; or the complaint is submitted anonymously or not in writing.

[180] The ICESCR Protocol vests the committee with the ability to request that the state party involved in a complaint take steps necessary to protect the life, integrity, and security of the complainant until there is a final decision on the complaint. Further, the protocol explicitly requires that states parties 'take all appropriate measures to ensure that individuals under its jurisdiction are not subjected to any form of ill-treatment or intimidation as a consequence of communicating with the Committee'. Additionally, the protocol vests the ICESCR Committee with the ability to consult UN and other relevant bodies to receive information appropriate to its determinations.

importance,' which under the protocol can act to soften the requirement that complainant proves individual harm. Crucially, the issue of causation would seem to be uniquely addressed through the notion of reasonableness, that is, the failure of a state to take reasonable steps to implement the covenant's rights, which then results in victims suffering 'a clear disadvantage' or raising 'a serious issue of general importance' that will trigger access to international mechanisms and afford victims, individuals or groups, redress.

Relevant to this book, the admissibility criteria and causation requirements found under the protocol (a legal document adopted by the United Nations General Assembly), in particular the notion of a *clear disadvantage*, *serious issue of general importance*, and the *test of reasonableness* can be replicated to operationalise a human rights approach to corruption, and utilised to probe the steps states parties to the African Charter are taking to implement their good faith (and voluntary) obligations These can potentially help to address the legal, substantive, procedural, and practical challenges (as highlighted above) that might undermine the potential of human rights law for combating corruption. That said, the opportunities that the protocol presents would appear not to be substantially different from those that already exist within the framework of the African Charter or even within sub-regional mechanisms, such as the ECOWAS supplementary protocol of 2005. These instruments grant individuals (and groups) access to the African Commission and the ECOWAS Court of Justice for violations of the human and peoples' rights under the African Charter; and in the case of the ECOWAS Court, even without having to first exhaust domestic remedies.

Nonetheless, the ICESCR Protocol (in paragraph 14(3)), unlike the African Charter or the ECOWAS Protocol, contemplates the establishment of a trust fund to provide expert and technical assistance to states parties (with the consent of the state party concerned) to implement the covenant's rights.[181] States are the direct beneficiaries of the fund, though vic-

[181] Several other human rights treaties make provision for the establishment of a fund. For instance, the Optional Protocol to CAT, 2002 (OP-CAT) establishes a fund to help finance the implementation of the recommendations made by the Sub-Committee on Prevention after a Visit to a State Party, as well as education programmes of the national preventive mechanisms. This fund is financed through voluntary contributions made by governments, intergovernmental organisations, NGOs, and other private or public entities. Also, the Rome Statute of the International Criminal Court (1998) established a fund for the benefit of victims of crimes within its jurisdiction and their families. This fund is financed through money and other property collected through fines or forfeiture to be transferred, by order of the Court, to the trust fund. The Rome Statute does not exclude the possibility that it might be financed from other sources, and it sketches the general outlines of the trust fund, leaving the Assembly of State Parties to decide on how to implement it in practice. However, practical and logistical challenges to the implementation and management of any established fund will need to be carefully addressed if any fund regime is to achieve its goal. The likely problems of linking violations to funding, and the chance that any such fund would involve high administrative costs and impose an additional burden on the Office of the High

tims were also beneficiaries in earlier drafts, and some states had indicated their support for providing assistance to victims. Moreover, the kind of assistance under the fund is not financial assistance, but expert and technical assistance. It is important to note that issues relating to the modalities of the fund have not been addressed in the protocol, but have been left to the General Assembly. The specific requirements of a clear disadvantage, serious issue of general importance, and reasonable steps are also absent from both the African Charter and the ECOWAS Protocol.

It should be pointed out that the ability of an individual or groups to bring such a complaint hinges first and foremost on whether the state alleged to have committed the violation is a state party to the individual complaint mechanism. Once this determination has been made, and the individual or group is able to satisfy the standing and justiciability – and causation requirements contained in the text of the instrument creating the individual complaint mechanism – they will have access to redress. Those that drafted the ICESCR protocol specifically and deliberately chose the term 'victim' to ensure that the individual complaint mechanism would not be read narrowly in terms of standing or causation, and to guarantee that the mechanism would have a broad construction into the future. In terms of standing, the ICESCR protocol provides that an agent is only allowed to submit a complaint on behalf of another person with that person's consent or, in the event that consent cannot be established, that the complainant provide a justification as to why consent is unavailable.

Thus, there is a discernible trend and increasing opportunities that improve the abilities of individuals and groups to assert and claim their human rights through the expansion of complaint mechanisms. This increased prominence is based generally on a sense of empowerment of individuals and groups, and on their identity as the holder of human rights and human dignity. In the same vein, the application of human rights law to combat corruption can also help to empower victims and allow them to have an important voice in the fight against corruption and the struggle to promote and protect human rights. Indeed, the increasing prominence of individuals and groups under human rights law shows the feasibility and workability of a human rights approach to corruption that is able to grant legal standing to victims and afford them effective remedies.

Commissioner for Human Rights (OHCHR) have been highlighted. Similarly, the funds administered by the UN Secretary-General and the OHCHR include a Voluntary Fund for Victims of Torture, Voluntary Trust Fund on Contemporary Forms of Slavery, Voluntary Fund for Indigenous Populations, and a Voluntary Fund for Technical Co-operation in the Field of Human Rights. These funds have a specific focus and are voluntary, and most either provide assistance to NGOs helping victims or assist representative organisations or communities to participate in meetings.

As noted, the evolution of human rights, and legal and judicial trends, show that the challenges posed by such doctrines as legal standing and causation are not insurmountable. In sum, the fact that the international community has used the framework of human rights (through the protocol and the covenant on economic, social, and cultural rights and case law) to address poverty and poverty-related issues suggests that the rights-based approach to corruption being put forward in this book, could, theoretically and practically, be a worthwhile tool to grant legal standing to victims, whether individuals or communities (or indeed public spirited individuals or groups), of human rights violations caused by corruption.[182] Overall, it would seem unquestionable that the individual and collective human rights violations suffered as a result of corruption are significant. Denying victims the right to sue in such circumstances simply on the ground that the violations may be 'intangible', and therefore not readily quantifiable, will allow these violations to go on without ever being remedied. As the preceding discussion also suggests, class actions may enhance the efficacy of private actions against corruption by permitting citizens to combine their limited resources to achieve a more powerful litigation posture. These human rights actions against corruption should be aided by the clear public interest that exists for all citizens to see acts of corruption combated.

Additionally, as observed, in many countries, the mechanisms of judicial review are available to citizens who challenge acts of official misconduct that cause harms. In these situations, exemplary damages may be awarded as an alternative to traditional compensatory damages. While exemplary damages can be paid directly to victims – for example through recovered stolen assets – affected communities and concerned members of the public can bring derivative proceedings (analogous to corporate shareholders' suits) to seek remedies for human rights violations caused by corruption and to recover stolen assets for the government. Independent

[182] While there are many points at which the ICESCR mirrors the ICCPR, it is still widely held that the terms of the ICCPR are quantifiable and thus subject to quasijudicial oversight, while the rights guaranteed under the ICESCR are more fluid and essentially aspirational, making them inappropriate for such oversight. Thankfully, civil society and a significant number of members of the international community, including committees of experts established to oversee the implementation of the covenant, have defied all odds to secure the adoption of the protocol. In particular, the ICESCR Committee asserted that an individual complaint mechanism was necessary in order to develop an understanding of the terms contained in the ICESCR, to establish how these terms should be implemented, and to create an effective method for and forum in which individuals and groups could voice alleged violations of their rights. Many of the initial issues associated with acceptance of an individual complaint mechanism focused on the collective or community-based nature of the rights provided for under the ICESCR. While there is still a good deal of debate as to whether this will be detrimental to the implementation of a respected and well-functioning individual complaint mechanism under the ICESCR, the adoption of the protocol has become a fait accompli, and the prospects for its justiciability and viability are strong.

public oversight of the spending of recovered assets will be crucial to ensure they are not re-stolen or mismanaged.

Finally, if it is accepted that Article 21 creates a constructive trust, and that states hold the natural wealth and resources in trust for the benefit of its individuals, communities (especially the economically and socially vulnerable), then these peoples should have the legal standing to ensure effective protection of the right and indeed other human rights and peoples' rights guaranteed by the African Charter when these rights are violated as a result of corruption. The idea of citizens' and public initiated actions is crucial where more effective law enforcement is desired, either because the crime involved (such as corruption) is serious enough to require extra attention or because existing remedies are inadequate. Victims and interested members of the public can thus seek discoveries or information through freedom of information laws on any subject matter relevant to human rights litigation. This will be an especially powerful tool to uncover complex allegations of corruption, will provide much needed evidence, and will assist the courts in the proper and fair administration of justice. In addition to facilitating the return of stolen assets for development programmes, citizens' and public initiated legal actions can improve public participation in the fight against corruption, encourage whistle-blowers, and enhance accountability of states, thus ultimately providing powerful incentives and deterrent measures.

### *Causation*

Generally, 'causation studies the relationships between causes and effects in the state of nature'.[183] The notion of causation was developed to determine attribution and responsibility (for example, in relation to human rights violations), and their limits. [184] Simply put, causation is a mechanism for determining whether a particular conduct plays some part in bringing about the harms or plays 'a sufficient part to count as a proximate or adequate cause of the harm'.[185] Nonetheless, causation analysis has been said to be 'densely political'.[186] In the first place, causation analysis is important to the system of attributing responsibility whether morally, legally, economically or politically.[187] Secondly, 'while it is not true that everything causes everything else, a large number of events and actions are, in some sense, causally connected to a particular outcome'.[188]

[183] León Castellanos-Jankiewicz, 'Causation and International State Responsibility', SHARES Research Paper 07 (2012), ACIL 2012-07, www.sharesproject.nl, 7.

[184] ibid.

[185] ibid, 8.

[186] Eric Tucker, 'The Westray Mine Disaster and its Aftermath: The Politics of Causation' (1995) 10 *Canadian Journal of Law Studies* 91, 94.

[187] ibid.

[188] ibid.

Another 'dimension of the politics of causation' relates to the fact that justice and political institutions operate within prevailing political and economic conditions, and as such, approaches to 'causation' may be dictated by these 'systemic conditions' and realities.[189] Accordingly, while scholars may broadly agree on the elimination of some relatively 'causal factors' in any sense; 'there is room for substantial disagreement about the relative significance of the many events that are causal in some sense'.[190] This suggests that various criteria (such as the purpose or goal being pursued) may be used to assess the relative significance of multiple causes. For instance, if the primary goal being pursued is to prevent corruption and the harms that it causes (in terms of human rights violations), the choice of significant causal factors is likely to be different than it would be if the sole goal were to be to directly pay compensation to victims of corruption. It has been stated that,

> Events typically have multiple causes. Usually, a combination of causes is necessary to produce a result and, in some cases, more than one causal factor is sufficient by itself. Moreover, one can trace the antecedents to an event back in an infinite regression. Because of this, different people can plausibly describe the cause(s) of a disaster in very different ways and disagree about whether an antecedent event or condition is properly considered causal. This condition of over-determination makes fertile the ground for disputes over causation that are more likely to be driven by politics than by science.[191]

Nonetheless, whereas there is little, if any, agreement on the notions of proximate cause or adequate cause, two general functions of the concept of causation can be identified. The first is that causation provides an account of the limits of responsibility by singling out the relevant facts to be considered in law.[192] Knowledge of these facts contributes to unravelling the conduct that is responsible for the harms caused, and whether the damage claimed is proximate to said conduct.[193] Second, the notion of causation suggests ways of fixing the limits of liability for the purposes of reparations.[194] In this respect, causal theories can help determine whether an obligation has been breached and if so, the extent to which a defendant is responsible.[195] However, while causation is an essential feature of domestic legal systems, the work of the United Nations International Law Commission would seem to suggest that it is 'irrelevant to determine the existence of an internationally wrongful act. Moreover, damage is not required for the purposes of attributing wrongful acts to a State.'[196]

[189] ibid, 95.
[190] ibid.
[191] ibid, 96.
[192] León Castellanos-Jankiewicz, 'Causation and International State Responsibility' (n 183) 8.
[193] ibid.
[194] ibid.
[195] ibid.
[196] ibid, 11.

In other words, while national legal systems require that damages in law amount to injury, and as such are capable of being compensated, the notion of an internationally wrongful act concerns itself with 'legal relationships arising from a determination of State responsibility',[197] regardless of damage or injury. Yet, the element of damage or injury may be said to be implicit in the failure to fulfil the obligation.[198] Accordingly, attribution of conduct to the state as a subject of international law is based on criteria determined by international law and not on the mere recognition of a link of factual causality.[199] This principle is built on another fundamental doctrine of international law: a state, as a subject of international law, is responsible for the acts of its agents, and as such the requirement of fault or malice on the part of the state is thus entirely unnecessary. This is exactly what makes international law different from domestic legal orders. León Castellanos-Jankiewicz stated:

> A finding of wrongfulness allows the law of responsibility to deploy its legal effects. Causation is superfluous in this process because of the operation of 'wrongfulness' in the determination of responsibility. Wrongfulness subsumes damage, thus rendering the causal relationship between damage and breach a superfluous one for the determination of international responsibility.[200]

While questions may be raised as to whether the concept of state responsibility can regulate the relationship between the state and its citizens, the application of the concept in such situation can well be justified in matters of human rights. On this account, the principles relating to state responsibility discussed above can be transposed (*mutatis mutandis*) to human rights law. In this respect, to prove causation in the context of the human rights violations stemming from corruption would imply establishing the nexus between a state behaviour and human rights violations suffered by the citizens, in particular the economically and socially vulnerable. The primary focus should be to interrogate and examine the routine business of government and state's behaviour in order to achieve the goal of accountability for corruption and associated human rights violations. If the goal is to protect citizens against corruption and its effects on human rights, then the attitude of states and the extent to which they have implemented their human rights obligations (including for example, obligation of prevention, vigilance and diligence), should be considered as major causation factors, if states and their high-ranking officials that perpetrate,

[197] ibid.

[198] ibid, 19.

[199] 'ILC Articles on State Responsibility of States for Internationally Wrongful Acts' in *Yearbook of the International Law Commission 2001*, Vol II (Pt 2) 31, annexed to UN Doc A/RES/56/83 of 12 December 2001, 38–39, para 4.

[200] León Castellanos-Jankiewicz, 'Causation and International State Responsibility' (n 183) 19.

facilitate or encourage corruption are not to continue to escape punishment or accountability for the corruption and its effects on human rights.

Yet, as already noted, the secrecy within which corruption takes place makes it especially difficult to obtain the necessary evidence to prove the crime. Even so, certain theories and principles such as the obligation of vigilance and diligence and the precautionary principle that have been discussed might help to address this challenge. Similarly, the existence of credible anticorruption indexes and measurement tools like the CPI might potentially help to address the challenge of establishing causation for human rights violations caused by corruption as such measurements will indicate a prima facie breach of obligation of vigilance and diligence in relation to human rights. And as already highlighted, courts are nowadays more willing to relax rigid requirements of locus standing and causation in human rights matters through the mechanism of public interest litigation. This approach underscores the legal and human rights consequences that arise when states violate human rights through failure to prevent corruption or to effectively investigate or prosecute high-ranking perpetrators.

As far as international law (including human rights law) is concerned, it is the obligations of state rather than the corrupt acts of its high-ranking officials that are considered to establish responsibility. Ideally, therefore, it should simply not be enough for states to accept international obligations and commitments, and for them not to be held to account for any such breach, especially where there is a clear evidence (which may, as the ECOWAS Court has said, be established through 'well-known facts') to suggest that the results contemplated by the assumption of these obligations and commitments (ie, relevant to the core thesis of this book, that corruption has been eradicated or minimised or effectively prosecuted, and that human rights violations have been prevented, and where they occurred, remedied), have not been achieved. Arguably, therefore, the failure of states to carry out their good faith and voluntary anti-corruption obligations and commitments, combined with the effects of this failure on the effective realisation and enjoyment of human rights especially by the economically and socially vulnerable, would impact a chain of human rights obligations, and ultimately, triggering accountability of states for any violations.

It is argued that a strict application of the concept of causation would not have been designed to thwart or undermine the pursuit of fairness, justice, and accountability in relation to such issue of public interest and importance like corruption and human rights violations. As such, outdated notion of causation should not be used as an excuse or escape route for states to avoid accountability. At any rate, the legal requirement of causation is about ensuring that it is *only* the party that has caused the harm or injury that is held to account for any such harm or injury, especially when several actors may have contributed to the harm or injury. Ultimately, the aim is to apportion appropriately, fairly, reasonably, and justly responsibility and accountability in specific cases. On this account, it should, ideally be sufficient for victims of human rights violations stemming from corruption to establish 'proximity' (simply called 'indirect' or 'contributory' causation) by proving that a nexus exists between the breach of obligation of vigilance an diligence, the corrupt acts of high-ranking officials, and consequently, the alleged human rights violations. This formula, alongside other fundamental principles that have been discussed throughout this book, should hopefully help victims to bring claims for violations of human rights stemming from corruption.

The proposals being put forward may be further justified given (as noted) the fact that the secrecy within which corruption takes place makes it extremely difficult to establish, and proving specific rather than general causation is harder and almost impossible given that multiple chains of factors lead to corruption, the frequency of the crime, and the near invisibility and impunity of perpetrators. In this instance, proving general causation would presumably require the establishment of a causal link between large-scale corruption, failure to exercise vigilance and diligence (ie, failing to put in place and/or effectively implement laws and policies to stem corruption and punish perpetrators), and the resulting human rights violations. Specific causation, on the other hand, would entail proving that a specific human rights violation was caused by a set of corrupt acts or by named or identified corrupt officials. It will certainly be unrealistic to expect victims of corruption, mostly the economically and socially vulnerable, to establish specific or direct causation in relation to human rights violations stemming from corruption.

Another justification for the use of indirect or contributory general causation might be that while corruption indexes and measurements exist, these may be disputed. However, better and more acceptable measurement tools can be developed to ensure that corruption in any state can reasonably be established, and such corruption indexes can then be made available for any potential victims to establish contribution of a given state to human rights violations. Even so, it will be extremely difficult if not impossible to find a measurement tool on controversial issues like corruption that will receive universal approval. Furthermore, indirect or contributory (and general) causation is relatively less controversial, and in fact, already an important feature of many legal systems, including those of African states. Since the majority of scholars and commentators would hardly disagree that corruption, especially large-scale corruption would weaken any state (let alone those with already limited resources), and cause serious human and social consequences, evidence of contribution of states to these problems should be sufficient to prove causation in human rights matters.

To apply, for example, the strict requirement of the 'but for' formula established in cases like *Donoghue v Stevenson*[201] is to be manifestly unfair and unjust to the economically and socially vulnerable, and to exacerbate their vulnerabilities and deepen inequalities, something that human rights law is designed to address (as this presumably would make them bear the burden of proving allegations of corruption they never committed). A fair and just approach would be to require states (rather than the victims) to prove that the acts or omissions of their agents (ie, corruption) had not contributed to the harms or injuries suffered by the victims. In any case, a state would arguably find it very difficult to explain away corrupt acts by its officials, and to assert that massive theft of the state's resources has had no contributory negative impact on human beings. As Judge Azevedo correctly stated in his judgment in the *Corfu Channel Case*,

> It would be going too far for an international court to insist on direct and visual evidence and to refuse to admit, after reflection, a reasonable amount of human presumptions with a view to reaching that state of moral, human certainty with which, despite the risks of occasional errors, a court of justice must be content.[202]

It is therefore realistic to expect that courts and human rights bodies like the African Court and the African Commission would be willing to apply the formula that this author is proposing (which would require that victims establish only a proof on the basis of balance of probabilities approach) to make sure that victims receive effective remedies (ie, that states prevent and end corruption, effectively punish perpetrators and recover stolen wealth, and remedy associated human rights violations, including by making reparation in some forms for the harms caused. This optimism would be justified in part by the reasonableness of the formula, and the growing jurisprudence in public interest litigation, some of which has already been discussed. It should be stressed, however, that the ultimate goal of the human rights approach to combat corruption is not necessarily to award monetary compensation to victims but rather to provide

[201] *Donoghue v Stevenson* [1932] AC 562, HL.

[202] *Corfu Channel Case (United Kingdom v Albania)* [1949] ICJ Rep 4, 17. See also *Massachusetts et al v Environmental Protection Agency et al* 549 US 497 (2007), where the US Supreme Court was required to determine whether or not the federal Environmental Protection Agency (EPA) possessed the statutory authority to regulate the greenhouse gas emissions from new motor vehicles under the federal Clean Air Act of 2004. The State of Massachusetts complained that the rising sea levels associated with global warning had caused harm to it, and would likely continue to cause even greater harm. The Supreme Court held that US motor vehicle emissions (accounting for around 6% of global CO2 emissions) made 'a meaningful contribution' to global warming, noting further that a 'reduction in domestic emissions would slow the pace of global emissions increases, no matter what happens elsewhere.' Ibid, 517–19. But contrast this with the minority opinion, which found that, 'in light of the bit-part domestic new motor vehicle greenhouse gas emissions have played in [global warming] . . . and the myriad additional factors bearing on the petitioners' alleged injury . . . the connection is far too speculative to establish causation.' Ibid, 507.

full, practical and effective remedies, which might also include administrative or other remedies. For example, while human rights courts and bodies will exercise (inherent) discretion whether or not to award compensation (or assess any other contributory factors that may be outside the control of the state) in specific cases, it may generally be enough for states to act to prevent acts of corruption, effectively prosecute perpetrators, and generally provide restitution in the form of identifiable projects to enhance access to justice for victims, and secure social, economic, political and other levels of development.

A compensation fund, in the form of a Trust Fund for Victims of Corruption (proposed in the Conclusion), drawn mostly from recovered stolen wealth and other interest that might be generated from this (as well as voluntary contribution from members of the international community), would be important to generate the funds to implement many of these initiatives. Funds (whether privately or publicly established) continue to be seen as plausible solution in similar cases of abuses by states or private actors (and if states like Mexico could establish national funds to deal with extreme weather events, and the European Union could establish a solidarity fund to address catastrophic losses), there is absolutely no theoretical, conceptual or logical basis not to follow similar path in cases of human rights violations stemming from corruption (a man-made problem). Since some countries might be unable to muster sufficient resources to set up a national funds of their own, private funds to augment public initiatives should be encouraged. Similarly, agencies like the Office of the High Commissioner for Human Rights should champion the establishment of an international fund for victims of corruption, combined with oversight functions, to deal with cases of victims of corruption. It should be noted that similar initiatives also exist to address cases of victims of international crimes in the context of the Rome Statute of the International Criminal Court, and to deal with terrorism, toxic torts, and damage to natural resources. It is to be hoped that such initiatives will be replicated to address the inequalities and injustice that is caused by corruption.

This way, human rights law can provide a powerful incentive for action, for instance, by triggering a mechanism that would ensure the effective implementation of international obligations, empowerment of victims, and remedies for individuals and communities (including by providing access to regional and international accountability mechanisms), and ultimately, the establishment of a rule of law-based society. As options based on international and regional human rights protection mechanisms will still have to be complemented and implemented on the domestic level, legal, judicial, administrative initiatives at this level will be crucial to achieve a sustainable system of law that is fair, just, transparent and protects the human rights of everyone. Yet, any domestic initiatives will succeed only if states show the necessary political will to reform critical institutions of governance, and their senior officials lead by example to show that corruption does not pay. Any reform of the justice system that ignores comprehensive (and root and branch) institutional, political, judicial and other social reforms will likely be marginal, and may prove to be insufficient long-term safeguards against corruption, impunity of perpetrators, inequalities, embedded injustice and the vulnerabilities that are entrenched as a result of corruption. Human rights law can provide the normative foundation to deliver a long-term, durable and sustainable reform as long as the required political will is present and civil society play their part, to make this happen. If this can be achieved, then the goal of human rights law approach to contribute to a multidisciplinary and comprehensive approach to corruption can be realised.

## VICTIMS OF CORRUPTION

Whereas 'the plight of the victims has been [historically] largely overlooked',[203] there is today an increasing focus on victims of violations of human rights. It is no coincidence that human rights instruments frequently refer to victims' right to effective remedies, including reparation, and treaty bodies such as the African Commission and the Human Rights Committee have consistently recognised the rights of victims, including to compensation and guarantee of non-repetition. Victims of human rights violations would be entitled to effective remedies regardless of whether they bring their claims against the state in an individual or collective capacity. As Theo van Boven has stated,

> It is obvious that gross violations of human rights and fundamental freedoms, particularly when committed on a massive scale, can by their nature and their scope hardly be repaired. In such instances, any remedy or redress granted stands in no proportional relationship to the grave injury inflicted upon the victims. It is nevertheless an imperative demand of justice that the responsibility of the perpetrators be clearly established and the rights of the victims sustained to the fullest possible extent.[204]

A victim can be defined as anyone who suffers individual or collective harm (or pain) such as physical or mental injury, emotional suffering, economic loss, or generally any impairment of human rights as a result of acts or omissions that constitute gross violations of human rights, or serious violations of humanitarian law norms.[205] A victim does not neces-

[203] Van Boven, 'The Relations between Peoples' Rights and Human Rights' (n 18) 194.
[204] ibid.
[205] See Basic Principles and Guidelines on the Right to a Remedy and Reparation for Survivors of Violations of International Human Rights and Humanitarian Law, GA Res 60/147, pmbl, Sec IX, UN Doc A/RES/60/147 (March 21, 2006), 8. The Principles and Guidelines are an important tool that would enhance the ability of states to fulfil their obli-

sarily have to be the person who has suffered the harm, as a dependant or a member of the immediate family or household of the person that has directly suffered harm can indirectly be characterised as a victim (as is anyone with a valid public interest to secure an end to human rights violations or a third party who has suffered consequences as a result of harm or injury to a direct victim). Indeed, the Basic Principles of Justice for Victims of Crime and Abuse of Power provides some guarantees for victims (including family members of direct victims), such as those that suffer 'substantial impairment of their fundamental rights' through acts or omissions, including abuse of power. Corruption must be included here as the ultimate abuse of power. As noted, victims have the right to redress, and are entitled to be informed about this right.

Under the declaration, states have a responsibility to pay restitution to anyone who suffers harm as a result of violations of national criminal law by public officials or other agents while acting in an official or quasi-official capacity. States are also responsible for any abuse of power that violates human rights norms and, as such, are required to provide effective remedies, including restitution and compensation to victims. According to Dinah Shelton,

> [T]he primary function of corrective or remedial justice is to rectify the wrong done to a victim. Compensation can only provide something equivalent in value to that which is lost; rectification or restitution restores precisely that which is taken. Where restitution or rectification is not possible, substitute remedies, including damages, are required..[206]

The ultimate aim is to wipe away all the consequences of a state's illegal act and to make the victims as whole as possible The question that arises, then, is: who are the victims of corruption? Answering this question is absolutely crucial to determining who might have the legal standing to seek redress for violations of human rights caused by corruption. As noted, both direct and indirect victims have standing to seek redress for violations of their human rights. On the one hand, the institutions of governance and the society as a whole are the victims. On the other hand,

gations to guarantee an effective remedy, including providing adequate reparations to victims, serve the rule of law, and to prevent future violations. Thus, 'an effectively functioning domestic system for providing redress is one of the best safeguards against impunity'. See Gabriela Echeverria, 'Codifying the Rights of Victims in International Law: Remedies and Reparation' in Permanent Court of Arbitration (ed), *Redressing Injustices Through Mass Claims Processes: Innovative Responses to Unique Challenges* 279. See also Final Report of the Special Rapporteur, MC Bassiouni, submitted in accordance with Commission resolution 1999/33, UN Doc E/CN 4/2000/62, 18 January 2000, annex, para 8.

[206] Dinah L Shelton, 'Reparations to Victims at the International Criminal Court', in The International Criminal Court Reparations to Victims of Crimes (Article 75 of the Rome Statute) and the Trust Fund (Aritcle 79) (Recommendations for the Court Rules of Procedure and Evidence), http://www.pict-pcti.org/publications/PICT_articles/REPARATIONS.PDF.

corruption disproportionately inflicts grave harms on the economically and socially vulnerable, who, in addition to violations of their specific human rights, are also denied access to effective institutions of government. As demonstrated through the comparative jurisprudence discussed earlier, victims of corruption would include the direct victims that have suffered *a clear disadvantage* as a result of violations of their human rights caused by corruption. Victims also would include anyone seeking to promote the public good or indicating 'an interest in the performance of a legal and human rights duty'. The term preferred by this author to characterise victims of corruption is 'economically and socially vulnerable'. As indicated in Chapter 2, this term is used very frequently in this book to refer to any individual or determinate class of persons, who by reason of poverty, or disability or socially or economically disadvantaged and vulnerable position, suffer most the immediate effects of violations of human rights caused by corruption. If victims of such human rights violations are not granted standing to seek redress (and when they are unable to do so, for any interested member of the public to seek redress on their behalf), the resulting harm and human suffering will continue unaddressed, and the rich few will continue to benefit from the poverty of the many, thus rendering the global fight against corruption and the struggle for the protection and promotion of human rights virtually inoperative.

While the harm caused to the economically and socially vulnerable (or even the public as a whole) by corruption may not necessarily be direct or precisely quantifiable or assessed in monetary terms, it is unreasonable to suggest, in the face of the conceptual foundations linking corruption with human rights violations, and the overwhelming evidence of loss of public revenue and weakened systems of rule of law, that corruption is a victimless crime. It is not that those who characterise corruption as victimless completely disagree that it causes harms, especially to the economically and socially vulnerable. On the contrary, the argument often put forward is that since no one victim suffers more harm than others, and that there may be no *direct victim*, it is probably pointless to labour in search of 'invisible victims'. This line of reasoning would appear weak and difficult to sustain, for the following reasons. First, as already argued, apart from causing both direct and indirect economic and other harms to its citizens and the public in the form of the loss of the common wealth and public revenue, corruption also causes non-monetary loss in the form of widespread and consistent denial of impartial application of the rule of law and the associated human rights violations. This proposition is also buttressed by the sound legal jurisprudence discussed in this chapter.

Moreover, while it may be difficult to quantify the harms that corruption causes, this does not make the harms less real, less destructive, or less corrosive. In fact, the manifestations and indicators of these harms can be easily recognised in the form of poverty and the systematic, gross human rights violations of the economically and socially vulnerable. Additionally, even though corruption may cause harms that cannot be measured in monetary terms, there are no legal, theoretical, or practical obstacles for using human rights law as a complementary framework to combat the problem. In fact, the use of human rights law may actually provide some tools to measure the harm that corruption causes in terms of human rights. A state should not escape accountability simply because it might be difficult to measure human rights violations caused by corruption. Any practical challenges that may arise when providing redress to large numbers of victims of corruption may also be addressed through strategies such as sampling, summary procedures, or designating a representative for the victims. This can assist in affording swifter resolution of claims for compensation or restitution and was the situation in the *Marcos* cases in the United States, in which due to the large number of victims in the class action suit, innovative procedures allowed the use of a statistical sample of the 10,059 claims to determine compensatory damages.

Courts may also seek a just and fair way of prorating access to remedies based, for example, on the severity of the harm. In terms of evidence and standards of proof, as already argued, fairness and justice will be best served, especially given the vulnerability and circumstances of most victims of corruption, if the appropriate standard for legal action seeking remedies in such cases is the preponderance of the evidence or balance of probabilities. Also, legal assistance can be provided to the victims (or their representatives) who may wish to seek redress but have no means to do this. Funds for this purpose could be drawn from the Trust Fund for Victims of Corruption, which this author proposes and discusses further in the next chapter.

Finally, it needs to be mentioned that the legal systems across African states (and elsewhere) often provide pecuniary compensation for victims of intangible harms, such as libel or false imprisonment. There is therefore no compelling reason why similar principle cannot apply by way of analogy to the human rights approach to corruption. At any rate, what is the point of guaranteeing a right if, when violated as a result of corruption, such rights cannot be directly or indirectly remedied by the victims? It is important to emphasise that while legal actions provide victims the independence, options, and authority to challenge violations of their human rights caused by corruption, governments can also move to devise policies and programmes to ensure, where appropriate, administrative and other remedies for victims and to address their vulnerability and disadvantage.

## HUMAN RIGHTS LAW AND CRIMINAL LAW APPROACHES TO CORRUPTION

Whereas there is nearly universal support among scholars and commentators for the idea of combating corruption through the framework of human rights law, a minority of opinions exists that (rather controversially) consider any such move a distraction and, in the words of probably the two most prominent opponents of a rights-based approach to corruption, 'an unwelcome addition to the development discourse'.[207] Although Morag Goodwin and Kate Rose-Sender acknowledge the harm that corruption poses, they claim that, 'corruption is not as straightforward a social evil as the anti-corruption crusaders would have us believe'.[208] Their claim essentially rests on three major planks: the first is that the move to connect corruption and human rights is an extension of the 'anti-corruptionism movement', and largely influenced by ideology. In turn, it is a form of 'neo-imperialism'.[209] The second plank is that while there may be some merit in the notion of fighting corruption through human rights law, 'there is at present no convincing argument to suggest it [is necessary]'.[210] The third is that even if it were possible to coherently connect corruption and human rights, this exercise will further the agenda of anti-corruptionism and exacerbate the 'colonisation of development discussions by human rights'.[211] They argue very strongly that any such move would be 'harmful to the notion of human rights and counterproductive to the stated aim of ending corruption'.[212] This author now responds to each of these points in turn.

In the first place, while it may be true that the anti-corruption movement has historically been influenced by some ideology, this assertion overlooks the growing clamour for transparency and accountability, especially by citizens of developing nations like Africa. For citizens of African

[207] Morag Goodwin and Kate Rose-Sender, 'Linking Corruption and Human Rights: An Unwelcome Addition to the Development Discourse' in Martine Boersma and Hans Nelen (eds), *Corruption and Human Rights: Interdisciplinary Perspectives* (Antwerp: Intersentia, 2010) 221. There are also scholars who simply question the necessity of the 'anti-corruption campaign' at all, suggesting that the campaign is a ploy, and an extension of a neo-colonialist agenda. See for example, David Kennedy, 'The International Anti-Corruption Campaign' (1999) 14 *Connecticut Journal of International Law* 455. According to Kennedy, 'I do oppose the international campaign against corruption, although I do not favour corruption. Perhaps we could describe this position as anti-anti-corruption': ibid, 456. Kennedy's 'anti-anti-corruption' theory is substantively similar to those by Goodwin and Rose-Sender and they will therefore be treated together.

[208] Morag Goodwin and Kate Rose-Sender, 'Linking Corruption and Human Rights: An Unwelcome Addition to the Development Discourse' (n 206).

[209] ibid, 239.

[210] ibid, 240.

[211] ibid, 240.

[212] ibid.

states, linking corruption and human rights is definitely not about ideology; it is rather an issue that is central to the survival and well-being of millions of poor women, men, and children in several African states. To use the excuse of ideology to criticise such a necessary and proportionate response to combat a grave problem like corruption, which has had decades of debilitating effects on human rights and which continues to overwhelm the continent is, to say the least, to be oblivious of the major issues and the need for a multidisciplinary approach. Such a restrictive analysis also does not do justice to the overreaching influence of human rights law as a branch of international law that cuts across all human endeavours. It has been pointed out that,

> [W]hilst those critical of making the connection between corruption and human rights are to be credited for challenging the *pensede unique* regarding the framework linking development, good governance, anti-corruption and human rights, they appear to overstate their claim. For one thing, the risk of human rights forfeiting their emancipatory potential when being made subservient to one particular development model appears to be exaggerated. Throughout history, ideologists have relied on legal tools and legal techniques to further their world view, without law (and more recently, without human rights) necessarily being discredited as an instrument of regulation or emancipation. Thus, arguably, human rights considerations can still inform alternative development models that highlight a global or Western responsibility for developmental problems.[213]

Secondly, the assertion that no convincing argument exists to link corruption with human rights is not supported, as there is a preponderance of evidence of such linkages in developing countries like Africa. Transparency International, the World Bank, and the United Nations, to cite just a few, have published reports based on thorough investigations and sound research methodologies to show that the relationship between corruption and human rights is not just a matter of theoretical conjecture but a practical issue that touches the lives of millions of vulnerable people in developing countries. For example, the UN Human Rights Council at its 23rd Session in 2013 organised a panel discussion on the effects of corruption on human rights.[214] At the meeting, the UN High Commissioner for

[213] See Jan Wouters, Cedric Ryngaertt and Ann Sofie Cloots, 'The International Legal Framework Against Corruption: Achievements And Challenges' (2013) 14 *Melbourne Journal of International Law* 205, 275.

[214] Annual report of the United Nations High Commissioner for Human Rights and reports of the Office of the High Commissioner and the Secretary-General, www.ohchr.org/Documents/HRBodies/HRCouncil/RegularSession/Session23/A.HRC.23.26_EN.pdf. The panel discussion aimed to draw attention to 'the manifold negative impacts of corruption on the enjoyment of human rights, particularly on the availability, accessibility, affordability and quality of human rights-relevant goods and services; to consider prospects and challenges from a gender perspective in relation to combating corruption as a human rights issue; and to make recommendations on ways to safeguard human rights by fighting corruption and strengthening anti-corruption efforts through the application of a human rights-based approach', para 3.

Human Rights Ms Navanethem Pillay stressed:

> Corruption is an enormous obstacle to the realization of all human rights – civil, political, economic, social and cultural, as well as the right to development. The money stolen through corruption every year was enough to feed the world's hungry 80 times over, and money siphoned from the public treasury could be spent to meet development needs; lift people out of poverty; provide children with education; bring to families essential medicine; and stop the hundreds of preventable deaths and injuries during pregnancy and childbirth that occurred every day. Corruption also denied access to justice for victims, exacerbated inequality, weakened governance and institutions, eroded public trust, fuelled impunity and undermined the rule of law.[215]

Ms Pillay reiterated that 'corruption violates the core human rights principles of transparency, accountability, non-discrimination and meaningful participation and that, conversely, those principles, when upheld and implemented, were the most effective means to fight corruption'. She concluded that, 'a human rights-based approach to anti-corruption efforts [will] deliver on the promises of "freedom from fear and want"',[216] a conclusion fully shared by the experts and UN member states represented at the meeting.[217] Subsequent to this meeting, the UN Human Rights Council has mandated a project to explore the relationship between corruption and human rights law.

It is clear that a human rights law response is neither an unnecessary nor imprudent addition to discussion of corruption. Yet, critics of a human rights law approach to corruption might also argue that the fact that corruption violates human rights is not by itself sufficient justification for using human rights to combat the problem. The contention might be that there are several other similar odious crimes with equally devastating effects on human rights, and as such there is no exceptional reason for singling out corruption. However, the fact that there are numerous crimes that infringe human rights is not a compelling enough reason not to apply human rights law to combat corruption. Probably no other crime carries with it the public indignation and a sense of injustice as corruption does. The pervading effects of corruption on society as a whole suggest that combating corruption might be the best solution for addressing similar crimes and thereby removing any threats they may pose to protection and promotion of human rights. The application of human rights law to other equally repugnant crimes may well be justified if it helps to improve efforts to combat the crimes and the harms they cause.

The third point Goodwin and Rose-Sender raised about colonisation of development and human rights discourse cannot stand the balancing of

[215] ibid, para 4.
[216] ibid, para 5.
[217] ibid, paras 5–14.

public interest tests that have been strongly put forward in this book. While it is true that Western governments may be in some ways complicit in fuelling corruption in developing countries including those in Africa, it is wrong to absolve African states (and corrupt senior state officials) of primary responsibility. Overall, there are a number of substantial legal and practical – and public interest – reasons for employing human rights law as a complementary framework to prevent and combat corruption in African states. Obviously, the strict economic and criminal law approaches have not helped to satisfactorily address and prevent the problem of corruption and its effects on human rights. Is it not then time to try a new approach that would potentially contribute to affording victims of corruption an effective remedy and at the same time improve the effective implementation and enforcement of the current framework against corruption? For those whose well-being suffers because of corruption, the application of human rights law to provide solutions is indeed clearly overdue. The potential of human rights law for addressing the depressing situation precipitated by corruption is aptly summarised by Dinah Shelton:

> Human rights law makes clear that while its primary objective is to protect individuals from abuse of power by state agents, including legislative representatives of the democratic majority, each state is also obliged to exercise due diligence to ensure that human rights are not violated by non-state actors. Due diligence requires measures to prevent abuses where possible, investigate violations that occur, prosecute the perpetrators as appropriate, and provide redress for victims.[218]

The application of human rights law to combat corruption has several advantages that are not available in the criminal law context. Whereas the sole purpose of the criminal law response to corruption is punishment, the application of human rights law underscores the fact that corruption causes measurable human rights violations, for which the victims should receive effective remedies. Simply put, the right to an effective remedy for victims of human rights violations is not available in the criminal law context. In this respect, it is noteworthy to mention that criminal law reform, *per se*, is inherently limited, and thus incapable of providing human rights remedies to victims of corruption. Although comprehensive criminal and justice systems reforms can contribute to better enforcement of anti-corruption laws, government enforcement efforts will inevitably remain limited in the long run because of the magnitude of the problem of corruption (for example, the fact that corruption in one area of government inevitably affects many other sectors), and the shortage of investigative

[218] Dinah Shelton, 'Human Rights And The Environment: What Specific Environmental Rights Have Been Recognized?' *Denver Journal Of International Law And Policy*, www.Highbeam.Com/Doc/1g1-177817178.html

and prosecutorial resources. The enormous costs of trying corruption cases may not always be commensurate with the actual number of cases prosecuted and assets recovered. Even if the resources allocated to enforcement agencies were increased, it would still most likely be insufficient to fight corruption as only a small fraction of the corruption cases involving high-ranking officials will be heard (especially given the sheer number of senior corrupt officials and the fact that to prosecute everyone may present other challenges to democracy and security of a nation). Ultimately, any impact of a criminal law approach to a social and human rights problem like corruption is bound to be marginal at best.

Besides, the notion of relying solely on a criminal law approach to corruption in states where corruption is the norms, and impunity is rife, is never going to be adequate or fully effective to address the problem. This can only be accomplished by empowering victims through legal and human rights frameworks and mechanisms that independently seek effective remedies, especially in cases where governments persistently fail to take preventive measures or take action to remedy any violations. Given these factors, governments will naturally continue to fail, at least in the short-term, until serious reforms are undertaken (through as it has been argued, entrenchment of human rights norms and standard), and allowed to take root. Furthermore, whereas criminal prosecutions of corruption are governed by the standard of 'beyond a reasonable doubt', which is a somewhat difficult task to accomplish given, as noted, the notorious secrecy surrounding corruption, human rights litigation is governed by a lower standard of proof: the preponderance of the evidence standard. Additionally, it has been observed that, 'human rights obligations only explicitly bind states whilst criminal prescriptions generally bind only private legal persons'.[219]

Yet, a criminal law response to corruption is neither undesirable nor unimportant. On the contrary, this book argues that the clear inadequacies of this approach (especially given the concentration of law enforcement in the hands of corrupt governments and officials), human rights law should be used as a complementary framework to augment the law enforcement efforts. Human rights law can also provide the normative standards with which to effectively reform the criminal justice system, and make any reforms more meaningful, tangible and sustainable. In addition to this, human rights law can serve to constrain or limit government misconduct or unchecked powers in the criminal process; for example, by helping to ensure the rights of those accused of corruption, including to the presumption of innocence, freedom from self-incrimination, and protection against arbitrary arrest and detention, and so on.

[219] Paul Arnell, 'Extraterritorial Human Rights: A Tool for Poverty Reduction' (2005) 38 *Comparative and International Law Journal of Southern Africa* 396, 404.

Whereas the merits for granting rights to those accused of corruption may be questioned, it needs to be said that corruption suspects may not be necessarily guilty of the charges against them regardless of the publicity and public interest that a corruption case can generate. Far from serving the interest of the accused, this notion of fairness actually serves to enhance the legitimacy of a justice system, and helps to command obedience to law. At the same time, human rights law can provide a balanced approach, as it will ensure that the rights of the victims are not sacrificed at the expense of securing the rights of the accused. Indeed, adhering to due process of law, justice, and fair trial principles is important regardless, and is crucial for improving the credibility and viability of human rights law, and for ending a culture of impunity.[220]

However, despite its potential, it has to be pointed out that human rights law faces important obstacles, which may provide some explanations in relation to the gaps still exit between human rights ideal and practice. Among the obstacles to the effectiveness and efficacy of human rights law are the lack of political will of many governments, the absence of 'coercive enforcement' at the international and regional levels, and the politicisation and selective use of economic or military interventions by powerful states to deal with alleged gross violations of human rights mostly in developing countries. While they may be justified on humanitarian grounds, such interventions often lead to claims and counter-claims of breach of national sovereignty. Nevertheless, these challenges do not vitiate the idea of human rights. Yet, the obstacles will need to be overcome if the international community is to enhance the effectiveness of human rights law, and ultimately, its promise for tackling corruption.

## CONCLUSION

A fundamental notion of contemporary human rights law is that victims of violations enjoy an independent right to effective remedies. This idea, which is now widely endorsed by legal scholars and states alike, is itself founded on another longstanding legal principle: *ubi ius ibi remedium* (there is no right without a remedy). Dinah Shelton put it succinctly, writing: 'Rights without remedies are ineffectual, rendering illusory the government's duty to respect such rights.'[221] Thus, the right to an effective remedy, either procedural or substantive, primarily aims to ensure, as far

[220] This point has been consistently emphasised, for example by the South African Constitutional Court. The court has stated that, 'In any democratic criminal justice system there is a tension between bringing criminals to book and ensuring that justice is manifestly done to all. But none of that means sympathy for crime and its perpetrators.' *S v Zuma* 1995 (2) SA 642 (CC).

[221] Shelton, *Remedies in International Human Rights Law* (n 217), 100.

as possible, that victims are made 'whole'.[222] Remedies logically should be proportionate to the gravity of the harm or violations caused by the state or its agents. Yet, the idea of an effective remedy is broad, all-encompassing, and not limited to judicial remedies or redress. Nonetheless, legal actions have remained an important avenue for securing remedies for human rights violations. This unique characteristic makes human rights law a satisfactory complementary framework to combat grave problems like corruption, which has long been regarded, rather erroneously, as a victimless crime. Furthermore, human rights law is inspired by a set of higher common values that centre on the protection of human dignity, are endowed with specific and arguably better and accessible supervisory mechanisms, and cover individual and collective guarantees. Human rights law also embodies both objective and positive obligations that sets them apart from other treaties, especially anticorruption treaties that emphasise only a limited criminal law.

Additionally, as has been shown, corruption unquestionably violates Article 21 of the African Charter, as well as other substantive human and peoples' rights in the charter. Not only is it the case that every dollar lost from corruption is one less than can be spent constructively, but also that the loss is often offset by government borrowing. These loans or international aid received from abroad may be considered part of the 'national cake' to be shared among high-ranking state officials, or, in plain language, stolen or mismanaged. Human and peoples' rights are seriously compromised because corruption undermines the integrity and impartiality of a government, the important values for the effective and efficient functioning of any state, and the enforcement of the rule of law and human rights. Clearly the public trust, confidence, and support on which every civilised government depends upon to discharge its duties and which is necessary for the effectiveness and survival of governments is lost without integrity and impartiality.

By undermining the rule of law, any abuse of the public trust turns the government itself into a lawbreaker and paves the way for citizens to take the law into their own hands. By advancing self-interest rather than the common good, corrupt public officials perpetrate unjust treatment of

[222] The foundational judicial authority for this proposition is the case of *Chorzow* (*Germany v Poland*), 1928 PCIJ (ser A) No 17 (Sept 13). In that case, the Permanent Court of International Justice, (which the International Court of Justice replaced) found: 'It is the principle of international law, and even a general conception of law, that any breach of an engagement involves an obligation to make reparation'. Ibid, 39. The ICJ has consistently followed this precedent. See, eg, *Armed Activities on the Territory of the Congo (Democratic Republic of the Congo v Uganda)*, Judgment, ICJ Reports (2005); and *Legal Consequences of the Construction of a Wall in the Occupied Palestinian Territory (Advisory Opinion)*, ICJ Reports (2004). Whereas these cases focus on the law of state responsibility generally governing disputes between states, the principles they advance provide the legal foundations for the remedies obtainable under human rights law.

the economically and socially vulnerable, and create distortions in their political decision-making process (also because outcomes are basically determined by political and other related considerations). This invariably leads to massive disparities in the distribution of wealth; creates disparities in political participation that unfairly reduces the political power of the poor, and ultimately destroys the climate of public trust in elected officials. Moreover, whereas effective prosecution of corruption involving high-ranking officials clearly has a powerful deterrent effect, criminal and law enforcement approach to corruption alone does not ensure ethical conduct of high-level state officials, accountability of states, or remedies for victims. Accordingly, human rights law can enhance the effectiveness of the criminal law regime, advance the goal of ending impunity for corruption, and ensure the continued viability of the criminal law dimension to corruption.

As its drafting history suggests, Article 21 was primarily directed towards multinationals, not high-level national officials stealing public funds. The aim was to reduce opportunities for multinationals and their officials to plunder Africa's wealth and resources. This proposition was fully justified, given that historically multinationals were primarily responsible for the theft of vast resources and wealth across the region. But times have changed, and the past decades have witnessed equal and sometimes greater levels of corruption by high-ranking state officials. These funds are transferred to developed economies, mostly through the use of 'shell banks' (see Chapter 2). Therefore, an expansive and evolutionary interpretation of broadly and generally phrased Article 21 to include corruption is necessary and can indeed encourage greater public-mindedness among public officials and eventually create a body of jurisprudence to serve as a human rights framework against corruption. This is not an unrealistic assessment of what the drafters of the African Charter might have meant by making Article 21 a fundamental feature of the African Charter. The charter, though, will only effectively and satisfactorily serve as a complementary framework for combating corruption if the African Commission and the African Court's interpretation of Article 21 is driven by the desire to ensure effectiveness, efficacy, and viability of the charter, as well as to align the intention of its drafters to meet the contemporary challenge of corruption and its effects on human rights across African states.

Although adopting a general comment is not the practice for which the African Commission is known, the commission might for instance, adopt a general comment on the relationship between corruption and the human rights recognised in the African Charter. While this may not entirely remove the textual ambiguities associated with Article 21, such an exercise will at least serve to direct and shape a clearer understanding of the issues, and thus facilitate a process for developing the normative contents of Article 21, in particular vis-à-vis its relevance for addressing corruption in Africa. The principle that human rights treaties such as the African Charter are to be interpreted maximally to advance the rights and freedoms of individuals and communities should provide a constant guide to the commission in this normative engagement.

Apart from the African Commission and the African Court, African human rights institutions and courts in general would need to be more aware of the substantive relevance of Article 21 for tackling corruption that affect human rights within their mandates and to undertake rigorous legal analysis to bring life to the provision in terms of the degree to which it (or other similar provisions) might contribute to preventing and combating corruption across Africa. It is to be hoped that the framework provided in this book would contribute to making this exercise possible.

Yet, despite the plain merits of deploying human rights law to combat corruption, questions may be asked that since corrupt acts are committed by individual state officials and therefore not attributable to a state, human rights law, being primarily regulated by treaties, only states parties to such treaties assume legal obligations to ensure and protect human rights. Thus, since only acts ascribable or attributable to a state can violate human rights (and the state does not directly engage in corruption), human rights law may not appropriately serve as the basis for curbing corruption. However, the simple response to such views is that, while individual public officials (or other individuals) are clearly not parties to human rights treaties, the duty of states to ensure human rights imposes obligations on states to protect citizens from non-state actor/individual conducts that violate human rights, and to provide effective remedies for the violations of the rights. Therefore, human rights law (in particular the African Charter) will indirectly regulate corrupt conducts of public officials, but *uniquely* attribute such conducts to states on the grounds of failure to exercise *due diligence* to prevent massive stealing of public resources which in turn violate human rights, and impose obligations on states to appropriately remedy those violations.

It needs to be stressed here that this book is not proposing the establishment of a new right to be free from corruption. Rather, it proposes, as will be discussed further in the Conclusion, a new protocol to the African Charter (and on the domestic level, similar national laws) to grant legal standing to victims of human rights violations and the concerned public to seek and obtain effective remedies for these violations under the African Charter, and other relevant treaties and national laws. The framework for the application of human rights law to combat corruption already exists in the form of the charter, although only implicitly. Of course, the rigorous and progressive interpretation of the charter and other similar treaties by national, regional, and global human rights institutions and courts, and where appropriate national human rights commissions, can help to accomplish this goal. Nonetheless, to effectively operationalise the existing framework, it is crucial to establish more specific normative frameworks that explicitly recognise corruption as a violation of human and peoples' rights in the charter and grants legal standing to victims and the concerned public. Yet, given the inherent limitations of litigation or a strict legal approach to problems generally, other preventive functions of human rights law ought to be fully explored and utilised.

Finally, while some commentators (such as Raj Kumar) have indeed proposed the establishment of a new human right to be free from corruption, it is unclear how any such right would operate coherently alongside existing human rights frameworks. The African Charter and other similar treaties are considerably developed and interpreted, so much so that today an impressive body of case law and jurisprudence exists on the meanings, contents, scope, and application of the human rights they guarantee. The proposal for a new human right in this apparently difficult political climate is less likely to be embraced by states, and may present daunting challenges such as the problems of definition and judicial adjudication. This author is therefore calling for the enhancement and greater use of existing human rights law to combat corruption, not new human rights.

# 7

# *Conclusions*

ALTHOUGH THE ANTI-CORRUPTION movement has made remarkable progress, when it is considered that the use of the word 'corruption' in international relations was once a taboo, questions remain as to the effectiveness of the traditional criminal law instruments that have been negotiated, adopted, and endorsed to combat corruption within African states (and internationally). Many countries in Africa have not made headway in the fight against corruption, despite the existence of a multitude of anti-corruption laws and instruments on the issue, because while states are vested with the *legal* capacity to implement these laws and instruments, they lack the *factual* capacity (because of corruption) necessary to discharge their responsibilities. Furthermore, apart from the fact that victims of corruption have no legal standing or right to effective remedies, not all the provisions of the four treaties studied in this book are mandatory; some are conditional, or subject to progressive development or national sovereignty. There are also a number of undefined escape clauses and 'blanket reservations' that states may use to truncate their implementation and enforcement of the treaties. While the escape clauses and reservations are not peculiar to the field of corruption, and are indeed part and parcel of international law, the specific inclusion in these treaties of the protection of national sovereignty as an overriding principle suggests that they are more likely to have negative effects on states and their obligations and commitments.

Part of the issue is that the legal instruments that have been examined in this book offer only a limited definition of corruption. The treatment of all kinds of corruption as the same, without considering the effects of the contemporary nature of large-scale corruption on the rule of law or on development and human rights, is perhaps the most significant foundational weakness of current criminal law instruments. Corruption is thus generally conceived as a victimless crime. However, this view unfortunately does not reflect the clear complexities, multidisciplinary nature, and varying effects of corruption on human rights. Although there are many definitions of corruption, of varying normative contents and significance, few capture the elements of the accountability of states for the human rights violations suffered by victims of large-scale corruption, most frequently the economically and socially vulnerable. The anonymity of the victims in the criminal process has meant that they are denied access to effective remedies.

Criminal law instruments against corruption are further weakened by the existence of several debilitating provisions such as sovereign immunity (which forbids jurisdictional review of official acts and shields corrupt senior officials from prosecution), constitutional and legislative immunity from criminal prosecution of certain high-ranking state officials, unbridled prosecutorial discretion (ie, *nolle prosequi*), plea-bargaining for corrupt suspects (who can then benefit from their crime), short limitation periods on the institution of criminal proceedings against corrupt suspects, and opaque, weak and non-independent anti-corruption institutions and agencies. Discriminatory and selective enforcement of anti-corruption laws, treaties and standards, and the shielding of corrupt officials from punishment and prosecution, combined with unfair targeting of low-level officials who commit petty corruption, provide additional explanations as to why the laws and instruments have shown little promise.

The weaknesses of these laws and instruments also illustrate why corruption cannot be effectively combated merely by reliance upon traditional criminal law instruments, and justify the application of human rights law, in particular the African Charter on Human and Peoples' Rights, as a complementary framework to address the problem. Such an approach based on human rights law and criminal law would not only improve the effectiveness of these instruments in many African states, but also enhance the promotion and protection of human rights. The application of human rights law to combat corruption may also be appreciated as a unique response to help correct the underlying structures, rather than just attending to the symptoms, while also improving the rule of law, reducing the cost of governance and important public services, increasing civil society participation in efforts to address the problem, and significantly, improving legal standing for victims of corruption, which in turn would grant them access to effective remedies.

Granted that a comprehensive reform of the criminal justice system may be one useful way to combat corruption, the limitation of this approach is however evident from the fact that it cannot by itself change human behaviour. Human rights law, in contrast, provides useful and comprehensive normative framework cutting virtually across all human affairs, enriching governance structure and institutions, and crucially, focusing on the provision of remedies for victims. However, application of human rights law itself will be imperilled without a corresponding improvement of national, regional and international human rights institutions, mechanisms and courts, in a manner that ensures that these institutions are not politicised or themselves corrupt. Beyond this, as noted earlier, the application of human rights law also faces other significant legal and practical challenges, the most significant of which are causation, legal standing for victims, identification of victims, and evidence-gathering. These challenges are not insurmountable, and can be addressed through appropriate legal and institutional reforms. The reality that corruption breeds terrorism (and other organised crimes), encourages money laundering (and vice versa), precipitates poverty, undermines the operation of the rule of law, the working of the institutions of governance and, ultimately, leads or contributes to violations of human rights mostly of the economically and socially vulnerable, should compel the world community to muster sufficient political will to begin to take steps in these directions.

It should be emphasised, however, that while a human rights approach to corruption is desirable, and in fact necessary, it would be unrealistic to expect that this will automatically and immediately end large-scale corruption and its associated human rights violations in countries across Africa. Nonetheless, while the problem of corruption (and human rights violations) will not and cannot be combated overnight, even with the invocation of human rights law, it does not mean that the international community's vision of curbing all forms of corruption is unattainable in the long run. The experience and achievements of the anti-slavery and anti-apartheid movements suggest that, with the appropriate strategy and requisite political will, the phenomenon of corruption can ultimately be surmounted, or at least considerably minimised and made negligible, in that it no longer constitutes much danger to individuals and communities (or worsens the already clearly precarious situation of the economically and socially vulnerable.

Furthermore, while human rights law (in particular the African Charter) can serve as an instrument to combat corruption through creative and dynamic and evolutionary interpretation of its various substantive provisions, it needs to be said that the charter neither explicitly refers to nor prohibits corruption. While dynamic and evolutionary interpretation rule is a proper part of judicial or interpretative duties, and obviously has its benefits, and is strongly encouraged (especially because of the broad and non-specific nature of many of the African Charter's provisions, which can be exploited to create novel results), ultimately, the extent to which the considerable potential of the African Charter is enhanced and realised for tackling corruption will be determined not by ascribing to its provisions 'a thousand and one interpretations', but by the development of a new instrument in the form of a protocol to the charter that explicitly recognises corruption as a violation of the rights in the charter, and thereby complementing the charter's provisions and giving them their full effect. This proposed protocol would ideally allow for better integration of human rights and criminal law instruments, grant explicit standing to victims (and NGOs or other interested parties) to approach the African

Commission and African Court for remedies, demonstrate states' intention to take their charter obligations and anti-corruption obligations and commitments seriously, and thus effectively contributing to the goal of a comprehensive and multidisciplinary approach to fighting corruption. This mechanism would enhance the credibility of the criminal law instruments against corruption and human rights law, by improving the prospect that a state will be held to account for any breach of the African Charter and the proposed protocol. It may also restrict states' sovereignty, which currently allows states to resist compliance. However, detailed rules of procedure would need to be established to determine issues such as admissibility criteria for potential complaints.

The proposed protocol would include provisions on the responsibility of financial institutions acting as havens for stolen funds, and principles that address the human rights dimension of corruption. A protocol to the charter does not require reinvention of the wheel, and would avoid the necessity of drafting a distinct human rights treaty on corruption and the creation of an acceptable enforcement mechanism. The human rights obligations of the African Charter have already been negotiated and its enforcement established. Thus, transforming the criminal law instruments against corruption into a human rights protocol would save time and resources, and would not require separate structures and institutions. Although the African Charter enforcement mechanisms at the moment are less than optimal, they nonetheless offer the fundamental utility of the charter itself, which is the best option for the creation of a regional human rights framework to tackle corruption. Indeed, the African Charter offers established mechanisms by which to enforce, monitor, and file complaints and to report on states' efforts to eliminate human rights violations arising from acts of corruption.

At the political level, the issues should be discussed among the various organs of the AU, and the effects of large-scale corruption on human rights must remain a permanent theme on the agenda of the AU Assembly and its Executive Council. The starting point, however, would be for these bodies to introduce a resolution recognising corruption as a violation of human rights recognised by the African Charter. While African states collectively and individually must demonstrate the requisite level of determination and capabilities to combat corruption, the UN and other members of the international community have to push for greater recognition of the impeding effects of corruption on the full and effective realisation of human rights in Africa, through, for example, improved technical assistance and cooperation, including in the areas of asset recovery. By doing so, the international community will indirectly contribute to the establishment of an environment in which African nations can reduce the flow of economic migrants to Western economies. In this respect, notable initiatives like the UN Human Rights Council round-table discussion on the negative effects of corruption on human rights should be welcomed, encouraged, and further developed.

At the domestic level, national courts and national human rights commissions, which exist in many countries, can play an important role in securing the enforcement of the protocol.[1] However, victims of human rights violations may be reluctant to bring complaints, out of fear of possible reprisals by various state authorities. Therefore, it is important for NGOs and national human rights commissions to encourage the establishment of mechanisms that protect complainants against any retaliation. They should also educate victims about any procedures and assist them in filling in and submitting complaints. However, given the general lack of interest of NGOs with observer status within the African Commission on the issue of corruption, and their lack of capacity to consider this from a human rights viewpoint, it is important for these groups and their funders and supporters to devote their own resources to improving their interest and work in this important field.

However, given the limited scope of the African-focused criminal law instruments against corruption, and the fact that the illicit movement of stolen public funds from many African states to developed economies in Europe and the Americas is not covered by the mandate of the African Commission, it will be necessary to develop, in the light of this author's proposed protocol to the African Charter, a rights-focused convention within the UN human rights mechanisms. Most of the countries that provide safe havens for stolen funds are already signatories to international human rights treaties, and are required to provide international cooperation and assistance in the fulfilment of human rights. Snidert and Won Kidanett stated that:

> In relation to the corruption that involves other continents, therefore, to avoid clapping with one hand, States Parties to the AU Corruption Convention and all other nations who wish to fight corruption through international law must accede to the UNCAC. That is the best way of addressing issues involved in the cross-continent corruption that is seriously affecting Africa's development today.[2]

[1] Indeed, some national human rights commissions such as Ghana's Commission on Human Rights and Administrative Justice have explicit competence to investigate corruption as recognised by the 1992 Constitution. Art 218(a) provides that the commission shall 'investigate complaints of violations of fundamental rights and freedoms, injustice, corruption, abuse of power and unfair treatment of any person by a public officer in the exercise of his [her] official duties'. See also Art 218(e), which requires the commission to 'investigate all instances of alleged or suspected corruption and the misappropriation of public moneys by officials and to take appropriate steps, including reports to the Attorney General and the Auditor-General, resulting from such investigations'. However, this mandate is somewhat limited and unsatisfactory, as the government officials referred to here may block investigations or prosecution, solely for political reasons.

[2] Thomas R Snider and Won Kidane, 'Combating Corruption through International Law in Africa: A Comparative Analysis' (2007) 40 *Cornell International Law Journal* 691, 747.

Further, an international convention or protocol in this field would provide the necessary level of coordination and harmonisation with important players from outside Africa, and would ensure that the resources and technical ability and technology of Western countries contribute much-needed support to fight corruption. The idea of an international agreement to provide effective remedies to victims is not a revolutionary one. W Michael Reisman proposed the drafting of an international declaration that would:

(1) characterise acts of corruption (what he called 'spoliation') by national officials as a breach of national trust and international law;
(2) impose on other governments an obligation of supplying information and cooperation; and
(3) characterise the failure of other governments to prevent such funds from being cached in their jurisdiction and to aid in their recapture as complicity, after the fact, and itself, an international delict.[3]

Reisman also suggested that the United Nations should consider forming an international high commission for the retrieval of diverted national wealth.[4] According to Reisman, the commission would be charged with responding to the requests of member governments to identify the location of purloined funds and to secure their return by negotiation or, where appropriate, by judicial action. The statute of the agency would grant it international legal personality and authorise it to cover its reasonable expenses from the funds regained.[5] While the four treaties above already contain provisions requiring governments to share information and cooperate and assist one another, most of the elements of Reisman's sensible proposal remain outstanding because they were not satisfactorily implemented at the time of the adoption of the UN Convention against Corruption, the AU Convention on Preventing and Combating Corruption, the SADC Protocol against Corruption, or the ECOWAS Protocol on the Fight against Corruption. However, Reisman's proposal should be implemented by way of a legally binding protocol (and not a declaration, as he has suggested) to the UNCAC, as it would be a major tool in addressing the problem of corruption and its effects on human rights in Africa.[6]

[3] W Michael Reisman, 'Harnessing International Law to Restrain and Recapture Indigenous Spoliations', (1989) 83 *American Journal of International Law 56,* 57.

[4] ibid.

[5] ibid.

[6] However, any such international agreement on large-scale corruption must be placed firmly and squarely within the human rights framework of the Office of the High Commissioner for Human Rights. Any such arrangement should take into account the role of Western states and their financial institutions that provide safe havens for stolen funds. It must also articulate norms necessary to comply with their obligations under international human rights treaties, and include accountability provisions for financial institutions and

One major challenge to the implementation of the idea of a protocol may be the lack of political will, especially given the slow pace of development of the anti-corruption movement and the reluctance of the international community to go the extra mile regarding corruption, despite recognising it as a serious problem. Other challenges may include the notorious principle of sovereignty associated with the fight against corruption; difficulty in obtaining agreement on the elements of corruption as a violation of human rights; limited resources; little appetite for additional normative standards, not least on the controversial issue of corruption; and the obstacles of privileges and immunities. Civil society and international NGOs such as Transparency International and Amnesty International would need to use their influence, global membership, and networks to mobilise African citizens and powerful Western countries if the idea of a regional (and global) protocol is to become a reality.

Even so, corruption can only be effectively and satisfactorily combated through a combination of approaches and strategies in the short, medium and long term, but given the serious harms that corruption has already caused (and continues to cause), it is clear that complementary legal, policy and other initiatives to address the problem and its effects on human rights should not be postponed or put aside indefinitely. The complementary initiatives suggested below would help to advance a human rights approach to corruption.

## COMPREHENSIVE LEGAL AND JUDICIAL REFORMS REQUIRED TO COMBAT CORRUPTION

### Constitutional and Legal Reforms

Constitutions are the supreme law of most countries including those across Africa. These documents usually elaborate the functions of key institutions of states, such as the executive, legislative, and judicial branches, and the importance of the separation of powers. Many constitutions also guarantee fundamental human rights for their citizens, remove the possibility of governmental abuse of those rights, pledge the independence and impartiality of the judiciary, and contain transparency and accountability provisions. However, experience has shown that in many cases the processes leading to the making of these constitutions have not been inclusive and participatory.[7] Apart from directly undermining the rule of law, such constitutions also breach citizens' internationally recognised human right to participate in their own government. Therefore, the

jurisdictions serving as havens to stolen funds from Africa.

[7] John Mukum Mbaku, 'The International Dimension of Africa's Struggle Against Corruption' (2010) 10 *Asper Review of International Business and Trade Law* 76.

starting point for countries to demonstrate a genuine intention to combat corruption (and its effects on human rights) is to begin a process of developing people-based and people-focused constitutions through real and genuine public consultation, negotiation, and participation.

Most of the existing constitutions in Africa need substantial rewriting to incorporate a comprehensive set of human rights – civil, political, economic, social, and cultural – to specifically recognise corruption as a violation of human rights, and to include provisions on mandatory, enforceable anti-poverty measures and commitments of governments. Preventing and combating corruption is possible only when the legal framework against corruption is rooted in the constitutional foundation of a state and is consistent with the fundamental principles of universal human rights and the rule of law. It is, in fact, the absence of constitutionalism as a tool of social engineering and a lack of effective human rights, governance institutions, and rule of law that contribute to corruption and citizens' apathy, lack of trust, and confidence in their government. Imposing strict sanctions against indicted corrupt public officials, preventing them from partaking in the political process for a specified period of time, can serve a powerful message of deterrence against corruption, as also can rewarding leaders who play by the rules and work to deliver the common good.

Other reforms must allow for public interest litigation, in particular, by facilitating requests for criminal investigations on public interest grounds and for asset recovery. Importantly, legal standing and right of the victims of corruption must be entrenched as part of the enforceable fundamental human rights. The need for a constitutional approach to tackle corruption has been aptly illustrated by John Hatchard:

> Suppose a judge, Judge Sisamnes, accepts money from a litigant, Tim, to rule in his favour in a civil case being brought by Colin. Both the payment and acceptance of the bribe constitute criminal offences. But law enforcement officers investigating the case may well face precisely the difficulties in obtaining admissible evidence for use at the criminal trial and the lack of any political will to prosecute serving judges. However, by viewing the matter as potentially raising a constitutional issue, new options become available and these focus particularly on enforcing the rights of individuals. In particular, this can assist individual victims of corruption and is an approach that is largely missing in other anti-corruption strategies. . .. Here it is the unsuccessful litigant, Colin, whose right to a fair hearing before an independent and impartial court has been infringed because of the corrupt judge. This raises a constitutional issue and enables Colin to bring a constitutional case before the courts to enforce his rights.[8]

[8] John Hatchard, 'Adopting a Human Rights Approach towards Combating Corruption' in Martine Boersma and Hans Nelen (eds), *Corruption and Human Rights: Interdisciplinary Perspectives* (Antwerp: Intersentia, 2010) 17–18. Hatchard identified some benefits of a constitutional solution to corruption as including the following: that it puts the matter effectively in the control of the claimant and thus reduces any possibility of political interference such

Additionally, the proposed constitutional reform must be complemented with equally comprehensive judicial, administrative, and institutional reforms in several areas of governance if corruption is to be satisfactorily combated. Tackling corruption effectively also requires enhancing the capacity, independence, autonomy, and indeed, accountability of specific anti-corruption institutions and other general law enforcement mechanisms.

It is useful to point out that genuine recognition of the seriousness of the problem of corruption at the highest level of political authorities, together with political commitment and comprehensive legal, administration, and institutional reforms, are responsible for the notable success of the fight against corruption in countries such as Singapore and Hong Kong, where corruption was once widespread. There is no reason why similar measures cannot be replicated in countries in Africa. In the case of Hong Kong, of particular importance was the institution of independent and motivated anti-corruption bodies separate from the police force and the civil service, with robust disciplinary codes and internal monitoring mechanisms. Hong Kong also created a corruption prevention advisory committee, with a dedicated community relations department that sought and garnered public support and offered public participation in prosecutor strategy and action.[9] In relation to Singapore, of special importance is the existence of tough deterrence measures, such as banning indicted corrupt contractors from obtaining public contracts; compulsory declaration of assets; prohibition of the use of information for personal benefit; strict conflict regulations on the acceptance of gifts; just and fair application of anti-corruption laws; and a genuine desire for fundamental changes in public attitudes.

Nonetheless, for countries in Africa, establishing anti-corruption bodies similar to those of Hong Kong and Singapore would require robust constitutional checks and balances to watch for potential abuses of powers and to prevent them from being used for political or unfair purposes to target opposition leaders and civil society. As Thomas T Snider and Won Kidane eloquently stated, 'Combating a phenomenon that is directly

as the power to file a *nolle prosequi*; that the application of the civil standard balance of probabilities and the relaxed rules of evidence will facilitate admissibility of evidence; that there is the possibility of assistance (including by civil society) for victims of corruption; and that the action is instituted against the state. Ibid, 18.

[9] However, Raj Kumar has stated that, 'In the context of Hong Kong, the successes achieved in combating corruption may not be sustained if it remains purely within the domain of law enforcement and public policy discourse. The fact that community education and participation of the people in generating an attitudinal change was deemed one of the initial goals of the ICAC's approach [means that] there is a need for the empowerment of the people of Hong Kong to fight against corruption on the basis of developing certain rights against corruption.' C Raj Kumar, 'Human Rights Approaches of Corruption Mechanisms – Enhancing the Hong Kong Experience of Corruption Prevention Strategies' (2004) 5 *San Diego International Law Journal* 350–51.

intertwined with the exercise of state power without appropriate institutional reform may be like putting the cart in front of the horse.'[10] And as John Mukum Mbaku wrote:

> A good start could and possibly should be made with corrupt legal systems and corrupt law enforcement because if these areas were clean and everyone was aware that they were, the corrupt would be fearful that they could no longer get away easily with what they do and are unlikely to enjoy their unjust desserts.[11]

In addition to constitutional reform, states must adopt and review national legislation to bring it in line with their international human rights and anti-corruption obligations and commitments, including under the African Charter and the UN Convention against Corruption. It should be stressed that such processes aim to complement constitutional guarantees. Any success in this regard will be short-lived and limited, without national political consensus by politicians and opposition leaders, and indeed without civil society recognising the seriousness of the problem. Consensus is also needed to develop a comprehensive and multidisciplinary framework to prevent and combat all forms of corruption and to improve the independence and freedom of the mechanisms mandated to fight corruption.[12]

## THE OFFICE OF INDEPENDENT SPECIAL COUNSEL

In light of wide prosecutorial discretion over corruption and constant political interference in the work of traditional anti-corruption commissions and agencies, states need to establish an independent investigatory and prosecutorial office dedicated to fighting large-scale corruption. Such an Office of Independent Special Counsel must be constitutionally created, and must be empowered to investigate and prosecute corruption among members of the cabinet and other high-ranking officials of government. The independence, integrity, and impartiality of the office must be constitutionally secured. A prevention unit could be established within the Office of the Independent Special Counsel to focus on public education on ethics, integrity, and leadership. At the same time, states should improve the mechanisms for fighting corruption in their countries in

[10] Thomas T Snider and Won Kidane, 'Combating Corruption through International Law in Africa: A Comparative Analysis' (2007) 40 *Cornell International Law Journal* 747. Snider and Kidane also suggest that the 'AU Convention's good governance and human rights approach must be encouraged and developed further in all implementation and enforcement stages.' Ibid, 746.

[11] John Mukum Mbaku, 'The International Dimension of Africa's Struggle Against Corruption' 10 *Asper Review of International Business & Trade Law* 35, 88.

[12] C Raj Kumar, 'Corruption and Human Rights: Promoting Transparency in Governance and the Fundamental Right to Corruption-Free Service in India' (2003–04) 31 *Columbia Journal of Asian Law* 71.

terms of the independence and resources – both human and materials – made available to these institutions. Unless the institutions and agencies established to combat corruption are guaranteed the necessary independence and freedom needed to discharge their mandates effectively and efficiently, the fight against corruption in many countries will remain tied to the political whims and caprices of senior public officials.[13]

## TRUST FUNDS FOR VICTIMS OF CORRUPTION

The notion of trust funds for victims of human rights violations is a well-established mechanism in international law and relations, such as under Article 75 of the Rome Statute of the International Criminal Court (which creates a fund for the benefit of victims of international crimes and their families, the assets of which may originate from money or property collected through fines or forfeiture imposed by the ICC on the individual perpetrator).[14] It is thus 'necessary that, in addition to individual means of reparation, adequate provision be made to entitle groups of victims or victimised communities to present collective claims for damages and to receive collective reparation accordingly'.[15] This novel mechanism to protect victims' rights indicates a willingness by the world nations to adopt innovative responses to serious challenges, and has contributed to the efforts to advance international law regarding reparations.

The idea of a trust fund is also frequently adopted in mass claims programmes (such as the Iran-United States Claims Tribunal of 1981) to provide 'effective remedies for numerous individuals who suffered losses, damage or injuries as a result of an armed conflict or a similar event caus-

[13] For anti-corruption agencies to be successful and effective, there must be strong political and public support, and strong political leadership and commitment on the part of elected government officials and opposition parties to make these agencies work. Importantly, any such agencies must be granted the necessary independence and freedom of action to operate and investigate allegations of corruption, no matter the people involved. Specifically, the power to appoint and dismiss, as well as to allocate material and human resources, should be exercised by a constitutionally established mechanism that is fully independent of the executive branch of government. It is useful to state that anti-corruption agencies themselves need to be accountable and corruption-free if they are to have the public trust and confidence essential for their credibility, legitimacy, and success.

[14] Under the Rome Statute, victims are entitled to present their views and concerns to the court (directly or through legal representation) where their interests are affected as long as this is not prejudicial or inconsistent with the rights of the accused or with a fair and impartial trial; and may even request the Prosecutor of the Court to initiate an investigation. The Court is also required to provide information to victims about their rights throughout proceedings.

[15] *Study Concerning the Right to Restitution, Compensation and Rehabilitation for Victims of Gross Violations of Human Rights and Fundamental Freedoms, final report submitted by Mr Theo van Boven, Special rapporteur to the Sub-Commission on Prevention of Discrimination and Protection of Minorities,* UN Human Rights Commission, 45th Sess, UN Doc E/CN 4/Sub 2/1993, s VII.

ing widespread damage'.[16] The existence of armed conflict is not a requirement for mass claims: 'similar types of claims would arise from environmental disasters, causing widespread damage or injury, or from systematic human rights violations in peacetime'.[17] The goal is presumably to achieve 'practical justice: that is, a justice that would be swift and efficient, yet not rough'.[18] Mass claims cases are clearly similar in kind to the adverse effects of corruption on human rights. If it is agreed that corruption violates human rights, then, it seems sensible, legitimate and appropriate for states to replicate the mass claims principles, and to work towards establishing their own trust funds (as an essential element of remedial justice) for victims of human rights violations that stem from corruption. The existence of clear links between corruption and violations of human rights demonstrates the need for effective remedies for victims nationally, regionally and internationally. By establishing such trust funds, states will also be signalling that victims will no longer be marginalised in the fight against corruption. The establishment of trust funds for victims of corruption is also justified on the grounds of fairness, because not all cases of violations of human rights stemming from corruption can reach the court, which will mean that without such trust funds, only some victims will receive compensation. While class action may be taken on behalf of victims, this alone may not be sufficient, given the magnitude of the problem and the logistical and other challenges that such actions often encounter.

Furthermore, each trust fund should be established initially on the domestic level, and then replicated and expanded to cover sub-regional, regional, national, and international levels. Part of the funds should be used to establish victims' assistance programmes to ensure the victims' perspective is fully integrated into the fight against corruption. The funds can be built and sustained through seized and repatriated stolen money, fines, and forfeiture proceeds of recovered wealth in key portfolios, and augmented by support from international development agencies and other relevant institutions. Drawing trust funds for victims mainly from fines imposed on corrupt officials is fully justified, given that the theft of large amounts of public money inevitably causes loss and suffering to the economically and socially vulnerable.

Thus, a 'victim of crime report' by the UN stated: '[I]f it is uncertain whether the budgetary means of the State will be sufficient to cover an unknown number of claimants, a fund should be established to limit the financial burden'. Given the limited resources available, fines should be imposed on corrupt officials, and such fines should be set aside as

[16] See Hans Das, 'The Concept of Mass Claims and the Specificity of Mass Claims Resolution' in Permanent Court of Arbitration (ed), *Redressing Injustices Through Mass Claims Processes: Innovative Responses to Unique Challenges* (Oxford: Oxford University Press, 2006) 5.

[17] ibid, 8–9.

[18] ibid, 10.

endowment for the trust funds. To prioritise areas of development, states also need to establish truth commissions on the costs and impact of corruption on communities and citizens. Of course, it is desirable for states to consider taking other necessary measures to mitigate the effects of corruption on victims. Increasingly, and in a myriad of ways, civil society organisations, including international and national NGOs, are positively pushing the boundaries of international law to achieve effective remedies for victims of human rights violations. In furtherance of this tradition (and given such NGOs' expertise and experiences and links to victims and families), they can play various meaningful roles such as demanding the establishment of funds for victims of corruption, and contributing to the modalities and implementation of these trust funds.

## ASSETS RECOVERY

The fight against corruption will mean little without a strong assets recovery programme to trace, seize, freeze, recover, and return the vast sums of stolen money. This process of assets recovery can also be a particularly powerful tool to stem the tide of corruption and thwart the ongoing impunity of perpetrators, while also improving the governance system, the rule of law, and respect for human rights. This money would improve the quality of life for a state's citizens, when it is returned to the programmes from which it was stolen. The UNCAC also encourages civil action over criminal action to recover stolen assets, because this requires the presence of corrupt officials in the courtroom and removes immunity of senior government officials, plus any complicit families and friends. For these reasons, even in cases where there is no need to obtain a criminal conviction, states should use this method more frequently.

Moreover, there is also the need for improved cooperation and better coordination between the World Bank and the United Nations, if the international assets recovery effort is to be successful in reversing the flow of corrupt funds into developed economies. Otherwise, corruption will continue to be a profitable business for many leaders of countries across Africa. However, given that any assets recovery initiative is capital-intensive, and that finding these required resources is exceedingly difficult for any country already destroyed by corruption, it is absolutely necessary, as described earlier, for the international community to establish trust funds for victims using recovered stolen wealth as the start-up money. Part of such funds can be used to trace stolen assets and to pursue civil suits and other relevant initiatives. Nonetheless, it is important for developed economies that are members of UNCAC to demonstrate a greater level of political will to improve international cooperation and mutual assistance by ensuring that their legal systems and financial institutions are not used to thwart or frustrate efforts to return stolen assets found in their jurisdictions.

Further, consistent with their commitments to combat corruption, developed economies that are home countries for multinational corporations carrying out business in countries across Africa need to amend their laws not only to make it easier for the prosecution of these corporations, but also support civil actions by the victim states. Developed countries should also allow the sharing of any damages and settlements with the host countries, whose people are the ultimate victims of multinationals' complicity. States with little or no capacity to undertake asset recovery initiatives[19] should be provided with appropriate technical assistance through international cooperation and mutual legal assistance. Similarly, corporations found guilty of bribery in African countries must be made, in the interest of justice, fairness and equity, to pay assessed compensation in settlement not only to their home countries but also to the victim states where they operate and offer bribes. African states, too, will need to show more willingness to fight corruption and work in a consistent and fair manner to recover stolen assets. At the moment, many African countries' commitment and action to pursue stolen assets from corrupt former government officials is limited or sporadic.

Additionally, the StAR Initiative has published important reports, a practitioners' handbook, and the *Asset Recovery Handbook*. The practitioners' handbook includes pioneering work on politically exposed persons (PEPs, discussed in Chapter 2), documents best practices, and makes recommendations for improving the capacity of financial institutions' obligations relating in particular to PEPs. The *Asset Recovery Handbook* also documents best practices in this field, addressing jurisdictional requirements, common challenges, and contemporary requirements for asset recovery. Nonetheless, significant challenges remain, particularly in terms of the limited resources, capacity, and reach of the StAR Initiative and its sporadic work with civil society groups in victim states. The StAR Initiative should work more with international and national civil society groups, especially those operating in the jurisdictions of victim states. It should also work to support development of legal and other infrastructure, and, importantly, victims and public-oriented alternatives to its own asset recovery and capacity-building projects. Accordingly, the StAR Initiative's *Asset Recovery Handbook* should be revised to incorporate latest developments and thinking, and be widely circulated. Further, the Open-ended Intergovernmental Working Group on Asset Recovery should collaborate more closely with the StAR Initiative and other appropriate

[19] For example, the StAR Initiative has stated that several developing countries, including across Africa, 'lack the capacity to prepare indictments, collect, preserve, and present evidence, properly adjudicate cases, and obtain convictions, as well as trace the proceeds of corruption and obtain valid freezing and confiscation orders'.

global and regional mechanisms, such as UNODC, the UN Office of the High Commissioner for Human Rights, and Interpol,[20] to develop synergies, enhance technical capacities, and share information on best practices on asset recovery efforts in Africa.

## MUTUAL PEER REVIEW MECHANISM FOR THE AU CONVENTION ON PREVENTING AND COMBATING CORRUPTION

None of the four anti-corruption treaties discussed in this book has a system of mutual peer review or any strong enforcement or accountability mechanisms. The fact that no mechanism exists within the anti-corruption legal framework to hold states accountable for failure to implement their obligations and commitments suggests that states are reluctant to relinquish sovereignty in this field. Therefore, it is absolutely imperative that states parties to these treaties consider the possibility of adopting the proposed mechanism, which has proved to be successful within the framework of the OECD Convention, not only in terms of facilitating the harmonisation of domestic laws with the provisions of the convention but also by ensuring effective implementation and enforcement.[21] Otherwise, it will be difficult for the treaties to achieve their fundamental objectives and purpose of preventing and combating corruption effectively. The mutual peer review mechanism should collaborate closely with the African Peer Review Mechanism, established within the framework of the New Partnership for Africa's Development. Further, as is practised by the Financial Action Task Force in relation to its efforts to combat money laundering, this mechanism should include a system of 'naming and shaming'. Most importantly is the coordination of pan-African and international organisations and their documents (SADC, ECOWAS, World Bank, OECD, United Nations, and so on).

The implementation and enforcement of the anti-corruption treaties can indeed be enhanced through the conduct of regular peer review evaluations. However, a government-to-government peer review process will be

[20] For example, the StAR Initiative could build on its partnership arrangement with Interpol's Asset Recovery Focal Point Database and Interpol's '24/7' emergency assistance contact list to increase the impact in Africa. Interpol's database aims to improve coordination of international investigations and provide technical assistance on the logistics of investigations in foreign jurisdictions. Its emergency assistance contact list includes contact details for initial inquiries into asset recovery procedure and the nature of evidence required for criminal investigations or civil action on stolen public funds in foreign jurisdictions, as well as providing immediate assistance and coordinating investigatory efforts. Interpol's work could enhance StAR Initiative's meagre resources, limited capacity, and absence of political will.

[21] Other useful best practices include the Committee of Experts of the Follow-Up Mechanism for the Inter-American Convention Against Corruption and the Group of States Against Corruption.

more effective if it is open to input from the private sector and civil society. A process that only provides for governments to monitor each other behind closed doors will have limited results, because officials may have other priorities that impede their willingness to criticise non-compliant governments. Important goals are served by a mutual evaluation system, including: increasing knowledge among signatories; promoting progress and consistency; identifying and addressing problems with compliance; and building momentum for corrective action. Mutual evaluation is increasingly turned to also because it minimises the need for new, permanent, and, perhaps, costly bureaucracies. It engages many more professional experts with credibility and expertise to address complex issues. Finally, periodic evaluation serves to maintain momentum for implementation of agreements. It also increases knowledge and understanding, for example, by facilitating exchange of information and disclosure on best practice in anti-corruption investigations, prosecution, and cases underway, as well as the progress that has been made on preventive measures.

However, while the concept of mutual evaluation has existed for some time, recent experience in the anti-money laundering area is probably the most useful example for understanding the concept of mutual peer review.[22] Such a mutual review system has been established under the OECD Convention, the Group of States against Corruption at the Council of Europe, the Caribbean Financial Action Task Force, and the Inter-American Drug Abuse Commission Mutual Evaluation Mechanism. The OECD Convention includes self-evaluation of implementing legislation via a detailed OECD questionnaire, peer review of those responses, on-site review of enforcement by a team of experts drawn from participating nations, and consideration of their reports at plenary meetings. As the Durban Commitment to Effective Action against Corruption declares, 'monitoring will be a vital element to promote consistency and cooperation'.[23]

[22] Essentially, mutual evaluation in this area has the following characteristics. First, representatives from all signatory countries meet regularly to discuss issues and review progress on implementing an agreed-upon set of recommendations. Each country is required to submit regular progress reports that are discussed in the meetings. Shortcomings and successes receive equal attention. Second, on a regular basis, a team of three to four experts from different professional backgrounds is drawn from each of the participating nations to conduct an in-depth, on-site evaluation of a nation's progress. This is important because simply examining laws and reports cannot assess actual compliance. Preliminary questionnaires are completed by the nation to serve as an aid in three- to four-day on-site assessment visits. A member of the secretariat is included on the team to ensure consistency and to assist in the final drafting of a report.

[23] Durban Commitment to Effective Action against Corruption.

## INTEGRATION AND HARMONISATION OF ANTI-CORRUPTION TREATIES AND MECHANISMS AND AFRICAN HUMAN RIGHTS TREATIES AND MECHANISMS

It is important for states to strive to integrate the implementation and enforcement procedures of the pan-African anti-corruption treaty – the AU Convention on Preventing and Combating Corruption – with the sub-regional instruments – the SADC Protocol and the ECOWAS Protocol – if the continent is to rid itself of corruption and its corrosive effects on human rights. These criminal law instruments should also be integrated and harmonised with African regional human rights mechanisms, especially the African Commission, the African Court, the ECOWAS Court of Justice, the SADC Tribunal, and the East African Court of Justice. The integration, harmonisation, and interaction could be achieved through dynamic and progressive interpretations of mandates and treaties and by exchanging information and joint missions.

The Office of the High Commissioner for Human Rights should actively promote and encourage interactions, collaboration and dialogue among human rights and anti-corruption institutions and NGOs, and come up with guidelines for facilitating mutual engagement and cooperation among them. The African Union should promote and encourage similar initiatives between the African Commission, the African Court, the Advisory Board established under the AU Convention on Preventing and Combating Corruption, and other similar bodies and agencies.

## IMPROVED AND EXPANDED ROLES FOR CIVIL SOCIETY AND INTERNATIONAL AND REGIONAL ANTI-CORRUPTION AND HUMAN RIGHTS NON-GOVERNMENT ORGANISATIONS

Civil society organisations, including human rights NGOs and anti-corruption activists, play important roles in the effective implementation and enforcement of anti-corruption laws, treaties, and standards, and in the protection and promotion of human and peoples' rights.[24] As Transparency International has stated:

> Experience in Africa teaches that civil society organizations have a key role to play in promoting anti-corruption conventions in all phases from negotiation to follow-up reviews. Civil society groups can press their governments to give priority to convention ratification and implementation through research, analysis and advocacy work. They can help translate the off-putting legal terminology

[24] See, generally, Transparency International, *Anti-Corruption Conventions in Africa: What Civil Society Can Do to Make Them Work, A Civil Society Advocacy Guide by Transparency International* (Transparency International, 2006).

> of conventions into language non-lawyers can understand and can explain to the public the usefulness of these conventions for addressing the corruption problem. They can keep track of their government's performance and make it public, adding an important independent perspective to the government's own assessment of its progress. Where they find deficiencies they can campaign for improvement, in coalition with supporters in government and the private sector. The more groups engaged in these activities, the stronger and more effective anti-corruption conventions and anti-corruption efforts in general are likely to be.[25]

Further, civil society groups can also do this through mobilising citizens against corruption and educating them on corruption's effects on human rights. They could also monitor and put pressure on states to effectively implement and enforce laws and standards on whistle-blowers to encourage and protect citizens who come forward with information on corrupt practices, as well as journalists whose investigative reports expose senior public officials engaging in large scale corruption. Anti-corruption NGOs should take advantage of the revolutionary idea of human rights, which has over the years demonstrated a strong capacity to serve as a mechanism for social mobilisation, while human rights NGOs develop their work and strategies to include collaboration with the anti-corruption movement to prevent and combat the effects of corruption on human rights. Influential international NGOs such as Transparency International and Amnesty International should vigorously support and promote this collaboration and synergy, and should themselves explore and work more closely together to advance the human rights approach to fight corruption on the national, sub-regional, regional, and international levels. The involvement of these two organisations would contribute to improved achievement of their goals and mandates in Africa.

## REGIONAL CENTRE FOR CIVIC EDUCATION

All the anti-corruption treaties discussed in this book underscore the central role education plays in the efforts to fight corruption and to build a culture of transparency, accountability, the rule of law, respect for human rights, and zero tolerance for corruption. Article 25 of the African Charter provides that, 'States parties to the present Charter shall have the duty to promote and ensure through teaching, education and publication, respect for the rights and freedoms contained in the present Charter and to see to it that these freedoms and rights as well as corresponding obligations and duties are understood'. Article 26 provides that, 'States parties to the present Charter shall have the duty to guarantee the independence of the

[25] ibid, 119.

Courts and shall allow the establishment and improvement of appropriate national institutions entrusted with the promotion and protection of the rights and freedoms guaranteed by the present Charter.' Education can include encouraging citizens to develop respect and trust for the public good and public interest, while creating awareness about corruption and its effects on society, communities, and individuals. The proposed regional centre for civic education would be ideal for achieving these important educational goals, and could help trigger the establishment of similar centres at the sub-regional or national level.

Civil society and the press must push for reforms and for the necessary political will to institute real changes. Both education and increased information are key instruments to gaining widespread support for reform. Civil society and the private sector must ensure that the fight against corruption is rooted in the building of both state and market institutions, and civil society and the press must support this work by creating checks and balances for government and the public sector. In the final analysis, the most potent force for change is the idea that corruption is morally repugnant and inimical to the rule of law, international development, and the welfare of citizens around Africa and around the world.

While the beneficiaries of corruption must be addressed before any real change can occur, ridding government of high-ranking officials on the grounds of corruption is not enough. Systems of checks and balances and democratic institutions, as well as civic education and social mobilisation, are key steps in ensuring that real change occurs and that democracy and governments are well-regarded among the general population. Citizens' education and empowerment is critical to enable them to contribute to addressing the problem, including by holding their own leaders accountable. Civil society, NGOs, and the business community should also be encouraged and supported to get involved in the efforts to combat corruption and the culture that allows it to persist and flourish.

It is also important to encourage lawyers and other professionals to be more involved in the fight against corruption. One way of achieving this is to entrench the teaching of issues relating to corruption and human rights in all educational institutions. In this respect, it is suggested that centres for the study of law, corruption and development be established in higher institutions and universities to educate and empower future lawyers and other professionals to be better able to track the problem of corruption and its deleterious effects. Students (and future leaders) should be encouraged to pursue issue-area specialisations, including multi-jurisdictional specialisations in the fields of anti-corruption and human rights. By gaining educational and practical skills in these fields, lawyers and others will also be more likely to contribute to the efforts to address corruption, and to advance professional goals, as well.

## REGIONAL LAW ENFORCEMENT ACADEMY

A Regional Law Enforcement Academy should be established within the AU Headquarters in Addis Ababa, to serve as a framework for providing training, support, and assistance to regional law enforcement communities, and to be able to effectively and satisfactorily address all forms of corruption. This academy could help to reduce cross-border effects of corruption, and stabilise the police environment regionally and domestically, which is critical not only to political, economic, and social stability but also to the development of individual states and respect for human rights across the region (and also internationally). The academy should be adequately resourced, so that it can offer technical assistance and other forms of bilateral and multilateral support to carry out its mandates. Collaboration with international agencies like the International Law Enforcement Academy and Interpol could contribute to the full achievement of this goal.

If Africa is to truly exercise its sovereignty – both political and economic – it must make as its utmost priority the betterment of its peoples without distinction of any kind. As the Polish lawyer Raphael Lemkin, who invented the term genocide in 1944, pointedly put it, 'Sovereignty implies conducting an independent foreign and internal policy, building of schools, construction of roads, in brief, all types of activity directed towards the welfare of people. Sovereignty cannot be conceived as the right to kill millions of innocent people.'[26] Likewise, one might add that sovereignty is not a licence for states and senior public officials to commit acts of corruption that imperil human dignity, and with it citizens' lives and hopes for a better future. Sovereignty should not (and cannot) be invoked to shield perpetrators of corruption from justice or victims from accessing effective remedies. The legal protection of human and peoples' rights should therefore be the primary aim of the African Union and its member states. Deploying human rights law as a complementary framework to prevent and combat corruption can contribute to continental (and global) efforts to improve both the effectiveness of the regional human rights mechanisms and the instruments against corruption.

Even so, 'the key to success is ensuring global implementation of [anti-corruption] instruments [and human rights law] at the national levels, and establishing effective mechanisms for the international community to enforce collectively the spirit and the letter of national commitments'.[27] Lori Ann Wanlin stated pointedly that, 'Promises [or expressed

[26] Mark Lattimer (ed), *Genocide and Human Rights* (Hampshire: Ashgate Publishing, 2007) xii, quoting from Lemkin's unpublished autobiography.

[27] Robert E Lutz, 'Combating the Culture of Corruption' (2003–04) 10 *Southwestern Journal of Law and Trade in the Americas* 268.

commitments] don't reduce corruption; actions do. Taking the public pledge gets you the headlines, but real people the world over [and in Africa] are waiting for those promises to be fulfilled.'[28] However, if any significant and sustainable success is to be recorded, African states will need to take creative, radical, evolutionary, and bold initiatives that address the enduring problem of corruption and its effects on human and peoples' rights. As Akin Oyebode, wrote, 'If [Africa] fails to stop corruption, corruption is most likely going to stop [Africa].'[29] It is to be hoped that this 'age of corruption' will give way to that of transparency, accountability, the rule of law, and full respect for human and peoples' rights throughout the continent.

[28] Lori Ann Wanlin, 'The Gap between Promise and Practice in the Global Fight against Corruption' (2006) 6 *Asper Review of International Business and Trade Law* 240.

[29] Akin Oyebode, 'An Overview of Corruption in Nigeria' in IA Ayua and DA Guobadia (eds), *Political Reform and Economic Recovery in Nigeria* (Lagos: NIALS, 2001) 560.

# *Select Bibliography*


Aceampong, Kenneth, 'Combating Grand Corruption: The Potential Impact of a United Nations Convention on Prevention and Punishment of the Crime of Economic Genocide' (1988) 7 *Revue Africaine des l'Homme*.

Akinnola, Richard, *The Politics of Corruption and Corruption of Politics* (Lagos, Nigeria: Rich Konsult, 2008).

Alston, Philip, 'Peoples' Rights: Their Rise and Fall' in Philip Alston (ed), *Peoples' Rights* (Oxford: Oxford University Press: 2001).

—— and Mary Robinson (eds), *Human Rights and Development: Towards Mutual Reinforcement* (Oxford: Oxford University Press, 2005).

Arnell, Paul, 'Extraterritorial Human Rights: A Tool for Poverty Reduction?' (2005) 38 *Comparative and International Law Journal of Southern Africa*.

Ashworth, Andrew, *Principles of Criminal Law*, 3rd edn (Oxford: Oxford University Press, 1999).

Bacio Terracino, Julio, *The International Legal Framework against Corruption: States' Obligations to Prevent and Repress Corruption* (Antwerp: Intersentia Publishing Ltd, 2012).

Baderin, Mashood, *International Human Rights and Islamic Law* (Oxford: Oxford University Press, 2003).

Baldwin, Clive, and Cynthia Morel, 'Group Rights' in Malcolm Evans and Rachel Murray (eds), *The African Charter on Human Rights and Peoples' Rights: The System in Practice, 1986–2006* (Cambridge: Cambridge University Press, 2008).

Baloro, John, 'Some International Legal Problems Arising from the Definition and Application of the Concept of "Permanent Sovereignty Over Wealth and Natural Resources" of States' (1987) 20 *Comparative & International Law Journal South Africa* 335.

Banda, Fareda, 'Protocol to the African Charter on the Rights of Women in Africa' in Malcolm Evans and Rachel Murray (eds), *The African Charter on Human Rights and Peoples' Rights: The System In Practice, 1986–2006* (Cambridge: Cambridge University Press, 2008).

Bayley, David, 'The Effects of Corruption in a Developing Nation' in Arnold J Heidenheimer (ed), *Political Corruption: Readings in Comparative Analysis* (New Brunswick, NJ: Transaction Publishers, 1978).

Bentham, Jeremy, *A Fragment On Government* [1776] (Cambridge: Cambridge University Press, 1988 ).

*Black's Law Dictionary*, 6th edn (St Paul, MN: West Publishing, 1996).

*Black's Law Dictionary*, 7th edn (St Paul, MN: West Group, 1999).

Bobdzie-Simpson, Ebow, 'A Critique of the African Charter on Human and Peoples' Rights' (1988) 31 *Howard Law Journal*.

Boersma, Martine, *Corruption: A Violation of Human Rights and a Crime Under International Law?* (Antwerp: Intersentia Publishing Ltd, 2012).

Brasz, HA, 'Sociology of Corruption' in Arnold J Heidenheimer (ed), *Political Corruption: Readings in Comparative Analysis* (New Brunswick, NJ: Transaction Publishers, 1978).

Brauch, Jeffrey A, 'The Margin of Appreciation and the Jurisprudence of the European Court of Human Rights: Threat to the Rule of Law' (2004) 11 *Columbia Journal of European Law*.

Brian, C Harms, 'Holding Public Officials Accountable in the International Realm: A New Multi-Layered Strategy to Combat Corruption' (2000) 33 *Cornell International Law Journal* 159.

Brown, Alexander Jonathan, 'What Are We Trying to Measure? Reviewing the Basics of Corruption Definition' in Charles Sampford, Arthur Shacklock and Carmel Connors (eds), *Measuring Corruption* (Aldershot: Ashgate, 2006).

Brownlie, Ian, *Principles of Public International Law*, 6th edn (Oxford: Oxford University Press, 2003).

Buergenthal, Thomas, 'The Normative and Institutional Evolution of International Human Rights' (1997) 19 *Human Rights Quarterly* 703–23.

——, Dinah Shelton and David Stewart, *International Human Rights in a Nutshell*, 3rd edn (St Paul, MN: West Group, 2002).

Cançado Trindade, Antonio A, 'La Justiciabilidad de los derechos económicos, sociales y culturales en el plano internacional' *Revista Lecciones y Ensayos, 1997–98* (Buenos Aires: Universidad de Buenos Aires, School of Law and Social Sciences, Abeledo-Perrot, 1998) 80.

Caney, Simon, 'Climate Change, Human Rights and Moral Threshold' in Stephen Humphreys (ed), *Human Rights and Climate Change* (Cambridge: Cambridge University Press, 2010).

Carozza, Paolo G, 'Human Dignity and Judicial Interpretation of Human Rights: A Reply' (2008) 19 *European Journal of International Law*.

Carr, Indira, 'Fighting Corruption through Regional and International Conventions: A Satisfactory Solution?' (2007) 15 *European Journal of Crime, Criminal Law and Criminal Justice*.

—— and Opi Outhwaite, 'The OECD Anti-Bribery Convention Ten Years On' (2008) 3 *Manchester Journal of International Economic Law*.

Cassese, Antonio, 'The Self-Determination of Peoples' in Louis Henkin (ed), *The International Bill of Human Rights: The Covenant on Civil and Political Rights* (New York: Columbia University Press, 1981).

Cecil, Sims, 'The Lawyer and the Classics' (1953–54) 8 *Arkansas Law Review*.

Coldham, Simon, 'Legal Responses to State Corruption in Commonwealth Africa' (1995) 39 *Journal of African Law*.

Craven, Matthew, *The International Covenant on Economic, Social and Cultural Rights (A Perspective On Its Development)* (Oxford: Oxford University Press, 1998).

Crawford, James (ed), 'The Rights of Peoples: Some Conclusions' in *The Rights of Peoples'* (Oxford: Clarendon Press, 1995).

Crutchfield George, Barbara, and Kathleen A Lacey, 'A Coalition of Industrialized Nations, Multilateral Development Banks, and Non-Governmental Organizations: A Pivotal Complement to Current Anti-Corruption Initiatives' (2000) 33 *Cornell International Law Journal*.

Das, Hans, 'The Concept of Mass Claims and the Specificity of Mass Claims Resolution' in Permanent Court of Arbitration (ed), *Redressing Injustices through*

*Mass Claims Processes: Innovative Responses to Unique Challenges* (Oxford: Oxford University Press).

de Albuquerque, Catarina, 'Chronicle of an Announced Birth: The Coming into Life of the Optional Protocol to the International Covenant on Economic, Social and Cultural Rights – The Missing Piece of the International Bill of Human Rights' (2010) 144 *Human Rights Quarterly*.

De Beco, Gauthier, 'Monitoring Corruption from a Human Rights Perspective' (2011) 15 *International Journal of Human Rights*.

De Villiers, Bertus, 'Directive Principles of State Policy and Fundamental Rights: The Indian Experience' (2011–12) 10 *Northwestern University Journal of International Human Rights*.

Demas, Reagan, 'Moment of Truth: Development in Sub-Saharan Africa and Critical Alterations Needed in Application of the Foreign Corrupt Practices Act and Other Anti-Corruption Initiatives' (2010–11) 26 *American University International Law Review*.

DeMott, Deborah A, 'Beyond Metaphor: An Analysis of Fiduciary Obligation' (1988) 37 *Duke Law Journal* 879.

Diersen, Kari Lynn, 'Foreign Corrupt Practices Act' (1999) 36 *American Criminal Law Review*.

Donaldson, Thomas, and Thomas W Dunfee, *Ties That Bind: A Social Contracts Approach to Business Ethics* (Boston, MA: Harvard Business School Press, 1999).

Duruigbo, Emeka, 'Realizing the People's Right to Natural Resources' (2011) 111 *Whitehead Journal of Diplomacy and International Relations*.

Ebobrah, Solomon T, 'African Charter on Democracy: Is Democracy Now an Issue in Africa? An Evaluation of the African Charter on Democracy, Elections and Governance' (2007) 1 *Malawi Law Journal*.

Echeverria, Gabriela, 'Codifying the Rights of Victims in International Law: Remedies and Reparation' in Permanent Court of Arbitration (ed), *Redressing Injustices through Mass Claims Processes: Innovative Responses to Unique Challenges* (Oxford: Oxford University Press).

Eide, Asbjørn, 'Study of the Right to Adequate Food as a Human Right' (United Nations Human Rights Study Series, No 1).

Eisler, Jacob, 'The Unspoken Institutional Battle over Anticorruption: Citizens United, Honest Services, and the Legislative-Judicial Divide' (2010–11) 9 *First Amendment Law*.

Elliot, Kimberly Ann, 'The Problem of Corruption: A Tale of Two Countries' (2008) 18 *Northwestern Journal of International Law and Business*.

Eric, L Lewis, 'Garnishing Graft: A Strategy for Recovering the Proceeds of Bribery' (1982) 92 *Yale Law Journal* 128.

Evans, Malcolm, and Rachel Murray (eds), *The African Charter on Human and Peoples' Rights: The System in Practice, 1986-2006*, 2nd edn (Cambridge: Cambridge University Press, 2008).

Falk, Richard, 'The Rights of Peoples (In Particular Indigenous Peoples)' in James Crawford (ed), *The Rights of Peoples* (Oxford: Clarendon Press, 1995).

Farmer, Paul, *Pathologies of Power: Health, Human Rights, and the New War on the Poor* (Berkeley, CA: University of California Press, 2003).

Findlay, Mark, 'Implementing Corruption Prevention Strategies through Codes of Conduct' (1991–92) 3 *Current Issues Criminal Justice*.

Fort, Timothy L, and James J Noone, 'Gifts, Bribes and Exchange: Relationships in Non-Market Economies and Lessons for Pax E-Commercial' (2000) 33 *Cornell International Law Journal*.

Fox, Hazel, *The Law of State Immunity* (Oxford: Oxford University Press, 2008).

Friedrich, Carl, 'Corruption Concepts in Historical Perspective' in Arnold J Heidenheimer, Michael Johnston, and Victor T LeVine (eds), *Political Corruption: A Handbook* (New Brunswick, NJ: Transaction Publishers, 1999).

Franck, Thomas M, 'The Emerging Right to Democratic Governance' (1992) 86 *American Journal of International Law*.

Gallant, MM, *Money Laundering and the Proceeds of Crime* (Cheltenham: Edward Elgar Publishing Ltd, 2005).

Gantz, David A, 'Globalizing Sanctions against Foreign Bribery: The Emergence of a New International Legal Consensus Citation' (1997–98) 18 *Northwestern Journal of International Law & Business*.

Gathii, James, 'A Critical Appraisal of the NEPAD Agenda in Light of Africa's Place in the World Trade Regime in an Era of Market Centered Development' (2003) 13 *Transnational Law and Contemporary Problems*.

Génaux, Maryvonne, 'Social Sciences and the Evolving Concept of Corruption' (2004) 42 *Crime, Law & Social Change* 13.

Gevurtz, Franklin A, 'Rethinking Corruption: An Introduction to a Symposium and a Few Additional Thoughts' (2007) 20 *Pacific McGeorge Global Business & Development Law Journal*.

Goldbarg, Andrea, 'The Foreign Corrupt Practices Act and Structural Corruption' (2000) 18 *Boston University International Law Journal*.

Goodwin, Morag, and Kate Rose-Sender, 'Linking Corruption and Human Rights: An Unwelcome Addition to the Development Discourse' in Martine Boersma and Hans Nelen (eds), *Corruption and Human Rights: Interdisciplinary Perspectives* (Antwerp: Intersentia Publishing Ltd, 2010).

Hannum, Hurst, 'The Right to Determination in the Twenty-First Century' (1998) 55 *Washington & Lee Law Review*.

—— 'Rethinking Self-Determination' (1993) 1 *Virginia Journal of International Law*.

Harrington, Alexandra R, 'Don't Mind The Gap: The Rise of Individual Complaint Mechanisms Within International Human Rights Treaties' (2011–12) 153 *Duke Journal of Comparative and International Law*.

Hassan, Parvez, 'The Word "Arbitrary" As Used in the Universal Declaration of Human Rights Illegal Or Unjust?' (1969) 10 *Harvard International Law Journal*.

Hatchard, John, 'Adopting a Human Rights Approach Towards Combating Corruption' in Martine Boersma and Hans Nelen (eds), *Corruption and Human Rights: Interdisciplinary Perspectives* (Antwerp: Intersentia Publishing Ltd, 2010).

Heidenheimer, Arnold J (ed), *Political Corruption: Readings in Comparative Analysis* (New Brunswick, NJ: Transaction Publishers, 1978).

—— et al (eds), *Political Corruption: A Handbook* (New Brunswick, NJ: Transaction Publishers, 1999).

Henkin, Louis (ed), 'Introduction' in *The International Bill of Rights* (New York: Colombia University Press, 1981).

Henning, Peter J, 'Public Corruption: A Comparative Analysis of International Corruption Conventions and United States Law' (2001) 18 *Arizona Journal of International & Comparative Law*.

Hess, David, and Thomas W Dunfee, 'Fighting Corruption: A Principled Approach: The C2 Principles (Combating Corruption)' (2000) 33 *Cornell International Law Journal.*

Huntington, Samuel, *Political Order in Changing Societies* (New Haven, CT: Yale University Press, 1968).

Igbinedion, Simeon Aisabor, 'A Critical Appraisal of the Mechanism for Prosecuting Systemic Corruption Offenders under the United Nations Convention against Corruption' (2003) 6 *Manchester Journal of International Economic Law.*

International Council on Human Rights Policy, *Corruption and Human Rights: Making the Connection* (Versoix, Switzerland: ICHRP, 2009).

Ionescu, Luminita, 'The Construction of Corruption as a Global Problem' (2011) 3 *Contemporary Readings Law and Social Justice.*

Jacobson , Sam and Maria Slavova, *Democracy Against Corruption: A New Way of Thinking About Public Administration* (Sofia, Bulgaria: Institute of Public Administration and European Integration, 2006)

Jenks, Wilfred, *The Common Law of Mankind* (New York: Frederick A Praeger, 1958).

Joseph, Sarah, Jenny Schultz, and Melissa Caston (eds), *The International Covenant on Civil and Political Rights, Cases, Materials and Commentary,* 2nd edn (Oxford: Oxford University Press, 2004).

Kennedy, David, 'The International Anti-Corruption Campaign' (1999) 14 *Connecticut Journal of International Law.*

Key Jr, VO, 'Techniques of Political Graft' in Arnold J Heidenheimer (ed), *Political Corruption* (New Brunswick, NJ: Transaction Publishers, 1970).

Kiwanuka, Richard N, 'The Meaning of "People" in the African Charter on Human and Peoples' Rights' (1988) 82 *American Society of International Law* 80.

Kofele-Kale, Ndiva, 'Change or the Illusion of Change' (2006) 38 *George Washington International Law Review* 697.

—— *The International Law of Responsibility for Economic Crimes* (Farnham: Ashgate Publishing, 2006).

Krause, C, 'The Right to Property' in A Eide (ed), *Economic, Social and Cultural Rights* (The Hague: Martinus Nijhoff, 1995).

Krevert, Tor, 'Curbing Corruption? The Efficacy of the Foreign Corrupt Practices Act' (2007–08) 33 *North Carolina Joint International Law and Commercial Regulation.*

Kumar, C Raj, 'Corruption and Human Rights: Promoting Transparency in Governance and the Fundamental Right to Corruption-Free Service in India' (2003–04) 31 *Columbia Journal of Asian Law.*

—— 'Human Rights Approaches of Corruption Control Mechanisms–Enhancing the Hong Kong Experience of Corruption Prevention Strategies' (2004) 5 *San Diego International Law Journal.*

—— *Corruption and Human Rights in India: Comparative Perspectives on Transparency and Good Governance* (India: Oxford University Press, 2011).

Lacey, Kathleen A, and Barbara Crutchfield George, 'Crackdown on Money Laundering: A Comparative Analysis of the Feasibility and Effectiveness of Domestic and Multilateral Policy Reforms' (2002–03) 23 *Northwestern Journal International Law and Business.*

Lattimer, Mark (ed), *Genocide and Human Rights* (Farnham: Ashgate Publishing, 2007).

Leff, Nathaniel H, 'Economic Development through Bureaucratic Corruption' (1964) 8 *American Behavioral Scientist*.

Levi, Michael, and Monty Raphael, 'Anti-corruption – A Signpost for Transactional Lawyers' (1999) 1 *Business Law International*.

Leys, Colin, 'What Is the Problem about Corruption' (1965) 3 *Journal of Modern African Studies*.

Lowenstein, Daniel Hays, 'For God, For Country, or For Me?' (1986) 74 *California Law Review*.

Lutz, Robert E, 'Combating the Culture of Corruption' (2003–04) 10 *Southwestern Journal of Law and Trade*.

Magen, Amichai, 'The Rule of Law and Its Promotion Abroad: Three Problems of Scope' (2009) 45 *Stanford Journal of International Law*.

Marks, Stephen, 'Poverty' in Daniel Moeckli, Sangeeta Shah, and Sandesh Sivakumaran (eds), *International Human Rights Law* (Oxford: Oxford University Press, 2010).

Marong, Alhaji BM, 'Toward a Normative Consensus against Corruption: Legal Effects of the Principles to Combat Corruption in Africa' (2002) 30 *Denver Journal of International Law and Policy*.

Mbaku, John Mukum, 'The International Dimension of Africa's Struggle Against Corruption' (2010) 10 *Asper Review of International Business & Trade Law*.

McLachlin, Beverly, 'Horchelaga Lecture: Criminal Law: Towards an International Legal Order' (1999) 29 *Hong Kong Law Journal*.

Medard, JF, 'Public Corruption in Africa: A Comparative Perspective' (1986) 1 *Corruption and Reform*.

Melnik, Steven, 'The Inadequate Utilization of the Accounting Profession in the United States Government's Fight Against Money Laundering' (2000–01) 143 *New York University Journal of Legislation and Public Policy*.

Milhizer, Eugene, 'So Help Me Allah: An Historical and Prudential Analysis of Oaths as Applied to the Current Controversy of the Bible and Quran in Oath Practices in America' (2009) 70 *Ohio State Law Journal*.

Miranda, Lillian Aponte, 'The Role of International Law in Intrastate Natural Resource Allocation: Sovereignty, Human Rights, and Peoples-Based Development' (2012) 45 *Vanderbilt Journal of Transnational Law*.

Moodie, Graeme, 'On Political Scandals and Corruption' (1980) 15 *Government and Opposition*.

Murray, Rachel, *Human Rights in Africa: From the OAU to the African Union* (Cambridge: Cambridge University Press, 2004).

—— and Steven Wheatley, 'Groups and the African Charter on Human and Peoples' Rights' (2003) 25 *Human Rights Quarterly* 213.

Mutua, W Makau, 'The Banjul Charter and the African Cultural Fingerprint: An Evaluation of the Language of Duties' (1995) 35 *Virginia Journal of International Law*.

Ndikumana, Léonce, and James K Boyce, *Africa's Odious Debts: How Foreign Loans and Capital Flight Bled a Continent* (London: Zed Books, 2011).

Nichols, Philip M, 'Regulating Transnational Bribery in Times of Globalization and Fragmentation' (1999) 24 *Yale Journal International Law*.

Noonan Jr, John T, *Bribes* (New York: Macmillan, 1984).

Nye, Joseph, 'Corruption and Political Development: A Cost-Benefit Analysis' (1967) 2 *American Political Science Review*.

O'Donnell, Thomas A, 'The Margin of Appreciation Doctrine: Standards in the Jurisprudence of the European Court of Human Rights' (1982) 4 *Human Rights Quarterly*.

Odinkalu, Chidi Anselm, 'Analysis of Paralysis or Paralysis by Analysis? Implementing Economic, Social and Cultural Rights under the African Charter on Human and Peoples' Rights' (2001) 23 *Human Rights Quarterly*.

Oloka-Onyango, Joseph, 'Reinforcing Marginalized Rights in an Age of Globalization: International Mechanisms, Non-State Actors, and the Struggle for Peoples' Rights in Africa' (2003) 18 *American University of International Review*.

*Oxford Advanced Learning's Dictionary*, 6th edn (Oxford: Oxford University Press, 2000).

Oyebode, Akin, 'An Overview of Corruption in Nigeria' in IA Ayua and DA Guobadia (eds), *Political Reform and Economic Recovery in Nigeria* (Lagos, Nigeria: NIALS, 2001).

Pearson, Zoe, 'An International Human Rights Approach to Corruption' in Peter Larmour and Nick Wolanin (eds), *Corruption and Anti-Corruption* (Canberra: Asia Pacific Press, 2001).

Peck, James, 'Measuring Justice for Nature: Issues in Evaluating and Litigating Natural Resources Damages' (1998–99) 14 *Journal of Land Use & Environmental Law*.

Peters, John G, and Susan Welch, 'Political Corruption in America: A Search for Definitions and a Theory' (1978) 72 *American Political Science Review*.

Pogge, Thomas, 'Recognized and Violated by International Law: The Human Rights of the Global Poor' (2005) 18 *Leiden Journal International Law*.

—— (ed), *Freedom from Poverty as a Human Rights: Who Owes What to the Very Poor?* (Oxford: Oxford University Press, 2007).

Posadas, Alejandro, 'Combating Corruption under International Law' (2000) 10 *Duke Journal of Comparative and International Law*.

Reisman, W Michael, *Folded Lies: Bribery, Crusades and Reforms* (New York: Free Press, 1979).

—— 'Harnessing International Law to Restrain and Recapture Indigenous Spoliations' (1989) 83 *American Journal of International Law*.

Robinson, Mary, 'Forward' in John Braithwaite (ed), *Yearbook of Women's Rights* (The Netherlands: BookWorld Publications, 2002).

Rose-Ackerman, Susan, *Corruption and Government: Causes, Consequences, and Reform* (Cambridge: Cambridge University Press, 1999).

—— 'Corruption and the Criminal Law' (2002) 2 *Forum on Crime and Society*.

Rossbacher, Henry H, and Tracy W Young, 'The Foreign Corrupt Practices Act: An American Response to Corruption' in Barry Rider (ed), *Corruption: The Enemy Within* (The Hague: Kluwer Law International, 1997).

Sachs, Jeffrey *The End of Poverty: Economic Possibilities for Our Time* (New York: Penguin Press, 2005).

Sandgren, Claes, 'Combating Corruption: The Misunderstood Role of Law' (2005) 39 *International Law*.

Scheinin, Martin, 'Impact on the Law of Treaties' in Menno Kamminga and Martin Scheinin (eds), *The Impact of Human Rights Law on General International Law* (Oxford: Oxford University Press, 2009).

Senturia, Joseph, 'Corruption, Political' in *Encyclopaedia of Social Sciences*, Part IV (New York: Crowell-Collier Macmillan, 1930–35).

Shelton, Dinah, 'Decision Regarding Communication 155/96 (*Social and Economic Rights Action Center/Center for Economic and Social Rights v. Nigeria*)' (2002) 96 *American Journal of International Law*.

—— *Remedies in International Human Rights Law*, 2nd edn (Oxford, Oxford University Press, 2005).

—— 'Human Rights and the Environment: What Specific Environmental Rights Have Been Recognized?' (2006) 35 *Denver Journal of International Law and Policy*.

—— 'Developing Substantive Environmental Rights' (2010) 1 *Journal of Human Rights and Environment*.

Simma, Bruno, and Philip Alston, 'The Sources of Human Rights Law: Custom, *Jus Cogens* and General Principles' (1992) 12 *Australian Year Book of International Law* 82.

Snider, Thomas R, and Won Kidane, 'Combating Corruption through International Law in Africa: A Comparative Analysis' (2007) 40 *Cornell International Law Journal*.

Sorensen, Juliet, 'Ideals Without Illusions: Corruption and the Future of a Democratic North Africa' (2012) 10 *Northwestern University Journal International Human Rights*.

Stessens, Guy, *Money Laundering: A New International Law Enforcement Model* (Cambridge: Cambridge University Press, 2000).

Stuart, George Moody, *Systemic Corruption: How Business Bribes Damage Developing Countries* (Oxford: WorldView Publishing, 1997).

Tanzi, Vito, 'Corruption Around the World Causes, Consequences, Scope, and Cures' *International Money Fund Staff Papers* (1998).

Transparency International, *Anti-Corruption Conventions in Africa: What Civil Society Can Do to Make Them Work, A Civil Society Advocacy Guide by Transparency International* (Berlin: Transparency International, 2006).

—— *The Anti-Corruption Catalyst: Realising The MDGs by 2015* (Berlin: Transparency International, 2010).

Tucker, Eric, 'The Westray Mine Disaster and its Aftermath: The Politics of Causation' (1955) 10 *Canadian Journal of Law and Society*.

Türk, Danilo, 'Study on the Realisation of Economic, Social, and Cultural Rights' (final report) United Nations Human Rights Study, E/CN 4/Sub 2/1992/16.

Udombana, Nsongurua J, 'Articulating the Right to Democratic Governance in Africa' (2003) 24 *Michigan Journal of International Law*.

—— 'Fighting Corruption Seriously? Africa's Anti-corruption Convention' (2003) 7 *Singapore Journal of International & Comparative Law* 452.

UNDP/Global Financial Integrity, *Illicit Financial Flows from the Least Developed Countries: 2002-2011* (New York: UNDP, 2013).

van Boven, Theo, 'The Relations Between Peoples' Rights and Human Rights in the African Charter' (1986) 7 *Human Rights Law Journal*.

—— 'Human Rights and Rights of Peoples' (1995) 6 *European Journal of International Law*.

van Duyne, P, 'Money Laundering: Pavlov's Dog and beyond' (1998) 37 *Howard Journal of Criminal Justice* 359.

van Klaveren, Jacob, 'Corruption as a Historical Phenomenon' in Arnold J Heidenheimer, Michael Johnston, and Victor T LeVine (eds), *Political Corruption: A Handbook* (New Brunswick, NJ: Transaction Publishers, 1999).

Vieira, Oscar Vilhena, 'Inequality and the Subversion of the Rule of Law' (2007) 27 *SUR International Journal on Human Rights.*

Viljoen, Frans, *International Human Rights Law in Africa,* 2nd edn (Oxford: Oxford University Press, 2012).

Vlasic, Mark V, and Jenae N Noel, 'Fighting Corruption to Improve Global Security: An Analysis of International Asset Recovery Systems' (2010) 5 *Yale Journal of International Affairs.*

Wanlin, Lori Ann, 'The Gap between Promise and Practice in the Global Fight against Corruption (2006) 6 *Asper Review of International Business and Trade Law.*

Webb, Philippa, 'The United Nations Convention against Corruption: Global Achievement or Missed Opportunity?' (2005) 8 *Journal of International Economic Law* 191.

Weber, Max, *Economy and Society* (New York: Bedminster Press, 1968).

Wilson, James Q, 'Corruption Is Not Always Scandalous' in John A Gardiner and David J Olson (eds), *Theft of the City: Readings on Corruption in Urban America* (Bloomington, IN: Indiana University Press, 1974).

World Bank, *Helping Countries Combat Corruption: The Role of the World Bank* (Washington, DC: World Bank, 1997).

—— *Africa Development Indicators 2012/13* (Washington, DC: World Bank, 2013).

World Health Organization, WHO Constitution, *Basic Documents of the World Health Organization* (37th edn) (Geneva: WHO, 1992).

Wouters, Jan, Cedric Ryngaertt, and Ann Sofie Cloots, 'The International Legal Framework against Corruption: Achievements and Challenges' (2013) 14 *Melbourne Journal of International Law.*

Zimring, Franklin E, and David T Johnson, 'On the Comparative Study of Corruption' (2007) 20 *Pacific McGeorge Global Business and Development Law Journal.*

# Index

www.ingramcontent.com/pod-product-compliance
Lightning Source LLC
LaVergne TN
LVHW052219200926
848481LV00001B/150